Social Problems

Social Problems

FIFTEENTH EDITION

William Kornblum
City University of New York
Graduate School and University Center

Fifteenth Edition Revised by:
Karen Seccombe
Portland State University

Joseph Julian, *Emeritus*
San Francisco State University

PEARSON

Boston   Columbus   Indianapolis   New York City   San Francisco
Amsterdam   Cape Town   Dubai   London   Madrid   Milan   Paris   Montréal   Toronto   Delhi
Mexico City   São Paulo   Sydney   Hong Kong   Seoul   Singapore   Taipei   Tokyo

VP, Product Development: Dickson Musslewhite
Publisher: Charlyce Jones Owen
Editorial Assistant: Laura Hernandez
Program Team Lead: Amber Mackey
Program Manager: Rob DeGeorge
Managing Editor: Denise Forlow
Project Manager: Lynne Breitfeller
Field Marketing Manager: Brittany
  Pogue-Mohammed

Product Marketing Manager: Tricia Murphy
Full Service Vendor: Integra Software Services, Inc.
Operations Supervisor: Mary Fischer
Operations Specialist: Mary Ann Gloriande
Cover Art Director: Maria Lange
Cover Designer: Lumina Datamatics
Cover Art: Neil Leslie/Alamy
Printer/Binder: Manufactured in the United States by RR Donnelley
Cover Printer: Phoenix Color/Hagerstown

Acknowledgements of third party content appear on pages 482–492, which constitutes an extension of this copyright page.

Library of Congress Cataloging-in-Publication Data

Kornblum, William, author.
  Social problems/William Kornblum and Karen Seccombe.—15th edition.
    pages cm
  ISBN 978-0-13-397458-4—ISBN 0-13-397458-8
1. Social problems—United States.   2. United States—Social conditions—1980–
I. Seccombe, Karen,   II. Title.
  HN59.2.K66 2017
  306.0973—dc23

                                        2015030686

10 9 8 7 6 5 4 3 2 1

V011

Student Version:
ISBN 10: 0-13-397458-8
ISBN 13: 978-0-13-397458-4

Books a la Carte:
ISBN 10: 0-13-397461-8
ISBN 13: 978-0-13-397461-4

Brief Contents

Contents

13 Population and Immigration 364

14 Technology and the Environment 395

15 Summing Up the Sociological Imagination: War and Global Insecurity 425

Special Features

Preface

This fifteenth edition of *Social Problems* appears as you are witnessing enormous turmoil in the Middle East, environmental devastation associated with climate change, continued acts of racism and sexism, growing income inequality, and terrorist acts at home and abroad. In Congress and elsewhere, Republicans warn of an impending debt crisis if public budgets are not cut, while Democrats fear that drastic cuts in spending will curtail the economic recovery and unfairly penalize those in the greatest need of social programs. During the life of this edition, the United States will have a presidential election and a new round of congressional and Senate elections in the states. For many voters these elections will represent a referendum on the Obama administration's wide-reaching healthcare reforms and its policies toward the environment, education, and international affairs to name only a few of the major social policy areas that a national election will test. Does that mean we can expect enormous progress toward solving domestic and global social problems? Not likely, because the problems discussed in this text have been with us for generations and do not admit of easy solutions. But no doubt there will be changes in policy based on trends that we can already determine.

Fortunately, for every major social problem there are groups of people dedicated to seeking a solution. Some of them are experts on particular social problems, like the members of the medical profession who each day confront the tragedies of infectious disease, or the teachers who work hard to educate all students, or the scientists who work to better understand climate change and how worst case scenarios can be avoided. Others are nonprofessionals, often citizens who have decided to devote themselves to doing something about a particular situation or problem. Among these activists are people who have experienced the condition they seek to improve—women who have suffered sexual assault, people who know what it is to be homeless, drug and alcohol abusers who want to help themselves and others, and neighbors confronted with the dumping of toxic wastes. Such groups may include elected officials and other political leaders who are expected to formulate sound social policies to address social problems. This book is written in an effort to make their work more effective and in the hope that some readers will be moved to take up their causes. We dedicate it to the citizens of the world who devote some of their precious time on earth to helping others.

Organization of the Book

The overarching goal of this text is to impart a sociological imagination—what students may initially see as individual issues are actually rooted in the social arrangements of society. Many personal troubles are really social problems, and these require social solutions to be resolved. This fifteenth edition uses four main themes to guide students as they learn to apply the sociological imagination. These themes include (1) using an empirical approach; (2) linking individual experience with social structure; (3) recognizing that social inequality contributes to social problems; and (4) using a comparative approach. Each of these themes are discussed in the opening chapter, revisited throughout the text, and then highlighted again in the concluding chapter.

The first few chapters of this book focus on seemingly individual behaviors, such as health care, drug use and crime. However, students will learn that these issues also have social roots. The social institutions and other factors that affect these behaviors are noted and described, and individual personal experience are clearly linked to structural factors. The middle chapters focus on inequality and discrimination, discussing such topics as poverty, racism, sexism, and ageism. Every attempt has been made to indicate the effects of discrimination on individuals, as well as to deal with the concept of institutionalized inequalities. Later chapters discuss problems that are common to many societies, such as those related to family life and work. The final chapters—on population and immigration, environmental pollution, and war and terrorism—focus on matters of great global significance. An attempt has been made throughout the text to identify how the different problems overlap and are interrelated.

Pedagogical Devices

Social Problems has been designed to be as helpful as possible to both students and teachers. Each problem is discussed in a well-organized and clear manner with personal vignettes and current examples. The treatment of each problem is analytical as well as descriptive and includes the most up-to-date examples and research findings available.

Each chapter begins with learning objectives and a personal opening vignette designed to grab student interest. Important terms within the chapter are boldfaced and listed at the end of the chapter, and their definitions are included in the glossary at the end of the book. In addition, boxed discussions in each chapter deal with current controversies or interesting solutions. In boxes, *A Personal View*, topics are first-person accounts, and include such topics as personal experiences with racism, illegal immigration, sex trafficking, poverty, fatherhood, and unemployment. Boxes entitled *A Closer Look* examine a problem that has been in the recent public spotlight, such as racial profiling, the outsourcing of jobs, or poverty, and show how controversies over the problem are addressed by research. Many chapters also include a box, entitled *A Global View*, that discusses a particular social problem from a global perspective, such as maternal and child health, female genital mutilation, or education in less developed countries.

In keeping with the book's effort to explore different solutions to social problems, there is a section at the end of each chapter called *Going Beyond Left and Right*. Its purpose is to help students think critically about the partisan debates over the problems discussed in the chapter they have just read.

Changes in the Fifteenth Edition

REVEL™
Educational technology designed for the way today's students read, think, and learn

When students are engaged deeply, they learn more effectively and perform better in their courses. This simple fact inspired the creation of REVEL: an immersive learning experience designed for the way today's students read, think, and learn. Built in collaboration with educators and students nationwide, REVEL is the newest, fully digital way to deliver respected Pearson content.

REVEL enlivens course content with media interactives and assessments—integrated directly within the authors' narrative—that provide opportunities for students to read about and practice course material in tandem. This immersive educational technology boosts student engagement, which leads to better understanding of concepts and improved performance throughout the course.

Learn more about REVEL

www.pearsonhighered.com/revel/

The fifteenth edition of Social Problems has taken on a new co-author, Karen Seccombe, who brings a fresh perspective to an already solid text. Each chapter has been extensively

revised with chapter objectives and current examples that resonate with students, such as the legalization of same-sex marriage, sexual assault among college students, excessive police force against unarmed Blacks, climate change, and terrorism. Throughout the text, greater emphasis is given to signature concepts such as gender, race, class, human rights, and globalization, reflecting the addition of new co-author Karen Seccombe.

The reception given to previous editions of *Social Problems* by both colleagues and students has been encouraging, and many of their suggestions and criticisms have been incorporated in this most recent revision. This fifteenth edition is both comprehensive and up-to-date. Our aim has been to retain the book's emphasis on the sociological analysis of social problems, as well as the policies designed to alleviate or eliminate them. Although policies change continually, we have attempted to update the discussions of policy to reflect the most recent thinking about solutions to social problems, using the most current data available.

- **Chapter 1**, Sociological Perspectives on Social Problems, introduces four main themes that run throughout the text to enhance students' sociological imagination: (1) Using an Empirical Approach; (2) Linking Individual Experience with Social Structure; (3) Recognizing That Social Inequality Contributes to Social Problems; and (4) Using a Comparative Approach. Our primary goal is to encourage students to think sociologically about the complex world around them, rather than to simply memorize a collection of random facts.

- **Chapter 2**, Problems of Health and Health Care, has been significantly expanded to examine the inequities and high cost of health care, which are important concerns that led to the passage of the Affordable Care Act (ACA). This historical legislation is discussed in depth. This chapter also contains expanded coverage of international health issues. New material has been added on the cultural and demographic factors affecting health and health care, such as obesity, smoking, and an aging population.

- **Chapter 3**, Problems with Mental Illness and Treatment, covers important issues related to mental illness and its treatment. This chapter is unique among social problem texts. This edition contains expanded coverage of suicide in the United States and worldwide. The chapter also contains new information on PTSD of military personnel, homelessness among those with mental illness, and current issues surrounding deinstitutionalization.

- **Chapter 4**, Alcohol and Other Drugs, contains several new features. First, it more thoroughly discusses alcohol and drug use among groups within the population. It also provides a detailed description of each of the more well-used substances. It elaborates on the social problems associated with alcohol and drug use, such as health issues, crime, and the consequences of driving while impaired. The chapter also contains a new section on the effects of alcohol on families, including codependency, enabling behaviors, and roles that children often adopt to cope with their parents alcohol use.

- **Chapter 5**, Crime and Violence, contains the most up-to-date statistics from the FBI and other national data sources. It also has expanded coverage of hate crimes and contains a new section on gender-based violence. Included is a policy discussion of gun control.

- **Chapter 6**, Poverty Amid Affluence, expands the discussion of the causes and consequences of poverty for both children and adults. Issues related to nutrition and food insecurity, inadequate housing, and health and well-being have added. The chapter now contains a more thorough discussion of welfare programs.

- **Chapter 7**, Race and Racism, provides recent data to demonstrate the changing racial composition of the United States. Recent research findings and current examples show that racism continues to persist. Content on institutional discrimination includes new information on education, income, housing, and the criminal justice system, including the death penalty.

- **Chapter 8**, Sex and Gender, focuses on sexism, male hegemony, and inequality internationally and in the United States. New to this edition is extensive coverage of female genital mutilation, sexist standards of beauty for women, sexual assault, and women's labor force experiences. A policy discussion of the Women's Movement has also been included.

- **Chapter 9**, An Aging Society, examines the structural and individual-level changes that accompany an aging population. Along with the most up-to-date statistics, the chapter contains new coverage of family issues, same-sex elders, long-term care, and death with dignity. This chapter also contains important international data on aging.

- **Chapter 10**, Changing Families, has been significantly revamped to identify the changing norms in marriage and intimate relationships, such as delayed marriage, the rise in cohabitation, the legalization of same-sex marriage, and the division of household labor. Also new to the text is a comparison of conservative, liberal, and feminist reactions to these changes. The chapter also reviews two critical issues in considerable depth: violence (among intimates and child abuse), and divorce.

- **Chapter 11**, Problems of Education, contains new data throughout, and a heightened discussion of differences in education across racial and ethnic groups and the unique barriers that groups face. The chapter also contains new international comparisons in educational achievement. Current challenges in providing high quality education to all students receive greater focus, including early childhood education.

- **Chapter 12**, Problems of Work and the Economy, contains several new or heightened discussions, including Americans' views of the economy and recession, global markets and sweatshops, and the effects of the changing economy on American workers, such as the growth in contingent jobs, the erosion of the purchasing power of the minimum wage, and the movement to raise the minimum wage to $15 an hour.

- **Chapter 13**, Population and Immigration, contains recent data on worldwide population trends. The chapter contains new information on rising expectations around the world and the realities of factors such as literacy, energy use, and food distribution and hunger. New information has been added on government population control efforts, comparing and contrasting China with Japan. Coverage of immigration has been expanded significantly, including a policy discussion of child immigrants from Central America fleeing gang violence.

- **Chapter 14**, Technology and the Environment, has been substantially updated. There is expanded coverage of environmental stress, including climate change, air pollution, water pollution, solid waste, and toxic wastes. Environmental racism is discussed. The latest scientific evidence is presented in a clear fashion, readily accessible to students.

- **Chapter 15**, Summing Up the Sociological Imagination: War and Global Insecurity, reviews the four themes of the text in the context of war and terrorism. This chapter has been revised given the state of the world in late 2015 as the book goes to press. Well-known recent terrorist attacks in the United States and abroad are discussed, and students are introduced to the major current terrorist groups. These issues are used to highlight the importance of the sociological imagination. While war is experienced on a personal level, it is also a social problem requiring large-scale social solutions.

Throughout the text, statistical material, figures, and tables have been updated, content is current, and recent research has been cited throughout. The *Social Policy* sections incorporate recent cutting-edge programs and proposals. Timely feature boxes have been included designed to enhance student interest.

Supplements

Instructors and students who use this textbook have access to a number of materials designed to complement the classroom lectures and activities and to enhance the students' learning experience. The following supplements can be downloaded by adopters from the Pearson Instructor Resource Center at www.pearsonhighered.com/irc.

Instructor's Manual Each chapter in the instructor's manual includes the following resources: learning objectives, lecture outline and suggestions, discussion questions, and class exercises. The instructor's manual is available for download at www.pearsonhighered.com/irc.

Test Bank The test bank includes multiple-choice and essay questions that focus on basic comprehension, and understanding and applying concepts. It is available for download at www.pearsonhighered.com/irc and in MyTest for generating tests electronically.

MyTest This computerized software allows instructors to create their own personalized exams, to edit any or all of the existing test questions, and to add new questions. Other special features of this program include random generation of test questions, creation of alternate versions of the same test, scrambling question sequence, and test preview before printing. For easy access, this software is available for download at www.pearsonhighered.com/irc.

PowerPoint Presentations The PowerPoint presentations are informed by instructional and design theory. The Lecture PowerPoint slides follow the chapter outline and learning objectives. Images from the textbook are also integrated within the slides. The PowerPoints are uniquely designed to present concepts in a clear and succinct manner. They are available for download at www.pearsonhighered.com/irc.

Acknowledgments

Revising and updating a social problems textbook is a formidable task, and new author Karen Seccombe learned a great deal in the process. Social Problems is a broad field with many critical issues that change rapidly. This edition has benefits from the reviews of many sociologists, all of whom have contributed useful comments and suggestions:

Donna Abrams, Georgia Gwinnette College
Tammie Foltz, Des Moines Area Community College
Laura Hansen, Western New England University
Kendra Murphey, University of Memphis
Ken Rudolph, Asheville-Buncombe Technical
    Community College
Patricia Sawyer, University of Bridgeport
Aleesa Young, Asheville-Buncombe Technical
    Community College

Many thanks are due to the keen publishing specialists who contributed their talents and energy to this edition. Mary Gawlik worked tirelessly as the developmental editor to ensure that this text was organized and expressed ideas with fluidity. The staff at Pearson–Rob DeGeorge, Program Manager, Lynne Breitfeller, Project Manager, Laura Hernandez, Editorial Assistant.

Finally, because a book is never a solo venture, it's important to acknowledge the assistance of Portland State University, and my friends and colleagues who offered support along the way, including those in the community of Friday Harbor, Washington. In particular, Richard, Natalie, Olivia, Bart, and Stella Meenan—my pack—have my eternal gratitude.

About the Author of Social Problems, Fifteenth Edition

Karen Seccombe is a Professor at Portland State University, in Portland, Oregon. A proud community college graduate, she received the mentoring and support to continue her education in sociology and social work. She earned her PhD at Washington State University, in Pullman. Karen is the author of several books, including, So You Think I Drive a Cadillac?; Families and Their Social Worlds; Exploring Marriages and Families; Families in Poverty; and Just Don't Get Sick. Her work focuses on the health and well-being of poor and vulnerable families. She is a Fellow in the National Council on Family Relationships, and is active in the American Sociological Association and in the Pacific Sociological Association. She is a Fulbright Scholar, and taught in Hangzhou, China. Karen is married to Richard Meenan, a health economist, and has two children, Natalie and Olivia, and two Australian Shepherds, Bart and Stella. She enjoys hiking, cycling, and relaxing with her pack in the San Juan islands off the coast of Washington. She enjoys hearing from students and faculty, so please send any comments her way: seccombe@pdx.edu

Chapter 1
Sociological Perspectives on Social Problems

 ## Learning Objectives

1.1 Explain the sociological imagination.

1.2 Discuss the definition of a social problem.

1.3 Compare and contrast the three main sociological perspectives on social problems.

1.4 Describe the process that reveals the natural history of social problems.

1.5 Review the four themes of the text.

1.6 Assess the social policy debates between conservatives and liberals.

Eleven-year-old Meghan sat wide-eyed in front of the television with her parents, watching the devastation in Nepal unfold after the 2015 major earthquake that rocked the region. She learned that thousands of people had been killed, and many more were injured, homeless, hungry, and without fresh water. She felt sad that so many people were suffering, and she wanted to help. "But what can one person do?", she thought. Almost embarrassed by the size of the contribution she had in mind, she turned to her mother and said, "Can we send my allowance to them?" Natural disasters like earthquakes, floods, droughts, and heat waves are usually not what we think of when someone is talking about "social problems." Yet natural disasters like these can be caused or exacerbated by broader structural problems in society. Poverty, social inequality, political corruption, racism, or environmental degradation can be a factor in natural disasters and can contribute to the untold suffering of millions in the aftermath. For example, patterns and the speed of emergency food and water distribution, medical supplies, and tents for makeshift housing are often related to these types of social problems. Yet, as big as these problems are, it is a combination of big and small efforts that can make a profound difference in the world, be it the devastating earthquake in Nepal, or the unforgiving drought in California.

Record droughts in California, the Ebola outbreaks in western Africa, unarmed blacks being killed by police officers, sexual assaults on college campuses, Islamic terrorists, record social inequality, continued discrimination, and millions of Americans without health insurance. In such difficult times, Americans may rightly wonder whether we are capable of successfully addressing our most severe problems, let alone the world's. This question is one that will arise in specific ways in this book's chapters, but you will also see that that there is little to be gained by giving in to failure. The history of efforts to address issues of environmental degradation, health problems, crime, racism and sexism, terrorism, poverty, and access to health care presents many bright spots and evidence that the more everyone understands the problems and the more citizens become engaged in seeking solutions, the more successfully society will address social problems.

The United States and other Western nations are experiencing more conflict about how to address social problems than was true in the decades after World War II. For a few decades after the devastation and collective sacrifices of World War II, there was far more consensus that government should play an important role in providing a "social safety net" for society's members who lacked the means to provide an adequate level of living for themselves and their children. Today, there is widespread debate about public versus private responsibility for addressing issues such as poverty, ill health, and environmental degradation. The ongoing "culture wars," as today's political ideological divisions and debates are often called, make it far more difficult for people to arrive at a broad consensus about which social policies and programs are most effective for dealing with major social problems. No doubt there will be many instances in which readers of this text will want to argue strongly for one set of policies versus another, and doing so is perfectly legitimate and desirable. This text utilizes a social-scientific approach to these problems, which can lead to progress in understanding their causes and arriving at policies to address them. As part of this strategy, every chapter in this book ends with a discussion of how social policies at different levels of government and in the private sector can address specific social problems.

The Sociological Imagination

1.1 Explain the sociological imagination.

We live in a world of more than 7.3 billion people, and we share a society with hundreds of millions. Despite the hugeness of humanity, most people think of themselves as unique individuals and as having distinctive experiences like no other. However, many of their personal experiences are not unique or exceptional. Instead, they are patterned and are shaped by **social structure**, which is the organized arrangements of relationships and institutions that together form the basis of society. For example, how has your sex influenced your life experience? Has being male or being female

social structure

The organized arrangements of relationships and institutions that together form the basis of society.

influenced your choice of a college major or your hobbies, interests, and relationships? Has your sex influenced your willingness to take drugs, commit crime, or enlist in the army and go to war? Has it influenced whether you have been sexually assaulted or battered by a partner? Perhaps another way of framing this question is how would your life be different if you were the "opposite sex"? In other words, there is a relatively organized set of arrangements associated with your sex.

Taking another example, how has your family affected you? You may have grown up with one parent, two parents, or with no parents at all. How did your family arrangement affect your financial well-being, your social capital, and overall opportunities? If your mother used drugs or alcohol, if your father was in jail, or if an uncle sexually abused you, how do you think those experiences may have affected your life? Families are a primary social institution in all societies and have a profound influence

A Personal View

Running Away to My Future

Jody is a vibrant 27-year-old single mother who has a bright future ahead of her after a rocky start in life. She was awarded a $7,500 annual scholarship that will help her to attend a four-year university next fall. The scholarship award committee noted "her steadfast determination and her potential to make a difference." These words are an apt description.

Jody was born to a single-mother who was poor and addicted to drugs. As a young child, Jody bounced from one home to another, often sleeping on the couch of her mother's latest boyfriend. Nourishing food was scarce, and Jody often went to school hungry. Her mother failed to fill out the forms for the school lunch program, but the school staff could see that Jody was hungry in the morning and let her eat breakfast with the other students who needed it. After school, Jody usually went home to an empty house, left on her own to do homework and make dinner.

Jody loved school, and diligently did her homework every day. School was her refuge. Because she excelled at school, was rarely absent or tardy, and completed her homework, the school assumed that Jody's home life was fine.

As the years went by, Jody did her best to hide the consequences of her family's poverty. She shopped for clothes at the Goodwill when she had a little extra money, and hunted for stylish clothes that would not reveal her secret. But one night her mother's latest live-in boyfriend crawled into bed with Jody, who was by then a budding 16-year-old girl, and tried to sexually assault her. Jody screamed, hit him, and ran out of the room, stumbling over her passed-out mother in the living room. Jody vowed to never go back home as long as he was living there. When she confronted her mother the next day, her mother insisted that the boyfriend was staying, and it was Jody who could leave.

Jody took some of her mother's drug money, which amounted to a few hundred dollars, a few clothes, and ran away. With her money, she bought a sleeping bag and supplies to camp out under a bridge with other homeless people. She got a job at a fast-food restaurant making minimum wage. All the while, she continued to go to school, cleaning herself up and washing her hair in the restroom at work. Despite her hardship, she graduated from high school with a B average.

Community college was her next step, but by this time, the stress of homelessness, a dead-end job, and schoolwork were taking their toll. She suffered from depression, which caused her to make a number of risky choices. She became pregnant. The father did not stick around, and the thought of raising a child in her circumstances depressed her even more. Jody decided to give the baby up for adoption. She cried for weeks before and after her decision, but knew in her heart it was the right thing to do. However, by this time, Jody was severely depressed, had dropped out of school, lost her job, and was begging on the street. She lived this way for several years, begging and earning just enough to buy food. Begging meant giving up her pride, but she said that part of living in poverty is blocking out how others might judge you.

By the time Jody was 22, she became pregnant a second time. However, on this occasion, she was determined to keep her baby and do whatever it would take to provide a good home. She sought out social service agencies and asked them for help. A counselor located low-income housing, arranged for medical care so Jody could get the depression medicine she needed, set her up with a part-time job, and helped her enroll back into community college. Jody began to flourish. She loved being a mother and felt that her son gave her life true meaning. She graduated from her community college with honors, and at the advice of the college's financial aid office, applied and received a scholarship to complete her degree. As she says it, "When I left home at 16, I had no idea that I was running away to my future. With the help that others have offered, I can do this."

Critical Thinking

Using a sociological imagination, how were Jody's choices and constraints shaped by larger social forces? Why do most people consider poverty a social problem rather than simply a personal experience of a few people like Jody?

on personal experiences. The box A Personal View—Running Away to My Future offers an example of the ways in which early family life can shape adulthood.

Using a sociological imagination reveals general patterns in what otherwise might be thought of as simple random events. C. Wright Mills stressed the importance of understanding the relationship between individuals and the society in which they live (Mills, 1959). Problems such as poverty, divorce, substance abuse, crime, and child abuse are more than just personal troubles experienced by a few people. They are issues that affect large numbers of people and originate in society's institutional arrangements. In other words, individual experiences are linked to the social structure.

Peter Berger elaborated on these ideas in his 1963 book *Invitation to Sociology*. Although we like to think of ourselves as individuals, much of our behavior (and others' behavior toward us) is actually patterned on the basis of what social categories we fall into, such as age, income, race, ethnicity, sex, and physical appearance. For example, men and women behave differently for reasons that often have nothing to do with biology. Many of these patterns are socially produced. In other words, boys and girls, men and women, are each taught and encouraged to think of themselves differently from one another and to behave in different ways. Society lends a hand in shaping people's lives. Why are over 85 percent of students in bachelor of science in nursing (BSN) programs female (National League for Nursing, 2015)? This demographic fact is obviously not the result of some biological imperative, some quirk of the occupation itself, or some random event. Rather, society even has a hand in shaping something as seemingly personal and individual as the choice of a college major.

Émile Durkheim (1897) conducted an early study on the subject of suicide, documenting how social structure affects human behavior. At first glance, what could be more private and individualized than the reasons that surround a person's decision to take his or her own life? The loss of a loving relationship, job troubles, financial worries, and low self-esteem are just a few of the many reasons that a person may have for suicide. Yet looking through official records and death certificates, Durkheim noted that suicide was not a completely random event and that there were several important patterns worthy of attention. He found that men were more likely to kill themselves than were women. He noted that Protestants were more likely to take their lives than were Catholics and Jews. He found that wealthy people were more likely to commit suicide than were the poor. Finally, it appeared that unmarried people were more likely to kill themselves than were married people.

Although his study was conducted over 100 years ago, recent research indicates that these patterns persist. Suicide today is a major social problem, with about 40,000 individuals taking their lives each year. It is the tenth leading cause of death for all Americans, and the second leading cause for youths ages 15 to 24 (Centers for Disease Control and Prevention, 2014).

The sociological imagination draws attention to the fact that seemingly private issues are often public ones (Mills, 1959). Moreover, when these issues affect the quality of life for a large number of people, they are called social problems.

What is a Social Problem?

1.2 Discuss the definition of a social problem.

When enough people in a society agree that a condition exists that threatens the quality of their lives and their most cherished values, *and* they agree that something should be done to remedy that condition, sociologists say that the society has defined that condition as a **social problem**. In other words, the society's members have reached a consensus that a condition that affects some people is a problem for the entire society, not just for those who are directly affected. Figure 1–1 illustrates trends in the issues considered to be the five top social problems between 2001 and 2014: the economy, unemployment, the government, health care, and immigration (Saul, 2015).

What Do You Think?

Evaluate your social class standing when you were a child. For example, did your parent(s) go to college? Did your parent(s) have a steady job? What type of house did you grow up in? Now describe how this social class standing has influenced your lifestyle and choices today.

---

social problem

Widespread agreement that a condition threatens the quality of life and cherished values and that something should be done to remedy that condition.

Figure 1-1 Most Important Problems Facing the United States by Percentage, 2001–2014

SOURCE: Saul, 2015.

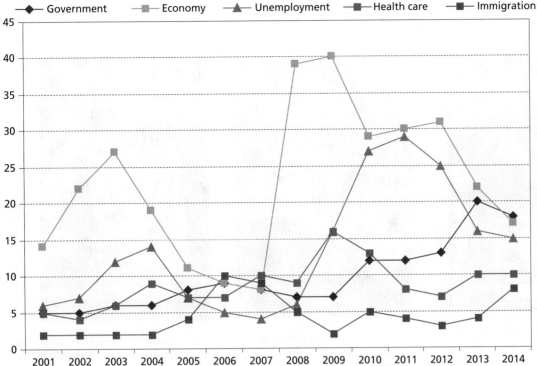

You will see, however, that for every social problem, arguments arise about the nature of the problem, its severity, and the best remedies—laws, social programs, or other policies—to address it. There must be enough consensus among people in a society that a problem exists for action to take place, but consensus on a problem does not indicate consensus on the solution. For example, most Americans are concerned about crime, but what to do about it is wide open to discussion. Some people favor mandatory sentencing for specific crimes, while others feel that a judge or jury should have some discretion. Some people support the death penalty for heinous crimes, while others oppose the death penalty and believe that life in prison without parole is the most appropriate punishment. Moreover, this text will also show that not all people have an equal ability to define social problems and to propose remedies; those with power often have more say in the matter.

Social problems are often closely interrelated. Crime, poverty, lack of medical care, violence, drug abuse, environmental degradation, and many other behaviors or situations that we commonly think of as social problems rarely exist in isolation. And for any one of the problems just named or others we could cite, the causes, responsibilities, and solutions are vigorously debated. Are we responsible, some ask, for the sins of others? For example, are not many people poor because they choose to drop out of school or have a baby before they were financially prepared to do so? Or are many people poor because of the erosion of the purchasing power of the minimum wage and social conditions like racism and sexism? These and similar arguments assert not only the causes of social problems but also what should be done about them. People may agree that certain conditions are social problems. Most members of society agree that these conditions ought to be remedied through intentional action. However, people disagree about, and politicize, what the causes are and what the precise intentional action should be.

For example, many Americans are appalled at the level of gun violence in their nation, but many others are equally appalled at the prospect of more government restrictions on their freedom to buy and use guns as they wish. Clearly, recognition

Slide Show

Where People Stand on Social Issues

Surveys based on representative samples of adults in the United States provide an important gauge of where people stand on social issues. A recent Gallup Poll survey reports that the top social problems in American society today are considered to be the economy, unemployment, the government, health care, and immigration. This slide show takes a look at these issues, with data provided by the Pew Research Center (June 2014) and Realty Trac (2015).

When housing prices began to tumble in the height of the recession, many people found that they owed more on their house than it was worth. Some people could no longer afford to make the payments and their house went into foreclosure. Although the economy has improved considerably since then, economic issues are still considered the top social problem. In May 2015—just one month—there were over 120,000 new foreclosure filings.

A national sample of adults ranked government third in a list of social problems. The majority of both conservatives and liberals say that they often or always do not trust the federal government, and that they feel angry toward it. The level of agreement is striking, given that these two groups see the role of government very differently.

Immigration is also ranked by Americans as a pressing social problem. However, the exact nature of the problem and what to do about it are not clear-cut. For example, the majority of Americans say that immigration actually strengthens our country through immigrants' hard work and talent. And most Americans believe that immigrants who live in the United States illegally should be eligible for citizenship if certain requirements are met.

Unemployment is more than a personal problem. At the height of the recession, when the national unemployment rate was over 10 percent, the federal government extended the amount of weeks a person could collect unemployment. That policy reflected the idea that unemployment is a social problem, not simply an individual issue.

Many Americans are concerned about health care. They see rapidly escalating costs and worry about a lack of access as fewer employers offer health insurance as a fringe benefit. The Affordable Care Act was created during President Obama's administration to decrease these problems and has met with some success. However, political backlash was swift, and today many people still oppose the Affordable Care Act.

Critical Thinking

Why do you think that these five social problems were rated as the most significant? What changes would you make in this list, and why?

that a social problem exists is far different from arriving at a consensus about a cause and a solution to the problem.

For better or worse, even in mature democracies like those of the United States and Europe, more powerful people have far greater influence in defining social problems than average citizens do. Rupert Murdoch, for example, is an Australian-born businessman who owns television and newspaper companies not only in the United States and Great Britain but also throughout the world. His media empire includes the Fox network and many others that adhere to his personal editorial views, which are strongly opposed to government intervention in the battle against poverty and lack of health care and very much in favor of a strong role for government in combating crime and pursuing the global "war" on terrorism.

The importance of power in the definition of social problems becomes clear if you consider one or two examples. In China, before the Communist revolution of the mid-twentieth century, opium use and addiction were widespread. In Shanghai alone, there were an estimated 400,000 opium addicts in the late 1940s. Everyone knew that the condition existed, and many responsible public figures deplored it, but few outside the revolutionary parties believed society should intervene in any way. After all, many of the country's richest and most powerful members had made their fortunes in the opium trade. However, the Chinese Communists believed society should take responsibility for eradicating opium addiction, and when they took power, they did so often through drastic and violent means. What had previously been seen as a social condition had been redefined as a social problem that had to be solved.

To take an example from our own society, before 1920, women in the United States did not have the right to vote. Many women objected to this condition, but most men and many women valued the traditional pattern of male dominance and female subservience. To them, there was nothing unusual about women's status as second-class citizens. It took many years of painstaking organization, persuasion, and demonstration by the leaders of the women's suffrage movement to convince significant numbers of Americans that women's lack of voting rights was a problem that society should remedy through revision of its laws. You will see later in the book, especially in Chapter 8, that many of the conditions affecting women's lives continue to be viewed by some members of society as natural and inevitable and by others as problems that require action by society as a whole.

It is worth noting that the idea that a society should intervene to remedy conditions that affect the lives of its citizens is a fairly recent innovation. Until the eighteenth century, for example, most people worked at exhausting tasks under poor conditions for long hours; they suffered from severe deprivation all their lives, and they often died young, sometimes of terrible diseases. But no one thought of these things as problems to be solved. They were accepted as natural, inevitable conditions of life. It was not until the so-called "enlightenment" of the late eighteenth century that philosophers began to argue that poverty is not inevitable, but a result of an unjust social system. As such, changing the system itself through means such as redistribution of wealth and elimination of inherited social status could alleviate many problems.

Sociological Perspectives on Social Problems

1.3 Compare and contrast the three main sociological perspectives on social problems.

Everyone has opinions about the causes of social problems and what should be done about them. In addition to Sociology, other disciplines in the social sciences are concerned with the analysis of human behavior, and sociologists often draw on the results

Table 1–1 Other Approaches to the Study of Social Problems

History

History is the study of the past. However, historical data can be used by sociologists to understand present social problems. In studying homelessness, for example, historians would focus on changes in how people obtained shelter in a society and what groups or individuals tended to be without shelter in different historical periods.

Cultural Anthropology

Cultural anthropologists study the social organization and development of smaller, nonindustrial societies, both past and present. Because cultural anthropology is closely related to sociology, many of the same techniques can be used in both fields, and the findings of cultural anthropologists regarding primitive and traditional cultures shed light on related phenomena in more complex, modern societies. An anthropological study of homelessness would look closely at one or a few groups of homeless people. The anthropologist might be interested in how the homeless and others in their communities understand their situation and what might be done about it.

Psychology and Social Psychology

Psychology focuses on human mental and emotional processes, primarily on individual experience. Rooted in biology, it is more experimental than the other social sciences. An understanding of the psychological pressures that underlie individual responses can illuminate social attitudes and behavior. Thus, a psychologist would tend to study the influences of homelessness on the individual's state of mind or, conversely, how the individual's personality and ways of looking at life might have contributed to his or her situation.

Social psychology involves the study of how psychological processes, behavior, and personalities of individuals influence or are influenced by social processes and social settings. It is of particular value for the study of social problems. A social psychologist would be likely to study how life on the streets damages the individual in various ways.

Economics

Economists study the levels of income in a society and the distribution of income among the society's members. To understand how the resources of society—its people and their talents, its land and other natural resources—can be allocated for the maximum benefit of that society, economists also study the relationship between the supply of resources and the demand for them. Confronted with the problem of homelessness, an economist would tend to study how the supply of and demand for different types of housing influence the number of homeless people in a given housing market.

Political Science

Political scientists study the workings of government at every level of society. As Harold Lasswell (1941), a leading American political scientist, put it, "Politics is the study of who gets what, when, and how." A political scientist, therefore, would be likely to see homelessness as a problem that results from the relative powerlessness of the homeless to influence the larger society to respond to their needs. The political scientist would tend to focus on ways in which the homeless could mobilize other political interest groups to urge legislators to deal with the problem.

of their research. The work of historians, for example, is vital to an understanding of the origins of many social problems. Anthropologists look at other societies and offer contrasting views of how humans have learned to cope with various kinds of social problems. Perhaps the greatest overlap is between sociology and political science, both of which are concerned with the development of social policies to curb social problems. Other social-scientific approaches to the study of social problems are described in Table 1–1.

Contemporary sociology is founded on three basic perspectives, or sets of ideas, that offer theories about why societies hang together and how and why they change. These perspectives are not the only sociological approaches to social problems, but they can be extremely powerful tools for understanding them. Each of these perspectives—functionalism, conflict theory, and symbolic interactionism—gives rise to a number of useful and distinctive approaches to the study of social problems, as identified in Table 1–2. The following sections explore these three approaches, using criminal deviance as an example to show the unique contributions of each perspective.

The Functionalist Perspective

From the day a person is born until the day that person dies, he or she holds a position—a **status**—in a variety of groups and organizations. In a hospital, for example, the patient, the nurse, the doctor, and the orderly are all members of a social group concerned with health care. Each of these individuals has a status that requires the

status

A social position.

Table 1–2 Major Sociological Perspectives on Social Problems

Perspective	View of Society and Social Problems	Origins of Social Problems	Proposed Solutions
Functionalist	Views society as a vast organism whose parts are interrelated; social problems are disruptions of this system. Also holds that problems of social institutions produce patterns of deviance and that institutions must address such patterns through strategic social change.	Social expectations fail, creating normlessness, culture conflict, and breakdown. Social problems also result from the impersonal operations of existing institutions, both now and in the past.	Engage in research and active intervention to improve social institutions. Create new organizations to address social problems.
Conflict	Views society as marked by conflicts due to inequalities in class, race, ethnicity, gender, age, and other divisions that produce conflicting values. Defines social problems as conditions that do not conform to society's values.	Groups with different values and differing amounts of power meet and compete.	Build stronger social movements among groups with grievances. The conflicting groups may then engage in negotiations and reach mutual accommodations.
Symbolic Interactionist	Holds that definitions of deviance or social problems are subjective; separates deviant and nondeviant people not by what they do but by how society reacts to what they do.	Society becomes aware that certain behaviors exist and labels them as social problems.	Resocializes deviants by increasing their contacts with accepted patterns of behavior; makes the social system less rigid. Changes the definition of what is considered deviant.

performance of a certain set of behaviors, known as a **role**. Taken together, the statuses and roles of the members of this medical team and other teams in hospitals throughout the country make up the social institution known as the health care system. An **institution** is a more or less stable structure of statuses and roles devoted to meeting the basic needs of people in a society. The health care system is an institution; hospitals, insurance companies, and private medical practices are examples of organizations within this institution.

The **functionalist perspective** looks at the way major social institutions like the family, the military, the health care system, and the police and courts actually operate. According to this perspective, the role behavior associated with any given status has evolved as a means of allowing a particular social institution to fulfill its function in society. Thus, the nurse's role requires specific knowledge and behaviors that involve treatment of the patient's immediate needs and administration of care according to the doctor's orders. The patient, in turn, is expected to cooperate in the administration of the treatment. When all members of the group perform their roles correctly, the group is said to be functioning well.

In a well-functioning group, there is general agreement about how roles are to be performed by each member. These expectations are reinforced by the society's basic values, from which are derived rules about how people should and should not behave toward one another in different situations. The Ten Commandments, the Golden Rule, the Bill of Rights, and the teachings of all of the world's religions are examples of sets of rules that specify how people should behave in different social roles.

But if a society is made up of groups in which people know their roles and adhere to the underlying values, why does that society have social problems like crime and warfare, and why does it seem so difficult to make social organizations function effectively? From the functionalist perspective, the main reason for the existence of social problems is that societies are always changing and having to adapt to new conditions; failure to adapt successfully leads to social problems.

The French social theorist Émile Durkheim observed that changes in a society can drastically alter the goals and functions of human groups and organizations. As a society undergoes a major change—say, from agricultural to industrial production—the statuses people assume and the roles they play also change, with far-reaching consequences. Thus, for example, the tendency for men and women from rural backgrounds

role
The performance of a certain set of behaviors that go with a status.

institution
A more or less stable structure of statuses and roles devoted to meeting the basic needs of people in a society, for example, the health care system.

functionalist perspective
A way of thinking that considers the way major social institutions such as the family, the military, the health care system, and the police and courts actually operate.

to have many children, which was functional in agrarian societies because it produced much-needed farmhands, can become a liability in an urban-industrial society, where housing space is limited and the types of jobs available are constantly changing. From the standpoint of society's smooth functioning, it can be said that the roles of the father and mother in the rural setting that stresses long periods of childbearing and many children become dysfunctional in an urban setting.

Wars; colonial conquest; disease and famine; population increases; changing technologies of production, communication, or health care—all these major social forces can change societies and thereby change the roles their members are expected to perform. As social groups strive to adapt to the new conditions, their members may feel that they are adrift—unsure of how to act or troubled by conflict over how to perform as parents or wage earners or citizens. They may question the values they learned as children and wonder what to teach their own children. This condition of social disequilibrium can lead to an increase in social problems like crime and mental illness as individuals seek their own, often antisocial, solutions to the dilemmas they face.

CRIMINAL DEVIANCE: A FUNCTIONALIST VIEW   From the functionalist perspective, all societies produce their own unique forms of crime and have their own ways of responding to them. All sociologists recognize that there are causes within the individual that help explain why one person becomes a criminal while another, who may have experienced the same conditions, does not. But for the sociologist, especially one who applies the functionalist perspective, the question of why particular crimes are committed and punished in some societies and not in others is an important research topic. Why is it that until quite recently a black man who was suspected of making advances to a white woman was often punished more severely than a black man who was suspected of stealing? Why was the theft of a horse punishable by immediate death on the early western frontier?

The functionalist answer is that societies fear most the crimes that seem to threaten their most cherished values, and individuals who dare to challenge those values will receive the most severe punishment. Thus, the freedom to allow one's horses to graze on common land was an essential aspect of early western frontier society that was threatened by the theft of horses. The possibility that a white woman could entice a black man and that their relationship could be interpreted as anything other than rape threatened the foundations of the American racial caste system, which held that blacks were inferior to whites. In both cases, immediate, sometimes brutal, punishment was used to reinforce the central values of the society.

SOCIAL PROBLEMS AS SOCIAL PATHOLOGY   In the late 1800s and early 1900s, functionalist theorists regarded crime and deviance as a form of "social disease" or social pathology. This view was rooted in the organic analogy that was popular at the time. Human society was seen as analogous to a vast organism, all of whose complex, interrelated parts function together to maintain the health and stability of the whole. Social problems arise when either individuals or social institutions fail to keep pace with changing conditions and thereby disrupt the healthy operation of the social organization; such individuals or institutions are considered "sick" (hence the term *social pathology*).

Although some people who comment on social problems today continue to use the organic analogy and the disease concept, most sociologists reject this notion. The social-pathology approach is not very useful in generating empirical research; its concepts of sickness and morality are too subjective to be meaningful to many sociologists. Moreover, it attempts to apply a biological analogy to social conditions even when there is no empirical justification for doing so. More important, it is associated with the idea that the poor and other "deviant" groups are less fit to survive from an evolutionary perspective and, hence, should not be encouraged to reproduce. The social-pathology approach therefore has been largely discredited. Modern functionalists do not focus on the behaviors and problems of individuals; instead, they see social problems as arising out of the failure of institutions like the family, the schools, and the economy to adapt to changing social conditions.

SOCIAL-DISORGANIZATION THEORY

Rates of immigration, urbanization, and industrialization increased rapidly after World War I. European immigrants, rural whites, and southern blacks were often crowded together in degrading slums and had trouble learning the language, manners, and norms of the dominant urban culture. Many of those who managed to adjust to the city were discriminated against because of their religion or race, and others lost their jobs because technological advances made their skills obsolete. Because of these conditions, many groups formed their own subcultures or devised other means of coping. Alcoholism, drug addiction, mental illness, crime, and delinquency rates rose drastically. Some sociologists believed the social-pathology viewpoint could not adequately explain the widespread existence of these social problems. They developed a new concept that eventually became known as social-disorganization theory.

A group of teenagers experience a sense of normlessness. They are neither adults nor children, and our culture has unclear expectations for people in this age group. They are told to go to high school, get good grades, play sports, and go to college. But this path is not of interest to all adolescents.

This theory views society as being organized by a set of expectations or rules. **Social disorganization** results when these expectations fail, and it is manifested in three major ways: (1) normlessness, which arises when people have no rules that tell them how to behave; (2) culture conflict, which occurs when people feel trapped by contradictory rules; and (3) breakdown, which takes place when obedience to a set of rules is not rewarded or is punished. Rapid social change, for example, might make traditional standards of behavior obsolete without providing new standards, thereby giving rise to normlessness. The children of immigrants might feel trapped between the expectations of their parents and those of their new society—an example of culture conflict. And the expectations of blacks might be frustrated when they do well in school but encounter job discrimination; their frustration, in turn, might lead to breakdown.

social disorganization

The result when rules break down; it is manifested in three major ways: normlessness, culture conflict, and breakdown.

The stress experienced by victims of social disorganization may result in a form of personal disorganization such as drug addiction or crime. The social system as a whole also feels the force of disorganization. It may respond by changing its rules, keeping contradictory rules in force, or breaking down. Disorganization can be halted or reversed if its causes are isolated and corrected.

MODERN FUNCTIONALISM: BUILDING INSTITUTIONS In this text, you will see many instances in which social-disorganization theory has been used to explain social problems. A more modern version of the functionalist perspective attempts to show how people reorganize their lives to cope with new conditions. Often this reorganization results in new kinds of organizations and sometimes in whole new institutions. This research focus is known as the institutional approach, or **institution building** (Caplan, 2005). Research on how to improve the organization of public schools to meet new educational demands is an example.

institution building

A modern version of the functionalist perspective, which attempts to show how people reorganize their lives to cope with new conditions.

The Conflict Perspective

conflict perspective

A way of thinking that is based on the belief that social problems arise out of major contradictions in the way societies are organized, contradictions that lead to large-scale conflict between those who have access to the good life and those who do not.

By no means do all sociologists adopt the functionalist view of society and social problems. A **conflict perspective** claims that the functionalist idea (that social problems can be corrected by reforming institutions that are not functioning well) is misleading because it ignores dimensions of power. The conflict perspective is based on the belief that social problems arise out of major contradictions in the way societies are organized, contradictions that lead to conflict between those who have access to the good life and those who do not. This perspective owes much of its early development to the writings of Karl Marx (1818–1883), the German social theorist who developed many of the central ideas of modern socialism.

In *Manifesto of the Communist Party* (Marx and Engels, 1848), *Capital* (Marx, 1867), and other works, Marx attempted to prove that social problems such as unemployment, poverty, crime, corruption, and warfare are not usually the fault of individuals or of poorly functioning organizations. Instead, he argued, their origins may be found in the way societies arrange access to wealth and power. According to Marx, the social problems of modern societies arise from capitalism. An inevitable outcome of capitalism is class conflict, especially conflict between those who own the means of production (factories, land, and so forth) and those who sell their labor for wages. In such a system, workers are exploited by their bosses, for whom the desire to make a profit outweighs any humanitarian impulse to take care of their employees.

In the capitalist system as Marx described it, the capitalist is driven by the profit motive to find ways to reduce labor costs—for example, through the purchase of new machinery that can do the work of several people or by building factories in places where people will work for less money. These actions continually threaten the livelihood of workers. Often they lose their jobs, and their lives are thrown into disarray. Sometimes they resort to crime or even begin revolutions to overturn the system in which they are the have-nots, and the owners of capital are the haves. In general, for Marx and modern Marxian sociologists, social problems may be attributed to the ways in which wealth and power become concentrated in the hands of a few people and to the many forms of conflict engendered by these inequalities.

Marxian conflict theory can be a powerful tool in the analysis of contemporary social problems. To illustrate this point, the following section looks at how this theory explains criminal deviance in societies like the United States.

DEVIANCE: A MARXIAN CONFLICT VIEW   Marxists believe that crime and deviance do not occur merely because such organizations as the police and the courts function in certain ways or do not function as they were intended to. Instead, Marxian theorists believe such situations are a result of differences in the power of various groups or classes in society. For example, top organized-crime figures have the money and power to influence law enforcement officials or to hire the best attorneys when they are arrested. Street drug dealers, in contrast, are relatively powerless to resist arrest. Moreover, they serve as convenient targets for an official show of force against drug trafficking. From the Marxian perspective, the rich and powerful are able to determine what kinds of behaviors are defined as social problems because they control major institutions such as the government, the schools, and the courts. They are also able to shift the blame for the conditions that produce those problems to groups that are less able to defend themselves, namely, the poor and the working class.

Scholars who adopt a Marxian perspective tend to be critical of proposals to reform existing institutions. Since they attribute most social problems to underlying patterns of class conflict and power differentials, they do not believe that existing institutions such as prisons and courts can address the basic causes of those problems. Usually, therefore, their research looks at the ways in which the material conditions of society, such as inequalities of wealth and power, seem to account for the distribution of social problems in a population. Or they conduct research on social movements among the poor and the working class in an attempt to understand how those movements might mobilize large numbers of people into a force that could bring about major changes in the way society is organized.

VALUE CONFLICT THEORY The Marxian theory of class conflict cannot explain all the kinds of conflict that occur around us every day. In families, for example, conflicts may range from seemingly trivial arguments over television programs to intense disputes over issues like drinking or drug use; in neighborhoods, conflicts may occur between landlords and tenants, between parents and school administrators, or between groups of parents who differ on matters of educational policy such as sex education or the rights of female athletes. Such conflict often focuses not on deep-seated class antagonisms but on differences in values. For most feminist groups, for example, abortion is a social problem if women cannot freely terminate a pregnancy. In contrast, many religious groups define legal abortion as a social problem. The debate over legalization versus criminalization of abortion reflects the conflicting values of important groups in society.

Value conflict theorists define social problems as "conditions that are incompatible with group values" (Rubington and Weinberg, 2003). Such problems are normal, they add, because in a complex society there are many groups whose interests and values are bound to differ. According to value conflict theory, social problems occur when groups with different values meet and compete. Returning to the example of criminal deviance, value conflict theorists would say that deviance from society's rules results from the fact that some groups do not agree with those rules and therefore feel free to break them if they can. For example, whenever a society prohibits substances like alcohol or drugs, some groups will break the rules to obtain the banned substance. This conflict stimulates the development of criminal organizations that employ gangsters and street peddlers to supply the needs of those who deviate. The underlying cause of the problem is conflicting values concerning the use of particular substances.

From the value conflict viewpoint, many social problems need to be understood in terms of which groups hold which values and which groups have the power to enforce them against the wishes of other groups. Once these distinctions have been determined, this approach leads to suggestions for adjustments, settlements, negotiations, and compromises that will alleviate the problem. These suggestions, in turn, may result in new policies, such as civilian review boards, arbitration of disputes, juvenile drug courts, and changes in existing laws to reflect a diversity of opinions (Larana, Johnston, and Gusfield, 1994).

THE IDEA OF A "CULTURE WAR" IN THE UNITED STATES When headlines claim conflict between different religious groups or communities about same-sex marriage or about school prayer, abortion, or any number of issues that arouse people's moral passions, it is easy to agree with some commentators that these conflicts are evidence of a "culture war." This supposed broad conflict over deeply held values is said to sway elections and determine the fate of many social policy issues, from gun control to "morning-after pills" and much more.

Recently, the Pew Research Center, a leader in survey research about social, political, and economic issues, examined the polarization in American society. The "political typology" they developed represents a unique approach to analyzing public values. The typology includes 23 questions on a

There has been increasing polarization in recent years over most political, social, and economic issues. Liberals and conservatives seem to be going in completely different directions.

broad set of topics, and instead of focusing on a single left–right dimension, it uses a cluster analysis to find groups of Americans with similar views across multiple dimensions. From these data, Pew identified eight political typologies. The two most resolute are the *Solidly Liberal* typology, which comprises 15 percent of the population, 17 percent of registered voters, and 21 percent of those who are politically engaged, and the *Steadfast Conservative* typology, which comprises 12 percent of the population, 15 percent of registered voters, and 17 percent of those who are engaged politically. These two groups stand wildly apart on social issues with very little middle ground, as shown in Table 1–3.

Interestingly, not all *Solid Liberals* or *Steadfast Conservatives* associated themselves with the political party that you might expect. Only 61 percent of Solid Liberals claimed they were Democrats. The others identified themselves as either Republicans or Independents. Similarly, only 57 percent of Steadfast Conservatives claimed that they were Republicans. The others said that they were either Democrats or Independents. Polarization is very real, but this polarization goes beyond the labels of "Democrat" or "Republican."

Table 1-3 Polarization on Social Issues, 2014*

U.S. SUCCESS IS DUE TO	Ability to change	Reliance on longstanding principles
Solid Liberals	79%	17%
Steadfast Conservatives	17%	78%
THE U.S ECONOMIC SYSTEM	Unfairly favors powerful interests	Is generally fair to most Americans
Solid Liberals	88%	9%
Steadfast Conservatives	48%	47%
ROLE OF GOVERNMENT	Government does too many things better left to businesses and individuals	Government should do more to solve problems
Solid Liberals	20%	73%
Steadfast Conservatives	87%	12%
GOVERNMENT AID TO POOR	Does more harm than good	Does more good than harm
Solid Liberals	7%	91%
Steadfast Conservatives	86%	10%
ENERGY PRIORITY	Focus on alternative energy	Expand oil/coal/natural gas
Solid Liberals	95%	1%
Steadfast Conservatives	26%	66%
MORE IMPORTANT GUN POLICY	Control gun ownership	Protect gun rights
Solid Liberals	81%	15%
Steadfast Conservatives	9%	89%
SAME-SEX MARRIAGE	Oppose	Favor
Solid Liberals	7%	89%
Steadfast Conservatives	84%	12%
ISLAMIC RELIGION	Not more likely than others to encourage violence	More likely than others to encourage violence
Solid Liberals	78%	13%
Steadfast Conservatives	20%	72%
ABORTION	Should be illegal in all/most cases	Should be legal in all/most cases
Solid Liberals	9%	87%
Steadfast Conservatives	70%	24%

*The Political Typology sorts people into groups based on their attitudes and values, not their partisan beliefs.

SOURCE: Pew Research Center, 2015

The Symbolic Interactionist Perspective

Why do certain people resort to crime while the vast majority seeks legitimate means to survive? A functionalist would point out that individuals who do not adhere to society's core values or have been uprooted by social change are most likely to become criminals. When they are caught, their punishment reinforces the desire of the majority to conform. But this explanation does not help us understand why a particular individual or group deviates.

Conflict theorists explain deviance as the result of conflict over access to wealth and power or over values. But how is that conflict channeled into deviant behavior? Why do some groups that experience value conflict act against the larger society while others do not? Why, for example, do some gays come out publicly while others hide their sexual preference? Presumably, both groups know that their sexual values may conflict with some people of the larger society, but what explains the difference in behavior? The conflict perspective cannot provide an adequate answer to this question.

The **symbolic interactionist perspective** offers an explanation that gets closer to the individual level of behavior by looking at the symbols people use in everyday interaction—words, gestures, appearances—and how these symbols are interpreted by others. People's interactions with others are based on how everyone interprets these symbols.

Research based on this perspective looks at the processes whereby different people become part of a situation that the larger society defines as a social problem. The interactionist approach focuses on the ways in which people actually take on the values of the group of which they are members. It also explores how different groups define their situation and in so doing "construct" a version of life that promotes certain values and behaviors and discourages others.

A key insight of the interactionist perspective originated in the research of W. I. Thomas and his colleagues in the early decades of the twentieth century. In their classic study of the problems of immigrants in the rapidly growing and changing city of Chicago, these pioneering sociologists found that some groups of Polish immigrant men believed it would be easier to rob banks than to survive in the mills and factories, where other immigrants worked long hours under dangerous conditions. The sociologists discovered that the uneducated young immigrants often did not realize how little chance they had of carrying out a successful bank robbery. They defined their situation in a particular way and acted accordingly. "Situations people define as real," Thomas stated, "are real in their consequences" (Thomas and Znaniecki, 1922). Thus, from the interactionist perspective, an individual's or group's definition of the situation is central to understanding the actions of that individual or group.

Another early line of interactionist research is associated with Charles Horton Cooley and George Herbert Mead. Cooley, Mead, and others realized that, although we learn our basic values and ways of behaving early in life, especially in our families, we also participate throughout our lives in groups made up of people like ourselves; these groups are known as peer groups. From these groups, we draw much of our identity and our sense of who we are, and within these groups, we learn many of our behaviors and values. Through our interactions in peer groups—be they teams, adolescent friendship groups, or work groups—we may be taught to act in ways that are different from those our parents taught us. Thus, when interactionists study social problems like crime, they focus on the ways in which people are recruited by criminal groups and learn to conform to the rules of those groups.

LABELING: AN INTERACTIONIST VIEW OF DEVIANCE Labeling theory is an application of the interactionist perspective that offers an explanation for certain kinds of social deviance. Labeling theorists think the label "deviant" reveals more about the society applying it than about the act or person being labeled. In certain societies, for

symbolic interactionist perspective

A way of thinking that offers an explanation that gets closer to the individual level of behavior by looking at the symbols people use in everyday interaction—words, gestures, appearances—and how these symbols are interpreted by others. People's interactions with others are based on how they interpret these symbols.

example, concern about climate change is far more accepted than it is in the United States. Labeling theorists suggest there are groups and organizations in American society that benefit from labeling climate change activists as deviant— the fossil fuel industries, for example. Similarly, deviant acts are not always judged in the same way; an analysis by the U.S. Sentencing Commission found that prison sentences for black offenders, for instance, tend to be about 20 percent longer than sentences for white offenders who commit the same crimes (Palazzolo, 2013). In short, labeling theory separates deviant and nondeviant people, not by what they do but by how society reacts to what they do.

According to labeling theorists, social problems are conditions under which certain behaviors or situations become defined as social problems. The cause of a social problem is simply society's awareness that a certain behavior or situation exists. A behavior or situation becomes a social problem when someone can profit in some way by applying the label "problematic" or "deviant" to it. Such labeling causes society to suffer in two ways. First, one group unfairly achieves power over another; "deviants" are repressed through discrimination, prejudice, or force. Second, those who are labeled deviant may accept this definition of themselves, and the label may become a self-fulfilling prophecy. The number and variety of deviant acts may be increased to reinforce the new role of deviant. A person who is labeled a drug addict, for example, may adopt elements of what is popularly viewed as a drug addict's lifestyle: resisting employment or treatment, engaging in crime, and so on. Sociologists term this behavior **secondary deviance**.

According to labeling theory, the way to solve social problems is to change the definition of what is considered deviant (Rubington and Weinberg, 2003). It is thought that the acceptance of a greater variety of acts and situations as normal would automatically eliminate concern about them. Decriminalization of the possession of small amounts of marijuana for personal use is an example of this approach. Note, however, that many people would consider marijuana use a social problem even if it were decriminalized. At the same time, discouraging the tendency to impose labels for gain would reduce the prevalence of labeling and cause certain problems to become less significant. Communism, for example, was a matter of great concern to Americans in the 1950s; many people won popularity or power by applying the label "Communist" to others. When it became clear that the label was being misapplied and that the fear it generated was unjustified, the label lost its significance and the "social problem" of internal Communist influence largely disappeared.

Labeling theory is only one of numerous applications of the interactionist perspective to social problems. Another common approach focuses on the processes of socialization that occur in groups and explores the possibility of resocialization through group interaction—as occurs, for example, in groups such as Alcoholics Anonymous. At many points, this book will discuss situations in which intentional resocialization has been used in efforts to address social problems.

THE SOCIAL CONSTRUCTION OF SOCIAL PROBLEMS The interactionist perspective also contributes to what is known as the **social construction** approach to social problems. This approach argues that some claims about social problems become dominant, and others remain weak or unheeded. Our perceptions of what claims about social problems should be heeded develop through the activities of powerful people and institutions in society that shape our consciousness of the social world. The press, television, radio, universities and colleges, government agencies, and civic voluntary associations are examples of institutions that often have a stake in defining what social problems are. Journalists, television commentators, editorial writers, professors who take public stands on issues, scientists who appear before the cameras, and many other lobbyists and "opinion makers" are in fact involved in selecting some claims and rejecting others. In so doing, they "construct" the way we think about the issues (Griswold, 2012).

secondary deviance

A state in which a person who is labeled "deviant" may then adopt elements of what is popularly viewed as a deviant lifestyle.

social construction

The process by which some claims about social problems become dominant and others remain weak or unheeded; these claims develop through the activities of actors and institutions in society that shape our consciousness of the social world.

Consider an example: Climate change research is extremely complex and requires knowledge that is too technical for most people to understand fully. But as members of the scientific community, along with the push of the media, develop a consensus that the atmosphere is warming because of pollution, the public begins to get that message and to share the opinion that climate change is occurring. Droughts and wildfires, which are becoming more common and more severe, come to be viewed as part of a social problem known as climate change.

Critics of the social construction view often argue that there are real trends and changes behind the emergence of social problems such as climate change or gun violence. Still, the influence of the media and other actors and social institutions do account for some tangible social construction of what we perceive as problematic in our society or in the world.

What Do You Think?

Identify a social problem, and using a social construction approach, describe how the media, certain people with power, and specific social institutions have framed this problem.

The Natural History of Social Problems

1.4   Describe the process that reveals the natural history of social problems.

To readers of daily websites and news sites, and to faithful watchers of television news, social problems may often resemble fads. People hear a great deal about a particular problem for a while, and then it fades from public attention, perhaps to reappear some time later if there are new developments in its incidence or control. With AIDS, crack cocaine, driving while intoxicated, serial killers, financial scandals, racial violence, terrorism, and so many other problems demanding attention, it is little wonder that the focus on any given subject by the press and the public tends to last only a few days or weeks.

To a large extent, the short attention span of the media can be explained by the need to attract large numbers of viewers or readers; the media can be expected to be rather fickle and to constantly pursue stories that will capture the attention of the public. However, sociologists distinguish between the nature of media coverage of a social problem and the way a problem is perceived by the public and political leaders. They have devoted considerable study to the question of how social problems develop from underlying conditions into publicly defined problems that engender social policies and sustained social movements. This subject is often referred to as the "natural history" of social problems.

Early in the twentieth century, sociologists recognized that social problems often seemed to develop in a series of phases or stages. They called the study of this process the **natural history approach** because their effort was analogous to the work of biologists who study the development of a great many individual organisms to chart the stages of development of a species (Edwards, 1927; Park, 1955; Shaw, 1929; Wirth, 1927). But whereas sociologists recognize that social problems often follow certain regular stages of development, they also know that there are many deviations from the usual sequence.

natural history approach
The idea that social problems develop in a series of phases or stages.

In a useful formulation of the natural history approach, Malcolm Spector and John Kitsuse (1987) outlined the following major stages that most social problems seem to go through.

- *Stage 1—Problem definition.*   Groups in society attempt to gain acknowledgment by a wider population (and the press and government) that some social condition is "offensive, harmful, or otherwise undesirable." These groups publicize their claims and attempt to turn the matter into a political issue.
- *Stage 2—Legitimacy.*   When the groups pressing their claims are considered credible and their assertions are accepted by official organizations, agencies, or institutions, there may be investigations, proposals for reform, and even the creation of new agencies to respond to claims and demands.
- *Stage 3—Reemergence of demands.*   Usually, the original groups are not satisfied with the steps taken by official agencies; they demand stronger measures,

A group of protesters is demonstrating for the right to bear arms, defending the Second Amendment to the Constitution. They believe that gun control violates their rights as Americans, and like the NRA, they do not believe that guns are the culprit in murder.

more funding for enforcement, speedier handling of claims, and so on. They renew their appeals to the wider public and the press.

- *Stage 4—Rejection and institution building.* The complainant groups usually decide that official responses to their demands are inadequate. They seek to develop their own organizations or counterinstitutions to press their claims and enact reforms.

This natural history approach can be applied to the idea that the easy availability of guns—especially handguns, automatic rifles and pistols, and assault weapons—contributes to higher murder rates. In the 1980s, musician John Lennon of the Beatles and President Ronald Reagan were victims of gun violence. Lennon was killed, and while President Reagan escaped serious harm, the bullets hit his press secretary, James Brady, who suffered a serious head injury and permanent disability.

Incidents like these, and many more, *defined the problem* of violence as being due to the easy availability of guns. This definition gained credibility and *legitimacy* as citizen groups pressed their lawmakers for gun control legislation. The Brady Bill, for example, was passed and required identity checks for gun purchasers and a ban on certain types of assault weapons. However, the National Rifle Association and other groups argued that guns are not the problem. The issue is mental illness, they claim, and legal gun owners should not be denied their rights because a few mentally ill people do the wrong thing.

Meanwhile, by the 1990s, mass shootings began to occur in public venues. Over the past several decades, there have been many of these horrific shootings. Sandy Hook elementary school: 26 elementary students, teachers, and staff were injured and killed. Virginia Tech University: 56 were killed or injured. Outside a Safeway shopping area where Congresswoman Gabriella Giffords was speaking: 19 people were injured or killed. An Army base in Texas: 43 people were killed or injured. These acts of violence have led to a *reemergence of demands* for more stringent gun control legislation. Gun control advocates have made their appeals publicly, but are growing frustrated by what they see as an inadequate response from the government. They are *rejecting and building their own institutions* to push their agendas and enact reforms.

Themes of this Text

1.5 **Review the four themes of the text.**

This text will introduce you to a wide variety of social problems experienced in American society today. However, you will learn more than a collection of random facts. Four themes are woven throughout the chapters to organize the discussion of social problems. These themes suggest that social problems can best be understood by (1) using an empirical approach; (2) linking individual experiences with social structure; (3) recognizing that social inequality contributes to social problems; and (4) acknowledging that understanding social problems requires a comparative perspective. Each of these themes is discussed below.

Using an Empirical Approach

empirical approach

A method that answers questions through a systematic collection and analysis of data.

A sociological understanding of social problems demands that one move beyond personal opinion and instead use an **empirical approach**, which is a method that answers questions through a systematic collection and analysis of data. Granted, most of you have commonsense ideas about social problems based on personal experience or habits, religious teachings, cultural customs, or societal laws. Because virtually everyone has some experience with social problems, they may think they are experts on the topic.

Historically, the commonsense view of violence among intimates was that it was okay for husbands to beat their wives—within reason. Supposedly, the term "rule of thumb" arises from the belief that the switch that a husband used to beat his wife should be no wider than his thumb. But common sense changes over time. Today, it is against the law in the United States for husbands to hit their wives (and vice versa). However, violence against an intimate partner is not illegal in many parts of the world. There, common sense suggests that violence can be justified and the husband has the prerogative to hit his wife, although again, usually within "reasonable" limits (e.g., a husband can beat, but not kill his wife). The World Health Organization takes violence against women very seriously. A study of 24,000 women in 10 countries found that the prevalence of physical and/or sexual violence by a partner varied from 15 percent in urban Japan to 71 percent in rural Ethiopia, with most areas being in the 30 to 60 percent range (Garcia-Moreno et al., 2015; World Health Organization, 2014).

If common sense is subject to historical and cultural whims, then what can researchers depend on to help them understand family dynamics? Sociologists use an empirical approach in collecting and analyzing data. The goals of empirical research can include the following.

- *Describe some phenomenon* (e.g., how many women have been physically assaulted by someone close to them; how does this number compare with the number of men who are assaulted by their partners each year; how do abused women and men interpret the reasons for the assault)
- *Examine the factors that predict or are associated with some phenomenon* (e.g., what factors are associated with violence among intimates; what factors predict whether a victim will report the assault to the police)
- *Explain cause-and-effect relationships or provide insight into why certain events do or do not occur* (e.g., what is the relationship between alcohol and violence among intimates; what is the relationship between attitudes of male dominance and domestic violence)
- *Understand the meanings attached to behavior or situations* (e.g., how do people interpret their roles as victims or perpetrators)

quantitative methods
A research strategy in which data can be measured numerically.

Empirical research has shown that violence is a serious and pervasive social problem. Somewhere between 1.4 and 4.3 million women are victims of intimate partner violence annually in the United States. Men can also be victims, but tend to be victims of the less severe types of violence. How can a sociological perspective help people who are battered by their partners? Family scholars conduct basic and applied research to understand the phenomenon, striving to reveal information about the incidence, predictors, social factors associated with violence, the experience of violence, and possible solutions. Psychologists, social workers, and politicians could use this information to develop programs to prevent violence, assist victims, and treat the perpetrators. Intimate partner violence is a social problem, not simply an individual one, and the goal is to uncover the social patterns that underlie it.

Sociologists and other social scientists use a variety of methods to collect and analyze data. A full discussion of these methods is beyond the scope of this text. However, Table 1–4 summarizes six primary methods of collecting data, outlining their strengths and weaknesses. These methods include surveys, in-depth interviews, experiments, focus groups, observational study, and secondary analysis.

Some researchers focus on **quantitative methods** in which the focus is on data that can be measured numerically. Examples are found in surveys, experiments, or doing

Violence among intimates is a serious social problem affecting millions of women and men. Sociological research provides a window into this phenomenon, including how often it occurs, who is most likely to be victimized, what types of violent acts are most common, and the effectiveness of different programs and policies to help victims.

Table 1–4 Six Research Methods: A Summary

Method	Application	Advantages	Limitations
Survey	For gathering information about issues that are not directly observed, such as values, opinions, and other self-reports. Can be conducted through mail or telephone or administered in person. Useful for descriptive or explanatory purposes; can generate quantitative or qualitative data.	Sampling methods can allow researcher to generalize findings to a larger population. Can provide open-ended questions or a fixed response.	Surveys must be carefully prepared to avoid bias. There is a potential for a low return or response rate. Can be expensive and time consuming. Self-reports may be biased.
In-depth Interview	For obtaining information about issues that are not directly observed, such as values, opinions, and other self-reports. Useful for getting in-depth information about a topic. Conducted in person, conversation is usually audiotaped and later transcribed. Generates qualitative data.	Can provide detailed and high-quality data. Interviewer can probe or ask follow-up questions for clarification or to encourage the respondent to elaborate. Can establish a genuine rapport with respondent.	Expensive and time-consuming to conduct and transcribe. Self-reports may be biased. Respondent may feel uncomfortable revealing personal information.
Experiment	For explanatory research that examines cause-and-effect relationship among variables. Several types: classical experimental design and quasi-experimental designs based on degree of controlling the environment. Generates quantitative data.	Provides greatest opportunity to assess cause and effect. Research design relatively easy to replicate.	The setting may have an artificial quality to it. Unless the experimental and control group are randomly assigned or matched on all relevant variables, and the environment is carefully controlled, bias may result.
Focus Groups	For obtaining information from small groups of people who are brought together to discuss a particular topic. Often exploratory in nature. Particularly useful for studying public perceptions. Facilitator may ask only a few questions; goal is to get group to interact with one another. Generates qualitative data.	Group interaction may produce more valuable insights than individual surveys or in-depth interviews. Research can obtain data quickly and inexpensively. Good for eliciting unanticipated information.	Setting is contrived. Some people may feel uncomfortable speaking in a group and others may dominate.
Observation	For exploratory and descriptive study of people in a natural setting. Researcher can be a participant or nonparticipant. Generates qualitative data.	Allows study of real behavior in a natural setting. Does not rely on self-reports. Researchers can often ask questions and take notes. Usually inexpensive.	Can be time-consuming. There could be ethical issues involved in certain types of observation studies, namely, observing without consent. Researcher must balance roles of participant and observer. Replication of research is difficult.
Secondary Analysis	For exploratory, descriptive, or explanatory research with data that were collected for some other purpose. Diverse. Can be large data sources based on national samples (e.g., U.S. Census) or can be historical documents or records. Generates quantitative or qualitative data, depending on the source of data used.	Saves the expense and time of original data collection. Can be longitudinal, with data collected at more than one point in time. Good for analyzing national attitudes or trends. Makes historical research possible.	Because data were collected for another purpose, the researcher cannot control what variables were included or excluded. Researcher has no control over sampling or other biases in the data.

qualitative methods

A research strategy that focuses on narrative description with words rather than numbers to analyze patterns and their underlying meanings.

further analyses on available government statistics (such as from the U.S. Census Bureau or U.S. Department of Justice) or another source (such as the United Nations). This research yields percentages and other statistics that can be easily interpreted.

Others use **qualitative methods** that focus on narrative description with words rather than numbers to analyze patterns and their underlying meanings. Examples of qualitative research methods include in-depth interviews, focus groups, observational studies, and in-depth analysis using narrative documents such as letters or diaries. Qualitative research does not usually offer statistics, but can reveal a rich description and understanding of some phenomena.

None of these methods are inherently better or worse than the others. The method used depends on the research questions that are posed. For example, if you want to better understand what family life was like in the nineteenth century, you would not want to conduct a survey today. How would people who are alive today best inform you of what happened 150 years ago? Obviously, the best method would be to conduct a further analysis of documents that were written during that time period. Diaries, letters or other lengthy correspondence between people, and other such qualitative data could help you understand the common everyday experiences within families. Likewise, you could analyze quantitative data from historical records to get an aggregate picture about, for example, immigration trends, age at first marriage, or the average length of time between marriage and first birth. Census records, birth, marriage, and death registers; immigration records; slave auctions and other transactions; church records; newspapers and magazine articles; employment ledgers; and tax records can also provide insight into the family lives of large numbers of ordinary people.

However, if you want to assess today's opinions or behaviors, perhaps a survey or in-depth interviews would be best. You may want to ask the same questions of everyone in your sample and offer a standard set of answers from which they can choose, such as "Have you ever been hit by a spouse or partner?" (yes, no). "If yes, would you say you have been hit 1–5 times, 6–10 times, more than 10 times?" You can easily quantify this information. Or, if you are interested in broader questions that allow each person in your study to elaborate in his or her own words (such as "How did you come to the decision to leave the violent spouse or partner?"), you would likely use in-depth interviews, which then yield qualitative data.

What Do You Think?

If you were conducting a study about violence, would you prefer qualitative or quantitative methods, and why? What could you hope to learn?

Linking Individual Experience with Social Structure

As the sociological imagination has revealed, most people are so embedded in their own lives that they fail to see the connections between their personal experiences and broader social concerns. By extension, many people perceive the lives of others around them also in this way: He's unemployed, and therefore he must not be working hard enough to get a job. She is stressed out from combining work and family, and therefore she needs better time management skills. He committed a crime; therefore, he should go to prison. Social scientists suggest that the best way to truly understand social problems is to see the connections between social structure and personal experience. Therefore, the second theme of this book emphasizes that, while people may initially think of experiences solely in personal terms, they are shaped in large part by the social structure in society, which is the patterns of social organization that guide one's interactions with others.

For example, many people are concerned about the number of poor single-parent households headed by women. People often wonder why women do not marry the men who father their children. Terry Lynn is one of these women, and if you look closer, you can see that her life choices are grounded in a social context.

Terry Lynn is a single mother who has never married and is raising a 6-year-old daughter alone, with the temporary help of cash welfare assistance (Seccombe, 2015). She is a shy young woman, yet at the same time, she is eager to tell her story. Terry Lynn works part-time at a bowling alley, a good job considering her weak reading and writing skills. She takes the bus to work, and various shifts sometimes keep her at work well into the night. She is savvy about the additional help she needs to support her child, and therefore deliberately keeps her employment hours below a certain threshold so that she and her daughter will continue to qualify for a childcare subsidy. Even at the age of 24, Terry Lynn knows that providing quality daycare for her daughter is vital. She and her daughter live with a sister in a cramped, rundown, two-bedroom apartment in an unfashionable part of town. The furniture is secondhand, and the couch is threadbare. Nonetheless, Terry Lynn is proud of herself and her daughter for "making it" on their own. You may wonder where the child's father is. He comes around now and then, she says, usually when he wants money or sex from her. Does Terry Lynn ever plan to marry him? Her answer is a definite "No."

Single-parent households have been blamed extensively for a wide variety of social ills. They are far more likely than other families to be poor (DeNavas-Walt and Proctor, 2014). Why are so many women, especially poor and low-income women like Terry Lynn, having children without marrying their children's fathers?

You might be tempted to look at individual-level factors and ask what is happening within intimate relationships, specifically the couple's values and choices. Certainly, these are important; but many people have found that poor women seem to value marriage quite highly. In fact, if anything, perhaps they value it *too* highly. They believe that their own relationships will never meet the "gold standard" they have set for themselves, such as a partner with a steady job, the chance to own their own home, and a reasonably lavish wedding ceremony. As a result, they shy away from marriage (Edin and Kefalas, 2005; Seccombe, 2015).

Therefore, you would need to look at structural factors to explain why poor women have children outside of marriage but are often hesitant to marry their partners. William Julius Wilson has suggested that the high unemployment rate of inner-city urban dwellers contributes to their low marriage rate. In his well-known books, *The Truly Disadvantaged* (Wilson, 1987) and *When Work Disappears* (Wilson, 1996), Wilson pointed out that many poor women see marriage to inner-city men as risky because the men cannot support families on their meager wages (Wilson, 1987, 1996). Furthermore, as factories and businesses move out to the suburbs or overseas, unemployment and poverty escalate. Consequently, there is a shortage of employed men whom these women see as good marriage prospects. Wilson shows that our changing economy (a structural condition) has a substantial effect on individual relationship choices.

In addition to high unemployment, or perhaps interrelated with it, are many other structural reasons why poor women often do not marry when they have children. For example, homicide, violence, drug addiction, and incarceration have all taken a tremendous toll on poor men, especially poor black men. In Terry Lynn's case, the father of her child was unemployed and had been in and out of jail, so she did not see him as a reliable "good catch." Although she cared for him, why would she want to marry him?

It is critical to move beyond just an individual perspective to really understand single parenthood among the poor. Social problems may be personally experienced, but they exist in a social context.

Recognizing That Social Inequality Contributes to Social Problems

A violent showdown erupted in Baltimore, Maryland, in April 2015, following the death of 25-year-old Freddie Gray, who died from a spinal injury while in police custody. He is the latest in a rash of incidents in which white police officers have killed or seriously injured black men.

A third theme of this text is that social inequality is a critical organizing feature in society and contributes mightily to social problems. Most Americans believe that the United States provides nearly equal opportunities for everyone. However, as detailed in upcoming chapters, American society is highly stratified on the basis of economics, power, and social status. Americans fantasize that they can be anything they want to be, but in reality, there is little substantial upward (or downward) social mobility. People usually live out their lives in generally the same social class in which they were born. Families pass on their wealth and social capital (or their lack of it) to their newest members, and this practice perpetuates social inequality. For example, because of the U.S. inheritance laws, affluent parents are able to distribute their wealth to their children after their death. Relatively little of the wealth is taxed and redistributed, as is the case in other countries. Consequently, some of America's richest people have only marginal employment histories. They do not need to work for a living, yet others who work relentlessly, often in the unglamorous but growing service sector, find no real route to a better life. Their wages are low; they may not receive health insurance or other benefits; and they live on

the margins, only one paycheck away from impoverishment. What type of wealth or social capital do these parents have to pass on to their children?

Inequality is woven into many basic social structures and institutions, and this inequality contributes to social problems, including poor health, immigration, mental illness, crime, poor race relations, overpopulation, violence among intimates, school dropout rates, war, discrimination against women, and environmental degradation.

For example, blacks, Hispanics, and American Indian/Alaska Native youths are less likely to finish high school than are their Asian and white counterparts. This educational disparity has serious long-term economic consequences, leading to higher poverty rates and more economic stress. But *why* are some groups more likely to quit high school?

One structural reason has to do with the quality of schools. Traditionally, schools reflect the socioeconomic and racial profile of the surrounding neighborhood; therefore, most schools have a long history of segregation. Desegregation effectively began with the Supreme Court's 1954 ruling in *Brown v. Board of Education of Topeka, Kansas*, which was based on the argument that segregation had negative effects on black students even when their school facilities were equal to those of white students. But many schools remained highly segregated because white or upper-income families transferred to private schools. Moreover, politicians often gerrymandered districts to change school attendance boundaries (Richards, 2014). Consequently, today's typical minority student attends school with fewer whites than his or her counterpart did in 1970 (Fiel, 2013).

Another structural reason has to do with the quality of the teachers in the schools. A teacher is estimated to have two to three times the impact of any other school factor on student performance on reading and math tests (RAND Education, 2012). Classrooms are often segregated into achievement levels, racial composition, and socioeconomic composition, and it is the teachers with less experience who tend to be assigned to the most challenging classes (Kalogrides, Loeb, and Béteille, 2013; Kalogrides and Loeb, 2013).

Patterns of social inequality filter down and shape all components of life—including educational achievement. This text examines the assumptions, values, and ideologies that are used to justify or explain social inequality and how inequality contributes to social problems.

Using a Comparative Perspective

The final theme of this text focuses on the importance of learning about other cultures and other historical periods to better understand American social problems. In the past, it was easier to ignore what was happening in the world beyond U.S. borders, but now, societies are becoming increasingly interconnected. New technologies, immigration, commerce across borders, and greater ease in world travel have increased visibility, and the United States can no longer remain isolated. Societies see other ways of doing things and sometimes adopt pieces of another's culture. One can now travel to many distant parts of the world and still find American fast food, such as McDonald's or Kentucky Fried Chicken. Likewise, the United States also has adopted foods and cultural artifacts from other countries. Tacos and pizza are staples in our diets today, but once were considered exotic or regional ethnic food. Social problems, too, move beyond borders. As shown in the box A Global View—World Population: 7.3 Billion and Counting, we are all affected by unchecked population growth.

Just as with culture, it is easy to ignore history and focus only on the here and now, yet many of our current social problems are rooted in the traditions of the past. For example, to better understand the current and heated debate over abortion, one should be aware that at one time, religious groups did not oppose abortion, including the Catholic Church. Likewise, to truly understand the high rate of divorce in the

A Global View

World Population: 7.3 Billion and Counting

As this box is being written on October 9, 2015, at 2:37 p.m., 7,372,738,852 people live on planet Earth. Is this a lot of people? Actually, all of these people could fit into the area the size of Los Angeles if they squeezed together. So space is not really the problem. This real issue is one of resources: food, water, energy, and overall use of environmental resources. How can all these people feed themselves nutritious food, drink clean water, heat their homes, drive to work, and dispose of their wastes? This question is an important one, and many people suspect that Earth has already exceeded its carrying capacity.

The United States overuses the Earth's resources, given the size of its population. Americans use a higher proportion of natural resources and live less sustainably than people in any other country. Americans have a uniquely high standard of living and have come to expect that cheap food, clean water, and gasoline will be available to us whenever we want it. Now, unsurprisingly, other countries want this standard of living, too. But the Earth would be in especially bad shape if everyone on Earth lived like an American.

Take energy, for example. Americans constitute 5 percent of the world's population, but they consume 24 percent of the energy. On average, 1 American uses as much energy as 2 Japanese, 6 Mexicans, 13 Chinese, 31 Indians, 128 Bangladeshis, 301 Tanzanians, and 370 Ethiopians (Mindfully. org, 2015). All the energy that Americans use pollutes the air, water, and soil. It also heats up the atmosphere. But China is right there with Americans, and, in fact the Chinese have eclipsed Americans in the use of fossil fuels. The Chinese do, however, have almost five times the population of the United States, so, per person, they still use considerably less than do Americans.

So, what does this mean? Simply put, the example that Americans have set will be copied by other countries around the world. Can the Earth support this many people if they live so unsustainably? How many people are we talking about? It's now 2:58 p.m., and the Earth's count is up to 7,372,742,189. In other words, in 21 minutes, the Earth's population grew by 3,337 people.

Critical Thinking

What do you think is the carrying capacity of Earth? If you think Earth has surpassed its carrying capacity, what do you propose be done about it? If you think that Earth has not surpassed its carrying capacity, when do you think that might happen, and with what effects?

United States, one should be aware of the ways in which the current notion of love, which evolved in the eighteenth century, changed the entire basis on which mates were chosen, and thereby increased the likelihood of couples ending an unhappy marriage (Coontz, 2005).

comparative perspective

A process to learn about other cultures and other historical periods to better understand social problems within one's own culture.

A **comparative perspective** helps enlighten a current situation because it reveals alternative social arrangements and presents new ways to frame an issue or policy solution. For example, how can a comparative perspective help people understand the nature and role of adolescence in U.S. culture? This concern is an important one because it is well known that adolescents commit a disproportionate number of crimes, experience higher-than-average unemployment, and face a host of other social problems, such as teen pregnancy or drug use.

A comparative perspective shows that adolescence, as it is known today, is largely a new social construction, originating in the West in the late nineteenth century as a result of newly created child labor laws and the changing nature of the labor market (Leeder, 2004; Mintz, 2004). Until then, children's labor was needed on farms and even young teenagers were considered mini-adults. However, with urbanization and industrialization in the late nineteenth century, a movement arose to increase the protection of young people. Social reformers known as "child savers" were particularly interested in developing social programs that were age-based and targeted toward children. Compulsory education increased the length of time children spent in school until well into their teenage years. Adolescence became a new period of transition between childhood and adulthood, but without clear-cut norms about what to expect during this period. By the twentieth century, the concept of adolescence as a separate stage of life had taken hold, and it now represents a substantial component of popular culture segregated from adult-oriented culture. Unique clothing, music, and food are directly marketed toward this relatively new consumer group. Nonetheless, it is not completely clear what the developmental tasks of this age group are and how adolescents can best serve the needs of society. Separating adolescents from adults, but giving them an unclear or unknown set of developmental tasks, has not necessarily served adolescents well.

How do other cultures construct this age period, and how do adolescents engage in society? How are these social constructions related to the level of technology or wealth in a society? A comparative perspective can shed light on our social problems and new ways to eliminate them.

What Do You Think?

Have you had the opportunity to travel to other cultures? If so, did you see anything that the United States could learn from?

Social Policy

1.6 Assess the social policy debates between conservatives and liberals.

Much of the research conducted by sociologists is designed to provide information to be used in formulating social policies as well as in evaluating existing policies and suggesting improvements and new directions. **Social policies** are formal procedures designed to remedy a social problem. Generally, they are designed by officials of government at the local, state, or federal level, but they can also be initiated by private citizens in voluntary associations, by corporations, and by nonprofit foundations.

social policies

Formal procedures designed to remedy a social problem; can be designed by officials of government at the local, state, or federal level or by private citizens in voluntary associations, by corporations, and by nonprofit foundations.

Social Policy Debates

There is generally a good deal of debate about any proposed social policy. Much of the debate consists of discussion and analysis of how well a proposed policy appears to address the problem. Such analysis tends to be considered technical in the sense that, although there is general agreement on the need to address the problem, the debate hinges on the adequacy of the proposed means to achieve the agreed-on ends. Increasingly, however, policy debates have become ideological rather than technical, and in the United States, such debates frequently pit conservatives against liberals.

Conservatives believe in limited government, free markets, individual liberty, personal responsibility, and a strong national defense. They believe the role of government should be to provide people the freedom necessary to pursue their own goals. Conservative policies generally emphasize empowerment of the individual to solve social problems, and they usually seek to limit the involvement of government in the solutions. Conservatives believe private firms, governed by the need to compete in markets and make profits, are the best type of organization for coping with most social problems.

In contrast, liberals believe government has a responsibility to address social problems. Liberals consider government action necessary to achieve equal opportunity and to protect civil liberties and human rights. Liberals are cautious of the dominance of the market (and, hence, the profit motive) and believe that it can be unfair and exploitive to certain groups in society. Therefore, the free market needs to be regulated to protect consumers, employees, and the environment, according to liberals. While liberals do not abdicate personal responsibility, they believe that the government has a responsibility to provide a structure that is fair to all.

Throughout the twentieth century and into the twenty-first, the government's role in attempting to solve social problems has increased steadily, despite the ideological stands of various administrations. For example, America's role as a world military power, along with new problems of terrorism, has required the continual expenditure of public funds on military goods and services. These costs have increased dramatically with every war and every major change in military technology. Similarly, the fight against drug commerce has added greatly to the cost of maintaining the society's judicial and penal institutions. Every function of government has a similar history of escalating costs because of increases in the scale of the society or the scope of the problem.

— CLIMATE CHANGE ?
NOW, THAT'S CRAZY TALK !

Climate change is one example of division between conservatives and liberals on important social problems. Many conservatives deny that the problem exists, or suggest that any change is due to natural fluctuations in the earth's temperature. The preponderance of scientific research, however, disputes this view.

Future Prospects

At this writing, the nation's voters have an increasingly ideological approach to social problems, at the expense of understanding and using empirical research. For example, public attitudes about climate change have become increasingly contentious. Despite near scientific consensus that the earth's climate is changing rapidly due to the emissions of fossil fuels, 25 percent of Americans do not believe that climate change is real (an increase from only 11 percent who denied climate change in 2009), and another 23 percent say that climate change is mostly caused by natural patterns in the earth's environment (Funk and Rainie, 2015). Even among young people who will experience the most severe effects during their lifetime of any group, only 57 percent agree that "global warming will seriously threaten one's way of life" (Jones, 2014). Furthermore, opinions about climate change are largely split along political party lines, with Republicans far more likely to deny climate change or attribute it to natural patterns than are Democrats.

This conflict is typical of many current controversies over the best ways to handle social issues, with conservatives stressing private or market solutions and liberals calling for public or government actions. These conflicting approaches are discussed in the Social Policy sections that conclude each chapter of this book.

Going Beyond Left and Right

The economic crash of 2008 and the recession experienced in subsequent years provide many lessons about how nations go awry in dealing with social problems. Above all, sociologists assert there are grave dangers in adopting policies based on unbending principles, whether they come from the left or the right of the ideological spectrum. For example, when he appeared before the Government Oversight Committee of the House of Representatives, Alan Greenspan, chair of the Federal Reserve, the nation's central bank and the most powerful regulator of interest rates, said that he was in a state of "shocked disbelief" that the financial markets had failed to regulate themselves. His firm belief in allowing markets to be as free as possible (a policy known as "laissez-faire," from the French for "let it be") had led him to believe that they would self-regulate. He admitted that the crash revealed "a flaw" in his laissez-faire principles and that the consequences turned out to have been "much broader than anything I could have imagined" (Alcaly, 2010, p. 43).

This belated quasi-apology from the Federal Reserve's fallen "economic guru" hardly solves the problems of millions of people who lost jobs and homes. It does, however, provide another lesson against relying on "single and sovereign" principles like laissez-faire market fundamentalism. But is the lesson from that experience that government should always step in and assume responsibility for losses or impose new and far stiffer regulations, as many on the left would argue? No doubt new regulations and stricter enforcement are vital to restoring balance between market processes and protection of vulnerable citizens, but social-scientific research almost always suggests that the key is in finding the right balance between these competing principles.

Summary

- The sociological imagination suggests that many of our personal experiences are patterned and are shaped by social structure. Using a sociological imagination reveals general patterns in what otherwise might be thought of as simple random events. Problems such as divorce, substance abuse, crime, and child abuse are more than just personal troubles experienced by a few people. They are issues that affect large numbers of people and originate in society's institutional arrangements. In other words, individual experiences are linked to the social structure.

- When enough people in a society agree that a condition exists that threatens the quality of their lives and their most cherished values, *and* they agree that something should be done to remedy that condition, sociologists say that the society has defined that condition as a social problem. Society's members have reached a consensus that a condition that affects some people is a problem for the entire society, not just for those who are directly affected.

- Contemporary sociology is founded on three basic perspectives, or sets of ideas, that offer theories about why societies hang together and how and why they change. These perspectives are not the only sociological approaches to social problems, but they can be extremely powerful tools for understanding them. Each of these perspectives—functionalism, conflict theory, and symbolic interactionism—gives rise to a number of useful and distinctive approaches to the study of social problems.

- Most social problems go through four major stages: (1) problem definition; (2) legitimacy; (3) reemergence of demands; and (4) rejection and institution building.

- This text has four themes: (1) a sociological understanding of social problems demands that one move beyond personal opinion and instead use an empirical approach, which is a method that answers questions through a systematic collection and analysis of data; (2) while people may initially think of experiences solely in personal terms, this text will show the importance of linking individual experience with social structure; (3) social inequality is a critical organizing feature in society and contributes to social problems; (4) it is important to learn about other cultures and other historical periods to develop a better understanding of American social problems today.

- Debates about many social problems are becoming increasingly polarized. Conservatives believe in limited government, free markets, individual liberty, personal responsibility, and a strong national defense. In contrast, liberals believe government has a responsibility not only to address social problems and consider government action necessary to achieve equal opportunity but also to protect civil liberties and human rights.

Chapter 2
Problems of Health
and Health Care

 Learning Objectives

2.1 Describe health care as a global social problem.

2.2 Identify the scope of health care problems in America.

2.3 Discuss Americans' unequal access to health care.

2.4 Review the reasons for the high costs of health care.

2.5 Summarize the ethical issues surrounding health care.

2.6 Classify explanations for health care problems.

2.7 Identify key issues in social policy, including the Affordable Care Act (ACA).

My son Marcus was complaining about a stomachache, and I just didn't take it very seriously. He's seventeen, and I figured he could just deal with it. But when he started to cry, I knew something was up. I can't remember when it was the last time he cried over pain—maybe when he broke his arm in fifth grade? But, a stomachache? I don't have any insurance so what am I supposed to do? I didn't want to pay for an emergency room visit over just a stomachache. I figured it would go away as they usually do. But as the night went on, I could tell that something was really wrong. He was rolling on the floor in pain, and at one point he seemed to be even losing consciousness. This had to be far more than just a stomachache, so I ended up taking him to the emergency room. It's a good thing I did because after they examined him they told me that his appendix had burst. Poisons were spewing in his body. The doctor told me that if I had waited much longer Marcus could have died. I feel horrible—risking my only son's life because I don't have any money to pay the bill. I know it sounds crazy, but I just didn't know what to do. I don't have any insurance.

Over the past few years, Americans and observers around the world witnessed the implementation of historic legislation to reform the health care system in the United States. After decades of mounting health care costs and increases in the number of people without access to health care, the U.S. Congress passed a compromise reform plan, the Patient Protection and Affordable Care Act (ACA), that promised to add at least 32 million people to those with health care insurance; people like Marcus who have often suffered without it. After a period of intense campaigning by President Obama and his supporters, and equally intense campaigning by ACA opponents, a bitterly divided Congress finally passed the historic health care reform bill in 2010 to be implemented over the next several years. Few legislators, and perhaps fewer American voters, were entirely pleased with the reforms, but the bill culminated many decades of effort to bring the U.S. health care system toward a par with those of other developed nations to which we often compare ourselves. It remains to be seen in the next few years, as the reforms are implemented and as Congress continues the work of making health care more accessible while controlling its costs, whether the efforts will have been worth the pain and political sacrifice of so many elected officials. But at this writing, it is safe to say that this bill is among the most significant legislation passed by Congress since the creation of the Medicare system in 1965. The Social Policy section of this chapter will guide you in analyzing this historic legislation. But first, we encourage you to look at the various ways in which health and inequalities of access to adequate health care are serious social problems on a global as well as national level.

Health Care as a Global Social Problem

2.1 Describe health care as a global social problem.

The lack of adequate health measures presents a variety of social problems to societies everywhere. In affluent regions like western Europe, North America, and Australia, problems associated with physical health often involve reducing unequal access to high-quality health care while controlling health care costs. In impoverished regions where high-quality medical care is often lacking, social problems associated with physical health are even more profound: the spread of infectious diseases, high rates of infant and maternal death, low life expectancy, scarcity of medical personnel and equipment, and inadequate sewage and water systems.

It is true that in the past half-century life expectancy has increased in most regions of the world. These improvements often reflect better water and sewage systems and adequate child vaccination programs. But recent reviews of the global health situation warn that continued improvements in public health systems and in delivery of medical services will be necessary, especially in poor regions, if these gains are to continue (Population Reference Bureau, 2015; United Nations Development Programme, 2013).

Slide Show

Health Care Needs in Less Developed Countries

Less developed countries face considerably different health issues, or face health issues on a significantly different magnitude than what is found in more developed nations. People in less developed countries fight for basic survival on a daily basis: access to food, clean water, and shelter. These pictures reveal some of the many issues faced by people in developing countries.

This woman from Malawi, Africa, looks much older than her 38 years. Her life has been hard and she has faced a number of health issues. She bore six children, only four of whom lived past the age of ten, and she had no prenatal care during her pregnancies. She has rarely been to a doctor and has never been to a dentist.

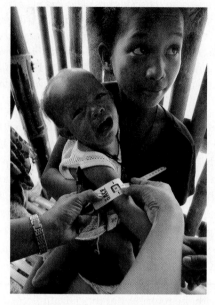

This little girl of 16 months cries while she is measured for signs of malnutrition. Regular natural disasters in the Philippines, an overreliance on rice, and a lack of breast-feeding have left Filipino children some of the most malnourished in Asia. Over 7 percent of children in the Philippines suffer from acute malnourishment.

A monk performs the last rites for a young woman before closing her coffin. She died from an AIDS-related illness shortly before this picture was taken. She was a sex worker who contracted the AIDS virus from a client.

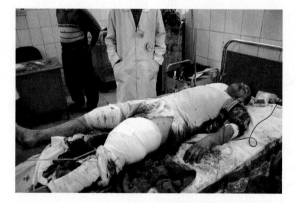

A wounded man lies in a hospital bed in Baghdad after a night of fighting, the victim of a bomb. The ongoing violence has left two of his cousins dead and several others wounded. Many developing nations are engaged in violence that kills, maims, and terrifies men, women, and children.

This thirsty young boy is drinking water from a pipe crossing an uncovered sewage canal. Access to clean drinking water is a serious social problem, and viruses and worms contained in dirty water kill millions of people every year.

Critical Thinking

What is the United States' responsibility to assist people in developing countries with the health crises they face? Should we be providing more aid? How will we ensure that aid gets to the people who really need it? Or should Americans focus on problems in our own country and let other countries take care of their own problems?

Table 2–1 Health Indicators for Selected Nations, 1970–2013

	Life Expectancy at Birth (years)		Infant Mortality Rate (per 1,000 live births)	
	1970	2013	1970	2013
Highly developed (1st world)				
United States	71	79	20	6
Sweden	74	82	11	3
Argentina	66	76	59	12
Costa Rica	67	79	58	9
Less developed (2nd world)				
Hungary	69	75	36	5
Mexico	61	77	79	15
China	62	75	85	16
India	49	66	130	44
Developing (3rd world)				
Nepal	42	68	156	46
Nigeria	43	52	120	97
Sierra Leone	34	45	206	128

SOURCE: Population Reference Bureau, 2015.

The United Nations rates nations on the basis of a series of indicators of health, education, equality of political participation, and many other factors. The nations are then grouped into high, medium, and low levels of human development for purposes of comparison. The numbers in Table 2–1 indicate how much or how little improvement various nations have made in two key health indicators: **life expectancy**, which is defined as how long a person can expect to live and is usually calculated at birth, and **infant mortality**, which is the number of deaths in a child's first year of life, for every 1,000 live births (Population Reference Bureau, 2015).

Life expectancy is highly correlated with a society's quality of health care. As a population's health improves because of better medical care and improved living conditions, the average age to which its members live (i.e., the life expectancy of the population) rises dramatically. For example, Table 2–1 indicates that a person born in Sierra Leone in 2013 (the most recent year for which international comparisons are available) can expect to live only about 45 years; in contrast, a person born in the United States in 2013 can expect to live about 79 years. Differences in life expectancy between developed (sometimes referred to as "industrialized") and less developed nations (sometimes referred to as "nonindustrialized") are largely due to the increasing chance that people in developed nations will survive the childhood diseases and parasites that cause such high death rates in less developed nations.

Table 2–1 also shows the wide gap between these countries in infant mortality rates, the most important comparative indicator of health. In Sierra Leone, the infant mortality rate is 128 per 1,000 live births, almost three times the rate in India, 21 times the rate in the United States, and 42 times the rate in Sweden.

Infant mortality rates and life expectancy are highly correlated with the number of health care professionals in a society, which serves as a measure of the quality of the health care available to its members. However, other factors besides the availability of health care professionals may affect a population's health. In the world's poorest regions, malnutrition, a decline in breastfeeding, and inadequate sanitation and health facilities are associated with high mortality. Poor maternal health and lack of prenatal care contribute even more to persistently high rates of infant mortality and other poor birth outcomes. A Global View: Fistulas on page 5 explains how obstructed labor can not

life expectancy

How long a person can expect to live, and is usually calculated at birth.

infant mortality

The number of deaths of children in their first year of life, for every 1,000 live births.

What Do You Think?

Realistically, what can be done about global health disparities? And if help is possible, why hasn't it been provided, or has it?

A Global View

Fistulas

Beza was a small Ethiopian girl of 15 when she married her husband. She had seen him only once before her wedding day, but they had never spoken to one another. Her father told her he was a good man, and so she quit school to become his wife. Five months later Beza was pregnant and she felt a combination of excitement and dread. She didn't see a doctor during her pregnancy because she had no money and the doctor was too far away. When labor began, she lay on the floor of the hut, but the pain was more than she could bear. Labor lasted for three days, but the baby wouldn't come. Finally, on the fourth day, with the help of a neighbor woman, the baby was delivered, but he was dead. As she healed from this trauma she noticed that she was leaking urine and had no ability to control it. Unknown to her at the time, the obstructed labor tore a hole in the tissue between her vagina and bladder. The smell was foul, and she was self-conscious about wetting herself. Her husband wanted nothing more to do with her—she killed his baby, as he saw it, and God was now punishing her—and he kicked her out of their home. She went back to live with her parents, but they too felt shame, so they built a hut for her in the back of their house where she could live, alone.

A story like this one plays out at least 100,000 times every year. Beza suffers from a fistula, a hole between her vagina and bladder caused by the many days of obstructed labor, when the pressure of the baby's head against her pelvis cut off blood supply to delicate tissues in the region. The dead tissue falls away, and Beza was left with a hole between her vagina and her bladder. Some women also have a hole between their vagina and rectum as well. This hole results in permanent incontinence of urine and/or feces. The World Health Organization estimates that approximately 2 million women have untreated fistulas.

Fistulas are most prevalent in sub-Saharan Africa and Asia. They once were present in the United States, but were largely eliminated in the latter nineteenth century with improved obstetric care and the use of C-sections to relieve obstructed labor. Yet, nearly half of women in developing countries give birth without any trained personnel, and when complications arise no one is available to assist the woman, leading to injuries such as fistula. Hospitals and personnel who can help them are often hundreds of miles away, and poor roads or a lack of transportation make travel difficult or impossible.

The majority of women who develop fistulas, like Beza, are abandoned by their husbands and ostracized by their communities because of their incontinence and foul smell. They fear going out in public because of the chronic leaking and smell.

The cause of fistulas may be obstructed labor, but the root causes are crushing poverty and the low status of girls and women. In developing nations, poverty and malnutrition stunt growth; a girl's skeleton, including her pelvis, does not fully mature. This stunted condition can contribute to obstructed labor, and therefore a fistula. Couple this condition with very early marriage and childbearing, and we can see why fistulas are an epidemic in the developing world. Very little money is spent on women's reproductive health care; women's needs are low priority.

Yet, fistula can be treated. A fistula can be easily closed with surgery, and the patient has a good chance of returning to a normal life with full control of her bodily functions. The cost of the surgery is about US$450, which includes the operation, high-quality postoperative care, and even a new dress and bus fare home. The Addis Ababa Fistula Hospital in Ethiopia has treated more than 20,000 women over the past several decades. Their cure rate is over 90 percent.

As for prevention, ready access to emergency obstetric care such as a C-section when complications arise could easily eliminate fistulas, as would delaying the age of first pregnancy. The bottom line for prevention is placing a greater value on women's lives.

SOURCES: Adapted from The Fistula Foundation, 2015; World Health Organization, March 2010.

Critical Thinking

Why do you think that so little attention has been given to this issue? Is the silence related to culture, shame, patriarchy, economics, or other factors? How are these factors sociological issues? Pretend you have unlimited resources and are asked by the World Health Organization to develop a program to curb, treat, and/or eliminate fistulas. What would your program look like? Be sure to address the root cause.

only lead to infant death but also leave the woman with a hole between her vagina and bladder (or rectum), otherwise known as a fistula (The Fistula Foundation, 2015; World Health Organization, 2014).

Moreover, the emergence of new and extremely deadly epidemics, especially AIDS and other sexually transmitted diseases, diverts scarce medical resources away from basic health care and preventive public health programs. In a later section of this chapter, we return to the special crisis in world health care presented by the growing AIDS epidemic.

The Scope of Health Care Problems in America

2.2   Identify the scope of health care problems in America.

Unlike in developing nations, our comparatively poor health in the United States is due largely to two social conditions: growing inequality and lifestyle problems. Inequality and increases in the poverty rate are associated with lack of health insurance and lack of access to high-quality medical care. Problems in the way we live include sedentary occupations; fattening, nonnutritious foods; and lack of proper exercise, all of which contribute to the high incidence of obesity, heart disease, and other ailments. Environmental pollution and cigarette smoking contribute to the high incidence of respiratory disease and cancer. There can be little doubt, however, that many of our health problems are aggravated by the kind of medical care that is—or is not—available.

Medical sociology is the subfield of sociology that specializes in research on the health care system and its impact on the public, especially access to health care (Cockerham, 2012; Weiss and Lonnquist, 2015) and the evolution of health care institutions (Starr, 2010). In describing problems of physical health, sociologists are particularly interested in understanding how a person's social class (as measured by income, education, and occupation) influences his or her access to medical care and its outcome. Sociologists also work with economists and health care planners in assessing the costs of different types of health care delivery systems.

medical sociology
The subfield of sociology that specializes in research on the health care system and its impact on the public, especially access to health care.

Medical sociologists often point out that health care institutions themselves are the source of many problems we associate with health in the United States. They emphasize that the health care system has evolved in such a way that doctors maintain private practices while society supports the hospitals and insurance systems that allow doctors to function (Cockerham, 2012; Weiss and Lonnquist, 2015). In other words, American health care never developed as a purely competitive industry or a regulated public service. Instead, as we will see shortly, it became a complex institution comprising many private and public organizations.

As great strides were made in the ability to treat illnesses—especially through the use of antibiotics—and to prevent those illnesses through improved public health practices, some doctors began to develop narrow specialties and to refer patients to hospitals with special facilities. This practice created a situation in which specialized doctors and hospital personnel became highly interdependent, and family doctors and preventive medical practices suffered in comparison (Starr, 2010). All efforts to change our health care system, to make it less costly, more efficient, or more humane, must deal with the power of insurance companies, doctors, and other health care providers, power that derives not from their wealth or their ownership of health care facilities but from their mode of relating to one another and to the public. This power is a subject that will become clear after discussing some of the specific problems of American health care.

The range of situations in which health care can be viewed as a social problem is extremely wide. At the micro, or individual, level, where family and friends are affected, such problems comprise issues such as whether the correct medical treatment is being applied, whether an elderly parent should be placed in a nursing home, or whether life support should be terminated. But as the Sociological Imagination reveals, people's experiences are influenced by larger forces that act throughout society and touch the lives of millions. These forces are the structural problems of health care. At the personal level, individuals may worry about care for elderly loved ones, but at the structural level the issue is how effectively health care is distributed among all people (including the elderly and the poor) and what can be done to improve the delivery of needed medical services.

This section explores several aspects of American health care that contribute to social problems at both the personal and structural levels. Unequal access to health services, the high cost of health care, and our own behaviors and use of technology are among the problems that must be addressed if more Americans are to receive more and better health care.

Unequal Access to Health Care

2.3 Discuss Americans' unequal access to health care.

To a large extent, health care as a social problem can be viewed in terms of unequal access to health care services. Marcus, introduced in the opening vignette, suffered unnecessary pain and almost died because his family had no health insurance. Unfortunately, he is not alone. Many Americans have trouble getting the health care they need when they are ill because they are without health insurance. Unfortunately, in 2010, 50 million Americans—over 15 percent of the population—had no insurance (Smith and Medalia, 2014), as shown in Figure 2–1. More recently, that figure has dropped substantially because of policy changes at the federal and state levels (which will be discussed later in this chapter), but the number of people who are uninsured remains at approximately 30 million (Garfield and Young, 2015). How could so many people be uninsured in a country as wealthy as the United States?

The short answer to this question is that the United States has traditionally had a **fee-for-service** health care system; in other words, if you get sick or injured, you must pay for medical care. Other countries roll the price of health care into their taxes so that there is little or no additional cost when a person is sick or injured.

fee-for-service

A type of health care system in which patients are expected to pay for their own medical care.

During World War II, when wage freezes were in effect, some large companies decided to offer health insurance as a fringe benefit of the job, and why not? Insurance was cheap to purchase because health care costs were relatively inexpensive and few drugs were available. To compete for labor, medium-sized and small businesses also decided to get into the act (Blumenthal 2006).

Figure 2–1 Number of Uninsured in the United States (millions)

SOURCES: Garfield and Young, 2015; Smith and Medalia, 2014.

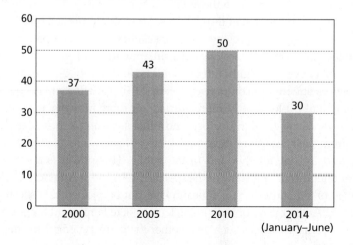

By the 1950s and 1960s, Americans began to equate health insurance with employment: you get a job and you get insurance. Americans forgot that this connection began through a simple historical accident (e.g., war-induced wage freezes led employers to offer health insurance instead), and they also forgot that no other developed nation ever tied health insurance to employment. In all developed nations (and many less developed ones), access to health care is a guaranteed right of citizenship, much like education or access to police protection. The result is that many Americans likely took jobs, or stayed in a job, simply because they needed the health insurance the job provided.

However, by the 1970s and 1980s, health care costs began to rise substantially. Small businesses were the first to say, "Hey, we cannot afford this." Today, companies of all sizes are dropping health insurance coverage completely or asking workers to pay more of the costs of the insurance plan. Only 62 percent of Americans now receive health insurance from an employer (Kaiser Family Foundation and Health Research and Educational Trust, 2014). Among low-income workers, only about one-third receives employer-sponsored insurance. Clearly, the connection between health insurance and employment is eroding.

Well, then, why not just purchase insurance yourself if you cannot get it from an employer? Many people in America cannot afford it because the average price of family coverage is now almost $17,000 per year (Kaiser Family Foundation and Health Research and Educational Trust, 2014). Also, until recent federal changes, just because a person applied for insurance there was no guarantee that he or she would be granted coverage; many people have been turned down by insurance companies because of a preexisting condition. Moreover, most Americans do not qualify for **Medicaid**, the federal-state health care program for certain categories of poor people.

The consequences of being without insurance can be devastating (Majerol, Newkirk, and Garlied, 2015; Tejada, 2013). Compared with those who have insurance, people without health insurance:

- are twice as likely to postpone seeking health care, are over four times as likely to forgo needed care, and are more than twice as likely to have a needed prescription go unfilled.
- pay large sums of their own money for their limited care, thereby reducing the amount of money for food, heat, and other necessities. One-third of uninsured patients and half of low-income uninsured patients say that doctors make them pay upfront before any health care is rendered. Medical bills are a major financial hardship, and they contribute to debt and bankruptcy.
- are less likely after an accidental injury to receive any care, are twice as likely to receive no recommended follow-up care, and are more likely to report not fully recovering.

Profile of the Uninsured

In 2014 approximately 30 million Americans were uninsured. This represents a significant decline in the number of people without insurance, largely because of changes in health care policy. A decline is something to celebrate. However, 30 million people represents a substantial portion of the American population. Who are these people? Some of the answers may surprise you.

First, almost half of the uninsured are in families where one or both parents are employed full-time, as shown in Figure 2–2a (Garfield and Young, 2015). Another 18 percent have a family member who is employed part-time. Their employers do not

Henry was suspicious of the job offer right from the beginning.

Unlike most countries, health insurance is designed to be a fringe benefit provided by employers. From the employers' perspective, the costs of health insurance are expensive and therefore many employers are reducing benefits or eliminating them altogether. It is as though they are saying, "You can have a salary, or you can have benefits. You choose."

Medicaid

The federal-state health care program for certain categories of people living in poverty.

Figure 2–2a Characteristics of the Non-Elderly Uninsured: Family Work Status, Fall 2014

SOURCE: Garfield and Young, 2015.

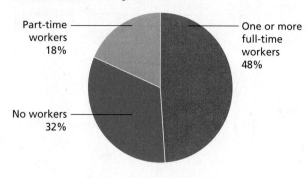

Part-time workers 18%

One or more full-time workers 48%

No workers 32%

Figure 2–2b Characteristics of the Non-Elderly Uninsured: Family Income, Fall 2014

NOTE: FPL (federal poverty level).
SOURCE: Garfield and Young, 2015.

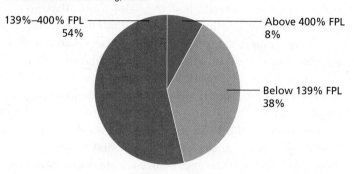

139%–400% FPL 54%

Above 400% FPL 8%

Below 139% FPL 38%

Figure 2–2c Characteristics of the Non-Elderly Uninsured: Race, Fall 2014

SOURCE: Garfield and Young, 2015.

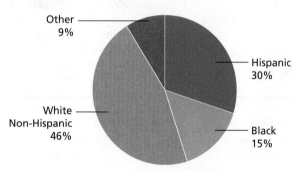

Other 9%

Hispanic 30%

White Non-Hispanic 46%

Black 15%

provide insurance for the worker or his or her dependents, and it costs too much for the family to purchase insurance privately.

Second, as you can see in Figure 2–2b, most uninsured people have low incomes. Thirty-eight percent have incomes below the threshold of Medicaid eligibility, which is below 139 percent of the Federal Poverty Line (FPL), or about $30,000 a year for a family of four (the FPL is adjusted for family size). Another 54 percent of uninsured people have incomes somewhere between 139 and 400 percent of the FPL, which is up to about $95,000 for a family of four. In addition, it is important to note that some high-income earners also do not have insurance. About 8 percent of uninsured people live in families with incomes of at least 400 percent of the poverty line, meaning that their incomes are over $95,000 (again, based on a family of four). So, while it is fair to say that many uninsured people have lower incomes, certainly not all do (Garfield and Young, 2015).

Finally, Figure 2–2c shows that non-Hispanic whites make up the largest uninsured group, but minority groups, especially Hispanics, are overrepresented among those who are uninsured, given the share of the population they represent (Garfield and Young, 2015). These findings are particularly disturbing because low-income people and racial and ethnic minorities tend overall to be in poorer health, as shown in Figures 2–3a, 2–3b, and 2–3c, and therefore need to have good access to health care services (National Center for Health Statistics, 2013).

Inequalities of Race and Ethnicity

Perhaps the most obvious sign of health status can be illustrated by life expectancy—on average, how long a person born today can expect to live. A comparison of life expectancy for whites and nonwhites reveals that white males can expect to live about five years longer than black males, while the gap between white and black females is over three years.

Figure 2–3a Major Health Indicators, by Race and Ethnicity: Life Expectancy in Years, 2012

SOURCE: National Center for Health Statistics, 2014.

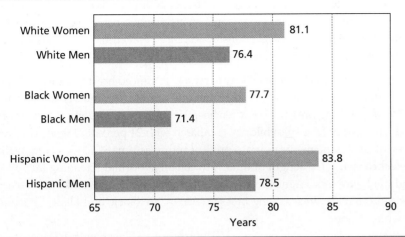

Figure 2–3b Major Health Indicators, by Race and Ethnicity: Infant Mortality Rate, 2012

SOURCE: National Center for Health Statistics, 2014.

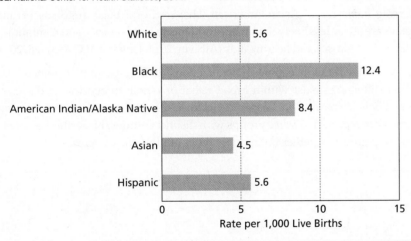

Figure 2–3c Major Health Indicators, by Race and Ethnicity: Percent Reporting Only Fair or Poor Health (Self-Assessment), 2012

SOURCE: National Center for Health Statistics, 2014.

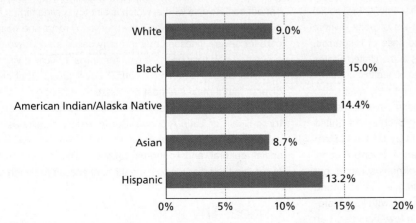

In addition, the infant mortality rate (number of deaths in the first year of life for all live births) for blacks is more than twice that for whites: 12.4 per 1,000 live births for blacks compared with 5.6 for whites (National Center for Health Statistics, 2014). Racial and ethnic minorities suffer proportionately more from almost every illness than do whites, and because they are less likely to have been immunized, nonwhites suffer higher rates of death from infectious diseases. Such differences cannot be ascribed to income differences alone because, even in cases in which income is the same, death rates remain higher for nonwhites. Even with respect to self-rated health, with the exception of Asians, minorities are far more likely to rate their health as only fair or poor (than as good or excellent).

The most comprehensive recent research on inequalities in health care for U.S. minorities shows that, even with equivalent insurance, racial and ethnic minorities are likely to receive less or inferior care compared with whites, especially for the following conditions:

- *Heart disease.* Blacks are less likely to receive advanced heart treatments; 13 percent fewer undergo coronary angioplasty and one-third fewer undergo bypass surgery.
- *Asthma.* Among preschool children hospitalized for asthma, only 7 percent of black and 2 percent of Hispanic children, compared with 21 percent of white children, are prescribed routine medications to prevent future asthma-related hospitalizations.
- *Breast cancer.* The length of time between an abnormal screening mammogram and the follow-up diagnostic test to determine whether a woman has breast cancer is more than twice as long in Asian American, black, and Hispanic women as in white women.
- *Human immunodeficiency virus (HIV) infection.* Blacks with HIV infection are less likely to be on antiretroviral therapy and less likely to be receiving protease inhibitors than are other people with HIV.
- *Nursing home care.* Asian American, Hispanic, and black residents of nursing homes are all far less likely than white residents to have sensory and communication aids such as glasses and hearing aids (Altman, 2014; Unger and O'Donnell, 2014).

Yet, as we make these sweeping generalizations, it is important to remember that significant differences exist within broad racial or ethnic categories, as discussed in A Closer Look–Disparities in Hispanic Health Care. After all, the terms *Hispanic* or *Asian American* represent diverse groups with distinct cultures. Nevertheless, most data sources lump groups together under these types of umbrella categories.

A Closer Look

Disparities in Hispanic Health Care

What is behind the statement that Hispanics in the United States are almost three times as likely as non-Hispanic whites to lack health insurance? The answer to this question requires that we explore the meaning of the term Hispanic. Often, social categories that lump together large numbers of quite diverse people can mask important trends. In the case of Hispanics, further analysis of the Hispanic subgroups in the United States reveals great variations in rates and sources of health insurance.

Health insurance coverage differs among the major Hispanic groups in the United States. Cuban Americans, the majority of whom live in Florida and have been in the United States since the 1960s if not earlier, have by far the highest rates of job-based or other private insurance. Puerto Ricans, like Cuban Americans, have lower rates of noninsurance, but they have the highest rates of public insurance (Medicaid and Medicare) because they are American citizens with long histories of job discrimination and residence in low-income urban ghettos. People of Central American or Mexican descent have the lowest rates of job-based insurance and, in consequence, extremely high rates of noninsurance. At the same time, they are most often found among the ranks of the working poor, in occupations like landscaping, dishwashing, and casual labor. Any improvements in coverage for the working poor would greatly benefit these Hispanic subgroups, but they would also benefit society as a whole, which is already paying higher hospital costs as poor people seek emergency room and hospital care for severe illnesses that in many cases could have been prevented had they been eligible for outpatient clinic visits.

The labels Hispanic (or Latino) cover groups that are so diverse that it makes almost no sense to lump them together. Theoretically, Hispanic refers to people who trace their ancestry to Spain or Latin America. But in reality, it includes people with roots all over the world who have widely different social, cultural, and economic patterns. These patterns help to explain their disparities in health and access to health care.

Critical Thinking

List the different groups classified as Hispanic. Can you identify ways in which they are culturally different? For example, describe any differences in food, language, or values. Do you think it is racist to lump groups together? Why or why not?

Inequalities of Social Class

From a socioeconomic point of view, there is a strong relationship between membership in a lower class and a higher rate of illness, as is clearly shown in Figures 2–4a, 2–4b, and 2–4c (National Center for Health Statistics, 2014). The wealthier people are, the more likely they are to feel, and to be, healthy. For example, 22 percent of people who live below the FPL (about $23,000 for a family of four) say that their health is only fair or poor, compared with only 4 percent of people who live at 400 percent of the FPL—a fivefold difference. The figure also points out significant income differences in terms of levels of serious psychological distress and the likelihood of disability among the elderly.

Low income affects the health of poor people from birth. The high rate of infant mortality among poor people is due to a number of factors associated with poverty. Inadequate nutrition appears to account for the high death rates among the newborn children of low-income mothers. The babies most at risk are those with a low birth weight. Among the causes of low birth weight are the low nutritional value of the mother's diet, smoking or other drug use by the mother during pregnancy, and lack of prenatal care. After the neonatal period (the first three months), the higher rate of infant

Figure 2–4a Major Health Indicators, by Income (Federal Poverty Level): Only Fair or Poor Health (Self-Assessment), 2014

NOTE: FPL (Federal Poverty Level).
SOURCE: National Center for Health Statistics, 2014.

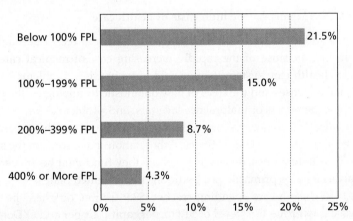

Figure 2–4b Major Health Indicators, by Income (Federal Poverty Level): Serious Psychological Distress, 2014

NOTE: FPL (Federal Poverty Level).
SOURCE: National Center for Health Statistics, 2014.

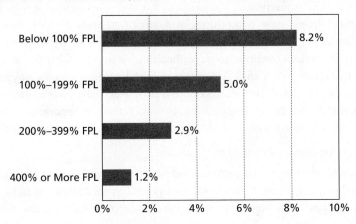

Figure 2–4c Major Health Indicators, by Income (Federal Poverty Level): Disability Among Elderly, 2013

NOTE: FPL (Federal Poverty Level).

SOURCE: National Center for Health Statistics, 2014.

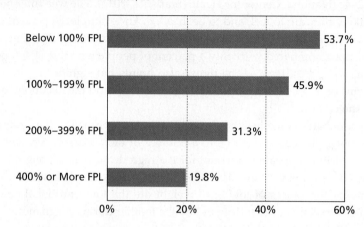

death among infants living in poverty is linked with a greater incidence of infectious diseases. Such diseases, in turn, are associated with poor sanitation and lack of access to high-quality medical care, as well as with drug use in some cases.

The High Cost of Health Care

2.4   Review the reasons for the high costs of health care.

Unequal access to health care is related to its cost, which in recent decades has been very high. In fact, because of the rapidly increasing cost of medical care in recent years, the U.S. health care system is often said to be in crisis. Problems such as containing hospital expenses and the costs of new diagnostic technologies, the cost of prescription drugs, the effects of malpractice lawsuits, and problems with managed care and other medical insurance systems are all specific aspects of the general crisis in health care economics in the United States. Other nations have some of the same problems and some different ones, depending on how they fund their health care systems, but this analysis focuses primarily on conditions in the United States.

In 2014, U.S. health care spending reached $2.9 trillion, or $9,255 per person, a ninefold increase over the 1980 level of $1,002 per capita (Unger and O'Donnell, 2014; Statistical Abstract, 2014). The good news is that, after skyrocketing increases for many years, 2014 was actually the fourth consecutive year of slower growth, averaging only 3 to 4 percent a year.

Yet, most Americans are likely to spend a higher proportion of their incomes on health care in coming years. Declining personal incomes due to global wage competition; dwindling government resources at the state and federal levels; the steady arrival of new drugs, new procedures, and advanced technologies; the continued profit motive in providing health care; and the difficulty of persuading people to change risky behaviors continue to make health care unaffordable for many people. As shown in Figure 2–5, 1 in 3 Americans report having difficulty paying medical bills, and ironically, almost two-thirds of these people actually have insurance (Pollitz, Cox, Lucia, and Keith, 2014). The problem is that, even with insurance, many people have to pay large sums of money to doctors and hospitals and for prescription drugs.

What are the consequences of medical debt?

Jackie, age 51, went for a routine checkup and mammogram, and the doctor was concerned about a lump in one of her breasts. Further tests revealed cancer. As Jackie tells it, she is not sure which caused her greater stress, the cancer or the continuous flow of *medical bills demanding immediate payment, which she refers to as "a complete night-mare." Jackie has insurance, but it covered only part of her very expensive and lengthy treatment. To help cover costs, she withdrew $48,000 out of her retirement account; it had taken her over 11 years to save that amount, and the withdrawal left her without any retirement cushion. But the bills continued to mount and the creditors began to call day and night, hounding her for payment. She sold her car and earned $14,000 for it, and the money went straight to medical bills. At one point, things were so dire that Jackie wondered whether she should go without treatment, risking possible death, but instead, a friend suggested that she ask her mortgage company whether they would revise her loan and lower the monthly payment on her house. They turned her down, and Jackie subsequently skipped a few payments. The skipped payments resulted in foreclosure proceedings. Jackie hoped she would be better able to pay past debts, as well as her ongoing care, if she didn't pay the mortgage so, as she put it, "I let them take the house."*

Jackie's story reveals that there are many consequences to the high cost of medicine and medical debt, including damaged credit, economic deprivation, depleted long-term assets, and housing instability. Some people file for bankruptcy, and others are forced to go without the care they need. These consequences can lead to grave emotional distress (Pollitz et al., 2014).

Specifically, what about health care costs so much? Many salient facts about and trends in health care costs can be gleaned from a careful look at Figure 2–6 (Kaiser Family Foundation, 2012). Notice that the largest expenditures are for hospital care and physicians' clinical services.

Hospitals

Until the mid-1980s, hospital costs rose at a dramatic pace, primarily because hospitals had little incentive to keep costs down. This situation was aggravated by health insurance programs like Blue Cross, which enabled hospitals to raise their fees almost at will. Expensive medical technologies are another important factor in the increase in hospital costs, as is the aging of the population, which increases the demand for hospital services.

In recent years, the rate of increase in hospital costs slowed somewhat, largely as a result of improvements in the efficiency of hospital administration that have been brought about largely by federal and state legislation. One technique used to reduce the level of hospital costs is to lower the average length of hospital stays. In addition, many procedures that previously were performed on an inpatient basis have been moved to outpatient and office settings. Other factors in the reduction of the overall

What Do You Think?

Why do you think medicine costs so much? This situation hasn't always been the case. Brainstorm to come up with at least five reasons why health care is so expensive. Then compare your answers with those provided in the text.

Figure 2–5 Percentage of Non-Elderly Adults with Difficulty Paying Medical Bills, 2012

SOURCE: Pollitz, Cox, Lucia, and Keith, 2014.

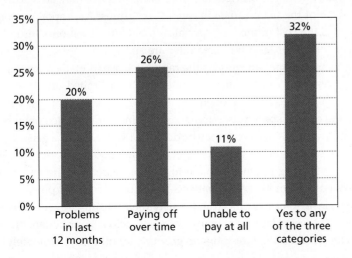

Figure 2–6 Distribution of National Health Expenditures, by Type of Service (in Billions), 2010

SOURCE: Kaiser Family Foundation, 2012.

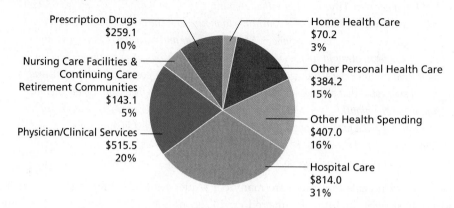

Prescription Drugs
$259.1
10%

Nursing Care Facilities &
Continuing Care
Retirement Communities
$143.1
5%

Physician/Clinical Services
$515.5
20%

Home Health Care
$70.2
3%

Other Personal Health Care
$384.2
15%

Other Health Spending
$407.0
16%

Hospital Care
$814.0
31%

level of hospital care are greater use of second opinions and an increase in care by nonhospital providers such as nursing homes and home health agencies.

Unfortunately, these various measures to control costs have not been fully successful. And as more patients are treated outside of hospitals or stay in hospitals for shorter periods, the costs of home care of the ill are rising rapidly. Another problem is that severe measures to reduce hospital costs disproportionately affect the poor and the elderly, who are more likely to suffer from chronic illnesses that may require hospitalization. These and similar situations illustrate the tendency of cost-control efforts in one area to result in higher costs elsewhere, and they provide an argument for comprehensive reform of the nation's health care system.

Physicians

During much of the twentieth century, a shortage of physicians, together with an increasing demand for medical services, helped doctors command high fees. The supply of doctors has grown significantly since 1950, but this growth has not necessarily led to improved access to medical care or to lower costs. Understanding the distribution of physicians will indicate why. People living in cities and suburbs can afford high-cost, specialized medical care. These places also tend to be more attractive than rural locales to physicians. As a result, physicians who engage in private practice tend to be clustered in metropolitan areas, producing shortages elsewhere. Even in densely settled urban areas, poor sections may have too few practicing physicians.

Contrary to what many Americans believe, the share of health care dollars that goes to doctors and clinical services has been declining, but they are and will remain a significant share of the nation's health care expenditures. An important component of these services is the cost of medical specialization. Only about one-third of physicians are general practitioners, and the remainder are specialists (AHRQ, 2011). One reason for the high degree of specialization is the rapid increase in medical knowledge, which means that physicians can become competent only in limited areas. Another reason is that high-quality medical care often requires the availability of specialists. The fact remains, however, that specialists command more income than doctors who engage in primary care. A specialist's income may be double or triple that of a general practitioner, although some effort is being made to limit Medicare and Medicaid payments to specialists while increasing payments made to primary care practitioners. Specialization also increases costs in another way; patients must consult several physicians for a variety of ailments instead of one physician for all of them. Visiting several different specialists multiplies the cost of treatment many times, whereas a primary care practitioner can coordinate care for the patent, resulting in greater continuity and ultimately better care.

Malpractice

A major factor in the high cost of physicians' services is the cost of malpractice insurance. Malpractice litigation has become more frequent for several reasons. Ineffective insurance programs play a significant role. If more people were adequately covered, they would be less likely to go to court to recover their health care costs. The increasing sophistication of medical technology also plays a part in the rise of malpractice litigation. Although recent advances enable doctors to perform treatments that once would have seemed miraculous, the treatments can be more hazardous for the patients if they are performed incorrectly or without sufficient skill and care. Public expectations about the powers of modern medicine also increase the likelihood of malpractice suits. A recent report by the American Hospital Administration estimates that 2014 medical malpractice claims will represent about 60 cents per every $100 of hospital revenue, or an average of $135 per hospital admission (Aon, November 7, 2013).

Medical Technologies

Steadily improving medical technologies, many of which can prolong life, are another reason for high medical costs. The list of advanced medical technologies that did not exist a few decades ago is impressive. It includes invasive cardiology (e.g., open heart surgery and angioplasty), renal dialysis, noninvasive imaging (e.g., sonograms, CAT scans, and MRI imaging), complex infertility treatments, organ transplantation, intraocular lens implants, motorized wheelchairs, and biotechnologies that are yielding new but costly drugs. Although some technologies may reduce the costs of health care, most studies indicate that they have caused total health care spending to rise (Kaiser Family Foundation, 2007; Rosenthal, 2014). For example, the Hastings Institute, a nonpartisan health research organization, claims that new or increased use of medical technology is responsible for at least 40 to 50 percent of the annual rise in health care costs. Although medical technology and expertise has dramatically deepened, it has not necessarily resulted in a higher quality of life for patients.

Prescription Drugs

The cost of prescription drugs is a large and growing factor in the high cost of health care. Even generic drugs, which consumers turn to because of their cost savings, have skyrocketed in price (Hirst, 2014). Throughout the industrialized world, advances in pharmaceutical research and technologies are bringing new and more effective drugs to market each year. These remedies often result in major savings for employers and individuals when measured in terms of lower rates of absence from work. But their costs threaten to accelerate the rate of increase in overall medical expenses. Total spending for prescription drugs increased over the past decade, due especially to the demand for new drugs to combat depression, allergies, arthritis, hypertension, and elevated cholesterol.

Demographic Factors

Another set of explanations for the high cost of American health care can be traced to demographic factors, which refer to aspects of population growth and change. Among the primary demographic factors influencing the cost of health care is the aging of the U.S. population, a phenomenon that is mirrored in many parts of the world, but is particularly salient in Western urban industrial nations (Centers for Disease Control and Prevention, 2013). The older population—people 65 years or older—numbered approximately 45 million in 2014 (Ortman, Velkoff and Hogan, 2014). They represented about 1 in every 8 Americans. Projections suggest that the number of elderly will more than double to approximately 92 million by 2060.

Marie and Gabrielle are twins celebrating their birthday. People who live to be 100 years old, centenarians, used to be rare, but that is no longer the case. However, these two may be the oldest twins on record.

Why is the number of older people in our society growing so quickly? The rapid aging of the U.S. population is being driven by two realities: Americans are living longer than in previous decades and, given the post–World War II baby boom, there are proportionately more older adults than in previous generations. Many Americans are now living into their seventies, eighties, and beyond. The leading edge of the baby boomers reached age 65 in 2011, launching an unparalleled phenomenon in the United States. Now, each and every day for the next 20 years, roughly 10,000 Americans will celebrate their sixty-fifth birthdays. By 2030, when the last baby boomer turns 65, the demographic landscape of our nation will have changed significantly.

The baby boom cohort, the generation of Americans born in the 15-year period after World War II, includes a disproportionately large number of dependent and working poor people. As this extremely large segment of the population passes through the life span, it exerts a strong influence on national social issues. Members of this cohort are living longer than previous generations and are likely to require costly medical services as they encounter the chronic illnesses of old age. Now entering their retirement years, they are becoming more concerned about health care and income security. The resulting pressure on the nation's health care system, according to some analysts, threatens to bankrupt the Social Security and Medicare systems unless changes are made in the taxation system that funds these entitlement programs.

Even more striking, the number of people often referred to as the "oldest-old"—those people age 85 and over—are the fastest growing cohort in the United States. Today they number about 5 million, but in 2050, they are estimated to number about 19 million (U.S. Census Bureau, 2014a). It is these people who will likely consume a great deal of costly health care in their last years of life.

Cultural Factors

Cultural factors also contribute to the high cost of health care in the United States. Cultural factors refer to specific ways of life, beliefs, and norms of behavior that may contribute to health or illness. Cultural factors that raise the cost of health care in the United States include aspects of lifestyle such as heavy use of tobacco and alcohol; unhealthy diet; high stress; and sedentary activities like driving and watching television and, at the opposite extreme, high-risk activities that increase the likelihood of broken bones and orthopedic surgery. The discussion here highlights several of these specific important factors that affect our health and well-being and contribute to health care costs.

OBESITY   It is strange to think that many people around the world are very sick or even dying because of lack of food, while here in the United States our trouble is that we consume too much food. Obesity is a social problem. It affects a large number of people and has serious consequences not only for the individuals involved but also for society as a whole.

For adults, overweight and obesity ranges are determined by using weight and height to calculate a number called the "body mass index" (BMI). For most people, BMI correlates with their amount of body fat.

- An adult who has a BMI between 25 and 29.9 is considered overweight.
- An adult who has a BMI of 30 or higher is considered obese.

See Table 2–2 for an example of BMI calculation.

Today, about 69 percent of Americans age 20 and over are overweight, including about 35 percent who are obese (CDC, 2014). Among children, nearly a third are overweight, and 1 in 5 is obese. However, we have not always been such an overweight group. In the past few decades, obesity has become much more prevalent among Americans than it was during the mid-twentieth century.

Obesity is a social problem because of the widespread nature of the epidemic, its considerable financial costs, the toll it takes on health, and the connections between obesity and food production and distribution in our country. Major health and social impacts of obesity include the following:

- Obesity increases the risk of illness from about thirty serious medical conditions.
- Obesity is associated with increases in deaths from all causes.
- Earlier onset of obesity-related diseases such as type 2 diabetes is being reported in obese children and adolescents.
- Obese individuals are at higher risk for impaired mobility.
- Overweight or obese individuals experience social stigmatization and discrimination in employment and academic situations.

The CDC estimates that about 280,000 Americans die each year as a direct consequence of obesity, although the immediate causes of death are quite varied. Heart disease, diabetes, and stroke are especially prevalent consequences of obesity. Second only to smoking as a cause of illness and death, obesity, like smoking, is directly related to trends in individual behavior—and, many critics would add, to the influence of corporations that market unhealthy foods to eager consumers. Conditions of overweight and obesity and their associated health problems have a significant economic impact on the health care system. Medical costs associated with overweight and obesity conditions may involve direct and indirect costs. Direct medical costs may include preventive, diagnostic, and treatment services related to obesity. Indirect costs relate to illness and mortality costs. Illness costs are defined as the value of income lost from decreased productivity, restricted activity, absenteeism,

Table 2–2 An Example of Calculating BMI to Determine Weight Category

Height	Weight Range	BMI	Considered
5'9"	124 lbs or less	Below 18.5	Underweight
5'9"	125 lbs to 168 lbs	18.5 to 24.9	Healthy weight
5'9"	169 lbs to 202 lbs	25.0 to 29.9	Overweight
5'9"	203 lbs or more	30 or higher	Obese

NOTE: BMI (body mass index).

SOURCE: CDC, 2012.

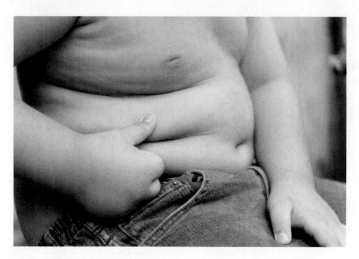

Obesity is a unique problem found primarily in developing countries. While many people in the world struggle to find enough food, Americans in particular face an obesity epidemic.

and bed days. Mortality costs are the value of future income lost by premature death (CDC, 2012).

SMOKING On January 11, 1964, Luther L. Terry, M.D., the ninth Surgeon General of the United States, released the first report on the health consequences of smoking: *Smoking and Health: Report of the Advisory Committee of the Surgeon General of the Public Health Service.* That report marked a major step to reduce the adverse impact of tobacco use on health worldwide by highlighting its many dangers and addictive qualities. The tobacco companies fought long and hard to discredit these findings (Proctor, 2012). Some catchy slogans they came up with to promote their products include the following (Stanford Research into the Impact of Advertising, 2014):

- "Smoke like a chimney? Who cares? Your mouth will taste clean as a whistle"
- "We don't try to scare you with medical claims"
- "Sensitive throats welcome Luckies"
- "Inhale to your heart's content"
- "More doctors smoke Camels than any other cigarette"

And perhaps the most famous slogan targeted women, tying smoking to liberation: "You've come a long way, baby."

Fifty years have now passed since that seminal report was published. During this period, thirty-one Surgeon General's reports have offered the latest available scientific evidence to demonstrate the negative health consequences of smoking and involuntary exposure to tobacco smoke. The conclusions from these reports have evolved from a few causal associations in 1964 to a robust body of evidence documenting the irrefutable health consequences from both active smoking and exposure to secondhand smoke across a wide range of diseases and vital organ systems (American Cancer Society, 2015; U.S. Department of Health and Human Services, 2014).

In a nutshell, smoking kills. Almost 21 million Americans have died as a result of smoking since the first Surgeon General's report on smoking and health was released in 1964, as you can see in Table 2–3. They died from smoking-related cancers, cardiovascular and pulmonary diseases, and even from house fires caused by the more than 25 trillion cigarettes they smoked. Most were adults with a history of smoking, but nearly 2.5 million were nonsmokers who died from heart disease or lung cancer caused by exposure to secondhand smoke. Another 100,000 were babies who died of sudden infant death syndrome (commonly referred to as SIDS) or

Table 2–3 Premature Deaths Caused by Smoking and Exposure to Secondhand Smoke, 1965–2014

Cause of Death	Total
Smoking-related cancers	6,587,000
Cardiovascular and metabolic diseases	7,787,000
Pulmonary diseases	3,804,000
Conditions related to pregnancy and birth	108,000
Residential fires	86,000
Lung cancers caused by exposure to secondhand smoke	263,000
Coronary heart disease caused by exposure to secondhand smoke	2,194,000
	20,829,000

SOURCE: U.S. Department of Health and Human Services, 2014.

complications from prematurity, low birth weight, or other conditions caused by the mother's smoking (U.S. Department of Health and Human Services, 2014).

Despite denials by the tobacco industry, people gradually listened to the official reports and public service announcements highlighting the dangers of smoking. The share of the adult population who smoke declined from 42 percent to 18 percent during the 50-year period between 1964 and 2014. Men were the first to decrease their smoking behaviors, and then women followed. Today there are actually more former than current smokers; however, the decline has slowed in recent years. Smoking remains popular among specific groups, as revealed in Table 2–4. In particular, men, Native Americans, those people with lower levels of education and income, adults between ages 18 and 44, and those who live in the Midwest are most likely to smoke (U.S. Department of Health and Human Services, 2014).

Smoking remains the leading high-risk behavior associated with poor health, untimely death, and extremely high health care costs. In fact, smoking-related issues account for somewhere between 7 and 9 percent of health care expenditures, at roughly $133–$176 billion. But there are also other costs, such as $151 billion on lost productivity due to premature death and $5.6 billion for lost productivity due to exposure to secondhand smoke (U.S. Department of Health and Human Services, 2014).

Most smokers begin as adolescents. In consequence, many health experts consider preventing tobacco use among young people, or getting them to quit, to be

What Do You Think?

Do you know someone who smokes? How does he or she justify it, given the scientific evidence outlining the health dangers?

Table 2–4 Who Is Most Likely to Smoke?

Sex	
Male	25%
Female	19%
Race/Ethnicity	
White	24%
Black	23%
Hispanic	15%
American Indian/Alaska Native	39%
Asian	8%
Education	
Less Than High School	32%
High School Graduate	27%
Some College	23%
College Graduate	10%
Age	
18–25	25%
26–44	27%
45–64	22%
65+	10%
Poverty Status	
At or Above Poverty Level	20%
Below Poverty Level	33%
Region	
Northeast	21%
Midwest	25%
South	23%
West	19%

SOURCE: U.S. Department of Health and Human Services, 2014.

among the nation's most important health challenges. School programs and public service announcements are specifically designed to target youth. Efforts have been somewhat successful, with smoking rates among young people declining by half since the 1990s. However, it remains that nearly 20 percent of high school males and 16 percent of high school females are regular smokers.

RISKY BEHAVIORS AND COSTLY PROCEDURES   Costly injuries due to skiing, rock climbing, mountain biking, skateboarding, and roller skating are associated with higher-income adolescents and young adults. Sports injuries are only one of many examples reflecting how features of American culture drive up the cost of medical care and health insurance. American culture, more than those of other highly developed societies, emphasizes seeking the most up-to-date medical treatments, even when those treatments have not always proven helpful. Bone marrow transplants to fight advanced cancers, hormone replacement therapy for women after menopause, and the indiscriminate use of MRI or CAT scans are all examples of expensive procedures or practices that increase costs for all health care consumers. At the same time, Americans have shown great reluctance to support any health care system that would limit their ability to seek whatever medical treatment they desire; this mindset drives up the cost of insurance and means that people who are less able to pay medical bills will postpone important preventive treatments.

Ethical Issues

2.5   Summarize the ethical issues surrounding health care.

As medical technology has improved and life-prolonging procedures have become more available and dependable, many complex ethical issues have arisen, and our society is only beginning to grapple with them. For example, some new technologies, such as heart and kidney transplants, are extremely costly and cannot be provided to all patients who might benefit from them. Thus, the question arises of how to choose the patients who will undergo these procedures.

The availability of life-prolonging equipment and procedures has also given rise to new questions about the meaning of life and death. State legislatures across the country have been debating the question of whether death occurs when the heart stops beating or when the brain stops functioning. Courts have been required to decide whether patients should have the right to die by terminating life-prolonging treatments.

END-OF-LIFE ISSUES   Few aspects of health care are as fraught with emotion and confusion as those dealing with how and under what circumstances loved ones die. On one side of the issue are people who believe in the "right to die." They claim that people should be able to commit suicide and have others assist them in doing so. Few societies in the world regard suicide as an acceptable individual act, so they make **euthanasia** (the painless killing of a patient suffering from a terminal illness or irreversible coma) illegal.

In recent years, a related issue, physician-assisted suicide, has come to the fore. Michigan doctor Jack Kevorkian became the personification of the right-to-die issue when he helped a 54-year-old woman with Alzheimer's disease kill herself, using an intravenous device that allowed the patient to receive a lethal drug by pressing a button. The doctor was arrested and charged with first-degree murder; later the charges were dropped, but the doctor was ordered to refrain from using the suicide device in the future. Kevorkian continued to defy the authorities in Michigan and eventually was sentenced to a term in prison. Although many doctors and health authorities condemn the practice, Kevorkian's sensational methods brought the right-to-die issue to national attention.

euthanasia

The painless killing of a patient suffering from a terminal illness or irreversible coma.

Only Oregon and a few European nations have laws that allow some form of legal suicide that involves the help of others:

1. Oregon (since 1997, physician-assisted suicide only)
2. Switzerland (1941, physician- and non-physician-assisted suicide only)
3. Belgium (2002, permits "euthanasia" but does not define the method)
4. Netherlands (voluntary euthanasia and physician-assisted suicide lawful since April 2002, but permitted by the courts since 1984)

Nothing in the 2010 health care reform plans suggested support for euthanasia or any form of assisted suicide, but opponents inferred from some proposed language in the ACA legislation that government bureaucrats would be heavily involved in patients' and families' decisions about end-of-life care. Sarah Palin, former governor of Alaska and vice presidential candidate, made headlines when she claimed that the reforms would subject dying people and their loved ones to federal "death panels" that would pressure them to make decisions that would reduce the cost of end-of-life medical care. She was referring to a clause in a draft of the reform bill (not included in the final law) that would have authorized advanced-care planning consultations for senior citizens on Medicare every five years, and more often "if there is a significant change in the health condition of the individual…or upon admission to a skilled nursing facility, a long-term care facility…or a hospice program." Although information about choices such as palliative care (designed to improve the quality of life for those who are suffering a life-threatening illness), home hospice care, and end-of-life directives can help allay fear and confusion about a loved one's last days, the potential value of such advice was immediately lost in the outcry against the idea of government "death panels."

The fear generated by false claims that bureaucrats on federal "death panels" would force people into end-of-life treatment modes reminded many citizens of the similar hysteria generated by the politicization of the tragic case of Terri Schiavo from 1990 until 2005. The controversy over removal of life support for Schiavo called attention to the problem of death with dignity in a situation in which a patient is on life support but has left no clear information about what their wishes are for handling the situation. To her parents and the lay public, Schiavo seemed to be responding to voices and other stimuli. But the neurologists who examined her believed that she had no awareness or other higher brain functions and that, with life support, she might live in a vegetative state for an indefinite length of time. Although individuals who are in a persistent vegetative state may appear somewhat normal, they do not speak and are unable to respond to commands. (For more on this subject, go to www.ninds.nih.gov/disorders/coma/coma.htm.)

Schiavo's family was divided on whether to remove life support, with her husband asserting that she had told him she would never want to live in such a hopeless condition. Right-to-life groups, along with political leaders, including President George W. Bush, former Governor Jeb Bush, then-House Majority Leader Tom DeLay, and many others, supported the right-to-life advocates and soon made Schiavo a national symbol of their desire to create a "culture of life" rather than of death. Every court, including the U.S. Supreme Court, ruled in favor of Schiavo's husband's assertion of his wife's right to die with dignity. Life support was removed, but demonstrations continued to be held outside her hospital until she finally expired. Every opinion poll conducted about how Americans actually felt about the case showed that strong majorities believed that the courts had acted wisely and that government should not interfere in what most people consider highly personal and extremely emotional issues.

As the populations of the urban industrial nations continue to age, and given the appearance of ever more sophisticated methods for prolonging life, the number of ethical, legal, and technical questions about life's end grows. Imagine that your elderly parent has had a stroke. Doctors express little hope that consciousness can be restored or that life-support systems could be removed without causing death. This scenario

advance directive
A written statement that explains the patient's wishes for medical care should the person be unable to communicate them to the physician.

is not a rare situation. Unless your family and the terminally ill parent have prepared **advance directives** (a written statement that explains the patient's wishes for medical care should the person be unable to communicate them to the physician) for dealing with the situation, much agony and prolonged suffering can ensue for everyone concerned. Advance directives have two parts: a living will, which tells doctors and hospitals how the patient wants to be cared for should he or she become terminally ill, and a health care proxy, which designates an advocate, usually a close family member, who can make sure that those wishes are honored.

PRIVACY AND PATIENTS' RIGHTS Another major medical-ethical issue in the United States concerns patients' right to privacy and control over their medical records. Insurance companies wish to share patients' medical records, and there are good medical reasons, as well as economic ones, for doing so. If hospitals, doctors, and insurance companies could draw on a single national database of patient records, the nation's medical system would benefit from faster processing and reduced waste. But patients' advocacy groups fear that systematic sharing of medical records would also allow insurance companies to deny coverage to people with serious medical conditions like AIDS and many other illnesses. In 2002, the George W. Bush administration ruled that patients did not need to give prior approval for their records to be shared, opening the way to both the positive and negative consequences of the flow of private medical information. Because the administration did not take any measures that would help fund the creation of a state-of-the-art medical database, critics argued that the ruling was primarily a gift to the major medical insurance corporations.

Explanations of Health Care Problems

2.6 Classify explanations for health care problems.

Why do we have such difficulty improving the quality of health care services and providing more equal access to them? The explanations offered by medical sociologists depend to a large extent on the perspective from which they view the problem. Conflict theorists, for example, tend to view the problem as an inherent feature of tensions associated with capitalism: The poor get less medical care because they get less of everything in American society. Those who approach this question from a functionalist perspective have sought the answers in medicine's development into a complex and costly social institution. And from an interactionist perspective, many of the problems of health care in the United States and other highly developed nations can be traced to cultural factors, including the way people are taught to interact with one another. (See Figure 2–7.) In this section, each of these approaches to the explanation of health care problems is briefly discussed.

Figure 2–7 Three Approaches to Explaining Social Problems in Health

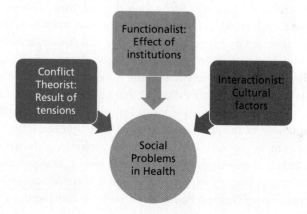

Class and Class Conflict

Sociologists often point out that social class, measured by the income and wealth a household has at its disposal, goes a long way toward explaining the types of illnesses experienced by members of that household and the kinds of health care they receive. We have already suggested that lack of access to good health care causes higher rates of illness and death among those who are poor. Until the early twentieth century, the ill health of poor people was caused largely by infectious diseases. Today, medical science can control and cure such diseases much more effectively, with the result that, by themselves, those diseases no longer account for tremendous differences in health between those who are poor and those who are not. Instead, the chief obstacles to good health in developed nations are lack of access to good health care, inadequate knowledge about health, failure to take preventive medical action, and delay in seeking treatment, all of which are especially prevalent among poor people (Cockerham, 2012; Weiss and Lonnquist, 2015).

In fact, as control of chronic diseases like cancer becomes more important, the differences between the health of those who are poor and those who are not are likely to increase; that is, poor people will still have higher rates of illness and death than people who are not poor because of their relative lack of access to high-quality health care.

In a classic analysis of the relationship between social class and ill health, Lee Rainwater (1974) introduced the idea that lack of access to health care is not the only factor that affects the health of poor people: Just being poor promotes poor health. Poor people, for example, cannot afford to eat properly, so they are likely to be weak. They often live in the most polluted areas and hence are susceptible to respiratory diseases. Because they cannot afford proper housing, they are exposed to disease-carrying refuse and rodents. Perhaps most important, their lives are filled with stress due to constant worry about getting enough money to pay for necessities. Such long-term stress can cause both physical and mental illness. Being poor also makes it difficult to react to minor signs of ill health. A cough is likely to be dismissed if one does not have enough to eat; only a much worse cough will prompt a visit to a clinic, and by then it may be too late. Poor people also seem to feel middle-aged earlier than those who are not poor.

Social scientists who see class conflict as a basic cause of social-class differences in health and unequal access to health care are skeptical of the increasing privatization of the American health care system. They point out that, as public hospitals are replaced by hospitals run for profit, there is a tendency to avoid treatment of less profitable patients (Wangsness, 2009).

Studies have shown that, as more hospitals are managed by for-profit corporations (as opposed to the public sector), they are indeed more likely to be concerned about earning money and less concerned with providing medical care for patients, particularly those less likely to be able to pay, who require more expensive treatments such as drug counseling, suicide prevention, and AIDS therapy (Ferdinand, Epane, and Menachemi, 2014; Gandhi, 2012; Kutscher, 2014). Both public and private hospitals share the duty to accept all patients who require emergency care, but private hospitals can decide to eliminate their emergency facilities altogether, and the requirement for emergency care does not extend to nonemergencies.

Social scientists who view health care problems from a conflict perspective often explain the outcomes of conflicts over medical policy in terms of conflict between classes. For example, in a study of the social, political, and psychological impact of AIDS in America, Dennis Altman (1987) showed that, as long as AIDS was perceived as a disease of homosexuals and intravenous drug users, members of the middle and upper classes did not put pressure on the government to invest heavily in its treatment and cure. Altman and others have pointed out that, because AIDS strikes disproportionately at less advantaged citizens and members of minority groups, it is often thought of as "their" disease, which was especially true in the beginning years of the epidemic.

Institutions and Health Care

Functionalist explanations of health care problems focus on features of health care institutions themselves. Sociologists with this institutional orientation point out that every society is faced with the problem of distributing health care services among its members. The United States uses a marketplace approach, which views health care as a commodity subject to the demands and spending power of consumers. Canada, by contrast, views health care as an entitlement of citizenship and extends full coverage to all its legal residents (HealthCanada, 2014).

Since health care costs are lower in Canada and many medical professionals believe the quality of care in that nation is at least equal to that of the United States, there are many advocates for a comparable "universal and single-payer" insurance system in the United States. Opponents of the Canadian system point out, however, that it deprives the well-off of the higher-quality health care they can afford. The broad sociological issue here is how to improve health care institutions to provide the best possible care for the greatest number of people. Most medical sociologists do not agree that health care should be treated as a commodity that is available in higher amounts and quality to those most able to afford it. But this position does not mean that they believe the Canadian model could be imported to the United States without a great deal of compromise.

There are a number of functionalist arguments for why a service that has come to be viewed as a basic human right, such as health care, should not be treated as a commodity:

- *Information.* A consumer is not in a position to shop for medical treatment in the same way that one shops for other products or services because the need for such treatment cannot be evaluated by the consumer.
- *Product uncertainty.* The consumer does not have sufficient knowledge to judge the effectiveness of sophisticated treatments.
- *Norms of treatment.* Health care is provided under the control of a physician. A patient does not direct his or her own treatment.
- *Lack of price competition.* Prices for doctors' services are not advertised and are not subject to true competition.
- *Restricted entry.* There are numerous barriers to entry to medical school. Many qualified applicants are turned down because of a limited number of places.
- *Professional dominance.* Many health care services restricted to physicians could be performed by trained technicians. This restriction has created a monopoly.
- *Misallocated supply.* An abundance of specialists encourages the use of expensive and sophisticated treatments when simpler ones would be just as effective (Dlugacz, 2006).

Health and Social Interaction

The relatively poor health of Americans is due in part to features of our lifestyle, including sedentary occupations, nonnutritious diets, lack of proper exercise, environmental pollution, and cigarette smoking (Cockerham, 2012). But if activities like smoking are detrimental to health, why do people engage in them? Interactionist explanations of social problems related to health care often draw on studies of patterns of sociability (i.e., interaction among people in groups) and the ways in which people are socialized in different societies and communities. Features of a society's lifestyle, such as smoking, drinking, and diet, are deeply ingrained in the way people interact with one another. Very often we eat, drink, or smoke as much to be sociable as to sustain ourselves.

Excessive eating, leading to obesity, and high rates of alcohol consumption are among the health problems related to patterns of sociability in an affluent society.

But as noted earlier, the most pervasive and serious problems are created by smoking. In addition, women often expose unborn infants to the negative effects of smoking, especially low birth weight.

Interactionist perspectives on issues like smoking and health typically focus on the way communications (e.g., advertising images and messages) seek to connect the use of tobacco with particular lifestyles. They may also take a more explicitly critical look at the way tobacco companies directly or indirectly influence those communications. For example, the cigarette brand Virginia Slims was specifically marketed to women, and ads featured a liberated young woman thoroughly enjoying her cigarette.

It is helpful to think of the major sociological perspectives as conceptual tools to be used in analyzing a complex social problem such as the prevention and treatment of physical illnesses. No single perspective explains all the important issues, but together they go a long way toward a full explanation. The functionalist view is most helpful in pointing out how social institutions like hospitals should function, why they do not function effectively, and how they could be improved. The conflict perspective allows for more insight into the influence of inequalities of wealth, education, and power on access to and quality of health care. The interactionist perspective points to the way differences in people's perception of social conditions such as the obesity epidemic influence their behavior toward others, as explored in A Personal View—My Experience with Obesity (below).

Mocking the famous Marlboro cigarette advertisements, this 1990s anti-smoking billboard is designed to make a point: smoking kills. During this time, cigarette manufacturers were trying to find ways out of costly lawsuits, and many cities began promoting anti-tobacco ads.

A Personal View

My Experience with Obesity

Like many overweight adults, I was also a very pudgy kid. I didn't know I was overweight until I went to school. Until then I was happy and enjoying all the rich and sugary foods my momma would make. "These will taste yummy," she used to say, as we devoured two-dozen chocolate chip cookies in one sitting. Momma was obese, weighing in at more than 300 pounds. But I never noticed. She was what you might call a binge eater. She said it calmed her nerves. And I learned this habit early in life.

By the time I went to kindergarten I weighed nearly 80 pounds. I was much heavier than any other child, but I continued not to notice. I did see that I was the slowest one at PE, and I seemed to huff and puff more than the others, but I didn't give it much thought. That is, until Brian Hemling, the class clown, called me "fatso" when I stood in line to get a drink of water. "Hey fatso, don't drink all the water. Save some for the rest of us." He laughed, and soon several other kids joined in. I'm sure my face turned red because I felt so embarrassed. I knew what the word fat meant; I just hadn't noticed that I fit the description. But that day changed my life, and not for the better.

Instead of being the happy child I used to be, I began a slow descent into depression. I hated school. A few people were mean to me, but most just ignored me. I didn't have any friends. I was always the last one picked for a team in PE, or the last one picked as a square-dancing partner in third grade. When the teacher decided to start assigning partners, all the boys had their eye on me, hoping that I would be assigned to someone else.

I consoled myself with food. This was easy to do because my momma continued to have fattening foods around the house, and together we would binge on what was available. A large bag of potato chips? No problem. I'd wash it down with a coke and ice cream. Of course, this only made my weight continue to skyrocket.

When I was in seventh grade I had to go to the doctor to get a physical for summer camp. I hadn't been to the doctor in years, and I was embarrassed to take off my clothes in front of her. At this point I weighed almost 190 pounds. But the doctor saw my shyness, and was actually really kind about it. However, she also told me directly that I was overweight and needed to be on a special weight loss program. She asked a lot of questions: What foods does my mom buy? What do we eat for dinner? Do we eat in front of the TV? What do I snack on? She called my mother into the room to discuss diet, exercise, and fitness. Then she made us agree to sign me up for a special class designed to help teens with weight loss. This day also changed my life, this time for the better.

I met new friends from the class and was now no longer lonely. Together we had weekly weigh-ins that were made into celebrations, not punishments. We socialized outdoors and exercised: We hiked, biked, and swam our way to fitness. We took cooking classes; if our parents didn't want to cook healthy foods, then we would do it ourselves. It worked! The pounds came off, and within eight months I was down to my desired weight.

Fortunately my mom supported my changes, although she did not incorporate them for herself. She remains obese, and now has diabetes, among other health problems. Her feet swell badly, which makes daily life difficult for her. Even working her eight-hour day is tough, and she has missed a lot of work because of health. I wish she would get serious about losing weight.

—Elise, Age 19

Critical Thinking

Why is there stigma surrounding obesity? Is it seen as a medical problem or a personal failing?

Social Policy

2.7 **Identify key issues in social policy, including the Affordable Care Act (ACA).**

When we compare ourselves with other advanced industrial nations, the United States is doing a relatively poor job of providing health care for its population (OECD, 2013). The Organisation for Economic Co-operation and Development (OECD) is a unique forum where the governments of thirty-four democracies with market economies work together and provide a setting in which governments can compare policy experiences. When we compare ourselves with these countries on basic health indicators like infant mortality rates or life expectancy, we pale in comparison with most of them. For example, while the average person in Sweden lives 82 years, the average American dies three years earlier. In fact, an average American dies a year and a half earlier than the OECD average. We fare no better in terms of how many babies die in their first year of life (OECD, 2013).

A primary reason our country's health registers so badly is that our low-income and minority populations have such poor health. More affluent individuals and families tend to get excellent care in the most up-to-date facilities, and they tend to say that they are satisfied with their care. In most other OECD countries the health gap between the rich and poor is significantly smaller than ours.

All major industrial nations are having difficulty coping with the demands on their health care systems, demands brought on by aging populations with more chronic illnesses. None of them has found easy solutions or avoided the need for compromises and less-than-perfect solutions. But in the United States—as compared with Canada, France, Germany, England, and the Scandinavian nations—there is an even greater lag in arriving at reforms of health care institutions that address the major problems.

The Single-Payer Nations

In Canada and some of the social democracies of Western Europe, the problems arising from aging populations, lack of coverage for the poor, the challenge of controlling health care costs, and a host of other issues are addressed through what is known as a single-payer system. In 1946, Canada introduced national legislation to extend health care to all, regardless of age, occupation, preexisting conditions, or income (HealthCanada, 2014). Today, all citizens and legal residents of Canada are covered by the Canadian "Medicare" system. Doctors are considered independent practitioners; however, there is only one official insurance company, and that is the government. Each Canadian province has its own system of health care providers, but to receive federal funding, the system must provide comprehensive services for anyone in the

Table 2–5 Canadians' Level of Satisfaction with Their Single-Payer Health Care System

Satisfied with wait times	76%
Satisfied with last doctor visit	84%
Confident that I or a family member were to become seriously ill, we would be able to access the necessary health care services	81%

SOURCE: EKOS Research Associates, Inc., 2011.

province. In this way, everyone is entitled to the same quality of services. Relatively few Canadians complain about the system or about lack of access to doctors, as shown in Table 2–5 (EKOS Research Associates, 2011). Overall, they seem quite satisfied with their health care system.

Yet, the Canadian system has some drawbacks. It is less well equipped with advanced medical technologies. As a result, there are usually longer waits than you would find in the United States for certain kinds of tests. (However, as shown in Table 2–5 over three-quarters of Canadians say that they are satisfied with the wait times.) Moreover, hospitals and doctors are allocated a fixed amount for their services, which keeps costs in check, but also results in longer hospital stays and a higher rate of hospital admissions than in the United States. However, with no insurance forms or billing procedures, the system employs far fewer clerks and other nonmedical service workers (Cockerham, 2012). Administrative costs are thus far lower than they are in the United States (less than 1 percent of all medical expenses compared with over 6 percent in the United States). In recent years, however, the rising costs of health care have placed strains on the Canadian system and have contributed to already high federal and provincial tax rates, something that frightens U.S. lawmakers who might otherwise be attracted to the more equitable Canadian system.

Health Care Reform in the United States: The Affordable Care Act (ACA)

With health costs spiraling upward far faster than the rate of inflation and the number of uninsured steadily increasing, there has long been debate about what to do. President Obama was not the first to tackle health care reform, but given his success, the reforms he championed will likely be his legacy. The **Affordable Care Act (ACA)** was passed in March 2010. "The bill I'm signing will set in motion reforms that generations of Americans have fought for and marched for and hungered to see," Mr. Obama said, adding, "Today we are affirming that essential truth, a truth every generation is called to rediscover for itself, that we are not a nation that scales back its aspirations" (quoted in Stolberg and Pear, 2010, p. 1).

With these comments, President Obama signed the bill mandating the first major overhaul of the U.S. health care system since the creation of Medicare and Medicaid in 1967. The signing capped over a year of extremely rancorous debate in Congress and throughout the United States. Republican leaders, who were unanimous in their opposition to the bill, were particularly angry at its passage. Liberals in Congress were also somewhat disappointed. They had hoped for a bill that would include even more of the uninsured and would also include a provision allowing citizens to choose a "public option," a form of public insurance like Medicare, which would be available to all. In the end, however, the bill represented a series of major compromises and will eventually extend the benefits of health insurance to millions of citizens.

The ACA is quite complex, but Table 2–6 outlines some of the major provisions (Kaiser Family Foundation, 2015).

In drafting the ACA, legislators had to balance a phasing-in of the bill's changes over multiple years—to allow time for hospitals, insurance companies, and a host of

Affordable Care Act (ACA)

Legislation developed by President Obama and passed in 2010 that is the first major overhaul of the U.S. health care system since the creation of Medicare and Medicaid in 1967.

What Do You Think?

Give an example of the arguments made by people who (a) think the ACA goes too far, (b) support the ACA, and (c) think the ACA does not go far enough.

Table 2–6 Key Components of the Affordable Care Act (ACA)

The ACA is a complex piece of legislation that affects individuals, employers, and insurance companies. In brief, below are some of the highlights of the ACA.

Most individuals were required to have health insurance by 2014.
Individuals without access to affordable employer coverage will be able to purchase coverage through a health insurance exchange with "credits" available to make coverage more affordable to some people.
Small businesses will be able to purchase coverage through a separate exchange.
Employers will be required to pay penalties for employees who receive credits.
New regulations will be imposed on health plans that will prevent health insurers from denying coverage to people for any reason, or for charging higher premiums based on health status or sex.
Young adults will be allowed to stay on their parents' plan until they are 26 years old.
Medicaid will be expanded to 133 percent of the federal poverty level (roughly $15,000 for an individual and $30,000 for a family of four).

SOURCE: Kaiser Family Foundation, 2015.

other actors to prepare and adjust—with the equally urgent need for citizens to gain some immediate benefits. And since the bill was being proposed during a severe economic recession, against a background of claims that the nation could not afford the cost of health care reform, compromises were also included that would pace the implementation of change over a time period during which the economy would be expected to improve.

As soon as the bill was passed, adults and children who were previously denied coverage due to preexisting conditions became eligible for access to health care. Insurance companies are required to allow these individuals to gain access to coverage. This especially significant change ends the ability of health insurance providers to reject coverage for people with preexisting conditions like AIDS, asthma, and other common but costly illnesses.

In an immediate and major change for families with college-age members, children up to age 26 can stay on their parents' health insurance plan. Small businesses that offer insurance to their employees can get a 35 percent tax credit from premiums paid, which will make it much easier for many small businesses to afford health insurance for their employees. New plans written during this time have to offer preventive care with no co-payments or deductibles. Retirees ages 55–64 are offered access to a reinsurance program—one of the many aspects of the bill that are intended to stimulate the economy as a whole.

By 2014, the bill's most significant measures went into effect, adding millions of citizens to the rolls of those with medical insurance and medical benefits, and reducing the number of people without insurance from 50 million in 2010 to 30 million in 2014. The ACA uses the strategy of the successful Massachusetts health care system, which requires all citizens to have medical insurance. This helps to keep the overall costs down. In 2014, an IRS penalty of $750 per individual or 2 percent of income—whichever is greater—went into effect for any citizen who is not covered by an employer or a public plan, such as Medicaid or Medicare, and who chooses not to

The Affordable Care Act is controversial. But the bottom line is that people with insurance are more likely to get quality health care than are people without it.

purchase health insurance. No one can be denied access to insurance for preexisting conditions, and annual caps on benefits are banned altogether.

By 2018, all insurance plans must offer preventive care with no co-payments or deductibles. The federal government will have established a subsidy program to help those with low incomes pay for the mandatory insurance if they have no existing insurance. The Congressional Budget Office estimates that by this time millions of American citizens will have been added to the total of those with adequate health benefits. Further, according to its early estimates, the total savings to the federal budget, due to cost controls, fewer catastrophic illnesses, and other improvements in health care, will offset the additional costs of the reforms and will have reduced the federal deficit by approximately $125 billion, with additional savings to be determined each year thereafter.

Future Prospects

Passage of the ACA in 2010 was the beginning of a new era in health care policy in the United States. Advances can be expected on many fronts, but how well costs will be controlled is the essential policy issue. The first benefits of the act should come with increased coverage and much greater access to primary care clinics and physicians. This new level of access is likely to reduce costs to society significantly, particularly by enabling more people to seek medical care at early stages. People without insurance are more likely to postpone seeking medical care because they cannot afford it. These delays often result in costly treatments that earlier detection could have prevented. For example, women without insurance are less likely to receive prenatal care in their pregnancies. When it is time to give birth, they may simply go to the emergency room at a local hospital. But because no information is known about the pregnancy, the emergency room staff treats the case as high risk, costing thousands of extra, often unnecessary, dollars. Likewise, people without insurance are far more likely than those with health insurance to have serious cancers diagnosed in late stages. Diagnosis at earlier stages not only can save lives but also can reduce the costs to society. The idea is that, spread over many different illnesses and conditions, the savings could amount to many billions of dollars annually.

Going Beyond Left and Right

At this writing, almost every major health initiative, either in the United States or globally, is fraught with issues that originate from deep ideological divisions and moral dilemmas. Among these issues, particularly in the United States, are end-of-life measures, research on stem cells taken from unused human embryos (i.e., ones not used in fertility clinics), funding for women's reproductive health, funding for safe-sex practices to reduce the spread of sexually transmitted diseases like AIDS, and reform of the health care system itself. These issues are all subjects of intense debates between staunch conservatives, who are opposed to any form of intervention in ending life and to any system that seems to resemble "socialized medicine," and liberals, who advocate health policies that stress individual choice and a role for government in providing more equal access to high-quality health care. The U.S. population is deeply divided on these issues, although most people believe individuals must be free to make their own final choices without governmental intervention. Over the next few years, it is likely that this belief, along with the shared perception that the nation must move beyond the current stalemate over controversial policies (such as whether to permit stem cell research), will break through the present ideological impasse.

Any attempt to reform the health care system generates intense political debate and lobbying efforts, either in Congress or in state legislatures. Current proposals, however, have been crafted so as to minimize such opposition and the accompanying ideological debate. One example is the popular reform measure that would require employers who do not provide health coverage to pay into a fund for working, but uninsured, families. Although opponents claim that it will force small companies to let some workers go, other companies that currently pay health benefits can counter with the argument that it is only fair for all employers to pay some share of the cost of providing health care for the nation's citizens. In other words, proposals that promise to increase health coverage but do not stimulate unified opposition have a much better chance of success than those that tend to deepen existing political and ideological divides.

Summary

- The lack of adequate health measures presents a variety of social problems to societies everywhere. In affluent regions like western Europe, North America, and Australia, problems associated with physical health often involve reducing unequal access to high-quality health care while controlling health care costs. In impoverished regions where high-quality medical care is often lacking, social problems associated with physical health are even more profound: the spread of infectious diseases, high rates of infant and maternal death, low life expectancy, scarcity of medical personnel and equipment, and inadequate sewage and water systems.

- Health care is considered a social problem when members of a society have unequal access to health care institutions and when the quality of the care provided is low relative to its cost.

- Health care is distributed very unequally in the United States. The use and availability of health care are directly related to socioeconomic class and race. People in the lower classes tend to have higher rates of untreated illnesses and disabilities and higher mortality rates for most diseases than do people in the middle and upper classes.

- Unequal access to health care is related to the cost of obtaining it. Health care costs have risen significantly. The cost of hospital care, physician fees, medical technology, and prescription drugs are major contributors to the high cost of American health care. Population demographics are changing, and the number of people who are elderly and need chronic care is increasing. Cultural factors that raise the cost of health care in the United States include aspects of lifestyle such as heavy use of tobacco and alcohol, unhealthful diet, and lack of exercise. Obesity is a major health problem in the United States and other affluent nations.

- As medical technology has improved and life-prolonging procedures have become more available and dependable, many complex ethical issues have arisen, and our society is only beginning to grapple with them. One example is end-of-life issues and the dilemmas surrounding "death with dignity."

- Conflict theorists believe social class goes a long way toward explaining the types of illnesses experienced by members of a household and the kinds of health care they receive. Functionalist explanations of health care problems focus on features of health care institutions themselves. The interactionist perspective on health care problems points to the role of lifestyle features such as poor diet, lack of exercise, and smoking–including passive smoking (breathing air that contains cigarette smoke).

- Many countries in western Europe and Canada offer single-payer health care systems for their citizens. The United States does not. In March 2010, Congress passed important health care reform legislation called the Affordable Care Act. It is designed to reduce the number of uninsured Americans and to lower health care costs.

Chapter 3
Problems of Mental Illness and Treatment

Learning Objectives

3.1 Identify the ways that mental illness is a social problem.

3.2 Discuss the social construction of mental illness.

3.3 Assess inequality and differences in mental illness.

3.4 Compare treatment options for mental illness.

3.5 Explain the institutional problems of providing treatment and care.

3.6 Analyze the policy implications of the Affordable Care Act for mental illness.

I have had issues with my weight since high school. I was your average nerdy 15-year-old, and I felt hopelessly inadequate. I felt like every girl at school was prettier than I was and more popular. I was painfully shy. I was self-conscious about everything and felt like people were laughing at me behind my back.

I cannot remember how I first heard about throwing up. But I do remember the first time I did it. I was depressed, and had eaten a bag of potato chips, and I wondered if I could do it. I made my way to the bathroom, and I was sweating as I approached the toilet, lifting the seat. I looked at the toilet bowl for … I'm not sure how long. But then I pulled my hair back, knelt over the toilet, stuck my finger down my throat, and gagged myself until I threw up. I was scared, started to cry, and felt more depressed than ever. I crawled into bed even though it was barely eight o'clock. A month or more passed until I tried it again.

That was eight years ago, and now, I can't seem to stop myself. I throw up at least twice a day. I eat only foods that will come up easily. I eat slowly and chew every bite carefully. It's like a ritual. I count the number of chews. I have a roommate so I have to be careful around her. I only eat alone. I don't like anyone to see me eating. And then, when I'm ready, I purge.

I know this is wrong, but I can't stop. It's all I think about … when can I eat … what should I eat … I need to get rid of what I ate. It's constant. I know this can be dangerous, and I feel so out of control.

mental health

A state of well-being in which the individual realizes his or her own abilities, can cope with the normal stresses of life, can work productively and fruitfully, and is able to make a contribution to his or her community.

mental illness

A mental, behavioral, or emotional disorder (excluding developmental or substance abuse disorders), diagnosable currently or within the past year and of sufficient duration to meet diagnostic criteria specified within the fifth edition of the *Diagnostic and Statistical Manual of Mental Disorders (DSM-V)*.

All people have days in which they feel blue, depressed, or anxious. However, for most people, these emotions are fleeting, and for the most part, they experience **mental health**, which is defined by the World Health Organization as "a state of well-being in which the individual realizes his or her own abilities, can cope with the normal stresses of life, can work productively and fruitfully, and is able to make a contribution to his or her community." In other words, despite a brief episode of feeling blue, a person continues to get up in the morning, go to work, take care of his or her family, and maintain his or her social roles (World Health Organization and the Calouste Gulbenkian Foundation, 2014).

Yet, for some people, this level of functioning is not possible. One of every five Americans age 18 and older has suffered, or continues to suffer, from some form of **mental illness**, defined by the National Institute of Mental Health as (National Institute of Mental Health, 2015):

- A mental, behavioral, or emotional disorder (excluding developmental or substance abuse disorders)
- Diagnosable currently, or within the past year; and
- Of sufficient duration to meet diagnostic criteria specified within the 5th edition of the *Diagnostic and Statistical Manual of Mental Disorders (DSM-V)*.

These disorders range from mild depression and anxiety to severely debilitating psychoses like schizophrenia and manic depression (National Institute of Mental Health, 2015). As you can see in Figure 3–1, women are significantly more likely to suffer mental illness than are men, and younger people are more likely to suffer mental illness than older age groups, although, if those age 70 and over were put in their own group, they would show higher rates of mental illness.

Many people believe that mental illness is rare. They see mental illness as something that happens only to people with life situations very different from their own, and they believe it will never affect them. People with this perception of mental illness are usually thinking of the most extreme types of mental illness, such as bipolar disorder or schizophrenia. These disorders are not very common, occurring in only 4 percent of Americans. Again, women and younger groups have the highest rates. Unfortunately, at least 40 percent of these individuals are not being treated for their illness (National Institute of Mental Health, 2015). Many of them are found among the homeless on the streets of the nation's cities (Kessler et al., 2005).

However, other forms of mental illness also exist. Many millions of women, men, and children suffer from depression, anxiety, autism, obsessive-compulsive disorder, Alzheimer's disease, and panic or eating disorders. These types of disorders are far more

Figure 3-1 Prevalence of Any Mental Illness Among U.S. Adults, 2012

SOURCE: National Institute of Mental Health, 2015.

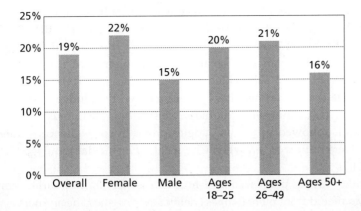

common than severe mental illness, and they are also considered forms of mental illness (National Alliance on Mental Illness, 2015; National Institute of Mental Health, 2015).

There is some positive news on the mental health front, however. In 2008, Congress had mandated that mental illnesses be covered under existing health insurance plans just as physical illnesses are. But that legislation did not address the needs of the uninsured, and it is estimated that rates of insurance coverage are significantly lower among those who are mentally ill than in the general population. The Affordable Care Act passed by the U.S. Congress in 2010 established a new level of parity in coverage and treatment benefits for mental health–related conditions. Now, with the Affordable Care Act, mental health advocates have more to celebrate. The new law expands parity to a much wider pool, making it possible for millions more people to obtain the same coverage for substance abuse disorders and major mental illnesses as they would for heart disease or cancer. The consequences of this major change in the situation of those with mental disorders will be examined later in this chapter.

Around the world, mental illness is a profoundly underestimated social problem. Approximately 80 percent of the world's 450 million people with mental illness live in developing nations (World Health Organization, 2010). While basic physical health has improved worldwide, mental health has remained stagnant or has deteriorated. Funding is low or nonexistent in many countries due to the lack of understanding of mental illness and the stigma associated with it.

Mental Illness As a Social Problem

3.1 Identify the ways that mental illness is a social problem.

The terms *mental disorder* and *mental illness* are often used interchangeably, and that is how they are used here. However, in formal social-scientific writing, mental illness is often reserved for mental disorders that require hospitalization or for which close medical supervision would normally be recommended. For the most part, people who seek help for mental illness are unlikely ever to be hospitalized.

Until the mid-twentieth century, a large proportion of people who were classified as mentally ill and admitted to mental hospitals were actually suffering from physical ailments like epilepsy and brain tumors (Barry, 2002). Today, researchers are learning about the biological origins of many mental illnesses, including schizophrenia, autism, and depression. Genes play a role, as do hormones. As researchers discover the biological bases of some mental illnesses, they also gain information about the social conditions—such as physical abuse, neglect, and severe stress—that may bring on the mental breakdowns that cause people to stop functioning "normally."

The specific relationships between biological factors and certain types of mental illness are considered in detail in psychology and genetics courses. In this text, it is

What Do You Think?

Close your eyes and picture a person who is "mentally ill." Carefully describe that person in detail. Do you picture a person who suffers from the more extreme forms of mental illness, or do you picture a person who suffers from the more common and less extreme forms?

enough to be aware that mental illness, whatever its causes, is a source of serious social problems not only because of the number of people affected but also because of the extent to which social institutions are strained by efforts to care for them.

The mental disorders that cause severe social problems are the most extreme forms. Of these, the most sensational are those that threaten the social order—sociopaths who become serial killers or severely mentally ill individuals with hostile and suicidal tendencies who are not receiving mental health treatment. The gunman, Seung-Hui Cho, who killed 32 people at Virginia Tech University in 2007, did not receive the mental health treatment ordered by a judge who declared him an imminent threat to himself and others. Neither the court nor community mental health officials followed up on the judge's order. In consequence, students at the university were not protected when Cho went on a suicidal rampage (Schulte and Jenkins, 2007).

In another highly publicized and horrific case in 2015, an airline copilot who apparently suffered from mental illness deliberately crashed the airliner he was piloting in France, killing himself and 149 other people on board. When the captain left the cockpit for a presumably brief bathroom visit, copilot Andreas Lubitz apparently locked the captain out of the cockpit and then activated a control causing the plane to descend toward rugged terrain. The plane dropped for about eight minutes from its cruising altitude of 38,000 feet before crashing. The authorities said that the flight recording indicated pounding on the cockpit door, Lubitz's steady breathing, and eventually, screaming passengers. The circumstances of the crash are under investigation as this book is written, but it appears that he suffered from a mental illness that he kept secret from his employer.

Certainly not all people who suffer serious mental illness are dangerous people or mass murderers. The number of these individuals with such disorders may be very small, but they constitute an especially serious social problem because they are so violent and irrational. These events receive international attention.

More widespread, and less threatening to public safety, are severely ill individuals who cannot care for themselves without specialized attention. This group includes people classified as mentally ill and perhaps chemically addicted, who are also especially likely to be indigent and homeless. These individuals may nap on park benches, wander the streets, and sleep under bridges. Many cities consider these mentally ill people a public nuisance rather than as people in critical need of medical attention.

For the mentally ill themselves, their problems pose a difficult personal challenge regardless of the severity of their individual condition. They may experience symptoms such as unimaginable fear, uncontrollable hallucinations, panic, crushing sadness, wild elation, roller-coaster mood swings, compulsive eating and then binging, exhaustion, and the inability to perform their social roles. For society as a whole, this group's illnesses present a range of social problems: stress in family life, heavy demands on health care institutions, moral and ethical problems (e.g., whether to permit the plea of insanity in criminal cases), and the cost of treatment to society. All of these social problems can be aggravated by the social stigma attached to mental illness. It can be said that those who are mentally ill suffer twice: They suffer from the illness itself, and they suffer rejection, as if their illness were their own fault. Social stigma is not nearly as likely for physical illness, and this factor alone qualifies mental illness for special consideration in the study of social problems.

Mental disorders are the leading cause of disability for people ages 15 to 44 in the United States and throughout the world (World Health Organization, 2012). To complicate matters, nearly half of those with any mental disorder meet the criteria for two or more disorders. Major depressive disorder affects approximately 16 million American adults, or about 7 percent of the population age 18 and older, in a given year. The disorder is more prevalent in women than in men (National Institute of

Mental Health, 2015). Extremely debilitating mental illnesses—especially bipolar disorder (sometimes called manic depression) and schizophrenia—affect far fewer than the number who suffer from major depression, but the consequences for society are far greater than the numbers would suggest.

A distressing aspect of the general problem of mental illness is the social impact of **deinstitutionalization**, or discharging patients from mental hospitals directly into the community. Some of these patients are not able to function as normal members of society, and the consequences can be painful both for them and for those who come into contact with them. For example, some severe disorders such as bipolar disorder, schizophrenia, and dissociative disorder are chronic conditions that must be managed with medication. Unfortunately, some people with those disorders find it difficult to manage staying on the medications, which creates a vicious cycle. It has been difficult to develop (or consistently fund) effective means of treating such individuals outside mental hospitals.

Policymakers at every level of society look to sociologists and other social scientists for basic research on the causes of mental illness and on the effects of major policy initiatives like deinstitutionalization or community treatment, as well as for recommendations on how to deal with trends in mental illness. Thus, in addition to sponsoring research on medical approaches to treatment and rehabilitation, the National Institute of Mental Health funds studies of the social epidemiology of mental illness—a concept that includes not simply its distribution in the population but also its impact on families, communities, and welfare institutions, as well as its relation to problems of homelessness and social dependency.

deinstitutionalization
The act of discharging patients from mental hospitals directly into the community.

Sociological Perspectives on Mental Illness

In studying social problems related to mental illness, basic sociological perspectives can help clarify the relevant issues and explain some aspects of the origins of mental disorders. The interactionist perspective focuses on the social construction of mental illness, that is, on how our definitions of "normal" and "deviant" behavior in social situations lead to definitions of mental disorders. To a large extent, the definition of mental illness is the province of psychologists and psychiatrists. Their diagnoses result in labels like "schizophrenic" or "depressed." Research by sociologists who have studied the interactions among people who are thought of as mentally ill suggests that such a label may cause one to define oneself as ill and to behave in ways that confirm the self-definition.

Conflict theorists tend to focus on how mental illness may be associated with deprivation and inequality, including unequal access to appropriate care. The emergence of a two-class system of mental health care in the United States is a central concern of this sociological perspective. Typically, more affluent patients with less severe mental illnesses receive higher quality private care, whereas severely ill patients, often reduced to poverty by their illnesses, are shunted into budget-starved public institutions.

From a functionalist perspective, mental illnesses constitute a social problem because they challenge our ability to provide effective treatment. This challenge is especially evident in societies marked by rapid social change, those in which people do not have long-standing attachments to others in their immediate social surroundings or are often separated from their families or those in which systems of treatment have been changing rapidly and it is not clear how people with mental disorders should be helped.

What Do You Think?

If you were going to study the topic of mental illness, which sociological perspective would you likely use, and why?

Suicide and Mental Illness

As I write, I can see the lower floors of the Empire State Building from my office window. Yesterday afternoon, a junior at Yale University threw himself from the building's 86th floor. Leaving a note of apology in his dorm for his loved ones, he came to New York, proceeded to that upper floor, climbed over a spiked barrier, and leaped to his death. His was the thirty-fourth such suicide since the building opened in 1931 (William Kornblum).

Every 13 minutes, someone commits suicide in the United States. Suicide is the tenth leading cause of death in the United States, with over 40,000 people killing themselves every year (and one million attempts). The rate of suicide, especially among teenagers and young adults, has been increasing steadily since 1950 and is now the second leading cause of death among younger people ages 10 to 24 (Centers for Disease Control and Prevention, 2015b). Men and women approach suicide differently. Women attempt suicide three times as often as do men, but men are four times more likely to actually kill themselves than are women. Women may attempt suicide as a cry for help, and they often use methods that are less lethal (poisoning, 37 percent) than those used by men (guns, 56 percent). Native Americans and Alaska Natives have suicide rates that are more than twice the national average.

Around the world, the World Health Organization estimates that about 800,000 people take their own lives every year, and 75 percent of these suicides occur in developing countries (World Health Organization, 2014). The link between suicide and mental disorders (in particular, depression and alcohol use disorders) is well established. Depression, for example, can be brought on by chronic anxieties over money and loss of work and by marital discord. Initial depression often engenders further depression or abusive behavior and substance abuse, which can accelerate a downward spiral toward suicide. Among the elderly, loss of mental capabilities (dementia) is associated with depression and suicidal tendencies.

But not all suicide is related to mental illness. Many suicides happen impulsively in moments of crisis, causing a breakdown in the ability to deal with life stresses such as financial problems, a relationship breakup, or chronic pain and illness. People commit suicide to avoid severe embarrassment, to escape debt, to express strong political protest, and to avoid severe suffering due to physical illness. In addition, experiencing conflict, disaster, violence, abuse, or loss, and a sense of isolation are strongly associated with suicidal behavior. Suicide rates are also high among vulnerable groups who experience discrimination, for example, refugees and migrants; indigenous peoples; lesbian, gay, bisexual, and transgender (LGBT) persons; and prisoners. In other words, the reasons for suicide are similar from country to country, although some may have greater importance in a particular society due to economic, social, or cultural considerations.

Over 40,000 people each year in the United States kill themselves. Suicide is among the leading causes of death in the United States, especially among men.

The continuing suicide bombings associated with terrorism and insurgency around the world call attention to the large number of people susceptible to the notion that their lives can gain meaning from suicidal acts of murder. This type of political suicide may draw on individuals with mental illnesses, but it is a form of suicide best considered separately, as you will see in Chapter 15. Many people might believe that anyone who commits suicide or murder is insane, but the causes of suicide are far more complex. Kay Redfield Jamison, an expert on the subject, notes that half of all people with bipolar disease (manic depression) will make a suicide attempt, as will about one in five people with major depression. People who have suffered neurological damage before birth, often because of alcohol or cocaine use by the mother, may experience severe mood disorders that can lead to suicide. And there is mounting evidence that genetic factors are responsible for some mental illnesses as well as for impulsiveness, aggression, and violence, which increase the risk of suicide. Unfortunately, our knowledge of the possible biological antecedents of suicide is still developing while the toll of suicide mounts. Although drugs like lithium and anti-depressants are somewhat effective in decreasing rates of suicide among risk-prone individuals with histories of mental disorders, there are as yet no therapies to correct genetic damage at the neurological level (Jamison, 2000).

Studies on college campuses and of school shootings inevitably raise questions about intervention and prevention. It is extremely difficult, however, to predict who will commit suicide among the far larger population of individuals who cope with suicidal thoughts. It is also true that suicide can produce localized suicide epidemics among peers. Strategies for peer counseling and suicide awareness, therefore, are extremely important.

The Social Construction of Mental Illness

3.2 **Discuss the social construction of mental illness.**

When social scientists say that mental illness is socially constructed, they are highlighting aspects of those illnesses that help define how both the mentally ill and "normal" people behave. The usefulness of this approach becomes clear if we consider some alternative views of mental illness. In this section, you will get a brief orientation to three different explanations of mental illness: (1) the medical model, which asserts that mental illness is a disease with physiological causes; (2) the deviance approach, which asserts that mental illness results from the way society treats people considered mentally ill; and (3) the controversial argument that mental illness is not a disease but a method governments use to define certain people as being in need of isolation and "treatment." You will also begin to see how social scientists use all three of these explanations as they consider mental illness.

The Medical Model

The most familiar school of thought holds that a mental disorder should be viewed as a disease with biological causes. That is, a mental disorder is primarily a disturbance of the normal personality that is analogous to the physiological disturbance caused by physical disease. It can be remedied primarily by treating the patient. Once this treatment has been done, the patient will be able to function adequately.

Research in the biological sciences, especially genetics, has uncovered strong evidence to support biological explanations of mental illnesses like schizophrenia, bipolar disorder, childhood autism, senility, and even alcoholism (covered more in Chapter 4). In addition to disorders that are classified as mental illnesses, many of which have been found to have somatic causes, a host of other mental disabilities can appear at birth, for example, Down syndrome, cerebral palsy, and brain damage caused by birth trauma; such disorders present unusual and difficult challenges to those afflicted by them. Other disorders do not become apparent until children are somewhat older, perhaps school age. The box A Personal View—My Brain Works Differently is based on an interview with Marshall, an 11-year-old boy who has been diagnosed with attention deficit disorder.

Research on the medical model of mental disorders arose in reaction to the earlier notion that mentally disturbed people are mad or "possessed" and should be locked up, beaten, or killed. This move away from that earlier notion made possible serious investigation of the causes and cures of mental disorders and was responsible for the development of virtually all the systems of mental health care and therapeutic

A Personal View

My Brain Works Differently

I'm 11 years old and for as long as I can remember, I've had two sides to myself. I'm told that I'm very smart and creative. But I also have to work really, really hard at things that seem much easier for other kids, like memorizing and paying attention.

Here's an example: In math, science, and art, I can figure things out faster than other kids. Like when my teacher tells us a new way to add fractions, it seems obvious to me but not to other kids. But when I'm trying to listen to someone talking or lecturing, my mind starts to wander.

For example, yesterday when my science teacher was talking about plants, it made me think about what I was going to plant in my garden next year. And that made me think about a new kind of chili pepper that I'm going to try to plant for my dad because he likes spicy things. And that made me think about the hot dishes he used to eat when we lived in China. And that made me think about the house we lived in when we were in China.

Pretty soon I didn't have a clue as to what the science teacher was talking about. Then she got mad at me for daydreaming. Sometimes my thoughts help me bring up new ideas that no one else has thought of. But I don't always fully get what the teacher is saying and she gets mad when she has to repeat herself.

When I'm doing something that's hard for me, like writing, I drift off easily and end up doing a quick job so I can do something else that I'm better at. But then I don't get a very good grade on my essay, and I feel bad. The problem is, there are so many interesting things to do in my house; things that I think are just as important as writing. I'd rather do chemistry and cooking experiments in the kitchen, or try out new kinds of seeds or soil mixtures in my garden, or watch the History Channel, or solve logic puzzles and games. My mom gets mad at me sometimes because it takes me a long time to do my homework and she has to remind me a lot, "Come on Marshall, stay on task," she says.

Sometimes I have complicated ideas that I can't explain to others. That really frustrates me, and I get upset with the person for not getting it! I guess you could say I cry pretty easily. It's embarrassing, but I just can't help it.

I've tried some medicine to help me with attention. Isn't it weird that they make medicine for that? One helped me concentrate and be more energetic about school. Another helps make me be more optimistic, but when it wears off, I feel less cheerful and drift more. My medicine helps some, but it doesn't completely solve the problem of attention. I still have to work at it, and sometimes I still drift off even with the medicine.

Medicine doesn't really help the problems I have memorizing and studying for tests. My tutor suggested that I draw pictures when I'm memorizing facts for my history test. For example, when we were studying the Lewis and Clark expedition in history, I drew a picture of a canoe, an Indian feather, and bison. That helped me remember those things for an exam. But it takes too long to study like that, so I wasn't able to get to everything and I got a bad grade. Sometimes it makes me want to give up when I realize how much harder I have to work at things that are not that hard for other kids. But my mom and dad told me that I'm smart; it's just that my brain works differently.

—Marshall, age 11

Critical Thinking

Drawing on the sociological imagination introduced in Chapter 1, analyze whether Marshall's concerns are a personal issue or a social problem.

treatment in existence today—systems that are still largely in the hands of medically oriented personnel. It has helped reduce the stigma and shame of mental disorder because, after all, "illness can happen to anyone."

Nevertheless, the concept of mental disorder as a disease has certain disadvantages. Because it concentrates on individuals and their immediate environment (often their childhood environment), it tends to disregard the wider social environment as a possible source of the problem. In addition, especially for hospitalized patients, the medical model can lead to impractical criteria of recovery—people may have gained considerable insight into their inner tensions but are still unable to function adequately when they return to the outer tensions of home, job, or society. It is also true that many mental illnesses, which may or may not be caused by an individual's physiology, may be brought on, alleviated, or worsened by conditions in that person's social environment.

Mental Illness as Deviance

Scientists do not know precisely what interactions among the multitude of physical and social conditions that affect human beings may cause mental illness in some cases, or lead to remission or recovery in others. We do know, however, that the way a mentally ill person is treated once the illness has been diagnosed can have a lasting impact on that person's behavior and on his or her chances of leading a happy and productive life.

The concept of mental disorder as a disease holds that something about a person is abnormal and that the fundamental problem lies in his or her emotional makeup, which was twisted, repressed, or otherwise wrongly developed as a result of genetic or chemical factors or events early in life. Although this theory seems to explain some mental disorders, many observers believe other factors need to be taken into account, especially the constant pressure exerted by modern society. Out of this broader effort has developed the view that mental disorder represents a departure from certain expectations of society—that it is a form of social deviance.

In this connection, the idea of residual deviance is useful. According to Thomas Scheff (1963), who formulated the concept, most social conventions are recognized as such, and violation of those conventions carries fairly clear labels: People who steal wallets are thieves, people who act haughtily toward the poor are snobs, and so on. But there is a large residual area of social convention that is so completely taken for granted that it is assumed to be part of human nature. To use Scheff's example, it seems natural for people holding a conversation to face each other rather than to look away. Violation of this norm seems contrary to human nature.

Scheff (1963) suggests that residual deviance occurs in most people at one time or another and usually passes without treatment. What causes it to become a mental disorder in some cases is that *society decides to label it as such*. When this labeling happens, the role of "mentally ill person" is suggested to the deviant individual. Because such people are often confused and frightened by their own behavior—as well as by other people's reactions to their behavior—during a time of stress, they are likely to be particularly impressionable and may accept the role suggested to them. Once they take on this role, it becomes difficult for them to change their behavior and return to their "normal" role.

If this labeling process is actually what occurs, then mental disorder may actually be a result of the attempts to respond to deviance. By treating a patient in a separate institution, the mental health profession certifies that the individual is indeed a patient and that he or she is mentally ill. The point of this concept of mental disorder as deviance is thus that the disorder may be a function not only of certain individuals' inability to comply with societal expectations but also of the label attached to those who deviate (Barry, 2002; Cockerham, 2006).

Problems in Living

A third approach to understanding mental disorder has been offered by Thomas Szasz, a psychiatrist who has generated considerable controversy by contending that mental illness is a myth. Although this view is not a widely accepted one, it does call attention to the relationship between diagnosis and repression. Szasz does not claim that the social and psychological disturbances referred to as mental illness do not exist; rather, he argues that it is dangerously misleading to call them illnesses. Instead, he believes, they should be regarded as manifestations of unresolved problems in living.

The significance of Szasz's basic argument is that it concerns justice and individual freedom. As he sees it, a diagnosis of mental disorder involves a value judgment based on the behavioral norms held by psychiatrists. Referring to certain behaviors as illnesses allows doctors to use medicine to correct what are essentially social, ethical, or legal deviations. This approach is not only logically absurd, Szasz contends but also dangerous.

Szasz (2003) believes that individual liberty can be unwittingly sacrificed through too great a concern for the "cure" of "mental illness." This issue has come to the fore in connection with the forcible removal of homeless individuals from city streets. The presence of homeless people, who are often shabby and dirty and may behave in bizarre ways, offends "normal" citizens. As we will see later in the chapter, the interpretation of this lifestyle as a sign of mental illness has been used to justify the involuntary placement of the homeless in shelters or hospitals, where they are out of sight. We will also see that sensational crimes by mentally ill people, such as incidents of sudden violence in which schizophrenic individuals push unsuspecting pedestrians off train platforms, along with public concern about links between mental illness and violent crimes in schools, have produced renewed efforts to enforce mandatory institutionalization (Salize, Schanda, and Dressing, 2008).

The Social Construction Process

When sociologists speak of the social construction of mental illness, they incorporate all these approaches into their explanations. They recognize that there is often a biological basis for mental illness. In fact, medical and genetic discoveries are making possible more effective treatments. But social-scientific research also finds that mental illness is often aggravated by the fact that mentally ill people are treated as social deviants. Sociologists therefore also study instances in which the label of mental illness is a convenient way of ridding society of people who are troublesome. (The nations of the former Soviet Union were notorious for this technique, but it has been used in societies all over the world at one time or another.) Most important, sociologists recognize that the classification of mental illnesses and decisions about how they should be treated is determined by how we think about the causes, consequences, and possibilities of treating mental disorders. Even the diagnosis of mental illness requires the emergence of a common set of perceptions among mental health professionals, a point that becomes clear if you look in more detail at the problems of diagnosis.

Classification of Mental Disorders

Clinicians and researchers need a common language to discuss mental disorders. It is impossible to plan a consistent program of treatment for a patient without an accurate diagnosis, and it is impossible to evaluate the effectiveness of various forms of treatment without clearly defined diagnostic terms.

There are many different kinds of mental illnesses. Some are relatively common, such as depression and anxiety, while others occur much less frequently, such as schizophrenia or psychosis. How do mental health practitioners keep track of the different types of illnesses? One important way is by using the book, *Diagnostic and Statistical Manual of Mental Disorders.*

In 1973, in an effort to deal with these problems, the American Psychiatric Association (APA) embarked on a controversial and ambitious revision of its manual of mental disorders. The new manual, released in 1980 and referred to as the *Diagnostic and Statistical Manual of Mental Disorders*, third edition, or simply as *DSM-III*, represented the work of hundreds of scientists and professionals in the field of mental health care. A revised edition, *DSM-IV*, was published in 1994, and the most recent revision, *DSM-V*, appeared in 2013 (American Psychiatric Association, 2015).

Widely regarded as a major advance in the scientific description and classification of mental disorders, the *DSM-III* had a significant impact on treatment when released. Among other things, it made an important contribution to the separation of mental disorders from behaviors (such as homosexuality) that deviated from societal norms at the time but were not a result of mental illness. In general, however, the manual continues to represent the illness model. To a large extent, it seeks to attribute mental dysfunctions to physiological, biochemical, genetic, or profound internal psychological causes.

The *DSM-V* contains a number of changes. For example, autism spectrum disorder (ASD) is a new *DSM-V* name that reflects a scientific consensus that four previously separate disorders are actually a single condition with different levels of symptom severity. ASD now encompasses the previous *DSM-IV* autistic disorder (autism), Asperger's disorder, childhood disintegrative disorder, and pervasive developmental disorder not otherwise specified.

A number of familiar terms are no longer used in *DSM-V*, such as *neurosis*, the older term for a wide range of disorders in which the individual suffers from severe anxiety but continues to attempt to function in the everyday world. The new classification system replaces this term with more specific ones such as *affective disorder, anxiety disorder, somatoform disorder*, and *psychosexual disorder*.

Diagnosis or Label?

Just as some physical illnesses may be culturally defined, so may certain mental disorders. The medical model assumes that patients present symptoms that can be classified into diagnosable categories of mental illness. But there is a growing belief that at least some psychiatric diagnoses are pigeonholes into which certain behaviors are placed arbitrarily. According to labeling theorists, the diagnosis of schizophrenia has been especially subject to misuse. Although there is little agreement about its origins, causes, and symptoms, it is the most commonly used diagnosis for severe mental illness. To labeling theorists, this trend suggests that diagnoses of mental illnesses tend to reflect cultural values, not scientific analysis. People are not "schizophrenic" in the sense that they manifest definite symptoms; instead, their behavior violates society's norms and expectations. For example, a person who sees visions might be considered perfectly normal, even admirable, in many cultures, although in the United States he or she would probably be regarded as disturbed.

The problem with labeling people as mentally ill is threefold: It makes us perceive certain behaviors as "sick," something to be eliminated rather than understood; it gives public agencies the right to incarcerate people against their will simply for not conforming; and it causes those people to define themselves as rule breakers and undesirables and allows them to fulfill that image. Many studies have demonstrated the influence of societal factors on the diagnosis of mental illness as well as the vagueness of such diagnoses. Rosenhan (1973), in a classic study that will be described more fully later in the chapter, found that psychologists and psychiatrists on the staffs of several mental hospitals were unable to determine accurately which of the people they interviewed were mentally healthy and which were mentally ill. Despite the undeniable influence of labeling on the diagnosis and treatment of mental illness, recent large-scale research has shown that interviewers with basic training in the diagnosis of mental illness can spot people with serious mental disorders like schizophrenia and severe depression quite accurately. Such research is vital to our knowledge of the extent of mental illness in a population (Kessler et al., 2005).

Post-Traumatic Stress Disorder Resulting from War and Terrorism

Even when research findings are available and widely publicized, there is no guarantee, especially with mental illnesses, that effective action will follow. A case in point is the gap that existed until quite recently between what is known about the incidence of mental illness among soldiers who have witnessed violent death and traumatic pressures on battlefields and the provision of adequate mental health services for them.

Once minimized as shell shock or combat fatigue, and frequently confused with cowardice or weakness, post-traumatic stress disorder (PTSD) has always been a consequence of war. Now, mental health researchers understand that an individual may develop PTSD after witnessing or experiencing any traumatic event. Service members are particularly vulnerable because they are often at high risk for death or injury. They may see others hurt or killed. They may have to kill or wound others. They are on alert around the clock. These and other factors can increase their chances of having PTSD or other mental health problems. The symptoms of this disorder may be quite severe and can include flashbacks, nightmares, feelings of detachment, irritability, trouble concentrating, sleeplessness, and in the most extreme cases, suicide (Schoenbaum et al., 2014; U.S. Department of Veterans Affairs, 2014).

The treatment of soldiers with PTSD may improve as a result of recent studies of the mental health needs of soldiers returning from Iraq and Afghanistan. For example, one large survey of nearly 2,000 recently returned service men and women, from all service branches, components, and unit types found that nearly one-third met the criteria for PTSD, depression, traumatic brain injury (TBI), or some combination during deployment, as shown in Figure 3–2 (RAND Center for Military Health Policy Research, 2008).

Only about half of returned soldiers with symptoms of PTSD seek help. Part of the reason for soldiers failing to seek care is related to a scarcity of providers in many regions of the country. Nearly 36,000 active component service members, and 230,000 National Guard and reserve members live more than a 30-minute drive from mental health professionals, including counselors, psychiatrists, and psychologists in military treatment facilities, community agencies, and private offices (Brown et al., 2015).

But another important reason for failing to seek care is more social in nature, indicated in Figure 3–3. Military service members report barriers to seeking care that are associated with fears about the negative consequences of using mental health services. The study results suggest that most of these concerns center on confidentiality and career issues,

Figure 3–2 Military Service Members with a Mental Health Condition or Who Reported Experiencing a Traumatic Brain Injury, 2008

SOURCE: RAND Center for Military Health Policy Research, 2008.

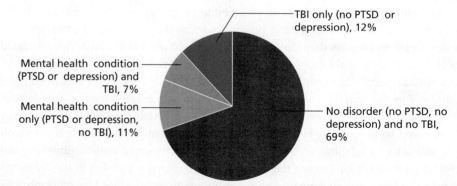

NOTE: TBI (traumatic brain injury); PTSD (post-traumatic stress disorder)

Figure 3–3 Top Five Barriers Among Military Service Members to Seeking Mental Health Care, 2008

SOURCE: RAND Center for Military Health Policy Research, 2008.

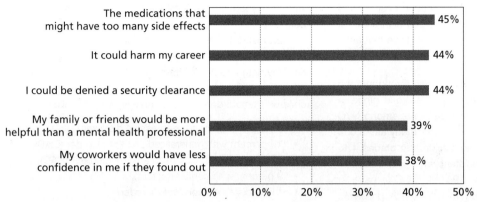

NOTE: Weighted percentage of those reporting barriers to care among those with a possible need for services

particularly relevant for those on active duty. Many also felt that seeking mental health care might have negative effects on career prospects or cause coworkers' trust to decline.

As a consequence of these findings, the U.S. Department of Defense has begun administering mental health questionnaires to all soldiers after they have returned home. A large current study called the Army Study to Assess Risk and Resilience in Service members (STARRS) is the largest study of mental health risk and resilience ever conducted among military personnel. The Army STARRS investigators are looking for factors that help protect a soldier's mental health and factors that put a soldier's mental health at risk. Army STARRS will run through June 2015; however, research findings are being reported as they become available so that they may be applied to ongoing health promotion, risk reduction, and suicide prevention efforts. Because promoting mental health and reducing suicide risk are important for all Americans, the findings from Army STARRS will benefit not only service members but also the nation as a whole (U.S. Army, National Institute of Mental Health, Uniformed Services University of Health Sciences, Harvard Medical School, University of Michigan, and University of California San Diego School of Medicine, 2015).

Another example of PTSD that has been ignored is that of the young schoolchildren who were going to school near the 9/11 terrorist attacks in New York City. As the box A Closer Look—9/11 and Schoolchildren shows, many children suffered from PTSD in the aftermath of the attacks, yet most of these children received no counseling to help them deal with the trauma they experienced.

A Closer Look

9/11 and Schoolchildren

Many people who watched in horror as the World Trade Center towers became a flaming death scene experienced symptoms of post-traumatic stress disorder (PTSD)—sleeplessness, attention problems, depression, recurring nightmares, and more—for days, weeks, or even months after the event. But children in New York City were especially prone to suffer one or more symptoms of PTSD long after the event. What follows are segments of the testimony of psychiatrist Christina W. Hoven, who directed a study for the New York Department of Education of children's lingering psychological difficulties as a consequence of their experiences on 9/11.

"To better appreciate the complexity and challenges faced by the New York City Board of Education, I want to identify a few issues that contributed to our conceptualizing the study the way we did, that is, to view the aftermath as a probable citywide phenomenon, not just a Ground Zero event:

1. There are approximately 1.2 million children enrolled in the New York City public schools.
2. Approximately 750,000 of them take public transportation every day, including subways, buses, and boats, pass-

ing through tunnels and going over bridges on their way to school.

3. Whereas only 35,000 people reside in the area surrounding Ground Zero, more than twenty times that number commute there to work each day. Similarly, the schools near Ground Zero, especially the specialized middle and high schools, are attended primarily by students living outside that area, coming every day from each of the boroughs of NYC.

Briefly summarizing our findings, we observed throughout the City a higher than expected prevalence of a broad range of mental health problems or psychiatric disorders among NYC public schoolchildren. It is estimated that as many as 75,000 (10.5%) New York City public schoolchildren in grades 4 to 12 have multiple symptoms consistent with post-traumatic stress disorder (PTSD); and that 190,000 (26.5%) have at least one of the seven assessed mental health problems (excluding alcohol abuse).

NYC public school students were exposed to the effects of the attack in different ways. Almost all the students in Ground Zero, and two-thirds of children in the remainder of the City, experienced some type of personal physical exposure to the attack, such as being near the cloud of smoke and dust, having fled to safety, having had difficulty getting home that day, and/or continuing to smell smoke after 9/11.

Having a family member exposed to the attack—that is, having a family member killed, injured, or in the World Trade Center at the time of the attack but who escaped unhurt—was more frequent among students in schools outside of Ground Zero than among students in schools near Ground Zero.

We know that previous exposure to trauma elevates an individual's response to any new trauma. We found that nearly two-thirds (64%) of New York City public schoolchildren had been exposed to one or more traumatic events *before* 9/11, including seeing someone killed or seriously injured, [or] seeing the violent/accidental death of a close friend or family member. Again, a disproportionate number of the children with previous exposure go to schools outside of the Ground Zero area.

Exposure to the media was also very high; almost two-thirds (62%) of the surveyed population spent a lot of their time learning about the attack from television.... Rates of the other psychiatric disorders [estimated for the city's 1.2 million children from random sample surveys] were as follows:

- 8 percent with major depressive disorder (MDD);
- 10 percent with generalized anxiety disorder (GAD);
- 12 percent with separation anxiety disorder (SAD);
- 9 percent with panic attacks;
- 11 percent with conduct disorder;
- 5 percent with alcohol abuse (grades 9–12 only).

All of these reported mental health problems were determined to be associated with impairment; that is, they were so severe as to indicate a need for immediate further assessment and appropriate intervention. Yet, at least two-thirds of children with probable PTSD following the 9/11 attacks have not sought any mental health services from school counselors or from mental health professionals outside of school."

SOURCE: Hoven et. al., 2005.

Critical Thinking

Why do you think that most of the children with probable PTSD from the 9/11 attack have not received any counseling inside or outside of school? Can you identify any structural reasons rather than just personal ones?

Inequality, Conflict, and Mental Illness

3.3 Assess inequality and differences in mental illness.

Sociologists and experts on mental health care have continually refined their research concepts and tools to trace the relationships between mental illness and inequalities of social class, race, ethnicity, gender, age, and other dimensions of social inequality. Sociologists are interested in the relationship between social factors like poverty and the incidence of mental disorders. Is mental disorder associated with social class and with conflicts over the distribution of social rewards? Does it occur more frequently in urban centers than in rural areas or suburbs? In what population groups is it most prevalent? Would changes in social conditions prevent or alleviate certain mental disorders?

Incidence Versus Prevalence of Mental Disorders

epidemiologists
Social scientists who study the course of diseases in human populations.

Epidemiologists—social scientists who study the course of diseases in human populations—make a distinction between the incidence of a disease or disorder and its prevalence in a given population. Incidence and prevalence are important concepts in studying how mental illness is related to social variables such as inequality, race, gender, and age. The *prevalence* of mental illness usually refers to the estimated population of people suffering from one or more mental illnesses at any given time. The term *incidence* refers to the annual diagnosis rate, or the number of new cases of mental illness diagnosed each year. The prevalence rate of childhood autism, for example, is about one in sixty-eight children, according to the Centers for Disease Control and Prevention (2015a). The rate of incidence of childhood autism is between one in one thousand and one in five hundred children, depending on the diagnostic criteria used.

The study of incidence and prevalence of mental disorders is complicated by the difficulty of determining an accurate calculation of mental disorders. We can count the number of patients in mental hospitals and, somewhat less accurately, those receiving treatment in clinics and other outpatient facilities. It is far more difficult to obtain reliable statistics on the number being treated in private practice. Moreover, an indeterminate number of people who would qualify as emotionally disturbed are not under treatment at all and therefore do not appear in most estimates of the incidence of mental disorders. Consequently, any statistics on treated mental disorders must be viewed as only a very rough estimate of the total number of people suffering from these problems.

Despite these difficulties, sociologists have reached several tentative conclusions about the relationship between mental disorders and patterns of inequality in a society. It should be noted that research on the impact of inequality is often conducted from a conflict perspective. Conflict theorists call attention to the ways in which inequalities of wealth and power produce inequalities in access to effective treatment for mental disorders. Underlying these inequalities is class conflict. For example, the poor demand more services and better care from public institutions, while those who are better off believe the poor bring their troubles on themselves and do not deserve expensive care facilities and treatment programs. Conflict theorists also emphasize that poverty itself is a social problem that can produce severe stress in those who experience it. Life in poverty is associated with higher exposure to crime and violence, which adds to the stress of everyday life. In some individuals, such extreme stress can precipitate mental illness (Elhai et al., 2009).

Social Class and Mental Disorder

Long before sociologists began to make systematic studies of social conditions and mental disorders, the connection between the two had been recognized. It was only in the 1930s, however, that serious sociological study of this relationship began, and although the research results are not in perfect agreement, they offer some useful information.

One pioneering study (Faris and Dunham, 1938) investigated the residential patterns of 35,000 hospitalized mental patients in Chicago. The highest rates of mental disorder were found near the center of the city, where the population was poor, of very mixed ethnic and racial background, and highly mobile. Although this number included many cases of organic psychosis due to syphilis and alcoholism in the skid row districts, it also included a significantly high rate of schizophrenia throughout the area. Conversely, the lowest rates of mental disorder were found in stable, higher-status residential areas.

We now know that the early research was somewhat misleading in suggesting that psychoses are more likely to occur among people who are poor and live in run-down areas. It has been shown that people with schizophrenia and drug-induced organic disorders tend to inhabit the poorer areas of cities, partly because they usually have limited incomes and because they feel more comfortable where there are people like themselves.

Another classic study, the Midtown Manhattan Study, went beyond treatment to include a random sample of 1,660 adult residents of midtown Manhattan (Srole et al., 1978). The researchers found that almost 23 percent were significantly impaired in mental functioning, including many people who were not under treatment. One of the factors investigated was socioeconomic status, not only that of the subjects but also that of their parents. Among subjects considered seriously impaired in mental functioning, the percentage with lower-class parents was twice the percentage of those with upper-class parents. This finding suggests that socioeconomic status is correlated with the mental health of children.

It should be kept in mind that studies like these tend to come up with widely divergent estimates of the proportion of mentally ill individuals in various populations. Some of these differences are due to the use of different data collection techniques and different definitions of mental illness. The studies are consistent, however, in reporting that only a minority of the cases observed have ever received treatment (Cokes and Kornblum, 2010).

All the studies just described agree that psychosis in general and schizophrenia in particular are much more common at the lowest socioeconomic level than at higher levels. They do not indicate, however, whether most schizophrenic individuals were originally in the lowest class or whether they drifted down to it as the disorder worsened. In other words, they fail to make clear whether low socioeconomic status is primarily a *cause* or an *effect* of serious mental disorder. Other research has attempted to address this question.

drift hypothesis
A concept that argues that social class is not a cause but a consequence of mental disorder.

Some researchers reject a poverty or social-stress hypothesis as an explanation of the preponderance of mental illness in the lower classes. Instead, they propose the **drift hypothesis**, which holds that social class is not a cause but a consequence of mental disorder (Cockerham, 2014; Hurst, 2013). In this view, people with mental disorders tend to be found in the lower classes because their illness has prevented them from functioning at a higher class level, and they have "drifted" downward to a lower class.

Studies do provide evidence that low social class does not cause mental illness (Hudson, 2005, 2012). Instead, a low social-class position is associated with mental disorders, most likely the result of a process in which the mentally ill drift downward in society. A review of existing studies on this subject, together with an analysis of new data from repeated interviews with a large sample of Americans, lends further support to the drift hypothesis. Sociologists and mental health experts find that a wide variety of mental illnesses impair individuals' ability to develop their skills and advance in the world of work and, thus, prevent them from attaining social mobility. In short, it is more often the case that mental disorders lead to low socioeconomic status than that low socioeconomic status leads to a mental disorder. The interconnectedness of social factors associated with mental illnesses can be represented as a "vicious cycle of poverty and mental disorders," as shown in Figure 3–4.

A variety of other factors have been investigated in an attempt to discover their relationship to mental disorder. Among these are demographic characteristics of race and ethnicity, sex, and age.

Race and Ethnicity

Rates of mental illness differ only slightly among most racial and ethnic groups with the exception of American Indians and Alaska Natives, who experience significantly more mental illness than do other groups, as shown in Figure 3–5 (National Institute of Mental Health, 2015). But are the differences really due to race or ethnicity per se, or can they be explained in terms of social class? People who are poor, of whom a large proportion are black or Hispanic, are more likely to suffer from mental illness or to be seen as needing hospitalization than are members of the middle and upper classes, more of whom are white. The latter are more likely to be seen as needing outpatient psychotherapy. The poor are also much more likely to deal with public agencies, including mental health centers, and to live in deteriorated urban environments (Cokes and Kornblum, 2010).

However, there is also some evidence that the experience of racial discrimination heightens stress and contributes to mental health problems (Pascoe and Richman, 2009). For example, a recent study based on data from over 4,000 African Americans and Caribbean blacks suggests that perceived experiences of discrimination in the form of disrespect and condescension (e.g., receiving poorer service at a store) do not by themselves increase risk for most mental disorders. However, hostile and

Figure 3–4 The Vicious Cycle of Poverty and Mental Disorders

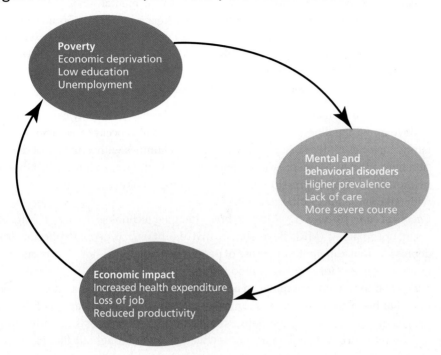

character-based discrimination (e.g., threats and harassment) in combination with disrespect and condescension does seem to place African American and Caribbean black adults at considerable risk for mental health problems (Clark et al., 2015).

Sex

Overall, men and women have different rates of mental illness for certain conditions. It appears that women are more likely to experience depression, anxiety, and phobias, whereas men are more likely to suffer from autism and schizophrenia.

Figure 3–5 Prevalence of Any Mental Illness Among U.S. Adults by Race/Ethnicity, 2012

SOURCE: National Institute of Mental Health, 2015.

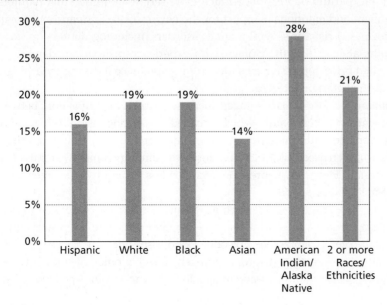

Women are much more likely than men to be diagnosed with severe depression, and because this disorder is the most common form of mental illness, it is worthy of extended discussion. Efforts to explain this difference in depression are ongoing as researchers explore many potential causes and contributing factors to women's increased risk for depression. It is likely that genetic, biological, chemical, hormonal, environmental, psychological, and social factors all intersect to contribute to depression (National Institute of Mental Health, 2015; World Health Organization, 2015):

- *Genetics.* If a woman has a family history of depression, she may be more at risk of developing the illness. However, depression can also occur in women without family histories of depression, and women from families with a history of depression may not develop depression themselves. Genetics research indicates that the risk for developing depression likely involves the combination of multiple genes with environmental or other factors.

- *Chemicals and Hormones.* Modern brain-imaging technologies such as magnetic resonance imaging (MRI) have shown that the brains of people suffering from depression look different from those of people without depression. The parts of the brain responsible for regulating mood, thinking, sleep, appetite, and behavior do not appear to function normally. In addition, important neurotransmitters—chemicals that brain cells use to communicate—appear to be out of balance. But these images do not reveal *why* the depression has occurred. Scientists are also studying the influence of female hormones, which change throughout life. Hormones directly affect the brain chemistry that controls emotions and mood.

- *Premenstrual Dysphoric Disorder.* Some women may be susceptible to a severe form of premenstrual syndrome called premenstrual dysphoric disorder (PMDD), which is associated with depression, anxiety, irritability, and mood swings the week before menstruation and that interferes with their normal functioning. Women with debilitating PMDD do not necessarily have unusual hormone changes, but they do have different responses to these changes. They may also have a history of other mood disorders and differences in brain chemistry that cause them to be more sensitive to menstruation-related hormone changes. Scientists are exploring how the cyclical rise and fall of estrogen and other hormones may affect the brain chemistry that is associated with depressive illness.

- *Postpartum Depression.* Women are particularly vulnerable to depression after giving birth, when hormonal and physical changes and the new responsibility of caring for a newborn can be overwhelming. Many new mothers experience a brief episode of mild mood changes known as the "baby blues," but some will suffer from postpartum depression, a much more serious condition that requires active treatment and emotional support for the new mother. Postpartum women are at an increased risk for several mental disorders, including depression, for several months after childbirth. Women who experience postpartum depression often have had prior depressive episodes. Some experience it during their pregnancies, but it often goes undetected.

- *Menopause.* Hormonal changes increase during the transition between pre-menopause to menopause, which is called perimenopause. While some women may transition into menopause without any problems with mood, others experience an increased risk for depression, even among women without a history of depression. However, depression becomes less common for women during the post-menopause period.

- *Stress.* Stressful life events such as trauma, loss of a loved one, a difficult relationship, or any stressful situation—whether welcome or unwelcome—often occur before a depressive episode. Gender-specific risk factors for common mental disorders that disproportionately affect women include gender-based violence, socioeconomic disadvantage, low income and income inequality, low or subordinate social status and rank, and unremitting responsibility for the care of others, including children and aging parents. Stress associated with these factors may trigger a depressive episode. A positive relationship exists between the frequency and severity of such social factors and the frequency and severity of mental health problems in women. Severe life events that cause a sense of loss, inferiority, humiliation, or entrapment can predict depression. However, it is unclear why some women faced with enormous challenges develop depression and some with similar challenges do not.

Age

In contrast to most severe and disabling physical diseases, many mental illnesses begin early in life. The most recent incidence research in the United States and worldwide shows that 50 percent of all lifetime cases of mental illness begin by age 14. Three-quarters have begun by age 24 (Kessler et al., 2005). Mental disorders therefore can be thought of as the chronic diseases of the young. Anxiety disorders such as panic attacks often begin in late childhood, eating and mood disorders in late adolescence, and substance abuse disorders in the early 20s. Table 3–1 reports the prevalence of specific mental health disorders among children. These rates are based on large, nationally representative samples—often more than one, which is why some disorders show a prevalence range rather than just one number. Overall, it is estimated that nearly one child in five is affected by some form of mental disorder (Perou et al., 2013).

Young people with mental disorders experience disability when they are in the prime of life, when they would normally be most productive, whereas extremely disabling physical illnesses like heart disease and cancer tend to strike adults in the later years of their working lives. The risk of mental disorders declines as people mature out of the high-risk age range. However, elderly people have increasing rates of depression after age 70, which is often due to loss of loved ones and to physical conditions such as progressive dementia manifested in Alzheimer's disease (National Institute of Mental Health, 2015).

The mental problems among the oldest-old population are a growing concern for researchers and policymakers and for millions of elderly people and their families. Alzheimer's disease, a degenerative brain disorder that destroys memory, has been increasing in prevalence (Alzheimer's Association, 2014). Recent progress in

Because of hormonal changes and fluctuations during pregnancy and after, some women experience depression while pregnant or, more commonly, experience depression after the baby is born. Stress likely also plays a significant role. Ask any parent about the work involved in caring for a new baby.

Table 3–1 Prevalence of Specific Mental Disorders Among Children, 2011

Mental Disorder	Prevalence among Children
Attention Deficit/Hyperactivity Disorder	7.6%–8.9%
Behavioral Conduct Problems	4.6%
Autism Spectrum Disorder	0.8%–1.1%
Depression	3.9%–12.8%
General Anxiety	4.7%
Post-Traumatic Stress Disorder	5.0%
Separation Anxiety	7.6%
Bipolar Disorder	2.9%

SOURCE: Perou et al., 2013.

What Do You Think?

Why do we know so little about what causes mental illness? When you compare mental illness across different groups, such as age or sex or race, do you think the causes of mental illness differ across these groups?

research and development of treatments for depression and possible treatments for Alzheimer's is encouraging, but the problems brought on by mental illnesses among the elderly are likely to increase as the elderly population grows, a subject to which you will return in Chapter 9.

Methods of Treatment

3.4 Compare treatment options for mental illness.

The treatment of mental disorders has undergone enormous changes in the past century and remains one of the most controversial aspects of mental health in all societies. This section reviews the major approaches to the treatment of mental illness and changes in mental health institutions. It will show that, although there has been a great deal of progress in treating mental illness, many problems remain, especially in creating and maintaining effective institutions for the treatment and care of the mentally ill (Cockerham, 2014).

The two major approaches to the treatment of mental disorders are medical treatment and psychotherapy. Although these approaches are sometimes used simultaneously, they involve different groups of mental health professionals who often have difficulty coordinating the diagnosis and treatment of their patients. The problem of coordination is discussed more fully in the Social Policy section of the chapter. In this section, we briefly review the most important methods of treatment.

Medical Approaches to Treatment

Medical treatments can help control most mental illnesses. These treatments are provided by physicians, including psychiatrists. Medications can play an important part in a treatment plan. The general consensus is that medicines are usually more effective when combined with psychotherapy. In some cases, medication can reduce symptoms so that other methods of a treatment plan can be more effective. For example, a medication may alleviate some significant symptoms of major depression, and then psychotherapy can help the patient change negative patterns of thinking (National Alliance on Mental Illness, 2015).

HISTORY OF MEDICAL APPROACHES Before the late 1930s, severe psychosis was treated in a variety of ways: by confining the patient in a straitjacket; by administering sedatives; by wrapping the patient in moist, cool sheets; or by immersing the patient in a continuous flow tub for hours at a time (Sheehan, 1982). Then a more drastic treatment was introduced: electroconvulsive therapy in which an electric shock produces a convulsion and brief unconsciousness. This frightening and dangerous treatment has produced dramatic results with deeply depressed patients and some schizophrenics. However, the effects tend to be temporary, and it is not clear how much brain damage the treatment causes. Moreover, it often results in long-term memory loss.

In the 1940s and early 1950s, shock treatment was used extensively, sometimes in coercive and excessive ways (Squire, 1987). The procedure was modified in the mid-1950s and made somewhat safer, but in the 1960s and 1970s, it fell into disfavor as drug therapies became increasingly popular.

COMMON MEDICAL APPROACHES TODAY The primary medical approach to managing mental illness today involves treating patients with a variety of drugs, ranging from mild tranquilizers to antidepressants and antipsychotic agents. Of all the recent innovations in drug therapy, the administration of antidepressants and anti-anxiety medications has had the greatest impact and has relieved severe and debilitating symptoms in millions of people. The current standard of treatment involves a drug class known as selective serotonin reuptake inhibitors (SSRIs). Scientists believe that depression can be triggered by a lack of the chemical serotonin, and these drugs essentially maintain higher levels of serotonin in the brain to correct the issue. In other words, these medications work by influencing the brain chemicals regulating emotions and thought patterns.

Prozac was the first SSRI, marketed in the 1980s. Newer related drugs have been developed and are advertised regularly on television with the brand names of Celexa, Wellbutrin, Cymbalta, and Abilify. Treatment typically consists of pills or capsules taken daily. A few medications are available as liquids, as injections, or as tablets that dissolve in the mouth. Most medications will start at a low dose and slowly increase dosages to therapeutic levels.

In addition to these antidepressants, the development of the antipsychotic drugs has made it possible to control the most incapacitating aspects of schizophrenia and paranoia. These medications reduce or eliminate the symptoms of psychosis (delusions and hallucinations) by affecting the brain chemical called dopamine. Newer, second-generation, or atypical antipsychotics can also treat acute mania, bipolar disorder, and treatment-resistant depression. Consistent use of these drugs often permits the patient to control his or her illness, allowing a normal life.

Mental illness is person-specific, and it is therefore important to find just the right drug that helps each person individually. For example, there is not one drug that works for all people who suffer from depression. Therefore, patients and providers work together, sometimes by trial and error, to find the correct treatment plan. It is generally believed that drugs should be used in conjunction with some other form of therapy for optimum results.

Nonmedical Forms of Treatment

There are many nonmedical forms of treatment for people with mental illness. Some are provided alone, and others are provided in conjunction with drug therapy. Of these nonmedical treatments, psychotherapy is most common, but other forms are also available.

PSYCHOTHERAPY   Patients who undergo **psychotherapy** are helped to understand the underlying reasons for their problems so that they can try to work out solutions. The process involves some form of interaction between the patient and the therapist or among patients in groups. Among the major forms of psychotherapy are psychoanalysis, client-centered therapy, and various types of therapy and support groups.

psychotherapy
Interaction between a patient and a therapist or among patients in groups that is intended to foster insight and change.

Developed by Sigmund Freud in the late nineteenth century, psychoanalysis seeks to uncover unconscious motives, memories, and fears that prevent the patient from functioning normally. Patients may use various methods of exploration and discovery, including dreams and free association.

Client-centered therapy was developed by Carl Rogers in the 1940s. This approach emphasizes current problems rather than unconscious motives and past experiences. The patient sets the course of the therapy, while the therapist provides support.

In therapy and support groups, people attempt to solve their problems through interaction with one another. Support groups are composed of people who have experienced the same problems as the other participants, for example, Alcoholics Anonymous, Overeaters Anonymous, and Gamblers Anonymous.

OTHER APPROACHES   Exercise is recommended for people who suffer from many mental illnesses. Research shows that exercise and physical activity can prevent or delay the onset of different mental illnesses, and they also have therapeutic benefits when used as sole or secondary treatment (Harvey et al., 2010; Zschucke, Gaudlitz, and Ströhle, 2013). For example, many people who have anxiety, depression, eating disorders, dementia, or schizophrenia receive significant relief from physical activity. On a neurochemical and physiological level, a number of acute

Slide Show

Treating Mental Illness

There are many different ways to treat mental illness. Unlike physical illnesses, which are more likely to be predictable

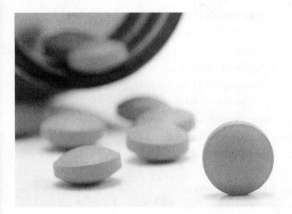

One of the more common treatments for mental disorders is drugs. However, the commonly used medicines work differently on people with the same condition. Sometimes people have to try several before they find the one that works well for them. Drugs are not without their controversy, but millions of people say they have been helped by them.

Social support from family or friends is also a key factor keeping many mental illnesses at bay and is an important tool of recovery from mental illness. Getting involved in social activities is also helpful, although many mental illnesses such as depression, phobias, or anxiety may keep people from socializing.

Socializing with others can happen in many different ways. This man receives support, warmth, and love from his border collie, "Zeke."

across patients, mental illness and the treatment for mental illness is very individualized. What works for one person does not necessarily work for another person, even if each are thought to suffer from the same disorder.

Psychotherapy is an important source of treatment, and psychotherapy is generally advised even if drugs are the primary treatment. Here, a teenage girl seeks help for her obsessive-compulsive disorder that involves repetitive and compulsive thoughts and behaviors.

Physical exercise is another nonmedical type of treatment that has had some success in preventing or treating mental illness, especially those disorders that are less severe. Exercise has positive effects both physiologically, such as by releasing endorphins, and socially by increasing a sense of mastery.

Critical Thinking

Using the sociological imagination, explain why mental health and mental health treatments are not simply personal problems.

changes occur during and following bouts of exercise. For instance, animal studies found exercise-induced changes in different neurotransmitters such as serotonin and endorphins that relate to mood and positive effects of exercise on stress reactivity. Potential psychological reactions associated with exercise include changes in body image, overall health attitudes, and behaviors; the potential for increased feelings of mastery and social reinforcement; and improved coping strategies, or simple distraction from personal problems.

Social support is also a key factor in mental health and well-being and is an important tool of recovery from mental illness. For example, a study with 153 persons ages 16 to 84 with serious mental health illnesses found that having a strong social support network, the size of the network, and engaging in social activities were related to higher scores on a commonly used "recovery assessment scale" (Hendryx, Green, and Perrin, 2009). The particular nature of the activities (more/less social, more/less physically active, inside/outside the home) was not important; rather, activities of any type were related to recovery. Furthermore, engagement in activities was more important as levels of social support declined. The results of this study suggest that both social support and activities may promote recovery, and that for persons with poor social support, engagement in a variety of individualized activities may be particularly beneficial.

> **What Do You Think?**
>
> Have you or someone you know closely ever suffered from a mental illness? If so, did this person receive any type of treatment? Describe the treatment.

Institutional Problems of Providing Treatment and Care

3.5 **Explain the institutional problems of providing treatment and care.**

The forms of treatment described earlier are carried out in a variety of settings. Psychotherapy and other nonmedical forms of treatment generally occur in nonhospital settings such as psychologists' offices. Medical treatments, in contrast, sometimes require hospitalization. In addition, some patients are so seriously ill that they cannot be cared for outside a hospital or asylum. In this section, we discuss issues related to the care of the mentally ill in hospitals and other institutions.

Mental Hospitals

In the late nineteenth and early twentieth centuries, care for patients with mental illness usually involved mental hospitals. The general thought was that mentally ill people belonged in institutions to receive appropriate treatment, and for their own safety and the safety of others. The number of mental hospitals and institutions increased substantially during this period. The role and conditions of mental hospitals was of concern to some, but the solutions proposed involved increasing the funding of hospitals, not the wholesale release of their patients.

During this period, the ties among members of extended families were being weakened as a result of increased mobility. The smaller nuclear family was less well equipped to care for its disabled members and began to look to the state for assistance (Curtis, 1986). Institutions like mental hospitals were developed to meet this need. In such institutions, those with mental illnesses were to be sheltered from a hostile world, kept from harming themselves or others, and given help and treatment. Hospitals were built in secluded spots and surrounded by high walls and locked gates. Within the walls, all the patient's needs were to be met. But the purpose of the hospital was not merely to protect patients from society and, if possible, to cure them; it was also to protect society from the patients. The old stereotype of the "raving lunatic" persisted, and eventually, security came to be considered more important than therapy.

For the sake of economy and efficiency, a system of enormous hospitals developed, each housing several thousand patients and staffed largely by aides whose

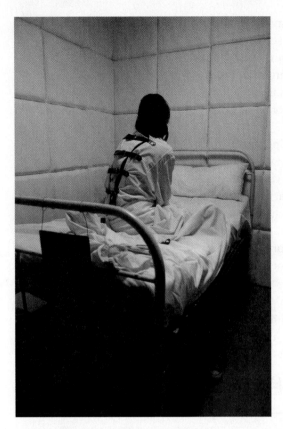

This woman is a patient in one of the remaining mental hospitals. She has a history of hurting herself, and in this picture she is wearing a straitjacket.

total institution
A place of residence and work where a large number of like-situated individuals are cut off from the wider society for an appreciable period of time and together lead an enclosed life.

main job is to keep things quiet on as low a budget as a state legislature can decently supply. Staffing these hospitals is a perennial problem. Salaries are usually low; working conditions are often unattractive or discouraging; and professionally trained personnel are almost irresistibly tempted away by private hospitals, clinics, or private practice, where the rewards, both monetary and in terms of visible therapeutic achievement, are much greater. Consequently, public institutions must depend heavily on partially trained personnel, particularly attendants or nursing aides. These attendants, though not fully qualified, have the most contact with the patients, and they typically control most aspects of the patients' daily life, including access to doctors.

There is evidence that hospitalization may not always be the best solution to mental illness, even in good hospitals. Long-term studies have shown that patients who do not improve enough to be discharged within a short period are likely to remain hospitalized for a very long time, if not indefinitely. This effect is due in part to the inadequacies of the hospital. It also seems to be a consequence of hospitalization itself, a position taken by Erving Goffman (1961). Goffman developed the concept of the **total institution**, which is defined as a place of residence and work where a large number of like-situated individuals are cut off from the wider society for an appreciable period of time and together lead an enclosed life. Mental hospitals are an example of a total institution, as are prisons and religious convents.

Goffman (1961) regarded the mental hospital as a prime example of a total institution. His field research and work in mental hospitals convinced him that, because inmates are constantly subject to its control, the hospital profoundly shapes their sense of self. In general, mental hospitals downgrade patients' desire for self-esteem and emphasize their failures and inadequacies. Uniform clothing and furniture, a regimented routine, and the custodial atmosphere of the hospital make patients docile and unassertive. Because the psychiatric approach requires cooperation, staff members often encourage patients to view themselves as sick and in need of help. Any act of self-assertion or rebellion may be interpreted as further evidence of illness, and patients will be expected to take that view of themselves. Release from the hospital is often contingent on the patient's accepting, or appearing to accept, the official interpretation of his or her hospital and prehospital life. Goffman concluded that, in most cases, there is a high probability that hospitalization will do more harm than good.

Goffman has received heavy criticism, particularly for not having conducted enough empirical research on enough hospitals to determine whether all mental hospitals could be called total institutions. Moreover, although Goffman's view has had a great influence on the way people think about mental hospitals (and jails), he is accused of having been influenced by the literary power of his ideas and images rather than by the force of empirical data (McEwen, 1988; Scull, 1988).

The classic study by Rosenhan (1973), mentioned earlier, illustrates the conditions prevailing in many mental hospitals. This research project involved eight "normal" people, or pseudopatients, who were admitted to several mental hospitals and diagnosed as schizophrenics. Their only symptom was a fabricated one: They said that they had heard voices on one occasion. Although the pseudopatients spent some time in the institutions and were recognized as normal by their fellow inmates, the staff continued to think of them as schizophrenic. Some were released with the diagnosis of "schizophrenia in remission," and none was ever thought to be cured. In a follow-up study, a hospital that had heard of these findings was informed that over a period of three months some pseudopatients would attempt to gain admission to the hospital, and staff members were asked to judge which applicants were faking illness. Over the three-month period at least 41 patients were judged to be pseudopatients. In fact, none of those patients was faking.

The results of this study were widely cited as supporting the labeling theory in that the diagnosis of illness—or health—was applied regardless of the actual condition of the patient. But also of interest here is what the pseudopatients observed while in the hospital. As much as possible, staff members were separated from patients by a glass enclosure; psychiatrists, in particular, almost never appeared on the wards. When pseudopatients approached staff members with questions, the most common response was to ignore the questions or mumble something—avoiding eye contact with the patient—and quickly move on. Patients were sometimes punished excessively for misbehavior, and in one case, a patient was beaten. Overall, the atmosphere for patients was one of powerlessness and depersonalization.

Community Psychology

The increased use of drugs in the treatment of mental disorders caused a revolution in mental health care. It began in the hospitals in the 1950s. As a result of the introduction of psychotropic drugs, thousands of patients who had been assaultive became docile. Many who had spent their days screaming subsided into talking to themselves. The decor of the wards could be improved: Chairs replaced wooden benches, curtains were hung on the windows. Razors and matches, once properly regarded as lethal, were given to patients who now were capable of shaving themselves and lighting their own cigarettes without injuring themselves or others or burning the hospital down (Sheehan, 1982, p. 10).

But the revolution went far beyond hospital care. New "wonder drugs" like Thorazine made it possible to release hundreds of thousands of hospitalized patients (Cockerham, 2006; Sperry, 1995), who were supposed to receive outpatient treatment in their own communities.

Outpatient treatment for mental disorders is far from new, but until the 1960s, it was confined largely to less severe disorders and to the upper and middle classes. By the mid-twentieth century, public attitudes had changed, and mental institutions were increasingly viewed as "warehouses" in which the mentally ill were shut away. In 1963, President Kennedy signed into law the Community Mental Health Act, which drastically altered the delivery of mental health services. The law led to the establishment of community mental health centers around the country. The idea of easily accessible, locally controlled facilities that could care for people in their own communities—**community psychology**—was established. The large mental hospitals began to close.

community psychology
The idea of easily accessible, locally controlled facilities that could care for mentally ill people in their own communities.

In 1955, there were 560,000 public mental hospital beds in the United States for use by mentally ill persons who needed care, but that number has shrunk to only 43,000 in 2010 (Treatment Advocacy Center, 2012). However, this dramatic decline of over 90 percent has not been offset by effective systems of community care (Drake and Latimer, 2012). Of the 2,000 community mental health centers planned in 1963, fewer than 1,000 have been established. As a result, hospital emergency rooms are often crowded with psychiatric patients. In addition, large numbers of former patients are in jail or prisons, or are homeless (Treatment Advocacy Center, 2015).

The community psychology movement arose from two basic sources: (1) awareness that social conditions and institutions must be taken into account in dealing with individual mental health problems; and (2) the idea that psychologists or psychiatrists should be able to contribute to the understanding and solution of social problems. The guidelines laid down for the centers provided for a wide range of mental health care in the community and for coordination with, and consultative assistance to, other community agencies.

halfway house

A small, privately run residential community, usually located in an urban area, in which ex-patients are helped to make the transition from the hospital to normal life.

The Community Mental Health Centers Construction Act set up a sophisticated support system to aid newly released patients, many of whom need considerable help in relearning the skills of everyday life and social interaction. The cornerstone of this system is the **halfway house**, a small residential community in which ex-patients are helped to make the transition from the hospital to normal life. They may receive therapy from a psychiatrist, they may be trained for a job and helped to obtain or keep one, and they are able to practice fitting into a community in which behavior is not subject to hospital regulations.

Under optimal conditions, halfway houses are capable of providing high-quality care; however, a variety of obstacles have prevented them from meeting the needs of many discharged mental patients. Operating almost in a vacuum—with no working relationship with the state mental hospitals from which they receive patients—many halfway houses soon found themselves with far more patients than they had staff or facilities to handle. This problem was exacerbated as hospitals rushed to reduce their patient loads long before community support systems were in place. In addition, halfway houses and other community mental health centers face the enormous problem of lack of funds. The insurance coverage of mentally ill patients tends to favor hospital care, and the coverage for mental problems is inferior to that available for physical illnesses. As a result, halfway houses, nursing homes, and other community mental health facilities have found it difficult to meet the growing demand for services (Hazlett et al., 2004).

To effectively address the needs of people with mental disorders, a variety of institutions and approaches, all working together, are required. Schools, hospitals, families, community centers, and law enforcement agencies need to become more aware of mental health problems and how to deal with them. In affluent nations, including the United States, part of the reason why so many cases of mental disorder go untreated has to do with lack of coordination and failure to overcome problems of stigma, discrimination, and lack of support in the person's social environment.

Deinstitutionalization and Homelessness

The preceding section noted that, beginning in the mid-1950s, large numbers of mental patients were deinstitutionalized, or released from mental hospitals, based on the belief that psychiatric patients would have a higher quality of life if treated in their communities rather than in mental hospitals.

Not all homeless people are mentally ill, but it is estimated that at least a quarter of homeless men, and nearly two-thirds of homeless women do suffer a serious mental illness. Deinstitutionalization has released many mentally ill people who would otherwise be in mental hospitals. Is this policy a good one or a bad one?

Throughout the 1960s and 1970s it was hoped that reductions in the hospital population would be accompanied by equivalent reductions in the incidence of mental disorders. This hope proved to be in vain. Far from decreasing, the incidence of mental disorders increased. At the same time, the funding of community mental health care was cut back. The presence of deinstitutionalized mental patients among the homeless is due partly to their tendency to congregate in central-city neighborhoods, which are unable to provide the services they need. It has also been caused, in part, by the passage of laws designed to protect the rights of the mentally ill. Because only patients who are demonstrably dangerous may be involuntarily committed to mental hospitals, most mentally ill patients receive only brief, episodic care. Chronically mentally ill people who are not dangerous to themselves or others are released into the community. Some find housing in single-room occupancy (SRO) hotels or cheap rooming houses, but these forms of housing are far less available today than they were in the 1950s and 1960s because landlords have either abandoned them or converted them into condominiums. As a result, mentally ill people often end up on the streets.

On a given night, nearly 600,000 people are homeless (U.S. Department of Housing and Urban Development, 2014). Most homeless people are not mentally ill, and the majority of the homeless are individuals or families who have been caught in either a cycle of unemployment or low-paying, dead-end jobs that fail to provide the means to get off the streets. Nontheless, somewhere between 25 and 33 percent of the homeless men are seriously mentally ill, as are nearly two-thirds of homeless women, which is a serious social problem (Treatment Advocacy Center, 2012).

Homelessness usually is the final stage in a long series of crises and missed opportunities, the result of a gradual process of disengagement from supportive relationships and institutions. The situation is especially severe for those who are mentally ill. They are isolated. Family members and friends have become tired and discouraged or are unable to help. Social workers are overburdened and cannot give them the attention they need, and the mentally ill themselves cannot communicate their needs adequately.

As a result of experiences like these, the homeless, especially those who are mentally ill, tend to be afraid of strangers, which is one reason why they often reject offers of shelter and efforts to help them. The fear experienced by some homeless people is so great that it can be overcome only with effort and patience. It should also be pointed out, however, that mental illness can be a consequence of homelessness as well as a cause of it. People who lose their homes suffer severe stress. They experience hunger, lack of sleep, and physical illnesses. In addition, they are "disorganized, depressed, disordered ... immobilized by pain and traumatized by fear" (Kozol, 1988).

What Do You Think?
Compare and contrast how a functionalist, conflict theorist, and symbolic interactionist would look at the issue of mental illness and homelessness.

Social Policy

3.6 Analyze the policy implications of the Affordable Care Act for mental illness.

In 2008, under the George W. Bush administration, Congress moved toward parity in insurance coverage between physical and mental illness. Before parity legislation, it was common for benefits policies issued by major corporations to impose a lifetime limit of benefits for mental illness to $50,000, whereas the limit for physical health care might range from $750,000 to $1 million. Health insurance experts feared that an unintended consequence of parity legislation would be that insurance companies would drop mental health coverage altogether, which would actually reduce the number of people covered by any form of mental health insurance.

The 2010 Affordable Care Act moved further toward parity for mental disorders and for those who suffer from them. By disallowing the insurance company practice of denying coverage for family members with prior illnesses, physical or mental, it ensures that millions of Americans will be eligible for coverage and treatment. This development can save society enormously—both in reducing the federal deficit and in reducing suffering—because the sooner mental illness is treated, the lower the cost to society in the long run.

Without adequate coverage for mental health care, people who suffer from severe mental illnesses are often forced into poverty. Once on the streets, they may be treated in public institutions, but in an era of shrinking budgets this approach also becomes problematic. State and municipal governments are often unwilling or unable to assume the burden of caring for the mentally ill. Some provide shelters for the homeless, but these facilities cannot hope to replace the mental hospital or the halfway house. Shelters offer minimal medical, psychological, and social services. Generally understaffed, they are open only at night and cannot provide the supervision and support needed by disturbed individuals.

Some reinstitutionalization has occurred as a result of the public outcry over the plight of the homeless mentally ill, particularly for patients under constant medication, who need careful monitoring because their tolerance of and need for psychotropic drugs are constantly changing. If they receive adequate treatment outside as well as inside the hospital, this revolving-door system is reasonably effective. However, such situations are rare.

An important problem in caring for those with mental illnesses is the lack of coordination of treatment. Because the mental health care field is divided between insight therapists and medical practitioners, there is a widespread tendency to see psychotherapy and medical treatment as mutually exclusive. Yet a patient who is on medication needs to have enough insight to be able to take the medicine in the prescribed dosage at the correct intervals. It follows that there must be a high level of coordination of treatment between social workers and others in the patient's social world, on one hand, and the clinical personnel who prescribe medication and decide whether patients should be hospitalized, on the other.

Without coordination of care, people suffering from mental disorders often fail to follow their medication regimes, or they may fail to get treatment as their conditions change, or in many instances they may fail to receive any treatment at all. Individualized treatment for mental illnesses can be complicated and require close coordination between patients and health care professionals. Some mental disorders can result in extremely high costs to the individuals involved and their families, as well as to society at large, when treatment is delayed or uncoordinated and intermittent. Bipolar disorder, for example, is the most expensive mental health care diagnosis, both for patients with the illness and for their health insurance plans, and it is the sixth most frequent cause of disability worldwide.

All untreated mental illness costs money. Although precise numbers are hard to pin down, it is estimated that untreated mental illness costs the U.S. economy at least $105 billion annually in absenteeism and reduced worker productivity (Giang, 2012). Millions of dollars more are spent on costly emergency room visits and additional doctor bills. The Affordable Care Act is moving toward an investment in a national system of electronic health records that should give mental health professionals improved capability to follow patients who move from one neighborhood or city to another and to continuously update their medical records so that everyone in the treatment network of a given individual can be kept current.

Mental illness can be controlled. With the right treatment, people who have a mental illness can lead happy, healthy, and productive lives. As Tremon says, Hey, I'm back!

Future Prospects

An emerging comprehensive approach to health care, including mental health care, is likely to bring vast improvements in the treatment conditions for people with severe mental illnesses. They are now more likely to have health insurance, and that insurance is more likely to cover mental health disorders. However, there is a flip side that is worthy of mention. Increasing insurance coverage will send more severely ill patients into an already heavily burdened public system. People with moderate mental illnesses like chronic depression, who do not need extensive rehabilitation or long-term care, will be likely to receive the care they need from their general practitioner, but patients with more severe chronic conditions such as schizophrenia may face delays in treatment as the hospitals adjust to increased demands on their services. More funding is needed to meet these demands. Ideally, as the number of treated cases increases, the savings to society will be measured in less suffering, lower treatment costs, fewer suicides, and earlier treatment.

Going Beyond Left And Right

Whose responsibility are the mentally ill? This question does not give rise to as many moral or ideological debates as some other social problems, but there are controversies nonetheless. In this chapter, for example, we have described the failure of the community mental health care movement. There is minimal ideological debate over the need to end the warehousing of mentally ill people in isolated state hospitals, especially when new drug therapies have made it possible for them to live more normal lives. But where are they to live? In whose communities should they reside? Do we all share the responsibility for their care, or must the communities where the mentally ill are most numerous bear a greater share of the burden?

On the right, there is a tendency to insist on the responsibility of families to care for their mentally ill members. On the left, one hears demands for public funding of mental health clinics. What are your views on the issue? Does the sociological analysis presented in this chapter help you go beyond the opposing viewpoints?

Family responsibility and adequate funding of public programs need not be incompatible policies. At some point the laws, which are based on social custom, insist that an adult person is no longer the sole responsibility of his or her family. However, lack of adequate funding for public mental health programs remains a serious obstacle to providing care for such individuals. And the tragic rampages at schools, shopping malls, movie theaters, sites of employment, and elsewhere call attention to the failure to enforce existing laws about selling guns to mentally ill individuals or to adequately monitor their activities and follow up on their treatment. Unfortunately, the likelihood of constructive action to address these problems is diminished by conservative opposition to restrictions on sales of firearms and liberal concerns about the restriction of civil rights. Still, lawmakers who wish to avoid ideological battles can remind the public of the consequences of inaction and invoke tragedies like the Virginia Tech University or Sandy Hook Elementary massacres, or a number of equally tragic cases, to make their case for effective measures to protect public safety.

Summary

- Mental illness is a social problem because of the large numbers of people who suffer emotionally and physically from mental disorders. Mental disorders are the leading cause of disability for people ages 15 to 44 in the United States and throughout the world. Mental illness is also a social problem because of the potential harm caused by people with unchecked serious mental illness, such as the mass shootings in schools.

- When social scientists say that mental illness is socially constructed, they are highlighting aspects of those illnesses that help define how both the mentally ill and "normal" people behave. There are three main approaches to constructing mental illness: (1) the medical model, which asserts that mental illness is a disease with physiological causes; (2) the deviance approach, which asserts that mental illness results from the way people considered mentally ill are treated; and (3) the controversial argument that mental illness is not a disease but a method governments use to define certain people as being in need of isolation and "treatment."

- Sociologists and experts on mental health care have continually refined their research concepts and tools to trace the relationships between mental illness and inequalities of social class, race, ethnicity, gender, age, and other dimensions of social inequality. There are significant differences among these groups. For example, women are far more likely than men to suffer from depression and anxiety, while men are more likely to suffer from autism or attention deficit disorder. Differences are likely due to a combination of genetic, hormonal, and social factors.

- The treatment of mental disorders has undergone enormous changes. The primary medical approach to managing mental illness today involves treating patients with a variety of drugs, ranging from mild tranquilizers to antidepressants and antipsychotic agents. The primary nonmedical approaches include psychotherapy, exercise, and social support. Although these approaches are sometimes used simultaneously, they involve different groups of mental health professionals, who often have difficulty coordinating the diagnosis and treatment of their patients.

- Mental hospitals and institutions were the primary method of dealing with persons with mental disorders until the mid-twentieth century. The development of drugs and a growing concern that large mental hospitals were essentially warehouses brought a reconsideration of how to best treat mentally ill people. Beginning in the mid-1950s, large numbers of mental patients were deinstitutionalized, or released from mental hospitals, based on the belief that psychiatric patients would have a higher quality of life if treated in their communities rather than in mental hospitals. The goal was to help these people through community mental health centers; however, some mentally ill persons are homeless and do not get the care they need.

- The Affordable Care Act (ACA) helps those people with mental illnesses because they can no longer be denied coverage for prior mental illnesses by insurance companies. The ACA ensures that millions of Americans will be eligible for coverage and treatment.

Chapter 4
Alcohol and Other Drugs

 ## Learning Objectives

4.1 Discuss the nature of the problem associated with alcohol and drugs, including definitions, abuse, and addiction.

4.2 Identify the perceptions toward alcohol and drinking patterns.

4.3 Assess several social problems related to alcohol.

4.4 Describe the effects of alcohol on the family.

4.5 Compare treatment options for alcoholism.

4.6 Summarize the nine most commonly used drugs that are abused.

4.7 Identify some of the patterns, problems, and treatments associated with drug abuse.

4.8 Review policy considerations of drug laws and enforcement.

Yeah, I like to get high. So what? How is it any business of yours? I'm basically a law-abiding citizen, but now and then I like to cut loose. A little cocaine never hurt anybody. The high makes me feel strong, powerful, on top of my game. I buy some on payday, but it's pretty expensive so I don't see how I could ever become addicted. I have a great Saturday night with my buddies, and then I'm done for two weeks until next payday. Or sometimes I skip a payday if my money needs to go somewhere else. Like, I'm saving for a snorkeling trip to Mexico, and that definitely cuts into my coke money. I've never had any problems with using coke, except when one guy last summer tried to steal some from me. That pissed me off and we roughed each other up a little. But he apologized, and quickly left the house after I bloodied his nose, and I haven't seen him around since. One of my buddies got a small inheritance from his grandmother when she died, and he bought four new tires for his car and I swear he spent the rest on coke. That's a little crazy if you ask me. He was going off on the deep end, but he pulled out of it. Well, I don't think I'll be getting any inheritances in the near future so I'm safe.

People use drugs, including alcohol, to ease pain, increase alertness, relax tension, lose weight, gain strength, fight depression, feel "high," and prevent pregnancy. Americans of all ages and at all socioeconomic levels consume vast quantities of chemical substances every year. Most of these drugs are socially acceptable, and most people use them for socially acceptable purposes. Alcohol is a drug, as are caffeine and nicotine; these substances are commonly and widely used as aids to sociability and ordinary activity. But some drugs and some users of drugs are socially defined as unacceptable, and it is these drugs and users that constitute the drug problem.

The uses and abuses of alcohol and other drugs are discussed together in this chapter for a number of reasons. Through its personal and social effects, alcohol abuse is as harmful as the abuse of less socially accepted drugs. Moreover, many drugs, including alcohol, offer satisfactions that make them attractive to many people, but they can be habit forming, sometimes with destructive consequences to both users and nonusers; thus, there are controversies over the causes, consequences, and moral implications of their use. Efforts to control drug use—particularly the "War on Drugs" that has been a cornerstone of American social policy against substance abuse for over 40 years—are increasingly controversial among political leaders and social scientists.

Strategies of interdiction and control are often associated with other social problems, such as violence, racism, and crime. Drastic measures to prevent drug cultivation and importation can also have negative effects on democratic institutions, both in the United States and abroad, with little evidence of success in diminishing drug supplies. Moreover, despite the nation's huge investments in antinarcotics policies, experts on addiction continually find that alcohol abuse is more prevalent and damaging to individuals and society than any other form of substance abuse.

Abuse of alcohol and other drugs is a growing problem throughout the world. Over 183,000 people died in 2012 in drug-related deaths (nonalcohol), amounting to 40 deaths per one million people between the ages of 15 and 64 (United Nations Office on Drugs and Crime, 2014). However, when 3.3 million alcohol-related deaths around the world are added to the picture, this number swells (World Health Organization, 2015).

Alcohol addiction has been a long-standing problem, but addiction to opiates and cocaine is a growing problem in China, Latin America, Russia, and many countries in Eastern Europe. Civil strife in drug-producing nations like Colombia and Afghanistan has multiple causes, but the importance of world drug markets as a cause of violence in these and other nations is undeniable. However, in its most recent survey of world drug use, the United Nations found that Americans use more drugs than people in other countries (United Nations Office on Drugs and Crime, 2014). Americans are also more likely to die from drug-related illness. The 2012 mortality rate of North Americans (which include Canadians) due to drugs was 142.1 per million persons, as indicated in Table 4–1. This rate is almost double that of the next highest region, Oceania, at 77.5 deaths per million persons, and is over three times the world average at 40 deaths per million. This global study did not deal with alcohol, which, as you

Table 4–1 Estimated Number of Drug-Related Deaths (Non-Alcohol) and Mortality Rates Per Million Persons Ages 15–64, 2012

Region	Number of Drug-Related Deaths	Mortality Rate Per Million, Ages 15–64
Africa	36,800	61.9
North America	44,600	142.1
Latin America and Caribbean	4,900	12.6
Asia	78,600	27.7
Western and Central Europe	7,500	23.2
Eastern and Southeastern Europe	8,700	37.9
Oceania	1,900	77.5
Global	**183,000**	**40.0**

SOURCE: United Nations Office on Drugs and Crime, 2014.

will see in this chapter, accounts for much of the cost and suffering that substance abuse causes in the United States and many other parts of the world. Although this chapter focuses primarily on alcohol and drug problems in the United States, much of what is learned in this nation also has a bearing on drug issues in other nations.

The Nature of the Problem

4.1   Discuss the nature of the problem associated with alcohol and drugs, including definitions, abuse, and addiction.

From a pharmacological viewpoint, a drug is any substance, other than food, that chemically alters the structure or function of a living organism. A definition this inclusive, however, encompasses not only medicines but also a huge range of substances from vitamins and hormones to herbs, snake and mosquito venom, antiperspirants, insecticides, and air pollutants. Obviously, this definition is too broad to be of practical value. Definitions that depend on context are more useful. Generally speaking, a **drug** is any substance, other than food, that chemically alters the structure or function of a living organism. However, in a medical context, a drug may be any substance prescribed by a physician or manufactured expressly to relieve pain or to treat and prevent disease. In a sociological context, the term *drug* denotes any chemical substance that affects physiological functions, mood, perception, or consciousness; has the potential for misuse; and may be harmful to the user or to society. In addition to the illicit drugs that attract so much attention, many pharmaceutical drugs are abused as narcotics (Centers for Disease Control and Prevention, 2015b).

Although the last definition is more satisfactory for our purposes than the original, much broader one, it omits the social bias that has traditionally determined what substances are labeled drugs. When members of a society have used a habit-forming substance for centuries, that substance may not be classified as a drug in that society, even if it has been proven to be harmful. Alcohol and tobacco (nicotine) are examples of such substances that we usually do not think of as drugs.

Subjective and Objective Dimensions

Like so many other social problems, drug use has both objective and subjective dimensions. The *objective aspect* is the degree to which a given substance causes physiological, psychological, or social problems for the individual or the social group—the family, the community, or the entire society. The *subjective aspect* is how people perceive the consequences of drug use and how their perceptions result in social action concerning drug use (such as norms, policies, laws, and programs).

drug

Any substance, other than food, that chemically alters the structure or function of a living organism.

Of course, these subjective perceptions may be based on objective evidence, but very often they are based on past practices and combinations of scientific and folk wisdom about a given substance. Aspirin, for example, is one of the most widely used drugs in the United States. From an objective standpoint, we know that aspirin is often taken in excessive dosages for every real or imagined physical or mental discomfort. Aspirin can cause ulcers, gastrointestinal bleeding, and other ailments. But most Americans believe—this is the subjective aspect—that aspirin is a harmless drug that is dangerous only when taken in massive doses. Thus, aspirin use is part of our overall drug problem in objective terms but not in subjective terms. For many Americans, the same failure to allow objective facts to shape subjective perceptions is true in the case of alcohol, which will be discussed later in the chapter.

Other drugs are part of the social problem of drug use because they are perceived as problems, even if the way they are used by certain people is not problematic in objective terms. Marijuana is an example. Objectively, there is little evidence that marijuana users damage themselves psychologically or physiologically, although researchers believe marijuana may decrease the user's motivation to concentrate and learn complex material. Yet the subjective view of many Americans, especially those in policymaking positions, is that marijuana is a dangerous drug. This subjective viewpoint is incorporated into laws against marijuana use, and these laws, in turn, foster the illegal traffic in marijuana.

The discrepancy between the subjective viewpoint and objective reality comes to prominence quite often in U.S. political affairs. In 1992, Bill Clinton's admission that he had tried marijuana as a student but had not inhaled became the subject of innumerable jokes during the presidential election campaign. The question of whether George W. Bush had used cocaine as a young man while "sowing his wild oats" was a persistent issue during the 2000 presidential primaries. President Obama, who admitted to trying marijuana as a younger man, put his administration clearly in the camp that opposes legalization of that and other drugs.

In the meantime, thousands of Americans are in jail for possession of marijuana, while small amounts are now legal in Colorado, Washington State, Oregon, and Alaska. Still, fearing a backlash from voters, only the bravest or most secure U.S. legislators would seriously consider supporting a national bill to legalize or decriminalize the substance for recreational use, as we will see in the Social Policy section of the chapter.

The point is that drugs such as marijuana are treated as social problems within our society's dominant system of norms and institutions. Other drugs, such as alcohol, caffeine, and nicotine, are much less sharply defined as problems even though in objective terms their harmful consequences have been fully documented (U.S. Department of Health and Human Services, 2014).

What Do You Think?

Do you think that marijuana for personal use should be legal in the United States? Why or why not? What about more harmful drugs, such as alcohol, caffeine, and nicotine? Why do you think that some of these drugs are legal, while others are not?

Abuse and Addiction

The difficulty of separating the subjective and objective dimensions of drug use causes a great many problems of definition for experts in the field. The term *drug abuse* is widely used, but it can refer to many things. First, it may to refer to the objectively harmful consumption of drugs that are subjectively approved of, such as alcohol and tranquilizers. Second, *drug abuse* also refers to the use—in any amount—of drugs that are subjectively disapproved of, such as marijuana, even if the objective facts about their effects in certain dosages do not indicate that they are particularly harmful. Third, almost all strongly addicting drugs, such as heroin or methamphetamine, are harmful both to the user and to society at any level of use and are usually included under the term *drug abuse*.

Despite this ambiguity, the National Institute on Drug Abuse continues to support the use of the term *drug abuse*, and we will use it in this chapter—except that we define

drug abuse as both the use of societally unacceptable drugs and/or the excessive or inappropriate use of acceptable drugs in ways that can lead to physical, psychological, or social harm.

The term **addiction** is often used rather loosely, but in fact it is a complex phenomenon that involves the drug user's physical and psychological dependence, the type of drug, and the amount and frequency of use. Physical dependence occurs when the body has adjusted to the presence of a drug and will suffer pain, discomfort, or illness—the symptoms of withdrawal—if its use is discontinued. Psychological dependence occurs when a user needs a drug for the feeling of well-being that it produces and the person may become anxious or agitated when the drug is unavailable.

In the diagnosis and treatment of alcoholism, the terms *dependence* and *abuse* have been combined into a single disorder in the *Diagnostic and Statistical Manual of Mental Disorders*, fifth edition (*DSM-V*) called alcohol use disorder (AUD) with mild, moderate, and severe subclassifications (National Institute on Alcohol Abuse and Alcoholism, 2013a). These definitions are used to determine health insurance payments for treatment and to legally determine the presence of alcohol problems. In addition, the *DSM-V* highlights the fact that symptoms of certain disorders, such as anxiety or depression, may be related to the use of alcohol or other drugs.

It is important to note that not all drug use is considered abuse in the sense that it impairs health. A person who is suffering from an illness that requires treatment with morphine, for example, might be addicted but would not be considered an abuser. However, there can be no doubt that some drugs are not only physically addicting but also dangerous to society because they compel their users to seek ever larger quantities to maintain a high.

These highly addictive drugs can be a major social problem in that thousands of otherwise productive people may disappear from the labor market or become involved in an underground drug economy. The classic example is the city of Shanghai before the Chinese Communist revolution of 1949. It has been estimated that almost 500,000 residents of Shanghai were addicted to opium and had to spend hours in smoking dens each day. Earlier in the twentieth century, thousands of Americans were addicted to a form of opium known as laudanum, which they used for headaches and menstrual cramps.

However one ultimately defines abuse and addiction, mere knowledge of patterns of use in the general population at a given moment and over time is an essential starting point. This point is where social-scientific data play an important role. Monitoring of drug use by people who are arrested, large-scale surveys of alcohol and drug use by adults and teens, and national surveys of the incidence of mental illness—including drug- and alcohol-related disorders—are designed and carried out by professional social scientists. At their most basic level, these surveys establish the prevalence of alcohol, tobacco, and illicit drug use in the general population. As discussed in Chapter 3, prevalence refers to the estimated population of people living with a given condition at any given time. Table 4–2 shows the proportion of high school seniors who have ever used a particular substance and those who have used it over the past month (National Institute on Drug Abuse, 2015a).

Drug prevalence data are especially helpful in comparing the popularity of specific drugs in a population or a segment of a population, such as teenagers. Questions that ask about the use of any illegal drugs over the lifetime, as reported in Figure 4–1, are especially helpful in tracking trends in drug consumption over time. The figure shows the trends among eighth-, tenth-, and twelfth-grade students between 1992 and 2014. Twenty percent of eighth graders tried an illegal drug in 2014, as did 37 percent of tenth graders and 49 percent of twelfth graders. Drug use by teenagers decreased significantly between the late 1990s and mid-2000s. Rates climbed somewhat in 2008, but have since stabilized (Johnston et al., 2015).

drug abuse
The use of societally unacceptable drugs and/or the excessive or inappropriate use of acceptable drugs in ways that can lead to physical, psychological, or social harm.

addiction
A complex phenomenon that involves the drug user's physical and psychological dependence, the type of drug, and the amount and frequency of use.

What Do You Think?
Why do you think that drug use among teenagers has stabilized since 2008? Consider economic, social, and cultural reasons.

Table 4–2 Lifetime Prevalence Rates of Use of Different Drugs among High School Seniors, 2014

Substance	Share Ever Using Drug	Share Having Used during Past Month
Alcohol	66%	37%
Cigarettes	34%	14%
Marijuana	44%	21%
Prescription Drugs	13%	0%
Cocaine	5%	1%
Hallucinogens	6%	2%
Heroin	1%	0.4%
Inhalants	7%	0.7%
MDMA	6%	1%
Methamphetamine	2%	0.5%
Steroids	2%	1%

SOURCE: National Institute on Drug Abuse, 2015b.

Figure 4–1 Trends in Lifetime Prevalence of Any Illegal Drug, 8th, 10th, and 12th Graders, 1992–2014

SOURCE: Johnston, O'Malley, Miech, Bachman, and Schulenberg, 2015.

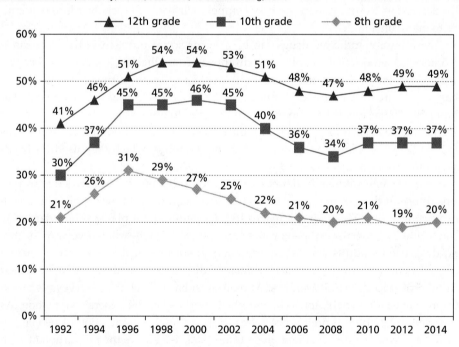

Alcohol Use, Abuse, and Alcoholism

4.2 Identify the perceptions toward alcohol and drinking patterns.

Because alcohol is the most commonly used drug and is capable of doing substantial harm to individuals, families, and communities, this section focuses on several aspects of alcohol use and abuse. On average, an American adult consumes about 21.8 gallons of beer, 2.5 gallons of wine, and 1.4 gallons of distilled spirits a year (U.S. Census Bureau, 2010).

Figure 4–2 Average Number of Drinks Per Person Consumed Weekly by Decile, Adults Age 18 and Over, 2014

SOURCE: Ingraham, 2014.

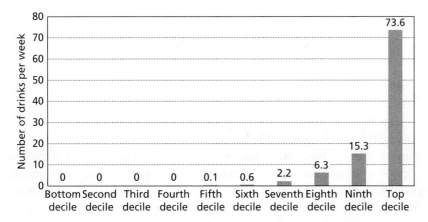

Granted, not all people consume alcohol, and some people consume far more than average amounts. Figure 4–2 breaks down the adult population into ten groups called deciles and examines how much each group drinks in an average week. As you can see, 40 percent of adults do not drink at all, and most groups drink very little. However, the top group—the top drinking 10 percent of the population consume an average of almost 74 drinks a week, or more than 10 drinks a day. The second highest group averages over two drinks a day (Ingraham, 2014).

Perceptions of Alcohol Use, Abuse, and Alcoholism

In our society, people have mixed feelings about alcohol. On one hand, alcohol creates warmth and high spirits and promotes interpersonal harmony and agreement ("Let's drink to that"). It has long been used in informal rituals (Christmas eggnog) and formal rites (wine as the blood of Christ) and has been important in the economies of many nations. The growing and harvesting of grapes, grain, and other crops used to produce alcoholic beverages, as well as the brewing, fermenting, distilling, and sale of alcoholic beverages, provide employment, trade, and tax revenues. On the other hand, the problems created by the abuse of alcohol are staggering. They include public drunkenness and disorderly behavior, traffic and industrial accidents, poor social functioning, broken marriages, child abuse, and aggravation of existing conditions such as poverty, mental and physical illness, and crime (National Institute on Alcohol Abuse and Alcoholism, 2015a).

According to the National Institute on Alcohol Abuse and Alcoholism (NIAAA), nearly 18 million adults, or one in twelve, suffer from **alcohol abuse** or **alcoholism** (National Institute on Alcohol Abuse and Alcoholism, 2015b). So-called alcohol abusers are those for whom alcohol interferes with normal social roles such as the roles of spouse, parent, or worker. These people may or may not be alcoholics.

alcohol abuse

An overuse of alcohol to an extent that interferes with normal social roles, such as the roles of spouse, parent, or worker.

alcoholism

The state of being addicted to alcohol with the following four symptoms: craving, loss of control, physical dependence, and tolerance.

Alcohol plays a prominent role in our society. Most people drink only occasionally and have only a couple of drinks at a time. However, for a small but significant portion of the population, alcohol poses a large problem.

Those people who are physically addicted to alcohol are considered alcoholics and have the following four symptoms of alcoholism.

- *Craving.* An uncontrollable urge for intoxication.
- *Loss of Control.* Not being able to stop drinking once drinking has begun.
- *Physical Dependence.* Acute withdrawal symptoms including uncontrollable trembling, nausea, rapid heartbeat, and heavy perspiration.
- *Tolerance.* The need to drink greater amounts of alcohol to get high.

Despite high rates of alcohol consumption by some people, the problems associated with alcohol abuse—especially chronic inebriation, vagrancy, missed days of work—seem to arouse less interest and concern than the abuse, or even the use, of other drugs. Alcohol is thoroughly integrated into Western culture. It is adapted to our complex lifestyle because, in addition to relieving tension and reducing sexual and aggressive inhibitions, alcohol seems to facilitate interpersonal relations, at least superficially, whereas other drug experiences, even in groups, are often highly private.

The perception of alcohol as a social problem varies with changes in American culture and increased knowledge about the effects of alcohol use. According to some sociologists, in the early decades of the twentieth century, alcohol was a symbol that masked the larger social conflict between the working class, with its large immigrant component, and the upper class, which sought to control the workers and increase their productivity (Szasz, 1992).

In recent years, the American public has become more aware of the dangers associated with drinking—for example, the extensive damage it can cause to a fetus and the high correlation between highway accidents and driving while intoxicated. In the United States, alcohol is implicated in about a third of all fatal highway accidents, approximately one-third of all homicides, and 20 to 25 percent of drownings and boating deaths (Centers for Disease Control and Prevention, 2015a, 2014e). These problems have led to crusades against excessive drinking rather than against alcohol itself. Both the Highway Safety Council and the Council for Accident Prevention note significant declines in traffic deaths due to drinking and in home accidents associated with alcohol consumption. These decreases seem to indicate that crusades against excessive drinking are having an impact, and their success will surely reinforce efforts to educate the public about its risks.

Alcohol Abusers and Alcoholics

Several factors seem to be related to whether, how much, and in what ways an individual uses alcohol and becomes an alcohol abuser or alcoholic. Among these factors are biological and socioeconomic factors, gender, age, religion, and cultural influences. Of particular interest are genetics, sex, and age.

GENETICS   Alcoholism and alcohol abuse appear to be due in part to biological factors and genetics (National Institute on Alcohol Abuse and Alcoholism, 2015a). How do researchers know this? One mechanism is to study people who were adopted or who are twins. For example, adoption studies allow researchers to separate the effects of genetic and environmental factors because adoptees receive their genetic heritage from one set of parents and their rearing environment from another set. The degree to which adoptees resemble their biological relatives is a direct measure of genetic influence. Conversely, the degree to which adoptees resemble their adoptive relatives is a measure of the influence of family environment. Five adoption studies of alcoholism in males and four studies in females have included adequate sample sizes to evaluate genetic influences on alcoholism. In all five studies of male adoptees, participants with a biological family history of alcoholism were at significantly higher (i.e., 1.6 to 3.6 times greater) risk for alcoholism than were participants without a family history of alcoholism. This finding suggests that genetics contributes substantially to the risk for alcoholism among males. The studies of female adoptees, in contrast, obtained mixed results, with only two of the four studies finding a significantly increased risk of alcoholism among females with a biological family history of alcoholism compared with females with a negative family history. These results provided some evidence of possible sex differences in heritability, but are inconclusive because of the small numbers of alcoholic female adoptees in the studies (Prescott, 2003).

So far, researchers who study the genetic factors linked to alcoholism are able to explain about half the risk for alcoholism faced by any given individual. Therefore, genes are important, but alone do not determine whether someone will become an alcoholic. Environmental factors, as well as gene and environment interactions, account for the remainder of the risk.

Nonetheless, neurological studies show that brain function is often different in alcohol abusers and their children. Studies of alcoholism and biogenetic factors also indicate that some ethnic groups, particularly Native Americans, have lower tolerances for alcohol than other groups do, putting them at greater risk for alcoholism, and that some Asian populations have highly negative physiological reactions to alcohol, which tend to diminish their risk of becoming alcoholics.

SEX   Compared with women, men are more likely to drink alcohol, and they drink in larger quantities, as indicated in Table 4–3. Seventy percent of men report having consumed an alcoholic beverage over the previous year, as compared with 61 percent of women. And, of those people who drank alcohol over the past year, 43 percent of men report usually having three or more drinks on their drinking day, as compared with only 22 percent of women who report doing so (National Institute on Alcohol Abuse and Alcoholism, 2013b).

Sex differences in body structure and chemistry, however, cause women to absorb more alcohol and take longer to break it down and remove it from their bodies (i.e., to metabolize it). In other words, after drinking equal amounts, women have higher alcohol levels in their blood than men, and the immediate effects of the alcohol occur more quickly and last longer. One reason is that, on average, women weigh less than men. In addition, alcohol resides predominantly in body water, and pound for pound, women have less water in their bodies than men do. Other biological differences, including hormones, also may contribute. These differences also make women more vulnerable to alcohol's long-term effects on their health, including higher rates of liver damage, breast cancer, and heart disease (Centers for Disease Control and Prevention, 2014a; National Institute on Alcohol Abuse and Alcoholism, 2013b; Wilsnack, Wilsnack, and Kantor, 2014).

Recent decades have seen a significant increase in alcohol abuse and alcoholism among adult women. Women are increasingly likely to be arrested for drunk

Table 4–3 Sex Differences in Alcohol Consumption, 2013

	Women	Men
Had At Least 1 Drink in Past Year	61%	70%
Usual Number of Drinks Consumed Per Drinking Day		
1	48%	29%
2	30%	29%
3 or more	22%	43%
Drank 4 or More Drinks on One Occasion		
Never in past year	71%	60%
1–11 times in past year	14%	15%
12 times or more in past year	15%	28%

SOURCE: National Institute on Alcohol Abuse and Alcoholism, 2013b.

driving and are showing up in emergency rooms dangerously drunk (Glaser, 2013; Grucza et al., 2008). For both sexes, social factors—the presence of alcoholism in the family, childhood unhappiness, and trauma—are important influences. But for women, increasing rates of alcohol abuse and alcoholism seem to go beyond these traditional factors. Some suggest it is related to their "liberation" in society—working and having a career, going to school, and remaining single—while others focus on the increased stress in women's lives as the culprit (Glaser, 2013). Today's women are supposed to "have it all"—a strong education, an exciting career, and a happy family life, and many choose to unwind from this stress with alcohol. Interestingly, it is upper-middle-class women and lower-middle-class men who are more likely to drink heavily.

Yet the statistics on female alcoholism may be misleading. As women have become more visible in society, their drinking patterns have become more visible. Perhaps researchers are only now learning to identify the female alcoholic, and many women may still be hiding their drinking problems at home. Moreover, even if there has been an increase in alcoholism among women, it remains true that women have far fewer drinking problems than men do.

fetal alcohol spectrum disorders (FASD)

A group of conditions that can occur in a person whose mother consumed alcohol during pregnancy. These effects can include physical abnormalities and problems with cognition, behavior, and learning that last a lifetime.

One particular issue among women involves drinking alcohol while pregnant. Alcohol can disrupt fetal development at any stage during a pregnancy—including at the earliest stages before a woman even knows she is pregnant. Alcohol passes easily from a mother's bloodstream into her developing baby's blood. Alcohol present in a developing baby's bloodstream can interfere with the development of critical organs and body parts, including the brain, leading to **fetal alcohol spectrum disorders (FASD)**, which are a group of conditions that can occur in a person whose mother consumed alcohol during pregnancy. These effects can include physical abnormalities and problems with cognition, behavior, and learning that last a lifetime. Prenatal alcohol exposure is the leading preventable cause of birth defects in the United States (Fetal Alcohol Spectrum Disorders Center for Excellence, 2015; National Institute on Alcohol Abuse and Alcoholism, 2015c).

It is not known precisely how much alcohol must be consumed during pregnancy for these results to occur, so pregnant women are advised to avoid alcohol entirely. Because the fetus is small, its blood-alcohol content will be much higher than that of the mother. A woman may hardly notice the effects of her drinking, but meanwhile her fetus is getting drunk.

AGE   Heavy drinking among men is most common at ages 21 to 30; among women, it occurs at ages 31 to 50. Nonetheless, drinking by teenagers and young adults is among the most serious aspect of alcohol use as a social problem, especially because so many lives are needlessly ended by alcohol-related deaths and because patterns of adult alcohol use are established during the teenage and young-adult years. Alcohol is by far the most frequently used illicit drug among teenagers, and it is consumed far more often than nicotine or marijuana (Johnston et al., 2015).

Teenagers who are defined as problem drinkers include those who have had confrontations with teachers or the police because of their drinking. Of these drinkers, only a relatively small percentage can be defined as an alcoholic with an actual physical dependency. Alcoholic teenagers differ from other adolescent drinkers in that they drink more often and consume greater quantities, often with the intention of getting drunk; they are also more likely to drink alone, to display aggressive or destructive behavior, and to have severe emotional problems.

The popularity of alcohol among young people is attributed to many factors, including the difficulty, expense, and danger of obtaining other drugs, and the manufacture and advertisement of alcoholic products that are especially appealing to the young, such as sweet wines and alcoholic beverages that resemble popular drinks such as lemonade.

Drinking among young people can also be construed as a rebellion against the adult world—an attempt to assert independence and imitate adult behavior. Some authorities believe strict regulations on drinking only make it more appealing. Moreover, prohibition of drinking by the young is extremely difficult in a society in which alcohol is widely used and relatively easy to procure. **Binge drinking**, defined as a pattern of drinking that brings blood alcohol concentration levels to 0.08 g/dL. This form of drinking amounts to a consumption of five or more drinks in a single session for males and four or more drinks for females. Binge drinking is a particularly dangerous behavior pattern because it often leads to violence, auto accidents, and other major problems. Yet, more than half of the alcohol consumed by adults in the United States is in the form of binge drinks, as is about 90 percent of the alcohol consumed by youth under the age of 21 (Centers for Disease Control and Prevention, 2014d).

Because binge drinking is found most commonly among young adults, it has been studied intensely by two nationwide surveys. The first one, *Monitoring the Future* survey, which focuses on high school drug and alcohol use, is conducted by the Institute of Survey Research at the University of Michigan. It is based on more than 16,000 high school seniors who are given a self-administered questionnaire (to encourage honesty) about their substance use. Conducted annually since 1975, this survey is an essential barometer of drug use among young Americans. Like all surveys, however, it has its limitations; in particular, it does not sample young people who have dropped out of school, an important population in the study of drug use. The second survey, the *Harvard School of Public Health College Alcohol Study* (CAS), is based on 50,000 college students attending 120 universities around the country. From these data, we know that, among high school students, binge drinking is on the decline, from about 32 percent of students acknowledging binge drinking over a two-week period in 1998, to less than 20 percent today (Johnston et al., 2015). The CAS survey of college students reports higher levels of binge drinking, with 43 percent of students reporting binge drinking at least once in a two-week period (Wechsler and Nelson, 2008).

binge drinking

A pattern of drinking that brings blood alcohol concentration (BAC) levels to 0.08 g/dL. Although the quantity of alcohol required to reach this level can vary, in general, it amounts to a consumption of five or more drinks in a single session for males, and to four or more drinks for females.

What Do You Think?

Why do many young college people binge drink? What are some of the consequences of binge drinking? Design a program to help combat binge drinking on your college campus.

Alcohol-Related Social Problems

4.3 Assess several social problems related to alcohol.

Excessive use of alcohol contributes to many different social problems: accidental injury, murder, family violence, divorce, suicide, ruined health, fetal harm, and many more. The United States spends approximately $224 billion annually on problems related to excessive drinking (Centers for Disease Control and Prevention, 2014b). In this section, we briefly describe a few of these problems (National Institute on Alcohol Abuse and Alcoholism, 2015a).

Health

Excessive drinking contributes to 88,000 deaths per year in the United States (Centers for Disease Control and Prevention, 2014c). On average, alcoholics can expect to live 10 to 12 fewer years than nonalcoholics.

There are several reasons for this shortened life span. Alcohol contains a high number of calories and no vital nutrients. Thus, alcoholics generally have a reduced appetite for nutritious food and inevitably suffer from vitamin deficiencies; as a result, their resistance to infectious diseases is lowered. Drinking can also damage the heart, causing problems such as stroke, high blood pressure, arrhythmias (irregular heartbeat) and cardiomyopathy (stretching and drooping of the heart muscle). Over a long period, large amounts of alcohol also destroys liver cells, which are replaced by scar tissue; this condition, called cirrhosis of the liver, is the cause of tens of thousands of deaths each year in the United States (U.S. Census Bureau, 2010). Other problems associated with the liver may include steatosis (fatty liver), alcoholic hepatitis, or fibrosis. Heavy drinking also contributes to the incidence of cancer, especially cancers of the mouth, esophagus, throat, liver, and breast (National Institute on Alcohol Abuse and Alcoholism, 2015a).

Drinking and Driving

After a hard night of partying, Nate hopped in his car for the drive home. "I'll drive slowly," he told himself, assuming that he could outwit the effects of six beers on his system. He was not successful. He didn't see the stop sign and ran right through it, totally oblivious. But he did feel the bump a minute later—"What was that?" He got out of the car, still wobbly, and saw that he had hit a cat, a black and white kitten, whose tuxedo face was now covered in blood and whose body was twisted in an awful position. He prayed the cat was dead so it wouldn't suffer, and he was thankful that he didn't hit a person. Two weeks later, he received a photo ticket in the mail, showing his car running the stop sign. He stared at the ticket, his stomach clenching, realizing that he could have paid far heavier penalties for driving while drunk.

There is a significant connection between alcohol use and vehicular accidents. Drivers whose alcohol level is over the legal limit of .08 are involved in nearly a third of traffic fatalities, accounting for 10,076 deaths in 2013 (National Highway Traffic Safety Administration, 2014). Body weight, length of time between drinks, type of alcohol, fatigue level, and medications or other drugs can all affect a person's blood alcohol level, so there is no set amount of alcohol that determines the legal limit. The good news, however, as you can see in Figure 4–3, is that there has been a steady decline in the rate of alcohol-related fatalities. These declines can be attributed to low rates of drinking by high school students and young adults, greater awareness of the consequences of drunk driving, and more rigorous social policies (e.g., raising the drinking age to 21 in all states), and enforcement of those policies. In particular, as states have adopted more uniform laws about driving under the influence of alcohol, and as more funding has been devoted to enforcement of these laws, declines in alcohol-related driving fatalities are evident.

Mothers Against Drunk Driving (MADD)
A nonprofit organization working to protect families from drunk driving and underage drinking through education and support of victims and survivors.

Drivers under the influence of alcohol kill about 10,000 people a year. This number represents a decline in recent years and is due to many factors, including an increase in the drinking age, more effective law enforcement, and widespread educational campaigns to highlight the risks of driving while intoxicated.

State police and other authorities credit much of this success to the activities of **Mothers Against Drunk Driving (MADD)**, a nonprofit organization working to protect families from drunk driving and underage drinking through education and support of victims and survivors. Candy Lightner founded MADD in 1980 after the death of her 13-year-old daughter Cari in California. Cari was walking to a school carnival when a drunk driver struck her from behind. The driver had three prior drunk driving convictions and was out on bail from a hit-and-run arrest two days earlier. Her daughter was not alone. Nearly 15 percent of the 200 children who are killed by alcohol-impaired drivers each year are children who are struck down while walking or riding their bicycles (National Highway Traffic Safety Administration, 2014).

Crime

At least one-third of crimes are committed by someone under the influence of alcohol. Some of these crimes are relatively minor offenses such as

Figure 4–3 Fatalities and Fatality Rate per 100 Million VMT in Alcohol-Impaired-Driving Crashes, 2004–2013

SOURCE: National Highway Traffic Safety Administration, 2014.

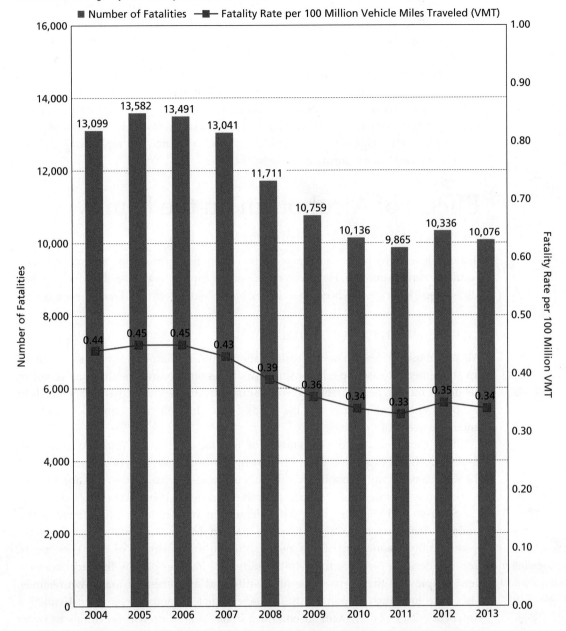

disorderly conduct or vagrancy. In arrests for serious violent crimes, drunkenness generally does not appear in the charges, although alcohol often contributes to criminal acts. Based on victim reports, alcohol use by the offender was a factor in (National Council on Alcohol and Drug Dependence, Inc., 2015a):

- 37 percent of rapes and sexual assaults,
- 15 percent of robberies,
- 27 percent of aggravated assaults, and
- 25 percent of simple assaults.

In many homicide cases, alcohol is found in the victim, the offender, or both. A significant percentage of male sex offenders are chronic alcoholics or were drinking at the time of the offense. The reasons for the high correlation of drinking with arrests for serious violent crimes are not fully understood. It has been pointed out that alcohol, by removing some inhibitions, may cause people to behave in unaccustomed ways. Also, as with other drugs, the need to obtain the substance may lead to theft or other property crimes and sometimes to violent crimes like armed robbery. Since chronic alcoholics may be unable to hold steady jobs, their financial difficulties are compounded, perhaps increasing the temptation to commit crimes. Also, the values and self-image of chronic heavy drinkers tend to change as their condition worsens. They are more likely to associate with delinquents or criminals, which may lead them to commit criminal acts themselves.

In addition to its link with serious crimes, alcoholism creates another problem; it places a major strain on the law enforcement system, which must process large numbers of petty offenders. Arrests, trials, and incarcerations of offenders cost taxpayers billions of dollars each year. And many of these arrests involve a small segment of the community—the neighborhood drunk or derelict who may be repeatedly arrested and imprisoned briefly during the course of a year.

Effects of Alcoholism on the Family

4.4   Describe the effects of alcohol on the family.

If the only victims of alcoholism were the alcoholics themselves, the social effects would be serious enough. However, other people, especially the families of alcoholics, also suffer. The home can become a chaotic battlefield, affecting all family members.

Consequences for Adults

Alcohol abuse can leave a marriage or relationship very shaky or may cause it to break up altogether because the relationship usually centers around the drinking member: his or her moods, health, feelings, work situation, stresses, and coping. The needs of the other spouse or partner and the needs of the children are ignored or subsumed under the needs of the alcoholic.

Two common interrelated sources of marital conflict are financial and work issues. Alcohol is expensive—and can cost upwards of thousands of dollars a year. At the same time, many alcoholics find it difficult to keep a job, or they are absent from work frequently, missing out on pay after their sick-leave benefits expire.

Spouses and partners deal with alcoholism in a number of different ways. **Codependency** refers to a relationship pattern in which a person assumes the responsibility for meeting others' needs, often to the detriment of their own needs. Codependency is far more than simply caring for another person. Instead, codependent people lose their own sense of identity and awareness of their own feelings. They take too much responsibility for their addicted spouse or partner. Usually, a codependent person engages in **enabling behaviors**. They will do things to cover for, support, and enable the alcoholic to continue to drink. For example, the codependent person might call an employer to claim that the drinker is sick when he or she is actually suffering from a hangover, might buy alcohol for the drinker, might excuse the drinker from doing domestic chores or participating in family life, might make up excuses to the children as to why their parent is not fulfilling his or her roles in the family, or might in other ways send messages to the drinker that it is okay to continue drinking.

Consequences for Children

Alcohol abuse in a family can strain children's lives. Children in families where one or both parents abuse alcohol are more likely to have problems with depression, aggression, peer relationships, delinquency, school performance, and emotional issues as compared with their peers whose parents do not have problems with alcohol. These problems stem from the painful emotional climate, dysfunction, and turmoil in the home

What Do You Think?

Identify a research question or hypothesis related to alcohol use and/or abuse that a functionalist, a conflict theorist, and an interactionist might pose. How are these research questions or hypotheses different from one another?

codependency

A relationship pattern in which a person assumes the responsibility for meeting others' needs, often to the detriment of their own needs.

enabling behaviors

Behaviors that a codependent person will do to cover for, support, and enable an alcoholic to continue to drink (or to enable another type of abuser to continue toxic behaviors).

(Dayton, 2011). Their environment is often unpredictable, chaotic, and filled with broken promises. Children may be asked to keep inappropriate secrets (e.g., "Don't tell Mommy that you saw Daddy drinking"); to live by arbitrary and rigid rules (e.g., going to bed unusually early so parents can drink); and to cope with chronic disappointment (e.g., parents making promises that they repeatedly do not keep). Many children in this kind of environment receive inadequate nurturing. Unlike a spouse who can choose to leave the situation, children in dysfunctional families are trapped. They cannot leave. Instead, they often play one of several roles to cope (McGaha, Stokes, and Nielson, 1990).

- *Chief Enabler.* A child may put aside his or her own personal feelings and become increasingly more responsible for control of the alcoholic and the family.
- *Family Hero.* This child tries to better the family situation by succeeding in the environment outside the home, such as school. Often, this behavior is a cry for positive recognition for the family or to increase self-worth.
- *Scapegoat.* Not willing to work as hard as the hero for recognition, the scapegoat pulls away in a destructive manner, bringing negative attention to the family.
- *Lost Child.* This child takes care of his or her personal problems quietly and avoids trouble. Often ignored by the family, this child faces problems inward, and is often lonely and quietly suffering.
- *Mascot.* To deal with personal pain and loneliness, this child is charming and funny in times of stress. This behavior relieves pain for some family members, but does not really help the mascot.

Many children experience long-term effects of their parent's alcohol abuse. For example, they may have little grasp of what is considered "normal" family behavior. Many suffer from low self-esteem, have trouble forming and maintaining close relationships, and experience other emotional difficulties (Dayton, 2011; McGaha, Stokes, and Nielson, 1990). These children have been referred to as suffering from post-traumatic stress disorder (PTSD) due to the trauma they endured (Dayton, 2010).

The box, A Personal View: My Dad Is an Alcoholic," chronicles a teenage girl's family life in which her father is an alcoholic. Can you identify the roles played out in the family?

A Personal View

"My Dad Is an Alcoholic"

My dad is an alcoholic. There, I said it. Do you know that this is the first time that I have talked about this issue to someone outside my family? He gets drunk every night after work, "I think I'll have a little scotch," he says, even when he is finishing a huge bottle. I hate it when he asks me to make him a drink.

I'm too ashamed to admit to my friends that my dad is an alcoholic, but they probably know because he is often drunk when they come over. And he gets loud when he is drunk. I don't even like my friends to come to my house anymore; I'll make excuses why it would be better for me to go over to their houses, or meet somewhere else. My sister, Rachel, doesn't bring her friends over either. One time Dad made a crude sexual joke in front of one of her friends, and that was that. She got mad at him and yelled, and he slapped her hard in front of her friend. He apologized the next day, as he usually does, but I don't think she will ever forgive him. She told me she hates him.

I just try to stay out from under his radar. I do really well in school so he doesn't have any reason to bother me. I like the

attention that I get from my teachers. They all think I'm really smart. I'm not so sure I'm smart, but it makes me feel good that they think so.

I tried talking to Mom about his drinking and how Rachel hates him, but my mom just said that it's natural for girls and their fathers to fight. She doesn't see the problem. It's weird. Sometimes she will come to Rachel and me at night crying about his drinking, but then at other times when we bring it up, she'll say "Oh, it's not that big of a deal." She even sometimes does both in the same conversation! A couple of weeks ago, Mom came to us crying and saying that she couldn't take it anymore, and a minute later, when Rachel said that she couldn't take it anymore either, Mom gave her a mean look and said, "Don't talk about your father like that! He's doing the best he can." It's like Mom just snapped. She can say it, but we can't. I hate what my father is doing to this family.

—Chris, age 13

Critical Thinking

When a parent is an alcoholic, other members of the family often play specific roles related to the alcoholism. What roles do you see being played out in this family?

Treatment of Alcoholism

4.5   Compare treatment options for alcoholism.

There are a number of treatment options for alcoholism, including rehabilitation, Alcoholics Anonymous, Antabuse, and other programs. These approaches differ from one another; there is not one option that is right for everyone.

Rehabilitation

Alcoholism is increasingly viewed as an illness with a variety of psychological and physiological components; therefore, it is possible to rehabilitate, but not completely cure, many alcoholics (Brick, 2004). A variety of nonpunitive attempts have been made to assist alcoholics in overcoming their addiction or habituation and to help alcoholism-prone individuals handle disturbing emotions and anxieties. The Comprehensive Alcohol Abuse and Alcoholism Prevention, Treatment and Rehabilitation Act of 1970 created the National Institute on Alcohol Abuse and Alcoholism to coordinate federal government activities. It also created the National Advisory Council on Alcohol Abuse and Alcoholism to recommend national policies. The act also provided grants to states for the development of comprehensive programs for alcoholism, for specific prevention and treatment projects, and incentives for private hospitals that admit patients with alcohol-related problems.

Traditionally, hospitals offered little beyond the "drying out" and release of alcoholic patients; they might treat a specific medical problem caused by alcohol but not alcoholism itself. The American Hospital Association now advocates hospital alcoholism programs and is attempting to utilize the resources of general hospitals in community treatment programs.

Alcoholics Anonymous

Some of the most impressive successes in coping with alcoholism have been achieved by Alcoholics Anonymous (AA). The effectiveness of this group in helping individual alcoholics is based on what amounts to a conversion. Alcoholics are led to this experience through fellowship with others like themselves, some of whom have already mastered their problem while others are in the process of doing so. There are nearly 115,000 AA groups throughout the world (Alcoholics Anonymous, 2012).

The organization insists that drinkers face up to their shortcomings and the realities of life and, when possible, make amends to people they have hurt in the past. The movement also concentrates on building up alcoholics' self-esteem and reassuring them of their basic worth as human beings. Since its founding in 1935, the group has evolved a technique in which recovered alcoholics support and comfort drinkers who are undergoing rehabilitation. This support is also available during crises when a relapse seems likely, and on a year-round basis through meetings that the alcoholic may attend as often as necessary.

Alcoholics Anonymous (AA), founded in 1935, has over 2 million members. The cornerstone of AA is a 12-step program based on faith in a "higher power."

AA has created special groups to deal with teenage and young adult drinkers. It has also established programs to aid nonalcoholic spouses and the children of alcoholics. Alateen, for example, is for young people whose lives have been affected by someone else's drinking. The alcoholic need not be a member of AA for relatives to participate in these offshoot programs, which developed out of the recognition that an entire family is psychologically involved in the alcohol-related problems of any of its members.

It appears that AA is the most successful large-scale program for dealing with alcoholism; it estimates its membership at over 2 million. According to the AA 12-step credo, it is essential for addicts to acknowledge their lack of control over alcohol use and to abstain from all alcoholic beverages for the rest of their lives. This approach sees alcoholism as an allergy in which even one drink can produce an intolerable reaction—a craving for more.

The voluntary nature of the program probably contributes to its success; however, it is unlikely that this approach, with its insistence on total abstinence, could be applied successfully to all alcoholics. In particular, alcoholics who reject the spiritual tenets of AA, which teach the recovering alcoholic to seek help from a "higher power," whatever that may mean to the individual, would not identify with many aspects of the AA approach. Alcoholics who are unwilling to accept these tenets can find programs that are related to the 12 steps of the AA program but eliminate the spiritual aspects.

Antabuse

Antabuse, a prescription drug, sensitizes the patient in such a way that consuming even a small quantity of alcohol causes strong and uncomfortable physical symptoms. Drinkers become intensely flushed, their pulse quickens, and they feel nauseated.

Before beginning treatment with Antabuse, the alcoholic goes through a process to **detoxify** (keep off alcohol until none shows in blood samples) his or her body. Then the drug is administered to the patient along with doses of alcohol for several consecutive days. The patient continues to take the drug for several more days, and at the close of the period another dose of alcohol is administered. The trial doses of alcohol condition the patient to recognize the relationship between drinking and the unpleasant symptoms. (Similar treatment programs depend on different nausea-producing drugs or electric shock to condition the patient against alcohol; this process is known as **aversion therapy** or **behavior conditioning**.)

Antabuse (or Disulfiram) has gained only limited acceptance in the treatment of alcoholics. Critics claim that its effect is too narrow and that this approach neglects the personality problems of the drinker. They also maintain that the drug does not work for people who are suspicious of treatment or have psychotic tendencies.

detoxify

To keep a person off alcohol or another substance until none shows in blood samples.

aversion therapy/behavior conditioning

A form of treatment that applies nausea-producing drugs or electric shock to condition the patient against alcohol.

Other Programs

A problem drinker or alcoholic who receives help while at home and on the job usually responds better than one who is institutionalized. Community care programs treat these problem drinkers, as well as their families, in an effort to improve their self-image and enhance their sense of security within the family.

Employee assistance programs, a relatively new development, have demonstrated considerable effectiveness in treating problem drinkers in the workplace. Their success depends on their availability on a scheduled basis and during crises, on the maintenance of absolute confidentiality, and on the development of rapport between the counselor and the patient as they explore underlying psychological problems such as loneliness, alienation, and poor self-image. Also important is the patient's desire to remain in the community and to continue working.

Illegal Drug Use and Abuse

4.6 Summarize the nine most commonly used drugs that are abused.

Although alcohol currently has a secure place in American social policy, it was made illegal during the Prohibition era in the early twentieth century. How does society respond to other drug use? The major categories of illegal drugs are constantly changing as culture and customs change. In eighteenth-century England, the use of tobacco was forbidden; anyone found guilty of consuming it could be punished by extreme measures such as amputation or splitting of the nose. In the United States, cocaine was introduced to the public early in the twentieth century as an additive to a new commercial soft drink, Coca-Cola.

Today the use of illegal drugs embraces an extremely diverse set of behaviors, ranging from recreational use of marijuana to heroin addiction. The most commonly used drugs today, in addition to alcohol, are marijuana, prescription drugs or cold medicines (for nonmedical purposes), hallucinogens (such as LSD), cocaine, inhalants, MDMA (which often goes by the names of Ecstasy or Molly), methamphetamine, crack cocaine, and heroin. The percentage of people ages 12 and over and 26 and over who have reported using these drugs at some point during their lifetime is reported in Table 4–4. Use ranges from nearly half of adults trying marijuana to only two percent trying heroin (National Institute on Drug Abuse, 2015b). This next section discusses each of these drugs.

Table 4–4 Percentage of Persons 12 or Over, and 26 or Over Who Have Used a Drug during Their Lifetime

	12 or Older	26 or Older
Marijuana	43.7%	45.7%
Prescription Drugs/Psychotherapeutics	20.3%	20.6%
Hallucinogens	15.1%	16.2%
Cocaine	14.3%	16.5%
Inhalants	8.0%	8.4%
MDMA (Ecstasy/Molly)	6.8%	6.4%
Methamphetamine	4.7%	5.5%
Crack Cocaine	3.4%	4.1%
Heroin	1.8%	2.0%

SOURCE: National Institute on Drug Abuse, 2015b.

Marijuana

Marijuana refers to the dried leaves, flowers, stems, and seeds from the hemp plant, *Cannabis sativa*. The plant contains the mind-altering chemical *delta-9-tetrahydrocannabinol* (THC) and other related compounds.

Like alcohol, marijuana is a social drug, one that is often used in social gatherings because it is thought to ease or enhance interaction. Because the use of marijuana is widespread and there is little evidence that it has detrimental long-term effects or leads to the use of stronger drugs, the federal government has shifted its enforcement efforts to the more clearly addicting drugs. About half of states now allow small amounts of marijuana to be used for medicinal purposes, such as helping with nausea.

Four states, Colorado, Washington, Oregon, and Alaska have legalized small amounts of marijuana for personal use. Meanwhile, possessing an eighth of an ounce of any grade marijuana is a misdemeanor in Texas and can land you in prison for up to 180 days. It carries a fine of up to $2,000. Possessing more than two ounces means an even harsher punishment (Boyette and Wilson, 2015).

Abuse of Prescription Drugs

Abuse of prescription drugs is becoming an ever more serious form of drug use and addiction. Opium-derived pain medicines such as Oxycontin and Vicodin; benzodiazepine tranquilizers such as Valium and Xanax; sedatives and sleeping pills such as Ambien and the barbiturates; and prescription amphetamines, often dispensed as diet pills, are among the most frequently abused of the widely available but heavily controlled prescription drugs. Pain relievers, which, because they are derived from opium, are among the most addictive prescription drugs, are also the most commonly abused.

Most adults over age 40 who abuse or become addicted to prescription drugs, first used the drug under a physician's supervision. But young adults and adolescents tend to obtain the drugs through friends and street dealers. The National Institute on Drug Abuse reports that, since the early 1990s, abuse of prescription-type drugs has "escalated substantially" across the nation, especially among people between the ages of 12 and 25 (National Institute on Drug Abuse, 2015b). The agency also warns that use of multiple drugs, known as polydrug use, is extremely common among abusers of prescription drugs. The mixing of drugs for nonmedical, recreational use has risks that are dangerously underestimated by users.

Hallucinogens

Hallucinogenic compounds found in some plants and mushrooms (or their extracts) have been used—mostly during religious rituals—for centuries. While the exact mechanisms by which hallucinogens exert their effects remain unclear, research suggests that these drugs work, at least partially, by temporarily interfering with neurotransmitter action or by binding to their receptor sites (National Institute on Drug Abuse, 2015a, 2015b).

Unlike most other drugs, the effects of hallucinogens are highly variable and unreliable, producing different effects in different people at different times. This changeability is mainly due to the significant variations in amount and composition of active compounds, particularly in the hallucinogens derived from plants and mushrooms. Because of their unpredictable nature, the use of hallucinogens can be particularly dangerous even though there is no evidence of hallucinogens being habit forming.

Cocaine

Cocaine is a powerfully addictive stimulant drug made from the leaves of the coca plant native to South America. It produces short-term euphoria, energy, talkativeness, and a feeling of increased intellectual power. Cocaine is a strong central nervous system stimulant that increases levels of the neurotransmitter dopamine in brain circuits

Slide Show

Legalizing Marijuana

Americans are ambivalent about marijuana. In the 1960s, the drug was popular among college students and other people "rebelling" against the norms of society. Today, as research shows the health effects of marijuana are significantly less serious than those of other drugs, including alcohol, many people are wondering why it is still illegal and lumped together with other "illicit" drugs.

Marijuana is the most commonly used illicit drug, tried by nearly half the population ages 12 and over. It is one of the few drugs whose use has been increasing in recent years.

There has been a move to allow marijuana to be used for medical purposes when prescribed by a physician. People who suffer from cancer or other painful illnesses, or whose medical treatment causes nausea, may find significant relief from their symptoms from marijuana. Currently, only about half of the states allow marijuana for medicinal purposes.

Other people oppose legalizing marijuana. They believe that it is a powerful drug with harmful side effects for the person using it, and for society as a whole. Why do we need another form of intoxication, they ask?

Some people oppose legalizing marijuana because they are concerned that it will lead to using other, more dangerous drugs. The popular view that marijuana is a stepping-stone or gateway to stronger drugs is not supported by research. It may be true that most people who abuse drugs first use alcohol and marijuana, but only a small percentage of people who use these drugs go on to use more dangerous and addicting drugs.

Some advocates of marijuana go even further, and suggest that it should be legal. Four states, Colorado, Washington, Oregon, and Alaska have legalized small amounts of marijuana for personal use.

Critical Thinking

Reflecting on the four themes of this text—the importance of using an empirical approach, linking individual experiences with social structure, understanding that social inequality contributes to social problems, and acknowledging that understanding social problems requires a comparative perspective—how do each of these themes inform your understanding of drug and alcohol use?

regulating pleasure and movement. Normally, dopamine is released by neurons in these circuits in response to potential rewards (like the smell of good food) and then recycled back into the cell that released it, thus shutting off the signal between neurons. Cocaine prevents the dopamine from being recycled, causing excessive amounts to build up in the synapse, or junction between neurons. This buildup amplifies the dopamine signal and ultimately disrupts normal brain communication. It is this flood of dopamine that causes cocaine's characteristic high.

With repeated use, cocaine can cause long-term changes in the brain's reward system as well as other brain systems, which may lead to addiction. With repeated use, tolerance to cocaine also can develop; many cocaine abusers report that they seek but fail to achieve as much pleasure as they did from their first exposure. Some users will increase their dose in an attempt to intensify and prolong their high, but this practice can also increase the risk of adverse psychological or physiological effects (National Institute on Drug Abuse, 2015b).

Inhalants

Many products readily found in the home or workplace—such as spray paints, markers, glues, and cleaning fluids—contain volatile substances that have mind-altering properties when inhaled. People do not typically think of these products as drugs because they were never intended for that purpose.

Abusers of inhalants breathe them in through the nose or mouth in a variety of ways (known as "huffing"). They may sniff or snort fumes from a container or dispenser (such as a glue bottle or a marking pen), spray aerosols (such as computer cleaning dusters) directly into their nose or mouth, or place a chemical-soaked rag in their mouth. Abusers may also inhale fumes from a balloon or a plastic or paper bag. Although the high produced by inhalants usually lasts just a few minutes, abusers often try to prolong it by continuing to inhale repeatedly over several hours.

Most abused inhalants depress the central nervous system in a manner not unlike alcohol. The effects are similar—including slurred speech, lack of coordination, euphoria, and dizziness. Inhalant abusers may also experience light-headedness, hallucinations, and delusions. With repeated inhalations, many users feel less inhibited and less in control. Some may feel drowsy for several hours and experience a lingering headache. Long-term use can damage the heart, liver, and muscles and can cause anemia and nerve damage.

MDMA

MDMA (3,4-methylenedioxy-methamphetamine), popularly known as ecstasy or, more recently, as Molly, is a synthetic mind-altering drug that has similarities to both the stimulant amphetamine and the hallucinogen mescaline. It produces feelings of increased energy, euphoria, emotional warmth and empathy toward others, and distortions in sensory and time perception. MDMA was initially popular among white adolescents and young adults in the nightclub scene or at "raves" (long dance parties), but the drug is now used by a broader segment of the population.

MDMA is taken orally, usually as a capsule or tablet. The popular term *Molly* (slang for "molecular") refers to the pure crystalline powder form of MDMA, usually sold in capsules. The drug's effects last approximately 3 to 6 hours, although it is not uncommon for users to take a second dose of the drug as the effects of the first dose begin to fade. It is commonly taken in combination with other drugs.

MDMA acts by increasing the activity of three neurotransmitters—serotonin, dopamine, and norepinephrine. The emotional and pro-social effects of MDMA are likely caused directly or indirectly by the release of large amounts of serotonin, which influences mood. The surge of serotonin caused by taking MDMA depletes the brain of this important chemical, however, causing negative after-effects—including

"Meth" can be used in a number of ways. Many people prefer to inject it into their veins because it produces an intense euphoria almost instantaneously.

confusion, depression, sleep problems, drug craving, and anxiety—that may occur soon after taking the drug or during the days or even weeks thereafter.

Methamphetamine

Methamphetamine (also called meth, crystal, chalk, and ice, among other terms) is an extremely addictive stimulant drug. It takes the form of a white, odorless, bitter-tasting crystalline powder. Methamphetamine is taken orally, smoked, snorted, or dissolved in water or alcohol and injected. Smoking or injecting the drug delivers it very quickly to the brain, where it produces an immediate, intense euphoria. Because the pleasure also fades quickly, users often take repeated doses, in a "binge and crash" pattern.

Methamphetamine is causing widespread concern among law enforcement officials and medical professionals. At present, this drug, which is often manufactured in makeshift "laboratories" in people's homes and garages, is making headlines and appears to be gaining in popularity among teenagers and young adults, especially in rural areas and small towns throughout the nation. Because the drug can be produced using some over-the-counter cold remedies, these cold medicines have been pulled from the market.

Crack Cocaine

Crack cocaine is a form of cocaine that can be smoked rather than ingested through the nasal passages. Commercial cocaine is "cooked" with ether or bicarbonate of soda to form a "rock" of crack. When it is smoked, crack produces an instant and extremely powerful rush that tends to last only about 15 minutes and to cause a strong desire for another rush. This form of cocaine is therefore highly addicting.

Crack is more expensive than cocaine in its powder form, and its use is often associated with an expensive lifestyle. Perhaps for this reason, some athletes, movie stars, and politicians who previously used cocaine have become addicted to crack, with disastrous consequences in some cases. Violence linked with the distribution and sale of crack continues. In addition, the birth of sickly, low-weight babies with cocaine addictions formed before birth is a serious problem in communities where the effects of the crack epidemic are still being felt.

Heroin

Heroin is an opioid drug that is synthesized from morphine, a naturally occurring substance extracted from the seedpod of the Asian opium poppy plant. Heroin can be injected, inhaled by snorting or sniffing, or smoked. All three routes of administration deliver the drug to the brain very rapidly. Most heroin users experience a sudden, intense feeling of pleasure; others may feel greater self-esteem and composure. But because heroin slows brain functions, the addict becomes lethargic after the initial euphoria.

Heroin has a very high risk for addiction, which can be characterized by uncontrollable drug-seeking no matter the consequences. The notorious relationship between crime and heroin addiction results not from the influence of the drug, per se, but from the suffering caused by the lack of it: Addicts avoid withdrawal symptoms at all costs. Because addicts are seldom employable and a single day's supply of heroin may cost well over $100, most of an addict's day is usually devoted to crime, especially property crimes.

A person addicted to heroin frequently suffers from malnutrition, as well as from hepatitis, AIDS, and other infections caused by intravenous injection of the drug. In communities where heroin addicts are numerous and visible, there is often conflict over the advisability of providing free needles so that addicts will not be forced to share illegally purchased hypodermics and risk the mixing of blood that may contain the HIV virus.

What Do You Think?
What types of drugs were popular in your high school? What was the general attitude toward these drugs and their health risks?

Patterns, Problems, and Treatment

4.7 Identify some of the patterns, problems, and treatments associated with drug abuse.

People who abuse drugs face many of the same issues as those who abuse alcohol (and some people abuse both simultaneously). But there are also substantial differences between who uses drugs, the problems they can bring, and treatment options.

Patterns of Drug Use

The study of drug use in the United States is a social-scientific undertaking of great magnitude. The data come from two major sources. The first source includes reports from public and private agencies that deal with arrest, hospitalization, treatment, or legal matters. These reports offer important evidence about trends in drug use among individuals arrested for crimes or admitted to hospital emergency rooms. But they do not tell us very much about the distribution of drug use in the general population. This information is obtained from large-scale national surveys, the second source.

For example, the annual survey of 16,000 high school seniors that was mentioned earlier, *Monitoring the Future*, gives a glimpse of drug (and alcohol) use among teenagers. Another important survey is the National Household Survey on Drug Abuse, which is sponsored by the National Institute on Drug Abuse, and which focuses on adults. Other surveys that collect information on various aspects of substance use and abuse are quite common, but these two allow researchers to track patterns of use from year to year.

WHO USES DRUGS? Data from the national surveys indicate that drug use among Americans has stabilized or is declining somewhat, except for a few drugs, most noticeably marijuana. As shown in Figure 4–4, after a decline in the early 2000s, marijuana use began to increase in 2007. By 2012, there were 18.9 million current people who had used it in the past month—about 7.3 percent of people ages 12 and over.

Surveys of drug use over time also provide information about its distribution by sex, socioeconomic status, and racial or ethnic background (National Institute on Drug Abuse, 2014). Men are more likely to use drugs, and they use more of them than do women. Drug use is found in all socioeconomic groups, although the type of drug used differs substantially due to the cost of the drug and the culture surrounding its use. For example, the abuse of prescription drugs is more likely to occur among the middle classes and those with more money because of the cost of the drugs or the likelihood of having health insurance to help pay for the drugs. Drug use is higher among Native Americans and blacks, least common among Asians, with whites and Hispanics falling somewhere between. Young adults use drugs more frequently than those who are older; however, use among young adults appears to have stabilized or declined, as shown in Figure 4–5. Meanwhile, drug use among older people is increasing.

HOW DOES DRUG USE SPREAD? Most sociologists and social psychologists agree that drug use is a learned behavior that spreads through groups of peers who influence one another. In a pioneering study, Howard S. Becker (1963) traced the career of a marijuana user, showing that users must learn how to smoke the drug and identify their reaction to it as pleasurable. If they are unable to make this identification, they stop using the drug. They also gradually learn that the social controls that work against marijuana use—limited supplies, the need to maintain secrecy, and the

Figure 4–4 Percentage of Persons Age 12 and Older Who Have Used the Most Common Drugs Over the Past Month, 2002–2012

SOURCE: National Institute on Drug Abuse, 2014.

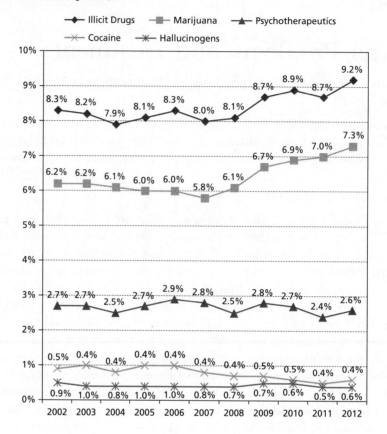

Figure 4–5 Percentage Using Drugs in Past Month, by Age, 2011–2012

NOTE: Percentages are rounded.

SOURCE: National Institute on Drug Abuse, 2014.

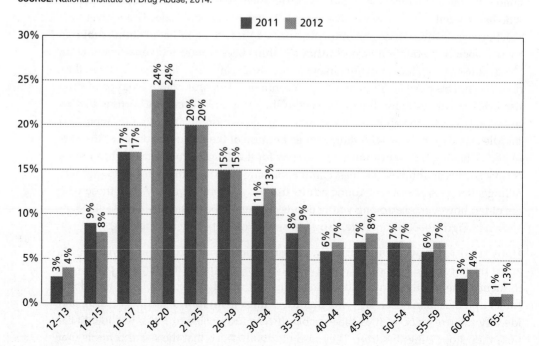

definition of drug use as immoral—either do not apply to the peer group or can be circumvented.

The most important direct influence on drug use is that of the peer group. However, other factors set the stage for involvement in drug-using peer groups, including the individual's socioeconomic status and neighborhood environment and the influences of family, religion, and school. For example, drug use is more likely when the family is not intact, when the young person has problems in school, or when the family is forced to live in a neighborhood where young people have ready access to drugs and are exposed to deviant role models (Green et al., 2010).

If the individual's social milieu contributes significantly to drug use, what effect might a change in milieu have? Most U.S. soldiers who were addicted to heroin in Vietnam were generally able to kick the habit rather easily when they returned home, which shows that people are able to abstain from an extremely addicting drug when their social milieu no longer supports it. This is also an example of the phenomenon that drug researchers term "maturing out," that is, the tendency of drug users to decrease their use of drugs of all kinds, including alcohol, beginning in their late 20s (Han, Gfroerer, and Colliver, 2010; Neff and Dassori, 1998).

Drug use is highest among young people ages 18–24. The peer group is an important influence on whether or not a young person will use drugs.

Problems Associated with Drug Abuse

A wide number of social and health problems are associated with drug abuse. Here we will examine two: crime and the spread of HIV.

CRIME Images of drugs and crime abound in the media. Popular television shows, such as *NCIS* or the now-ended *Breaking Bad*, vividly illustrate how drugs and crime are interrelated. However, the nature of drug-related crimes varies with the type of drug involved. Neither marijuana nor low-to-moderate use of barbiturates are likely to promote violence. Users of other drugs, such as heroin, crack cocaine, or methamphetamine, in contrast, seem disproportionately involved in crime. The connection of these drugs with crime occurs because people who abuse these drugs can rarely support their habit on their own without resorting to crime. In addition, many abusers already have a criminal history (Inciardi, 1999; National Council on Alcohol and Drug Dependence, Inc., 2015b).

The crimes committed to support a drug habit tend to be money-seeking crimes such as burglary, prostitution, and shoplifting. Although these crimes may provide 40 to 50 percent of the addict's income for drug purchases, one study estimated that almost half the annual consumption of heroin in New York City is financed by selling the drug itself along with the equipment needed to inject it (Inciardi, 1999). All these crimes, considered nonviolent in themselves, nevertheless are often accompanied by violence such as muggings or armed robberies.

Jail or prison time alone has little effect on the reduction of drug addiction or in promoting recovery. Sixty to 80 percent of those who abuse drugs commit a new crime (typically a drug-driven crime) after release from jail or prison (National Council on Alcohol and Drug Dependence, 2015b). Incarceration without access to treatment or without specific plans for treatment after the person's discharge is not particularly effective.

DRUG USE AND AIDS A primary means by which AIDS spreads among heterosexual populations is the sharing of needles and syringes by intravenous drug users. Public health officials were slow to realize the extent of AIDS transmission among intravenous drug users. Hence, they were also slow to initiate educational and other programs that might hinder the spread of the disease in this population.

Efforts to reach addicts must overcome a number of obstacles. Because their activity is illegal, addicts are reluctant to come forward to be tested for AIDS. Public health workers lack credibility in the eyes of addicts, but attempts to employ ex-addicts in outreach programs have had more success. Needle exchange programs have been tried successfully in many cities. The World Health Organization sponsored a study of HIV prevalence in 103 cities throughout the world. In 36 cities with needle exchange programs, HIV infections declined by 19 percent annually, but in 67 cities without such programs infection rates increased by 8 percent each year (Campbell, 2005). Remarkable results like these provide strong support for needle exchange and other "harm reduction" programs that seek to reduce the ravages of drug addiction. However, public opposition to programs that appear to condone drug use limits their impact.

Treatment of Drug Abuse

Efforts to rehabilitate those who abuse drugs have been impeded by the notion that "once an addict, always an addict." Until recently, statistical evidence supported this belief, and the prospects for returning addicts to normal living were bleak. However, drug use spreads through the peer group and may be reversed with a change in social milieu. And drug use does not necessarily follow a predictable course from experimentation to addiction; instead, it encompasses a wide range of behaviors that may include experimentation, occasional use, regular use, and heavy use. These behaviors stem from the interaction of many complex factors, and efforts to rehabilitate addicts have not always addressed all of them. Two types of treatment programs are discussed here: therapeutic communities and methadone maintenance.

THERAPEUTIC COMMUNITIES Therapeutic communities are a way to attack the high relapse rate of addicts who are detoxified and returned to the larger society. They enable individuals to reenter social life gradually and at their own pace. This controlled reentry reduces the shock of moving from a protective institutional environment to the much greater freedom of the outside world.

Phoenix House operates one of the most highly developed therapeutic community programs around the country. In the Phoenix program, addicts who have completed their treatment are transferred to a Re-Entry House for gradual reintegration into everyday life. Educational facilities are part of the program and include training in vocational skills and preparation for entry into other educational programs.

The Phoenix House approach rests on two key precepts: that addicts must assume responsibility for their own actions and that treatment should address psychological as well as physical difficulties. Phoenix House relies on ex-addicts, who are often more effective in breaking through the barriers of isolation and hostility. In addition, ex-addicts provide living proof that addiction can be overcome. In operation since 1968, the Phoenix House program has helped many addicts recover permanently.

METHADONE MAINTENANCE Methadone, a synthetic narcotic, has been tested extensively and is now used regularly in treatment programs for heroin addicts. In prescribed amounts, it satisfies the addict's physical craving, preventing the agonizing symptoms of withdrawal. Although it does not produce a high, methadone is addicting and therefore offers not a cure but a maintenance treatment for addicts who do not respond to other types of therapy.

Many people, including addicts themselves, believe methadone keeps addicts dependent on drugs and hence is useful only for a short time while the addict is weaned from heroin. Methadone treatment can be regarded as a form of social control imposed by the dominant culture. The substance is legally available only through approved programs, which require addicts to report to the treatment center for their daily dosage. Nonetheless, these ambivalent attitudes toward methadone treatment do not seem to deter potential clients.

Social Policy

4.8 Review policy considerations of drug laws and enforcement.

Social policies that address drug and alcohol abuse take two main forms. One consists of control strategies—that is, attempts to help individuals or groups control their own behavior—coupled with efforts to build local institutions (e.g., residential treatment centers) that provide helping services. The second is law enforcement, meaning attempts to tighten the enforcement of existing laws or to enact new laws designed to deal with the problem more effectively. Control strategies such as rehabilitation and other efforts were discussed earlier in the sections on treatment, and this section focuses on law enforcement.

Law Enforcement

One approach to a problem like drug abuse is to crack down on the sale or use of the drug. This rationale was used for Prohibition, an era in which the manufacture, sale, or transportation of alcoholic beverages was banned beginning in 1919 by an amendment to the U.S. Constitution. Although Prohibition was repealed in 1933, the attitudes that gave rise to this approach are still in evidence. Chronic drinkers are still thrown in jail to dry out; people are still arrested in most states for possession of a single marijuana cigarette; drug addicts still receive heavy jail sentences. In many places "treatment" is simply incarceration.

Yet, repeated arrests of chronic alcoholics or drug abusers merely perpetuate a revolving-door cycle. Offenders are arrested, processed, released, and then arrested again, sometimes only hours after their previous release. Each such arrest, which involves police, court, and correctional time, is expensive and may actually contribute to the labeling process in which an excessive drinker becomes an alcoholic and behaves accordingly.

Drug Law Reform

Many observers believe that revising drug laws so that they deal with issues more realistically and consistently can ease the drug problem. The most insistent demands for reform have focused on marijuana. It is considered unfair to classify marijuana with the far more dangerous hard drugs, and even people who do not favor legalization of marijuana may support reductions in the penalties for its possession and sale.

The legalization of marijuana for medical uses has created a major rift between states and the federal government. Marijuana can significantly reduce the pain and nausea associated with cancer, cancer treatments, and other serious illnesses. Critics see the use of marijuana for medicinal purposes as a first push toward legalizing marijuana more generally. After some states objected to this push, in 2005 the Supreme Court, in a 6 to 3 ruling, decided that doctors can be barred from prescribing marijuana for patients. The ruling gave clear precedence to federal antidrug legislation over "medical marijuana" laws passed by the states. Yet, the number of states allowing marijuana to be used for medical purposes, as well as allowing it for personal use, is quickly growing.

With regard to other drugs, some experts advocate revision of drug laws and, in some cases, they propose outright legalization. For example, one argument for the legalization of heroin is that it would drive down the price of the drug so that addicts would no longer be compelled to engage in crime to support their habit. The British system is cited in support of this position. The British view drug addiction as a disease that requires treatment, and they regulate the distribution of narcotics through physicians and government-run clinics. This system does not give addicts unlimited access to narcotics, but it eases the problem of supply. Those who oppose this approach fear that it might tempt people to experiment with drugs.

Issues of foreign policy complicate the problem of enforcement at the national level. Through economic and military aid, the United States supports the governments of countries that are major suppliers of illegal drugs, particularly Colombia, Peru, and Bolivia. It has been suggested that the United States should suspend foreign aid to governments that do not cooperate with efforts to stop the flow of drugs into the U.S. market. Other suggestions include imposing trade sanctions on those countries or reducing military assistance.

An issue that has generated a great deal of controversy is the testing of public employees for drug use. Appeals court rulings have reversed lower court decisions that such testing violates the Fourth Amendment to the Constitution, which protects citizens against "unreasonable searches and seizures." Many private firms are imposing drug (including alcohol) testing on employees in sensitive positions.

Future Prospects

It is extremely difficult to bring about change in drug policies in the United States. No elected official wants to look "soft" on drugs, even when the majority of constituents ask for a softer approach. For example, the majority of Americans now favor legalizing marijuana for personal use, as illustrated in Figure 4–6 (Swift, 2013). Moreover, about

---

Figure 4-6 Americans' Views on Legalizing Marijuana

SOURCE: Swift, 2013.

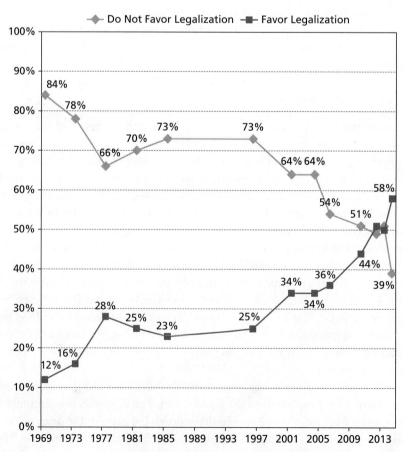

seven in ten American adults believe that alcohol is more harmful than marijuana (Motel, 2015).

Canada and Great Britain are ahead of the United States in reexamining drug laws, although they, too, must move slowly in making reforms in the direction of harm reduction because of efforts by opponents of any liberalization efforts. In England, the influential Police Foundation has developed the following stance toward marijuana, for example:

> *Our conclusion is that the present law on cannabis produces more harm than it prevents. It is very expensive of the time and resources of the criminal justice system and especially of the police. It inevitably bears more heavily on young people in the streets of inner cities, who are also more likely to be from minority ethnic communities, and as such is inimical to police-community relations. It criminalizes large numbers of otherwise law-abiding, mainly young, people to the detriment of their futures. It has become a proxy for the control of public order; and it inhibits accurate education about the relative risks of different drugs including the risks of cannabis itself. (Police Foundation of the United Kingdom, 2000)*

Yet, in the United States, many elected officials see the political stakes as being too high for them to reconsider their stance on drugs.

Going Beyond Left and Right

Is there really a difference between the views of those people on the left and those on the right about drug and alcohol use and abuse? In fact, there are many differences, although there are no monolithic views on either side of the political spectrum. Too many people have had direct experiences with drug and alcohol problems for this issue to be a partisan one. Nevertheless, there are some clear differences among major segments of the population. Think about these issues and choose among the following beliefs:

A. You believe that all kinds of mind-altering substances, from alcohol to most illegal drugs, are immoral and must be strongly prohibited.

B. You believe that what people want to drink or ingest is their own business, and the state should have no role in saying what they may buy or use.

C. You believe that mind-altering drugs like marijuana and LSD and the opiates and amphetamines are dangerous and need to be controlled, but you approve of moderate social drinking.

D. You believe that many drugs that are now illegal are no more or less dangerous than alcohol and should not be prohibited.

Do you agree with any of these strong but commonly held opinions? No doubt you do. Someone who agrees with choice A is likely to be a religious conservative, for example, a Southern Baptist or a follower of Islam. Someone agreeing with choice B could well be a libertarian who mainly desires less government and regulation; a person choosing B could also be a conservative who is more tolerant of different behaviors than is someone choosing A. People who select C could be on the right or the left. The majority of Americans, spanning all political divisions, drink in moderation but think that society needs to control access to other illegal substances. Someone who agrees with D, who argues against the criminalization of marijuana and other mind-altering drugs, is likely to be on the political left. But some conservatives also support this position.

To go beyond all these differences and divisions, one needs to go back to the facts about alcoholism and drug addiction. One needs to consider the ravages of alcohol in families and entire peoples, such as Native Americans. One needs to see the associations between alcohol and drug abuse and poverty and discrimination. These considerations lead to the idea that society as a whole, through its governmental institutions or its civic and community institutions, has a responsibility to devise policies to deal with the problems of alcohol and drug abuse.

Many conservatives believe that prisons should not "pamper" inmates and that offering them education, rehabilitative treatment, and counseling should not be substituted for "hard time" spent on prison chores and work programs. Many more liberal observers plead for more rehabilitation and drug counseling and in the past have favored "softer" prison terms. Yet, when one considers the costs to society of repeat offenders with drug and alcohol problems, it is clear that whatever our political beliefs, we all stand to benefit from drug and alcohol treatment programs in prisons.

Summary

- Like so many other social problems, drug use has both objective and subjective dimensions. The term *drug abuse* is widely used, but it can refer to many things. In this chapter, the term *drug abuse* is defined as both the use of societally unacceptable drugs and/or the excessive or inappropriate use of acceptable drugs in ways that can lead to physical, psychological, or social harm. The term *addiction* is often used rather loosely, but in fact is a complex phenomenon that involves the drug user's physical and psychological dependence, the type of drug, and the amount and frequency of use.

- In our society, people have mixed feelings about alcohol. Despite high rates of alcohol consumption by some people, the problems associated with alcohol abuse—especially chronic inebriation, vagrancy, missed days of work—arouse less interest and concern than the abuse, or even the use, of other drugs. Several factors seem to be related to whether, how much, and in what ways an individual uses alcohol and becomes an alcohol abuser or alcoholic. Among these factors are biological and socioeconomic factors, gender, age, religion, and cultural influences.

- Excessive drinking contributes to health problems, accidental deaths and injury through drunk driving and crime. For example, alcohol is a factor in 88,000 deaths per year; Mothers Against Drunk Driving (MADD) has waged a large campaign to reduce the number of drivers who are impaired; and about one-third of all crimes are committed by someone under the influence of alcohol.

- Alcohol abuse can leave a marriage or relationship very shaky or may cause it to break up altogether because the relationship usually centers on the drinking member and his or her moods, health, feelings, work situation, stresses, and coping. Partners and children often take specific roles within the family to cope with living with the alcoholic and engage in enabling behaviors.

- There are a number of treatment options for alcoholism, including rehabilitation, Alcoholics Anonymous, Antabuse, and other programs. Rehabilitation is often done through hospitals and clinics, allowing a person to "dry out" while under care. Alcoholics Anonymous focuses on fellowship with others like themselves, some of whom have already mastered their problem while others are in the process of doing so. Antabuse, a prescription drug, sensitizes the patient in such a way that consuming even a small quantity of alcohol causes strong and uncomfortable physical symptoms.

- In addition to alcohol, the nine most commonly abused drugs are, in order of their use, marijuana, prescription medicines, hallucinogens, cocaine, inhalants, MDMA, methamphetamine, crack cocaine, and heroin.

- Data from national surveys indicate that drug use among Americans has stabilized or is declining somewhat—except for a few drugs, most noticeably, marijuana. Drug use is higher among males, Native Americans, and young adults. Drugs are associated with a number of social problems, including crime and the spread of HIV. There are several treatment options, including therapeutic communities and methadone maintenance.

- Social policies that address drug and alcohol abuse take two main forms. One consists of control strategies—that is, attempts to help individuals or groups control their own behavior—coupled with efforts to build local institutions (e.g., residential treatment centers) that provide helping services. The second is law enforcement, meaning attempts to tighten the enforcement of existing laws or to enact new laws designed to deal with the problem more effectively. It is extremely difficult to bring about change in drug policies or create a more relaxed enforcement of certain policies. No elected official wants to look as though he or she is "soft" on drugs.

Chapter 5
Crime and Violence

 Learning Objectives

5.1 Describe the nature of crime and crime statistics, including police discretion and problems of accuracy.

5.2 Compare different types of crimes and the people who commit them.

5.3 Evaluate biological explanations for crime and violence.

5.4 Contrast the sociological explanations for crime and violence.

5.5 Identify ways to control crime and violence.

5.6 Explain the policy considerations surrounding gun control.

Clay just got himself in big trouble. Never one to do very well in school, and tired of being a loner, 16-year-old Clay has been hanging around a group of older kids who think school is a waste of time and would rather hang out on the streets. He looks up to these kids, "Man, they do want they want to do… they don't just go with a crowd and stay in school because they are supposed to… they think for themselves," he says. One day, they decided to dare one another to break into a house in the neighborhood and steal some small items that they could easily pawn, "You know, jewelry and stuff like that, nothing too big or fancy." Clay wasn't very sure about this idea; he had never done anything like this before. But he didn't want his new friends to think poorly of him so he remained quiet. They walked by a few houses, but something didn't look right in them. Maybe someone was home, or a dog was barking, or a radio was on. Finally, they found a house that looked empty, and it had a side window sized just right for one of the smaller guys to crawl through. After his friend made it inside and opened the door for the rest of the group, the search began for jewelry, prescription drugs, silverware, and other small items. Clay even found a stash of money, at least a hundred dollars worth! All seemed cool. As they were leaving and about to jump into the car, a neighbor yelled at them, "Hey, what are you doing? What's going on?" They sped away, but apparently the neighbor had a good look at the license plate. Eventually, the police caught up with all of them, and now they all face counts of burglary. Clay, along with the others, will face jail time.

Americans consistently rank crime as among the most serious social problems in the United States. Depending on their concerns about issues such as health care or the state of the economy, they may rank any of these problems as more serious at a given moment. But for many decades, crime has been ranked at or very near the top of the list of major social problems. During the past few years, some crime rates have decreased. At the same time, as you will see in this chapter, governments at all levels continue to invest heavily in crime control (although not necessarily crime prevention). As a result, the prison population in the United States has reached record proportions.

It is important to realize that at least some crime has existed in virtually all societies. As the French sociologist Émile Durkheim (1897/1951) pointed out, wherever there are people and laws, there are crime and criminals:

> *Crime is present … in all societies of all types. There is no society that is not confronted with the problem of criminality. Its form changes; the acts thus characterized are not the same everywhere; but, everywhere and always, there have been men who have behaved in such a way as to draw upon themselves penal repression. … What is normal, simply, is the existence of criminality. (p. 65)*

According to the Uniform Crime Reports (UCR) of the Federal Bureau of Investigation (FBI) there has been a steady decline in the number and the rate (which is adjusted for the size of the population) in violent crime. This decline is shown in Table 5–1. For example, the rate of violent crimes has dropped by nearly half between 1994 and 2013, from 714 to 368 crimes per 100,000 people in the population (FBI, 2014c).

Table 5–1 Number of Violent Crimes, and Rate of Violent Crime per 100,000 People, 1994, 2000, 2013

Year	Number of Violent Crimes	Violent Crime Rate (per 100,000 people)
1994	1,857,670	713.6
2000	1,425,486	506.5
2013	1,163,146	367.9

SOURCE: FBI Uniform Crime Reports, 2014a.

Table 5–2 Number of Property Crimes, and Rate of Property Crime per 100,000 People, 1994, 2000, 2013

Year	Number of Property Crimes	Property Crime Rate (per 100,000 people)
1994	12,131,873	4,660.2
2000	10,182,584	3,618.3
2013	8,632,512	2,730.7

SOURCE: FBI Uniform Crime Reports, 2014b.

The FBI also reported that the number of property crimes has been decreasing substantially, as reported in Table 5–2. Property crimes include burglary, larceny-theft, and motor vehicle theft. Property crimes since 1994 have dropped 40 percent (FBI, 2014b). These numbers are somewhat surprising because, even during severe economic recession, property crime continued to decline.

While these numbers are quite encouraging, it is also true that the United States has far higher rates of crime than do most other developed nations. It also is a leader in rates of imprisonment of its citizens, despite falling crime rates, a subject to which we return later in the chapter.

In this chapter, we examine these and other trends in crime and violence more fully. You will see that there is a good deal of argument among experts about whether these trends are likely to continue. Another problem is that the statistics used are based on reports provided by local police departments and often contain errors.

One reason for the disagreement is that it is difficult to measure actual crime rates. An annual survey of U.S. households by the U.S. Department of Justice asks respondents detailed questions about their experiences with crime. This survey, known as the National Crime Victimization Survey of the Bureau of Justice Statistics, reveals that the actual rates of violent personal and property crime are two to three times higher than the official rates presented in the UCR, which are based on crimes reported to the police, as shown in Table 5–3 (Truman and Langton, 2014). Many victims do not report crimes to the police because they believe nothing can be done.

Official statistics, of course, do not tell the whole story. It has never been easy, for example, to assess accurately the extent of organized and occupational (white-collar) crime. Exposures of scandals in government and business show that these types of crimes are far more widespread and pervasive than is generally realized.

Fear of crime, especially in large cities, significantly affects the lives of many people. Large numbers of Americans feel unsafe in their homes, neighborhoods, or workplaces. Sociologists who study the effects of media coverage of crime report

Table 5–3 Percentage of Victimizations That Are Reported to the Police, 2013

Violent Crime	46%
Rape	35%
Robbery	68%
Assault	43%
Intimate Partner Violence	57%
Property Crime	**36%**
Household Burglary	57%
Motor Vehicle Theft	76%
Theft	29%

SOURCE: Truman and Langton, 2014.

that attitudes about safety in one's neighborhood and about going out at night in the city in which one resides vary directly with the rate of crimes in that city; however, reports of crimes in other cities can make people feel safe in comparison. The reports that are most closely correlated with fear of crime are those describing sensational murders in one's own city, that is, murders reported on the front pages of newspapers and on television. Less sensational murders, even in one's own city, do not have a measurable impact (Schmalleger, 2000). Of course, the crimes that are most likely to generate fear are those that directly affect one's family and friends, even if they are relatively minor.

The Nature of Crime and Crime Statistics

5.1 Describe the nature of crime and crime statistics, including police discretion and problems of accuracy.

There is no single, universally agreed-on definition of crime. In the words of one of the world's foremost historians of crime, the late Sir Leon Radzinowicz, crime

> is something that threatens serious harm to the community, or something generally believed to do so, or something committed with evil intent, or something forbidden in the interests of the most powerful sections of society. But there are crimes that elude each of these definitions and there are forms of behavior under each of them that escape the label of crime. The argument that crime is anything forbidden, or punishable, under the criminal law is open to the objection that it is circular. But at least it is clear cut, it refers not to what ought to be but to what is, and it is an essential starting point. (Radzinowicz and King, 1977, p. 17)

crime

Any act or omission of an act for which the state can apply sanctions.

According to this argument, a **crime** is any act or omission of an act for which the state can apply sanctions. This definition is most frequently used to define crime and the one we will use in this chapter. However, keep in mind that what activities constitute crime are subject to changing values and public sentiments; moreover, as you will see shortly, factors such as police discretion play a major role in the interpretation of particular behaviors as crimes.

criminal law

The practice wherein society prohibits certain acts and prescribes the punishments to be meted out to violators.

The **criminal law** in any society prohibits certain acts and prescribes the punishments to be meted out to violators. Confusion frequently arises because, although the criminal law prescribes certain rules for living in society, not all violations of social rules are violations of criminal laws. A swimmer's failure to come to the aid of a drowning stranger, for example, would not constitute a criminal act, although it might be considered morally wrong not to have done whatever possible to save the victim, short of risking one's own life.

civil law

Laws that deal with noncriminal acts in which one individual injures another.

Many acts that are regarded as immoral are ignored in criminal law but are considered to be civil offenses. Under **civil law**—laws that deal with noncriminal acts in which one individual injures another—the state arbitrates between the aggrieved party and the offender. For example, civil law is involved when a person whose car was destroyed in an accident sues the driver responsible for the accident to recover the cost of the car. The driver at fault is not considered a criminal unless he or she can be shown to have broken a criminal law, for instance, to have been driving while intoxicated.

Police Discretion

In addition to problems of definition, such as ambiguity about whether loitering is a crime, certain other factors contribute to the difficulty of knowing what crimes are committed in a particular society. A significant factor is the role of police discretion.

In practice, the definition of criminality changes according to what the police believe criminal behavior to be. Given the thousands of laws on the books, police officers have considerable discretion about which laws to ignore, which laws to enforce, and how strongly to enforce them. This discretionary power, in turn, gives them many opportunities to exercise their own concept of lawful behavior in decisions about what complaints merit attention, whom they should arrest, and who should be released (Lee, Vaughn, and Lim, 2014).

In an important study of police discretion, Michael K. Brown (Brown, 1988) compared police activities in two Los Angeles Police Department (LAPD) districts and three suburban towns in the Los Angeles metropolitan region. On the basis of interviews with patrol officers and their supervisors, Brown concluded that "a police bureaucracy has a significant impact on the behavior of patrolmen. … Patrolmen in the two divisions of the LAPD are formalistic and more willing to make an arrest in a variety of incidents than patrolmen in small departments, who are consistently more lenient and less willing to invoke the force of the law in the same circumstances" (p. 275). When asked whether they would normally arrest disorderly juveniles on their beat, for example, 28 percent of veteran police officers with five years or more experience in the smaller departments said that they would arrest the offenders, whereas 65 percent of the LAPD veteran officers said that they would arrest disorderly juveniles.

In another well-known study of two groups of adolescents in the same high school, William Chambliss (Chambliss, 1973) examined how the biases of the local police affected their treatment of middle- and lower-class delinquents. A group of middle-class boys (the Saints) had been truant almost every day of the two-year period during which they were studied. They drove recklessly, drank excessively, and openly cheated on exams. Yet only twice were members of the Saints stopped by police officers; even then, nothing appeared on their school records. The members of the other group (the Roughnecks) all came from lower-class families. Unlike the Saints, who had cars and could "sow their wild oats" in parts of town where they were not known, the Roughnecks were confined to an area where they could be easily recognized; they therefore developed a reputation for being delinquent.

The demeanor of the two groups of boys differed markedly when the police apprehended them. The Saints, who were apologetic, penitent, and generally respectful of middle-class values, were treated as harmless pranksters. The Roughnecks, who were openly hostile and disdainful toward the police, were labeled deviant. These results demonstrate that factors such as low income, unemployment, or minority status are not the only ones that have a bearing on the commission of juvenile crimes. Although these factors did account for a higher rate of detection and punishment, the rates of actual misbehavior in Chambliss's study were virtually the same for both groups. Differences in the official records of the two groups reflect the discretionary power of the police (Chambliss, 2000).

Problems of Accuracy

Another issue that contributes to the problem of determining the level of crime in a society is that police statistics depend on police reports, which in turn depend on the level and quality of police personnel in a given area. Because police are assigned to lower-income communities in greater numbers, there is a tendency for police records to show higher crime rates for those communities and lower rates for more affluent areas.

If official data on crime are less than fully accurate on a local level, it is possible that similar problems undermine the accuracy of national crime statistics. The standard index of criminal activity in the United States, the UCR, supplies racial and economic profiles of people arrested for crimes such as murder, rape, assault, and

What Do You Think?

The study involving the Roughnecks and the Saints was conducted over 40 years ago. Describe how things have changed, or how they have remained the same.

robbery. Recent data support the long-held assumption that minority group members and poor people are more likely than nonminority and wealthier individuals to be involved in crimes. Yet it must be remembered that UCR statistics cite only individuals who are apprehended. If adult offenders in middle- and upper-class groups are less likely to caught or punished, like the Saints in the Chambliss (1973) study, then UCR-based data become inaccurate. Because those data do not profile those who successfully evade apprehension and prosecution, the UCR fails to reveal the entire range of criminal activity in the United States.

Acting on this idea, researchers attempted to devise more reliable ways of tracking criminal activity. Self-report studies, such as the National Crime Victimization studies introduced earlier, provide alternative data. Whereas higher crime rates occur among minorities and poor people when judged by official data, self-reporting techniques indicate that rates of criminal activity are more similar among people of different race or income groups than originally imagined (Dunaway et al., 2000). Thus, the idea that race or income is a primary factor in criminality is called into question when different standards of measurement are used.

Types of Crimes and Criminals

5.2   Compare different types of crimes and the people who commit them.

This section reviews several major types of crimes and criminals. These categories include (a) violent personal crimes such as murder; (b) occasional property crimes such as theft; (c) occupational crimes, which are sometimes nicknamed white-collar crimes and include acts such as embezzlement; (d) corporate crimes, which can include offenses such as defrauding employees or falsifying company records; (e) organized crime, which might include global crime syndicates; (f) public order crimes such as gambling or prostitution; (g) hate crimes, which are the commission of a traditional offense like murder, arson, or vandalism with an added element of bias; and (h) gender-based violence (slow to be recognized as hate crimes), which are offenses such as sexual assault or sex trafficking that are targeted primarily toward women.

The murder rate in the United States has been on a steady decline for many years; however, it remains among the highest of any developed nation.

Violent Personal Crimes

Violent personal crimes include rape, assault, robbery, and various types of homicide—acts in which physical injury or death is inflicted or threatened. Their frequency within the U.S. population is shown in Figure 5–1, represented as a rate per 100,000 people. As you can see, the most serious crimes occur less frequently than those that are less serious. For example, the murder/homicide rate in 2013 was 4.5 per 100,000 people, while the rate for aggravated assault was over 229 per 100,000 people (FBI, 2014c).

Although robbery and assaults occur most often between strangers, rapes and murders are very often perpetrated on "friends," acquaintances, or relatives. For example, federal sources reveal that at least 60 percent of rape victims know their attacker, and about 75 percent of all homicide victims are related to or acquainted with their assailants (Harrell, 2012; National Institute of Justice, 2010).

Criminal homicide takes two forms: **murder** is defined as the unlawful killing of a human being with malice aforethought; **manslaughter** is unlawful homicide without malice

Figure 5–1 Violent Crime Rate, per 100,000 People, 2013

SOURCE: FBI Uniform Crime Reports, 2014a.

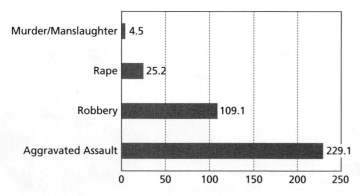

aforethought. In practice, it is often difficult to distinguish between them. Someone may attack another person without intending to kill, but the attack may result in death. Depending on the circumstances, one case might be judged to be murder and another to be manslaughter. Often the deciding factor is the extent to which the victim is believed to have provoked the assailant. In this discussion of violence, we will use the term *murder* for both terms without distinguishing the degree of malice afore-thought, as does the FBI when they record statistics.

Paradoxically, most murderers do not have a criminal record. Of course, there are those who use actual or threatened violence as tools in a criminal career, but these individuals are exceptions. Murderers do not conform to any criminal stereotype, and murder is not usually part of a criminal career. As a rule, professional criminals try to keep murder to a "necessary" minimum because of the "heat" it would bring from the law. Instead, most murderers do not see themselves as real criminals, and until the murder occurs, neither does society.

Murder does, however, follow certain social and geographic patterns. Guns tend to be the weapon of choice: guns were used in 69 percent of all murders in 2013. The FBI reports that murders occur most often in large cities. There are also regional dif-ferences; for example, murder is more likely to occur in the southern United States, even though it is one of the more rural parts of the country (FBI, 2014c). This tendency seems to be a result of the culture of the region, which tends to legitimize personal violence and the use of weapons, coupled with high levels of gun ownership. For example, in Louisiana, which has a murder rate that is four times the national average, almost half of all households own at least one gun. In contrast to Louisiana, in Hawaii, which has a murder rate only about half of the national average, less than 10 percent of households have guns (Violence Policy Center, 2015).

Men are more likely to commit murder than are women. Men are socialized to be more violent than women and may have more experience with guns because of recreation or military use. More than half of all people who murder are members of minority groups, most commonly blacks. Likewise, murder victims also tend to be members of minority groups, most often blacks. Most of the time, the killer and the victim are of the same race. Approximately 85 percent of white murder victims were slain by white offenders, and about 90 percent of black victims were slain by black offenders (FBI, 2013b). For black men in the United States, the chances of living beyond age 40 are worse than in the poorest nations of the world, mainly because of the toll taken by gun violence.

More significant than the demographic characteristics of murderers and their victims is the relationship between them. Several studies have indicated that this rela-tionship is generally close; often, the victim is a member of their killer's family or is an

murder

Unlawful killing of a human being with malice aforethought.

manslaughter

Unlawful homicide without malice aforethought.

Figure 5–2 Murder Victims By Relationship.

SOURCE: FBI, 2013b.

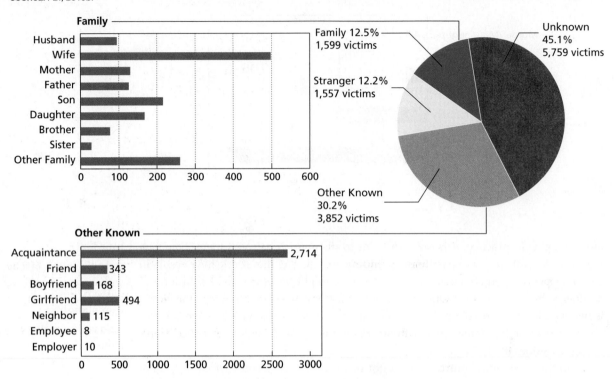

intimate friend. These relationships between murderers and their victims are clearly shown in Figure 5–2. Note the disproportionate number of wives and girlfriends among victims.

Most murders occur during a quarrel between two people who know each other well. Often, the murderer and the victim may have been drinking, perhaps together, before the event. Even though many homicides occur during the commission of other crimes, these killings, too, are usually unpremeditated, for example, deaths that occur when a thief is surprised by a security officer or when a bank robber is confronted by an armed guard.

As you learned earlier, violent crime, including murder, is on the decline. Despite this progress, the level of deadly violence remains higher in the United States than in any other urban industrial nation (United Nations Office on Drugs and Crime, 2013), as illustrated in Map 5-1. Although rates of interpersonal violence are higher in some poorer nations that are riddled with gang or drug violence, no major industrialized nation has murder rates as high as those in the United States.

The widespread availability of guns and the contribution of drugs to violence are important factors in this situation, but those who study the problem also point to the pervasiveness of violence in our culture. Increasingly frequent incidents of aggressive driving, often referred to as "road rage," increases in fights at sports events and school outings, high rates of family violence, and outbreaks of deadly violence in workplaces have drawn attention to the underlying levels of interpersonal violence.

Occasional Property Crimes

Occasional property crimes include vandalism, check forgery, shoplifting, and some kinds of automobile theft. These crimes are usually unsophisticated, and the offenders lack the skills of the professional criminal. Because occasional offenders commit their crimes at irregular intervals, they are not likely to associate with habitual lawbreakers.

Map 5-1 Homicide Rates, by Country or Territory, 2012 or Latest Year

SOURCE: UNDOC Homicide to Statistics, 2013.

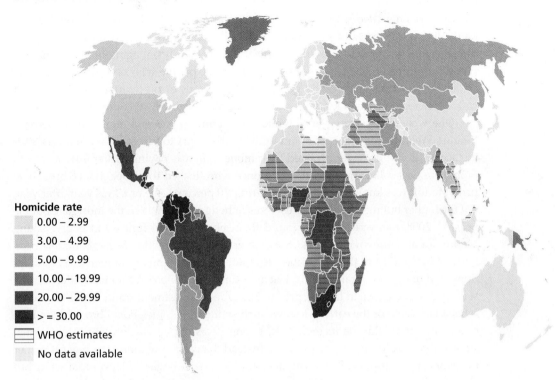

Homicide rate
- 0.00 – 2.99
- 3.00 – 4.99
- 5.00 – 9.99
- 10.00 – 19.99
- 20.00 – 29.99
- > = 30.00
- WHO estimates
- No data available

Nonprofessional shoplifters, for example, view themselves as respectable law-abiders who steal articles from stores only for their own use. They excuse their behavior on the grounds that what they steal has relatively little value and that the "victim" is usually a large, impersonal organization that can easily replace the stolen article.

Neither nonprofessional shoplifters nor nonprofessional check forgers are likely to have a criminal record. Like vandals and car thieves, they usually work alone and are not part of a criminal subculture; they do not seek to earn a living from crime.

Occupational (White-Collar) Crimes

The phenomenon of occupational crime was defined and popularized by sociologist Edwin H. Sutherland, first in a 1940 article and then in his 1961 book *White Collar Crime*. Sutherland analyzed the behavior of people who break the law as part of their normal business activity: corporate directors who use their inside knowledge to sell large blocks of stock at tremendous profits; accountants who juggle books to conceal the hundreds of dollars of company funds that they have pocketed; firms that make false statements about their profits to avoid paying taxes. Such acts tend to be ignored by society. They rarely come to the criminal courts, and even then, they are rarely judged as severely as other kinds of criminal activities. Since Sutherland first described it, the category of occupational crime has broadened to include both individuals committing illegal acts in the course of their jobs and entire corporations circumventing the law. It has come to include acts such as embezzlement, fraud, false advertising, violations of labor laws, insurance fraud, money laundering, and black-market activities.

The occupational offender is far removed from the popular stereotype of a criminal. Few people imagine that a lawyer or stockbroker is likely to engage in illegal activities. Because of their respectable appearance, it is difficult to think of these offenders as criminals. In fact, occupational offenders often consider themselves respectable citizens and do everything possible to avoid being labeled as lawbreakers—even by themselves.

Sutherland's theory of differential association asserts that occupational criminality, like other forms of systematic criminal behavior, is learned through frequent direct or indirect association with people who are already engaging in such behavior. (We discuss this theory later in the chapter.) Thus, people who become occupational criminals may do so simply by going into businesses or occupations in which their colleagues regard certain kinds of crime as the standard way of conducting business.

One well-known example of white-collar crime involves a man named Bernard Madoff. Wealthy investors gave him millions of dollars to invest for them in his trading accounts. But he never invested their money. He was paying earlier investors with money he was collecting from the new ones who flocked to his legendary brokerage firm. Madoff was known to pay "safe returns, 10 percent, give or take," year after year, not the higher but more fickle interest rates of hedge funds. When the mortgage bubble burst in 2008, many rich people found themselves short of funds and began asking Madoff for amounts that he could not deliver. Shortly thereafter, facing complete ruin, he gave himself up to the authorities. Investors, including many universities, foundations, and nonprofit organizations, lost an estimated total of $52 billion. Madoff is now serving a life sentence in federal prison. His type of investment fraud is called a Ponzi scheme after one of the earliest known such swindles. Charles Ponzi brought the idea to America from Europe in the 1920s, telling investors he was buying international stamps that would appreciate in value. Instead, he used new money to pay off earlier investors and to support his lavish lifestyle. All Ponzi schemes will eventually fail, but along the way, many people lose a great deal of money. It must be said, however, that investors in Ponzi schemes almost always have the hope of unrealistic gain, which makes them prone to be taken in (Matulich and Currie, 2008).

Corporate Crimes

Related to white-collar crime and organized crime (see next section) are corporate crimes, that is, crimes that are committed by a corporation or an individual working on behalf of an organization (rather than an individual working on his or her own behalf), usually for monetary gain. Corporate crime may include acts such as defrauding of employee pension plans, clandestine environmental pollution, illegal labor practices, falsification of company records, price-fixing, antitrust violations, or bribery of public officials. Recent disclosures of corporate crime in the tobacco and food industries commanded large headlines and large lawsuits. The financial and housing crises also have a basis in corporate crime. Attorney General Eric H. Holder proclaimed in 2015, "We have never hesitated to investigate and prosecute any individual, institution or organization that attempted to exploit our markets and take advantage of the American people." He made this claim when the Justice Department announced that Standard & Poor's (the ratings agency) had agreed to pay $1.4 billion to settle civil charges that it inflated ratings on mortgage-backed securities at the heart of the financial crisis (Stewart, 2015). But who are the specific individuals involved? As is the case with most corporate crimes, low-level employees are often charged with crimes, but higher-level executives manage to skirt prosecution.

Recently, a researcher from the University of Virginia law school analyzed 303 cases with corporations from 2001 to 2014 in which companies avoided guilty pleas by paying fines and agreeing to other measures. His results are found in his book *Too Big to Jail* (Garrett, 2014). It would seem obvious that, *individuals* actually committed the crimes, since corporations are legal entities and cannot be charged unless their employees engaged in wrongdoing. Yet the researcher found that

Slide Show

Examples of Corporate Crime

Corporate crimes are those crimes that are committed by a corporation, or an individual working on behalf of a corporation, for monetary gain. When caught, the corporation may have to pay a fine, which often is little more than a slap on the wrist, or underlings are punished while key executives go free. This slideshow illustrates some recent examples of corporate crime in the United States.

Thousands of construction companies broke employment laws and cheated on their taxes to gobble up a slice of the federal stimulus money that kept the building industry afloat during the recession. Thousands of companies avoided state and federal taxes, cheated on vulnerable workers, and undercut law-abiding competitors.

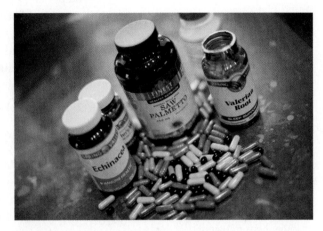

An investigation by the New York State attorney general's office into store-brand supplements being sold at Walmart, Walgreens, GNC, and Target found that many did not contain the herbs shown on their labels and some included potential allergens not identified in the ingredients list.

Pfizer, a large pharmaceutical company has had repeated violations and many nonprosecution agreements that resulted in large fines. However, to a multibillion-dollar company, the fines are relatively minor.

Critical Thinking

What type of penalties should be levied on corporations who are found guilty of committing high-level crimes? Is fining the corporation sufficient? Why or why not?

U.S. Attorney General Eric Holder takes a question as Acting Associate Attorney General Stuart Delery looks on during a news conference to make a major financial fraud announcement in 2015 at the Justice Department in Washington, D.C. Rating agency Standard and Poor's (S&P) has agreed to pay a $1.37 billion fine to resolve allegations that S&P had engaged in a scheme to defraud investors in structured financial products known as Residential Mortgage-Backed Securities (RMBS) and Collateralized Debt Obligations (CDOs).

individuals were charged in only 34 percent of the cases. And of those, only 42 percent received any jail time.

One particularly grievous case involves Pfizer, the large pharmaceutical company that has a string of nonprosecution agreements and guilty pleas. In the most recent instance, Pfizer paid $2.3 billion, including a criminal fine of $1.2 billion, for bribing doctors to prescribe an off-label painkiller and an antipsychotic drug. Despite the company's recidivism, none of its senior executives have ever been charged or convicted (Garrett, 2014).

In another recent case, Tyson Foods entered into a deferred prosecution agreement and paid a $4 million fine after disclosing what would seem to be a clear-cut case of bribery at its Mexican subsidiary. Yet no individuals were charged or even named. Meanwhile, the highest-ranking executive involved took early retirement and got a send-off of $1 million in cash, a multi-million dollar consulting deal, reimbursement of his country club dues, and use of the corporate jet (Stewart, 2015).

Organized Crime

organized crime

Crime that is committed by various types of criminal organizations, from large global crime syndicates to smaller local organizations whose membership may be more transient.

Organized crime is a term that includes many types of criminal organizations, from large global crime syndicates that originated in Sicily and Italy (the Mafia) and, more recently in Russia, to smaller local organizations whose membership may be more transient.

The groups that we usually think of as representing organized crime tend to be large and diversified regional or national units. They may organize initially to carry on a particular crime such as drug trafficking, extortion, prostitution, or gambling. Later, they may seek to control this activity in a given city or neighborhood, destroying or absorbing the competition. Eventually, they may expand into other types of crime, protecting their members from arrest through intimidation or bribery of public officials (Salinger, 2004).

Unlike other types of crime, organized crime is a system in which illegal activities are carried out as part of a rational plan devised by a large, often global organization that is attempting to maximize its overall profit. To operate most efficiently, organized crime relies on the division of labor in the performance of numerous diverse roles. Within a typical organized crime syndicate in a large metropolitan area, there will be groups in the stolen car and parts business, others in gambling, and still others in labor rackets. In each of these and other businesses, there will be specific occupations such as enforcer, driver, accountant, lawyer, and so on. Another major feature of organized crime is that the crime syndicate supplies goods and services that a large segment of the public wants but cannot obtain legally. Without the public's desire for gambling or drugs, for example, organized crime's basic means of existence would collapse.

In recent years, the FBI has investigated not only large and well-organized crime syndicates on the Mexican border that deal in international drug smuggling but also a growing number of Russian crime syndicates that have been caught moving large amounts of illegally gained money through U.S. and European banks (von Lampe, 2009). These large, globally organized crime organizations derive huge profits from supplying illegal goods and services to the public. Their major source of profit is illegal gambling in the form of lotteries, numbers games, off-track betting, illegal casinos, and dice games. Organized crime syndicates that operate through elaborate hierarchies control much of the illegal gambling. Money is transferred up the hierarchy from the small operator, who takes the customer's bet, through several other levels until it finally reaches the syndicate's headquarters. This complex system protects the leaders, whose identities remain concealed from those below them. The centralized organization of gambling also increases efficiency, enlarges markets, and provides a systematic way of paying graft to public officials.

Closely related to gambling and a major source of revenue for organized crime is loan sharking, or lending money at interest rates above the legal limit. These rates can be as high as 150 percent a week, and rates of more than 20 percent are common. Profits from gambling operations provide organized crime syndicates with large amounts of cash to lend, and they can ensure repayment by threatening violence. Most loans are made to gamblers who need to repay debts, to drug users, and to small businesses unable to obtain credit from legitimate sources.

Drug trafficking is organized crime's third major source of revenue. Its direct dealings in narcotics tend to be limited to imports from abroad and wholesale distribution. Lower-level operations are considered too risky and unprofitable and are left to others.

A large and growing source of revenue for organized crime focuses on human trafficking, particularly selling and buying women and girls for sexual servitude. Overall, 21 million persons, mostly girls and women, have been forced into sexual slavery, although not all of this is related to organized crime, of course. Human trafficking is discussed in depth later in this chapter.

It is particularly hard to fight organized crime, for several reasons. A major one is the difficulty of obtaining proof of syndicate activities that will be accepted in court. Witnesses rarely come forward; either they fear retaliation or they themselves are too deeply implicated. Since the top levels of the syndicate's hierarchy are so well insulated from those below them, witnesses are rarely able to testify against them. Documentary evidence is equally rare, since the transactions of organized crime are seldom written down. Finally, corruption of government officials hinders effective prosecution of organized crime.

Despite these obstacles, in recent decades, the FBI has made immense progress in its battle against organized crime; today, numerous reputed syndicate leaders are under indictment or in jail. Experts credit this breakthrough to a number of factors, the most prominent of which is that the FBI now devotes about one-quarter of its personnel to combating organized crime. Other important factors are using undercover agents in long-term investigations, pooling the resources of agencies that formerly competed with one another, and giving the FBI jurisdiction in narcotics cases. Especially significant has been the use of sophisticated surveillance techniques and computer technology. The witness protection program, in which witnesses are offered new identities, support, and protection in moving away from their organized-crime contacts, has also proven successful in a number of instances.

Public-Order Crimes

In terms of sheer numbers, public-order offenders constitute the largest category of criminals; their activities far exceed reported crimes of any other type. Public-order offenses include prostitution, gambling, use of illegal substances, drunkenness, vagrancy, disorderly conduct, and traffic violations. These offenses are often called victimless crimes because some people believe that they cause no harm to anyone but the offenders themselves. Society considers them crimes because they violate the order or customs of the community.

Public-order offenders rarely consider themselves criminals or view their actions as crimes. The behavior and activities of prostitutes and drug users, however, tend to isolate and segregate them from other members of society, and these individuals may find themselves drawn into criminal roles.

Prostitution is a particularly relevant example of public-order crime because of the way young women (and young men or adolescents) are exploited by older adults in the sex trade, both in the United States and in developing countries (Kristof and WuDunn, 2009, 2014). Prostitution is illegal everywhere in the United States except in some counties of Nevada. There is little pressure on other states to follow Nevada's example; however, proponents of legalization claim that prostitution will continue to exist regardless of the law and that recognizing this fact would bring many benefits: Legalization would make prostitutes' incomes taxable; it could eliminate or reduce the frequent connection of prostitution with crime and government corruption; and health regulations for prostitutes could be enacted and enforced, reducing the incidence of sexually transmitted diseases. They argue that prostitution is a victimless crime and that the legalization of brothels would result in a reduction of streetwalking and public solicitation, which disturb residents of the neighborhoods where they occur.

However, others say that prostitution does indeed have a victim: the prostitute. Many prostitutes have been trafficked for sex and are not working of their own free will. Prostitutes do not keep the money they earn, and they are subject to manipulation, violence, and the control of a pimp. Those against legalized prostitution also believe that society is the ultimate victim of prostitution and that legalization would not necessarily remove the prostitute from exploitation by pimps or organized crime figures. Moreover, legalizing prostitution might increasingly make it seen as normative, which might encourage more young women to enter "the life" and encourage more men to exploit these women.

Hate Crimes

Marcus was attacked by a group of white supremacists, targeted simply because he was black and walking in "their" neighborhood.

Colton was accosted by a group of men shouting "Die faggot," as he was leaving a gay bar. They chased Colton down as he tried to run away and they stabbed him.

Mohammad had his car spray-painted with the word "terrorist", while it was parked at the mall.

Lindsey walked up to a Sikh teen in the school hallway and said, "I'm going to cut your hair!" The Sikh teen replied, "For what? It is against my religion to cut my hair!" Lindsey replied, "I don't care," and later snuck up behind the Sikh teen and cut the victim's hair.

A hate crime is a traditional offense like murder, arson, or vandalism with an added element of bias. For the purposes of collecting statistics, the FBI Uniform Crime Reporting (UCR) Program collects hate crime data regarding criminal offenses motivated, in whole or in part, by the offender's bias against a race, religion, disability, sexual orientation, ethnicity, sex, or gender identity (FBI, 2014a, 2015). Only recently has the FBI begun keeping data on crimes motivated by bias related to gender (sex) and gender identity (transgender and gender nonconforming). Because determining the offender's subjective motivation is difficult to do, bias is to be reported only if investigation reveals sufficient objective facts to lead a reasonable person to conclude that the offender's actions were motivated, in whole or in part, by bias.

The FBI investigated the types of crimes that we now call hate crimes as far back as World War I; however, the FBI began to look at the issue more closely after the Civil Rights Act of 1964 was passed. This legislation moved the protection of civil rights from a local to a federal function. In particular, the murder of civil rights workers Andrew Goodman, James Chaney, and Michael Schwerner in Mississippi in June 1964 provided the impetus for a stronger federal effort to protect and foster civil rights for black Americans. The case was called MIBURN (for Mississippi Burning), and became the largest federal investigation ever conducted in Mississippi. Three years later, seven men were convicted of conspiring to violate the civil rights of the murdered civil rights workers and were sentenced to prison.

Even when hate crimes do not result in murder and mayhem, these criminal acts reveal hatreds and violent propensities that go far beyond what we usually see

Figure 5-3 Types of Hate Crimes (*N* = 6,933), 2013

SOURCE: FBI, 2014a.

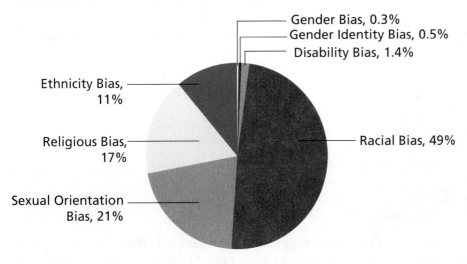

in violent or property crimes. Hatred of gays or people of other races and religions is widespread in all societies, but the propensity to express it through violent acts tends to be a phenomenon primarily of youth and young adults. Nevertheless, the emotions that motivate the deeds are taken from the adults who socialize young people. Throughout the world—in Kosovo, Rwanda, Northern Ireland, Israel, Pakistan, Russia, the United States, and elsewhere—adult hatreds spawn violence, which is often carried out by the young.

In an exhaustive study of hate crimes, the FBI concluded that 49 percent of such incidents in 2013 were racially motivated, 21 percent resulted from sexual orientation bias, and 17 percent were motivated from biases against religion, as shown in Figure 5-3. Almost two-thirds of hate crimes are against people; the other third involve crimes against property. Of those crimes against people, intimidation was the single most frequently reported hate crime offense, accounting for 44 percent of the total, and close behind were simple assault at 37 percent and aggravated assault at 17 percent (FBI, 2014a).

Gender-Based Violence

Cutiyo lives in a camp for internally displaced persons (IDPs) with her four children near Somalia's capital city, Mogadishu. Last night, she heard a woman being attacked, and the screams brought back the trauma of her own experiences of rape. Cutiyo believes that rape has become more pervasive at the camp and the situation for women and girls has deteriorated since she herself was first raped two years ago. "When we saw someone, we used to say, 'How are you.' Now when we see each other we ask, 'Were you raped today?'" The first time Cutiyo was raped she was asleep in her make-shift shelter with two of her youngest children. "The men took terms raping me while one of them stood guard outside. There were five of them. I struggled and screamed, but no one came to help me. My children were terrified." The next day, as word of the assault spread, the camp manager came to check on her and took her to the police station. As she explained the details of the assault, she got sick and vomited. They told her to go home and forget about the assault, but before they let her go, they made her clean the floor. She never returned to the police station to pursue the case. She was afraid the assailants would come after her and "do something worse." Four months later, Cutiyo was raped again at night in her tent by a different gang of assailants. Two months after that, her oldest daughter was raped. She was eleven years old.

gender-based violence

Any act of gender violence that results in or is likely to result in physical, sexual, or psychological harm and suffering to women, including threats of such acts, coercion, or arbitrary deprivations of liberty, whether occurring in public or private life.

Violence is a widespread problem around the world, and women and girls are overwhelmingly its victims. Because violence against women and girls is so common, it is often described as **gender-based violence**, defined by the United Nations General Assembly as any act of gender violence that results in or is likely to result in physical, sexual, or psychological harm and suffering to women, including threats of such acts, coercion, or arbitrary deprivations of liberty, whether occurring in public or private life.

Gender violence would include, among other things:

- Intimate partner violence
- Sexual abuse
- Forced prostitution
- Female genital mutilation
- Rape
- Honor killings
- Selective malnourishing or infanticide of female children

Gender-based violence is an epidemic and occurs in both developed and developing nations (Kristof and WuDunn, 2009; United Nations Population Fund, 2013). It causes more death and disability in women between the ages of 15 and 44 than cancer, malaria, traffic accidents, and war combined. Human Rights Watch (Human Rights Watch, 2014c) and the United Nations (UN Women, 2015), both international organizations dedicated to protecting the human rights of people around the world, report that many countries have horrendous records on addressing violence against women and girls. For example, in sub-Saharan Africa, many women are infected with HIV and will eventually die because the government has failed in any meaningful way to condemn, criminalize, or prosecute violence against women in the home. In Malawi, which has one of the highest rates of child marriage in the world, half of all girls will be married by their eighteenth birthday, and usually not by choice (Human Rights Watch, 2014b). In Somalia, rape is so common that it has been reported as "normal" (Human Rights Watch, 2014a). Women in Ecuador face prison sentences of one to five years for securing an abortion that results from a rape (Human Rights Watch, 2013). Some 42 percent of all women older than 15 in Turkey and 47 percent of women living in the country's rural areas—approximately 11 million women in total—have experienced physical or sexual violence at the hands of a husband or partner at some point in their lives (Human Rights Watch, 2011). In the United States, many women are sexually assaulted and raped, which is discussed further in Chapter 8, or abused by a spouse or intimate partner, discussed in Chapter 10.

Another important form of gender-based violence found all over the world is sex trafficking. **Human trafficking** (the illegal and highly profitable business of recruitment, transport, or sale of human beings into all forms of forced labor and servitude) is a tragic human rights issue. At least 21 million adults and children are in forced labor or sexual servitude at any given time, although precise numbers are impossible to know (U.S. Department of State, 2014). Some victims are forced into manual, military, or domestic labor, but many become sexual slaves. They are coerced, kidnapped, sold, deceived, or otherwise trafficked into sexual encounters, as illustrated in the story of Anu and Reeta in the box A Global View: Anu and Reeta. Increasingly around the world, girls are sought out in the mistaken belief that they are less likely to be HIV-positive. In reality, they are most vulnerable to HIV infections because their bodies are physically unready for sex and may tear more easily.

Human sex trafficking is not only slavery but also big business (Kristof and WuDunn, 2009, 2014). In fact, it is the fastest-growing business of organized crime and the third-largest criminal enterprise in the world. Most sex trafficking is international, with victims taken from places such as South and Southeast Asia, the former Soviet

human trafficking

The illegal and highly profitable business of recruitment, transport, or sale of human beings into all forms of forced labor and servitude.

Union, Central and South America, and other less developed areas. They are then moved to more developed nations, including Asia, the Middle East, Western Europe, and North America, including the United States (Walker-Rodriguez and Hill, 2011). Victims of sex trafficking can include not only girls and women but also boys and men.

Sexual trafficking results from a broad range of factors, including poverty, inequality, and economic crises. Globalization has triggered an influx of money and

A Global View

Anu and Reeta

For millions of people, Bombay is a city of dreams. It was the land of plenty, where the rich people lived. Among these people who harbored such ideas were Anu and Reeta, who were two teenage mountain girls from a small mountainous village about 105 kilometers northwest of the Nepalese capital, Kathmandu. Life was very difficult in their poor village where hardship, starvation, and scarcity was a villager's daily way of life. Sensing that their only hope was to run away, one spring day, the two girls left their village along with a group of other young girls and two men. Their journey brought them to a large market center for hand-made woolen carpets. Anu and Reeta got jobs in one of these factories and joined other carpet weavers, most of whom had come from the mountain regions to start a new life.

After about three months, an old woman who lived in Bombay offered to take them there. For the girls, it was as if their dreams had come true! The silk sarees and golden ornaments of the women returning from Bombay, and most of all their prestige, had made a deep impression on Anu and Reeta.

They eagerly agreed to go with the woman on the trip, having no idea what was in store for them. After many days of travel, when the girls were lost and confused, the woman sold them to an infamous brothel in Calcutta for 25,000 rupees each. Anu and Reeta were imprisoned by the man who bought them and were beaten, raped, and tortured. Once "broken," they were forced to become sex slaves in one of the largest red-light areas in the world, where dozens of young girls are brought every day through trickery, just like Anu and Reeta. The majority of the 40,000-plus prostitutes in this area of Calcutta are from Nepal.

After three cruel years of being forced to service men sexually, a seemingly magical change happened in their lives. Two of their regular customers rescued and married them. As it turned out, little changed in their lives; their husbands brought "customers" home and insisted that Anu and Reeta have sex with them. Their husbands beat and tortured their wives if they refused and kept all the money earned for themselves.

One day, Anu's husband told her they were leaving to go to Bombay. This long-held dream was now a nightmare because it separated her from her best friend, Reeta. Anu begged to stay put, but her husband ignored her pleas. After arriving in Bombay, her husband immediately sold her to a brothel for 12,000 rupees in another large red-light area in Asia, harboring around 100,000 prostitutes. Her husband disappeared. Anu met several other Nepali women in the brothel where she lived and worked and learned that all of them had a more or less similar story to tell.

Anu spent about 18 months in a dark room of this brothel receiving, on the average, four or five customers daily. She was let out of the room for only 20 minutes a day for "exercise." Anu was forced to entertain all types of customers, regardless of what they wanted from her. For her services, she received nothing but two meals a day and, occasionally, small tips given to her by kind customers. Bombay, once her land of dreams, was now nothing more than the dark room and filth of the brothel area.

She became infected with several sexually transmitted diseases and was admitted to a hospital where she was treated for several months. A sympathetic doctor was able to get her released her from the brothel, realizing that Anu was dying and had little time left to live.

She returned to her village after leaving the hospital, now having been gone for almost five years. Some of her relatives sympathized with her and her tragic situation and took her in. Others were less sympathetic, but left her alone. She died soon after.

As for Reeta, no one knows what happened to her.

Critical Thinking

Why didn't Anu and Reeta simply leave the brothel in Calcutta if they were unhappy there? If you were in Anu's position, what would you have done differently, if anything? What can be done to eliminate human trafficking?

goods to certain groups, further aggravating disparities between rich and poor and promoting new levels of consumerism. Influenced by patriarchal norms in which women and girls are disvalued, some families sell their daughters to traffickers or put them in vulnerable positions as domestic workers in far-off urban locations. Husbands, who have virtually complete control over their wives, may sell or "rent" them out for money.

Women and children who are trafficked into prostitution face many dangers (Territo and Kirkham, 2010; U.S. Department of State, 2014). In addition to injuries and disease associated with multiple sexual encounters, they become dangerously attached to pimps and brothel operators and become financially indebted to them. Moreover, they may become addicted to drugs that have been given to subdue them. If women and children do manage to escape and return to their families, they may be rejected because of the stigma associated with prostitution.

Biological Explanations of Crime

5.3   Evaluate biological explanations for crime and violence.

A medieval law stated that "if two persons fell under suspicion of crime the uglier or more deformed was to be regarded as more probably guilty" (Ellis, 1914; quoted in Wilson and Herrnstein, 1985, p. 71). This law and others like it illustrate the age-old and deep-seated belief that criminality can be explained in terms of certain physical characteristics of the criminal. An example of this point of view is the theory of crime advanced by an Italian physician, Cesare Lombroso, in the late nineteenth century.

Lombroso was convinced that there is a "criminal man," a type of human being who is physically distinct from ordinary human beings. In the course of his examinations of convicts both before and after their deaths, he developed the concept of criminal atavism—the notion that criminality is associated with physical characteristics that resemble those of primitive humans and lower primates: a sloping forehead, long arms, a primitive brain, and the like. Lombroso believed, in short, that there was such a thing as a "born criminal." Although this explanation was wrong, it served to initiate scientific inquiry into the causes of crime.

In the twentieth century, Lombroso's theory and other biologically based explanations of crime have been discredited and supplanted by sociological theories. However, some theorists (e.g., Wilson and Herrnstein, 1985) defend the identification of biological characteristics that appear to be predisposing factors in criminal behavior rather than full explanations of it. They believe certain inherited traits, such as an extra Y chromosome or a particularly athletic physique, may be correlated with a greater than average tendency to engage in criminal behavior. Research on the possibility of a link between criminality and an extra Y chromosome has consistently failed to demonstrate such a relationship.

Biology, Violence, and Criminality

Is violence simply part of human nature? Because it is such a common occurrence, some social scientists have argued that human aggressive tendencies are inherent or instinctual. According to this view, social organization helps to keep violent tendencies under control. Other experts argue that aggression is natural, but violence is not. In an exhaustive review of research on the causes of interpersonal violence, a panel of experts convened by the National Academy of Sciences concluded that there is no solid evidence to support the early neurological or biological explanations of violent behavior among men. The panel did note, however, that findings from studies of animals and humans point to several features of the nervous system as possible sources of such explanations and recommended continued research (Reiss and Roth, 1993).

Given the weight of evidence in favor of social and psychological explanations of violent behavior, this recommendation drew considerable criticism from social scientists.

In her response to the report, Dorothy Nelkin (1995), a well-known evaluator of scientific panels, argued that "biology is not destiny" and "it is not necessary to explain through biology why a child exposed to poverty and racism might become violent." The real source of violence, she believes, can be found in the growing inequality in the United States and other societies (Duster, 2003). This argument is an important sociological viewpoint, to which we will return in later chapters.

Sex Differences and Crime

Since nations began collecting systematic statistics on crime, analysts have realized that men are far more likely than women to commit crimes. Indeed, sex is one of the most obvious correlates of criminality (FBI, 2014b, 2014c). The different arrest rates for men and women may be a result of biological differences between men and women, along with different patterns of socialization. On average, males are biologically more aggressive than females. Higher levels of testosterone and androgens play a large part in this aggression.

However, in our society, men have been raised to be more aggressive than women, and they have therefore been more likely to commit certain crimes. Women generally have been regarded more protectively by the police and the courts; therefore, they have been less likely to be arrested and, if arrested, less likely to be punished severely, especially if they are wives or mothers. Despite the persistent differences in arrest rates of women and men, with men more than eight times more likely to appear in official crime statistics, rates of crime by women increased rapidly in the second half of the twentieth century. As more women are socialized under conditions of deprivation and abuse, we can expect that larger numbers will be recruited into street hustling, prostitution, and shoplifting, which in turn will account for increasing numbers of arrests. Indeed, today women make up about 12 percent of the total prison population in the United States, compared with only 7.7 percent in 1997 (U.S. Census Bureau, 2006).

Here is the cast of *Orange Is the New Black*, the popular television show that profiles female inmates in a women's federal prison. The lead character, Piper Chapman, is a woman in her thirties who is sentenced to fifteen months in prison after being convicted of a decade-old crime of transporting money for her drug-dealing girlfriend.

Sociological Explanations of Crime

5.4   Contrast the sociological explanations for crime and violence.

Demographic factors do not offer a complete explanation of crime. They do not, for example, explain why some juveniles and young adults drift into long-term criminal careers or why some young people never commit crimes. Nor do they tell us why some individuals, such as white-collar criminals, begin breaking laws during adulthood and middle age (Barlow and Kauzlarich, 2002). Thus, in addition to demographic analyses of crime, sociologists have proposed a number of theoretical approaches to explain why some people become criminals and others do not.

The first theoretical approach discussed here has evolved from conflict theory; it claims that most crime is either a form of rebellion by disadvantaged groups or a form of illegal exploitation by the rich and powerful. A second approach, derived from the functionalist perspective, holds that crime stems from the uncertainty about norms of proper conduct that accompanies rapid social change and social disorganization. A third major explanation applies the interactionist perspective to the study of how people drift toward criminal subcultures and become socialized for criminal careers.

Conflict Approaches

Conflict theorists identify inequalities of wealth, status, and power as the underlying conditions that produce criminal behavior. The groups in society that are more disadvantaged than other groups, such as the poor and racial minorities who experience discrimination, are thought to be likely to rebel against their situation. Criminality, in this view, is one way in which disadvantaged individuals act out their rebellion against society (Quinney, 1979).

INEQUALITY AND CRIME   As noted earlier in the chapter, official statistics show a high incidence of crime among members of the lower socioeconomic classes. Those statistics have fueled a sociological debate over the relationship between social class and criminality. For much of the twentieth century, many sociologists believed that people in lower socioeconomic classes were more likely than those in higher classes to commit crimes. Current research suggests that crime is distributed among all the social classes, but arrests are most often made in lower-class neighborhoods and prosecuted most strictly where defendants have limited access to legal help (Sanchez-Jankowski, 2008). While that finding may be true, social inequality—that is, the gap between haves and have-nots in a society—seems also to produce its own incentives for crime.

CROSS-CULTURAL RESEARCH   The United States has experienced tremendous increases in economic inequality in the past several decades. In comparison with other advanced nations to which it compares itself, the United States has developed one of the largest gaps between the rich and the poor segments of its population. Worldwide, there is a correlation between social inequality and homicide rates. This correlation does not prove that inequality causes homicide, but it suggests that the anger and resentment of people who do not share in the benefits of a rich society often find violent, even murderous, ways to vent their frustrations (Wilkinson and Pickett, 2010). In the nations of the former Soviet Union, for example, there have been rapid increases in poverty and in the number of wealthy individuals, many of whom have made their fortunes in connection with organized crime or other criminal activity. This rapid social change, in which it is no longer clear what the rules of behavior are or whether laws will be enforced, tends to produce lawlessness, corruption, and crime.

In the past few decades, as the total U.S. prison population has grown to record levels, the conflict perspective on crime has gained new adherents. Joseph Califano, former U.S. Secretary of Health and Human Services, is an example. Califano (1998) is highly critical of theories of crime that claim punishment will deter people from committing crimes. He sees the failure of U.S. drug policy and the failure to provide adequate rehabilitation as major causes of the boom in prison populations—which, he believes, only increases the chances that people in prison will become criminal recidivists later in their lives. In other words, in Califano's view, conflicts in U.S. society over how to deal with drug and alcohol abuse result in some types of crime and, more important, in the dramatic increases in the prison population. Other critical theorists, however, point to differences in income in a society as the most important contributor to crime (Wacquant, 2003).

RACE, ETHNICITY, AND CRIME   Every study of crime based on official data shows that blacks are overrepresented among those who are arrested, convicted, and imprisoned for street crimes. According to official statistics, blacks are arrested at higher rates than whites on charges of murder, rape, robbery, and other index crimes.

In any society, one can find differences in crime rates among various racial and ethnic groups. Chinese and Japanese Americans have lower crime rates than other Americans; Hungarian immigrants to Sweden have higher crime rates than native Swedes; Scandinavian immigrants to the United States get into less trouble with the police than do Americans of Anglo-Saxon descent. In the case of black Americans, however, the differences are pronounced (FBI, 2014b, 2014c).

It is possible that the overrepresentation of blacks in official crime statistics is partly due to greater surveillance of black communities by the police and to the greater likelihood that blacks who commit crimes will be arrested and imprisoned. The recent cases of Freddie Gray, a 25-year-old black man from Maryland who died of a spinal injury while in police custody; Michael Brown, a young unarmed black man who was shot and killed by a white police officer in Ferguson, Missouri; and Eric Garner in New York City who, while selling untaxed cigarettes, was placed in a chokehold by a white police officer, which resulted in Garner's death, demonstrate the possibility that race continues to be an influencing factor in how blacks are treated by the police. As shown in Figure 5–4, blacks are far more likely than whites to say that race is a factor in the juries' decisions not to press charges in these cases. For example, almost two-thirds of blacks believe that race was a "major factor" in these decisions, as compared with only 16 percent of whites who think this way.

However, victimization surveys show that police and court bias cannot be the sole cause of high rates of crime among blacks. Blacks are far more likely than whites to be victims of crime, and it is unlikely that these higher victimization rates are caused by whites who enter black neighborhoods to commit crimes (Wilson and Herrnstein, 1985).

A more plausible explanation is the disproportionately high percentage of blacks in the lower classes that, as you saw earlier, is associated with higher crime rates. Research by William Julius Wilson (1996) points to the growing isolation of some black communities from sources of jobs and income. This trend is especially marked in and around cities that have lost large numbers of manufacturing jobs, which once provided a relatively decent livelihood for black and other minority workers. In communities where legal employment is in short supply, people often turn to illegal activities.

The Functionalist View and Anomie Theory

Functionalists focus on issues to explain crime that are different from those proposed by conflict theorists. Anomie theory, also known as the goals-and-opportunities approach, is favored by many scholars who seek explanations of crime. Robert K. Merton (1968) argued that a society has both approved goals and approved ways of attaining them. When some members of the society accept the goals (e.g., home ownership) but do not have access to the approved means of attaining them (e.g., earned income), their adherence to the approved norms is likely to be weakened, and they may try to attain the goals by other, socially unacceptable means (e.g., fraud). In other words, criminal behavior occurs when socially approved means are not available for the realization of highly desired goals.

Anomie, the feeling of being adrift that arises from the disparity between goals and means, may vary with nationality, ethnic background, bias, religion, and other social characteristics. Some societies emphasize strict adherence to behavioral norms—the case in Japan, for example—and for those societies, the degree of anomie may be fairly low. Other societies place relatively more emphasis on the attainment of goals and less on their being attained in socially approved ways. Merton (1968) maintains that the United States is such a society. Identifying anomie as a basic characteristic of U.S. society, he lists several kinds of common adaptations. One of these, innovation, consists of rejecting approved practices while retaining the desired goals, which seems to characterize the

anomie

The feeling of being adrift that arises from the disparity between goals and means.

Figure 5–4 Public response to Jury's Decision Not to Charge in the Michael Brown (Ferguson) and Eric Garner Cases, by Race, 2014

SOURCE: Pew Research Center/*USA Today*, December 8, 2014.

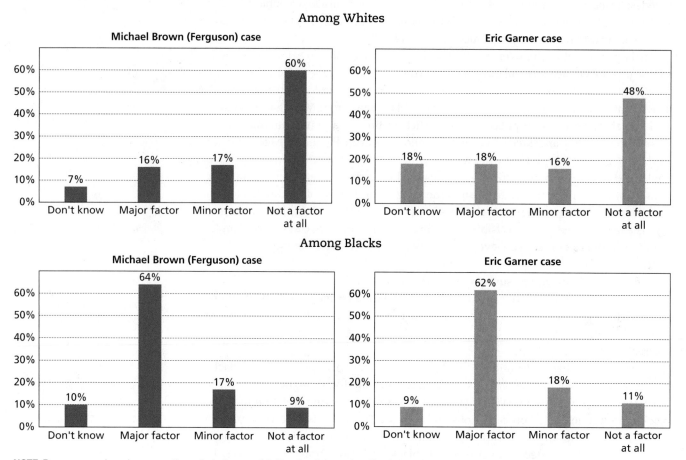

NOTE: Responses are based on perceptions of whether race (of either the victim or the officer) was a factor in the jury's decision.

behavior of certain lower-class gang members who have adopted socially approved goals but have abandoned socially approved methods of attaining them.

This rejection of approved practices occurs widely in groups with the greatest disjuncture among goals, norms, and opportunities. In this country, anomie of this type is most often found among those who have the greatest difficulty in obtaining a good education or training for high-paying jobs, particularly members of disadvantaged minority groups. Higher crime rates among such groups are not automatic, but they can happen when society erects barriers to the attainment of valued goals. If more attainable goals were set for people in lower socioeconomic classes, presumably there would be less disjuncture between goals and means and hence less anomie. For example, if low-cost rental housing were more widely available as a goal, more poor people could see how even low-wage jobs would improve their lives. When only luxury homes are available (and shown as models on television), then poor people sense the futility of conventional jobs or other approved means.

Research has provided some support for the premise on anomie, although there are types of crimes that it fails to explain adequately, such as assault for purposes other than monetary gain. This inability of the theory to explain certain crimes is related to the question most frequently raised about Merton's theory: Are financial success and material possessions only middle-class goals? Do members of the lower classes have different values and aspirations? Many sociologists believe that people in the lower classes tend to hold two sets of beliefs simultaneously. That is, they share the norms and values of the larger society but are forced to develop standards and expectations of their own so that they can deal realistically with their particular circumstances. For example, people in the lower classes share the view with the affluent that crime is bad, but they lack conventional means to attain goals such as secure jobs. They may consider illegal "hustles" as an alternative means to some goals, especially when these crimes seem justified by the behavior of others outside their communities whom they observe buying drugs or sex or other illicit goods and services. It is not surprising, therefore, that studies have supported Merton's view that anomie, rather than poverty itself, is a major cause of crime and delinquency (Conklin, 2007).

Interactionist Approaches

Interactionist explanations of criminal behavior focus on the processes by which individuals actually internalize the norms that encourage criminality. This internalization results from the everyday interaction that occurs in social groups. Interactionist theories differ in this respect from anomie theory, which sees criminal behavior as the result of certain aspects of social structure or from conflict theory which sees income inequality as the primary culprit of crime. Two examples of interactionist theories of criminality are (1) Edwin Sutherland's theory of differential association and (2) the subcultural approach to the study of juvenile delinquency.

Anomie is a feeling of being lost or adrift that can result from the disparity between goals and means. Jackson wants a better life than the one he was dealt, but how does he get there?

DIFFERENTIAL ASSOCIATION Introduced by Sutherland in 1939, the approach known as **differential association**, with some later modifications, still seems to explain the widest range of criminal acts. According to this theory, criminal behavior is a result of a learning process that occurs chiefly within small, intimate groups—family, friends, neighborhood peer groups, and the like. The lessons learned include both the techniques for committing crimes and, more important, the motives for criminal behavior. Law is defined not as a set of rules to be followed but as a hindrance to be avoided or overcome.

Briefly stated, the basic principle of differential association is that "a person becomes delinquent because of the excess of definitions favorable to violation of law over definitions unfavorable to violation of law" (Sutherland and Cressey, 1960, p. 28). People internalize the values of the surrounding culture, and when their environment includes frequent contact with criminal elements and relative isolation from noncriminal elements, they are likely to become delinquent or criminal. The boy whose most admired model is another member of his gang or a successful neighborhood pimp will try to emulate that model and will receive encouragement and approval when he does so successfully.

differential association

A theory that suggests that criminal behavior is a result of a learning process that occurs chiefly within small, intimate groups—family, friends, neighborhood peer groups, and the like.

DELINQUENT SUBCULTURES AND CONFLICTING VALUES The legal definition of crime ignores the effect of social values in determining which laws are enforced. Although judges and prosecutors use criminal law to determine the criminality of certain acts, the process of applying the law involves status and political power.

The issue of status is especially relevant to the study of delinquent subcultures. Albert K. Cohen (1971), for example, viewed the formation of delinquent gangs as an effort to alleviate the difficulties that gang members encounter at the bottom of the status ladder. Gang members typically come from working-class homes and find themselves measured, as Cohen put it, with a "middle-class measuring rod" by those who control access to the larger society, including teachers, businesspeople, the police, and public officials. Untrained in "middle-class virtues" such as ambition, ability to defer gratification, self-discipline, and academic skills, and therefore poorly prepared to compete in a middle-class world, they form a subculture whose standards they can meet. This delinquent subculture, which Cohen described as nonutilitarian, malicious, and negativistic, "takes its norms from the larger culture, but turns them upside down. The delinquents consider something right, by the standards of their subculture, precisely because it is wrong by the norms of the larger culture" (p. 28).

Other sociologists do not believe that the formation of delinquent subcultures is a frustrated reaction to exclusion by the dominant culture. Instead, they see delinquency as a product of lower-class culture. A study of street gangs by Walter Miller (2001), for example, identified six "focal concerns" of lower-class culture that often lead to the violation of middle-class social and legal norms:

- *Trouble.* Trouble is important to the individual's status in the community, whether it is seen as something to be kept out of or as something to be gotten into. Usually there is less worry about legal or moral questions than about difficulties that result from the involvement of police, welfare investigators, and other agents of the larger society.
- *Toughness.* Toughness comprises an emphasis on masculinity, physical strength, and the ability to "take it," coupled with a rejection of art, literature, and anything else that is considered feminine. This concept is partly a reaction to female-dominated households and the lack of male role models both at home and in school.
- *Smartness.* In the street sense of the term, smartness denotes the ability to outwit, dupe, or "con" someone. A successful pimp, for example, would be considered smarter than a bank clerk.
- *Excitement.* To relieve the crushing boredom of ghetto life, residents of lower-class communities often seek out situations of danger or excitement, such as gambling or high-speed joyrides in stolen automobiles.
- *Fate.* Fate is a major concern because lower-class citizens frequently feel that important events in life are beyond their control. They often resort to semimagical resources such as "readers and advisers" as a way to change their luck.
- *Autonomy.* Members of this group are likely to express strong resentment toward any external controls or exercise of coercive authority over their behavior. At the same time, however, they frequently seem to seek out restrictive environments, perhaps even engineering their own committal to mental hospitals or prisons.

Research by Gerald Suttles (1970) and Elijah Anderson (1992) on the street-corner culture of delinquents and other groups provides evidence of continuity in these values. Anderson, for example, writes that lower-class life has an internal coherence that is seldom appreciated by the casual observer. Both researchers show that teenagers and young adults in lower-class street corner groups make careful distinctions based on trust and confidence. They may be labeled street people by the larger society, but among themselves, they continually rank each other according to notions of respect and trust derived from their life on the street.

Controlling Crime

5.5 Identify ways to control crime and violence.

Efforts by the police, courts, and other agencies to control crime need to be understood as part of society's much larger system of social control (Conklin, 2007). In its broadest sociological sense, **social control** is the capacity of a social group, which could be an entire society, to regulate itself according to a set of "higher moral principles beyond those of self-interest" (Janowitz, 1978, p. 3). The Ten Commandments are a good example of what is meant by such values as they are translated into norms of everyday life. All of a society's ways of teaching the young to conform to its values and norms (i.e., socialization), together with the ways in which people in a society reward one another

---

What Do You Think?

Pick a specific type of crime, and compare and contrast what a conflict theorist, a functionalist, and a symbolic interactionist would see as the causes of that crime. What would they see as a solution to that crime?

---

social control

The capacity of a social group, which could be an entire society, to regulate itself according to a set of higher moral principles beyond those of self-interest.

for desired behaviors, contribute to social control. But every society also includes members who deviate from its norms, even strongly held norms like the prohibition against murder or thievery.

Techniques of social control range from informal processes such as gossip, ridicule, advice, and shunning to the formal processes embodied in the actions of the police, courts, corrections officers, and others who work in the criminal-justice system and in related systems such as the mental-health and juvenile-justice systems. It is important to recognize that, without the great array of informal controls that exist in every community and society, none of the formal systems would be of much use. If the police and the courts and other formal institutions of social control are at all effective, it is because most people are law-abiding and these institutions need deal with only a relatively small minority (which may still be a very large number in absolute terms).

Prison is primarily designed as a way to punish lawbreakers. The thought is that, if the punishment is severe enough, it will deter others from engaging in criminal behavior.

Most formal systems of social control rely on coercion rather than on reward. Surely this approach is true of courts and prisons. However, it is not true entirely; even in a prison or other correctional facility, a person can be rewarded for behavior that is defined as positive and as having favorable consequences for the individual and for society. The fact that coercion and punishment often far outweigh persuasion and reward reflects the different goals society has incorporated into its institutions of criminal law, that is, police, prosecution, and corrections (Garland, 2005). In examining how these formal institutions of social control operate (and sometimes fail to operate), it is important to remember that formal efforts to control crime can be classified under three headings: (a) retribution-deterrence; (b) rehabilitation; and (c) prevention.

Retribution-Deterrence

Retribution and deterrence—"paying back" the guilty for their misdeeds and discouraging them and others from committing similar acts in the future—have historically been the primary focus of efforts to control crime. Although retribution no longer follows the "eye for an eye, tooth for a tooth" formula (in which in earlier times slanderers had their tongues cut out, thieves had their hands amputated, and rapists were castrated), today's retributive orientation can be seen in public demands for longer sentences for such crimes as murder.

The punishments meted out to murderers, forgers, and other offenders are meant to serve several purposes. Besides the often-cited goals of preventing crime and rehabilitating offenders, punishment serves to sustain the morale of those who conform to society's rules. In other words, law-abiding members of society demand that offenders be punished partly to reinforce their own ambivalent feelings about conformity. They believe that, if they must make sacrifices to obey the law, then someone who does not make such sacrifices should not be allowed to "get away with it." Even those who view criminals as sick rather than evil, and who call for the "treatment" of offenders to correct an organic or psychological disorder, are essentially demanding retribution (Barlow and Kauzlarich, 2002).

Some criminologists, such as James Q. Wilson (1977, 1993), have suggested that society needs the firm moral authority derived from stigmatizing and punishing crime. Although Wilson grants that prisoners must "pay their debts" without being deprived of their civil rights after release from prison and without suffering the continued indignities of parole supervision and unemployment, he stresses the moral value of stigmatizing crime and those who commit it: "To destigmatize crime would be to lift from it the weight of moral judgment and to make crime simply a particular occupation or avocation which society has chosen to reward less (or perhaps more) than other pursuits. If there is no stigma attached to an activity, then society has no business making it a crime" (1977, p. 230).

Laws that establish penalties for crimes are enacted by the states and by the federal government. But concern for the rights of citizens who face the power of the state to enforce laws and inflict punishment is a prominent feature of the U.S. Constitution. The Fourth Amendment guarantees protection against "unreasonable searches and seizures"; the Fifth Amendment guarantees that citizens shall not be compelled to testify against themselves, be tried more than once for the same crime (double jeopardy), or be deprived of due process of law; the Sixth Amendment guarantees the right to a public trial by an impartial jury, the right to subpoena and confront witnesses, and the right to legal counsel; the Eighth Amendment prohibits "cruel and unusual punishment" and "excessive" bail or fines.

It is important to note these points because they are at the heart of conflicts about how fairly laws are enforced and how impartially justice is meted out. In the controversy over capital punishment, for example, opponents argue that it has become a form of cruel and unusual punishment. Others argue that because those who are condemned are often unable to afford adequate counsel, they have been deprived of their rights under the Sixth Amendment. Whatever one believes about such controversies, it is clear that the Constitution establishes the basis for protection of individual rights, but also leaves much discretion to citizens and lawmakers to establish the ground rules for how justice is to be carried out.

The role of the sociologist in these debates is to help establish a scientific basis for decision making. Empirical data collected by social scientists and government statisticians can be used to compare homicide rates in states that have the death penalty and states that do not. When this comparison is done, the results provide dramatic support for the contention that the death penalty does not deter murderers. As a form of retribution, it allows victims' family members to feel that justice has been done, but the data show that murder rates in states like Texas and Louisiana, where the death penalty is legal and executions routine, remain higher than average despite capital punishment.

Many social scientists also cite the negative effects of the severe anti-drug-dealing and anti-gun-possession laws put into effect in New York during the 1970s. In the years since these laws were passed, there have been significant increases in rates of drug dealing and arrests on drug and gun possession charges, despite much higher penalties for these offenses (Califano, 1998). Critics of such findings point out that seldom do criminals ask themselves before committing a crime, "Will I be punished if I am caught, and how severe will the punishment be?"

Research on the deterrent effects of punishment for crimes other than murder is made extremely difficult by the fact that few perpetrators of these crimes are actually caught and sentenced. For many decades, researchers have been able to show that whatever the punishment, a high likelihood of arrest is the greatest deterrent to crime. However, the arrest rate for property crimes is only about 20 percent (FBI, 2013a). These rates are based on crimes reported to the police. Because far more crimes are committed than are known to the police, the actual rates are even lower.

Rehabilitation

The idea of rehabilitating offenders, which has developed only during the past century and a half, rests on the concept of crime as a social aberration and the offender as a social misfit whose aberrant behavior can be modified to conform to society's norms—in other words, "cured." As yet, there are no clear guidelines concerning the form of rehabilitation that will be most effective with a particular kind of offender. Rehabilitation usually includes varying amounts of counseling, educational and training programs, and work experience. In the past, the programs that have had the most success have been those that prepare criminals to enter the world of legitimate work and help them actually secure and hold jobs after incarceration. However, such ambitious programs are unlikely to be implemented on a large scale.

By the 1990s, both the ideal and the practice of rehabilitation in prisons and among paroled offenders had reached a low point in what has historically been a cyclical process. Efforts to institute rehabilitation programs often follow efforts to increase the severity of sentencing. When it is shown that longer sentences and harsher punishment do not prevent crime or repeated offenses, society tends to shift toward efforts to rehabilitate criminals (Conklin, 2007).

Studies of **recidivism**—the tendency that a former inmate will break the law after release and be arrested again—have found no conclusive evidence that various approaches to rehabilitation, such as prison counseling programs or outright discharge, are more effective in reducing recidivism rates than more punitive alternatives. All that can be said is that some of the rehabilitation experiments undertaken to date—in particular, those that include extensive job training and job placement—have been more successful than others.

recidivism

The tendency that a former inmate will break the law after release and be arrested again.

In an in-depth study of the juvenile justice system and rehabilitation, sociologist Mark Jacobs (1990) found that rehabilitation is hampered by a maze of organizations and regulations. Juveniles are shuttled from one jurisdiction or program to another and are often the victims of inadequately funded training programs and haphazard supervision by overburdened caseworkers. Given the extreme splintering of the system—family courts, juvenile courts, schools, parents, parole officers, correctional officers, psychologists, and many more—the young offender is often deprived of the rehabilitation to which he or she is entitled. And no coherent set of laws holds anyone in the system accountable for the youth's rehabilitation; that is, no single institution, group, or person can be said to be at fault. In such a no-fault society, Jacobs argues, rehabilitation will remain a distant ideal.

The nature of the prison system itself is a major hindrance to rehabilitative efforts. Prisons remove offenders from virtually all contact with society and its norms, then subject them to almost continual contact with people who have committed crimes ranging from petty larceny and fraud to homosexual rape and murder (Garland, 2005). Often, inmates are abused by their guards. Within prison walls, offenders are punished by being deprived of liberty, autonomy, heterosexual contacts, goods and services, and the security normally obtained from participation in ordinary social institutions. At the same time, prisoners create a social order of their own. Adherence to the norms of prison life, which may be necessary for both mental and physical well-being, further separates inmates' goals and motivations from those of the larger society and makes it more difficult for them to benefit from whatever rehabilitative measures are available.

The most common type of rehabilitation program consists of work training. However, prison work is generally menial and unsatisfying, involving jobs such as kitchen helper or janitor. The difficulty of rehabilitating offenders in prison has led to various attempts to reform them outside prison walls. Perhaps the oldest and most widely used system of this kind is the work-release program, in which prisoners are allowed to leave the institution for part of the day or week to work at an outside job. Although this type of program was first authorized in Wisconsin in 1913, it has become widely used only since the mid-1950s. Today, many states and the federal government have authorized various kinds of work-release programs.

The idea of releasing convicted felons into society, even for limited periods, has met with considerable opposition, but in general, such programs seem to work well. Besides removing convicts from the criminal society in the prison, work-release programs reimburse the state for some of the costs of supporting them and allow the prisoners to support their dependents, thereby helping them stay off the welfare rolls. In addition, a work-release program is a practical step toward reintegrating offenders into society because many of those who successfully complete the program retain their jobs after release. In fact, in a classic study, Martinson (1972) found that the most effective single factor in rehabilitating offenders is a program of training for work following release; work during the prison term itself; and above all, job placement and training during probation.

The controversy over youthful offenders raises further questions about what kinds of corrections are most appropriate for this segment of the criminal population. So far, it does not appear that more punitive programs, or "boot camps," are more effective than others. In addition, it is extremely costly to keep teenagers in prison or detention; the costs range from $20,000 to $90,000 per year, depending on the state and the particular form of incarceration (Belluck, 1996). Many states, therefore, are experimenting with programs in which youthful offenders can attend school or job training while in prison or in lieu of prison (Barlow and Kauzlarich, 2002).

Programs like these involving school or job training are controversial because violent offenders are expected to do "hard time." Even so, a few states (New Jersey, Texas, Florida, and California) have created residential training schools for juvenile offenders. This approach involves an old concept that is being modified with new techniques for supervision, mentoring, and training (Snyder and Sickmund, 2006). Although such programs may not work for the most violent or hardened young criminals, many penologists believe that, when young inmates can be released to their communities with new skills and education, more positive options are open to them and they are less likely to drift back into a criminal lifestyle. But many young offenders return to extremely troubled families and peer groups. The more contact they have with professionals who can help them find alternatives to a violent home or neighborhood group, the better their chances—and society's—of avoiding crime and violence (Belluck, 1996; Gardner, 2005).

Prevention

The idea of preventing crime and delinquency before they occur is an attractive one, but like rehabilitation, it is difficult to implement. Crime prevention is customarily defined in three different ways: (1) the total of all influences and activities that contribute to the development of a nondeviant personality; (2) attempts to deal with conditions in a person's environment that are believed to lead to crime and delinquency; and (3) specific services or programs designed to prevent further crime and delinquency.

Programs based on the first definition include measures designed to improve the social environment, such as improved housing and job opportunities for those who live in low-income neighborhoods. Although one of their goals may be the reduction of crime and delinquency in the target area, it is rarely their primary goal. Moreover, studies of youths involved in antipoverty programs have not demonstrated a positive correlation between such participation and reduced delinquency rates. The most positive results are found in evaluations of Job Corps and other education, job training, and social skills programs in which young people at risk are given a chance to leave their neighborhood peer groups.

The second definition includes efforts based on Sutherland's theory of differential association (Sutherland and Cressey, 1960), such as efforts to reduce children's exposure to the antisocial and/or illegal activities of people around them, to improve their family life, and to create a viable and conforming social order in the community itself. Several projects of this sort have been attempted; some, like the Chicago Area Project (discussed shortly), have had notable success.

Most crime prevention programs attempt to work within the third definition—prevention of further delinquency and crime. They include not only well-established approaches such as parole, probation, and training schools but also more experimental programs. It is difficult to compare these approaches with those attempted under the other two definitions because they deal with quite different sets of circumstances.

An early prevention program, the Chicago Area Project, was established in the mid-1930s in the Chicago slums, where immigrant families were no longer able to control their children because of a weakening social order. The project sought to develop youth welfare programs that would be viable after the project leaders had left. It was assumed that local youths would have more success than outside workers in establishing recreation programs (including summer camping), community improvement campaigns, and programs devoted to teaching and assisting delinquent youths and even some adults who were returning to the community after release from prison. The project not only demonstrated the feasibility of using untrained local youths to establish welfare programs but also indicated a possible decrease in the delinquency rate (Kobrin, 1959). This model has been used successfully in many communities to diminish gang violence.

What Do You Think?

Develop a crime prevention program based on at least one of the dimensions listed above. What theory best informs your program: conflict theory, functionalism, or symbolic interactionism?

Social Policy

5.6 Explain the policy considerations surrounding gun control.

The fact that violent crimes and property crimes have declined in recent years has not been noted by most Americans; instead, they tend to believe that crime is on the upswing. Almost two-thirds of Americans believe that there is more crime today in the nation than there was one year ago (Gallup, 2014). This widespread misperception may be partly the result of sensational episodes of violence that dominate cable television stations, the fact that more people are incarcerated than ever before, as well as a widespread fear of identity theft, which polls show is the crime that is currently most feared. This persistent fear despite the facts likely influences attitudes toward gun ownership and gun control.

Gun Control

In recent decades, there has been a heated discussion between those calling for stricter federal supervision of the purchase and sale of firearms, particularly the cheap handguns that are readily available in many areas, and those who believe that Americans have the right to own guns with minimal interference from the government. In 1993, in response to what had come to be perceived as a national epidemic of gunshot injuries and deaths, as well as the earlier shooting of President Reagan and his press secretary James Brady, Congress finally passed the Brady Act and other legislation to limit the access of felons to handguns and assault weapons. In 1996, Congress attempted to repeal the ban on assault weapons, but President Clinton vetoed the repeal. During the George W. Bush administration, support for gun control, and even the ban on assault weapons, declined as the National Rifle Association (NRA) and its allies continued to hold sway over a majority of Republican elected officials.

Demonstrators take part in a rally against gun violence and ask for stricter policies regarding who can buy guns and where guns can be purchased. The rally in New York City is a combined effort of health care providers, victims and their families, youth organizations, union members, and faith leaders.

The shootings at Virginia Technical University in Blacksburg in 2007 and Sandy Hook Elementary School in 2012, among many other mass shootings, led to renewed calls for better enforcement of existing laws requiring background checks for gun buyers. But even these devastating mass murders did not result in a strong push for gun control among Democrats, who, unlike the Republicans, tend to fear the influence of gun advocates.

Opponents of gun control legislation include the outspoken NRA, which constitute one of the most powerful interest groups in the nation. The NRA draws much of its strength from areas of the nation where hunting is popular and where there is a strong feeling that people need to protect themselves and their families. Members of the NRA claim that gun control measures would violate the "right to bear arms" that is contained in the Second Amendment to the United States Constitution. This position is a strong one—and one that most political leaders are unwilling to challenge directly. Opponents of gun control claim that the decision to commit murder has nothing to do with possession of a gun; a killer can stab, strangle, poison, or batter a victim to death. Gun control, therefore, would make little difference.

Although this argument sounds logical, it ignores the lethal potential of guns, which are about five times more likely to kill than knives (the next most commonly used murder weapon), according to those who advocate greater controls and protections against guns. And since most murders are spontaneous results of passion rather than carefully planned acts, it follows that the easy availability of guns is likely to increase the death rate in criminal assaults. In most cases, murders are a result of three factors: impulse, the lethal capacity of the weapon, and the availability of the weapon. Limiting guns would eliminate or at least reduce the latter two factors.

Future Prospects

Fifty years ago, the majority of the U.S. public favored tighter controls over firearms that stop short of a complete ban on handguns. That support has greatly diminished, as shown in Figure 5–5. By 2014, 52 percent agreed that it is more important to protect the rights of Americans to own guns, versus 46 percent who say that it is more important to control gun ownership (Pew Research Center, 2014).

Support for gun control measures usually correlates closely with the nation's murder rate. Throughout the 1980s and 1990s the murder rate varied between about 8 and 10 per 100,000, and support for stricter laws was more popular. As the murder rate declined through the 1990s and early 2000s, so did support for gun control. However, as recent school shootings bring media attention to the horrific

Figure 5–5 Percentage of Adults Expressing Support for Protecting Rights of Americans to Own Guns vs. Greater Importance Controlling Gun Ownership

SOURCE: Pew Research Center, December 10, 2014.

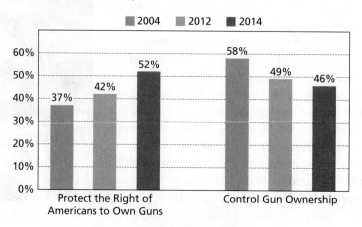

consequences of guns in the wrong hands, the NRA has become more vocal in their campaign that "guns don't kill … people do." The NRA promotes the idea that greater gun ownership (in the right hands, of course) actually promotes safety. The NRA has experienced its largest jump in membership ever, and public opinion is swinging in their direction.

Going Beyond Left and Right

No one likes crime, except perhaps the criminals themselves. All Americans are concerned about crime and violence, regardless of political persuasion. However, what differs between conservatives and liberals is the opinion on the best ways to tackle crime and violence in the community. Conservatives are less likely to support gun control and see gun ownership as a potential solution to crime, while liberals are more likely to believe that access to guns is a cause of crime, particularly violent crime.

While the political debate continues, there have been some efforts to decrease the number of available guns in high-risk communities—that is, places where there have been recent histories of high murder rates and deaths of bystanders. Congress and the Justice Department have cooperated in instituting a number of programs such as the Kansas City experiment that attempted to show a relationship between seizures of guns and reduced numbers of crimes committed with guns. A target police beat covering a neighborhood where homicides were twenty times above the national average was selected. Officers with special training in detecting people who were carrying weapons patrolled the beat. On another beat, similar in demographic and crime characteristics, the police continued to use their traditional methods. After 29 weeks of operations, statistics revealed that gun crimes had dropped significantly on the beat with the special patrols. Drive-by shootings also decreased, as did homicides of all kinds. Programs like this one can appeal to both liberals and conservatives, if the price is right.

Summary

- A crime is any act or omission of an act for which the state can apply sanctions. According to the Uniform Crime Reports (UCR) of the Federal Bureau of Investigation (FBI) there has been a steady decline in the number and the rate of violent and property crime in the United States. However, exact statistics are difficult because of ambiguity about whether certain acts are crimes, police discretion regarding what laws to ignore and which ones to enforce, and reporting accuracy.

- Violent personal crimes include rape, assault, robbery, and various types of homicide—acts in which physical injury is inflicted or threatened. Occasional property crimes include vandalism, check forgery, shoplifting, and some kinds of automobile theft. White-collar crimes are those in which people break the law as part of their normal business activity. Corporate crimes are committed by a corporation or an individual working on behalf of an organization (rather than an individual working on his or her own behalf), usually for monetary gain.

- Organized crime is a term that includes many types of criminal organizations, from large global crime syndicates to smaller local organizations whose membership may be more transient. Public-order offenses include prostitution, gambling, use of illegal substances, drunkenness, vagrancy, disorderly conduct, and traffic violations. Hate crimes include traditional offenses such as murder, arson, or vandalism with an added element of bias against a race, religion, disability, sexual orientation, ethnicity, gender, or gender identity. Gender-based violence includes acts likely to result in physical, sexual, or psychological harm and suffering to women, including threats of such acts, coercion, or arbitrary deprivations of liberty, whether occurring in public or private life.

- Early criminologists proposed that crime and violence had a biological basis in some people; however, most experts now argue that, although aggression is natural, violence is not. Men commit far more crime than do women, which may be explained by men's greater level of aggression and the different ways that men and women are socialized.

- Conflict theory proposes that most crime is either a form of rebellion by members of disadvantaged groups or a form of illegal exploitation by those who are rich and powerful. The functionalist perspective holds that crime stems from the uncertainty about norms of proper conduct that accompanies rapid social change and social disorganization. The interactionist perspective tends to focus on the study of how people drift toward criminal subcultures and become socialized for criminal careers.

- Efforts by the police, courts, and other agencies to control crime include (a) retribution and deterrence, (b) rehabilitating offenders, and (c) crime prevention.

- Support for gun control usually correlates closely with the nation's murder rate. However, with the recent media attention around mass shootings, the NRA has become more vocal in their campaign that "guns don't kill … people do."

Chapter 6
Poverty amid Affluence

Learning Objectives

6.1 Discuss the extent of social inequality in the United States.

6.2 Recognize the importance of wealth.

6.3 Summarize how poverty is measured, and identify who are poor.

6.4 Compare and contrast Marxian and Weberian approaches to social stratification and class.

6.5 Identify the consequences of poverty for children and adults.

6.6 Analyze the individualistic, structural, and cultural explanations for poverty.

6.7 Assess the implications of social policy in terms of welfare reform.

Sheila could be considered "poster material" for poverty. Unlike the popular stereotypes, she is not a teenager, she is not lazy, she is not unwilling to work, and she doesn't have eight children by eight different fathers. Instead, she is a quiet, unassuming 40-year-old, trying to raise her 12-year-old daughter on her own after her husband walked out on them. He pays no child support and never has, and she has great difficulty supporting her daughter on the meager income she earns from her housecleaning job. Sheila and her daughter live in a small, dank, one-bedroom apartment "on the other side of the tracks," as it is known to those in the relatively well-off community. Her daughter never invites over friends from school; she is too embarrassed for them to see her home. They have a car, but it is 16 years old, and it often doesn't work. Right now it needs a new battery, but there is no money to buy one, so it sits in the driveway while they both walk to where they need to go. Once payday comes again, they will have a little extra money to ride the bus, shaving hours off their commute time.

A few years ago, Sheila turned to welfare programs for financial help. She received $241 a month for the two of them, about $300 in food stamps, and the security of having Medicaid if a health problem arose. But she is no longer eligible for welfare because she no longer meets the strict time limits and work requirements of the program. Instead, she makes do on her labor-intensive housecleaning job—cleaning toilets and mopping floors—that pays $9 an hour. Her daughter now babysits on weekends and turns her money over to her mother to help pay the rent.

As Sheila tells it, there is always a stressful undercurrent in their lives. Will they have enough money to live on? Will they be able to pay their rent or have to risk eviction? Will they ever be able to fix their car? Despite her careful planning, something unexpected comes up almost every month. Last month, both of them needed winter coats, and even the used ones at the Goodwill set them back $30. Now her daughter has outgrown her athletic shoes, and Sheila shudders when she thinks how much they may cost. To make up the difference in the budget this month, she decided to turn the heat down in the house to 58 degrees. They simply cannot afford both heat and shoes.

The stress of not having enough money is always gnawing at Sheila, and she believes it is responsible for her poor health. She has seen a doctor to find what is ailing her, but they cannot pinpoint the problem. It is probably stress, they tell her. Sheila knows that a better-paying job would alleviate this stress, but her reading, writing, and math skills are low, typical for someone who did not complete high school. Sheila has always worked, usually at housekeeping jobs, and has always been poor. But she values education, and knows that it is her daughter's ticket out of poverty. "Do good in school," she tells her daughter.

In the United States and throughout the world, the gap between those who are rich and those who are poor is widening. Of the 7.3 billion people on the planet, 2.4 billion are so poor that they must subsist on the equivalent of two dollars a day or less (The World Bank, 2014). Although poor people in the United States, including Sheila and her daughter, do not routinely face starvation like poor people might elsewhere, the decline in their nutrition, health, and overall well-being is of serious concern. Many Americans go to bed hungry; live in substandard, rat-infested housing; and live in neighborhoods that are too dangerous to go outside. This level of poverty and social inequality, challenging enough on its own, can also contribute to a wide array of other social problems.

Why does poverty exist? What can people do about it? This chapter offers many different explanations for the persistence of poverty amid growing affluence. It also highlights the wide ideological differences in policies proposed for dealing with poverty. You might wonder how something that is so obviously harmful could have solutions that are so controversial.

By almost any standard measure, the United States ranks as one of the wealthiest nations in the world. Its gross domestic product (GDP)—the total market value of all final goods and services produced within the United States in one year—was over $15 trillion at the end of 2013. Dividing the GDP by the total population to derive the per capita GDP (a crude but commonly used measure of the comparative wealth of nations) shows that the United States ranks well above most other countries, with a GDP of over $50,000 per person. Other advanced industrial nations such as France, Germany, Denmark, and the United Kingdom fall below this figure by $10,000 or more

A Global View

Adeola's Story

Adeola, who is only 13, is already known as a thief in his rural community located in northern Nigeria. He steals whatever he can: fresh eggs from the neighbors' chickens, vegetables from the gardens, or trinkets from old ladies at the Saturday market that he can later sell for a profit. When people see him, they shoo him away like he is a fly—annoying but inevitable. But when they catch him stealing, they often let him keep some of the goods, even though they tell him, "Adeola! Stop that! Thieving is no way to live!"

They tolerate some of Adeola's antics because he is responsible for taking care of his younger sister and brother, who are only 10 and 7 years old. They are three of the millions of children who have been orphaned by AIDS (see Figure 6–1). Like most of the other orphans, Adeola and his siblings live in sub-Saharan Africa, which is notoriously poor and ravaged by HIV and AIDS. Their father died last year from the disease that everyone whispers about, but won't discuss aloud. Their mother soon fell weak and died earlier this year. Adeola, the dutiful older brother, quit school when his father became too ill to work and tended to their small farm. But, now with his mother gone too, keeping up the farm is too much for him, and there is no money to invest in new crops. Instead, to provide for himself and his siblings, he steals what he can. But the community is poor, and therefore Adeola, like the rest of the community, struggles for the basics of food, shelter, and clothing.

Poverty is especially severe in rural areas of Nigeria, where up to 80 percent of the population lives below the

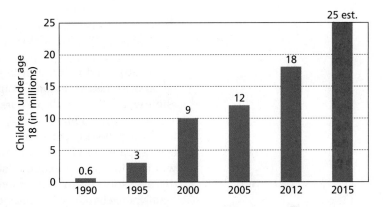

Figure 6–1 Increase in Children Orphaned by AIDS in Sub-Saharan Africa, 1990–2015

NOTE: "Orphaned" includes children who lost at least one parent to an AIDS-related cause.
SOURCES: AVERT, 2015; United Nations Children's Fund and UNAIDS, 2006.

poverty line. The country's rural women and men who are poor depend on agriculture for food and income. About 90 percent of Nigeria's food is produced by small-scale farmers who cultivate small plots of land and depend on rainfall rather than irrigation systems. The poorest groups barely eke out a subsistence living and are often low on food. Drought, deforestation, and overgrazing are ongoing problems. Rural infrastructure in Nigeria has long been neglected. Investments in health, education, and water supply have been focused largely on the cities. As a result, the rural population has extremely limited access to services such as schools and health centers, and about half of the population lacks access to safe drinking water. This neglect affects agricultural production. The lack of rural roads impedes the marketing of agricultural commodities, prevents farmers from selling their produce at reasonable prices, and leads to spoilage. The farmers' isolation also limits their access to new equipment and technology, further reducing their yields.

The productivity of the rural population is further hindered by ill health, particularly HIV and AIDS, tuberculosis, and malaria. Parents become ill and either can no longer care for their crops or die, leaving hungry children like Adeola and his siblings in their wake.

SOURCES: International Fund for Agricultural Development, 2014; United Nations Children's Fund and UNAIDS, 2006.

Critical Thinking

Why should Americans be concerned about poverty in developing nations like Nigeria? If countries like Nigeria are so poor, why do they continue to engage in risky behaviors such as unprotected sex, which jeopardizes their livelihood (and lives) even further?

(International Monetary Fund World Economic Outlook Database, 2014). Meanwhile, many countries in Africa have a GDP of less than $1,000 per person. Since a large part of this money goes for food, many people around the world have very little in the way of food or material goods.

You will see in this chapter that the gap between those who are rich and those who are poor has widened all over the world. In the world today, there are a record-breaking 2,089 billionaires and 17 million millionaires, but there are hundreds of millions of homeless people (Matthews, 2015; Withnall, 2015). While hunger and malnourishment are widespread in the developing world, Americans spend upwards of $60 billion per year on ways to lose weight and to lower their caloric intake (Williams, 2013). These growing disparities between rich and poor throughout the world have direct effects on the situation of the poor population in the United States because many jobs are "exported" to countries where extremely poor people will accept work at almost any wage. The increase in world poverty also contributes to environmental degradation and political instability and violence, which drain resources that might be used to meet a nation's domestic needs. A Global View: Adeola's Story gives a glimpse into these multiple harsh consequences of poverty.

In the United States, the standard of living for most Americans has been declining, while the concentration of wealth in the hands of a few fortunate people has been expanding (Thompson and Smeeding, 2014). As you read this chapter, you will first look at the extent of social inequality in the United States. Then you will discover some of the consequences of the inequality that characterizes U.S. society. Finally, the chapter will present several theories to explain the presence of poverty in one of the world's most affluent nations and some social policies designed to reduce or eliminate poverty.

Although this chapter focuses on poverty in the United States, you will have a chance to also make appropriate comparisons to other countries. However, it is important to note that the experience of poverty is based on conditions in one's own society. People like Sheila and her daughter feel poor (or rich) with reference to others around them, not with reference to very poor or very rich people elsewhere in the world. The experience of living in the United States as a teenager in a family for which every penny counts—there is rarely enough money for new clothes or a family car or out-of-town trips—can be as emotionally difficult to bear as life in poverty anywhere. An American who is poor draws little comfort from the fact that poor people in the United States are relatively better off than poor people in Bangladesh.

Social Inequality: The Haves and the Have-Nots

6.1   **Discuss the extent of social inequality in the United States.**

Although equality of opportunity is a central value of U.S. society, equality of outcome is not. In other words, most Americans believe everyone should have the same *opportunity* to achieve material well-being, but they do not object much to inequality in the *actual situation* of different groups in society. The middle-class standard of living is portrayed over and over again in media representations of American lifestyles. But this image ignores both the handful of extremely rich Americans and the tens of millions who share only minimally in the nation's affluence. To observe inequality and understand its impact, you need only compare a few aspects of the lives led by the affluent and the poor in our society.

The affluent live longer and better and can afford the best medical care in the world, the finest education, and the most elegant possessions (Burgard and King, 2014; Reardon, 2014; Wolff, 2014). In addition, by discreetly influencing politicians, police officers, and other public officials to promote or defend their interests, they can obtain social preference and shape government policies. This capacity to purchase both possessions and influence gives those who are extremely wealthy a potential power that is grossly out of proportion to their numbers.

For those who are poor, the situation is reversed. Although America's poor people seldom die of starvation and generally have more resources than the hopelessly poor populations of the developing world, they lead lives of serious deprivation compared with others in their own culture. This relative deprivation profoundly affects the style and quality of their lives. It extends beyond the mere distribution of income and includes inequality in education, health care, police protection, job opportunities, legal justice, housing, and many other areas. Poor people require more medical treatment and have longer and more serious illnesses. Their children are more likely to die than those who are more affluent, and their life expectancy is below the national average. They are more apt to live in deteriorating neighborhoods located near toxic waste sites. Given their despair, they are more likely to become criminals or juvenile delinquents, and they contribute more teenage pregnancy, alcoholism, and violence to U.S. society than any other socioeconomic group.

Those Who Are Rich

6.2 Recognize the importance of wealth.

What does being "rich" mean? It is more than just the size of a paycheck that makes a person rich because many rich people do not even work or have salaries. Instead, it is important to consider **net worth**, a frequently used measure of wealth, which refers to the value of savings and checking accounts, real estate, automobiles, stocks and bonds, and other assets (minus debts). Inequality, when considered in terms of net worth, is staggering: 1 percent of all households hold over one-third of all personal wealth. The distribution of income, just one slice of wealth, is also unequal: The wealthiest 20 percent of households receive almost 60 percent of all income, while the poorest 20 percent receive less than 4 percent (Domhoff, 2013). And the gap between the haves and have-nots has widened in recent years (Fry and Taylor, 2013).

The United States has a long history of attempting to redistribute wealth through taxation and other policies. These policies have been instituted for three reasons: (1) Those who are wealthy get more out of the economic system and can afford to pay more taxes; (2) the wealthy have a greater investment in the economic system and should pay more to maintain it; and (3) redistributing some income from the rich people to the poor people is fair and just in a democratic society. Ideas such as these led to the establishment in the 1930s of President Franklin D. Roosevelt's New Deal, which, together with the Great Society legislation proposed by President Lyndon B. Johnson in the 1960s, created most of this country's welfare institutions and programs.

The United States is considered a **welfare state**, meaning that a significant portion of the GDP is taken by the government to provide certain minimum levels of social welfare for those who are poor, elderly, disabled, and vulnerable in other ways. In a welfare state, governments at all levels attempt to smooth out the effects of recessions through programs such as unemployment insurance, and the transfer of some wealth from the rich segments of the population to the poor segments through programs like Medicaid or through cash welfare, known as Temporary Assistance to Needy Families (TANF). However, these programs are often stigmatized, and those who receive them are looked down upon (Seccombe, 2015).

In general, the competition for resources—not only income and wealth but also what money can buy (e.g., exclusive vacations,

What Do You Think?

Why are poor people more likely to have a mental illness than those who are not poor? What is the cause and what is the effect? That is, does poverty contribute to mental illness, or does mental illness contribute to poverty?

net worth

For a person or entity, the value of savings and checking accounts, real estate, automobiles, stocks and bonds, and other assets (minus debts).

welfare state

A type of country in which a significant portion of the GDP is taken by the government to provide certain minimum levels of social welfare for those who are poor, elderly, or disabled, among others.

A debutante and guests attend the Sixtieth International Debutante Ball at the posh Waldorf-Astoria hotel in New York. She and her guest typify the upper class, and, like most people, tend to socialize with other people who are of similar economic standing.

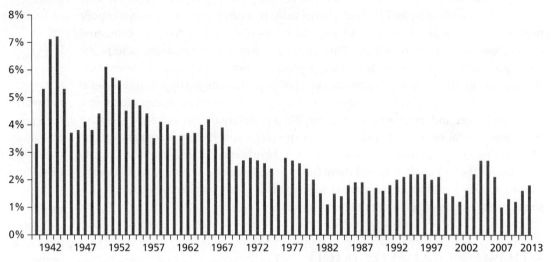

Figure 6–2 Corporate Income Taxes as a Percentage of Gross Domestic Product, 1942–2013

SOURCE: Tax Policy Center, 2013.

comfortable housing, top-quality education)—heavily favors those who are rich. For example, people in upper income brackets have many legal ways to avoid taxes. If they purchase real estate, they can obtain substantial tax reductions for mortgage interest payments at the same time that the property is increasing in value.

However, several other aspects of the welfare state's programs have escaped stigmatization. These programs have been nicknamed "wealthfare," and consist of subsidies for rich people. For example, government import–export policies are designed to protect certain industries such as textiles or steel and the jobs of their employees from foreign competition. However, when the government limits imports of a certain product, competition is stifled and consumers must pay the prices demanded by domestic manufacturers. Similarly, when the government agrees to rescue failing corporations, as it has done with railroads, banks, and aerospace companies, the owners of substantial portions of the corporations' capital are most likely to benefit. It can be argued that the poor segments of the population are relative losers in these situations since, as a result, less government money is available for social programs. Likewise, when government revenues are raised through such means as sales taxes on gasoline, those with less money effectively bear a greater share of the burden because the proportion of tax they pay is higher relative to their smaller incomes than it is for those who are rich. Corporations are heavy users of the nation's resources but pay a declining share of taxes to help support roads, education, improvements in air quality, and the like. Figure 6–2 shows this decline, expressed as a percentage of the nation's GDP from 1942 to 2013. As you can see, during World War II, corporate income taxes equaled about 7 percent of GDP, but have been declining since then. During the 1950s through 1970s, corporate taxes averaged about 3 percent of GDP. Today, they hover around 1 to 1.5 percent. Who is picking up the slack?

Are Rich People a Social Problem?

By the turn of the twenty-first century, the ten richest Americans had amassed a total net worth of $333 billion (Kroll and Dolan, 2013). At the same time, increasing numbers of low-wage workers had seen the value of their earnings diminish even in a period of low inflation. The gains of the rich segment of the population and the losses of the nonrich segment are clearly shown in Tables 6–1 and 6–2 (DeNavas-Walt and Proctor, 2015). Note the extraordinary growth in income of the top one-fifth of American households.

Table 6–1 Share of Income Received by Each Fifth and Top 5 Percent of Households

	1990	2000	2014
One-fifth with lowest income	4%	4%	3%
Next lowest one-fifth	10%	9%	8%
Middle one-fifth	16%	15%	14%
Next highest one-fifth	24%	23%	23%
One-fifth with highest income	47%	50%	51%
Top 5 percent	19%	22%	22%

SOURCE: DeNavas-Walt and Proctor, 2015.

Table 6–2 Mean Household Income Received by Each Fifth and Top 5 Percent, 2014

Lowest One-Fifth	$11,676
Next Lowest One-Fifth	$31,087
Middle One-Fifth	$54,041
Next Highest One-Fifth	$87,834
Highest One-Fifth	$194,053
Top 5 Percent	$332,347

SOURCE: DeNavas-Walt and Proctor, 2015.

Today, that group earns about 51 percent of all income, up from 46.6 percent in 1990. The average income for a household in this upper income bracket is $194,053. A quick look at the top-earning 5 percent shows that the richest Americans have fared particularly well over the past few decades. The top 5 percent earned 22 percent of all income, up from 18.5 percent in 1990, averaging $332,347. In contrast, the average household income for the 20 percent of American households in the lowest income group is only $11,676, and their share of income has declined from 3.8 percent to only 3 percent. Note, too, that earned income is likely a small portion of the rich's entire set of financial resources. It is likely that this top group also holds substantial wealth. The recession years ushered in greater wealth inequality than had existed since 1980, in large part because home values, which plummeted during this time, make up a large part of middle-class wealth, but only a small part of the portfolios of the wealthiest 1 percent (Wolff, 2014). In other words, the rich are getting richer, and the poor are getting poorer.

But are those who are rich really a *social problem*? Remember how Chapter 1 defines this concept. Here, it is sufficient to point out that, although there is no consensus in American society that rich people themselves are a social problem, there is evidence of concern that the ethic of individual success and enrichment may actually hamper efforts to develop new policies to address the problems of poverty (Reich, 1998).

What Do You Think?

Do you know anyone from a household that would be classified in the top 5 percent in terms of wealth, or would you classify yourself as being in that group? Does that person (or do you, if applicable) stay separate from others in lower-income groups?

Those Who Are Poor

6.3   **Summarize how poverty is measured, and identify who are poor.**

Although those who are rich are able to take advantage of various ways of improving their situation, those who are poor face an entirely different set of circumstances. *Poverty* is a deceptively simple term to define. Certainly those who are poor have less money than other people. In addition, the money they do have buys them less. Poor people must often purchase necessities as soon as they have cash (e.g., when a welfare check or paycheck arrives). They cannot shop around for sales or bargains, and they can be taken advantage of by shopkeepers who raise their prices the day welfare checks are delivered. When they buy on credit, poor people must accept higher interest rates because they take longer to pay and are considered poor credit risks. Inflationary price increases affect poor people first, and more severely. The cost of essential consumer goods may rise suddenly (e.g., when energy costs increase as a result of a crisis in the Middle East), but the wages of the lowest-paid people and government income assistance payments rise slowly if at all.

For most people, poverty simply means not having enough money to buy things that are considered necessary and desirable. Various formal definitions of poverty have been offered. John Kenneth Galbraith (1958) stressed the sense of degradation felt by those who are poor and concluded that "people are poverty stricken when their income, even if adequate for survival, falls markedly behind that of the community" (p. 245). Poverty may mean a condition of near starvation, bare subsistence, or any standard of living measurably beneath the national average. A generally agreed-on, scientifically based, and more specific definition of *poverty* is needed to deal more effectively with poverty as a social problem.

The Poverty Line

Official U.S. government definitions of poverty are based on the calculation of a minimum family food budget. The U.S. Department of Agriculture regularly prepares estimates of the cost of achieving a minimum level of nutrition, based on average food prices. It is assumed that an average low-income family must spend one-third of its total income on food; thus, by multiplying the family food budget by three, the government arrives at a poverty income that can be adjusted for the number of people in the household and for changes in the cost of food. The official measure is also corrected at least annually for changes in the cost of living as measured by the consumer price index (CPI). In 2014, this inflation-corrected, official poverty line for a family of four was $24,230. By this measure, 46.7 million people, or 14.8 percent of the U.S. population, were below the poverty line as shown in Figures 6–3a and 6–3b (DeNavas-Walt and Proctor, 2015).

This official poverty measure was developed in 1965 by Mollie Orshansky, an economist at the Social Security Administration, who reasoned that the primary measure of the adequacy of a person's level of living is food consumption. However, although this definition was accepted as the official means of establishing a poverty line, there has been continuing controversy and debate over definitions of poverty and their implications for social policy.

Some conservative social scientists and policymakers are critical of the way poverty is measured. In particular, they have argued that if benefits provided to poor people, such as reduced-price school lunch programs, Medicaid, and subsidized housing, are included in the calculation of income, then the extent of poverty is much less than is generally believed. These differences in measurement could affect whether millions of Americans are classified as being above or below the official poverty line.

Figure 6–3a Number of People in Poverty, 1959–2014 (Millions)

SOURCE: DeNavas-Walt and Proctor, 2015.

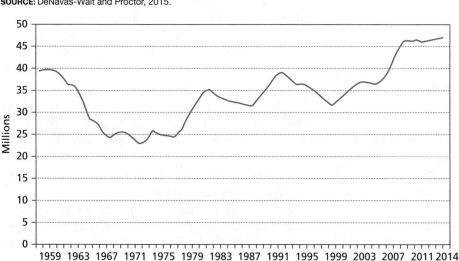

Figure 6–3b Percentage of U.S. Population in Poverty Rate, 1959–2014

SOURCE: DeNavas-Walt and Proctor, 2015.

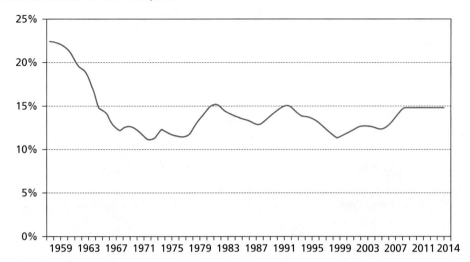

But those who believe that existing poverty measures actually underestimate the size of the poor population also have strong arguments on their side. First, when the poverty line was first created, it averaged about half the median income of Americans; however, it has eroded and now only represents about one-third of the median household income. In addition to the cost of food, other costs such as childcare, home heating, and housing also have increased substantially over the past few decades. In other words, not only are there more poor people than officially counted, these people are considerably poorer than those who were counted decades ago.

Second, there is the argument that taxes, alimony, out-of-pocket health care expenses, and many work-related expenses should be excluded from the income figures used to determine poverty status because this money cannot be used to purchase food and other necessities of life.

Third, the official poverty definition does not take into account regional differences in the cost of living and therefore neglects hundreds of thousands of poor people in high-cost cities like Washington, D.C., while overestimating the number of poor people in smaller towns, where the cost of living is lower. Finally, many researchers and advocates for poor people note that the poverty threshold is extremely low and that people living above that level are still quite poor.

When the poverty formula was first developed, conveniences such as telephones and indoor plumbing were not necessarily part of Americans' expectations of a minimally adequate level of living. And at that time, far fewer children lived with only one parent and far fewer women were employed. Childcare, a significant expense for most working families (and essential if a single parent is to work), was not the major and necessary expense it is today. With these factors in mind, many suggest that the poverty line is far too low, and underrepresents the real number of needy people in America.

Who Is Living in Poverty, and Why?

The 14.8 percent of the population living in poverty represents many people across different types of family structures, races, ages, and personal situations, as shown in Table 6–3. For many people, poverty is a short-term event caused by a single, temporary crisis, for example, an unexpected job loss, an accident or illness, or a divorce. For others like Sheila, introduced in the opening vignette, poverty is a longer-term event. Both situations can cause suffering and hardship, and it is estimated that about half of Americans will experience a bout of poverty sometime in their lives. The following sections take a closer look at who is living in poverty and why.

Table 6–3 People and Families in Poverty (15 Percent of Total Population) by Selected Characteristics, 2014

Characteristic	Percentage of Those in Poverty
Age	
Under 18	21% ·
18–64	14%
65 and over	10%
Race	
White (Non-Hispanic)	13%
Black	26%
Asian and Pacific Islander	12%
Hispanic	24%
Family Type	
Married Couple	6%
Female-Headed	32%
Male-Headed	16%

SOURCE: DeNavas-Walt and Proctor, 2015.

SINGLE-PARENT FAMILIES Of all children under the age of 18 in the United States, 21 percent are living in poverty. Put another way, more than one child in five lives in a family with a household income so low that they are considered poor. The situation is especially common for children in single-parent families headed by women. Today, nearly one-third of female-headed families live below the poverty threshold (DeNavas-Walt and Proctor, 2015).

One reason for such high levels of poverty among these families is the decrease in subsidies for low-income children and their mothers. For example, food assistance benefits from SNAP (formerly known as the Food Stamp Program) are the nation's most important anti-hunger program. It helps more than 47 million low-income Americans afford nutritional food each month. Nearly three-quarters of SNAP participants are in families, most often single-mother families (Bean, 2011).

> Some nights were really hard. The hunger would be gripping my stomach and all I could think about was food. We just didn't have enough of it at the end of the month. Simple as that. What we did have we gave to the little ones because you can't let babies go hungry. (Tania, age 15)

In late 2013, Congress significantly cut the funding for SNAP. This cut resulted in fewer people now eligible for SNAP and a reduction in the size of a SNAP benefit (Bolen, 2015; Dean and Rosenbaum, 2014). The amount of SNAP money received by a family of four dropped from $668 to $632 a month, a decrease of $36, or $432 a year (Sherter, 2013). Thirty-six dollars a month may not sound like much, but these critical dollars can make the difference between a child getting enough food to eat and going hungry. The declines in food aid to poor children highlight the stark differences between the United States and most other affluent nations in the efforts made at the national level to combat child poverty.

CHILDREN One out of five American children lives in poverty. The United States leads all affluent nations in the proportion of its children it allows to live in poverty, according to a recent UNICEF study (UNICEF Innocenti Research Centre, 2013), as illustrated in Figure 6–4. Of 35 nations reviewed by UNICEF, only Romania has a higher percentage of children in poverty (internationally defined as living in a household below half of the median income). Why does the United States fare so

Figure 6–4 Relative Child Poverty Rates, Percentage of Children Aged 0-17 Living in Households with Equivalent Incomes Below 50% of National Median

SOURCE: UNICEF Innocenti Research Centre, April 2013.

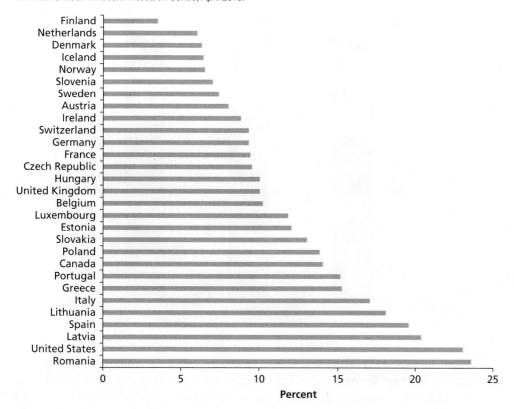

poorly? Most other affluent industrial nations have far more effective and generous social safety nets, welfare systems that assist significant proportions of children and their families in their efforts to escape poverty (Ermisch et al., 2012).

Most industrial nations do a far better job helping parents in low-income families obtain quality childcare services that will allow them to work steadily while their children are adequately cared for. In the United States, in contrast, childcare is often a major obstacle for low-income single mothers who want to work and could be successfully employed. Their jobs may have split shifts or night hours, which make it difficult to find and afford childcare (Laughlin, 2013). The stress and fatigue associated with nonstandard hours or evening and night shifts may adversely affect parenting, contributing to less responsiveness and sensitivity toward the children (Li et al., 2012). Yet, quality childcare for children, especially poor children, is crucial to their social and cognitive development. Substandard childcare, in contrast, can have devastating and long-lasting results.

A study by the National Institute of Child Health and Human Development illustrates this point. Researchers had tracked more than 1,300 children since 1991. The results showed that obedience and academic problems among children who received low-quality care in their first 4½ years of life persisted through their fifteenth birthdays. Researchers and experts who commented on the study agreed that these results point to the likelihood of lifelong problems, which would include higher than expected rates of school failure and dropping out, higher rates of incarceration, and greater likelihood of teenage parenthood (Stein, 2010).

Father involvement and child support enforcement are other major areas of concern for poor mothers struggling to work and raise children simultaneously. Noncustodial parents (who are mostly, but not exclusively fathers) have a legal

What Do You Think?

Why do you think that other countries are more helpful to their low-income families than the United States is to its? Do you think the United States should be more like those countries, or should those countries be more like us?

Figure 6–5 Level of Child Support Payment Among Custodial Parents with a Formal Agreement or Court Order, 1995, 2005, 2011

SOURCE: Grall, 2013.

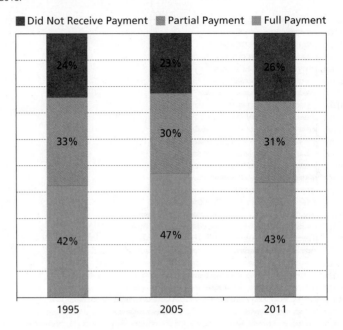

responsibility to support their children. In the past, these payments were arranged privately between the parents, and not surprisingly, the amount of these awards varied widely. More recently, the federal government has mandated child support and will prosecute a person who willfully avoids paying, but still, the data remain unimpressive. Too often, men are unwilling or unable to pay court-ordered child support payments. Only about half of custodial parents have some type of formal agreement or court award. And among those who do, less than half of custodial parents receive the full amount of the award, as shown in Figure 6–5 (Grall, 2013).

MINORITY GROUPS It should be noted that although whites are by far the largest group among poor families, blacks and Hispanics are overrepresented, given their size in the population. For example, about 27 percent of blacks and 26 percent of Hispanics have incomes below the official poverty level, compared with about 10 percent of the non-Hispanic white population and 12 percent of Asian Americans. In other words, a larger proportion of the black and Hispanic populations have incomes below the poverty level than do whites and Asian Americans, but in terms of actual numbers of individuals, more whites can be counted as being in poverty (DeNavas-Walt and Proctor, 2014).

Several factors are thought to be responsible for the lower earning power of blacks and Hispanic workers and their higher rates of poverty. Among the most important are low wages, discrimination, and educational deficits. The proportion of people of black or Hispanic background working at low-wage and minimum-wage jobs is higher than the proportion of whites in such jobs. The minimum wage was raised from $5.15 per hour to $7.25 per hour in three increments beginning in 2006, but has now fallen far behind the poverty threshold. There is a movement under way to raise the minimum wage, and in fact several cities, including Los Angeles, San Francisco, Seattle, and New York have opted to raise their minimum wage to $15 an hour over the course of a few years (Luckerson, 2015; Patel, 2014).

The discrimination experienced by blacks, Chicanos, Puerto Ricans, Native Americans, and other minority groups in housing, education, and health care exacerbates the effects of low income. In fact, discrimination often accounts for their inability

Figure 6–6 Educational Extremes, by Race and Ethnicity, Age 18 and Older, 2014

SOURCE: U.S. Census Bureau, January 5, 2015 (Educational Attainment in the United States: 2014 Detailed Tables).

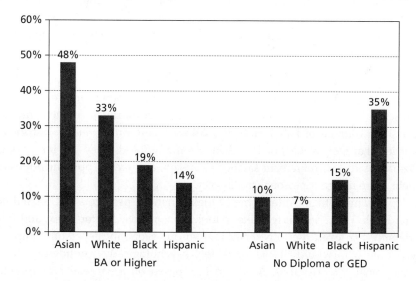

to find higher-paying employment. Members of these groups are often forced to pay higher rents and to live in dilapidated or deteriorating dwellings, and the quality of predominantly minority schools is often inferior to that of predominantly white schools. In these and other areas, the disparity between blacks and whites in both opportunity and treatment is evident.

Although the education gap between minorities and whites is narrowing, members of minority groups who have low levels of education encounter greater difficulty finding jobs that will lift them out of poverty than do whites with the same low levels of education. Figure 6–6 shows this education gap quite clearly by looking at both ends of the education spectrum. Whites and Asian Americans are much more likely than blacks or Hispanics to have achieved a bachelor's degree or higher, whereas blacks and Hispanics are overrepresented in the lower rungs of education.

THOSE WITH DISABILITIES Americans have an ambivalent attitude toward poverty (Jansson, 2012). We recognize that poor people are not always responsible for their situation, yet those who must turn to public assistance (sometimes referred to as the "dependent poor") are often pictured as lazy, shiftless, or dishonest. Their private lives are scrutinized because those who have more money are often suspicious of them and worry that they may be taking advantage of the rest of society.

However, a significant proportion of those who are poor are people who have struggled with disabilities from childhood. A serious disability may beget poverty because jobs are limited and other aspects of life may be hampered. However, poverty itself may beget further disabilities, especially in children. Although disabilities are not unique to poor families, children in low-income households are more likely to be chronically ill or disabled because of the environmental risks of substandard housing and low-income neighborhoods and because of deficiencies in nutrition and health care. Moreover, childhood disability not only correlates highly with later adult dependence, but also can create extreme hardship for single parents already burdened by the basic effects of poverty.

Event Poverty

Some families are prone to what is known as *event poverty*. In the event of illness, loss of one of the jobs, marital discord, or pregnancy, for example, the family could easily lose half its income and then plunge well below the official poverty level. When a

What Do You Think?

Asian Americans have been nicknamed "model minorities." Why are they so financially successful compared with other minorities?

manufacturing plant or other place of employment closes abruptly, hundreds of workers may be thrown out of work. Or a family may become impoverished because of high medical bills (we will return to this subject shortly) or, as Americans have seen so dramatically in the last decade, because they have lost everything in a storm or other natural disaster. The following sections discuss some of the events and situations that can lead to poverty.

A SEVERE RECESSION   The recession that began in 2008 has largely abated at this writing in late 2015. Today, unemployment rates hover around 5 percent for all U.S. residents and around 10 percent for blacks, but in 2010, unemployment rates were twice as high (Bureau of Labor Statistics, 2015b). Many breadwinners lost their jobs (or worried that they would) or had their income reduced. They lost their homes to foreclosure, used their retirement savings to live on, and racked up tremendous credit card debt, often filing for personal bankruptcy.

Take a moment to consider some of these financial problems and related issues in more depth. What does it feel like to look for work week after week, and find no job offers? When even the lowest-tier jobs in our economy have stiff competition, many people who would like to work feel psychologically wounded by the lack of employment opportunities. A Gallup Poll based on a nationally representative sample found that people who have been unemployed more than six months are far more likely than those who are employed to feel stress, sadness, and worry (Marlar, 2010).

"Rhonda" is one of many people who are looking for a good job with good pay (Seccombe, 2015). She has a high school diploma, but does not have a college degree. She is a single mother, and would like to raise her young son Bobby without relying on government assistance. Rhonda, who wants a permanent full-time job but has been stymied by the tremendous growth in part-time, temporary positions, explains (Seccombe, 2015, p. 177):

> *Hopefully I can get me a job. A permanent job. My sister's trying to get me a job where she works. I put my application in last week. And it would be a permanent job. When you go through those agencies, it's just temporary work. It's just whenever they need you, and it's unfair too. Every job I've found is through this temporary agency, like Manpower, but it's only temporary. And they cut my check and my food stamps, and when my job ends, it's like you're stuck again. So I'm trying to find a permanent steady job. But it's hard around here. I've been out looking for work, and hoping that something comes through.*

Rhonda may be surprised to learn that temporary agencies are doing very well in this recessionary economy. Manpower is one of the largest private employers in the United States, ranked 129 in the Fortune 500 list of large companies, and has revenues of about $21 billion worldwide. It serves over 400,000 employer clients and has placed 12 million workers in more than 80 countries and territories (ManpowerGroup, 2015). Rhonda's experience with temporary agencies is not unique, however, and the success of these agencies reflects the growing divide between the haves and the have-nots.

As the recession begins to improve, it is also apparent that immigration and the fate of the nation's immigrants also hinge to a large degree on the changing feelings of economically pinched Americans and their elected officials.

IMMIGRATION   Immigration is a different kind of life event that may be associated with poverty or with efforts to escape from it. In many of the world's wealthier nations, particularly in the United States, an increasing proportion of poor people are immigrants. Almost 25 percent of the increase in poverty since the early

---

What Do You Think?

Do you know anyone who has been hit hard by the recession? How did the recession affect him or her?

1970s has occurred among recent immigrants and their children. Although it is important to remember that the majority of Hispanics and Asians are neither impoverished nor immigrants, poor people from Mexico, Central America, the Caribbean, and Southeast Asia are among the largest immigrant groups today (Motel and Patten, 2013; Pew Research Center, April 4, 2013). Many live in the poorest city neighborhoods and rural counties. Most of the adults work full-time, often in the lowest-paying and most undesirable jobs. Most lack health insurance, and many fear that changes in welfare laws will make it impossible for them to send their children to school or to receive the same benefits as others who pay taxes.

The issue of whether poor and unskilled immigrants drive down the wages of those who are working and poor and represent a burden to taxpayers generates a great deal of controversy. Politicians who wish to capitalize on the resentment some Americans already feel toward immigrants often use this argument. For example, Arizona passed a law giving police authorization to check on the immigration status of anyone they reasonably suspect of being in the United States illegally. The failure to carry identification of one's legal status would be a crime. Opponents argue that such a law violates civil liberties and encourages racial profiling.

LOW WAGES   We see poor people working all around us, in restaurant kitchens, on landscaping crews, installing roofs in the hot sun, and taking care of our loved ones. According to the U.S. Department of Labor, the "**working poor**" are individuals who spent at least 27 weeks in the labor force (working or looking for work), but whose incomes fell below the official poverty level. Of all the people in the labor force for at least 27 weeks, about 10 million people, or about 7 percent of the nation's labor force, are working at wages so low that they remain below the official poverty threshold (Bureau of Labor Statistics, 2014). The majority of the working poor are women.

working poor

Individuals who, within a year, spent at least 27 weeks in the labor force (working or looking for work), but whose incomes fell below the official poverty level.

The situation of those who are working and poor has deteriorated over the past few decades. There are several reasons for this downhill slide, including technological changes that eliminate certain kinds of jobs, globalization (which exports jobs to lower-wage regions of the world), the reluctance of the middle and upper classes to share their wealth with less fortunate members of society, and the general attitude of Americans toward poverty.

UNEMPLOYMENT OR LIMITED PART-TIME WORK   In addition to those who are working but cannot escape from poverty because of low wages, an increasing proportion of people in the United States either are working part-time or are out of the labor force and receiving minimal benefits. These people live on a bare-bones budget and have difficulty providing for the basics in life. Their numbers are growing at a rapid rate. Sociologists often consider "extremely" poor people or households to be those living at 50 percent of the poverty threshold, which would amount to roughly $13,000 a year for a family of four or about $6,000 for one person. Using this definition, over 20 million Americans, 7 million of whom are children, live in extreme poverty.

Others apply the criterion used by the World Bank in international work: A person is described as living in extreme poverty if he or she lives on less than $2 a day (Shaefer and Edin, 2012). In recent years, the percentage of the population considered extremely poor has reached the highest point in four decades. A University of Michigan study notes that 1.5 million U.S. households, comprising about 2.8 million children, were living on $2 or less in income per person per day in a given month. This figure represents almost 20 percent of all poor non-elderly households with children. About 866,000 households appear to live in extreme poverty across a full calendar quarter.

Poverty and Social Class

6.4 **Compare and contrast Marxian and Weberian approaches to social stratification and class.**

In every society, people are grouped according to their access to the things that are considered valuable. This phenomenon is **social stratification**—a pattern in which individuals and groups find themselves in different positions in the social order, positions that enjoy varying amounts of access to desirable goods and services.

The stratification of individuals and groups according to their access to various occupations, incomes, and skills is called social **class stratification**. A social class is a large number of people who have roughly the same degree of economic standing; to varying degrees, depending on the culture, people may enter or leave a given class as their economic fortunes change. Marxian social theory emphasizes a form of this stratification. For Marx and his followers, the basic classes of society are determined by ownership or nonownership of the means of production of goods and services. The owners are called capitalists, and those who must sell their labor to the capitalists are the workers.

Marx referred to members of capitalist societies who are poor and not in the labor force as the **lumpenproletariat**. This class is made up of people at the margins of society who either have dropped out of the capitalist system of employment or have never been part of it at all. Marx thought of the lumpenproletariat as comprising the criminal underworld, street people, the homeless, and all the other categories that make up the marginal members of humanity. He believed capitalism would always impoverish the working class because the owners of capital would seek to exploit the workers to the fullest extent possible, and as a result, the lumpenproletariat would expand and become ever more dangerous to the stability of capitalist societies.

The German sociologist and historian Max Weber was critical of the Marxian perspective. Weber accepted most of the Marxian analysis of economic classes, but he did not believe capitalism would inevitably cause the expansion of the lumpenproletariat. Moreover, he pointed out that other valued things besides wealth are distributed unequally in modern societies. For example, status (or prestige) and power are both highly valued, and their distribution throughout society does not always coincide with the distribution of wealth. People who have made their money recently, for example, are often accorded little prestige by capitalists who made their money much earlier.

In their studies of the American system of social stratification, social scientists have developed a synthesis of the Marxian and Weberian approaches. They have devised designations like upper class, upper middle class, middle class, working class, and poor class, which combine the Marxian concept of economic class with the Weberian concept of status.

Sociologists have pointed out that the ways in which people distinguish among these class levels have both *objective dimensions*, which can be measured by quantifiable variables such as income or by membership in certain clubs, and *subjective dimensions*, which are the ways in which individuals

social stratification

A pattern in which individuals and groups find themselves in different positions in the social order, positions that enjoy varying amounts of access to desirable goods and services.

class stratification

The stratification of individuals and groups according to their access to various occupations, incomes, skills, and opportunities.

lumpenproletariat

Members of capitalist societies who are poor and not in the labor force, according to Karl Marx.

The hit PBS television series, *Downton Abbey*, vividly illustrates the concept of social stratification. In early twentieth-century England, some people were born to be aristocrats, and others were born to be servants.

evaluate themselves and others (and the way they feel about people in the various objective classes). Objectively, Americans base their estimations of social class position more or less on the Marxian model. Major employers, powerful political leaders, and very wealthy people are assigned to the upper class. Managers of large firms and relatively well-off people with successful businesses and professional practices (e.g., physicians) are in the upper middle class. People who are employed as middle-level managers and averagely paid professionals (e.g., teachers) are in the middle class. People who earn lower salaries or depend on hourly wages make up the working class (e.g., janitors). People who lack steady work or drift back and forth between legitimate employment and other ways of obtaining income are considered the poor class.

The subjective dimension of social class becomes evident when people are asked to identify the class to which they belong. For example, the proportion of people who classify themselves as poor is considerably lower than the proportion that is classified as such by the Census Bureau. Part of the reason for this difference is the stigma associated with poverty. Many poor people have low-paying jobs and hesitate to identify themselves as poor even when they are; instead, they place themselves in the working class.

All of these social class categories are extremely difficult to define precisely. The designations "middle class" and "working class" are especially problematic. In the booming 1950s and 1960s, when the GDP doubled each decade, it appeared that the distinctions between the working and middle classes were becoming blurred and meaningless. For a period of about 20 years, more people shared in the benefits of expanding wealth. Lower-income workers were adopting lifestyles that seemed to make them indistinguishable from the middle class of salaried employees and professionals. In that period, only the extremes of social stratification were easy to identify: the wealthy at the top and the poor at the bottom. Otherwise, the incomes of most Americans were giving them access to what sociologist David Riesman called the "standard package" of goods and services available in a wealthy society (Riesman, Glazer, and Denney, 1950). That package included a home, a car, and consumer goods such as TV sets, air conditioners, and washing machines (Blumberg, 1980).

The growing strength of labor unions allowed workers to bargain for higher wages and better benefits than ever before. The growth of public educational institutions made education available to more people and provided training for new jobs and professions. Social welfare programs like Social Security, workfare, food stamps, Medicare and Medicaid, affirmative-action programs, youth programs, unemployment insurance, and many other kinds of government support seemed to offer the hope that the degree of inequality in American society would be reduced still further. However, events of recent decades have reversed the trend toward greater affluence for all, and the gap between those who are poor and those who are affluent has increased. Further discussion of this subject will continue in later sections of the chapter.

Consequences of Poverty

6.5   Identify the consequences of poverty for children and adults.

Poor families face a higher degree of stress, disorganization, and other problems in their lives. Poverty is difficult for everyone, but weighs especially heavily on children's physical, social, and emotional health.

How Poverty Can Affect Children

Poor children are vulnerable. They tend to exhibit more antisocial behavior and are more likely to drop out of school or become teenage parents, are more likely to suffer from depression, and are in poorer health (Bloom, Jones, and Freeman, 2013). Naturally, not all poor children suffer these outcomes; many poor children are the models of success. However, they are more likely than other children to face a host of serious challenges. How does poverty exert its influence? Figure 6–7 summarizes the pathways through which poverty hurts children (Seccombe, 2007). Poverty contributes to:

- Inadequate health and nutrition
- Lower-quality home environment
- Parental stress and mental health problems
- Fewer resources for learning
- Housing problems
- Poor-quality neighborhoods

Figure 6–7 Pathways from Poverty to Adverse Child Outcomes

SOURCES: Adapted from Children's Defense Fund, 2005; Brooks-Gunn and Duncan, 1997; and Seccombe, *Families and Their Social Worlds*, 3e. © 2016 Pearson.

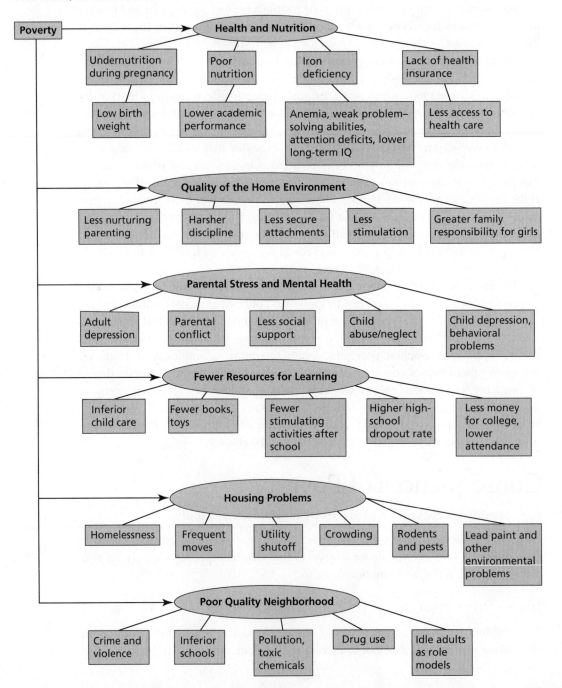

Slide Show

Growing Up Poor

Poor children are vulnerable. They face many challenges as they grow. This slideshow illustrates some of the difficulties of growing up poor.

Hunger and malnutrition are not just problems in the developing world. Many American adults and children are also food insecure and are at risk for a number of health problems. Here, people are handed bread during a food distribution by a local food bank.

Parents living in poverty face a high level of stress, depression, and mental health problems related to their situation. Finding enough money for food, shelter, and clothing is a constant struggle.

Poor children generally have fewer resources for learning. There are fewer books available at home, and they are less likely to go to preschool because of the cost. Consequently, many children who are poor begin school already academically behind their peers.

This 3-year-old and her mother just received shoes and school supplies during a charity event to help more than 4,000 underprivileged children at a mission in the Skid Row area of Los Angeles. Skid Row contains one of the largest populations of homeless people in the United States. This mother and her daughter stay at a shelter when room is available, but must often resort to staying under bridges.

A pedestrian walks through a neighborhood with run-down homes in Selma, Alabama 50 years after the historic civil rights march from Selma to Montgomery where marchers were beaten by state police officers as they crossed the Edmund Pettus Bridge. Selma struggles economically and is one of the poorest cities in Alabama, with over 40 percent of its residents living below the poverty level.

Critical Thinking

Of all these possible difficulties that children who are poor face, which do you think are most serious, and why? Can you identify any solutions to these problems?

food insecurity

A condition, defined by the United States Department of Agriculture (USDA), as not having enough nourishing food available on a regular basis.

INADEQUATE HEALTH AND NUTRITION   Research is clear about the relationship between poverty and health. Poverty puts the health of children at risk in many ways, including the likelihood of having low birth weight, which in turn increases chances of serious chronic and acute illness, along with emotional and behavioral problems (Bloom, Jones, and Freeman, 2013). Children who are poor may also receive inadequate food and nutrition. Nearly 15 percent of households experienced **food insecurity** at some point, defined by the United States Department of Agriculture (USDA) as not having enough nourishing food available on a regular basis (Coleman-Jensen et al., 2014). Twenty-one percent of households with children are food insecure. Children suffer the immediate pain of hunger and the longer-term consequences of malnutrition. They run the risk of more frequent colds, ear infections and other infectious diseases, impaired brain function, and stunted growth, and they are more vulnerable to lead poisoning and other environmental toxins.

LOWER-QUALITY HOME ENVIRONMENT   Warm loving relationships with parents, in conjunction with rich opportunities for learning, help children thrive. The Home Observation of the Measurement of the Environment (HOME) is a widely used interview and observation tool assessing parent–child interaction. The HOME shows that poverty has a significant negative effect on the quality and stimulation of the home environment (Crosnoe, Leventhal, Wirth, Pierce, Pianta, and NICHD Early Child Care Research Network, 2010; Yeung, Linver, and Brooks-Gunn, 2002). One study of the linguistic capabilities of young children found that children between the ages of 13 and 36 months who are poor and on welfare have exposure to only half as many words per hour as the average working-class child, and less than one-third the average of a typical child in a professional family (Children's Defense Fund, 2005). Obviously, parents cannot teach their children what they themselves do not know. There are also other differences. For example, parents who are poor are less nurturing and more authoritarian, and they use more inconsistent and harsh physical discipline.

PARENTAL STRESS AND MENTAL HEALTH PROBLEMS   What else about an impoverished family environment increases the likelihood of negative outcomes for children? Parents living in poverty face a high level of stress, depression, and mental health problems related to their situation. For example, high levels of male unemployment are significantly associated with child abuse and deprivation. While child abuse occurs in many different types of households, poor children have a higher probability of being abused, neglected, and more severely injured by abuse than do children in more affluent households (Cancian, Slack, and Yang, 2010; Centers for Disease Control and Prevention, 2015).

FEWER RESOURCES FOR LEARNING   In every respect, poor children get less education than those born into more affluent families. They receive fewer years of schooling, have less chance of graduating from high school, and are much less likely to go to college. On average, children living in poverty have fewer resources for learning in the home, including books and educational toys. Therefore, high-quality childcare and preschool programs become very important to helping them overcome the disadvantages in their home environment. Unfortunately, childcare and preschool are very expensive, as Chapter 10 makes clear, and fewer and fewer subsidized spots are available. Full-time childcare can easily cost over $10,000 per year for each child (ChildCare Aware of America, 2014). Consequently, many children living in poverty start school academically behind their peers. This disadvantage often continues throughout life. Generally, children who are poor receive lower grades and lower scores on standardized tests, they are less likely to finish high school, and are less likely to attend or graduate from college than are other children (Federal Interagency Forum on Child and Family Statistics, 2014). The low educational attainment of poor children tends to perpetuate poverty. In general, those who are less educated have lower incomes, less secure jobs, and more difficulty in improving their economic condition. Children of parents with less than a high school education generally do not do as well in school as children whose parents have completed high school. Thus, the cycle in which poverty and education are linked may be passed from one generation to the next if interventions are not available.

HOUSING PROBLEMS   The 2015 fair market rent for a two-bedroom apartment, according to the U.S. Department of Housing and Urban Development, was $908 in Phoenix, $1,093 in Chicago, and $1,162 in Miami (U.S. Department of Housing and Urban Development, 2015). Because many poor people cannot afford these levels of cost, they end up living in housing that is overcrowded, infested with vermin, in need of major repairs, lacking basic plumbing facilities, without needed appliances, and inadequately heated (Siebens, 2013). For example, Table 6–4 compares the likelihood of some of these deficits among those with household incomes in the lowest quintile (20 percent of the population) versus the highest quintile. As the table shows, families with the lowest incomes are far less likely to have appliances such as clothes washers, dishwashers, or computers in the home; are more likely to have housing with pests or in poor repair; and are more likely to live in unsafe homes or neighborhoods.

Many children who are poor experience frequent moves, live in crowded conditions, or have utilities in their homes shut off. It is difficult to do homework when there are no lights in your home. Some poor families are homeless, and a 2013 survey of 25 U.S. cities found that most of these cities reported a rise in homelessness over the previous year (U.S. Conference of Mayors, 2014). People who live in their cars while they work at jobs that do not pay enough for them to afford local housing are homeless—so are people sleeping over the warm air of exhaust grates in the alleys of urban office buildings. Women seeking safety from abusive spouses by sleeping with their children in a local women's shelter may have a home, but during the time they are in the shelter, they too are homeless. As these examples suggest, it is extremely difficult to actually count those who are homeless or even to adequately describe all the forms homelessness can take.

POOR-QUALITY NEIGHBORHOODS   Children living in poverty are increasingly isolated from those who are not poor in their communities, and they tend to live in inner cities where violence, crime, truancy, loitering, and a sense of despair predominate (Massey and Denton, 1993; Wilkenfeld, Moore, and Lippman, 2008). Guns killed 2,500

Table 6–4 Comparisons of Home and Neighborhood by Income

	Lowest Quintile	Highest Quintile
Appliances Lacking in Home		
Clothes washer	31%	4%
Dishwasher	55%	10%
Computer	47%	4%
Housing Condition		
Pests	13%	6%
Dissatisfied with repair of home	10%	3%
Dissatisfied with overall housing	6%	1%
Neighborhood Conditions		
Stay at home for safety	16%	5%
Consider home safe	4%	1%
Consider neighborhood safe	11%	3%

SOURCE: Siebens, 2013.

A Personal View

"All I Want Is a Fish"

When I was a little girl, I always wanted a pet. I begged my mom to get a dog. I knew someone who had one, and I thought it would be cool to have one too. My mom looked at me as if I was crazy. "How am I supposed to feed you AND a dog?" she shrieked. "I can feed one of you, but I can't afford to feed you both. So you choose."

I knew that she meant what she said. We didn't have much money, and after paying rent on our trailer and trying to scrape up the money to pay the utility bill, there just wasn't much left over. Sometimes we'd keep the trailer ice cold in the winter to save money. At night, Mom and I slept together to stay warm. I know Mom even sold her food stamps a few times to gather up a little more cash. We ate noodles for a week, but at least it was hot, filled our bellies, and it paid our bills for the month.

I hated always scrimping on things. Kids at school would tease me sometimes because of the clothes I wore. Hey, those clothes were not the latest style, but that coat kept me warm anyway. But really, I just wanted to be like every other girl at school—having new shoes now and then, feeling pretty, and having a friend. It's no fun being poor. People notice what you're wearing, or where you're living, or what you're eating for lunch, and it's embarrassing. But I didn't talk about these things with Mom much. She said it gave her migraines.

That's why I wanted a pet. Mom never let me play outside in our neighborhood—it's too dangerous—and I was lonely cooped up in the house alone when she worked. I wanted someone to cuddle, to talk with, someone who would not judge me, and would think I was beautiful. I imagined that a dog would offer these things. But every time I asked her about it, Mom would give me that look, and start talking about food again—how much I eat, how much a dog eats.

Finally it came to me—a fish! They don't eat much, do they? Really, how much can those tiny little grains of food cost? One of those little containers must last a whole year. So I begged mom for a fish—someone whose container I could cuddle, who I could talk with, someone who would not judge me, and who would think I was beautiful. Again, all my mom could talk about was the stress of it all and my constant begging for things she could not afford. "But please Mom," I pleaded. "All I want is a fish."—Cassandra

Critical Thinking

As you think about the poverty pathways, which specific ones come to mind as you read this short story? What makes child poverty a social problem rather than an individual one for this particular family?

What Do You Think?

Create a program to help eliminate or decrease the effects of poverty on children. How would you intervene in each of these pathways?

children and teens, and homicide is the second leading cause of death among children ages 1 to 19. It is the leading cause of death among black children and teens (Children's Defense Fund, 2014).

A Personal View: "All I Want Is a Fish" reveals how these different pathways of poverty play out in a child's life. As you read Cassandra's simple story of wanting a pet, put yourself in her shoes and visualize her experience.

Consequences of Poverty for Adults

The effects of poverty on the lives of children are clear; similarly, the potentially harmful health effects of poverty on adults are also numerous. For example, adults living in poverty have significantly higher morbidity (sickness) and a lower life expectancy than other adults (Bloom, Jones, and Freeman, 2013). They are more likely to work in dangerous occupations and live in unsafe neighborhoods, and their homes are more likely to be located near toxic sites.

One issue with far-reaching consequences for families is that men and women living in poverty are less likely to marry (Edin and Kefalas, 2005; White and Rogers, 2000). Poverty undermines economic security and makes men less attractive marriage partners. For example, Wilson (1987) suggests that the key factor in explaining the falling marriage rate among inner-city blacks is their declining employment opportunities as jobs move to the suburbs or overseas.

Poverty also undermines marital stability and leads to greater marital conflict. Poverty increases stress or depression, which can then lead to anger, resentment, and hostility between partners, and difficulties among children (Conger and Conger, 2008; Scaramella et al., 2008).

Why Does Poverty Persist?

6.6 **Analyze the individualistic, structural, and cultural explanations for poverty.**

Many theories are offered to explain the nature of poverty and account for why so many people are impoverished in the United States. Here we will discuss individualistic, structural, and cultural explanations.

Individualistic Explanations

"Rags to riches" stories are popular in the United States. Americans like to believe that anyone can pull him- or herself up by the bootstraps with hard work, and that people in the United States can be anything they want to be. From that perspective, it follows that those who are poor, particularly welfare recipients, are blatant examples of those who have failed to work hard. An individualistic explanation argues that poverty is primarily the result of laziness or lack of motivation, and those who are poor generally have only themselves to blame. It asserts that the United States is largely a land of meritocracy, and that hard work will reap social and financial rewards.

Individualistic explanations are popular in America. There is great ambivalence toward those who are poor (Browning, 2008; Pew Research Center for People and the Press, 2012). Almost two-thirds of Americans believe that people can create their own fate through their own efforts (National Opinion Research Center, 2009). People who are more likely to espouse individualistic explanations are white, live in the southern and north-central regions of the United States, are older than 50, and have moderate levels of education. Perhaps surprisingly, even welfare recipients tend to denigrate those who are poor. They distance themselves from other people on welfare, despite the fact that their circumstances are not altogether different (Seccombe, 2015). As "Sheri," a 27-year-old mother of three who had received welfare for seven years, said:

> I think a lot of them are on it just to be on it. Lazy. Don't want to do nothing. A lot of them are on it because a lot of them are on drugs. Keep having kids to get more money, more food stamps. Now that's abusing the system. And a lot of women are abusing the system.

Structural Explanations

Structural explanations of poverty incorporate elements of both the functionalist and the conflict perspectives described in Chapter 1. These explanations attribute poverty to the functioning of the dominant institutions of society, such as markets and corporations. In contrast to individualism, a social structural explanation assumes that poverty is a result of economic or social imbalances within the social structure that restrict opportunities for some individuals (Swedberg, 2007). For example, the U.S. economy has been changing over the last several decades, resulting in erosion of the purchasing power of the minimum wage, a growth in low-paying service jobs, and job relocation from inner cities to the suburbs. About 3.6 million hourly workers earn the minimum wage (or less). Half of these people are age 25 or older. These low-wage workers are distributed evenly across racial and ethnic groups (except for Asians, who are more likely to have higher wages). Women are more likely to earn minimum wage (or less) than are men, and it is likely that many of these women

Individualistic explanations are popular in American society. Many people believe that anyone can be rich if he or she is willing to work hard, and that the poor have primarily themselves to blame.

are supporting children as well as themselves (Bureau of Labor Statistics, 2015a). Although low wages may be enough to support a single person, a family trying to make ends meet would be living near or below the poverty threshold. Moreover, low-wage jobs often fail to provide families with important benefits like sick leave, health insurance, or retirement benefits.

Closely related are those structural explanations that emphasize the dual market for labor. In studies of the migrations of blacks and other groups to the cities, sociologists have found that there is a dual labor market in which favored groups are given access to the better jobs—those that offer secure employment and good benefits. Other groups, usually minority groups and migrants, are shunted into another segment of the labor market in which the jobs pay extremely poorly and offer no security or benefits (Lister, 2004; Wilson, 1987).

These inequalities are social problems, not simply personal ones. People may find themselves vulnerable because of their social location and relationship to the social structure. A changing economy, a drive for profit inherent in capitalism, racism, sexism, and an eroding safety net have greater deleterious effects on some than on others. One woman highlights the value of this safety net as she compares what is available to families in Hungary with what is available to those in the United States.

> *I am an American and my husband is Hungarian, and we made a deliberate choice to have our children in Hungary. I'm happy to live here because the benefits for families surpass those of just about any other country I've heard of. For example, when I had a baby, my maternity leave was three years. She went to daycare and preschool, which are free. Elementary school has optional aftercare if you want it. Most schools also offer wonderful activities after school, like music lessons, dance, computer clubs, and sports. All families receive a monthly family supplement grant until the child turns 18. The more children, the larger the grant. When the child turns six, we get an additional $100 or so at the beginning of each school year to cover school supplies. All children have medical coverage through the age of 18, or even longer if they are in college. Pediatricians make house calls—just try to find that in the U.S.! A friend of mine has a child with a disability and she receives the minimum wage to stay home and take care of him. When you compare Hungary with the U.S., there is no question that the U.S. needs more generous benefits for families. Sometimes I get homesick, but then I think of my overworked, stressed-out friends back home and think: No way. I think parents everywhere should have the same opportunities we've got here in Hungary to make life easier for families.*

Her point is that families need programs and policies in place to remain socially and economically healthy. Families without these benefits are more likely to slip into poverty.

Cultural Explanations

Cultural explanations of poverty are based on the interactionist perspective in sociology. In this view, people become adapted to certain ways of life because of the way they were raised, including adapting to poverty.

Proponents of the cultural approach argue that a "culture of poverty" arises among people who experience extended periods of economic deprivation. Under these conditions, new norms, values, and aspirations emerge and eventually become independent of the situations that produced them, so that eliminating the problem does not eliminate the behaviors that have been developed to deal with it. The result is a self-sustaining system of values and behaviors that is handed down from one generation to the next (Lewis, 1968; Murray, 1984).

The idea that there is a culture of poverty that arises among chronically poor individuals and families is controversial. William J. Wilson (1987), a noted expert on inner-city poverty, rejects the concept, claiming that it is a general label that does not fit in many instances. But he recognizes that long spells of poverty may have long-term consequences for children and grandchildren. He attributes this decline in family norms to the despair felt by those living in poverty, especially impoverished men. This despair also leads to higher rates of suicide, homicide, incarceration, and addiction, which in turn decrease the pool of eligible men in poor communities.

Overall, he suggests that poor people in inner-city ghettos and elsewhere share the same values and express the same aspirations as more affluent Americans, but their confidence in attaining them is greatly diminished by their negative life experiences. They may develop certain styles of language and expression that look like a separate culture to outsiders, but these differences, according to Wilson, hardly qualify as a culture of poverty.

Sociologist Herbert J. Gans (1995) is also critical of the culture-of-poverty thesis. Gans stresses the heterogeneity of those who are poor, noting that some are in families that have been poor for generations, while others are poor only periodically; some have become so used to coping with deprivation that they have trouble adapting to new opportunities; and some are beset by physical and emotional illnesses. He is critical of the idea that culture is holistic, that no element of it can be changed unless the entire culture is altered. Instead, he argues that behavior results from a combination of cultural and situational influences.

Gans (1995) maintains that the ultimate solution to the problem of poverty lies in discovering the specific factors that constrain those who are poor as they react to new opportunities when these opportunities conflict with their present cultural values. He believes that Americans must examine the kinds of changes needed in our economic system, social order, and power structure and in the norms and aspirations of the affluent majority that permit a poor class to exist. These themes will all emerge again in considerations of social policy and poverty.

Social Policy

6.7 Assess the implications of social policy in terms of welfare reform.

As is evident throughout this chapter, the extent of poverty in the world's most affluent society is a matter of continuing controversy, and so are the questions of what can be done about it. These questions are intimately bound up with attitudes toward those who are poor: Are the poor to blame for their own poverty? Do they avoid work? Would providing more jobs for the poor do any good? One's views on these issues have a lot to do with one's opinions about government intervention on behalf of the poor. Many myths surround poverty, and these are summarized in A Closer Look: Myths about Poverty in the United States.

Many people believe that those who are poor are largely to blame for their own poverty (Pew Research Center, 2014; McClam, 2013; Seccombe, 2015). The argument goes this way: As a group, most of those who are poor are unemployed. They are responsible for their own condition because they will not work. If they could be persuaded to work for a living or were forced to take jobs, poverty could be eliminated. What we have now is a group of freeloaders who are getting by on welfare, and welfare does more harm than good. A recent national survey asked adults (McClam, 2013), "Which of the following reasons do you think is most responsible for the continuing problem of poverty: lack of government funding and programs, the lack of job opportunities, racial discrimination, the breakdown of families, drugs, the lack of a work ethic, the lack of good educational opportunities, or too much government welfare that prevents initiative?" Which answer do you think scored the most votes? See Table 6–5 for the answer.

What Do You Think?

Which of these three explanations for persisting poverty makes the most sense to you, and why? Do you think most people your age feel as you do?

A Closer Look

Myths about Poverty in the United States

As if they did not have enough to cope with, those who are poor are often stigmatized as lazy, dishonest, and unable to help themselves. In fact, as you have seen, people living in poverty are an extremely diverse population, and many are among the hardest-working people in the nation. Here are seven common myths and the facts that debunk them:

Myth 1: The vast majority of those living in poverty are blacks or Hispanics. Poverty rates are higher among blacks and Hispanics than among other racial/ethnic groups, but they do not make up the majority of the poor. Non-Hispanic whites are the most numerous racial/ethnic group in the poverty population.

Myth 2: People are poor because they do not want to work. Half of those who are poor are not of working age: Many living in poverty are under age 18, and another group is age 65 and older. Is expecting them to work realistic? As for adults, many do have jobs but earn below-poverty wages. Numerous individuals who are poor cannot work because of a serious disability or because they must care for family members.

Myth 3: Poor families are trapped in a cycle of poverty that few escape. The poverty population is dynamic—people move in and out of poverty every year. Less than 15 percent of those who are poor remain in poverty for five or more consecutive years.

Myth 4: Welfare programs for those who are poor are straining the federal budget. Social assistance programs for low-income families and individuals accounted for less than 12 percent of federal expenditures. A much larger share of the budget goes to other types of social assistance (such as Social Security), which mainly go to middle-class Americans.

Myth 5: The majority of people who are poor live in inner-city neighborhoods. Less than half of the people in poverty live in central-city areas, and less than one-quarter live in high-poverty inner-city areas. Over one-third of those who are poor live in the suburbs, and more than one-fifth live outside metropolitan areas.

Myth 6: People who are poor live off government welfare. Under the new rules for public assistance, which require welfare recipients to work after two years of public assistance, welfare itself accounts for a diminishing proportion of the income of adults who are poor. Well over half of the income received by adults in poverty comes from wages or other work-related activity. Perhaps the most pernicious myth about those who are poor is that they do not share the work ethic of the middle class—that they are lazy or shiftless and would much rather be on welfare than work. Many studies have shown that people living in poverty have a strong work ethic and regret being on welfare (Seccombe, 2015). The research indicates that, in terms of life goals and willingness to work, there are no differences between those who are poor and those who are not; the differences are that those who are poor lack opportunities and confidence to succeed, and hence, they accept welfare or low-wage work as a necessity.

Myth 7: Most of the people who are poor are single mothers and their children. Female-headed families represent less than half of those who are poor. About a third of those in poverty live in married-couple families.

Critical Thinking

How many of these myths did you believe before reading this chapter? Why are these myths so widespread? What myths exist about people who are rich? Do these myths tend to be more positive, negative, or about the same as the ones that attempt to describe those who are poor? As a budding sociologist, how do you interpret any differences in the myths?

The inaccuracy of this argument is evident when one examines the data on poverty and work. Many families in poverty, including those on welfare, do work, often full-time, but minimum wage does not pull a family out of poverty. Moreover, other people who are poor cannot work because of physical or mental problems or because they are children or elderly. Welfare and other antipoverty programs help to keep many families safe and secure, although they do not cover the true extent of need (Jusko and Weisshaar, 2014).

Table 6–5 Reasons for Poverty, 2013

Which of the following reasons do you think is most responsible for the continuing problem of poverty?

Reason	Percentage
Too much government welfare that prevents initiative	24%
Lack of job opportunities	18%
Lack of good educational opportunities	13%
Breakdown of families	13%
Lack of work ethic	10%
Lack of government funding	4%
Drugs	3%
Racial discrimination	2%
Other	4%
All reasons equally	8%
Not sure	1%

SOURCE: McClam, 2013.

Reform of "Welfare as We Know It"

In 1996, Congress passed the Personal Responsibility and Work Opportunity Reconciliation Act, more widely known as "welfare reform." This landmark legislation targets the parents of children in households whose incomes fall below the poverty line. Poor parents who were formerly entitled to monthly payments or assistance are now required to obtain jobs or enroll in work training programs to qualify for supplemental assistance through their state governments. These state payments are subsidized by federal government grants. Few policy changes have received more attention or generated more confusion or ideological controversy.

Advocates of welfare reform, including both Republicans and Democrats, point to a dramatic decline in the number of people, especially female single parents, receiving various types of "welfare" payments under the Temporary Assistance to Needy Families program after welfare was reformed. Since the passage of welfare reform, many people have left welfare, usually for low-wage work. From 1994 to 2014, national caseloads fell by two-thirds, declining from 5 million to about 1.5 million families (Administration for Children and Families, Office of Family Assistance, 2015). Advocates of welfare reform also cite abundant examples of people who have succeeded in finding real employment. The individuals showcased are ones who have gained greater self-esteem and pride from their jobs.

However, have these far-reaching changes actually improved the lives of poor families? Although declining caseload numbers are often seen as a sign of success, families leaving welfare for work are not necessarily better off financially (Schott and Pavetti, 2011; Seccombe and Hoffman, 2007; Trisi and Pavetti, 2012). Commonly, families have difficulty paying their rent or utilities; have experienced bouts of food insecurity (i.e., they did not have money to purchase food for their family) or used a food bank; and have no reliable transportation, making it more difficult to work or take children to school. In the past, these vulnerable families could rely on TANF, but with the reforms of the 1990s, receiving this support is often no longer the case. As Figure 6–8 reveals, for every 100 families with children in poverty, only 27 of them even receive TANF benefits, a significant decline from the time before welfare was reformed. Are these children really better off now that their parent (or parents) work? Probably not. They are still in poverty.

Figure 6–8 Number of Families Receiving Cash Welfare Benefits for Every 100 Families with Children in Poverty

SOURCE: Trisi and Pavetti, 2012.

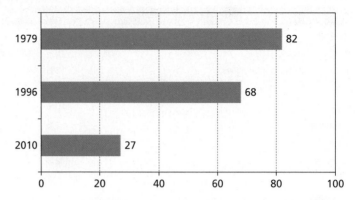

Part of the reason that families leaving welfare sometimes fare poorly is that many face one or more significant barriers to securing employment. The most common work barriers that TANF recipients face include low levels of education and a lack of work experience, mental and physical health challenges, and the necessity to care for a child with special needs. Other TANF recipients report domestic violence, which can make it difficult to work, and some have criminal records, which can severely limit work opportunities.

Statewide studies of families leaving welfare agree with national reports. For example, a study in Oregon, which followed 552 former welfare recipients for 18 months after leaving TANF, found that recipients' average income hovered near the poverty line, but their income rendered them ineligible for a number of important services (Seccombe and Hoffman, 2007). Forty percent had no health insurance, and 21 percent had at least one child uninsured. Thirty-two percent had cut or skipped meals entirely because of a lack of money, and 8 percent had cut or skipped their children's meals. Most reported outstanding debt, including 54 percent who had medical debts averaging nearly $2,500, a sum nearly impossible to repay given their inadequate incomes.

The study included women like "Molly" who suffered a tubal pregnancy, yet tried to avoid seeking health care because she had no insurance and no way to pay the medical bill (Seccombe and Hoffman, 2007, p. 4). Finally, after enduring pain for nearly two weeks, she went to the emergency room of her local hospital and was immediately taken to surgery. Her fallopian tube was removed at a cost of $14,000. She discusses her debt:

> *There's all these doctor's offices that I owe money to, and I had to set up payment plans with all of them. But, you know, it's like paying as much as rent every month to each doctor's office. I'm never going to come up with the money. I mean, I can try to make my payments, but it's never going to happen. I make eleven bucks an hour. I have to pay rent, gas, utilities, groceries, diapers, and, you know, daycare is way expensive. That's like 400 bucks a month, and now they want me to pay 400 bucks a month to different offices. And I'm like, dude, I'm not made of money. The next time something like that happens, I'm just going to dig a grave in the backyard. Fourteen grand's not worth it.*
>
> —Molly

So what is the truth about welfare reform? The answer is that there is no single truth. Instead of a national program and set of policies dealing with cash assistance, the United States now has 51 different systems across all states and the District of Columbia. This hodgepodge makes it extremely difficult to analyze which mix of financial incentives, work supports, and work obligations is most effective (Kaplan, 2002). Different state policies are still being evaluated. Positive claims based only on reduction of the welfare rolls should never be taken as the full measure of the program's success, nor should claims based on the experience of the poorest of those who are poor. Far more careful evaluation of the actual conditions experienced by parents and children in the new welfare systems is required. In the meantime, social scientists need to conduct politically neutral analyses of the empirical facts.

It is important to remember that the United States also attempts to provide a safety net of social insurance programs for *all* taxpayers and their dependents, not only those who are already quite poor. Some social insurance programs are intended to compensate for loss of income, regardless of income level or need. Through unemployment insurance, for example, cash benefits are paid for short periods to insured workers who are involuntarily unemployed. Unemployment insurance was created by the same act of Congress that established the Social Security system; however, the responsibility for administering unemployment insurance was delegated to the states, which were given broad latitude in setting eligibility standards and levels of benefits. As a result, the amount and duration of unemployment benefits vary greatly across states.

Other forms of social insurance include workers' compensation programs, which provide wage replacements to insured workers who suffer occupational injuries, and veterans' compensation plans, which issue benefits to disabled veterans to make up for their loss of earning potential. Social Security payments to elderly people also fall into this category. Cash income-support programs are provided for unemployable people, those who are not covered by any form of social insurance, and those with special needs, such as veterans.

Other programs provide "goods and services," such as food, housing, and health care, rather than income. These programs include public housing and urban renewal, health plans like Medicare and Medicaid, and food supplements like the commodity distribution program (which distributes surplus farm products to poor households). You could even say that police and fire departments are a form of social insurance; we pay taxes for these programs, and they are there for us if we need them. However, note that the specific programs that those who are poor use (e.g., Medicaid) are likely to be stigmatized, whereas the program that cuts across income levels (e.g., Medicare) is not stigmatized.

Families who leave welfare for work usually earn low pay, and at the same time, they may lose critical benefits that helped them make ends meet. To save costs, some skimp or go without food.

What Do You Think?

Why are poor people more likely to have a mental illness than those who are not poor? What is the cause and what is the effect? That is, does poverty contribute to mental illness, or does mental illness contribute to poverty?

Future Prospects

One of the most difficult problems in attempting to improve the condition of those who are poor is what to do about people living in highly concentrated or segregated poor neighborhoods. As long as large numbers of people live in inner-city neighborhoods where there has been a drastic loss of jobs and opportunity, it will be difficult for workfare or any other training and work approaches to make much of a difference because employment opportunities do not exist.

A policy innovation that holds promise is a set of experimental programs designed to move people from areas of concentrated poverty to communities where they will have more opportunity. These programs were motivated in large part by an important court decision about what is known as the Gautreaux project in Chicago. The city of Chicago and the state of Illinois were ordered to assist residents of public housing in an extremely poor neighborhood to move to better neighborhoods outside the inner city. Evaluations of how the families who moved fared in the job market and in schools were generally favorable (Briggs, Popkin, and Goering, 2010). As a result, the U.S.

Department of Housing and Urban Development has developed a program known as Moving to Opportunity. Families that are selected to move to new housing in neighborhoods with better job and educational opportunities are showing statistically significant gains in important social indicators, especially family income. Unfortunately, the experimental results also show that many people who were helped to move to better neighborhoods could not improve their economic condition over the full five years of the experiment, primarily because the weak economic recovery of recent years reduced the numbers of jobs that might have been available in the areas where they moved.

Recent research shows some promising results and some important disappointments that reveal how complex the problems are. Among teenagers whose families participated in the Moving to Opportunity experiments, girls did much better than boys as measured by educational achievement, staying out of trouble (and jail), and rate of non-sports-related personal injuries. In fact, boys whose families moved to higher-income neighborhoods actually showed negative changes as measured by these variables (Clampet-Lundquist et al., 2006; Ludwig and Kling, 2006; Turney et al., 2006).

During the recent recession in which the United States lost more than 1 million jobs, more U.S. residents sought help from federal and state welfare programs—especially through SNAP (food stamp support) and from voluntary agencies running food banks and soup kitchens. SNAP use has been at record highs the last several years. Often scorned as a failed welfare scheme by critics opposed to government programs to help those in poverty, the food stamp program administered by the Department of Agriculture now helps feed one in eight Americans and one in four children; nevertheless, it is experiencing deep cuts (Dean and Rosenbaum, 2014; USDA, 2014).

Going Beyond Left and Right

Referring to earlier antipoverty policies, former Republican President Ronald Reagan said, "We fought a war on poverty, and poverty won." People on the left often claim that, unlike the war on drugs or the war on terrorism, the war on poverty was abandoned too soon. This point was driven home, to the shock of many Americans, in the aftermath of Hurricane Katrina. Twenty-eight percent of New Orleans residents lived below the poverty threshold, and this group was by far the least likely to have cars or other means of transportation to safety during that catastrophe.

There is broad agreement among both Democrats (68 percent) and Republicans (61 percent) that economic inequality has grown over the past decade (Pew Research Center, 2014). Although they may differ on poverty's causes or the best approaches to dealing with it, most Americans can agree that the sight of children and their parents who are poor and living on the streets, either because of a natural disaster or because of homelessness caused by other forces, is unacceptable.

As vulnerable people on the margins of an enormously affluent society, those who are poor often have to suffer before wiser policies are formulated to meet their needs. But any opportunities for adequate childcare, decent education, and job training do not negate the widely shared desire to end welfare dependency by asking people who are able to do so to work for their incomes. Americans can begin to go beyond the left–right impasse by achieving a better balance between work requirements and opportunities to meet those requirements and by doing far more to address the housing, education, and health care needs of children and families who are living in poverty.

Summary

- Although the United States ranks among the wealthiest nations in the world, many Americans are living in poverty. In the past two decades, the gap between those who are rich and those who are poor has widened.

- The United States has a long history of attempting to redistribute wealth through taxation and other policies. In so doing, however, it has actually provided more opportunities for those who are rich to get richer than for those who are poor to escape from poverty.

- About 15 percent of Americans live below the official poverty line. They include children, elderly people, single mothers, ill or disabled individuals, students, and people who work either full- or part-time at poverty-level wages.

- The stratification of individuals and groups according to occupation, income, and skills is called class stratification. The Marxian view of stratification holds that classes are determined by economic measures. This view has been supplemented by those of Weber and his followers, who pointed out that other valued things besides wealth, such as status and power, are distributed unequally in modern societies. American society can be divided into five main classes: the upper class, the upper middle class, the middle class, the working class, and the poor class.

- Consequences of poverty can be severe, especially to children, and include poor health and unequal access to health services, substandard home environment, parental stress, inadequate education, substandard housing and homelessness, and neighborhoods of poor quality.

- Individualistic explanations for poverty place the blame on the person; structural explanations of poverty attribute it to dominant social institutions; and the cultural explanation holds that extended economic deprivation creates a culture of poverty with its own norms and values.

- The 1996 welfare reform bill requires able-bodied recipients to enroll in a training program or find work. Evaluations of the new system find that more parents are working, but are not necessarily better off.

Chapter 7
Racism, Prejudice, and Discrimination

 ## Learning Objectives

7.1 Describe the growing diversity of the American population.

7.2 Sequence the continuing struggle for minority civil rights.

7.3 Explain the social construction of minority groups.

7.4 Contrast racism, prejudice, and discrimination.

7.5 Summarize the origins of prejudice and discrimination.

7.6 Identify examples of institutional discrimination.

7.7 Discuss some of the consequences of prejudice and discrimination.

7.8 Analyze the policy of affirmative action.

Michael Brown was an unarmed black teenager in Ferguson, Missouri, who was shot and killed by a white police officer. What do we know about this case? Brown and his friend were walking down the street on a Saturday afternoon. According to Brown's friend, a police officer drove up to them and said "get the f—k on the sidewalk" and then braked in front of Brown. The officer threatened to shoot, then fired multiple shots, and Brown ran for his life. At one point Brown stopped, with his hands up in surrender, yelling "I don't have a gun, stop shooting!" But Brown was then shot, and collapsed onto the ground. Other witnesses corroborated that Brown had his hands up while the police officer shot at him repeatedly. The police, in contrast, tell a different story. They say that a fight broke out after the police officer asked the two boys to step aside. The gun went off in the police car. The officer was not indicted. A few months after Brown's death, Eric Garner, a black man, died in New York after a police officer put him in a chokehold, despite the fact the New York City Police Department prohibits the use of chokeholds. Garner was accused of selling single cigarettes from packs without tax stamps. When the police officer took Garner's wrist behind his back, Garner swatted his arm away. The officer then put his arm around Garner's neck and pulled him backwards onto the ground. After releasing his arm from Garner's neck, the officer pushed Garner's head into the ground while four other officers moved to restrain Garner, who repeated "I can't breathe" eleven times while lying face down on the sidewalk. Garner lost consciousness, and officers turned him onto his side to ease his breathing while waiting seven minutes for an ambulance to arrive. Garner remained lying on the sidewalk the entire time. The police contend Garner was not put in a headlock and that no choking took place. The officer was not indicted. And then there is the story of Freddie Gray in Baltimore … The stories go on and on.

In many ways, the United States prides itself on its ethnic and racial diversity and on the progress it has made since the Civil War toward greater tolerance and racial harmony. The election of Barack Obama in 2008 was rightfully marked as a historic first of which the nation could be proud. The global response to Obama's victory was amazement that a nation that had fought a civil war largely over slavery could have come so far. At the time, over two-thirds of Americans said in polls that his election as president was either the most important advance for blacks in the past 100 years or among the two or three most important such advances (Newport, 2008).

However, the realities of a sputtering economy, ecological disasters, international conflicts, and signs of racism have lowered the sense of optimism. Both blacks' and whites' views on achieving racial equality have become more pessimistic since the inauguration, returning nearly to their pre-election levels, as shown in Figure 7–1 (Pew Research Center, 2013). Events in 2014 and 2015 of unarmed black men being shot or put into illegal chokeholds by white police officers adds to the concerns of many people that tolerance and harmony may be an illusion.

Figure 7–1 Percentage Saying Situation of Black People Is Better Today Than Five Years Ago, 2007, 2009, 2013

SOURCE: Pew Research Center, August 22, 2013.

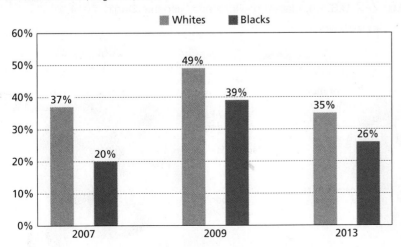

As the population continues to diversify, with growing numbers of people of Latin American descent and Asians from different regions of that vast continent, problems involving race relations and racial inequalities take ever-newer turns. At the same time, conditions in the nation's inner-city ghettos and Indian reservations, for better and worse, reveal the continuing struggle against racial and ethnic hatreds.

"We have a choice in this country," President Obama said in his famous speech on race during the presidential campaign of 2008. "We can accept a politics that breeds division, and conflict, and cynicism. We can tackle race only as spectacle—as we did in the O. J. Simpson trial—or in the wake of tragedy, as we did in the aftermath of Katrina—or as fodder for the nightly news." Or we can take real action "by investing in our schools and our communities; by enforcing our civil rights laws and ensuring fairness in our criminal justice system; by providing this generation with ladders of opportunity that were unavailable for previous generations. It requires all Americans to realize that your dreams do not have to come at the expense of my dreams; that investing in the health, welfare, and education of black and brown and white children will ultimately help all of America prosper."

It is important to note that indeed the nation has made significant progress in addressing social problems related to racial inequality over the past century. In the early twentieth century, the United States was still characterized by deep racial and ethnic divisions. Its educational and economic institutions were marked by sharp patterns of racial and ethnic exclusion, its communities rigidly segregated along racial lines. Indeed, when he surveyed the situation of prejudice and discrimination in the 1930s and 1940s, the eminent Swedish social scientist Gunnar Myrdal called the situation of "poor and suppressed" minorities in the land of freedom and opportunity "the American dilemma." Although much has changed since that time, racial and ethnic prejudice is still a significant social problem in many areas of American life. You will see in this chapter that many aspects of inequality in our society are the results of past patterns of racial and ethnic discrimination.

A More Diverse Nation

7.1 **Describe the growing diversity of the American population.**

Anyone who takes a quick look at the United States cannot help but notice the nation's diversity. An assortment of ethnic restaurants is available from which to choose, within schools many languages may be spoken, and a trip to the mall reveals people dressed quite differently from one another. The United States is quickly becoming more diverse every year due to immigration patterns and birthrates among specific groups, as shown in Figure 7–2. Currently, a little more than one person in three is a member of a minority group, but in Hawaii, New Mexico, California, and Texas, minorities outnumber whites. However, by 2060, minority groups are likely to comprise about 56 percent

Figure 7–2 U.S. Population by Race and Hispanic Origin, 2014, 2060

SOURCE: Colby and Ortman, 2015.

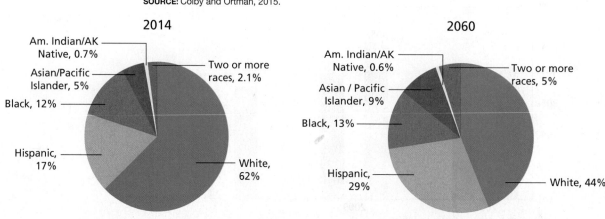

of the U.S. population. The percentage of blacks and American Indians will remain relatively stable, Asian Americans and Pacific Islanders will nearly double but remain a small group, and the growth of Hispanic groups will be considerable. Although now making up 17 percent of the population, Hispanics are expected to grow to 29 percent by the year 2060 (Colby and Ortman, 2015).

What Do You Think?

What types of cultural changes do you expect in American society in the future as whites become the minority in number? Do you believe that these potential cultural changes will be good or bad (or neutral) for America, and why?

The Continuing Struggle for Minority Civil Rights

7.2 Sequence the continuing struggle for minority civil rights.

Although the constitutional bases for racial equality were established in the 1860s and 1870s with the ratification of the Thirteenth, Fourteenth, and Fifteenth Amendments, it was not until the mid-twentieth century that the rights guaranteed by these amendments began to be exercised effectively (Parrillo, 2016; Schaefer, 2016). Starting with Supreme Court decisions that affected specific, small areas of life, black Americans began to work their way toward equality. A major legal breakthrough came in 1954 with the historic decision in *Brown v. Board of Education of Topeka* that "separate educational facilities are inherently unequal." The Supreme Court later applied this "separate cannot be equal" doctrine to a wide range of public facilities.

The Civil Rights Act of 1964 was another important step. Unlike the civil rights acts passed in 1957 and 1960, the 1964 act provided a means for fighting discrimination in employment and public accommodations and for denying federal funds to local government units that permitted discrimination. Eventually, the comprehensive Voting Rights Act of 1965 followed, as well as a federal prohibition against housing discrimination in the Civil Rights Act of 1968. Subsequent affirmative-action orders by President Lyndon B. Johnson aided the enforcement of these new laws; in addition, the Johnson administration set up new programs, such as the Head Start preschool program, to counter the effects of discrimination.

But in 1964, when the discrepancy between legal equality and actual inequality was clear, the impatience of some American blacks developed into anger, and in August 1964, a riot erupted in Watts, a black section of Los Angeles. By the time the wave of violent protest set off by the Watts riot subsided, it had struck almost every major urban center in the country. In 1967, after especially destructive riots in Newark and Detroit, President Johnson appointed the National Advisory Commission on Civil Disorders to investigate the origins of the disturbances and to recommend ways to prevent or control them in the future. Its findings suggested that there had been very little change since Myrdal's study. Describing the basic causes of the disorders, the commission stated,

> The first is surely the continuing exclusion of great numbers of Negroes from the benefits of economic progress through discrimination in employment and education, and their enforced segregated housing and schools. The corrosive and degrading effects of this condition and the attitudes that underlie it are the source of the deepest bitterness and at the center of the problem of racial disorder. (p. 203)

The commission concluded that "our nation is moving toward two societies, one black, one white—separate and unequal" (p. 1).

Although the situations of other minority groups—Native Americans, Chicanos (Mexican Americans), Hispanic Americans (especially Puerto Ricans and Cubans), Asian Americans, and some white ethnic groups—have received less intensive study, they are similar to that of black Americans. One form of discrimination to which these other groups are particularly vulnerable is harassment at the voting booth, largely because of some individuals' inadequate command of English. The 1975 extension of the Voting Rights Act attempted to alleviate this problem by requiring cities with sizable "language minority" populations to provide bilingual ballots in elections; it also permanently banned the use of literacy tests as a prerequisite for voting.

In recent years, there has been a major influx of immigrants from Asian countries, especially Korea, Vietnam, Cambodia, India, and Pakistan. The experiences of these immigrants have shown that small groups with education, business experience, and some funds, coupled with cultural values that stress family cohesion and extremely hard work, have less difficulty in adapting to their new environment. In contrast, large populations that gather in concentrated settlements, as Vietnamese immigrants have done in Texas and California, have been targets of racial hostility. Thus, it appears that the larger a group and the more segregated it is, the more hostility it encounters.

In the same vein, Stanley Lieberson (1990) argued that when an immigrant group is small, it is relatively easy for it to develop an occupational niche or specialty, as the Greeks and the Chinese have done in the restaurant industry. He cites a study showing that 15 percent of Greek immigrants were working in the restaurant industry and 9 percent of Swedish immigrants were carpenters. But when an immigrant population grows, it becomes far more difficult for the group to retain control of an occupational niche and expand it enough to accommodate newcomers. Later arrivals, therefore, are more dependent than earlier immigrants on the general labor market.

The terrorist attacks on the United States in 2001 showed quite vividly how national and world events can quickly change the fortunes of particular minority groups. According to the U.S. Commission on Civil Rights, Ohio Advisory Committee (2001),

> For those of Middle Eastern descent or appearance, September 11 ushered in fear of reprisal and concern for personal safety. Some Muslims, Arab Americans, and Southeast Asians have paid a high price for sharing a similar appearance or cultural and religious background of the accused terrorists. In the months after the attacks, reports of harassment and assaults against these groups soared, as did complaints of workplace bias and allegations of racial profiling by law enforcement and airline personnel.

The situation of immigrant groups highlights the problems of minority status in the United States. But before discussing these problems in detail, it is important to gain a clearer understanding of the meaning of the term *minority* as it is commonly used today.

The Social Construction of Minorities

7.3 Explain the social construction of minority groups.

One often hears the claim that, due to immigration and differences in the birthrates of various groups within the population, the United States is rapidly becoming a "nation of minorities." This claim refers especially to the increasing numbers of Hispanics, Asians, and other groups, but it does not address the more important sociological aspects of the term *minority*. From the standpoint of social problems, minorities are those that do not receive the same treatment as other groups in society. But how and why does such a situation come about? Arriving at answers to these questions depends on understanding three terms that are central to the discussion: *racial minorities*, *ethnic minorities*, and *assimilation*.

racial minorities

Groups of people who share certain inherited characteristics, such as eye folds or brown skin.

Racial minorities are groups of people who share certain inherited characteristics, such as eye folds or brown skin. Most experts believe that the biologically determined racial groups into which humanity is divided—caucasoid, mongoloid, and negroid—are strictly social categories and that the actual hereditary differences among them are meaningless. This perspective is known as the "social constructionist" explanation for the existence of racial minorities. Race is a socially constructed concept in that people take what are actually rather trivial biological distinctions and "construct" ideas about more general differences among groups. Historically, when it is convenient for those in power to do so, they have used socially constructed ideas about racial superiority and inferiority to justify slavery or other extreme forms of racial dominance.

Ethnic minorities are made up of people who share cultural features, such as language, religion, national origin, dietary practices, and a common history, and who regard themselves as a distinct group. They, too, have been victims of socially constructed ideas about superiority and inferiority. For example, 6 million Jews were killed by the Nazis because of the socially constructed ideas about them: Jews were thought not only to have abhorrent religious views, and too much economic and political influence, but also to be biologically distinct. From this perspective, there was a biological component to the struggle between Jews and everyone else, and the only way to win the struggle was to exterminate all Jews.

Since this time, there have been other cases of genocide with the intention of eliminating ethnic groups. In Rwanda, it is estimated that anywhere from 500,000 to 1,000,000 people were slaughtered in a 100-day period from April 7, 1994, to mid-July of that year. The Hutu majority, incited by top government officials to kill all Tutsi, brutally murdered their neighbors and fellow villagers with machetes and other weapons. Seventy percent of all Tutsi living in Rwanda were killed as the world watched in horror, too stunned to intervene. Former President Bill Clinton referred to America's lack of intervention as one of his biggest regrets while in office.

Sometimes members of either a racial or an ethnic minority slowly cease being "different" by taking on the characteristics of the mainstream culture. This process is called **assimilation**. Members of a minority group may adapt their own unique cultural patterns to those of the majority, or intermarry, and over time, the group ceases to be singled out as a minority. Many Caucasian immigrant groups in the nineteenth century fit this pattern: The Irish, Greeks, or Italians may have been considered distinct groups, living in their own enclaves, speaking their own language, and eating traditional foods. But over time, they assimilated, and today they do not receive a lot of attention for being an ethnic group. It is easier for Caucasians to assimilate because they usually do not have distinctive physical features.

It should be noted that the term *minority* as used here does not refer to a group's numerical size in the population. For example, blacks in South Africa are a minority. Women around the world are often considered a minority. All minority groups have their own particular characteristics, but the following characteristics are sociologically significant (Feagin, 2013; Simpson and Yinger, 1985):

- Minorities are subordinate segments of a complex society.
- Minorities tend to have special physical or cultural traits that are seen as undesirable by the dominant segments of the society.
- Minorities develop a group consciousness or "we feeling."
- Membership in a minority is transmitted by a rule of descent—one is born into it—which can impose the minority status on future generations even if by then its special physical or cultural traits have disappeared.
- Members of a minority, whether by choice or by necessity, tend to marry within their group.

There is no clear line between totally dominant and totally minority groups; rather, any given group can be placed at some point along a continuum of "minorityness." Sociologist Michele Lamont (2003) compared racism in the United States and France, two highly developed nations, and asked the question, "Who counts as 'them'?" Lamont interviewed 150 white, working-class men living in the suburbs of

Ethnic groups, just like racial groups, have been victims of social constructivism. Here we see bodies of prisoners who were transported to Dachau, Germany, from another concentration camp in 1945, dying in route. This freight car is only one of fifty similar cars.

ethnic minorities

Groups of people who share cultural features, such as language, religion, national origin, dietary practices, and a common history, and who regard themselves as a distinct group.

assimilation

A process through which a racial or an ethnic minority group slowly ceases being "different" by taking on the characteristics of the mainstream culture.

What Do You Think?

Assimilation is controversial. Is it a good idea for all Americans to eventually look and sound alike, or should Americans keep their distinct racial and ethnic differences? Which view would make a stronger America in your opinion, and why?

Paris and New York. Instead of asking directly about racism, respondents were asked to describe the kinds of people they like and dislike, the kinds of people they feel similar to and different from, and the types of people to whom they feel inferior or superior. The Americans were much more likely than the French to mention race or skin color as a deciding factor. In particular, blacks emerged most often as the group disdained by the white New Yorkers as "them"; yet in France, blacks were not of concern. The French "them" were Muslim immigrants (Lamont, 2003).

Various immigrant groups in the United States have moved along this continuum, edging progressively closer to equality and shedding some or all of their distinctive minority characteristics. It should be emphasized, however, that the physical distinctiveness of racial minorities has made the attainment of assimilation and equality much more difficult for them than for other immigrant groups that are defined largely by cultural traits. Thus, racial minorities have tended to remain minorities much longer than nonracial minorities.

Subordinate status is the principal characteristic of a minority group. In almost any society, the desire for some goods, whether tangible or intangible, exceeds the supply, and groups within the society are likely to compete for them and for the power to control them. The groups that gain the most power dominate the other groups, controlling their access to the desired goods and often also to other goods—social, economic, political, and personal. The dominant group need not be the most numerous; it must merely be able to prevent other groups from effectively challenging its power (Feagin, 2013).

Once established, however, the dominant–subordinate relationship is not fixed for all time. Either through the efforts of the subordinate group itself or as a result of changing legal or economic conditions, power relationships can be altered. You can see in American society, for example, that women are not as subordinate as they were only a generation ago. Similarly, in southern counties where blacks considerably outnumber whites, extensive voter registration has enabled blacks to become politically significant. On a broader scale, most of the former colonial areas of Africa and Asia are now independent nations, and some countries that formerly lacked influence, such as Japan and China, are now world powers.

Despite these examples of long-term change, it is usually very difficult for members of a subordinate group to attain a share of power and influence. The dominant group naturally wants to protect its privileged position. Among the weapons it uses to do so are prejudice and discrimination.

Defining Racism, Prejudice, and Discrimination

7.4 Contrast racism, prejudice, and discrimination.

Racism is behavior, in word or deed, that is motivated by the belief that human races have distinctive characteristics that determine abilities. Racists believe in this erroneous concept of race; they also believe that their own race is superior and therefore ought to dominate or rule other races. Racism may be an attribute of an individual, or it may be incorporated into the institutions (social structures and laws) of an entire society. Nazi Germany, South Africa under apartheid, and the United States before the civil rights era of the mid-twentieth century are examples of societies and nations that incorporated racist beliefs within their social institutions. Societies that have attempted to eliminate racism from their institutions continue to struggle with the legacies of their racist histories.

Prejudice is an emotional, rigid attitude toward members of the subordinate group. But while prejudices are attitudes, not all attitudes are prejudices. Both share

racism

Behavior, in word or deed, that is motivated by the belief that human races have distinctive characteristics that determine abilities and cultures.

prejudice

An emotional, rigid attitude toward members of the subordinate group.

the element of *pre*judgment—the tendency to decide in advance how to think about a situation or event. Unlike other attitudes, however, prejudice involves an emotional investment that strongly resists change. Prejudiced people tend to be so committed to their prejudgments about a particular category of people that even in the face of rational evidence that the prejudgment is wrong, they will maintain their prejudice, even defend it strongly, and denounce the evidence.

It is important to note that prejudice need not always involve antipathy. One can be prejudiced in favor of a person or group, with a similar degree of disregard for objective evidence. Prejudice is based on attitude; it is a tendency to think about people in a categorical, predetermined way: *My daughter Ashley has a new boyfriend, a Chinese boy. He's a good catch. You know how smart those Chinese people are.*

Discrimination is the differential treatment of individuals considered to belong to a particular social group. To treat a member of a subordinate group as inferior is to discriminate against that person. Members of the dominant group tend to use one standard of behavior among themselves and a different standard for any member of a subordinate group.

Discrimination is overt behavior, although it may sometimes be difficult to observe—as in tacit agreements among real estate agents to steer members of minority groups to particular blocks or neighborhoods. To justify the behavior to themselves, people tend to rationalize it on the grounds that those whom they discriminate against are less worthy of respect or fair treatment than people like themselves. Moreover, people tend to be ethnocentric—to see their own behavioral patterns and belief structures as desirable and natural and those of others as less so.

It may be easy to say that discrimination is a thing of the past, but it would be untrue. Sociologists and others have conducted many natural experiments and found that, despite what people say they would do, many do discriminate. For example, sociologists at Harvard sent people to apply for low-wage jobs. The applicants were given identical resumes and similar interview training. The black applicants were offered jobs much less often than the white applicants. In fact, blacks with no criminal record were offered jobs at about the same rate as white applicants who had criminal records (Pager, Western, and Bonikowski, 2009).

Likewise, in another study, people seeking to discuss research opportunities before applying to a doctoral program contacted over 6,500 professors. The names of the students were randomly assigned to signal sex and race (Caucasian, black, Hispanic, Indian, and Chinese), but the students were otherwise identical. The researchers found that university faculty were significantly more responsive to Caucasian males than to all other categories of students. This bias was especially strong in higher-paying disciplines, but was also found in disciplines that contain higher numbers of women and minorities in them (Milkman, Akinola, and Chugh, 2014).

Discrimination occurs among our state legislators, who researchers found were less likely to respond to constituents with black-sounding names than to those with white-sounding names (Butler and Brockman, 2011); on eBay auctions in which an iPod held by a white hand received 21 percent more offers than one held by a black hand (Doleac and Stein, 2013); and landlords posting on Craigslist who were less likely to respond to e-mails with stereotypical black-sounding names than to their white counterparts (U.S. Department of Housing and Urban Development, 2013).

Prejudice and discrimination are closely related, and both are often present in a given situation. But this pairing is not always the case. Robert Merton (1949) outlined

This illustration is of Cassius Clay (now known as Muhammad Ali) and a friend after they returned from the Rome Olympic games. They were refused service by a waitress because of their race.

discrimination

The differential treatment of individuals considered to belong to a particular social group.

Table 7–1 A Typology of Prejudice and Discrimination

Prejudice (the Attitude)	Discrimination (the Behavior)	
	Yes	**No**
Yes	Outright bigotry	Latent bigotry
No	Institutional discrimination	Integration (both psychological and institutional)

four possible relationships between prejudice and discrimination: unprejudiced and nondiscriminatory (integration), unprejudiced and discriminatory (institutional discrimination), prejudiced and nondiscriminatory (latent bigotry), and prejudiced and discriminatory (outright bigotry) (see Table 7–1). Although it is possible to be both completely free of prejudice and completely nondiscriminatory—or to be a complete bigot—most people fall somewhere between these two extremes. It is possible to be prejudiced against a particular group but not to discriminate against it; it is also possible to discriminate against a particular group but not to be prejudiced against it.

For example, the builders of a new, expensive cooperative apartment house may not be personally prejudiced against Arabs, but they may refuse to sell apartments to Arab families (i.e., they may discriminate against Arabs) out of fear that the presence of Arab families would make it more difficult to sell the remaining apartments. This example is a clear case of institutional discrimination (the lower-left cell in Table 7–1). Or the reverse may occur: In a corporation that holds a government contract, and hence is subject to federal equal employment opportunity regulations, the personnel director may be very prejudiced personally against Blacks but may hire a Black woman as a management trainee—that is, not discriminate—to comply with the law. This behavior is an example of latent bigotry (the upper-right cell).

Suppose the builders were confronted with a different situation: a Hispanic family attempting to buy one of their apartments. On the one hand, they might very well discriminate out of both personal prejudice and concern for profits—a case of outright bigotry (the upper-left cell). On the other hand, there can be situations in which legal controls prevent latent bigotry from affecting such behaviors as the sale of a house to a Hispanic family, but those controls cannot prevent social isolation of the family after the sale. These examples illustrate the difficulty of keeping personal prejudices from leading, sooner or later, to some form of discrimination, particularly if a significant number of people share the same prejudice (Ore, 2006).

Origins of Prejudice and Discrimination

7.5 Summarize the origins of prejudice and discrimination.

Although prejudice and discrimination are weapons used by a dominant group to maintain its dominance, it would be a mistake to see them as always, or even usually, weapons that are used consciously. Unless the subordinate group mounts a serious challenge to the dominant group, prejudice and discrimination often seem to be part of the natural order of things. Their origins are numerous and complex, and to explain them, it is necessary to consider both the individual and the structural organization of society. Do patterns of prejudice and discrimination result from the aggregation of individual attitudes and behaviors, or do prejudice and discrimination arise from the society? In fact, neither argument excludes the other; both are possible. To blame prejudice and discrimination wholly on warped personalities or wholly on oppressive social structures is to oversimplify (Plous, 2003).

Prejudice and Bigotry in the Individual

There are a number of ways that prejudice and bigotry may manifest in individuals. Two are discussed below, frustration-aggression, and projection.

FRUSTRATION-AGGRESSION   At one time or another, most human beings feel frustrated. They want something, but because of events or other people they cannot get it. This can lead to anger and to aggression, which may be expressed in any of several ways. The most obvious way is to strike at the source of the frustration, but often that action is impossible; frustrated individuals may not know the source, or are subjectively unable to recognize it, or are in a position in which they cannot risk such an action. Whatever the reason, the results are the same: They are unable to vent their anger on the real source of their frustration.

Instead, the aggression is often directed at a safer and more convenient target, usually one that somewhat resembles the real source of the frustration. In other words, the aggression is displaced onto a scapegoat. When this displacement is not limited to a particular person but is extended to include all similar people, it may produce prejudice.

For example, suppose a middle-aged man who has been working for 20 years at the same job is told by his young supervisor that his job will soon be eliminated as a result of automation. The man is understandably angry and frightened. But if he were to vent his aggression on the supervisor, he would almost certainly be fired. That evening, as he is telling his woes to friends at the local bar, a young man comes in for a beer. The middle-aged man accuses the youth, and "all you lazy kids," of being a good-for-nothing and ruining the country, and only the intervention of the bartender prevents him from assaulting the young man.

It is fairly clear that this man has displaced his aggression toward his young supervisor onto all young people. Rather than deal with the supervisor and the whole range of factors that led to the elimination of his job, he blames the problems of the country on young people; that is, he uses them as a scapegoat.

PROJECTION   Another source of prejudice and discrimination is **projection**. Many people have personal traits that they consider undesirable. They wish to rid themselves of those traits, but they cannot always do it directly—either because they find the effort too difficult or because they are unable to admit to themselves that they possess those traits. They may relieve their tension by attributing the unwanted traits to others, often members of another group. This behavior makes it possible for them to

projection
The act of attributing the unwanted traits of themselves onto others.

Protesters in California demonstrate against illegal immigration and amnesty for undocumented immigrants. The frustration-aggression perspective suggests that the real frustration among protesters is the lack of jobs, low pay, and high unemployment. The protesters use illegal immigrants as a scapegoat.

reject and condemn the traits without rejecting and condemning themselves. Since the emotional pressures underlying projection can be very intense, it is difficult to counter them with rational arguments.

An often-cited example of projection is white attitudes toward black sexuality. Historically, many whites saw blacks as extremely promiscuous and uninhibited in their sexual relations, and there was much concern about protecting white women from sexual attacks by black men. Actually, it was white men who enjoyed virtually unlimited sexual access to black women, particularly slaves. White society, however, regarded overt sexuality as unacceptable, and it is likely that white men felt some guilt about their sexual desires and assaults on black women. To alleviate their guilt, they projected their own lust and sexuality onto black men—a much easier course than admitting the discrepancy between their own values and behavior.

Prejudice and Bigotry in Social Structures

The emotional needs of insecure individuals do not fully explain why certain groups become objects of prejudice and discrimination. To understand this behavior, you will need to look at larger social processes.

POLITICAL DOMINANCE AND ECONOMIC EXPLOITATION In many societies, the demand for more than the available supply of certain goods gives rise to a competitive struggle, which usually results in the dominance of one group and the subordination of others. Even if the initial competition is for economic goods, the contest is ultimately a struggle for power and, hence, a political process. Once established, political dominance is likely to be reinforced by economic exploitation. Slavery and serfdom are the most obvious forms of exploitation, but "free" workers may also be exploited. Migrant farmworkers are an example. They work in dirty jobs in the hot sun, stooped over for hours, and receive low pay and no benefits.

Economic exploitation is one form of discrimination practiced by the dominant group against a subordinate group. Historically, the subordinate group has consisted of unskilled workers. In the case of blacks, for example, unskilled jobs were plentiful and available (at low wages) before the 1940s. With the development of protective labor legislation (e.g., minimum wage, antidiscrimination, and workers' compensation laws), employers could no longer use the subordinate group as a source of cheap labor. Blacks were then systematically denied jobs as white-dominated unions maintained control over skilled jobs and employers sought cheaper unskilled labor by transferring basic manufacturing operations abroad (Sears, Sidanius, and Bobo, 2000).

LAWS AND POLICIES Discrimination can take many other forms. Members of the subordinate group may be legally prevented from owning property or voting, or may be terrorized into submission. Some legal forms of discrimination are symbolic measures to keep the subordinate people "in their place," such as the severe immigration control law passed in the Arizona State Legislature in 2010 and signed into law by the state's governor, Jan Brewer. The law, nicknamed the "show me your papers law," requires state troopers to ask for identification and proof of citizenship or legal status in the United States from anyone they stop who, in their judgment, might be an illegal immigrant. It was unclear how a state trooper would make such a judgment, and it was left to the troopers' discretion. After much controversy and court hearings, the law was enforced beginning in 2012. The law is an example of many initiatives in the Southwest that are designed to address what advocates regard as a crime wave by illegal immigrants. In the meantime, one very immediate effect is the rise of protests throughout the nation, and especially in cities with large numbers of immigrants of Hispanic origin.

social norm

A commonly accepted standard that specifies the kind of behavior appropriate in a given situation.

SOCIAL NORMS A **social norm** is a commonly accepted standard that specifies the kind of behavior appropriate in a given situation. It is relevant to this discussion because, although it does not clarify why prejudice and discrimination begin, it helps explain how and why they are perpetuated.

Social norms are learned in a process that begins almost at birth. Small children soon learn what kind of behavior elicits the approval of their parents and what kind is likely to elicit a rebuke. The same process continues as they encounter other significant adults. Gradually, children internalize the values and norms of their society. They receive approval from parents and other adults, and later from their peers, when they behave in socially acceptable ways; they experience disapproval when they do not.

A good example of a social norm that pertains to minority–majority relations is **homogamy**, the requirement or expectation that one must marry a person similar to oneself with respect to such characteristics as religion, social class, and race or ethnicity. This expectation has been a particularly strong norm in the United States for race. The early U.S. censuses included a category called *mulatto* to describe people of multiple races. **Antimiscegenation laws** banning marriage between whites and other races were common well into the latter half of the twentieth century. Racially mixed couples often encountered severe hostility, and many felt compelled to move to places like Greenwich Village in New York City or Hyde Park in Chicago, where there were similar couples and they could feel less "deviant." The U.S. Supreme Court struck down such laws in 1967; however, Alabama was the last state to formally repeal its antimiscegenation law through a state constitutional amendment as late as 2000.

The norm of homogamy is far weaker today than it was even a generation ago. Today, interracial couples account for over 8 percent of all married couples and 15 percent of newly married couples (Wang, 2012). In 1958, only 4 percent of the population approved of interracial dating. By 2013, that number had jumped to 87 percent and is even higher among people under age 30, as you can see in Table 7–2 (Newport, 2013). Younger adults have grown up in an environment immersed with multicultural images including those in music, art, sports, and television. They saw a biracial man as president when many of them were still children. On the contrary, older Americans grew up with the notion that segregation was normal, justifiable, and the appropriate way for Americans to live their lives. Even so, the views of many elderly persons have evolved over time.

STEREOTYPES   Still another source of prejudice and discrimination is **stereotyping**, or attributing a fixed and usually unfavorable or inaccurate conception to a category of people. Whereas social norms are concerned primarily with behavior and only indirectly with attitudes, stereotyping is a matter of attitude.

Usually a stereotype contains (or once contained) some truth, but it is exaggerated, distorted, or somehow taken out of context. Stereotyping has much to do with the way humans normally think. We tend to perceive and understand things in categories, and we apply the same mental process to people. We build up mental pictures of various groups, pictures made from overgeneralized impressions and selected bits of information, and we use them to define all members of a group regardless of their individual differences. Thus, we come to assume that all Native Americans are warriors, all African Americans are good at sports, all residents of Appalachia or the Ozarks are hillbillies, all Puerto Ricans are short, all Italians

homogamy

The expectation that one must marry a person similar to oneself with respect to such characteristics as religion, social class, and race or ethnicity.

antimiscegenation laws

Laws banning marriage between whites and other races.

stereotyping

Attributing a fixed and usually unfavorable or inaccurate conception to a category of people.

Table 7–2 Percentage Who Approve of Racial Intermarriage, 2013

Total	87%
18–29 years	96%
30–49 years	93%
50–64 years	84%
65 and older	70%

SOURCE: Newport, 2013.

Slide Show
Ethnic and Racial Stereotypes

Stereotypes are exaggerations of some small element of truth, grossly distorted and taken out of context. They are usually negative in nature, but not always. Nonetheless, whether positive or negative, stereotypes are harmful because they treat people as one homogeneous group and ignore personality and other individual differences.

Asian Americans are stereotyped as smart and as having professional, well-paying careers. Although the median income of Asians is the highest among all racial and ethnic groups, it is not fair to say that all Asians are doing well financially. Many Asians, especially those from Vietnam, Cambodia, and Laos, work in poorly paid service work or in factories.

The image of the Mexican bandit, wearing a sombrero, red bandana, a vest, and boots with spurs is widespread. The "Frito Bandito" was a classic image in advertising. However, most Mexican men do not look like this, are definitely not bandits, and could be highly offended by the stereotype.

One of the many stereotypes about blacks, especially black men, is that they are good in sports. Yes, a look at professional sports teams usually shows an overrepresentation of blacks, but that observation is a far cry from assuming that most blacks are good athletes. Black people come in all shapes, sizes, and abilities.

Stereotypes of Native Americans are less than flattering. Images like this one do not represent the lives of Native Americans, and yet, these images are common, including as mascots for sports teams. Many teams have changed their mascots, but others such as the Washington Redskins, have resisted changes despite some degree of public outcry.

Stereotypes also abound regarding white people; they have the world in the palm of their hands! However, race and ethnicity are also interwoven with class and sex. Rich white men may be overrepresented among the powerful, but poor whites, and poor white women in particular, generally do not have the same opportunities.

Critical Thinking

What other racial or ethnic stereotypes exist? Make a list of stereotypes for each primary racial and ethnic group.

Compare and contrast these stereotypes; is the list longer for some groups than others? Do some groups have more positive (or negative) stereotypes than other groups?

are gangsters, all Jews are religious, all Asians are smart, all Swedes are blond, all Frenchmen are amorous, all old people are senile, and so forth. None of these generalizations will stand up to even perfunctory analysis, yet many people habitually use them in thinking about minority groups. The slide show reveals some common stereotypes about racial and ethnic groups.

Institutional Discrimination

7.6   Identify examples of institutional discrimination.

If discrimination is a socially learned behavior of members of dominant groups, designed to support and justify their continued dominance, it is reasonable to expect that it will be built into the structure of society. When members of a society are socialized to believe that certain groups are naturally to be treated as inferiors, it would seem perfectly reasonable to formulate public policies and build public institutions that discriminate against them.

To some extent, this type of socialization is exactly what has happened in the United States. When many Hispanics, blacks, Native Americans, Asians, women, and members of other minority groups are not treated fairly, it is not necessarily because of the conscious prejudices of individual public officials. It often is not a case of "I don't like your kind, so I am not going to hire you." There are laws in place designed to protect people from discrimination of that nature.

These laws are not always successful, however, as evidenced by the over 43,000 individual filings of discrimination based on race, national origin, or skin color to the U.S. Equal Employment Opportunity Commission in 2014. As you can see in Table 7–3, these types of filings have increased since 2000 (U.S. Equal Employment Opportunity Commission, 2015). Nonetheless, there is another type of discrimination that is even more difficult to prove.

> *As a Native American student in the public school system in Oklahoma, I always felt a bit offended when we celebrated Columbus Day, or when we learned that Columbus "discovered" America. Oh really? My forbearers were here long before Columbus sailed over in his funky boats. Yes, Columbus opened up North America for white people, but he also brought death and destruction to MY people. I didn't like celebrating that.—Tiva, 18-year-old recent high school graduate*

Institutional discrimination is an unconscious result of the structure and functioning of the public institutions and policies themselves. It often goes unnoticed by the dominant group because it is woven into the cultural fabric of society. Our culture celebrates Christopher Columbus; Southern culture celebrates the Confederate flag (although as of July 2015 it no longer flies over the statehouse in South Carolina); and Arkansas, Mississippi, and Alabama continue to celebrate Robert E. Lee (the leader of the Confederate army) on the same day as the Martin Luther King Jr. federal holiday, despite the obvious conflict of interest. Practices such as these are rarely noticed as racist or discriminatory until a crisis occurs, such as the gunning down of nine black church-goers in South Carolina in 2015, which began the national outcry to remove the Confederate flag from South Carolina's state capital.

institutional discrimination

An unconscious result of the structure and functioning of the public institutions and policies themselves.

Table 7–3 Number of Individual Filings of Discrimination Based on Race, National Origin, or Color, 2000, 2014

	2000	2014
Race	28,945	31,073
National Origin	7,792	9,579
Color	1,303	2,756

SOURCE: U.S. Equal Employment Opportunity Commission, 2015.

Racial profiling provides another example. It refers to the practice—by law enforcement personnel, security agents, or any person in a position of authority—of disproportionately selecting people of color for investigations or other forms of discrimination, which often include invasions of privacy. To a large degree, racial profiling is a form of institutional discrimination because representatives of social institutions, such as the police or intelligence organizations, unfairly single out certain groups, distinguished by racial characteristics, in seeking to enforce rules or laws. From the authorities' viewpoint, this behavior may be justified by the belief that their suspicions correspond to realistic probabilities of wrongdoing by members of those groups. Thus, after 9/11, Arab Americans and Indian American Sikhs wearing turbans—in fact, anyone with swarthy skin and a beard—have been far more likely than lighter-skinned individuals to be searched at airports. Many Muslim immigrants and Americans, and Arab Americans of any religion, have accepted this behavior as the inevitable consequence of heightened

A Closer Look

Driving while Black

Many blacks assert that they are unfairly singled out for traffic stops and other investigations, which, if initiated because of their race, are violations of their civil rights. Data from studies that have been done on who is stopped by the police tell identical stories: Racial minorities are stopped at significantly higher rates than whites. A recent survey of 2,329 drivers in and around Kansas City sheds light on this issue (Epp, Maynard-Moody, and Haider-Harkel, 2014). The data collected allowed the researchers to distinguish between two types of stops— those stops to enforce traffic safety laws such as speeding, and those stops designed to investigate the driver. One of the researchers' key findings is that these two types of stops differ from start to finish. Traffic safety stops are based on clear violations of the law, and the officer tends to quickly issue a ticket or warning, and the driver is let go. Investigatory stops last much longer. The officers drag out the stop as they ask questions, try to look inside the vehicle, and seek consent for a search.

The researchers found that, in traffic safety stops, being black had no influence. Blacks were not more likely than whites to be stopped for clear traffic safety law violations. But in investigatory stops, the issue is *who you are* rather than *what you have done*, and being black is a primary factor in the likelihood of being stopped. For example, the researchers found that a black man age 25 or younger had a 28 percent chance of being stopped for an investigatory reason over the course of the year, while a similarly aged white man had only a 12.5 percent chance. Police in investigatory stops tend to pull over young people, but a black man must reach age 50 before his risk falls below that of a white man under age 25. Overall, black drivers are nearly three times more likely than whites to be subjected to investigatory stops.

Being black is also the primary influence on how far police officers pursue their inquisition in these investigatory stops. Black drivers were five times more likely than whites to be subject to searches. One man, "Billy," explained how he was pulled over on his way to a job interview by a highway patrolman for speeding even though he was going only two miles over the speed limit. The trooper made Billy get out of his

car and put his hands on the hood while the trooper searched the car. Finding nothing, the trooper explained that the reason why he checks the car is because the police have been having problems with people trafficking drugs up and down the highway—the assumption being that it is okay to stop a black person because of the (extremely slim) chance that he will be smuggling drugs. This stop was not Billy's only time being pulled over. On another occasion, Billy, his wife, and his cousin were stopped while on their way to visit an ill relative and their rental van was searched for drugs by a sheriff's deputy.

It comes as no surprise that black people view investigative stops more harshly than whites. These stops impart feelings that the police are trying to hurt racial minorities, not help them. Investigative stops like Billy's undermine confidence in the policy, which is why three times as many blacks as whites responded in the survey that you cannot always trust police to do the right thing. Likewise, black respondents were five times more likely than whites to agree with the statement, "The police are out to get people like me."

As the discriminatory practice of investigative stops comes to light, many people are demanding change. New York City is taking a close look. A judge there ruled that the New York City's stop and frisks, as practiced, violate the Constitution. She ordered that police be better trained in what kinds of justifications for these stops are constitutional, and all police officers must explain, in writing, any stops of this nature that they instigated. She also appointed a lawyer to monitor the police department's implementation of these directives. At this writing, her decision was suspended by the appellate court.

Critical Thinking

Have you, or someone you know, ever been stopped by the police for an investigative issue? If you answered yes, do you believe your race or ethnicity was a factor? What information would you need to help you decide whether race was, or was not, a factor? Can you identify other social institutions in which discrimination is likely to occur?

security after the terrorist attacks. But others cannot help feeling that their status in the United States is diminished and threatened (Bozorgmehr and Bakalian, 2009).

Racial profiling has also been a major subject of controversy among blacks and other people of color who are disproportionately stopped while driving and searched for possible drug possession. According to the theory among law enforcement personnel, such people are more likely than others to be involved in drug use and drug dealing (Epp, Maynard-Moody, and Haider-Harkel, 2014). Conservative social scientists, such as Heather MacDonald (2001), argue that racial profiling is justified because the facts show that blacks and Hispanics are indeed disproportionately more likely to drive fast and also to be carrying drugs than whites. But as we see in A Closer Look: Driving while Black, the best research on this issue to date has convinced judges in many courts that indeed racial profiling violates the civil rights of innocent people and must be curtailed.

Since it would be difficult to discuss all categories of institutional discrimination against all minority groups, this discussion focuses on four major categories: education, housing, employment and income, and social justice.

Education

Americans take public school systems very seriously. Undoubtedly, one reason is that, in this country, education has generally been seen as the road to social and economic advancement. It is almost an article of faith that American children should get more education than their parents and achieve higher social and economic status.

Since the 1940 census, which was the first to ask about educational attainment, the average number of years of school completed by all Americans has increased steadily (National Center for Education Statistics, 2014). Despite these gains, members of minority groups remain less likely to finish high school or attend college than are whites. In 2012, the graduation rate for public high school students averaged 85 percent for whites and 93 percent for Asian/Pacific Islanders, yet hovered only around 68 percent among blacks and Native Americans and 76 percent for Hispanics (Kena et al., 2014). Likewise, although the likelihood of receiving a bachelor's degree or higher has doubled, or nearly so, for blacks and Hispanics, it remains that only 21 percent of blacks and 16 percent of Hispanics, as compared with 40 percent of whites, have achieved this credential. Thus, although there has been a significant gain in educational parity since World War II, large differences remain.

In an important early study of how minority achievement in education and in the labor force is related to parents' wealth, Dalton Conley (1999) found that the level of education of one's parents and their net worth (not only income but also the total of all owned assets, or wealth) are the two best predictors of the quality of higher education their children will receive. Since black students tend to come from far less wealthy homes than white students do, their ability to go to the prestigious universities and colleges that produce the most entrants into the professions and the world of finance and business is far more limited. Consequently, although as we have seen blacks and other minority persons increase their educational attainment substantially, their inability to pay the costs of an elite higher education presents a major barrier to their full equality in a labor market that demands increasingly sophisticated skills and in which success often hinges on personal contacts established in college.

There is no doubt that the more highly educated usually receive substantially higher salaries than those with little education. However, blacks and Hispanic people at all levels of education earn less than their white counterparts (National Center for Education Statistics, 2013). Figure 7–3 compares the median annual earnings of full-time workers ages 25–34 by their educational levels. The figure shows that whites earn the most money at lower levels of education (high school diploma or less), and Asians earn the most at higher levels of education. Meanwhile, blacks and Hispanics earn significantly less than whites or Asians at all levels of education.

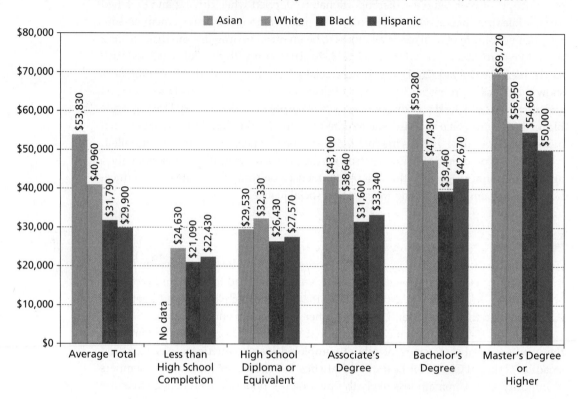

Figure 7–3 Median Annual Earnings of Full-Time Year-Round Workers, Ages 25–34, by Educational Attainment and Race/Ethnicity, 2012

SOURCE: National Center for Education Statistics, Digest of Education Statistics, Table 502.30, October, 2013.

de jure segregation

Segregation that is required by law.

de facto segregation

Segregation that is not required by law, but results from housing patterns, economic inequalities, or gerrymandered school districts.

What Do You Think?

Describe the level of de facto segregation in the neighborhood in which you grew up. What specific factors contributed to its racial and ethnic makeup?

One explanation for these differences in educational achievement and earnings has to do with the quality of schooling that different groups experience. Throughout the United States, school administrations are under pressure to raise standards and increase performance, especially in underachieving schools. These schools are often found in communities with high proportions of low-income black and Hispanic households. The causes of this situation and policies to address it have been hotly contested issues. Relevant here is the issue of minority segregation and poor schools, along with the retreat from policies to achieve school desegregation.

In its 1954 *Brown v. Board of Education* decision, the Supreme Court mandated integration "with all deliberate speed" but was vague on actual remedies to be used. The decision effectively wiped out **de jure segregation**—segregation required by law—and by finding that "separate but equal" schooling was inherently unequal, it set in motion decades of sporadic efforts to achieve more racially balanced classrooms. To do so, states and municipalities had to address **de facto segregation**, segregation resulting from housing patterns, economic inequalities, gerrymandered school districts, and the departure of middle-class families from communities with increasing rates of minority households and poor or mediocre schools.

Throughout much of the 1970s and 1980s, busing of students, primarily minority students, to schools outside their neighborhoods was the primary remedy for desegregation. Today, however, busing is largely considered to have been a failure. White families tend to move to suburban areas, leaving minorities behind in the central cities. At the same time, no alternative strategies have been implemented to achieve school desegregation. Demands for higher standards and higher achievement are not generally matched with increases in funding for schools in lower-income minority neighborhoods. Public schools in the United States are typically funded from local property taxes or local levies, so wealthier communities can afford to pay higher salaries to teachers and hire more experienced teachers than can financially strapped inner-city schools.

A study by the Civil Rights Project on school desegregation found that resegregation of the races is increasing. For example, as shown in Figure 7–4, in 2011, only 23 percent of black students attended schools in which whites were the majority group (the same percentage as in 1968), down from almost 44 percent in 1988, despite the fact that whites are the majority of the population overall.

The situation among Hispanic students is even more alarming. In the southern, northeastern, and western United States, almost half of all Hispanic school children attend a school referred to as "intensely segregated," meaning that fewer than 10 percent of the students at the school are white. Again, as shown in Figure 7–5, this segregation has accelerated rather than declined, especially in the western United States where the majority of Hispanic children live.

What is the "big deal" about segregated schools? Schools that serve predominately black and Hispanic students usually receive fewer property tax dollars. They have a harder time hiring, retaining, and paying good teachers. Classrooms have a higher turnover of students and teachers, a greater number of students with special needs, and less parental involvement. Students have less access to Advanced Placement classes, new books, the latest science equipment, and other resources that cost money. But perhaps most of all, segregated schools deprive both whites and minorities the opportunity to meet people of other backgrounds and to expand their views (Badger, 2014).

School busing was a commonly used method of school integration in the 1970s and 1980s. Children were bussed from one school to another so schools would have racial parity. However, the result was "white flight"; white families moved out to the suburbs to avoid busing.

Housing

School desegregation is an extremely difficult issue to address when such a high proportion of minority and nonminority people live in segregated neighborhoods to begin with. Housing segregation—the separation of minority groups into different regions, cities, neighborhoods, blocks, and even buildings—has diminished somewhat in recent years, but it remains a serious problem (Badger, 2014; Glink, 2012; Logan, 2011).

Figure 7–4 Percentage of Black Students in Majority-White Schools, 1954-2011

SOURCE: Orfield, Frankenberg, Ee, and Kuscera, 2014.

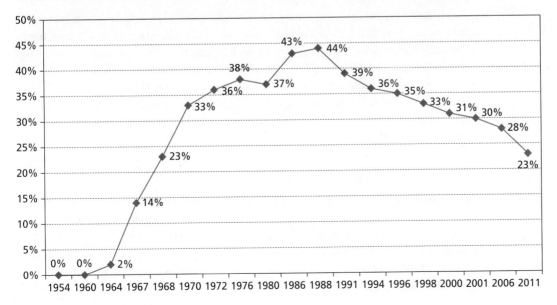

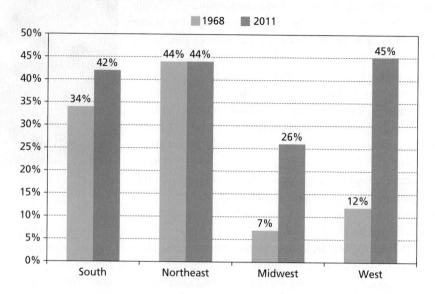

Figure 7–5 Percentage of Hispanics Enrolled in "Intensely Segregated" Schools (90%–100% Minority), 1968, 2011

SOURCE: Orfield, Frankenberg, Ee, and Kuscera, 2014.

An analysis of recent census data shows that black people have become less isolated from Hispanics and Asians over time, but their exposure to whites has changed very little (Logan, 2011). This situation is true regardless of income. In other words, affluent blacks have only marginally higher contact with whites than do blacks who are poor. Analyses also show that minorities at every income level live in poorer neighborhoods than do whites with comparable incomes (with the exception of the most affluent Asians). In fact, the average *affluent* black or Hispanic household lives in a poorer neighborhood than the average *lower-income* white resident.

A practice that contributes to high rates of segregation is racial steering, a practice in which real estate brokers refuse to show houses outside of specific areas to minority buyers. Before the landmark judicial decisions of the 1950s, racial steering was enforced through restrictive covenants—agreements among homeowners not to sell their property to people designated as undesirable. Although restrictive covenants are now illegal, racial and ethnic steering still occurs unofficially in many all-white neighborhoods. Because it operates below the surface, with no written agreements, racial steering is difficult to prevent.

Massey and others who study racial and ethnic segregation assert that more audit research is needed to show lawmakers that racial steering and other forms of discrimination exist and that laws against them must be enforced far more rigorously (Massey and Fischer, 2004). In audit research, a black or minority couple is sent to real estate agents and shown (or not shown) certain types of housing. Then a white couple is sent to the same agents and the results are compared; this process is repeated many times with different agents to determine whether a systematic pattern of discrimination exists.

Employment and Income

The idea that work will improve one's social status is deeply ingrained in U.S. culture. Although it is no longer as pervasive as it once was before the recession, the work ethic still holds that, if you really want a job, you can find one, and that, if you work hard, you will make money. The corollary to this idea is the notion that, if you are wealthy, you deserve your wealth because you worked for it, and if you are poor, it is largely because you are lazy or unmotivated (Seccombe, 2015). This view

Table 7–4 Percentage of Employed People (age 16 and over) Who Are Members of Unions, by Race/Ethnicity, 2000, 2014

	2000	2014
White		
Men	14.8%	11.5%
Women	10.9%	10.1%
Black		
Men	19.3%	14.5%
Women	13.6%	12.2%
Hispanic		
Men	10.3%	9.4%
Women	9.9%	9.4%
Asian		
Men	11.7%	9.2%
Women	11.1%	11.8%

SOURCES: Bureau of Labor Statistics, 2007; 2015.

ignores the fact that discrimination is no less prevalent in employment than it is in education and housing.

In some ways, discrimination in employment is a direct result of discrimination in education. We have already noted the relationship between income and education. Today, since the chances of finding even an entry-level job without a high school diploma are slim, low levels of education means that many minority group members will spend their lives underemployed or unemployed. This situation, in turn, leads to a low income, resulting in inferior housing, with the likelihood of a poor education for the next generation, and so on—a cycle of discrimination that is built into the system.

Is there any escape from this situation? What about jobs that do not require much formal education, jobs that one learns mostly through apprenticeship and are represented by many labor unions? Historically, labor unions have been in the forefront of battles for civil rights, and for wages and benefits that can support a family, but unions and union membership have declined substantially (Bureau of Labor Statistics, 2007, 2015).

Table 7–4 compares the percentage of employed people who are members of unions by race and ethnicity between 2000 and 2014. Union membership has declined among all racial and ethnic groups, with Asian women being the lone exception.

The employment problem is particularly devastating for young black and Hispanic men. Their unemployment rate is higher than that of their white and Asian counterparts; their wages are lower; they are less likely to have fringe benefits on the job such as sick leave, retirement pensions, or vacation pay; and they have fewer assets. In the absence of legitimate means of getting ahead, some of these youth turn to various forms of illegal activity (FBI, 2013).

In addition to illegal activity, without hope for a steady income, young men often find it economically impossible to form stable families (Edin and Kafalas, 2005; Seccombe, 2015). Poor women (like most women) want marriage to a man who has strong employment prospects rather than weak ones. And this situation shows few signs of changing.

> *I want a house with a nice yard and a picket fence before I even think of marrying him. Why would I go and marry a man if he can't take care of me? I can take care of myself just fine, but I ain't taking care of no man, that's for sure.*
>
> —*Leila, age 24, mother of a 2-year-old son*

There is a considerable gap in income between whites and most minority groups. On average, white households have twice the income of black, Hispanic, or Native American households (DeNavas-Walt and Proctor, 2015). However, focusing on income differences can be deceptive (McKernan et al., 2013). Although it is true that in the past 30 years there has been a trend toward income parity among groups, the same is not true for assets, such as homes, cars, saving accounts, retirement savings, stocks, or other capital-generating investments. Asset inequality has a profound impact on intergenerational inequality. People with property and investments can will their estates to their children so that they have some material advantages as they establish homes of their own. This benefit is not possible for those without assets, whatever their ethnic or racial background.

The gap in assets between whites and most minority groups is large and growing. On average, white families have six times the wealth of black and Hispanic families, at $632,000 among whites, and $98,000 and $110,000 among blacks and Hispanics, respectively (McKernan and Ratcliffe, 2013). However, this comparison takes all people into account, including those whose incomes are most extreme. If we look only at typical people, that is, use the median income (the midpoint, with an equal number above and below this amount), we find that the wealth gap actually increases rather than decreases.

How do white people accumulate all this wealth? First, their incomes are significantly higher than most minorities, which allow them greater purchasing and saving power. Second, many of the tax laws are in favor of those with more money. For example, a tax subsidy for a home mortgage helps those people, largely white, who have enough wealth to buy a home in the first place. It does little or nothing for those who cannot afford such a purchase. Likewise, subsidies for retirement savings also largely assist those who are already financially well off enough to save for retirement. Meanwhile, policies for providing aid to lower-income people actually discourage them from saving. A low-income person will lose important social supports such as food assistance or cash welfare if he or she is even one dollar above the asset allowance threshold (Seccombe, 2015).

What Do You Think?

What amount and types of assets do you think you will inherit from your parents? How will these assets shape your future?

Justice

Philosopher and social theorist Cornel West (1994) recounts an all-too-familiar tale of the daily injustices faced by those who are racial and ethnic minorities. While driving to a college lecture, he remembers, "I was stopped on fake charges of trafficking cocaine. When I told the police officer I was a professor of religion, he replied, 'Yeh, and I'm the Flying Nun. Let's go, nigger!' " (p. xv). Such degrading experiences with the police and other street-level authorities enrage members of minority groups, who know that those who are poor and powerless may receive far worse treatment in the justice system. This kind of treatment is seen in the recent publicized cases in 2014 and 2015 of unarmed black men being mistreated, even to the point of death, by police officers, as shown in the opening vignette.

The U.S. system of justice is based on two premises that are relevant to this issue: (1) Justice is blind; that is, racial, ethnic, economic, or social considerations are irrelevant in the eyes of the law, and (2) any accused person is considered innocent until proven guilty in a court of law. But do these assumptions apply equally to everyone?

As noted in Chapter 5, minority groups are overrepresented in official arrest records, and it seems probable that in general they are more likely to be arrested and charged with a crime, regardless of whether they are guilty. The higher arrest rates among minorities are partly due to the higher arrest rates among the poor in general (who, as noted earlier, include a disproportionate number of minority group members), but there is considerable evidence that discrimination plays a role in who is arrested. For example, blacks use marijuana at a rate 1.3 times that of whites. However, blacks are arrested for marijuana possession at a rate 3.7 times that of whites (The Sentencing Project, 2015). Why the difference?

After arrest, the obstacle of the bail system must be overcome. It is here that the criminal justice system may be most discriminatory. To begin with, bail involves money; those who have it can usually arrange to be released after arrest and await their trial in freedom, subject only to the limitations of the bail agreement. Those who do not have money are punished, in effect, because of the long delay between arrest and trial in many jurisdictions (particularly in big cities). They are compelled to wait in jail until their case comes up. Even those who can pay bail can rarely afford costly legal counsel, and those who are detained have little opportunity to prepare a defense. This inequality in the administration of justice extends to the sentencing process. Although blacks and Hispanics account for less than a third of the population, they make up almost 60 percent of the prison population (NAACP, 2015).

Racial differences do not stop there, however. They continue into the more extreme realms within our criminal justice system.

RACIAL INEQUALITIES IN CAPITAL PUNISHMENT   The U.S. Supreme Court banned the death penalty for many decades, in part, because of the recognition that the effects of prejudice and the inability to afford good legal counsel would discriminate against minority people. In 1977, however, the Court reversed its position and the death penalty was reinstated. There have been nearly 1,500 executions since that time (Death Penalty Information Center, 2015). The number of executions peaked in 1999 with 98 executions and has been declining since, with 35 executions in 2014.

Since 1977, the issue of racial bias in the application of the death penalty has reappeared. Figures 7–6a and 7–6b show the racial and ethnic background of defendants who have been executed and those who are currently on Death Row. As you can see, the majority of people executed are white, although blacks are greatly overrepresented, given their size in the population. The situation for blacks is even more extreme among those on Death Row. However, some people argue that this disparity does not represent bias because black people are overrepresented among those who commit capital crimes. If blacks commit more capital crimes, then it follows that they are put to death at higher rates, the argument goes.

However, David C. Baldus, a leading expert on the subject and the author of numerous studies that have influenced the courts, notes, "Some people are being sentenced to death based on race, and I find that morally and legally objectionable" (quoted in Eckholm, 1995, p. B1). For example, consider the following:

- Jurors in Washington State are three times more likely to recommend a death sentence for a black defendant than for a white defendant in a similar case (Beckett and Evans, 2014).

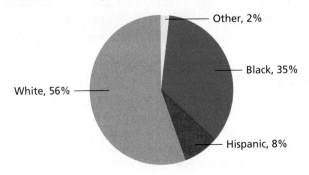

Figure 7–6a Race and Ethnicity of U.S. Defendants Executed, 1976–2015

SOURCE: Death Penalty Information Center, 2015.

Other, 2%
Black, 35%
White, 56%
Hispanic, 8%

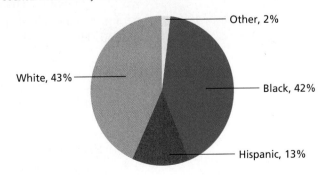

Figure 7–6b U.S. Death Row Inmates by Race, 1976–2015

SOURCE: Death Penalty Information Center, 2015.

Other, 2%
White, 43%
Black, 42%
Hispanic, 13%

- In Louisiana, the odds of a death sentence were 97 percent higher for those whose victim was white than for those whose victim was black (Pierce and Radelet, 2011).
- A study in California found that those who killed whites were over three times more likely to be sentenced to death than those who killed blacks, and over four times more likely than those who killed Hispanics (Pierce and Radelet, 2005).
- In the case of interracial murders, those cases with a black defendant and a white victim were almost ten times more likely to involve execution than those cases with a white defendant and a black victim (Death Penalty Information Center, 2015).

FELONY DISENFRANCHISEMENT In many states, people convicted of a felony may lose the right to vote (sometimes permanently), which is known as felony disenfranchisement. With the world's highest rates of imprisonment, the United States is also the world's leader in felony disenfranchisement, a dubious distinction that has an enormous impact on the political fate of minority groups. Approximately 5.8 million Americans have currently or permanently lost the ability to vote because of a felony conviction, and most of these people are black Americans. As a result, 1 in 13 black people is unable to vote (The Sentencing Project, 2013).

Some Consequences of Prejudice and Discrimination

7.7 **Discuss some of the consequences of prejudice and discrimination.**

The harmful effects of prejudice and discrimination are not limited to minority groups. As the Supreme Court noted in its decision in *Brown v. Board of Education of Topeka*, the lives of members of the dominant group are also stunted by the artificial barriers and warped perceptions that such social divisions create. Here, however, we will consider the effects on the subordinate group, since the effects are usually more serious.

What happens to people who must live with institutionalized discrimination and the prejudice that accompanies it? First, there are, of course, effects on the individual personalities of minority group members. Second, both individuals and groups develop protective reactions against prejudice and discrimination.

Consider the effects of discrimination on individual personalities. In his groundbreaking work, *Children of Crisis*, Robert Coles (2003) documented some of the effects on the first black children to attend desegregated schools in the South. These children were subjected to blatant discrimination and bitter prejudice, including mob action against them and their parents. Coles observed the children for several months after desegregation, focusing on how they depicted themselves and their world in drawings. His account of the drawings of one black girl, Ruby, is fascinating. For months Ruby would never use brown or black except to indicate the ground. However, she distinguished between white and black people. As Coles describes:

> *She drew white people larger and more lifelike. Negroes were smaller, their bodies less intact. A white girl we both knew to be her own size appeared several times taller. While Ruby's own face lacked an eye in one drawing, an ear in another, the white girl never lacked any features. Moreover, Ruby drew the white girl's hands and legs carefully, always making sure that they had the proper number of fingers and toes. Not so with her own limbs, or those of any other Negro children she chose (or was asked) to picture. A thumb or forefinger might be missing, or a whole set of toes. The arms were shorter, even absent or truncated. (p. 47)*

At the same time, Jimmy, a white classmate, always depicted blacks as somehow related to animals or extremely dirty and dangerous. However, Coles noted that, over time, blacks' self-image improved, and whites became less prejudiced. For example, after about two years of contact with Ruby and other black children in his school in New Orleans, Jimmy grew less fearful of blacks, and the change was reflected in his drawings. Coles concluded that children were conditioned to fear and distrust members of the other race, but that with continuing friendly contact, these prejudices were broken down. He also found that children eventually helped change their parents' attitudes.

This pioneering work has set the stage for more recent studies that focus on the ways in which racism affects individuals. More recent studies find that people who experience racism are more likely to be depressed and discouraged, have more negative images about their racial or ethnic group, do more poorly in school, and experience greater stress and physical ailments (Gaylord-Harden and Cunningham, 2009; Kwate and Goodman, 2015; National Association of School Psychologists, 2012). A Personal View: Everyday Racism highlights one girl's story about the racism that she experiences.

In addition to individual responses to prejudice and discrimination, larger group responses also may occur, such as public protest. After the success of the Montgomery bus boycott of 1955 and 1956 (when blacks stopped riding buses until discriminatory seating rules were eliminated), a broad social movement for desegregation emerged. Initially led by Martin Luther King, Jr., the movement was directed against laws that enforced or created a statutory inequality—that is, an obstruction maintained for the purpose of denying minority groups the rights and privileges enjoyed by other Americans. In the 1960s, however, as hopes were high, progress was slow. As white resistance increased, minority protests sometimes took violent forms. Anger, frustration, and rage provoked urban riots across the country. At no time, however, did a majority of blacks approve of the violent protests (National Advisory Commission on Civil Disorders, 1968).

The Martin Luther King, Jr. Memorial in Washington, D.C., pays tribute to the leader of the modern civil rights movement. He was an advocate for nonviolent, peaceful demonstrations.

A Personal View

Everyday Racism

I've gotten to know my biology lab partner pretty well in middle school and we've had some interesting conversations. I think she was trying to show me how cool she is when she said the other day, "I don't know what the big deal is about race; we're all the same." All the same? Oh really? I wanted to tell that girl a thing or two about race. First of all, the simple fact that she can see it as no big deal is an example of white privilege. As a dark-skinned Latina, I don't have that same privilege. I have to think about race every day whether I want to or not. Last week, I went into a grocery store and the clerk at the counter told me I had to leave my backpack at the counter; I saw plenty of other white folks and they were able to keep their purses or backpacks with them. A few months ago when I went to the movies with my older sister, the ticket clerk was speaking very loudly and slowly to us. He assumed that we didn't speak English well! Last year, my older brother was driving home from work and was stopped by the police for no reason at all. They made him get out of his car and they searched his vehicle. He didn't do a thing! I'm guessing they thought he had drugs. A few months before that, my cousin was stopped by police, and the same thing happened to him. My other brother liked this certain girl and asked her out, but she told him no because her father doesn't want her to date Mexicans. My sister, brothers, and I were all born here! So, when my biology lab partner downplayed race and said it was no big deal, I debated whether or not to tell her all of this. I ended up keeping quiet, which to be honest, is another example of racism. I was afraid to tell her the truth.

—Gabriela, age 14

Critical Thinking

If you were Gabriela, how would you have responded to her biology lab partner? How would you explain white privilege and racism? How do you think her lab partner would respond?

Social Policy

7.8 **Analyze the policy of affirmative action.**

Another example of a group response is the development of affirmative action policies. In response to the demands of blacks and other minority groups for a more equal share in the benefits of the American way of life, leaders have instituted various programs to alleviate the effects of prejudice and discrimination. For the most part, these programs tend to have more support among liberals and Democrats, which helps explain why such initiatives tend to wax and wane in different presidential administrations. One of these approaches is affirmative action.

Affirmative action

affirmative action

Controversial policies that require institutions that have engaged in discriminatory practices to increase opportunities for women and members of minority groups.

Affirmative action programs have successfully increased the number of minorities in professional positions. Mariana is a second-year law student at the University of California, Berkeley. She graduated in the top 10 percent of her high school class and graduated with a B+ average from a state university in central California that served predominantly low-income students, most of whom were first-generation college students. Her goal is to practice family law in minority communities.

The most controversial policy designed to redress past institutional discrimination is **affirmative action**. This term refers to policies based on a body of federal law originating in the 1964 Civil Rights Act that bans discrimination on the basis of race, religion, sex, or national origin in areas such as employment, education, and housing (Kelley, 2010; National Conference of State Legislatures, 2014). Affirmative action programs require institutions that have engaged in discriminatory practices to increase opportunities for women and members of minority groups. The policy is controversial because, with the goal of correcting past patterns of discrimination, institutions such as universities and businesses must make special efforts to recruit minority applicants, and those efforts may affect white applicants.

Proponents see affirmative action as proactive measures to remedy inequality, fight discrimination, and have an integrated society with equal opportunities for all members. Opponents believe it is misguided social engineering that uses quotas and preferences to replace qualified people with unqualified minorities and women. They claim it promotes "reverse discrimination," and is harmful to those it is trying to help. In fact, John Roberts, Chief Justice of America's Supreme Court, takes a dim view of affirmative action. "The best way to stop discrimination on the basis of race," he says, "is to stop discriminating on the basis of race" (*The Economist*, 2013).

HISTORY OF AFFIRMATIVE ACTION   Until the mid-1960s, minorities were barred from certain jobs, some universities would not admit them, and many employers

would not hire them. The Civil Rights Act of 1964 made discrimination illegal in the workplace, in federally funded programs, and in privately owned facilities open to the public. The original goal of the civil rights movement had been "color-blind" laws; however, many people were concerned that simply ending a long-standing policy of discrimination did not go far enough. One year later, Congress passed the Voting Rights Act, which gave the U.S. Department of Justice the power to take "affirmative" steps to eliminate discrimination. President Lyndon B. Johnson gave the U.S. Department of Labor the responsibility of enforcing affirmative action. In that role, the Labor Department began requiring government contractors to analyze the demographics of their workforce and to take proactive measures to remedy inequalities.

Over time, the U.S. Supreme Court has defined the scope of affirmative action policy through a series of legislative initiatives and decisions. Overall, the Court has upheld the constitutionality of affirmative action in principle, but has placed restrictions on how it is implemented. One of the major restrictions on affirmative action has to do with quotas. By way of background, in an effort to enable members of minority groups to receive the same educational opportunities as whites, beginning in 1965, the federal government required schools to establish goals for minority enrollment and in some cases to set quotas that specify the number of minority students to be admitted each year. These policies met with considerable opposition. Charging that affirmative action is reverse discrimination, critics focused on the Supreme Court case of Allan Bakke, a white student who was refused admission to the medical school of the University of California at Davis even though his grades were higher than those of many black students who were admitted under an affirmative action program.

TESTING AFFIRMATIVE ACTION IN THE COURTS   Allan Bakke was a 35-year-old white male who applied to a number of medical schools in 1976. He was a strong applicant with a solid grade point average and high test scores, but was denied admissions by several universities because of his age (age discrimination was legal at that time). Bakke was also denied entrance to the medical school at the University of California, Davis, for two years in a row, but he noted that a number of minority candidates were admitted with lower grades or test scores than his. Feeling that this treatment was unfair, Bakke sued the university. He sought an order admitting him on the grounds that the special admissions programs for minorities violated the U.S. and California constitutions and Title VI of the Civil Rights Act. In 1976, the case was argued before the state supreme court. The court at the time was thought to be liberal, and it was assumed that the court would support the university and uphold the idea of special preferential treatment of minorities. However, this action did not occur. The court barred the university from using race in the admissions process and ordered it to provide evidence that Bakke would not have been admitted under a race-neutral program. The university conceded that it could not do so, and the court ordered Bakke's admission.

The story does not end there. The university requested that the U.S. Supreme Court review the case and in the meantime halt the order requiring Bakke's admission. In 1978, the majority of the U.S. Supreme Court found that the special quota program, which earmarked a specific number of seats for minorities, did discriminate against Bakke. However, they also ruled that less restrictive programs, such as making race one of several factors in admission, would not be discriminatory. Justice Powell offered the example of the admissions program at Harvard University as one he believed would pass constitutional muster: Harvard did not set rigid quotas for minorities, but actively recruited them and sought to include them as more than a token part of a racially and culturally diverse student body. Although a white student might still lose out to a minority student with lesser academic qualifications, the admissions program at Harvard could theoretically help (or hurt) any student by reviewing other factors that would contribute to a diverse student body, such as the ability to play sports or a musical instrument. The Supreme Court saw no constitutional violation in using race as one of several factors used to enhance diversity. Yet, Justice Powell noted that, because the university had admitted that it could not prove that Bakke would not have been admitted under a race-neutral admissions program, the portion of the California Supreme Court's decision ordering Bakke's admission was upheld. In 1980, Bakke entered medical school, eventually becoming an anesthesiologist.

A number of other test cases have redefined the scope of affirmative action. In a 2003 case at the University of Michigan, the Supreme Court ruled that the school's point system that gave minority applicants a better chance of acceptance was unconstitutional. The justices affirmed the law school's more individualized method of reviewing applicants, which allows race to be one of many factors in deciding whom to admit. The point system was considered by the majority of the Supreme Court justices to be too "mechanistic" and was considered tantamount to a quota system.

Opponents were not satisfied and felt the ruling did not go far enough, and in 2006, they put affirmative action to a state vote. The people voted 58 to 42 to amend the State Constitution to prohibit preferential treatment in public education, government contracting, and public employment. Groups favoring affirmative action sued to block the part of the law concerning higher education. They noted that the number of minority students admitted to the most selective schools declined in those states that forbid affirmative action. They wanted the Supreme Court to intervene.

In 2014, Michigan was once again in the limelight on affirmative action. The Supreme Court upheld the Michigan constitutional amendment passed in 2006 that banned affirmative action in admissions to the state's public universities. In the 6 to 2 ruling (with Justice Sotomayor and Justice Ginsburg dissenting), the majority claimed that there were no legal grounds for overruling the will of the voters in that state. Their ruling effectively endorsed similar measures in seven other states and may encourage more states to enact measures banning the use of race in admissions. Justice Sotomayor's written dissent touched on the personal importance of affirmative action (Lempert, 2014):

> [R]ace matters for reasons that really are only skin deep, that cannot be discussed any other way, and that cannot be wished away. Race matters to a young man's view of society when he spends his teenage years watching others tense up as he passes, no matter the neighborhood where he grew up. Race matters to a young woman's sense of self when she states her hometown, and then is pressed, "No, where are you really from?" regardless of how many generations her family has been in the country. Race matters to a young person addressed by a stranger in a foreign language, which he does not understand because only English was spoken at home. Race matters because of the slights, the snickers, the silent judgments that reinforce that most crippling of thoughts: "I do not belong here."

What Do You Think?

Referring to Justice Sotomayor's comment, have you ever felt "I do not belong here," for reasons related to race, ethnicity, sex, age, gender orientation, income, or some other reason? How did it make you feel? What did you do about it?

Future Prospects

Despite the legislative challenges, the Supreme Court has established the value of affirmative action programs in schools and work settings. The need is not expected to last forever: "We expect that 25 years from now, the use of racial preferences will no longer be necessary to further the interest approved today," former Justice O'Connor wrote in 2003. Doing the math, this prediction would suggest that affirmative action programs will no longer be needed by 2028. Whether that situation will indeed be the case is a matter of speculation.

Although it is too soon to know the fate of affirmative action policies in the current presidential administration, national surveys reveal that most Americans support affirmative action programs on campus. As shown in Figure 7–7, 63 percent of adults in 2014 believed that "in general affirmative action programs designed to increase the number of black and minority students on college campuses" were a good thing. Nonetheless, it seems likely that preferential selection systems of any kind will continue to come under attack by a ferocious group of dissenters, at least in public institutions like universities and agencies of government. The same is not entirely true of private businesses. Major corporations like Texaco and Verizon have affirmative action recruitment policies for women and minorities and will maintain those policies because they fear negative publicity and wish to please the vast markets they serve. This approach may not be true of all corporations, but it has been a pattern for many large corporations that operate in global markets.

Figure 7–7 Share of Americans Supporting Affirmative Action on College Campuses, 2014

SOURCE: Drake, 2014.

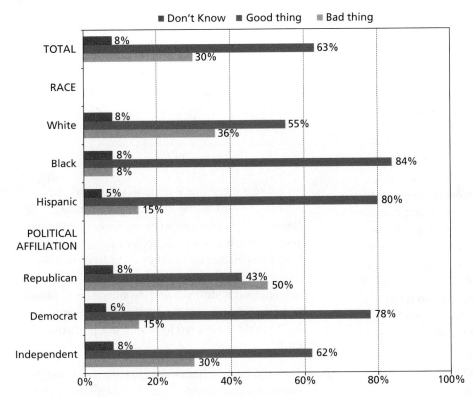

Going Beyond Left and Right

Conservatives tend to dislike affirmative action because they believe that it discriminates against individuals who themselves are not responsible for past patterns of racism and discrimination. Liberals want to redress old patterns of racial and ethnic inequality and argue that, when other considerations are equal, race or descent may be valid criteria for allocating scarce resources like scholarships. However, it is best not to overgeneralize. As you saw in Figure 7–7, although 50 percent of Republicans believe that affirmative action on college campus was a "bad thing," 43 percent of Republicans reported that it was actually a "good thing." In other words, the number of Republicans opposing affirmative action at universities is not much larger than the number of Republicans who support it.

Where do you stand on these issues? You may be among the majority who would like to see less racism and discrimination and more equality, but you may also have some concerns about whether affirmative action is reverse discrimination. Sociologists are also concerned, and prominent sociologist William J. Wilson and many others argue for race-blind social policies that will not create reverse discrimination but will address past patterns of racism and the inequalities they engendered. Such policies would create jobs where there is high unemployment and increase educational and training opportunities wherever people need them, thus dealing with the needs of people on a class basis rather than in terms of their race or ethnic status. Many conservatives have doubts about any government-sponsored program to deal with inequality, but they are more willing to entertain such race-blind policies than those directed at particular groups.

An example of race-blind social policy in the interests of increasing diversity and equality of opportunity is the practice recently instituted by Harvard and other private universities of awarding full scholarships to students who have been accepted by the university but whose families earn less than $50,000 per year. Since more minority students than white students fall into this category, this strategy is showing some success at encouraging minority enrollments. Other universities have taken note, and offer similar programs.

No one really knows whether former Justice O'Connor's prediction about affirmative action being unnecessary by 2028 will come true. It does remain, however, that eliminating individual and institutional racism is a very long process, and while America has made many significant strides, it still has a long way to go on its journey.

Summary

- The United States is becoming more diverse due to immigration patterns and birthrates among minority groups. Currently a little more than one person in three is a member of a minority group; however, by 2060, minority groups are likely to comprise about 56 percent of the U.S. population. The percentage of blacks and American Indians will remain relatively stable, Asian Americans/Pacific Islanders will nearly double but remain a small group, and the growth of Hispanic groups will be considerable.

- The Thirteenth, Fourteenth, and Fifteenth Amendments to the Constitution were ratified in the 1860s and 1870s, but it was not until the mid-twentieth century that the rights guaranteed by these amendments began to be exercised. It took further legislation, such as the Civil Rights Act passed in 1964, to make discrimination illegal. But the discrepancy between legal equality and actual inequality remains and progress is slow.

- There is no clear line between totally dominant and totally minority groups; rather, any given group can be placed at some point along a continuum of "minorityness," and this continuum can shift historically and cross-culturally. What is defined as a minority group at one point in time, or in one particular culture, may not be seen as a minority elsewhere.

- Racism is behavior, in word or deed, that is motivated by the belief that human races have distinctive characteristics that determine abilities. Racists believe in this erroneous concept of race; they also believe that their own race is superior and therefore ought to dominate or rule other races. Racism may be an attribute of an individual, or it may be incorporated into the institutions (social structures and laws) of

an entire society. Prejudice is an emotional, rigid attitude toward members of the subordinate group. Prejudiced people tend to be so committed to their prejudgments about a particular category of people that, even in the face of rational evidence that the prejudgment is wrong, they will maintain their prejudice, even defend it strongly, and denounce the evidence. Discrimination is the overt differential treatment of individuals considered to belong to a particular social group.

- The origins of prejudice and discrimination are numerous and complex, and to explain them, it is necessary to consider both the individuals and the structural organization of society.

- Institutional discrimination is an unconscious result of the structure and functioning of the public institutions and policies themselves. It is more difficult to prove than other forms of individual discrimination. There are many types of institutional discrimination, including in education, housing, employment and earnings, and justice.

- There are two types of general responses to prejudice and discrimination. The first response focuses on the individual, and the second focuses on the larger group's protective reactions against prejudice and discrimination.

- Affirmative action refers to policies based on a body of federal law originating in the 1964 Civil Rights Act that bans discrimination on the basis of race, religion, sex, or national origin in such areas as employment, education, and housing. Affirmative action programs require institutions that have engaged in discriminatory practices to increase opportunities for women and members of minority groups.

Chapter 8
Sex and Gender

Learning Objectives

8.1 Analyze the distinction between sex and gender.

8.2 Define traditional gender roles.

8.3 Examine the roots of sexism and inequality.

8.4 Identify several examples of sexism and inequality today.

8.5 Assess the sources of sexism.

8.6 Describe the Women's Movement and its policy agenda.

Joelle Taylor is getting married next month. In the whirlwind of final preparations for a large wedding, she almost forgot about gathering all the documents she will need to revise once she changes her last name to Robson. Joelle Robson! Joelle asked her maid of honor for some assistance in coordinating her name change, knowing that there will be a lot of forms to fill out. Her maid of honor gave her an odd look, and responded "What? You're not going to change your name, are you? That's so old-fashioned ... so sexist ... so ugh." Joelle was shocked by her friend's response. Don't all women change their name when they get married? What's the big deal, she wondered? With the help of her maid of honor, Joelle did a little investigating and found that most women today do change their last names when they marry. Joelle also found out that several hundred years ago, married women had no surnames at all. They were simply the wives of so-and-so. By the sixteenth century, women began to routinely take the surnames of their husbands because they were considered his property, and religious doctrine of the time considered husband and wife to be a single person. That single person was the man; the woman could not hold property, vote, or speak out in a public assembly. Legally, wives virtually ceased to exist. In more modern times, most women continued to take their husband's names when they married, but the likelihood of doing so shifted somewhat from one decade to the next. But as if the name change quandary wasn't enough, Joelle's investigation also identified other aspects of weddings and married life that surprised her. Her engagement ring is a carryover from a custom designed to take women off the marriage market; the practice of a father giving his daughter away and handing her to the groom is exactly how it sounds; the tradition of a bride's parents paying for the wedding is reminiscent of dowry; the woman's white wedding dress symbolizes virginity; and her husband's lifting of the veil symbolizes his right to consummate the marriage. "Hmmm," said Joelle, "I just had no idea. Why do these sexist customs persist?"

Personal questions like Joelle's have sociological significance. Have you noticed that most women routinely change their last name when they marry, whereas men virtually never do so? There have been times in history when it was common for women to keep their last names, but over the past generation that trend has been declining. Why do women change their last names when they marry? Some may argue, "It's just easier this way ...", but look at macro-explanations: Changing of wives' names is a carryover from older patriarchal and patrilineal customs where upon marriage a woman became the legal property of her husband. It was important to name the child after the father so that he could identify and establish "ownership" of his heirs. Surnames (last names) were created to codify inheritance rules and thereby bolster tax revenues (Stevens, 1999). But why does the tradition continue today? Much of what people do in marriage is simply done out of habit, even when the tradition has no legal or financial basis. There is a powerful pull toward reproducing tradition. Yet, these persistent traditions tell something about women's continued roles in our society.

Virtually all social institutions—whether political, religious, economic, educational, or familial—distinguish between men and women in fundamental ways. Throughout the world, people are virtually obsessed with perceived sex differences, and these differences become the basis on which power is distributed. Perceptions about differences between men and women are sometimes used to deny women equal rights under the law or equal opportunities in work or education.

Yes, it is true that, over the past several decades women in the United States and around the world have made many notable gains. Rates of literacy are increasing; more women are gaining political rights in more nations; and there is an increasingly active global array of women's organizations working to achieve the rights and empowerment goals set forth at the historic Beijing Conference in 1995 in which 189 countries signed a declaration to promote women's rights. In many impoverished regions, it is women who form economic cooperatives, develop women's reproductive health clinics, carry forward the fight for women's political rights, and provide the greatest impetus to positive social change and economic development.

In Western countries, women are increasingly gaining education and entering occupations that were traditionally dominated by men. For example, in the United States, about one-third of lawyers and physicians are now women (American Bar Association, 2014; Association of American Medical Colleges, 2013). Moreover, the gap between the earnings of men and women is narrowing. In early 2015, the median earnings of women who worked full-time were about 82 percent of those of men, compared with 68 percent in 1985, just a generation ago (Bureau of Labor Statistics, 2015).

Despite the gains of recent decades, however, sex discrimination and stereotyping continue to limit the opportunities of women. The extent to which women remain subordinate to men remains a severe obstacle to further development. From a global perspective, women face an array of daunting social problems, including dire poverty, severe lack of rights in many nations and cultures, forced marriage, rape and other violence, enslavement in sex industries, and societal failure to recognize and develop their full human potential (Kristof and WuDunn, 2010, 2014). Globally, women are beset by hunger and violence far more than are men.

In the United States, working women are still shunted into the "girl's ghetto": housekeeping; retail trades; insurance; real estate; and service positions such as secretary, receptionist, telephone operator, and clerk (Bureau of Labor Statistics, 2014). Even when women are in the same professions or occupations as men, their salaries are lower; subtle and persistent discrimination in employment and salaries is still widespread.

Furthermore, at this writing, there are only 20 women senators and 82 women in the U.S. House of Representatives, representing 20 percent and 19 percent, respectively. While these percentages represent significant boosts within a generation, few think the present proportions are sufficient given that women make up more than 50 percent of the population.

This chapter explores the relevance of sex and gender in our lives—within our societies, our culture, our social institutions, and our families and close relationships. Sex and gender are major organizing constructs within societies, cultures, social institutions, and personal relationships. You may be thinking that the two concepts are the same, but they are quite different.

Is It Sex or Gender?

8.1 Analyze the distinction between sex and gender.

The term **sex** refers to biological differences and one's role in reproduction, as indicated in Table 8–1. Typically, people think of sex in terms of genitalia: male and female, or man and woman. However, anatomical categories are not always easily identifiable, as is the case with **intersexed** individuals. The ambiguity is often the result of chromosomal or hormonal imbalances during the prenatal stage. It is difficult to get a firm number of intersexed individuals because sexual ambiguities occur along a continuum and not everyone agrees on what exactly constitutes an intersexed person. The frequency of surgery needed to normalize the genital appearance runs about 1 or 2 for every 1,000 births. The genitals are usually surgically reconstructed to adhere to the child's genetic chromosomes, either XX for a female or XY for a male.

In contrast to sex, which is rooted in biology, **gender** refers to the culturally and socially constructed differences between males and females, which are found in the meanings, beliefs, and practices associated with femininity and masculinity. These concepts are learned attitudes and behaviors, not biological or physical qualities. Gender is socially constructed; expectations about gender differ around the globe. People may be born male or female, but they learn the culturally and socially prescribed traits associated with masculine or feminine patterns of behavior.

sex

Biological differences and one's role in reproduction.

intersexed

Individuals with anatomical categories that are not easily identifiable.

gender

The culturally and socially constructed differences between males and females, which are found in the meanings, beliefs, and practices associated with femininity and masculinity.

Table 8–1 Summary of Sex and Gender

Sex
• Biological differences and role in reproduction
• Usually "male" or "female," although some people are intersexed

Gender
• Culturally and socially constructed differences associated with men and women
• "Masculinity" or "femininity" is learned

Gender Is Socially Constructed

In most societies throughout the world today, and certainly throughout history, men and women have been viewed as far more different than alike. Men and women even refer to one another as "the opposite sex." Men are often assumed to be more aggressive, sexual, unemotional, rational, and task oriented than women, whereas women are assumed to be more nurturing, passive, and dependent. Many social roles played out in families every day reflect these presumed characteristics. For example, research shows that mothers spend far more time than do fathers on childcare, even when both work outside the home for pay, because women are thought to be more innately nurturing (Parker and Wang, 2013).

However, the suggestion that men and women are the opposite of one another is seriously flawed. Modern social science and biological researchers note that men and women are far more alike than different (Eliot, 2009; Lindsey, 2011). Both men and women express aggression, passivity, nurturance, rationality, instrumentality, and other gender-typed behaviors. All people possess both so-called masculine and feminine traits, although to varying degrees.

Expectations about gender are in large part socially constructed (Ward and Edelstein, 2014). They are variable across and within cultures, are historically situated, and reflect broad social patterns. Gender is not completely innate or instinctive. Rather, much of it is socially and culturally produced.

Sex Differences

Even though men and women are far more alike than they are different from one another, it is important to note that the biological differences between men and women extend beyond the ones necessary for reproduction (Helgeson, 2012). Although using human subjects in this line of research presents a set of particular challenges, many studies suggest that males are biologically stronger, more active, and more aggressive than females, on average. However, in other ways, males are more fragile. Males suffer from a wider variety of physical illnesses; infant mortality rates are higher among males; and their life expectancy is shorter in almost all countries, including the United States (Ward et al., 2014; Population Reference Bureau, 2015). Males are afflicted with more genetic disorders and suffer from accidents at a higher rate than do females. Depression, however, is far more common among women, as learned in Chapter 3. Certainly, many men suffer from depression and many women deal with physical illness. However, scientists tend to be interested in statistically typical behaviors rather than exceptions.

There is also some scientific evidence that males and females may solve intellectual problems somewhat differently (Mosley, 2014). Although most research points to no overall differences in average levels of intelligence (measured with IQ tests), men tend to perform better at certain spatial tasks and mathematical reasoning tests. Meanwhile, women tend to outperform men in terms of the precision with which they perform certain manual tasks. Women also tend to excel on tests that measure recall of words or matching items.

What is the cause of these differences? Originally, the assumption was that these were innate biological differences. Then more recently, it was popular to attribute sex differences exclusively, or nearly so, to social learning. The argument was that males and females are treated differently because of stereotyping, and therefore, they come to behave differently and develop different skill sets. Evidence of stereotyping is overwhelming, whether in the family (Endendijk et al., 2013; Parker and Wang, 2013), in schools (Riegle-Crumb and Humphries, 2012), in the media (England, Descartes, and Collier-Meek, 2011; Peter and Valkenburg, 2007), or in work (Kaufman, 2010).

However, the most recent accumulating evidence now suggests that some cognitive and skill differences may be present at very early ages. These differences may result from hormones such as women's higher levels of estrogen and progesterone and men's higher levels of androgens, including testosterone. Exposure to different hormones begins in the uterus and may have implications for the way the brain is "wired" (McCarthy et al.,

Olympic champion athlete Bruce Jenner was born male; however, he was uncomfortable as a male from earliest memories. She has now transitioned to Caitlyn, and finally feels that she is her authentic self. In contrast, Chastity Bono, the daughter of the famous duo "Sonny and Cher," never felt quite right as a girl. Today, he lives his life comfortably as Chaz.

2012). Studies of female fetuses who had been exposed to abnormally large quantities of androgens because of a genetic defect called congenital adrenal hyperplasia (CAH) showed that the girls exposed to CAH as children were more likely to prefer playing with typically masculine toys, such as construction or transportation toys, as compared with the other girls who preferred typically feminine toys (Kimura, 2002).

Although brain research is still in its infancy, there is some evidence that the size, shape, and use of the brain may differ somewhat by sex in regions involved in language, memory, emotion, vision, hearing, and navigation (Becker et al., 2008; Hines, 2005). Some studies suggest that women may use more parts of their brain at once, while men are more inclined to have focused responses (Onion, 2005). One study conducted with mice has shown that, as mammals develop in the womb, testosterone and related hormones trigger cell death in some regions of the male brain and foster cell development in other regions (Forger et al., 2004). Removing or adding testosterone in mice shortly after birth causes their brains to develop according to the presence or absence of the hormone, regardless of their sex.

Given these intriguing studies, what is the role of nature versus nurture, and how would this relationship play out in personal relationships, social institutions, cultures, and societies? Social scientists suggest that most sex differences are probably a result of both biological and social influences, with social factors powerfully shaping biological ones (Eliot, 2009; Etaugh and Bridges, 2013; Fine, 2010). This process becomes clear when examining the wide variety of sex and gendered expectations cross-culturally. What one culture defines as distinctly feminine behavior or activities, another culture may see as quite masculine, as the research by the famous anthropologist George Murdock (1949, 1957) has shown. Are females more emotional—or are males? Answers to questions like this one are not universal; they vary across different cultures.

Although all people may possess both masculine and feminine traits, most people display primarily the gendered traits that are associated with their sex in a particular culture. Females are indeed usually more "feminine" and tend to behave in culturally prescribed feminine ways, and males are more "masculine." This tendency is likely due to both the strong cultural messages received throughout our lives as well as various biological forces.

Incongruence between Sex and Gender

Most people (but certainly not all) have a binary view of sex and gender; that is, you are either male and expected to behave in masculine ways or female and expected to behave in feminine ways. An interesting exception to this expectation occurs on a cultural level in Native American culture, in which berdache, or Two-Spirit, men assume a woman's social roles in virtually every respect. They are considered a third gender and not necessarily gay or lesbian.

What Do You Think?

How would your life be different if you were the "opposite" sex? Put yourself in the same family and general social setting, but as the opposite of the sex you are now. Describe the changes that might take place.

Transgender people manifest characteristics, behaviors, or self-expressions associated typically with the other sex (American Psychological Association, 2011; Pardo, 2008; PFLAG, 2013). They may feel that inside that they are truly the other sex. A man may feel more relaxed, comfortable, and normal engaging in feminine behaviors—such as wearing certain clothing (dresses), engaging in particular grooming practices (painting nails), or having typically feminine hobbies—than he does in engaging in masculine ones. Transgender women are not usually as obvious in Western cultures because women are allowed more leeway to behave in traditionally masculine ways, such as wearing men's clothing or acting aggressively.

Transgender issues have been largely ignored historically, but this situation is beginning to change as more transgender people speak out. Caitlyn Jenner, who was a male Olympic athlete in the 1970s, and Chaz Bono, a writer and musician and who was the daughter of the famous singers Sonny and Cher, are examples of celebrities who have been transitioned. Because of the long-held stigma associated with being transgender, no one knows the exact number of transgender men and women. The most frequently cited estimate in the United States is around 700,000 people, or 0.2 to 0.3 percent of the population (Lewis, 2015).

Some transgender individuals harbor a deep sense of discomfort about their sex and wish to live fully as members of the other sex (Shipherd, Green, and Abramovitz, 2010). These persons may undergo sex reassignment surgery and hormone treatments, either male-to-female or female-to-male. Surgery is very expensive, and the preparation is time-consuming. It is estimated that between 100 and 500 sex reassignment surgeries are conducted each year in the United States, and 2 to 5 times this many worldwide. Perhaps 25,000 U.S. adults have undergone sex reassignment surgery (*Encyclopedia of Surgery*, 2015).

The Social Evaluation of Sex and Gender

What should be clear by now is that men and women are somewhat different and somewhat alike and that the gender roles associated with sex are socially constructed and vary not only from one place to another but also from one historical time period to another. Why is this information important for the study of social problems?

It is important because societies, cultures, social institutions, and personal relationships *evaluate* these sex and gender differences, and guess what? Women very often come up short. Around the globe, women are often considered "less than" men. Women are trafficked as sex slaves, are mutilated by having their clitorises cut out from their bodies, are denied access to schools, are forbidden the right to vote, are raped on college campuses (among other places), are paid less than men for equal work, are subjected to the rule of their husbands, and are forced to marry, because women have been deemed as less important, less valuable, less intelligent, and less morally righteous than men. *This* oppression is a social problem, indeed.

What Do You Think?

Can you identify a specific personal experience situation in which you felt that men and women (or masculinity and femininity) were evaluated differently? How did this make you feel?

Traditional Gender Roles

8.2 Define traditional gender roles.

In Chapter 7, we suggested that prejudice—a predisposition to regard a certain group in a certain way—often becomes the justification for discriminatory behavior. That is, if people believe that a certain group is "inferior" or "different," they can easily justify less-than-equal treatment of its members. It is also suggested that the norms of society are an important source of prejudice and discrimination. If an entire society is prejudiced against a certain group and discriminates against it, then most members of that society will accept such actions as natural and right.

Until the early 1970s or so, it was widely accepted that the primary desirable roles for a woman were wife, mother, and homemaker and that her entire life should revolve around these roles. Women were expected to be nurturing and skilled in the emotional aspects of personal relationships. They were considered too delicate to do "men's work" and therefore were legally denied many career and job opportunities. In contrast, men were expected to be leaders and providers, highly rational and able to not let emotions get in the way of action. They were taught to "act like a man" and that "big boys don't cry." These expectations often caused men to deny their emotions and thus made them less able to enjoy many aspects of life in their families and communities. Women and men were thought to be different and hence were treated differently by social institutions–including the government and legal system.

Today many people think of the traditional roles of women and men as somewhat outdated. However, as you will see later in this chapter, vestiges of these roles remain. You can see them in personal relationships and in social institutions. Nonetheless, it is also true that in many countries, such as in Latin America, the Middle East, and Africa, the status of women is far more subordinate than in our own country. Women in those societies face substantial restrictions on their lives and few are able to pursue careers outside the home. Although women in Eastern European countries have greater equality with men, disparities exist there as well. For example, most physicians in Russia are women, but they receive lower pay than male physicians.

This traditional hierarchy is extremely resistant to change. Women and men are shaped by the culture in which they are raised, so that most adults are thoroughly indoctrinated or socialized for the roles their culture has prescribed for them. Change is suspect because it threatens their identity.

Within this hierarchy, there is considerable variation in the types of behavior that are considered appropriate for men and for women. These behaviors often reflect the values of a particular society more than any innate or "natural" qualities. Whereas it was once supposed that behavioral differences between men and women are innate, today it is clear that many of these differences are learned through socialization. And, although it was once believed that there are universal standards of masculine and feminine behavior, in fact the standards in other societies vary a great deal.

The Roots of Sexism and Inequality

8.3   Examine the roots of sexism and inequality.

Sexism is the counterpart of racism and ageism, which are discussed in Chapters 7 and 9, respectively. It may be defined as the "entire range of attitudes, beliefs, policies, laws, and behaviors discriminating against women (or against men) on the basis of their [sex or] gender" (Safilios-Rothschild, 1974, p. 1). In this section we describe several factors that contribute to sexism around the world and in the United States.

sexism
The entire range of attitudes, beliefs, policies, laws, and behaviors discriminating against women (or against men) on the basis of their sex or gender.

Power, Male Hegemony, and Patriarchy

Sociologists who study gender relations call attention to persistent patterns of male dominance throughout the institutions of modern societies. R. W. Connell (1995), for example, has analyzed how dramatic inequalities in the distribution of power in societies often deprive women of opportunities to realize their full potential. Connell's research shows that, wherever possible, males attempt to preserve their hegemony (controlling power) over women. In relations marked by hegemony, domination by one group, class, or sex over another is achieved by a combination of political and ideological means. Although political power or coercion is always important, ideologies can be equally important. In relationships between men and women, these ideologies differ from one culture to another. In parts of the Islamic world, male dominance is enforced by religious principles that emphasize female dominance over the home and male dominance over the world outside the home.

Connell's (1995) work shows that, in much of the industrialized world, men still have much greater access than women to cultural prestige, political authority, corporate power, individual wealth, and material comforts. Individual men or small groups may be confused or insecure about these inequalities. Men with feminist ideals may join with women in rejecting male hegemony. But despite all the recent feminist criticism and despite all the documented struggles by women to assert their equality and make political and economic gains in the workplace, men continue to be dominant. With some notable exceptions (the occasional female boss or political leader), male–female relations are structured so that women are subordinate. This subordination is reinforced by the symbolic equation of masculinity and power.

An unfortunate aspect of ideologies that support male dominance is that even people victimized by them tend to believe that they are true. Thus, many women are prejudicial to other women, undervalue the work of other women, and encourage the sexual objectification of women. Research on the influence of stereotypes focuses on how women may become obsessed with their appearance and their efforts to please males or live up to an image of femininity largely created by men. Many researchers attribute the rise of problems like anorexia and compulsive dieting to the commercialization of images of women's bodies and the prevalent notion that one cannot be too thin (DeBraganza and Hausenblas, 2010).

Stereotyping

As you saw in Chapter 7, one source of prejudice and discrimination is stereotyping—attributing a fixed and usually unfavorable and inaccurate conception to a category of people. Stereotypes often make it easier to justify unequal treatment of the stereotyped person or group.

We've discussed the ways that women are stereotyped; however, there are also a set of stereotypes about men that limits their ability to function fully and effectively. The masculine stereotype is that all men are tough, unemotional, and dominant; yet however unrealistic and inaccurate this stereotype is, many men (and women) believe it. Men may try to avoid performing traditionally "female" tasks, such as washing dishes in the home or working as a secretary or nurse, for fear that their masculinity will be questioned. And many men who might prefer the role of homemaker feel compelled to seek careers in business because they have been socialized to believe that domestic work is not really very masculine.

The masculine stereotype not only limits the freedom of men to engage in any activity or occupation they choose but also limits their personal relationships. They are uncomfortable discussing their feelings with other men, and instead, their relationships are more competitive in nature.

Examples of Sexism and Inequality Today

8.4   Identify several examples of sexism and inequality today.

Sexism is widespread and is found in virtually every society; however, it is obviously more pronounced in some societies than in others. In many places in the world today, women cannot drive, vote, divorce, or own property in their own name. In virtually every society, women's activities and jobs carry less prestige and pay than those that are primarily held by men. Even when men and women work in identical or comparable jobs, women are paid significantly less for their effort overall. Moreover, women are underrepresented in public office, and men primarily make the laws that women must follow, including those on issues that affect women in particular, such as abortion, birth control, or guaranteed family leave. These inequities are justified on the basis of biology ("it's human nature"), religion ("it's God's will"), economics ("that's not a budget priority"), or cultural customs ("that's the way we do things here"). These views are representative of **patriarchy**, a form of social organization which supports male authority.

patriarchy

A form of social organization that supports male authority.

We begin this discussion of sexism and inequality by illustrating an extreme example of patriarchy experienced in the world today. Sometimes it is easier to see how patriarchy operates by examining the most glaring example because it is often easier to identify patriarchy elsewhere than it is within our own borders. We will then turn to gendered experiences in the United States and other developed nations: Does patriarchy operate here also?

Female Genital Mutilation

The young girl introduced in A Global View: Female Genital Mutilation, like 100–140 million others, suffers as she tries to recover from the dangerous practice of female genital mutilation (FGM), also known as female genital cutting. In an excruciatingly painful procedure, often without anesthesia, a woman's clitoris, and possibly also part of her vagina, is cut and removed with a knife, razor blade, or broken glass. She is then sewn up to ensure virginity for her future husband.

A Global View

Female Genital Mutilation

Shani is a young woman born and raised in a rural village in Egypt. Like most females there, she has undergone female genital mutilation. This is her story.

My genitals were mutilated at the age of nine. I was told by my grandmother that they were taking me down to the river to perform a certain ceremony, and afterwards I would be given a lot of food to eat. As an innocent child, I did not know what was ahead of me and the pain that I would endure for the rest of my life.

Once I entered the secret area behind the bushes, I was taken to a very dark room and was told to undress. I was scared, and therefore just stood there unable to move. But an old woman blindfolded me and stripped me naked. Four strong women carried me to the site for the operation. I was forced to lie flat on my back while two women held tight to each leg, and another woman sat on my chest to prevent my upper body from squirming away. A piece of cloth was forced in my mouth to stop me screaming.

When the cutting began, I put up a big fight. I was genitally mutilated with a blunt penknife. They stabbed and cut and ripped at my body. I was not given any anesthetic in the operation and the pain was terrible and unbearable. I lost a lot of blood and it was everywhere. I kept telling them, "You're going to kill me." Yet those who took part in the operation were happy. They ignored my screams. Some of them had alcohol to drink. I saw a few other women were dancing and singing.

After the operation, they tied my legs together so I could not move. I laid this way for nearly two weeks. The medicine they put on my wound stank and was painful. When I wanted to urinate, I was forced to stand upright. The urine would spray over the wound and would cause agonizing pain all over again. Sometimes I tried not to urinate because of the terrible pain. They did not give me any antibiotics to fight against infection. Afterwards, I hemorrhaged and became anemic. I suffered for a long time from acute vaginal infections.

When I married, my husband had to rip me open again. He tried not to hurt me, but I nearly passed out from the pain.

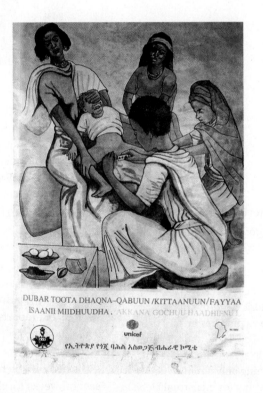

DUBAR TOOTA DHAQNA–QABUUN /KITTAANUUN/FAYYAA ISAANII MIIDHUUDHA . AKKANA GOCHUU HAADHIFNU I

He is a good man, but I hate sex, I'll always hate sex. But I know that it did not have to be this way. I've heard of other girls who were not cut. A health worker came to our village and said that cutting is no good. She urged us to leave our daughters alone. I believe her, and I will try to keep my daughter away from this.

Critical Thinking

Why do women put up with this procedure? Why don't they just say no? What obstacles might the health worker face when she goes into a village or community to tell people that "cutting is no good"? Can you design a public health strategy for eliminating, or at least reducing, female genital mutilation?

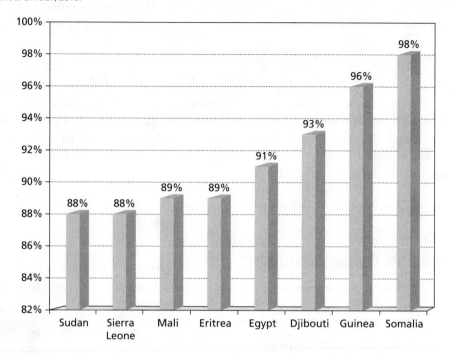

Figure 8–1 Percentage of Girls and Women in Selected African Countries Who Have Undergone Female Genital Mutilation/Cutting

SOURCE: UNICEF, 2013.

Among countries with adequate national data, Somalia, Guinea, and Djibouti have the highest prevalence of FGM; at least 90 percent to 98 percent of women ages 15–49 have had their genitals cut, as shown in Figure 8–1. In addition, the practice of FGM and its harmful consequences concerns a growing number of women and girls in Europe, North America, Australia, and New Zealand as a result of international migration. It is estimated that about 500,000 women living in Europe have had their genitals cut (World Health Organization, 2011).

In one form of genital cutting, **clitoridectomy**, the clitoris is cut out of the body. In the more extreme form, **infibulation**, the vaginal lips are also cut or scraped away, and the outer labia are stitched together, leaving only a miniscule opening for menstrual blood and urine to escape the body. The procedure is done crudely; a layperson rather than a physician usually conducts it. One study of nearly 2,000 women living in Egypt who had their genitals cut reports that only 14 percent of the cutting was performed by a doctor (Yount, 2002). In an excruciatingly painful procedure, often without anesthesia, the girl is tied or held down and the instrument used may be a knife, razor blade, or broken glass. Often, the girl's body is stitched together with thorn or catgut, and her knees are bound together for several weeks for the incision to heal itself and not tear open again when she walks.

The health consequences of genital mutilation are swift, long-lasting, and severe, and they include much more than a loss of sexual pleasure. Immediate consequences include possible shock, hemorrhaging, or bleeding to death. Soon afterwards, women face possible pelvic infection, dangerous scarring, and internal pain from urination and menstrual fluids that cannot properly escape the body. As they mature, they may experience infertility, a greater likelihood of miscarriage, recurrent urinary tract infections, anal incontinence, and fissures. Intercourse will be painful, childbirth will be prolonged and obstructed, it is likely that the perineal area will be lacerated, and there is a greater chance of stillborn births (World Health Organization, 2014).

In those countries where FGM is practiced, it has widespread support; in fact, most women intend to continue the practice with their own daughters (Williams and Sobieszczyk, 1997; Yount, 2002). One national study in Sudan revealed that close to 90 percent of all women surveyed either had the procedure performed on their daughters

clitoridectomy

A procedure in which the clitoris is cut out of the body.

infibulation

A procedure in which the clitoris is cut out of the body, the vaginal lips are cut or scraped away, and the outer labia are stitched together, leaving only a miniscule opening for menstrual blood and urine to escape the body.

or planned to do so. Nearly one-half of women who were in support of cutting favored infibulation, the most extreme form (Williams and Sobieszczyk, 1997). Even better-educated women often support it. Failure to do so will make their daughters "different" or "promiscuous" and perhaps unable to marry (Leonard, 2000; Mackie, 2000).

Why is this practice so popular, and why has it continued for so many years? It is deeply rooted in the patriarchal traditions (rather than religious teachings) in these societies (Panet, 2013). Women are expected to be subject to the social and sexual control of men at all times. They are expected to be virgins at the time of marriage and must remain sexually faithful thereafter. Removing the clitoris, the source of women's sexual pleasure, ensures that they will not experience orgasm, and thus the likelihood of engaging in or enjoying sexual relationships outside of marriage is lessened. Among women whose entire external genital area has been removed, the opening that remains is so small as to forbid penetration. Husbands are virtually guaranteed that their wives are virgins.

FGM persists, and is endorsed, perpetuated, and often conducted by other women, because their status is low and their options are few. Marriage and motherhood are the primary ways in which women receive recognition. Without marriage, they bring shame to themselves and to their families. Virginity is highly valued, and this procedure helps to ensure that women's sexuality will be muted. Mothers have been taught to believe that if they do not have their daughter's clitoris removed or have her infibulated, the chances of finding a husband will be reduced considerably and their daughter will bear considerable shame.

Sexist Standards of Beauty

After reading about FGM, it's easy to say, "Whew, I'm glad I live in the United States." However, the United States has its own set of patriarchal norms and sexist customs. Do any come to mind? How many U.S. presidents have been women? Vice presidents? Senators? How many heads of Fortune 500 companies are women? How does women's pay compare with men's? Where did you get your last name? How do standards of beauty vary for men and women—some with potentially dangerous or painful repercussions (hint: think cosmetic surgery, breast implants, waxing, or even high-heeled shoes)?

Over 1.6 million cosmetic surgery procedures are performed each year. Table 8–2 reveals the top five surgical cosmetic procedures in 2014 (American Society of Plastic Surgeons, 2015). Interestingly, all of these procedures have actually declined since 2000 with the exception of breast augmentation, which increased by over 30 percent. These procedures should be cause for concern because they are not risk-free and can have short- and long-term side effects. Women who have cosmetic surgery have internalized the media messages about "ideal" women's body image and are dissatisfied with their own bodies (Markey and Markey, 2009). The slide show illustrates the harsh standards of beauty for women throughout the world.

Women in the Labor Force

In addition to unrealistic standards of beauty, sexism is also evident in women's employment situations. Women are concentrated in lower-status jobs at the low end of the pay scale. The vast majority of retail clerks, typists, and secretaries are women, whereas men

What Do You Think?

How would you develop a campaign to eliminate female genital cutting? Who would you involve, and how would you get your message across? How would you take into account the culture in which people live?

Table 8–2 Top Five Surgical Cosmetic Procedures in 2014

Type of Procedure	Number of Procedures
Breast Augmentation	286,000
Nose Reshaping	217,000
Liposuction	211,000
Eyelid Surgery	207,000
Facelift	128,000

SOURCE: American Society of Plastic Surgeons, 2015.

Slide Show

Beauty Ideals for Women

The United States is not the only country that has harsh beauty ideals for women. Historically, and around the world today, women have endured painful procedures and have been maimed in the quest to be beautiful in the eyes of men. As you look at the photos in this slideshow, reflect on the societal pressures that women face to be beautiful.

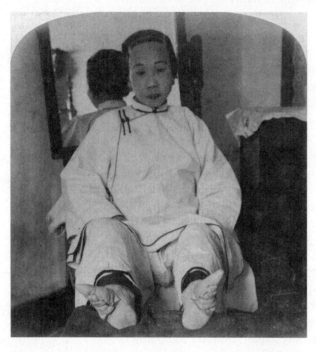

This woman, like millions of other women in China, was told that big feet are ugly on a woman. To secure a proper husband, she submitted to a procedure that slowly and painfully broke all the bones in her feet, so they could heal in a bent, deformed shape, referred to as "golden lilies" or "bound feet." Throughout the rest of her life, she could barely walk, and her dependency was considered a further attraction.

The goal of this apparatus is to give the impression of an elongated neck, a sign of a woman's maturity and beauty. Girls may begin to wear small coils at the age of 2 and gradually increase the number of coils as they grow older. The weight of the coils will eventually place sufficient pressure on the clavicles to cause them to deform and create an impression of a longer neck.

When a Suri girl in Ethiopia is about to be married, usually in her teens (around 14 or 15), the gap between her lower lip and the flesh below is pierced and gradually stretched. In the beginning a hole is made in the lip with a wooden stick. The stretch continues as successively bigger discs of clay or wood are accommodated by the disfigured lip. Generally, the two lower front teeth are pulled (or knocked) out to aid the process. The final size of the plates determines how many cattle the woman will receive as a dowry, so the more stretched her lip the better, and the more cattle the woman is worth. Some women have stretched their lips so as to allow plates up to 20 cm in diameter. Having a lip plate is considered a sign of beauty.

Singer Taylor Swift illustrates the emphasis on thinness in American culture. The desire to be unnaturally thin is related to a wide variety of dangerous eating disorders among women, including anorexia and bulimia. Why is such extreme thinness considered beautiful?

Breast augmentation is a leading form of cosmetic surgery. Very few women with low body fat would have large breasts naturally; instead, they are turning to surgery. But surgery is risky, and women could face a number of side effects. But risks notwithstanding, why do so many women want to add uncomfortable weight onto their bodies? Why do they conform to unrealistic fantasies?

Critical Thinking

Drawing on what you have learned in this chapter, why are standards of beauty for women often so extreme, and why do women go along with these standards?

account for the largest proportions of corporate directors, white-collar administrators, and blue-collar supervisors (U.S. Department of Labor, Women's Bureau, 2014). Some people may try to claim that these differences are due to men's greater educational attainment. However, that claim is not the case. On average, women have more education than do men.

HISTORY OF WOMEN'S EMPLOYMENT   Today, most women work outside the home for pay, whether or not they are married and whether or not they have children. But this practice has not always been the case. In early colonial America, most families worked closely with the land. Their lives revolved around the seasonal work necessary for farming and ranching. The labor of men, women, and children was needed and was considered invaluable to the success of the family enterprise.

In the nineteenth century, the U.S. economy was evolving from an emphasis on agriculture to an emphasis on industrialization. During this century, work was often done away from home, and people were paid wages for their labor. New industries needed expanding numbers of laborers, so, in addition to recruiting men, young, poor, minority, and immigrant women and children were hired. By 1890, 17 percent of women were in the labor force (Coontz, 2000). Much of the work in these factories was dangerous and dirty, and there were minimal occupational safety standards compared to today. Women's roles became increasingly intertwined with class and race: Poor or minority women *had* to work, whereas white middle-class women stayed far away from the outside world of work.

This pattern continued for many years. During the 1940s through the mid-1970s (except briefly during WWII), most employed women were either single, married without children, or had husbands that did not earn enough to support the family. Married mothers worked outside the home in small numbers and tended to organize their labor force participation around childbearing and childrearing. In the 1940s and 1950s, they tried to wait until their children had grown up before returning to work; in the 1960s, mothers tried to wait until their children were in high school; and by the 1970s, it had dropped to when children were in middle school. Nonetheless, the general convention was, unless a mother had to work because of dire economic circumstances, employment was secondary to the bearing and rearing of children.

By the mid-1970s, a new pattern of mothers' labor force participation emerged and has continued today: Over two-thirds of married mothers and three-quarters of unmarried mothers (i.e., never married, divorced, separated, or widowed) are employed for pay (Bureau of Labor Statistics, 2014). However, instead of continuing to adapt work to fit childbearing, the reverse has occurred. Childbearing and childrearing are being adapted to fit the demands of work. Families have delayed having children and have had fewer of them, and an increasing number of women and men have chosen not to have children at all (Martin, Hamilton, and Osterman, 2014). Thus, a macro-level condition of changing norms surrounding women's employment has led to micro-level changes in the structure of families.

Beginning in earnest in the 1970s, Americans have witnessed a restructuring of the U.S. economy. Whereas the country was once heavily dependent on raw materials and manufacturing, today the U.S. economy is heavily geared toward the provision of a wide range of services from medical care to food and entertainment. Wages have declined, and most families rely on two paychecks to make ends meet. Women contribute nearly 40 percent to the family income, up from only 27 percent a generation ago, and nearly 40 percent of married women earn more than their husbands do (Bureau of Labor Statistics, 2014).

HOW DO WOMEN WORKERS FARE?   How do female workers fare compared with their male counterparts? Table 8–3 reports women's earnings as a percentage of men's earnings among people who work full-time over an entire year (Bureau of Labor Statistics, 2014). The table compares data for whites, blacks, Asians, and Hispanics. As you can see, there has been considerable movement toward greater equality over time. The data also reveal that black and Hispanic women earn incomes closest to their male counterparts, whereas the gender gap for whites and Asians is the widest. Why do you think this is the case?

What Do You Think?

If young women between the ages of 25 and 34 earn 90 percent of men's wages (while older women earn less), do you think these young women will retain this advantage as they age, or will they see their advantage start to decline?

Interestingly, pay differences continue even among those who are most educated, as shown in Table 8–4. Women without a high school diploma earn about 81 percent of their male counterparts' salaries, whereas women with a PhD earn roughly 78 percent of men's salaries (Bureau of Labor Statistics, 2014). However, differences in pay between men and women are smaller among younger workers than they are among those who are older. For example, employed women between the ages of 25 and 34 earn about 90 percent of men's wages, while those ages 35 to 44 earn only 78 percent.

Table 8–3 Women's Earnings as a Percentage of Men's Earnings

	Total	White	Black	Asian	Hispanic
1980	64%	63%	76%	–	74%
1985	68%	67%	83%	–	78%
1990	72%	72%	85%	–	87%
1995	76%	73%	86%	–	87%
2000	77%	76%	84%	80%	88%
2005	81%	80%	89%	81%	88%
2013	82%	82%	91%	77%	91%

SOURCE: Bureau of Labor Statistics, 2014. Highlights of Women's Earnings in 2013. December. Accessed 25 September 2015. http://www.bls.gov/opub/reports/cps/highlights-of-womens-earnings-in-2013.pdf

Table 8–4 Median Weekly Earnings of Full-Time Workers, by Sex and Educational Attainment

	Women (weekly pay)	Men (weekly pay)	Women's Earnings as a Percentage of Men's Earnings
Less Than High School Diploma	$395	$488	81%
High School Graduate	$554	$720	77%
Some College/Associate's Degree	$645	$840	77%
Bachelor's Degree	$930	$1,199	78%
Master's Degree	$1,125	$1,515	74%
Professional	$1,415	$1,836	77%
Doctorate	$1,371	$1,734	79%

SOURCE: Bureau of Labor Statistics, 2014.

WHAT ACCOUNTS FOR THESE GENDER DIFFERENCES?   Realistically, differentials could be due to several factors. One explanation offered is the different work habits of men and women. For example, among full-time workers, men tend to work a greater number of hours, which could boost pay. But, as a sociologist, look at the social context of this fact—why is it men tend to work longer hours on average? Could it be because women are responsible for the majority of household labor and childcare? Many women might say that they would work longer hours if their spouse or partner made dinner, picked up the kids after school, and did the laundry. We see that, as the division of household labor has become more equitable in recent years, the amount of time women spend working has also increased.

A second and more significant explanation for pay differences is labor market segmentation in which men and women usually work in different types of jobs with distinct working conditions and pay. Women tend to work in less prestigious, nonunionized, and lower-paying jobs than men. They are found working as secretaries, registered nurses, elementary and middle school teachers, and in service work. Table 8–5 lists the 20 most common occupations for women and shows the share of female workers in the occupation as a whole. As you can see, the most common occupations that women work in tend to be dominated by women, with only a few exceptions (U.S. Department of Labor, Women's Bureau, 2014). To eliminate sex-segregated jobs in the United States, about half of male (or female) workers would have to change occupations.

A third explanation for wage differences is discrimination: Women are paid less for doing the same job as men. In virtually every job category provided by the Department of Labor, men are paid more than women. Even in occupations in which women are the large majority of workers—such as housecleaners, nurses, or clerical workers—men in these occupations earn more, as measured by average weekly earnings for full-time workers and by the earnings ratio, which divides women's earnings by those of men. The differences are particularly striking in occupations such as physicians, lawyers, and judges, which require years of professional education and experience.

Wage and job discrimination are illegal under the Equal Pay Act of 1963 and the Civil Rights Act of 1964, yet they continue to exist. Over 27,000 charges of sex discrimination were filed with the Equal Employment Opportunity Commission (EEOC) in 2014, which represents an increase of 20 percent compared with 2000. In a major sex discrimination settlement, more than 5,000 women who formerly worked for the Rent-A-Center Corporation of Plano, Texas, the nation's largest rent-to-own company, were awarded a total of $47 million in damages. Over many years, the company had systematically promoted men instead of women, and the women, finding themselves in dead-end jobs, typically left the company and found new jobs with different employers. After a suit was

Table 8–5 Twenty Most Prevalent Occupations for Employed Women

Occupation	Total Number of Women in the Occupation	Share of Female Workers in Occupation
1. Elementary and middle school teachers	2,138,000	81%
2. Secretaries and administrative assistants	2,113,000	94%
3. Registered nurses	2,023,000	90%
4. Nursing, psychiatric, and home health aides	1,207,000	89%
5. Customer service representatives	1,068,000	66%
6. First-line supervisors/managers of retail sales workers	981,000	43%
7. Accountants and auditors	945,000	62%
8. Cashiers	932,000	72%
9. Managers, all others	905,000	34%
10. First-line supervisors of office and administrative support workers	828,000	70%
11. Receptionists and information clerks	828,000	92%
12. Retail salespersons	737,000	50%
13. Office clerks, general	734,000	84%
14. Bookkeeping, accounting, and auditing clerks	702,000	89%
15. Financial managers	613,000	55%
16. Maids and housekeeping cleaners	605,000	88%
17. Waiters and waitresses	558,000	70%
18. Personal care aids	539,000	84%
19. Secondary school teachers	529,000	57%
20. Social workers	507,000	80%

SOURCE: U.S. Department of Labor, Women's Bureau, 2014.

filed with the EEOC, the company eventually settled with the plaintiffs. Unfortunately, however, hundreds of such claims are pending before the Commission, and many others have never been filed because of fear or lack of knowledge on the part of those women who have been discriminated against. But large awards such as the one involving Rent-A-Center serve to remind large employers that such discrimination is illegal.

Rape, Sexual Assault, and Harassment

Rape

Penetration, no matter how slight, of the vagina or anus with any body part or object, or oral penetration by a sex organ of another person, without the consent of the victim.

Sexual assault

An act that may include rape, but which also includes other types of behavior, such as unwanted physical contact or noncontact, unwanted sexual experiences.

Other forms of sexism are obvious in American culture. Among the most persistent and difficult aspects of sexism are rape, sexual assault, and sexual harassment. On January 1, 2013, the official legal definition of **rape** was changed from "the carnal knowledge of a female forcibly and against her will," to "penetration, no matter how slight, of the vagina or anus with any body part or object, or oral penetration by a sex organ of another person, without the consent of the victim." This expanded definition now is gender neutral and includes sodomy (oral and anal penetration) and use of an object. Rape is still rape if the victim is drunk, high, drugged, or passed out and unable to consent. Nearly 1 in 5 women in the United States has been raped in her lifetime, as compared with 1 in 71 men (Black et al., 2011).

Sexual assault may include rape, but it also includes other types of behavior, such as unwanted physical contact (e.g., grabbing or pinching a woman's breasts) or noncontact, unwanted sexual experiences (e.g., flashing or masturbating in front of the victim). More than one woman in four has experienced unwanted sexual contact, as has one in nine men. Noncontact, unwanted sexual experiences have occurred to one in three women, and one in eight men (Black et al., 2011).

Perpetrators tend to differ across these crimes, as shown in Figure 8–2. For example, rape is most likely committed by a current or former intimate partner, or by an

Figure 8-2 Lifetime Reports of Sexual Violence Among Female Victims by Type of Perpetrator, 2010

SOURCE: Black et al., 2011.

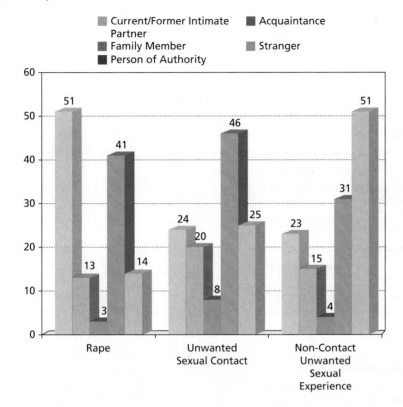

acquaintance. Unwanted sexual contact is most often committed by an acquaintance, whereas noncontact, unwanted sexual experiences tend to be initiated by strangers (Black et al., 2011). These crimes are often not reported to the police out of fear or shame.

The tumultuous 1991 Senate hearings on the confirmation of Clarence Thomas as a Supreme Court justice focused national attention on the range of behaviors that may be viewed as forms of sexual harassment. The charges leveled against Thomas by Anita Hill, a former employee and law professor, included making lewd and suggestive comments and requesting sexual favors. Partly as a result of the Hill–Thomas controversy and partly as a consequence of women's continual struggle against harassment, people throughout the nation have been drawn into a national debate over its nature and significance (Chancer, 2005).

It is illegal to harass a person because of that person's sex. Sexual harassment includes unwelcome sexual advances, requests for sexual favors, and other verbal or physical harassment of a sexual nature. Although the law does not prohibit simple teasing, offhand comments, or isolated incidents that are not very serious, harassment is illegal when it is so frequent or severe that it creates fear or creates a hostile or offensive environment (Equal Employment Opportunity Commission, 2014).

Nowadays, sexual harassment is likely to occur electronically. A large study of teenagers found that one in four dating teens is abused or harassed online or through texts by their partner. Given the importance of computers, cell phones, text messages, social networking sites, and e-mail in everyday life, abusers have another way to harass, control, degrade, and frighten their partners. Table 8–6 shows the type of electronic harassment that teens report having experienced (Zweig and Dank, 2013).

Stalking, another type of harassment, has received greater attention since California passed the first anti-stalking law in 1990. **Stalking** consists of repeated and obsessive contact or tracking of another person—attention that is unwanted and causes a reasonable concern for one's safety (Black et al., 2011). It is a combination of

What Do You Think?

Have you or someone that you know ever been abused or sexually harassed through technology? How did you (or they) respond? How does this type of harassment differ from that which is done in person?

stalking

Obsessive contact or tracking of another person—attention that is unwanted and causes a reasonable concern for one's safety.

Table 8–6 Percentage of Teenage Respondents Who Have Been Abused and Sexually Harassed Through Technology

Type of Technological Harassment	Percentage of Teenage Respondents Who Report Being Harassed
Used my social networking account without permission	8.7%
Sent me texts/e-mails/etc. to engage in **sexual acts I did not want**	7.4%
Pressured me to send a sexual or naked photo of myself	6.8%
Sent threatening messages to me	6.1%
Sent me so many messages it **made me feel unsafe**	5.5%
Posted embarrassing photos of me online	5.5%
Wrote nasty things about me on his or her profile page	5.1%
Spread rumors about me using a cell phone/e-mail/networking site, etc.	5.0%
Made me afraid when I did not respond to my cell phone/text/etc.	4.2%
Sent sexual or naked photos I did not want	3.8%
Used information from my social networking site to harass me	3.7%
Sent me instant messages or chats that **made me feel scared**	3.4%
Used a cell phone/text/etc. to **threaten to harm me physically**	2.7%
Took a video of me and sent it to his or her friends **without my permission**	2.6%
Threatened me if I did not send a sexual or naked photo of myself	2.6%
Created a profile page about me **knowing it would upset me**	1.3%

many unwanted acts that, by themselves, are not necessarily abusive—for example, sending flowers or gifts, calling on the telephone, or sending a text or e-mail—but, when taken together, may constitute a form of mental abuse. Stalking exists on a continuum. It may be so subtle that the victim is not even aware it is happening or, in contrast, the perpetrator may purposefully try to instill terror in the victim (Logan and Walker, 2009).

Some stalkers harass or threaten their victims electronically, a phenomenon known as **cyberstalking**. Repeated unwanted attention could come in the form of e-mail, texts, bulletin boards, chat rooms, or other types of media (Stalking Resource Center, 2012). One factor that distinguishes cyberstalking from other forms of stalking is ease; one can repeatedly threaten and harass a person by a simple click or swipe. In fact, programs can be set up that send messages at random times when the sender is not even physically present at the computer. Similarly, private information or rumors can be posted for others to see. Although the contact may be indirect, it can be threatening nonetheless. Table 8–6 reports the frequency with which teenagers report being victimized by technology.

THE COLLEGE ENVIRONMENT College students are particularly vulnerable to rape, sexual assault, harassment, and stalking, in part because of their age, but also because of the group living quarters and the party atmosphere at many universities. In a study of female undergraduates, 19 percent, or nearly one in five, experienced attempted or completed sexual assault since entering college. And many of the respondents in this study still had several years of college ahead of them (Centers for Disease Control and Prevention, 2012).

cyberstalking

Stalking and harassment that occurs electronically, such as through e-mail, texts, bulletin boards, chat rooms, or other types of media.

Another study by the U.S. Department of Justice reveals that 3 percent of college women are raped in a given nine-month academic year. Although that figure might not sound like a lot of women when you first read the number, ponder it more carefully. For a campus with 1,000 incoming freshmen women, it means 30 of them could be raped over the nine-month period. Over a typical five-year college career, that share translates to about 150 rapes in this cohort—and that does not even include the risk in the other three months of summer (Fisher, Cullen, and Turner, 2000).

Who is being raped, and who is doing the raping? Among college students, about 80 percent of victims and perpetrators know each other; they are intimate partners, "friends," roommates, acquaintances, and classmates. Women are raped by their study partner on the way to the library, by the guy they just met at the party in the dorm, by their roommate's brother, or by the partner they are involved with.

The pioneering work of Mary Koss and her colleagues (Koss and Cook, 1993; Koss, Gidycz, and Wisniewski, 1987) sheds some interesting light on college-age perpetrators. In a survey of 32 college campuses, they found that although fully 12 percent of men had committed acts that would fit the legal definition of rape or attempted rape, only 1 percent thought their actions were criminal. Many made a distinction between "forcing a girl to have sex" and "rape," as though they are different. The law, of course, makes no such distinction.

"DATE-RAPE" DRUGS   Alcohol or drugs are often involved in a sexual assault (Roudsari, Leahy, and Walters, 2009). **Date-rape drugs** such as gamma hydroxybutyrate (GHB), Rohypnol (popularly known as "roofies" or "roofenol"), or ketamine hydrochloride (ketamine) can immobilize a person to facilitate an assault (U.S. Department of Health & Human Services, Office of Women's Health, 2012). The effects of these drugs cause people to be physically helpless, lose muscle control, feel very drunk, or lose consciousness, and they often can't remember what happened. The drugs usually have no color, smell, or taste and can be easily added to flavored drinks without the victim's knowledge. How can you protect yourself? Don't accept drinks from other people; open containers yourself; keep your drink with you at all times, even when you go to the bathroom; don't share drinks; don't drink from punch bowls or other large, common, open containers because they may already have drugs in them; don't drink anything that tastes or smells strange (sometimes GHB tastes salty); and have a designated nondrinking friend with you to make sure you stay safe.

Sources of Sexism

8.5   **Assess the sources of sexism.**

We have described some of the causes of the subordination of women and indicated some of the major inequities that women face in our society. In this section, we discuss in some detail the processes by which American institutions reinforce and perpetuate sexism.

Socialization

If much of gendered behavior is socially constructed and learned, where do people learn it? **Gender socialization** is the process whereby people learn to behave according to the gendered norms of a culture. They are taught the norms associated with being male or female (Helgeson, 2012; Ward and Edelstein, 2014). Gender socialization may be a conscious effort such as a teacher criticizing a young girl for being rowdy and "unladylike" in the classroom or scolding a young boy for displaying his emotions because "big boys don't cry." It also may occur on a less conscious level, for example, parents providing different toys for their children—dress-up clothes for their daughters and war toys for their sons. The **agents**

What Do You Think?

What is it about a college environment that makes rape and sexual assault so prevalent? What do you think is happening at your college? What can or should be done about it? How can feminist theory or conflict theory guide you?

date-rape drugs

Drugs such as gamma hydroxybutyrate (GHB), Rohypnol (popularly known as "roofies" or "roofenol"), or ketamine hydrochloride (ketamine), which can immobilize a person to facilitate an assault.

gender socialization

A process whereby people learn to behave according to the gendered norms of a culture.

Table 8–7 Agents of Socialization and How They Work

Family Members

- Parents and other family members have the initial responsibility for introducing the gendered norms and expectations of their culture.

Toys

- Books show boys as leading characters and girls in stereotypical roles; toys are sex-typed.

Schools

- The "hidden curriculum" traditionally encouraged sex-typed behavior and taught girls to fear academic success. However, things are changing, and now girls are experiencing greater success at school than boys. Yet, training for many occupations remains sex-typed.

Peers

- Same-sex play reinforces different interaction styles that carry over into adulthood.

Media

- Television, music videos, and electronic games tend to focus more on boys and present girls in stereotypical and sexist ways.

agents of socialization

The people, social institutions, and organizations that teach boys and girls their gendered expectations.

Toys for boys and girls differ and perpetuate gendered stereotypes. Dolls for boys are called "action figures" and usually emphasize toughness, whereas dolls for girls emphasize domesticity.

of socialization, summarized in Table 8–7, include the people, social institutions, and organizations that teach boys and girls their gendered expectations. Through socialization, people internalize to varying degrees the roles, norms, and values of their culture and subculture, which become their guides to behavior and shape their deepest beliefs.

FAMILY MEMBERS Parents and other family members have the initial responsibility for introducing the gendered norms and expectations of their culture (Endendijk et al., 2013; Marks, Lam, and McHale, 2009). They teach a child about what to wear, how to behave, what toys to play with, what the child's status is, and what the overall expectations are for the child. Consciously or not, parents, especially fathers, often treat their sons and daughters differently. They hold baby girls more gently and cuddle them more than they do boys. Parents of girls describe their children as more dainty and delicate than do parents of boys, and the choice of dress usually reflects these perceptions (Leaper and Friedman, 2006). This different treatment might help to explain why many parents hold a specific preference for their child's sex, as discussed in A Closer Look: A Son or a Daughter?

TOYS Children's toys and games are also differentiated on the basis of sex (Auster and Mansbach, 2012). Toys for boys often emphasize rough-and-tumble play (e.g., sports, guns, vehicles, action figures), whereas toys for girls often focus on quiet or nurturing activities (e.g., dolls, arts and crafts, kitchens and cooking).

An analysis of virtually any children's toy store will reveal that pink aisles specialize in girl toys whereas others are reserved for toys for boys. Toy websites are equally gendered (Auster and Mansbach, 2012). A toy as seemingly gender-neutral as a bicycle takes on great gender significance by its color: pink for girls, blue for boys. Books, too, give a lopsided view of the world and reinforce traditional stereotypes. A review of the 200 best-selling children's books and a seven-year sample of Caldecott award-winning books revealed that there were nearly twice as many male as female title and main characters; male characters appeared in illustrations 53 percent more than female characters; and female characters nurtured others more than did male characters, were seen in more indoor than outdoor scenes, and were more likely than male characters to have no paid occupation (Anderson and Hamilton, 2006).

A Closer Look

A Son or a Daughter?

If you could have only one child, would you prefer to have a son or a daughter?

Around the world, many couples are answering this question with a resounding "son!" The preference for sons over daughters has dramatically shifted the sex ratio in countries like China and India, where strict birth control is encouraged but patriarchal norms are prominent. Preference for boys is also found in many other cultures throughout the world. This preference could lead to a worldwide shortage of girls now that various techniques for detecting the sex of a fetus can be assessed. But what about the United States? Is there a preference for sons over daughters here?

The Gallup Poll conducts research on a variety of social, economic, and political issues, using large, nationally representative samples of adults in the United States, and the data collected can be compared over time to assess how things are (or are not) changing. Gallup has conducted telephone interviews with over 1,000 adults ages 18 and older, living in all 50 states and the District of Columbia. Americans have been asked about their preferences for a boy or girl—using slightly different wordings over the years—since 1941. The findings are generally consistent: If Americans could have only one child, they would prefer that it be a boy rather than a girl by a 40 percent to 28 percent margin (Newport, 2011). The preference for sons is highest among men, and, rather surprisingly, highest among younger adults. Younger men ages 18 to 49 prefer boys to girls by a 54 percent to 19 percent margin, as you can see in Table 8–8. Republicans, conservatives, and those with less education also tend to prefer a son.

Think about the sociological implications of these data. Why do men most starkly want sons, but women do not seem to care? Why are younger people, who are usually more liberal on social issues, more likely to want sons than are older people? And finally, do Americans deliberately attempt to select the sex of their child? The answer to that last question might depend on the power relationships between men and women, because it is young males, not their female wives and partners,

Table 8–8 Preference for a Son versus a Daughter, Responses to *"Suppose you could only have one child. Would you prefer that it be a boy or a girl?"*

	Boy	Girl	Doesn't matter/ Unsure/No opinion
Total	**40%**	**28%**	**32%**
Men	49%	22%	28%
Women	31%	33%	36%
Age 18–29	54%	27%	18%
Age 30–49	39%	27%	34%
Age 50–64	34%	29%	37%
Age 65 and over	31%	29%	40%
Men 18–49	54%	19%	26%
Women 18–49	36%	35%	28%
Men 50 and over	41%	26%	33%
Women 50 and over	25%	32%	42%
Postgraduate	32%	33%	35%
College Graduate	35%	29%	36%
Some College	39%	28%	33%
High School or less	44%	25%	30%
Republicans/Leaners	43%	25%	30%
Democrats/Leaners	39%	33%	28%
Conservative	41%	25%	34%
Moderate	40%	27%	33%
Liberal	36%	37%	28%

who clearly prefer sons over daughters. This trend is certainly one to watch.

Critical Thinking

Why do men most starkly want sons, but women do not seem to care? Why are younger people, who are usually more liberal on social issues, more likely to want sons than are older persons? Do Americans deliberately attempt to select the sex of their child?

SCHOOLS Schools represent a more formal type of socialization. Considering how much time children spend in school, the socialization they receive there inevitably affects how they behave. Daycare centers, preschools, elementary schools, secondary schools, and even college classrooms are important arenas in which gender socialization occurs. Research a decade or two ago revealed that teachers called on boys to answer questions more often than girls and that boys were given more public praise by teachers. The **hidden curriculum** informally teaches gendered norms, and in this case, taught girls that academic achievement could mean forfeiting popularity (Orenstein, 1994). Consequently, although girls tended to excel in elementary school, by the time they reached middle and upper school, they lost confidence and tested more poorly than boys (Kenney-Benson et al., 2006).

What Do You Think?

Reflect on the toys you played with as a child or the books you read. Were they sex-typed? If so, why did you have sex-typed toys?

hidden curriculum

An undocumented teaching approach that informally teaches gendered norms.

But something has changed. In recent years, much emphasis has been placed on ridding the schools of bias against female achievement and gender equality. Today, it appears that many girls and young women have a strong achievement ethic, are doing well in school, and are surpassing boys and young men. More girls apply to, attend, and graduate from college now than boys (Gonzales, Allum, and Sowell, 2013; National Center for Education Statistics, 2014). And over half (53 percent) of doctorates, the highest achievement, are now awarded to women. Many college majors, however, remain sex-typed. Students in nursing, elementary education, and social work are overwhelmingly female, whereas students in engineering and computer science are primarily male. At the doctoral level, women are overrepresented in the fields of education, health sciences, and the social and behavioral sciences. Women remain underrepresented in math, computer science, and the physical sciences.

PEERS Peer groups, an important source of socialization, grow in importance as a child ages (Mulvey and Killen, 2014; Kwon, Lease, and Hoffman, 2012). However, even young children are socialized by their same-sex peers to conform to traditional gender expectations. Psychologist Eleanor Maccoby (1998), in her seminal study of children's play groups, found that children between the ages of 2 and 3 tend to prefer same-sex peer play groups when provided with the opportunity to do so. She also noted that when girls were playing with other girls, they were as active as were boys playing with other boys. However, when girls were playing with boys, they frequently stood back and let the boys dominate the toys or games. Maccoby speculated that the boys' rougher play and greater focus on competition was unattractive to girls, and girls responded by pulling back rather than by trying to exert their own play style. Maccoby suggests that these peer groups reinforce different interaction styles that carry over into adulthood: Boys' groups reinforce a more competitive, dominance-oriented style of interaction, which carries over into adult male communication patterns that include greater interrupting, contradicting, or boasting. Girls' cooperative groups reinforce a style that contributes to adult female communication patterns, including expressing agreement and acknowledging the comments of others and asking questions rather than making bold pronouncements. A study in Texas found that children who engage in more same-sex play were better liked by peers and were viewed by teachers as being socially competent (Colwell and Lindsey, 2005).

MASS MEDIA The mass media, including television, radio and video games, are an important mechanism for socializing children. Video games are an increasing part of children and teen's entertainment, and consumers spent over $20 billion on games, hardware, and accessories in 2014 (Entertainment Software Association, 2015). Women and girls are portrayed in these games much less frequently than are men and boys, and when they are included, are often shown in subordinate or "hypersexualized" ways (Downs and Smith, 2010; Near, 2013; Terlecki et al., 2011). In videos with ratings of Teen or Mature, women's bodies are often artificially thin with exaggerated breasts. They are also considerably more attractive than most of the male characters and are often portrayed with revealing clothing.

Boys, especially middle-class white boys, are at the center of most children's television programming, playing the most roles and engaging in the most activity (Gerding and Signorielli, 2014). Reviews of recent children's television shows reveal that male characters are still more likely than female characters to answer questions, boss or order others, show ingenuity, and achieve a goal. A study of morning commercials showed that half of the commercials targeted to girls spoke about physical attractiveness, whereas none of the commercials targeted to boys mentioned attractiveness (National Institute on Media and the Family, 2009). Incidentally, females are less likely than males to be shown eating, not an insignificant finding given the higher rates of eating disorders among girls and women (National Institute of Mental Health, 2013).

Recent advertising campaigns have sought to attract the growing population of educated females by presenting successful businesswomen and female scientists to endorse products. But the patterns of sexism in advertising remain strong: Sex appeal and sexual stereotypes are still used to sell many products.

Socialization reinforces sexism, as do many social institutions. In particular, organized religion and the legal system contribute to sexism in our society.

Organized Religion

Women attend church more frequently, pray more often, hold firmer beliefs, and cooperate more in church programs than men do; yet, organized religion is dominated by men (Giroux, 2005; Mills, 1972). In their theological doctrines and religious hierarchies, churches and synagogues tend to reinforce women's subordinate role. Explicit instructions to do so can be found in the Bible: "A woman must be a learner, listening quietly and with due submission. I do not permit a woman to be a teacher, nor must woman domineer over man; she should be quiet. For Adam was created first, and Eve afterwards; and it was not Adam who was deceived; it was woman who, yielding to deception, fell into sin" (Timothy 2:11–15).

Historically, organized religion has reinforced many secular traditions and norms, including the traditional views that men are primary and women secondary, and that a woman's most important role is procreation. In Judaism, women are required to obey fewer religious precepts than are men because less is expected of them. Orthodox Jewish males recite a prayer each morning in which they thank God that they are not women. The Catholic Church still assumes authority over a woman's sexual behavior, forbidding the use of birth control devices because they prevent reproduction.

In recent decades there have been some changes. The movement to allow women to hold leadership positions in churches and synagogues has had some success: In more liberal denominations (such as Episcopalians, Presbyterians, and Reformed Jews), women may be ordained as ministers and rabbis. Within the Catholic Church, there are groups of women devoted to changing the norm against female priests, but they encounter resistance from traditionalists in the Catholic hierarchy (Carbine, 2010).

The Government and Legal System

There have been many legal barriers to sexual equality throughout history. For example, a 1919 study by the Women's Bureau (a federal bureau created by Congress) found that women were explicitly barred from applying for 60 percent of all civil-service positions, notably those involving scientific or other professional work. Women were placed in a separate employment category, and their salaries were limited. Many labor laws were also implemented for women during the early and mid-1900s, such as those that set shorter work hours, allowed lower wages, regulated how much a woman could lift, and required breaks from work for lunch or bathroom use (Stansell, 2010). These laws were ostensibly to protect women, but in effect kept them from a variety of jobs. As late as 1965, the EEOC stated that laws designed to protect women (but not men) were not discriminatory. Labor laws have now changed, but they have left behind a legacy that says it is okay to treat men and women differently under the law.

As another example, it took until 1938 for a judge to lift the ban on birth control, a ruling that involved Margaret Sanger, a leading crusader for the rights of all women to have access to contraceptives. However, it took until 1965 for the Supreme Court (in *Griswold v. Connecticut*) to guarantee married couples the right to use birth control, ruling that it was protected in the Constitution as a right to privacy. Meanwhile, millions of unmarried women living in 26 states were still denied the right to buy birth control to protect themselves from an unwanted pregnancy. It took until 1972 for the Supreme Court (in *Baird v. Eisenstadt*) to find birth control to be legal for all citizens, regardless of marital status. Again, while laws surrounding birth control have changed, women have more recently fought for their reproductive self-determination.

As a final, more modern-day example, in the United States, men are 15 times as likely to be incarcerated as are women. What explains this gap? Is it due to sex differences in the frequency and type of criminal behavior, or are courts or prosecutors treating genuinely equivalent cases differently on the basis of sex? According to research, both are operating. Men do indeed commit a greater number of serious crimes, but women and men who commit identical crimes are treated differently under the criminal justice system, with far greater leniency for women (Stacey and Spohn, 2006; Starr, 2012). Using information gleaned from four national data sources, Sonja B. Starr, a researcher from the University of Michigan Law School, found that women are twice as likely as men to avoid incarceration if convicted of the same crime. Moreover, if incarcerated, men receive sentences that average 63 percent longer than women do (Starr, 2012). She speculates on the factors that may explain the leniency afforded to women.

> *Girlfriend Theory:* Women might be viewed as minor players—perhaps mere accessories of their male romantic partners. Prosecutors and judges may consider such women less dangerous, less morally culpable.
>
> *Parental Responsibilities:* Prosecutors and/or judges worry about the effect of maternal incarceration on children, and therefore give women lighter sentences.
>
> *Cooperativeness:* Female defendants receive leniency because they are more cooperative with the government.
>
> *Sympathetic Life Circumstances:* Female defendants may be seen as having more troubled life circumstances, such as poverty, mental illness, addiction, and abuse histories. If so, they may be perceived as less morally culpable or as candidates for rehabilitation.

Starr's research allowed her to test these theories statistically. She found that these theories were important and explained part, but not all, of the sex differences in punishments for identical crimes. She speculates that sex discrimination may be a remaining factor due to chivalry, paternalism, and trivializing women.

Social Policy

8.6 Describe the women's movement and its policy agenda.

There are many social policies that touch on sex and gender. This section looks at a broad issue, the women's movement, describing its history and policy agenda.

The Women's Movement

The women's movement in the United States was officially founded in 1848, when a women's rights convention held in Seneca, New York, was attended by 300 women and men, many of whom, like Elizabeth Cady Stanton and Lucretia Mott, were active in the abolitionist movement. The Seneca convention endorsed a platform that called for the right of women to vote, to control their own property, and to obtain custody of their children after divorce, all thought to be heresy at the time. After women won the right to vote in the 1920s, considered to be a major political victory, the women's movement receded from public consciousness. This consciousness was awakened again in the 1960s, a decade characterized by considerable activism and numerous social movements (Banaszak, 2006).

The resurgence of the movement in the 1960s occurred in a context of widespread social change. In 1963, the year in which Betty Friedan's book, *The Feminine Mystique*, appeared, the President's Commission on the Status of Women published its recommendations for equal opportunity in employment. In 1964, Congress passed the Civil Rights Act, which included a provision (Title VII) that made it illegal to discriminate against women in promotion and hiring. But the Equal Employment Opportunity Commission

In 1970, enthusiastic and resolute women march in a parade down Fifth Avenue in New York on the fiftieth anniversary of the passage of the Nineteenth Amendment, which granted women the right to vote.

(EEOC), established to enforce Title VII, was unwilling to serve as a watchdog for women's rights. As a result, in 1966, a pressure group, the National Organization for Women (NOW), was founded. Its stated purpose was "to take action to bring women into full participation in the mainstream of American society *now*, exercising all the privileges and responsibilities thereof in truly equal partnership with men."

Attitudes about gender roles have undergone a major transformation since the resurgence of the women's movement. Although as we have seen, significant inequalities and double standards continue to exist, they are far less sharply defined than they were in earlier decades.

Changes in Men's Roles

The issues of women's rights have often eclipsed the need for men to examine and change their own gendered roles. Inspired by the successes of women, however, many men are exploring the roles that have also limited them in the past, and they are discovering a new freedom in moving toward sex-role egalitarianism, as shown in A Personal View: What Does It Take to Be a "Good Father"?

Some people suggest that, although both boys and girls receive gender messages, perhaps boys experience even more pressure to conform to cultural stereotypes (Kimmel and Messner, 2013; Messner, 2009; Pascoe, 2011). Girls are allowed more leeway. They can behave in ways that have been considered masculine; for example, there is little social stigma in being a "tomboy," whereas boys are not allowed to behave in ways that are deemed feminine. To be told that "you throw like a girl" or to be labeled a "sissy" (which is the opposite of a tomboy) is tantamount to social suicide. Likewise, women have moved into many occupations traditionally held by men (such as doctor or lawyer), whereas men may still face scrutiny if they want to become a nurse, childcare worker, secretary or stay-at-home dad. And finally, while women are allowed, even encouraged, to express their emotions, the cultural imperative for men is to remain stoic and strong.

The result of suppressing emotions is well noted. Problem behaviors of young boys, including use of alcohol and drugs, police detainment, fighting and other acts of aggression against their peers, school suspension, or forcing someone to have sex against her will, are all associated with heightened traditional masculine ideals. Consequently, numerous books have been published over the past decade about the "boy crisis"—how

A Personal View

What Does It Take to Be a "Good Father"?

In this essay, 51-year-old Patrick, father of three, compares what it takes to be a good father today with what it meant for his father's generation.

When I was a young boy living at home with my parents, my father was not very involved in day-to-day activities around the house. We all understood that his job was to earn a living and support us. He did so with gusto and was generally gone from home from 7 in the morning until at least 7 at night, and sometimes all day on Saturdays, too. Sunday was our primary family day, and we usually did something special—took a drive to the beach, visited our relatives, or had a special Sunday dinner. Although my dad wasn't around much, my sisters and I all considered him to be a "good father." When he was at home in the evening after work, usually he was catching up on the evening news on television or reading the newspaper. Sometimes he helped us with our homework, but usually we had it done well before he came home in the evening. My mom always said, "Try not to bother your dad with things like homework. He's tired when he comes home and needs to relax." This is just how it was in the 1960s.

Fast forward to today. I am 51 years old and have three children of my own. I cannot imagine my wife saying to them, "Try not to bother your dad with things like homework. He's tired when he comes home and needs to relax." It just wouldn't happen. Why? First, we both work. Unlike my mom, who was a homemaker, my wife Katie is a nurse, and

therefore we both need to take care of the children. Second, I actually want to be involved in the day-to-day activities around the house. No offense to my father—I understand that he was just doing what was expected of him at the time—but I want a different path. I don't want to just earn money, but I want to help spend it too! I like hanging out with the kids, helping them with homework, taking them fun places, and watching them grow and become the best they can be. Third, even if I wanted to just be a breadwinner, I don't know whether society would let me do that. I think I would be labeled a "bad father" if I just went to work and then came home and read the newspaper while my wife did all the housework and childcare. Men, at least in my circles, are looked down on if they don't pitch in fully. In only one generation we have completely redefined what it means to be a "good father."

—Patrick

Critical Thinking

On a societal level, what accounts for the changes in how we define a good father? How do you think Patrick's father would interpret the changes associated with what is expected of fathers? Patrick says, "Men, at least in my circles, are looked down on if they don't pitch in fully." Do you think that is the case for all men today? What types of men are more likely to agree with Patrick? What types of men are less likely to agree with him?

to raise emotionally healthy, well-balanced, and achievement-oriented boys (Biddulph and Stanish, 2008; Kindlon and Thompson, 2000).

There is evidence of a beginning shift in male gender roles, especially among educated men in their twenties and thirties. The growing presence of women in the workforce is leading to greater egalitarianism as women become breadwinners and men participate more freely (although not equally) in childrearing and housework.

Future Prospects

In coming years, the women's movement is likely to continue its focus on strengthening families and, within this group, the special needs of low-income, female-headed families. With many marriages ending in divorce and about one-fourth of all households headed by single parents or unrelated individuals, it is certain that the politics of childcare and aid to children will be at the forefront of feminist concern. There will also be greater emphasis on family and work policies, including pressure to extend family leave policies so that both men and women can take time off when a new baby comes. Will that leave be paid, as it is in so many European nations? Such a policy is unlikely to be approved in the United States, since, as with healthcare, employers rather than the state or federal governments would be expected to pay for it (Banaszak, 2006). Childcare and early childhood education, however, are likely to be the subjects of significant new initiatives and funding, a reflection of the new, more women-friendly Congress. Likewise, the opening up of fields that have traditionally been "male" or "female" to members of both sexes is likely to remain an important goal of the women's movement and civil rights organizations throughout the United States.

On a global level, what Jessie Bernard (1987) refers to as the "feminist enlightenment" has made significant progress in recent years. Women throughout the world have benefited in many ways, ranging from improved health and education to expanded economic and political opportunities. Much of this progress can be attributed to the role of the United Nations as a platform for women's issues. Throughout the late 1970s and the 1980s, women became increasingly skilled at using the United Nations' information and communication systems effectively. These efforts continue to build momentum throughout the developing world (Susser and Patterson, 2001).

Going Beyond Left and Right

This chapter has focused on sex and gender issues, highlighting historical and contemporary gendered roles, sexism and social inequality. The old saying "You've come a long way, baby" could apply to some of the changes that have taken place. In a 1936 Gallup Poll, only 30 percent of Americans said they would vote for a woman for president even if she were qualified for the job and represented their interests. However, in contrast, today nearly 100 percent of Americans express a willingness to have a woman in the highest office in the country. Many seemingly radical ideas have now come to pass, or even if they haven't, they don't really seem so radical anymore. They have been embraced by the mainstream. For example, while the fight over equal pay for equal work continues, it would be a lonely person who would stand up and say "I oppose!"

Is it safe to say, then, that sexism is a thing of the past? No, not really. For example, a set of researchers used the Implicit Association Test (IAT) to assess gender biases. The IAT measures how quickly a person can pair two concepts, in this case, women and leadership, or men and leadership. The researchers looked for unconscious gender biases in the notion of leadership and then observed whether these biases affect how a person would vote. Despite "political correctness," the average person did, indeed, find it easier to pair words like *president, governor,* and *executive* with male names. Meanwhile, people were also more likely to pair words like *secretary, assistant,* and *aid* with female-sounding names. It appears that many people had an unconscious gender bias in that they had more difficulty associating leadership positions with women than they did with men. Moreover, this finding is important because these biases reflected how people voted. The more difficulty a person had in classifying a woman as a leader using the IAT, the less likely the person was to vote for a woman candidate, regardless of "political correctness" (Mo, 2012).

Summary

- Virtually all social institutions—whether political, religious, economic, educational, or familial—distinguish between men and women in fundamental ways, and these differences become the basis on which power is distributed. The term sex refers to biological differences and one's role in reproduction. Gender refers to the culturally and socially constructed differences between males and females found in the meanings, beliefs, and practices associated with femininity and masculinity.

- Until the early 1970s, it was widely accepted that the primary desirable roles for a woman were wife, mother, and homemaker and that her entire life should revolve around them. In contrast, a man was expected to be a leader and provider, a highly rational person who would not let emotions get in the way of action.

- Sexism is the counterpart of racism and ageism, and it can be defined as the entire range of attitudes, beliefs, policies, laws, and behaviors discriminating against women (or against men) on the basis of their sex or gender. Power, male hegemony, and stereotyping are the roots of patriarchy.

- Sexism is widespread and is found in virtually every society. One example of sexism is female genital mutilation, which affects 100 to 140 million women and girls today. Sexism is also evident in the United States. One example of sexism can be seen in employment status of women. Women workers earn considerably less than men. Another set of examples of sexism include rape, sexual assault, sexual harassment, and stalking.

- Sources of sexism include gender socialization, which is the process whereby people learn to behave according to the gendered norms of a culture. Agents of socialization that teach people about gender include family members, toys, schools, peers, and the mass media. Organized religion and the government and legal system also reinforce sex and gender inequality.

- The women's movement in the United States was officially founded in 1848, with a women's rights convention held in Seneca, New York, endorsing a platform that called for the right of women to vote, to control their own property, and to obtain custody of their children after divorce. After women won the right to vote in the 1920s, the women's movement receded from public consciousness until the 1960s. Since then a number of laws have passed, the National Organization for Women was created, and many men are also exploring the ways that they have been limited by traditional gender roles.

Chapter 9
An Aging Society

Learning Objectives

9.1 Evaluate the degree to which aging is a social problem.

9.2 Compare the growth of the elderly population in developed and developing countries, and assess the reasons for this growth.

9.3 Discuss the growth in the elderly population in the United States and the consequences of this growth.

9.4 Contrast the physiological, psychological, and social and cultural aspects of aging.

9.5 Analyze the economics of aging, including distribution of income and assets among the elderly population, economic discrimination, and the consequences of having multiple jeopardies.

9.6 Describe the unique issues that families with older members may face.

9.7 Identify the health concerns common among the elderly, and describe the primary program that pays for their health care.

9.8 Summarize the Social Security program.

I have a birthday coming up and I'm looking forward to celebrating it with my family and friends. For a while there I didn't really like birthdays. They made me feel old. I remember turning 35 and thinking, "I remember when my parents were this age." It bothered me a lot. I remember turning 50. My youngest child left for college that year. I was an "empty-nester" and entering a new chapter in life. I remember turning 65 and became officially "an elderly person." That one stung. But now birthdays make me feel young! This one is particularly special, so all my kids and their young ones will be there. Some are even traveling from as far away as Alaska. I wish Lyle could be here with me. I remember the fun and romance we had! He was a part of my life beginning in high school. (Sigh) We met when a few kids from school gathered for a bonfire and hot dogs. I miss Lyle terribly. We'll be together one day, but not this day. This day is all about me. I hope my hair looks okay. I had it fixed yesterday so I could look my best for the pictures. After all, not everyone gets to turn 108, do they?

One hundred years ago, not many understood a lot about the physical and social aspects of aging. Those who were elderly made up such a small proportion of the population that most researchers did not spend time studying them. Most people assumed that old age meant deterioration. Few people worried about dementia or Alzheimer's disease as we do today; instead, a person who was elderly and seemed deranged was simply called "old," as though senility was automatic.

Today, more people know far more about aging than they did in the past, mainly because more people are entering that age category called "elderly." The demographics of the United States, as well as those around the world, are quickly changing; in fact, the proportion of people classified as elderly within the global population is increasing faster than any other age group (Ortman, Velkoff, and Hogan, 2014). The elderly population are a force to be reckoned with because political clout often accompanies size. Yet, in many ways, aging is a social construction, not simply a biological phenomenon. Yes, everyone grows older, but how aging is defined, how it is perceived by other members of the culture, and the policy implications that come from these definitions and perceptions can vary quite a lot.

In social terms, age is a major factor in determining groupings and role assignments in a society. Age plays a large part in how people feel about themselves and what society expects of them. And the way in which a society thinks about its aged members depends very much on the value its culture attaches to age as opposed to youth. The American culture places a high value on youth and youthful attractiveness; consequently, Americans tend to devalue aging because it is associated with changes in physical appearance that detract from the image of youth.

This chapter examines the demographic changes under way in the United States and around the world. It explores what it means to have increasing numbers of older people in the population. The issues that older people face and how Americans choose to address these issues—retirement, Social Security, widowhood, health, and family caregiving—are bound to become concerns for all members of society.

Aging as a Social Problem

9.1 Evaluate the degree to which aging is a social problem.

Why is aging a social problem, you ask? There are two primary reasons. One has to do with social structure. Aging places stress on society as well as on the individual, as we will show later in the chapter. For example, as the American aging population continues to grow, and the country's number of younger workers does not keep up, how will Americans pay for the programs that older people use? Economic programs such as Social Security and health programs such as Medicare are a large and growing part of the federal budget. Are these programs sustainable as is, or will Americans need to make some changes, and if so, what type of changes? Should the country tax workers even more? Should the country cut the funding for these programs? Should society restrict eligibility only to those who are elderly and poor or low-income? Should society raise the age at which people become eligible for these programs? These types of questions show that the large and growing number of elderly persons is a social problem.

The second reason aging can be viewed through a social problem lens involves a more micro, or individual, approach. It has to do with the way that elders live their lives and are treated in society. For example, many elders are widowed, live alone, and experience food insecurity or poor health. In the future, the number of people facing these issues will be quite large. Should Americans try to improve the quality of life for their elderly population, and if so, returning to the issues above, how do they achieve this goal?

Sociological Perspectives on Aging

Aging is often studied from the point of view of one or more of the basic perspectives introduced in Chapter 1. From the functionalist perspective, for example, aging is a problem because the institutions of modern society are not working well enough to serve the needs of those who are dependent and aged. The extended family, which once allowed elders to live out their lives among kin, has been weakened by greater social mobility and a shift to the nuclear family as the basic kinship unit. (See Chapter 10.) Those who are elderly are rendered useless as their functions are replaced by those of other social institutions. As grandparents, for example, older people once played an important part in socializing those who were young, teaching them the skills, values, and ways of life of their people. Now those functions are performed by schools and colleges; it is assumed that those who are elderly cannot understand or master the skills required in today's fast-changing world. Instead, they must be cared for either at home or in institutions such as residential care facilities or nursing homes (Achenbaum, 2010).

Interactionists take a different view. They see the term *elderly* often used as a stigmatizing label; older people are less valuable because they do not conform to the norms of a youth-oriented culture. Interactionists acknowledge elderly people may be victims of ageism, which comprises forms of prejudice and discrimination that are directed at them not only by individuals but also by social institutions. The remedy, according to interactionists, is to fight ageism in all its forms. A Global View: HIV Is Not Just a Young Person's Disease shows that ageism prevents many older people from accessing information or treatment about HIV, leading to a growing world health crisis.

Finally, conflict theorists focus on elders' status and power to shape social institutions to meet the unique needs of older persons. In this view, elders must resist the effects of labeling and the loss of their roles by banding together in organizations, communities, and voting blocs that will assert their need for meaningful lives and adequate social services. In this regard, elderly persons have been very successful. They represent a large and relatively organized group. Which legislator, for example, would dare rise up and ask that Social Security or Medicare be eliminated, or even significantly reduced? If any legislator proposed such a thing, they would likely be quickly removed from office. Table 9–1 summarizes the major sociological perspectives on aging.

What Do You Think?

Can you think of some aspect of aging that places stress primarily on society? Can you think of another aspect of aging that places stress primarily on the individual? Finally, can you think of another aspect of aging that places stress squarely on both?

A Global View

HIV Is Not Just a Young Person's Disease

Namukasa was born a long time ago—she does not remember when—in the southwest corner of Uganda. She is an old woman, with a wrinkled face and gray hair. She bore six children, and four of them are still alive. They live nearby with their own families and help take care of her. Her husband has long since passed away. One of her daughters died in childhood from a sickness that she is unsure of. Another daughter died from AIDS as a young adult. *That* sickness Namukasa is very sure of. HIV and AIDS are commonplace in Uganda, although no one speaks much of them publicly. It is considered shameful and not something spoken of beyond a whisper in the confines of home.

Namukasa is also infected with HIV. But unlike her daughter who caught the dreaded disease as a young adult, Namukasa caught it as an old woman. She met a man, and he seemed nice enough. She is past the age at which she could get pregnant. If there is no risk of having a baby, why not have sex, she asked herself? Namukasa—old, wrinkled, and gray—now has HIV, which she contracted at the age of 59. She does not want to go to a doctor. "HIV is a young person's disease," she says.

Despite the global attention being paid to HIV and AIDS, most people knew very little about infection among those who are elderly until recently. There is a common misperception that older people are not sexually active; therefore, there is little need for research or programs specifically tailored to older adults. However, a 2012 study in South Africa revealed that HIV prevalence was 12 percent among women and 7 percent among men who were between the ages of 55 and 59 years. An estimated 100,000 people ages 50 and over in low- and middle-income countries acquire HIV every year. Of these, three-quarters live in sub-Saharan Africa. UNAIDS now estimates that the 50-and-over cohort contracts HIV at a higher frequency than do younger groups (UNAIDS, 2013).

Apparently, those who are elderly are indeed sexually active. Because they are beyond the age of reproduction, they often take risks and have sex without using condoms. Furthermore, several biological and cultural factors put older people at an added risk of becoming infected with HIV. The thinning of the vaginal wall after menopause increases the risk of HIV transmission during sex. And practices such as wife inheritance and ritual cleansing, in which a widow is expected to either marry or have sex with relatives of the deceased husband, can increase older women's exposure to the virus.

This Kenyan woman stands in line to get a health checkup for HIV/AIDS. Most of the people in line are young, but there are several women about her age who contracted HIV later in life.

HIV prevention programs must expand to include the considerations and needs of older persons. Ageist stereotypes about sex and those who are elderly must be put aside so that fewer people like Namukasa are infected, and if infected, they receive the treatment they need.

Critical Thinking

Create an HIV/AIDS prevention program that would be targeted toward older people such as Namukasa. What would be the main features of this program? Would it differ from programs targeted toward younger people? How would you market your program? What types of challenges would your program face?

Table 9–1 Major Sociological Perspectives on Aging

Perspective	Why Aging Is a Social Problem
Functionalist	Social institutions do not adequately serve people as they grow older (e.g., the family is no longer capable of providing adequate care).
Interactionist	The elderly are stigmatized and are victims of ageism because they do not conform to the norms of a culture that emphasizes youthfulness.
Conflict	The problem of the elderly is their relative lack of power; when they organize for political action, they can combat ageism.

Changing Demographics around the World

9.2 Compare the growth of the elderly population in developed and developing countries, and assess the reasons for this growth.

Learning more about aging is important because the world is in the midst of a powerful revolution—a *demographic* revolution. The changes that an aging population brings will be felt by all of us, from the richest nations to the poorest ones. The world population is aging at an unprecedented rate. The number of people who are elderly is expected to more than double from about 850 million today, to over 2 billion in 2050. It is difficult to imagine, but the number of older people will then exceed the number of children in the world (United Nations, Department of Economic and Social Affairs, Population Division, 2015).

Developed versus Less Developed Countries

You may assume that this growth in the number of older people is occurring primarily in developed nations like the United States or within Europe. But this assumption is *wrong*. Yes, it is true that most developed nations have a high and growing *proportion* of elderly people, such as Japan with one-quarter of its population age 65 and over, and one-third age 60 and over (*Japan Times News*, 2014; United Nations, Department of Economic and Social Affairs, Population Division, 2015). Compare Japan's proportion of elderly people with Uganda or Gambia, where less than 4 percent of the population is over age 60, as shown in Table 9–2. But there is an important difference between proportions (percentages) and actual numbers.

Populations of developed countries may have higher *proportions* of those who are elderly, but the actual *numbers* of the elderly in LDCs are very large, and they are increasing at a staggering rate that far exceeds the rate in developed countries, as you can see in Maps 9–1 and 9–2. In many countries, the population of the elderly is expected to double or even triple, including Singapore, Colombia, Brazil, Costa Rica, the Philippines, Indonesia, Mexico, South Korea, Egypt, Bangladesh, China, and Peru (Kinsella and He, 2009; Population Reference Bureau, 2015).

These countries tend to be poorer and often are without economic or health care provisions for the elderly. The question of how to care for these elders will become one of the most vexing policy issues in the coming decades. The effects will be felt

> **What Do You Think?**
>
> Do you think those who are elderly have higher status and are treated better in developed or less developed countries?

Table 9–2 Top Five and Bottom Five Countries with Population Age 60 and Over

Top Five Countries	Share of the Population	Rank
Japan	32%	1
Italy	27%	2
Germany	27%	3
Bulgaria	26%	4
Finland	26%	5
Bottom Five Countries	**Share of the Population**	**Rank**
Gambia	4%	197
Uganda	4%	198
Bahrain	4%	199
Qatar	2%	200
United Arab Emirates	1%	201

SOURCE: United Nations, Department of Economic and Social Affairs, Population Division, 2015.

Map 9–1 Comparative Aging—Percent of the Population Age 65 and Over, 2015

SOURCES: Kinsella and Velkoff, 2001; Kinsella and He, 2009; Population Reference Bureau, 2015.

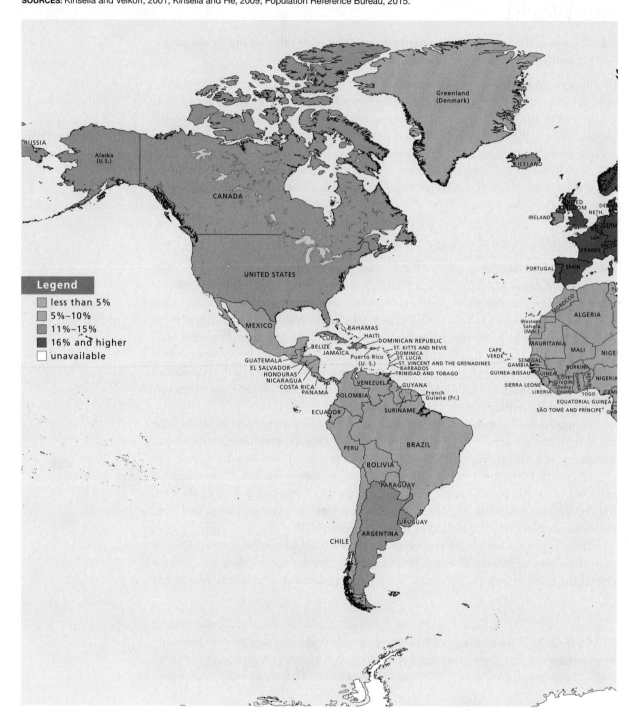

Legend

- less than 5%
- 5%–10%
- 11%–15%
- 16% and higher
- unavailable

far beyond the borders of individual nations; they will spread throughout the global economy.

Among the elderly, the largest increase around the world is in the "oldest-old" cohort—those age 80 and over (sometimes defined as age 85 and over). The oldest-old cohort currently constitute about one in five elders, but will grow quickly, given the large number of births in the 1940s and 1950s, and the fact that people are living longer lives due to better nutrition, sanitation, and health care developments. Granted, these developments have been more readily available in developed countries, and

therefore, the groups of those who are among the oldest-old are heavily concentrated there. Nonetheless, there will be large increases among the oldest-old around the world, as shown in Figure 9–1. For example, in Mexico in 2013, only 1.5 percent of the population was age 80 and over, but by 2050, this proportion will jump to 5.7 percent (U.S. Census Bureau, 2013).

An age of 80 or 85 years used to be considered very old, but now, a large number of people are even living to age 100 or beyond. These people are called centenarians. Even as recently as a generation ago, one rarely met anyone who was 100 or 101 years

Map 9–2 Comparative Aging—Percent of Population age 65 and Over, 2040

SOURCES: Kinsella and Velkoff, 2001; Kinsella and He, 2009; Population Reference Bureau, 2015.

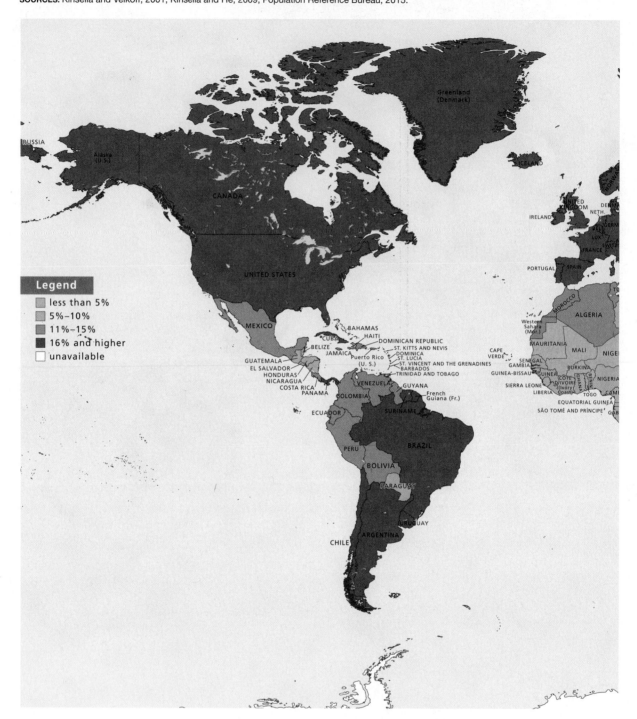

old. But today it is not uncommon, and it seems like everyone has an old-age story to tell. (Author Karen Seccombe's grandmother lived to be 108 and a half! You can learn more about her life in A Personal View: Celebrating My Grandmother's 105th Birthday.) As you can see in Figure 9–2, the largest population growth by far between the years 2010 and 2015 is expected to be among centenarians.

On one hand, it seems that living longer is a good thing because it provides more time for families and loved ones to be together. But on the other hand, this unprecedented rise in the number of the oldest-old and centenarians can also be considered a social

problem because as more people live to the oldest ages, we will see more chronic conditions such as arthritis, osteoporosis, and dementia. These types of conditions require more medical care and more personal help with cooking, cleaning, bathing, and home repair. Who will provide this care? Most countries have few government agencies or private facilities to provide this care. Furthermore, among the oldest cohorts, most are widowed and an increasing number live alone (United Nations, Department of Economic and Social Affairs, Population Division, 2015). Who then will care for these older people? The vast majority of elderly people around the world will be cared for by their adult children, and chances are, these adult children will be in their sixties or seventies themselves.

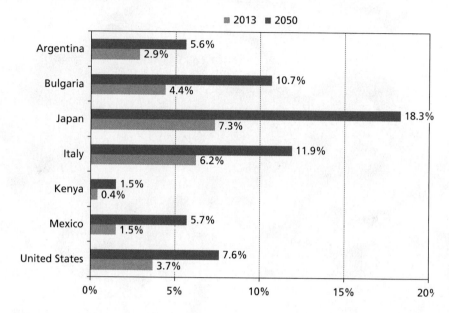

Figure 9–1 Oldest-Old as a Percentage of All People, 2013 and 2050

SOURCE: U.S. Census Bureau, 2013.

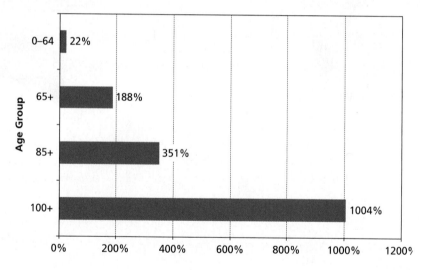

Figure 9–2 Percentage Change in the World's Population by Age, 2010–2050

SOURCE: United Nations, 2011.

Reasons for the Rapid Growth in the Elderly Population

Why is the world's population aging so quickly? There are two primary reasons: (1) people are living longer and (2) fewer babies are being born.

Obviously, the first reason for the rapid growth in the elderly population is that more people are living longer. Life expectancy (how long a person can expect to live) can be calculated at any age, but the most common way is to calculate it from birth: For a girl or boy born today, how long on average can she or he be expected to live? Extraordinary strides have been made in extending life expectancy in much of the world. In 1900, U.S. life expectancy was 48 years for males and 51 years for females. Today, it has increased to 76 for males and 81 for females (Central Intelligence Agency, 2014; Population Reference Bureau, 2015). Other countries have made even greater advances because of improved nutrition, sanitation, health care, and other scientific

A Personal View

Celebrating My Grandmother's 105th Birthday

As more adults are living past 100, many families now are celebrating birthdays that would have been unheard of a generation or two ago. The essay below asks you to ponder what such a birthday could mean.

My extended family gathered in Montana for my grandmother's birthday—who had just turned 105. Yes, you read that correctly—105! We celebrated the marvelous and very long life of this amazing woman. But wait, that was three and a half years ago. She is now over 108! She was born in 1901, and just imagine the changes she has witnessed:

- William McKinley was president of the United States when she was born.
- Henry Ford showcased the first model T for $950 when she was 7 years old.
- World War I began when she was 13.
- Women did not receive the right to vote until she was 19.
- The Roaring Twenties occurred when she was in her twenties.
- World War II, the deadliest war in history, began when she was 38.
- The case of *Brown v. Board of Education*, which decided that separate schools for black children were inherently unequal, was not settled until she was in her fifties.
- Medicare, the health insurance program for those who are elderly, was created when she was 64—just in time!
- Personal computers were not readily available until she was in her eighties.
- Cell phones were not commonplace until she was well into her nineties.

- Her youngest great-grandchild, Olivia, was born when she was 102; her youngest great-great-grandchild (to date), Crosby, was born when she was 107.

Here's to you, Grandma!
Love,
Karen

Note: Karen Seccombe is one of the authors of this textbook. Her grandmother Blanche Coy Seccombe died peacefully at the age of 108 and a half only a few years ago.

Critical Thinking

If you lived to be 105, what type of social, technological, environmental, and political changes do you think could occur during your lifetime? Do you see these changes as good or bad for society?

---

discoveries. Infectious diseases such as influenza, smallpox, or measles that killed many people in the past have been controlled in many parts of the world.

However, a few countries have experienced no substantial gains in life expectancy, and others have actually experienced a decline. Most of these countries are in Africa. The most prominent reason is that HIV/AIDS is still a fatal disease in many African countries and thereby reduces life expectancy.

A second reason for the tremendous growth in the elderly population around the world is a decline in fertility rates; fewer babies are being born. Countries with low fertility rates such as Japan and Western Europe tend to have high proportions of people who are elderly. With fewer births over an extended period of time, cohorts of older people make up an increasing proportion of the population. Demographers use the term **demographic transition** to refer to the process in which a society moves from a situation of high fertility rates and low life expectancy to one of low fertility rates and high life expectancy.

Figure 9–3 shows three population pyramids from 1950, 1990, and projections for 2030. The pyramids show the population by age, by sex, and by the countries' level of development. In 1950, birthrates were high. This age group, including those born

demographic transition

The process in which a society moves from a situation of high fertility rates and low life expectancy to one of low fertility rates and high life expectancy.

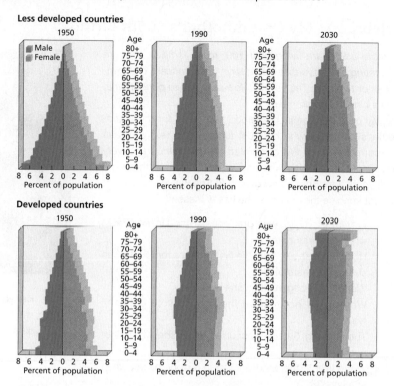

Figure 9–3 Population Pyramids

1950, 1990, 2030 for Less Developed Countries and for Developed Countries.

from 1947 through the early 1960s, is known as the post–World War II **baby-boom generation**. At the same time, life expectancy was relatively low, and the number and proportion of those who were elderly in the population were small, particularly in developing nations. However, 40 years later in 1990, the population distribution in developed nations had changed. Birthrates were lower; therefore, a noticeably large "bulge" appeared in the pyramid among the baby-boom generation, who by that time were ages 25–45. In another 40 years, projecting out to 2030, patterns are expected to shift as birthrates continue to decline and life expectancy increases; at this point, the baby-boom generation will be elderly (Population Reference Bureau, 2014). By 2030, you can see that the "pyramids" are no longer pyramids, especially in more developed countries.

Aging and Modernization

Research on nomadic societies has found that, in some situations, especially in times of scarcity or when they impeded the group's mobility, elderly persons were often badly mistreated and even encouraged to die (Hooyman, Kawamoto, and Kiyak, 2015; Hooyman and Kiyak, 2011). Explorers and anthropologists have also cited instances of mistreatment in some tribal societies. But in many settled agrarian societies, the status of adults actually increases with age. In many African and Asian nations, for example, decisions about land tenure, kinship, and ceremonial affairs are the province of those who are elderly. In the United States and most Western countries, the productive and cultural roles of those who are aged have been weakened by industrialization and by the migration of family members to cities. In this sense, the problems of those who are aged are part of the larger complex of social changes known as modernization, which typically describes three characteristics: (1) the transformation of societies to urbanized and industrialized ways of life based on scientific technologies, (2) individualized rather than communal or collective roles, and (3) a cosmopolitan outlook that values efficiency and progress. Thus, many problems faced by elderly persons in the United States today are social problems that arise from the nature of modern Western society.

Modernization produces far-reaching changes in societies, but clearly, the terms *modernization* and *progress* are not equivalent. With modernization come new social problems and sometimes, new solutions. Modernization is usually associated with increasing length of life, but longer life is a positive change only when the quality of life is also enhanced. For many people, however, as the life span increases, so do the pain and suffering associated with old age.

Technological and scientific advances have reduced the infant mortality rate and eliminated or provided cures for many formerly fatal diseases. Because many of these advances, such as antiseptics, vaccines, and antibiotics, occurred within a short time, record numbers of people began living much longer. As the population of people who were elderly increased, modern societies across the globe began to deal with poverty and illness among their elderly citizens. Pension plans, Social Security, and health care systems were developed to address their needs.

From the earliest periods of human prehistory (before written evidence of human civilization appeared) to the present, the average life expectancy has increased by about 40 years. In prehistoric times, a person could expect to live into his or her early forties; now, life expectancy is approaching 80 in many societies. Great surges in life expectancy occurred with the transition from hunting-and-gathering to agrarian societies, with the development of modern techniques of sanitation and water supply, and with the discovery of the causes of diseases and of antibiotics and techniques for preventing many major illnesses. In the past 20 or 30 years, however, the rate of increase in life expectancy has decelerated. There are biological limits to how long humans can live, and although there may be small shifts in life expectancy in the future, we cannot expect advances at the same rate as in the past indefinitely.

We can expect, however, that the number of older people who are alive but unwell will increase. As more people live longer, the proportion with major medical problems increases, as does the need for costly health care. Although most people wish to live longer lives, the negative side is that they are likely to experience pain and suffering. Thus, society as a whole faces an increased need to improve the quality of life of and to find ways to care for a growing number of elderly people who are frail and ill.

The Elderly Population in the United States

9.3   Discuss the growth in the elderly population in the United States and the consequences of this growth.

The number of elderly people in the United States is growing rapidly, which is bound to shape our culture, family relationships, and political and economic systems. This next section examines the growth of the elderly population, the consequences of this growth, and some of the challenges that elderly people may face.

The number of elderly people in the United States is strong and growing rapidly. Today there are about 45 million people age 65 and over, but that number could jump to over 90 million by 2060.

Who Are Included in the Elderly Population?

Only a century ago, people did not live very long, even in the United States. Many younger Americans probably spent long portions of their lives rarely seeing a person who was elderly.

Figure 9–4 Number of Persons 65+, 1960–2060, United States (Millions)

SOURCE: Administration on Aging, 2014.

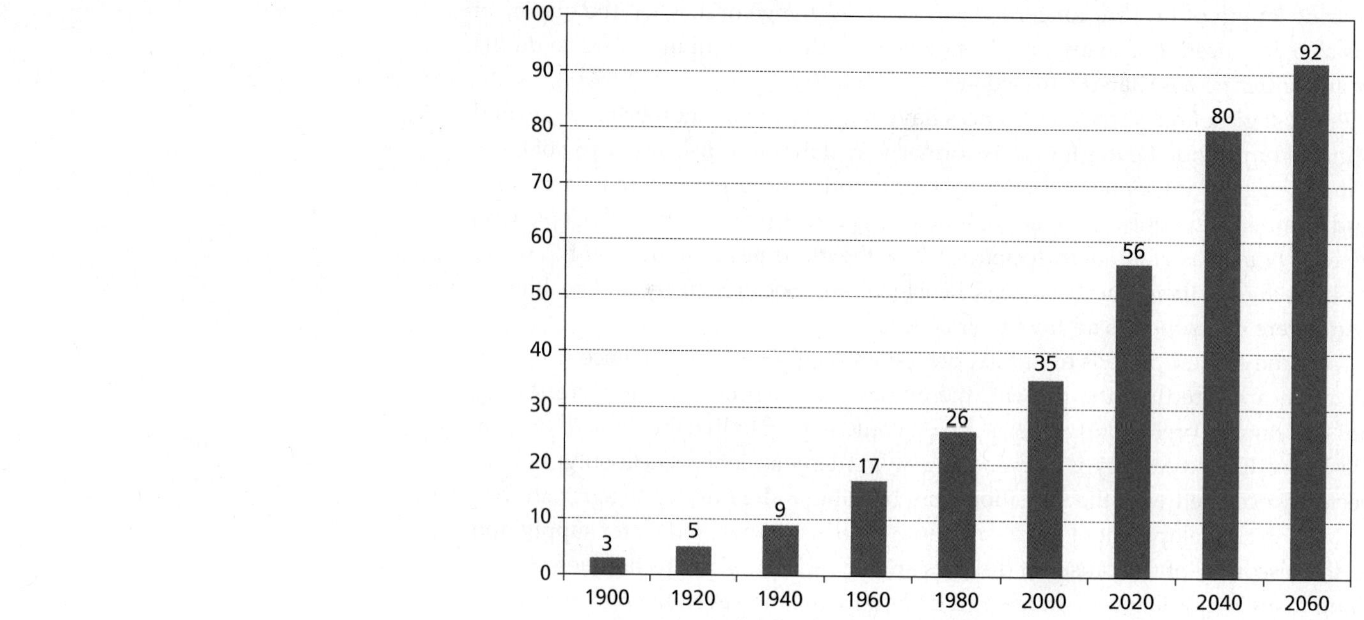

More recently, the elderly population in the United States has been increasing almost four times as fast as the population as a whole, and seniors now constitute one of every eight Americans (Administration on Aging, 2014). Today, there are nearly 50 million people age 65 and older in the United States, and as you can see in Figure 9–4, the numbers are quickly rising. By 2020, which is just around the corner, there are likely to be another 6 million elders, and by 2060, the number could be about 92 million. Much of the growth between 2010 and 2060 in the elderly cohort will occur as the baby-boom generation ages. And like the rest of the world, Americans will see the number of the oldest-old and centenarians increase.

However, not all groups are equally likely to reach old age. Minorities are under-represented in the aging population, in part due to their lower life expectancy. For example, a white girl born today can anticipate living an average of 81 years, 4 years longer than a black girl.

Two-thirds of the elderly live in urban areas, many in central cities. For them, problems of aging are complicated by problems of the urban environment: crime, decaying neighborhoods, the shortage of affordable housing, and congestion. Yet, although most elderly people live in urban areas, they also represent the highest proportion of the population of small towns. This phenomenon is a result of the patterns of migration that have occurred since World War II, when many people moved from farms to small towns. Many of those people are now elderly. In turn, their children have relocated from these small towns to suburbs or cities. The resulting migration has led to varied concentrations of elderly and younger people in different parts of the nation. Map 9–3 shows the distribution of elderly people throughout the United States. As you can see, certain states such as Kansas, Nebraska, and Florida contain large proportions of elderly people, while other states such as Utah, Illinois, or Georgia have a more youthful population.

In counties with high proportions of elderly residents, there is a need for creative entrepreneurs who are willing to help their elderly neighbors remain independent as long as possible. In many rural counties in the Midwest, elderly people can access a variety of services such as minor home repairs, errands, and monitoring of medical needs. These services enable older people to live happily on their own and may be harbingers of trends elsewhere in the nation (Heumann, McCall, and Boldy, 2001).

Map 9–3 Map of the United States by County

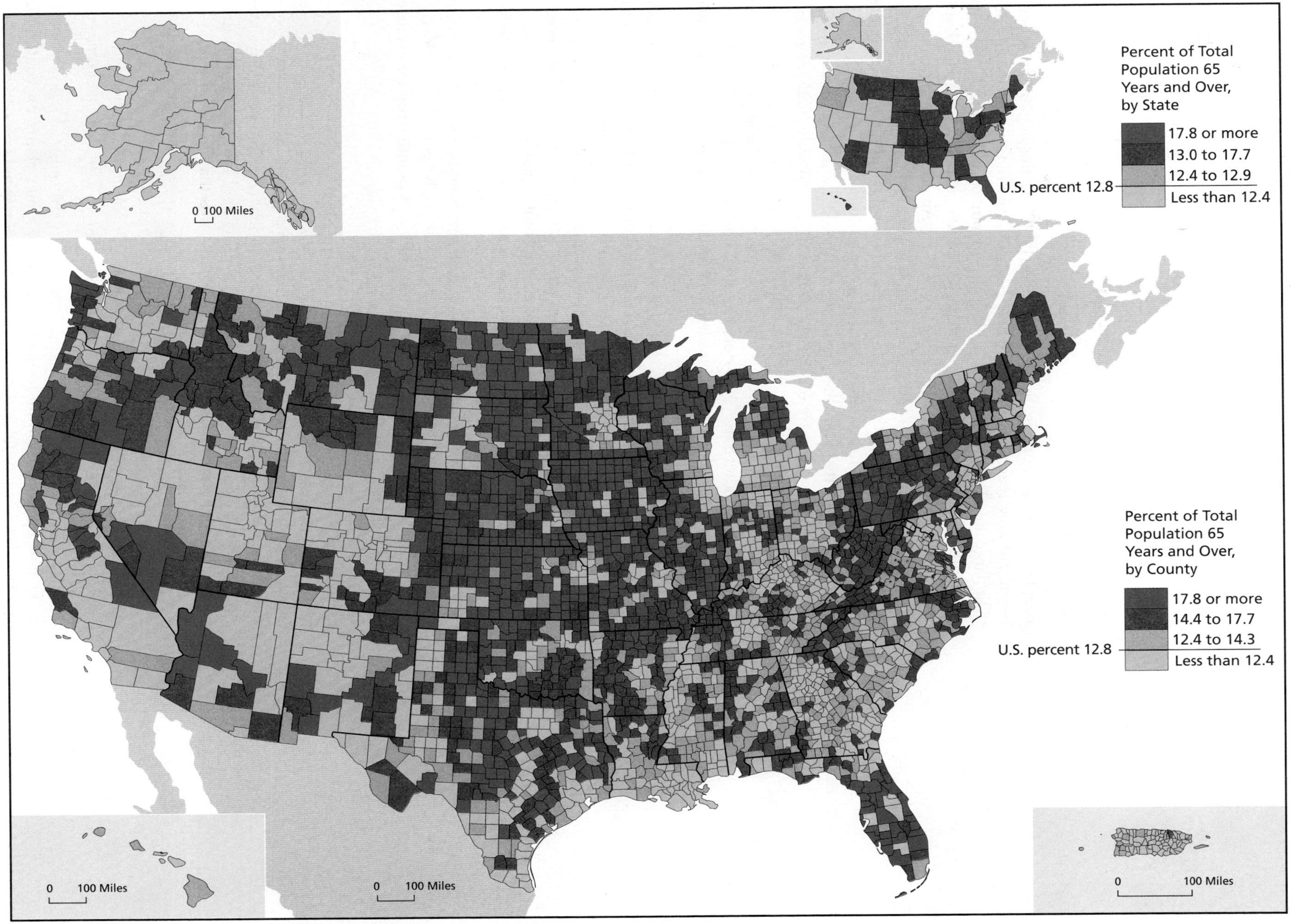

Percent of Total
Population 65
Years and Over,
by State

17.8 or more
13.0 to 17.7
12.4 to 12.9
Less than 12.4

U.S. percent 12.8

Percent of Total
Population 65
Years and Over,
by County

17.8 or more
14.4 to 17.7
12.4 to 14.3
Less than 12.4

U.S. percent 12.8

0 100 Miles

0 100 Miles

0 100 Miles

0 100 Miles

Yet, not all elderly people have stayed put in small towns. Another important pattern of migration is the movement of retired people to the West and South. As people age, some move to communities where the climate is warmer and an infrastructure of services and institutions (elder-care residential developments, hospitals, and nursing care facilities) exists. In some parts of the United States, such as south Florida and parts of Arizona and southern California, they have become a large group and exert considerable political influence.

Consequences of the Growth in the Elderly Population

People who were born in the 1940s and early 1950s, the beginning of the baby boom, are now reaching retirement age. As they grow old, physically and socially, their large numbers exert major influences on our society (Riley, 1996). Among these influences is the likelihood of increased conflict between the generations over scarce public resources. AARP (formerly called the American Association for Retired Persons) has a very active and well-funded lobbying group, and they spend considerable resources on assuring that the needs and interests of elderly people are well represented in Congress. Is there a parallel organization with similar clout for other age groups? Not really. In these lean times, should the federal government fund programs such as Medicare for elderly people, or should they fund programs such as Medicaid for children (Quadagno, 2002)? As can be seen from their turnout at elections, the elderly population is a political force to be reckoned with. People over age 65 vote at higher rates than does the total voting-age population. Thus, as the population grows older, political leaders will be unable to ignore the power wielded by elderly people at the ballot box.

Another consequence is the changing cultural attitudes toward youth and old age. For example, think about fashion. I tell my college students that they can thank baby boomers for such things as designer eyewear, spandex in jeans, and comfortable "everyday" walking shoes. These were not readily available before baby boomers made them fashionable. Instead, people wore unattractive glasses ("boys never make passes at girls who wear glasses" was a classic taunt); girls and women wore male Levi denim jeans with unflattering fits; and shoes were not designed for the athleticism of females. But, the large numbers of baby boomers who now need glasses, have expanding waistlines, and have bunions on their feet from uncomfortable shoes have demanded change, and the fashion industry listened. The point is that elderly people exert an increasing influence over social policy and popular culture in large part because of their size in the population.

What Do You Think?

We have listed several trends that baby boomers are responsible for, including stretch jeans, designer eyewear, and comfy shoes. Can you think of any others? Are all the trends positive, or are any negative?

Ageism

Elderly people are growing in numbers and are making their voices heard. Yet, at the same time, many prevalent attitudes in modern society contribute to ageism. Western cultures tend to value youth, associating it with vitality and beauty. This theme is reflected throughout the culture, even in greeting cards that mock older people (Ellis and Morrison, 2005):

- *60?! Don't worry—we're still just kids ... trapped inside the bodies of old people.*
- *There's a reason "sixty" and "sexy" sound alike! The hearing is starting to go.*
- *60 is when you start asking yourself life's big questions. Like "why did I come into this room? I knew a minute ago ..."*

One of these ageist attitudes is the inordinate value placed on youthful looks, especially for women. Older adults do not meet the standards of youthful beauty (Slevin, 2010).

Table 9–3 Surgical Cosmetic Procedures for Middle Age and Elderly People in the United States in 2014

	Total Number	Number Age 51–64	Share of Total Surgeries	Age 65+	Share of Total Surgeries
Eyelid Surgery	165,714	73,979	45%	35,736	22%
Facelift	126,713	70,344	56%	38,668	31%
Liposuction	342,495	73,395	22%	12,330	4%

Adapted From: American Society for Aesthetic Plastic Surgery, 2015.

Over 3,500,000 people, mostly women, had Botox injections in 2014 to ease the wrinkle lines in their faces. Cosmetic surgery is at an all-time high as many older women opt for facelifts or other ways to look younger. Between 1997 and 2014, the number of facelifts has increased 28 percent, and the number of liposuctions performed in the United States has increased 94 percent. These three procedures are the most common ones for those who are elderly (American Society for Aesthetic Plastic Surgery, 2015). For example, as shown in Table 9–3, in 2014 alone there were over 35,000 eyelid surgeries, 38,000 facelifts, and 12,000 liposuction surgeries done on people ages 65 or older, representing 22 percent, 31 percent, and 4 percent of the total procedures, respectively. And if we include people between the ages of 51 and 64 who also have these procedures, then over 110,000 each of eyelid surgeries and facelifts and approximately 85,000 liposuction procedures are done on middle-age or older persons every year, mostly women. These procedures cost thousands of dollars and are not without risk, but the quest for a youthful appearance apparently outweighs the cost and risk for many. Ageism as a social problem is also confounded with sexism, the focus of Chapter 8. Feminist social scientists ask, with reason, whether ageism would be the problem it is in American society if men outlived women instead of the reverse (Friedan, 1993).

The mass media play a part in promoting ageism. Just as women and minority groups must contend with negative images in the media, so must older people. Television often portrays the elderly as weak in both body and mind, and as a burden on their relatives—or else as unnaturally wise or kindhearted. Direct-to-consumer advertising on television leaves the impression that all people who are elderly suffer from sexual dysfunction, heartburn, constipation, and arthritis. Because ageism is so deeply rooted in the social and psychological fabric of our culture, it is extremely difficult to eliminate.

The difficulties of those who are old in modern societies are reflected in the much higher-than-average suicide rate in the elderly population (American Foundation for Suicide Prevention, 2014). Overall, about 12 people of every 100,000 kill themselves in a given year, but among the elderly, that figure rises to about 15 people per 100,000. Interestingly, although women's likelihood of committing suicide does not rise significantly with age, men's likelihood does. Particularly at risk are elderly men who are over age 85; the suicide rate jumps to about 47 deaths per 100,000 in that age group (Span, 2013). Although declining health, loss of status, and reduced income play a part in suicides by the elderly, a lack of relationships with family, friends, and coworkers seems to exert the most consistent influence (Hooyman and Kiyak, 2011). An analysis of suicides by elderly people over a period of nine years in Pinellas County, Florida, indicated that widowed males were more likely to commit suicide than any other group of old people. Elderly women were more likely to have extended family ties, friends, and club memberships that provided social restraints against suicide. Elderly men who enjoyed these kinds of contact were less likely to commit suicide. This finding mirrors the classic finding by Émile Durkheim

(1897/1951), one of sociology's founders, that people of any age who lack social attachments are more likely to commit suicide than are people with active social lives among family and friends.

Dimensions of the Aging Process

9.4 **Contrast the physiological, psychological, and social and cultural aspects of aging.**

There are different ways to think about the aging process, including physiological, psychological, and social/cultural aspects. These perspectives on aging are discussed in the following sections.

Physiological Aspects of Aging

CHRONOLOGICAL AGING   Chronological aging, the simple accumulation of years, is an automatic process. You may have observed, however, that not everyone seems to age at the same rate. Some people look and act middle-aged while still in their twenties, whereas some 60-year-olds radiate the vitality and health that are usually associated with youth. The actual age associated with being "old" has shifted in recent years. As the saying goes, "Sixty-five is the new fifty."

PRIMARY AND SECONDARY AGING   There are two categories in the aging process: (1) primary aging, the result of molecular and cellular changes, and (2) secondary aging, which is an accelerated version of normal aging (Whitbourne, 2005) that is caused by environmental factors such as lack of exercise, stress, trauma, poor diet, disease, and even sun exposure.

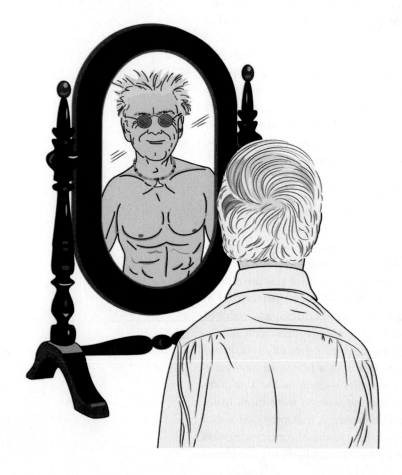

The effects of primary aging are seen in the characteristics that we associate with advancing years, including gray hair, balding, wrinkles, and increased susceptibility to disease. As the body ages, its systems degenerate. The brain, for example, loses thousands of cells daily from birth onward. Some of the body's organs such as the skin can regenerate their cells, although they do so less effectively with each passing year. Others such as the kidneys lack regenerative powers and eventually wear out. More significant, however, is a general decline in the body's immune defenses, which fight off infections such as pneumonia. As a result, elderly people often die of diseases that would not usually be fatal to younger people (Quadagno, 2002).

Aging is a gradual process; not all of the body's systems age at the same rate. The process of decline usually starts relatively early in life. By the mid-twenties, the skin begins to lose its elasticity and starts to dry out and wrinkle; by 30, the muscles have begun to shrink and decrease in strength. As time passes, the capacity of the lungs is reduced, and less and less air is drawn into the body; circulation slows, and the blood supply decreases; bones become brittle and thin; hormonal activity ebbs; and reflexes become slower. This is a natural process. Aging is not a disease in itself, but it does increase susceptibility to disease.

Some researchers are convinced that each of us carries a personal "timetable" for aging within our cells, a timetable controlled by our genes. Others believe that secondary aging factors are also involved. The role of stress is particularly important. One of the most salient age-related changes is the decline in homeostatic capacity—the ability to tolerate stress. This type of decline makes older people more susceptible to stress, and it takes them longer to return to normal after being exposed to a stressful situation.

The reduced capacity to cope with stress is a result of primary aging, but stress itself is an agent of secondary aging. Together, stress and the declining capacity to cope with it may be responsible for many illnesses that plague elderly people. Older people are confronted by numerous stress-producing situations, including widowhood, the death of friends and family members, and loss of status and productivity. Illnesses such as leukemia, cancer, and heart disease often strike in the wake of stress-producing life changes.

Psychological Dimensions of Aging

The aging process produces not only physical effects but also psychological ones. Self-concept and status are particularly important as aging occurs. One theory observes older people living in a shrinking social environment. Their world grows smaller and smaller as they leave work, as their friends and relatives die, and as their mobility decreases; at the same time, their social status changes and they become less influential.

New roles always require some adjustment, but this adjustment is complicated for the elderly because their new roles are poorly defined; there are few role models or reference groups on which they can pattern their behavior. In our society the labels applied to those who are old are often negative because they are based on an ethic that equates personal worth with economic productivity (Hooyman and Kiyak, 2011). However, as the cohort of babyboomers begins to age, their large numbers are commanding changes in the way the elderly view themselves, the way others see them, and the way society responds to them. For example, there has been a tremendous growth of housing communities, senior centers, and social groups that emphasize friendship, fun, and support. Rather than a shrinking world, many look forward to retirement as a new chapter in life, one that can be exciting and full of promise and new experiences.

Social and Cultural Dimensions of Aging: Aged People as a Minority Group

Social gerontologists frequently refer to those who are aged as a minority group, pointing out that the elderly cohort exhibits many characteristics of such groups, as described in Chapter 7. Like members of racial and ethnic minorities, elderly people can be victims of prejudice, stereotyping, and discrimination. However, some social scientists argue that, although elderly people share many characteristics of minorities, they are not a true minority group. Unlike traditional minority groups—such as blacks, Native Americans, and Jews—those who are elderly do not exist as an independent subgroup; everyone has the potential to become old. Some suggest that it would be more accurate to describe the elderly cohort as a "quasi-minority," reflecting their unique position in our society (Quadagno, 2002).

The potential power of this quasi-minority is enormous. Those who are elderly are not only increasing as a proportion of the population but are also changing significantly. They are more politically active than ever before, and many older persons remain active in voluntary associations even into their eighties. They play a much larger role in organizational life than many younger people assume (Riley and Riley, 2000).

What Do You Think?

How do television and movies portray those who are elderly? Are there differences in the ways that older men and older women are portrayed in the media?

The Economics of Aging

9.5 Analyze the economics of aging, including distribution of income and assets among the elderly population, economic discrimination, and the consequences of having multiple jeopardies.

Two contrasting images emerge in discussions of the economic conditions and well-being of the elderly. One projects an image of retired tycoons living in mansions on the Florida coast. In stark contrast, the other image projects elders as poor, alone, living in ramshackle housing, and eating dog food to stay alive. Although some elderly people fit each of these stereotypes, the reality is that most are somewhere in the middle of these two extremes.

Income and Assets: How Those Who Are Elderly Fare

The median household income of a person age 65 or older in the United States is about $37,000, which is well above the poverty line, according to Census Bureau data (DeNavas-Walt and Proctor, 2015). This income comes from a number of sources, such as earnings, pensions, or retirement savings, but the largest single source, at nearly 40 percent, comes from Social Security (Social Security Administration, 2014). Earnings comprise about a quarter of the average income of elders, and pensions account for 20 percent. Assets, such as stocks, bonds, or income from rented real estate, and other income sources make up the remainder.

Many Americans are (or should be) concerned about having sufficient income during retirement. Over one-third of the workforce has no savings set aside specifically for retirement (Social Security Administration, 2014). In addition, they cannot necessarily rely on a pension. Employers are moving away from offering pension plans that provide periodic payments over the life of the retiree and his or her spouse. In the early 1990s, about 35 percent of private industry employees had a traditional pension plan from their employer, but today it is down to only 18 percent, as shown in Figure 9–5, and most of these employees work for very large firms. In fact, only 10 percent of private industry establishments even offer a pension (Bureau of Labor Statistics, 2014). Instead, a firm may put some money into a retirement account for each employee to manage themselves, or may do nothing at all.

Figure 9–5 Percentage of Private Industry Employees Participating in Defined Benefit Pension Plans, Selected Years, 1990–2011

SOURCE: Bureau of Labor Statistics, 2013.

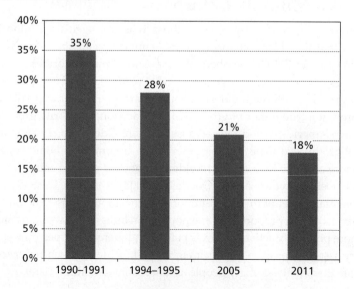

The result is that many elderly people rely primarily, or even exclusively, on Social Security, and this program was never intended to be the major or sole source of retirement income (Waid, 2014). Nearly half of older Americans rely on Social Security for at least 50 percent of their family income, and nearly one elder in four relies on it for at least 90 percent. As a result, many of them are hovering just barely above the poverty line. The Census Bureau may not count them as poor, but for all practical purposes, their lives are quite impoverished.

Economic Discrimination

With limited pensions and little retirement savings, older people are putting off the age at which they retire. At the same time, older workers can be targets of job discrimination. The U.S. Equal Employment Opportunity Commission received 22,000 complaints of age-based discrimination in 2013 (U.S. Equal Employment Opportunity Commission, 2014).

One of the most common forms of discrimination at work is "forced" retirement, which is a life-altering experience with social, economic, and emotional effects. The practice of forced, or mandatory, retirement at a certain age is against the law in most industries (airline pilots, as one example, however, are not covered by this law and are required to retire at 65). Nevertheless, some companies try to circumvent the law and find ways to oust older workers because it gives companies a tool for cutting labor costs. In a tight economy, a company may try to retire its older employees, who earn higher salaries, and replace them with younger workers who usually are paid less.

Older workers may also encounter job discrimination when seeking new employment. The 1967 Age Discrimination in Employment Act is designed to protect workers between the ages of 40 and 65, but it has not succeeded in eliminating discrimination against those over 65. Employers can no longer advertise for applicants "under 30," but a phrase such as "one to three years' experience" accomplishes the same goal of targeting younger workers. When they do obtain interviews, older workers may be rejected as "overqualified," a euphemism for "too old." For these reasons, older unemployed workers remain jobless longer than younger ones.

Multiple Jeopardy

Overall, elderly persons are less likely than any other age group to live in poverty, largely because of income programs such as Social Security (DeNavas-Walt and Proctor, 2014). Nonetheless, certain groups of elderly persons are vulnerable to becoming impoverished. To be old, female, and black (or Hispanic or Native American) in American society is to experience **multiple jeopardy**—to face more hardships than one would face if one were in just one or two of these categories. The cumulative disadvantages minorities and women have experienced throughout their lives put them at greater risk to live in poverty. For example, because older women's salaries are lower than those of men, their pensions and Social Security benefits are also lower. The Social Security system gives no credit for homemaking, the principal occupation of most women until recent decades. Many employed older women suffer the double burdens of age and sex discrimination. Factor in the disadvantages experienced by most minority groups, and the basis for multiple jeopardy becomes clear.

Retirement

Retirement is a fairly recent concept. Before the advent of Social Security and pension plans, few workers could afford to stop working. As a result, people worked well into old age, often modifying the nature of their work to match their diminished strength. This is the situation in many less developed countries today.

What Do You Think?
What would a conflict theorist have to say about why such a large number of older people are nearly poor?

multiple jeopardy
Having multiple minority statuses that include being old, female, and black (or Hispanic or Native American), which may cause more hardships than a person would face if he or she were in just one or two of these categories.

Four conditions must be met for significant numbers of elderly people to be able to withdraw from the labor force (Morgan and Kunkel, 1998):

- A society must produce an economic surplus that is large enough to support its nonemployed members.
- There must be a mechanism in place to divert some of that surplus to the nonemployed members, such as through a pension or government transfer program.
- Nonemployed members should be viewed positively by the rest of society, and their activities or leisure must be seen as legitimate.
- The nonemployed members must have accumulated an acceptable number of years of productivity to warrant support by the other members of society.

These conditions materialized in the United States after industrialization during the nineteenth and twentieth centuries. However, today, these four conditions are under threat. The cost of caring for the elderly population—Social Security, health care programs, and private retirement plans—is consuming a greater share of our country's income. Furthermore, these programs compete with funding for other groups. Programs for children, for example, have received a declining proportion of federal spending (Uhlenberg, 2009), and federal spending on the elderly population is now eight times that of what is spent on children (Klein, 2013).

Work provides us with more than an income. It is also an important part of our identity. People commonly say, "I *am* a high school teacher," "I *am* a dentist," "I *am* a police officer," as though they *are* the occupation. Retirement is an important event because it not only reduces income but also alters a major identity.

Still, many people eagerly await this change and see retirement as a legitimate, earned privilege. They look forward to extended time with friends and family, and having the opportunity to pursue other hobbies and interests. The average age at retirement fell from 69 years in 1950 to 59 years in 2002, but has since risen to age 62. Additionally, the age at which younger people now *expect* to retire is also on the rise, as shown in Figure 9–6 (Employee Benefit Research Institute, 2014; Munnell, 2011; Riffkin, 2014).

Figure 9–6 Trends in Actual and Expected Age at Retirement, 2002–2014 (Age In Years)
SOURCE: Adapted from Riffkin, 2014.

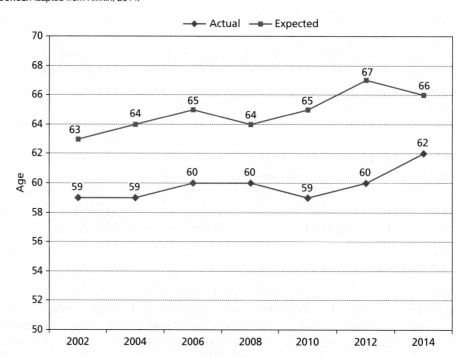

The rise in the age of retirement is likely due to several factors, including the following (Munnell, 2011):

- *Social Security.* Changes to Social Security have created many incentives to continue working, and have made work more attractive relative to retirement. For example, the delayed retirement credit, which increases benefits for each year that claiming is delayed between the full retirement age and age 70, has improved incentives to keep working.
- *Improved health and longevity.* Life expectancy for men at 65 has increased about 3.5 years since 1980, and much of the evidence suggests that people are also healthier. The correlation between health and labor force activity is very strong.
- *Pension type.* The shift from a regular pension to 401(k) plans eliminated built-in incentives to retire. Studies show that workers covered by 401(k) plans retire a year or two later on average than similarly situated workers covered by a defined benefit plan.
- *Less physically demanding jobs.* With the shift away from manufacturing, jobs now involve more knowledge-based activities, which put less strain on older bodies.
- *Decline of retiree health insurance.* Combine the decline of employer-provided retiree health insurance with the rise in health care costs, and workers have a strong incentive to keep working and maintain their employer's health coverage until they qualify for Medicare at 65.
- *Joint decision making.* More women are working; wives on average are three years younger than their husbands; and husbands and wives usually like to coordinate their retirement.
- *The recession of the 2000s and poor economy.* Some elders sustained significant losses to their retirement funds, or were forced to take pay cuts during the recession, and now work longer to make up the difference.

We also see that many older workers are now retiring in stages rather than all at once (Calvo, Haverstick, and Sass, 2009). The recent recession and low interest rates on retirement savings forced many older people to go back to work part-time. Fewer Americans are confident that they will have the necessary money needed for retirement (Morin and Fry, 2012).

From the point of view of society as a whole, large-scale retirement creates social problems because those who are no longer in the labor force are dependent on the wealth produced by those who are still working. Over the next 25 years, the ratio of retirement-age people to working-age adults will increase considerably around the world. In fact, the United States will fare rather better than nations like Japan, Austria, and Germany, where the number of retirees may severely overstretch the ability of the working population to produce adequate surpluses. But even in the United States, the problem of increasing dependency ratios poses a threat to the Social Security and Medicare systems, a problem you will be able to consider further in the social policy section of this chapter.

Family Relationships

9.6 **Describe the unique issues families with older members may face.**

Most married older couples have a relationship that has endured many years. Newspapers are full of stories of couples celebrating their fiftieth or sixtieth wedding anniversaries. Together, the couple has faced life and its transitions: the birth of a child, job opportunities, disappointments, the effort to balance work and family, the departure of children from home, and their living as just a couple once again.

Over three-quarters of men ages 65–74 are married, as are more than half of women. However, as people age, the likelihood of being married begins to decline, particularly for women (U.S. Census Bureau, 2014). Among those ages 85 and over, less than one in five women are married, compared with one in two men in the same age group.

Family relationships grow and change over the years. In families with children, older parents and their adult children remain emotionally linked to one another and have feelings of connectedness. This attachment usually grows when grandchildren are born.

Lesbian, Gay, Bisexual, and Transgender Couples

When most people think of a person who is lesbian, gay, bisexual, or transgender (LGBT), chances are they do not envision a senior citizen. Nonetheless, somewhere between 1.4 and 3.8 million elderly people are LGBT, a population that may number 7 million by 2030 (Grant, 2009). Although they face many of the same issues that other elders face, such as health problems or the need for reliable transportation or housing assistance, they also have many unique concerns. For example, older gay men are aging in a context sharply shaped by HIV and AIDS (Rosenfeld, Bartlam, and Smith, 2012). Likewise, older transgender adults have significantly higher risk of poor health, disability, depressive symptoms, and stress, as compared with those who are not transgender (Fredriksen-Goldsen et al., 2014).

A recent study conducted with over 2,400 LGBT older adults ages 50 and over reviewed their health status and identified both the risk factors contributing to poorer health and the protective factors to health outcomes. The findings showed that among those in the study group, lifetime victimization, internalized stigma, financial barriers, obesity, and limited physical activity contribute to poor general health, disability, and depression. In contrast, social support and a social network of adequate size served as protective factors, decreasing the odds of poor health, disability, and depression. In other words, those LGBT elders who had strong and extensive support systems were doing better than those without (Fredriksen-Goldsen et al., 2013).

Only recently have same-sex couples been allowed to marry in all states. Until this change, most federal programs and laws treated same-sex couples differently from married heterosexual couples, as discussed in Chapter 10 (Human Rights Campaign, 2015). For example:

- Social Security pays survivor benefits to widows and widowers, but not to the surviving same-sex life partner of someone who dies. This different treatment may cost LGBT elders $124 million per year in lost benefits.
- Married couples are eligible for Social Security spousal benefits, which can allow spouses to earn half their spouse's Social Security benefit if it is larger than their own. Unmarried partners in lifelong relationships are not eligible for spousal benefits.
- Medicaid regulations protect the assets and homes of married spouses when the other spouse enters a nursing home or long-term care facility; no such protections are offered to same-sex partners.
- Tax laws and other regulations of 401(k)s and pensions discriminate against same-sex partners, costing the surviving partner in a same-sex relationship tens of thousands of dollars a year, and possibly more than $1 million over a lifetime. For example, if a person with a 401(k) pension plan dies, the money rolls over to a *legal spouse* without any tax penalty. However, since gays and lesbians cannot legally marry in most states, the surviving partner would have to pay a 20 percent federal tax.

It is easy to see why many same-sex couples rallied for marriage because the effect of this unequal treatment is striking. Assume Samantha dies at age 60 with $100,000 in her retirement account, which she leaves to her life partner, Jennifer, also age 60. Jennifer will receive the inherited money, less taxes (at least $20,000), for a total of no more than $80,000. Jennifer cannot roll the money over into a tax-free IRA. If Jennifer

Slide Show

Family Experiences of Older People

Family relationships continue into old age and they can grow in size and complexity. This slideshow introduces you to some of the many family experiences of older people.

Joan and Carson have been married for 68 years. The romance has never gone out of their relationship. Like most elderly persons with a spouse or partner still alive, they enjoy regular sexual relations.

Rita and Kay have been married for 9 years; however, if you were to ask them when they married, they would tell you it was 42 years ago when they became college sweethearts. State and federal law prohibited them from legally marrying until recently.

Most grandparents report that their relationships with their grandchildren are meaningful and fun. Grandfathers are now more likely to recognize the importance of having close emotional involvement with young children and have opportunities to participate in ways that seemed unavailable to them when they were fathers.

Many older people do not have a spouse, or they may not live near their adult children or grandchildren. Their friends may become "fictive kin." This group of men meets twice a week for cards at the Senior Center, and they enjoy the camaraderie and friendship that has developed over the years.

Grandparents take on parent-like roles in many parts of the world. This grandmother lives with her son, daughter-in-law, and grandson. Both parents work and lead busy lives, and therefore she gladly considers herself as her grandson's primary caregiver.

Critical Thinking

How do you think that family relationships in old age differ across social class and race/ethnicity? What might account for any differences?

were a man—let's call him James—then as Samantha's widower, James would receive the full $100,000 and could shield it from taxes until age 70½. In other words, the survivor of the legally married couple has a nest egg to invest that is roughly 20 percent larger than that of the surviving partner in the same-sex couple. The nest egg can grow in a tax-deferred account until the maximum age of disbursement for the surviving spouse in a legally married couple.

Even basic rights such as hospital visitation or the right to die in the same nursing home as one's partner are regularly denied to unmarried couples. These policies have social, economic, and health consequences for gay and lesbian elders (Human Rights Campaign, 2015). They may hide their sexual orientation from their health care and social service providers out of fear, further compromising their ability to get needed care and assistance. Many gay and lesbian seniors remain hidden, reinforcing isolation and forgoing services they may truly need.

Widowhood

The death of a spouse or partner stands as one of life's most stressful events (Holmes and Rahe, 1967). It often means the loss of a companion and friend, perhaps the loss of income, and the ending of a familiar way of life. Widowhood can occur at any point in the life cycle, but because it is most likely to occur among older people, research tends to focus on that population.

Over 14 million persons are classified as widowed in the United States, and over three-quarters of them are women (U.S. Census Bureau, 2014).The number of people who have *experienced* widowhood, however, is much larger than that because some have remarried.

Women are more likely to be widowed than are men for three primary reasons. First, mortality rates among females are lower than for males; therefore, they live to older ages. The life expectancy of females at age 65 exceeds that of males of that age by nearly 7 years. Second, wives are typically 2 to 3 years younger than their husbands and consequently have a greater chance of outliving them. Third, widowed women are less likely to remarry than are widowed men. There is a lack of eligible men because cultural norms encourage older men to date and marry younger women, but not the reverse (Berardo and Berardo, 2000; He et al., 2005).

You may have heard others suggest that an elderly person often dies soon after his or her spouse dies. "He just gave up …"; "She died of sadness …"; "He saw no reason to go on after Rose died…." But is there any truth to this so-called "widow effect"; that is, is there really an increased probability of death among new widows and widowers? Two Harvard sociology professors decided to answer this question by following nearly 4,500 U.S. couples age 67 and older for five years (Elwert and Christakis, 2006). They found some truth to the "widow effect"; the likelihood of death does increase slightly after a spouse dies. The effect, however, does not occur equally among racial and ethnic groups. White men were 18 percent more likely to die shortly after their spouses' deaths, as were 16 percent of white women. But among blacks, a spouse's death had no effect on the mortality of the survivor.

Why would widowhood contribute to an early death for whites, but not for blacks? On marrying, blacks and whites appear to receive many of the same health, financial, and socioemotional benefits, such as emotional support, caretaking when ill, and enhanced social support, so what could account for the variations in the "widow effect"? Research shows that blacks are almost twice as likely to live with other relatives (Pew Research Center, 2010), are more active in religious groups, and when married are less likely to adhere to a traditional gendered division of labor, which may reduce dependence on a spouse. It seems that blacks may somehow manage to extend the benefits of marriage into widowhood and are therefore less likely than whites to die soon after their spouse passes on (Elwert and Christakis, 2006).

Grief and Bereavement

People handle their grief over the death of a loved one in a variety of ways. Some try to remain stoic; others cry out in despair. Some people fear death, whereas others, perhaps because of a strong religious faith, see it as part of a larger "master plan." Those widows and widowers in poor health at the time of widowhood had significantly higher risks of complicated grief and depression (Utz, Caserta, and Lund, 2012).

One of the more well-known perspectives on death and dying is based on the work of Elizabeth Kübler-Ross (1969). Her work with 200 primarily middle-aged cancer patients suggested five somewhat distinct stages that dying people and their loved ones experience. Although some critics say that not everyone experiences these stages, or in a particular order, Kübler-Ross's work is useful nonetheless. The five stages are:

- *Denial*—Many people first refuse to believe that they or a loved one is dying. They may ask for additional medical tests, desire a second or third opinion, or in other ways deny that death is near.
- *Anger*—When coming to grips with the truth, some people become angry. They may project this anger toward friends, family, people who are well, or medical personnel.
- *Bargaining*—The dying person or loved one may try to forestall death by striking a bargain with God.
- *Depression*—Depression may set in when the dying person or his or her loved ones realize that winning the fight against the illness or disease is not possible. Those who are dying may be depressed over the symptoms of their condition (e.g., chronic pain) or effects of their treatment (e.g., hair loss). As they see and plan for their future, the loss they face can feel overwhelming.
- *Acceptance*—Eventually, a patient and/or loved one may come to accept the approaching death. In this stage, each may reflect on their lives together.

These five stages are highly individualized. No two people pass through them at exactly the same pace, and many people may go back and forth between stages before finally reaching acceptance.

Health and Health Care among the Elderly

9.7 Identify the health concerns common among those who are elderly, and describe the primary program that pays for their health care.

Most elderly people report their health as good or excellent. Only about a quarter assess their health as fair or poor. Elderly men and women report only a small difference in health, and the gap has narrowed in recent years. However, older blacks are more likely to describe their health as only fair or poor than are whites or Asian Americans (National Center for Health Statistics, 2013).

Health Problems

Despite various improvements in the general way of life, there is no denying that as people age their health declines in a number of ways.

Despite images to the contrary, most elderly people are in good health and stay active. This man swims for 30 minutes almost daily, as he has done for years. Community centers often have special exercise programs that cater to elderly people.

If people live long enough, everyone is likely to lose some of his or her vision and hearing; to develop chronic conditions such as arthritis, heart disease, or diabetes; and to suffer some degree of memory impairment (National Center for Health Statistics, 2013). The health status of older adults is a result of a complex set of factors, including individual factors such as diet, exercise, and heredity, and structural factors such as socioeconomic status, racism, and access to health care. People may need someone to help with many things that they used to do for themselves: cooking, cleaning, home repairs, and perhaps even personal care.

Researchers have measured the degree of physical impairment by using a common set of activities of daily living (ADLs) such as bathing, dressing, eating, getting into and out of bed, walking indoors, and using the toilet. Instrumental activities of daily living (IADLs) include meal preparation, shopping, managing money, and taking medication. By using a common set of measures, gerontologists can track elders' degree of impairment and can make some comparisons across different samples. Millions of elderly people cannot perform ADLs and IADLs. As people age, they may become more disabled. Gerontologists estimate that the number of older people needing long-term care will increase over the next 50 years as the oldest-old cohort expands: 14 million elders may need this care by 2020 and 24 million by 2060.

Severe Memory Loss

dementia
An overall term that describes a wide range of symptoms associated with a decline in memory or other thinking skills severe enough to reduce a person's ability to perform everyday activities.

Perhaps one of the most difficult disabilities facing some elders, and those who care for them, is severe memory loss, known as dementia. **Dementia** is not a specific disease. It is an overall term that describes a wide range of symptoms associated with a decline in memory or other thinking skills severe enough to reduce a person's ability to perform everyday activities such as:

- the ability to generate coherent speech and understand spoken or written language;
- the ability to recognize or identify objects, assuming intact sensory function;
- the ability to execute motor activities, assuming intact motor abilities, sensory function, and comprehension of the required task; and
- the ability to think abstractly, make sound judgments, and plan and carry out complex tasks.

Alzheimer's disease is by far the most common form of dementia, affecting over 5 million persons. It is the seventh leading cause of death for people of all ages and the fifth leading cause of death among people age 65 and over (Alzheimer's Association, 2015b). The disease starts subtly; a person may have difficulty remembering names or recent events. It progresses over the course of years, and later symptoms include impaired judgment; disorientation; confusion; behavior changes; lack of recognition of loved ones; and eventually the inability to walk, speak, and even swallow. Alzheimer's is ultimately fatal. Given the changing demographics of our country, and the growing size of the oldest old cohort, Americans will see a large increase in people with Alzheimer's: 10 million baby boomers are expected to eventually develop it.

Alzheimer's disease takes a large toll on the individual, the family, and the community. Annually, about 16 million caregivers provide 18 billion hours of unpaid care valued at over $200 billion (Alzheimer's Association, 2015a). It also takes a toll on our communities. Alzheimer's cost the nation about $214 billion for health care, long-term care, and hospice for people each year, and the amount is expected to rise to $1.2 trillion by 2050 as the number of Alzheimer's patients continues to grow (Alzheimer's Association, 2015a). Given that the direct and indirect costs of Alzheimer's and other dementias, not to mention the cost in terms of families' heartache and despair, it is no wonder researchers are vigorously pursuing an agenda of prevention, treatment, and cure.

Medicare

Today, most people in developed countries do not encounter the infectious diseases such as tuberculosis or measles that used to be deadly, and if they do, they survive them. Instead, they live longer and become more prone to chronic illnesses such as arthritis, which develop over a long period and are often expensive to treat. Thus, the elderly tend to require increasing amounts of costly medical care, which they may be unable to afford.

Because elderly people require more medical care than others, and because the cost of medical care was impoverishing many elderly people, the Medicare program was created in 1965. **Medicare** is a federal health insurance program for people age 65 and older (and for younger people receiving Social Security Disability Insurance payments or suffering from a few specified conditions).

Medicare has kept millions of elderly people from impoverishing themselves to pay for their health care costs by making health insurance far more affordable and available. Because it is a universal program (available to virtually all citizens age 65 and over), rather than a program only for low-income people, it carries no stigma. And because virtually all elderly people qualify, administrative costs are significantly lower than other programs that have stringent income requirements.

Medicare, however, has some problems with it. First of all, Medicare does not provide elders with "free" health care. It covers most hospital costs but only part of physicians' bills, and the charges that are not covered can quickly become an enormous financial burden. Moreover, most nursing home care is not covered, nor are dental care, hearing aids, eyeglasses, and many other important and often used health services. Given high deductibles, co-payments, and payments for things not covered under Medicare, elderly persons spend an average of over $4,700 of their own dollars each year on medical care (Cubanski et al., 2014). Consequently, most elders have some form of additional insurance, as shown in Figure 9–7, which they often pay for themselves. Only the poorest, about 16 percent, may also qualify for Medicaid, the federal–state health care program designed to serve poor people, regardless of age. Medicaid also covers long-term care, but again, only for those who are poor enough to qualify (McArdle, Neuman, and Huang, 2014).

Medicare
A federal health insurance program for people age 65 and older (and for younger people receiving Social Security Disability Insurance payments or suffering from specified conditions).

Figure 9–7 Ways in Which Medicare Beneficiaries Supplement Their Medicare, 2010

NOTE: Medigap is private health insurance sold to supplement Medicare insurance in the United States. Medicare Advantage is a U.S. health insurance program of managed health care (preferred provider organization (PPO) or health maintenance organization (HMO)) that substitutes for regular Parts A (hospital) and B (physician and outpatient) Medicare benefits.

SOURCE: McArdle, Neuman, and Huang, 2014.

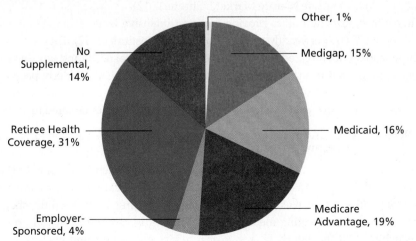

- Other, 1%
- Medigap, 15%
- No Supplemental, 14%
- Medicaid, 16%
- Retiree Health Coverage, 31%
- Medicare Advantage, 19%
- Employer-Sponsored, 4%

A second criticism of Medicare is that the health care providers are usually reimbursed by the government at a lower rate than they would be if they were seeing patients with private insurance. Providers complain that reimbursement is too low and cumbersome. They are not required by law to see Medicare patients, and therefore, many providers refuse to do so. Consequently, of those Medicare patients who reported looking for a new primary care physician, 28 percent reported a problem finding one who would see them (MedPAC, 2014).

A third concern of Medicare points to the changing U.S. demographic structure, which has some distressing repercussions for the Medicare program. Medicare is primarily funded through taxes; working people pay taxes today for programs used by those who are elderly today. In the future, as the U.S. population ages, there will be fewer working adults paying taxes relative to the number of elderly people needing Medicare services. There were about 4 workers for each Medicare user in 2001, but there will be only 2.3 workers by 2030 (Heritage Foundation, 2013). This trend coupled with rising health care costs clearly signals that the country faces a serious challenge. The Medicare program costs about $520 billion, and this cost is estimated to grow to $680 billion by 2020, and to $850 billion by 2024 (Kaiser Family Foundation, 2014). To deal with this problem, Congress could modify the program in several ways, such as increasing the amount that elders pay by raising deductibles and co-payments, covering fewer services, or even raising the age at which people are eligible for Medicare services, similar to what has been done with Social Security. The goal is to keep Medicare solvent well into the future because our society recognizes that the health of seniors is a social concern, not merely an individual problem.

Long-Term Care

long-term care
Care for chronic physical or mental conditions that will likely never go away.

As people live longer, and their health deteriorates, many need **long-term care**, which is care for their chronic physical or mental conditions that will likely never go away. How do we care for the growing numbers of elderly people who can no longer care for themselves?

FORMAL CARE Some who are elderly in the United States rely on formal care provided by social service agencies on a paid or volunteer basis. This care could include a variety of types: paid visiting nurses, meals or housecleaning programs, a paid personal attendant, assisted living, or nursing home care.

Assisted-living facilities are a booming business, with over 40,000 operating throughout the country (MetLife Mature Market Institute, 2012). They vary in scope: Some assisted-living facilities are little more than apartments for seniors with optional food, housekeeping, and entertainment services, and others provide more skilled nursing care. The price varies by what is included, but averages approximately $40,000 per year (MetLife Mature Market Institute, 2012).

In contrast, nursing homes provide the most intensive level of care, at an average cost of about $75,000 per year (MetLife Mature Market Institute, 2012). They are available for those who cannot be cared for at home because of medical needs and who have likely moved beyond what most assisted-living centers can provide. Few elderly people actually live in nursing homes, although that number rises with age. Most people do not need the intense level of care, cannot afford such care, and would rather be cared for at home.

INFORMAL CARE In contrast to formal care, most elders in the United States rely primarily on informal care, which is unpaid care by someone close to the care recipient, such as a spouse, daughter, son, or even a grandchild, friend, or neighbor (Family Caregiver Alliance, 2012; Fox and Brenner, 2012). These caregivers provide a wide variety of hands-on care, such as cooking, cleaning, bathing, housekeeping, shopping, administering and managing medications, coordinating care with medical providers, and watching over the elderly person to ensure his or her safety and well-being.

Caring for elderly parents or a spouse can be a labor of love, but it is also time-in-tensive, potentially expensive, and often stressful. Historically, tending to the elderly was the task of daughters or daughters-in-law who were full-time homemakers. As more women work outside the home, they are less available to care for elderly parents and therefore sons or other relatives may chip in. Some of these adult caregivers also have their own children to care for and are therefore described as the **sandwich generation**. Because most adult caregivers are employed, they may make substantial sacrifices at work to accommodate caregiving, including going in work late or leaving early, working fewer hours, taking a leave of absence, turning down a promotion, choosing early retirement, or giving up work completely. Caregivers often spend their own money to provide medicines, groceries, or other supplies to the person they are caring for.

As society continues to age, the United States could benefit from an explicit plan for caring for frail elders. If caregiving is indeed a personal responsibility to be provided by family members, then families should be strengthened by a variety of financial and policy benefits, such as tax credits, paid family leave, free or low-cost senior day care, or respite care. Moreover, although the Family Medical Leave Act allows for 12 weeks of leave from employment to allow a person to care for a sick or disabled relative (in qualifying workplaces), the time off is unpaid, which makes it prohibitive for many people.

Death with Dignity

"Death with dignity" has become a popular phrase as people confront the issues of relegating those who are old and those who are terminally ill to institutions and possibly to a life sustained by machines. Often, the use of these technologies prolongs the dying process rather than maintains life.

Although old people have always died, those who are dying have not always been old. Only in recent decades has death occurred mainly among the elderly. Because of this new link between old age and death, the social issues related to death also involve aging. It is becoming increasingly important *how* we die. Dying is not a medical condition; it is a personally experienced, lived condition (Hospice Foundation of America, 2014). And many people are finding that current practices in hospitals and nursing homes offer little possibility of a good and meaningful death.

In contrast, **hospice** offers medical care with a different goal: maintaining or improving quality of life for someone whose illness, disease, or condition is terminal. The focus is on caring, not curing. Each patient's individualized care plan is designed to address the physical, emotional, and spiritual pain that often accompanies terminal illness. Hospice care also offers practical support for the caregiver(s) during the illness and grief support after the death (Hospice Foundation of America, 2014).

Hospices can be located in health facilities made to be as homelike as possible. But increasingly, hospice emphasizes health services at home for those who are dying, including visiting nurses, on-call physicians, and counselors. This kind of service enables many

sandwich generation

Adults who are caring for an aging parent while also caring for their own children under age 18.

What Do You Think?

Look into the future to a time when your parent(s) need long-term care. What will you do? How will this care be provided? Will you rely on formal or informal care, and how will you integrate this care with your own work, family, and leisure?

hospice

Offers care to a dying person, with the goal of maintaining or improving quality of life; the focus is on caring, not curing.

Many people no longer want their last living days to be spent in a hospital, hooked up to machines. They would prefer to die at home, which they see as a more dignified way to pass.

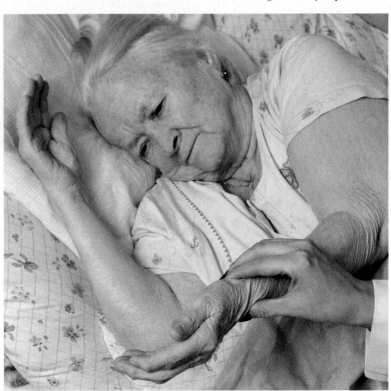

Table 9–4 Characteristics of Hospice Users

Sex		
	Female	56%
	Male	44%
Age		
	Under 65	17%
	65–74	16%
	75–84	28%
	85+	41%
Race/Ethnicity		
	White	82%
	Black	9%
	Asian/Pacific Islander	3%
	American Indian	0.3%
	Hispanic (either White or Black)	7%
	Multiracial or Other	7%
Location of Death		
	Private Residence	42%
	Nursing Home	17%
	Other Residential Facility	7%
	Hospice Inpatient Facility	27%
	Acute Care Hospital	7%

SOURCE: Adapted from National Hospice and Palliative Care Organization, 2014.

people to live their final days in the familiar surroundings of their own home, surrounded by their loved ones. As reported in Table 9–4, almost half of hospice patients die at home (National Hospice and Palliative Care Organization, 2014). Being at home with one's family seems to provide a greater chance for "death with dignity"; being institutionalized implies loss of control and individuality.

The hospice movement has had an astounding impact on how people actually experience death. Over a third of all deaths in the United States now occur to patients who are in the care of a hospice program, and the total number of patients served either in hospice facilities or hospice home care exceeds 1.5 million.

One of the most unusual episodes in the sociology of old age is the story of Brandeis University professor Morris Schwartz. Much to his surprise, Schwartz became one of the most respected contemporary voices on issues of life and death. And it is all because a former student took the trouble to renew their friendship and to listen to what his former professor had to say.

The student, Mitch Albom (1998), visited the terminally ill Schwartz, whom everyone called Morrie, every Tuesday for several months. He recorded his insights about life and death, and compiled them into a book titled *Tuesdays with Morrie*, which became a best seller. It was featured on the *Oprah Winfrey Show*, and a television movie of the story was made. By now the book has reached millions of people with its message.

Morrie Schwartz had many lessons to teach about confronting death. Chief among them is that death is part of life and must be experienced fully. It is not something to be ashamed of, to be whispered about, as is too often the case. For Schwartz, the end of life is a time to dwell on "love, responsibility, spirituality, awareness." To do so, despite his increasing weakness and pain, the former professor surrounded himself with the people and things he loved and, according to Albom, essentially wrapped himself in a cocoon of human activities, conversation, interaction, and affection. He even hosted his own "living funeral" to give his family and himself the rare opportunity to hear and say the things that they all felt needed to be said. Schwartz's criticism of the American way of death was thus countered by his loving and deeply personal example of how death can be dignified, spiritual, and enlightening.

Social Policy

9.8   Summarize the Social Security program.

There are many social policy issues that are important to the elderly, including the quality and cost of Medicare, long-term care, affordable senior housing, and adequate transportation options, to name just a few. The issues around Social Security are particularly important because it is the largest source of income for those who are elderly.

The History Behind Social Security

The United States is one of over 150 countries that have some sort of financial program for elders. Each program operates somewhat differently but provides at least some financial benefit to help the elderly make ends meet.

In the United States during the late nineteenth and early twentieth centuries, few companies had private pensions for seniors, and the government did not provide public pensions. Consequently, elderly people who could still work usually continued to do so. Public pensions were introduced many times in the U.S. Congress between 1900 and 1935 with no success. But during the Great Depression, it became obvious that those who were elderly could not rely on jobs, private pensions, savings, or their families for financial support. By 1935, unemployment rates among those 65 and older were well above 50 percent (Hardy and Shuey, 2000), and a federal commission determined that nearly half of all seniors in the United States could not support themselves.

The Social Security Act was passed in 1935, creating many different kinds of assistance programs. One of them, Old Age, Survivor, and Disability Insurance (OASDI), is the program Americans have come to know as "Social Security." It offered seniors public pensions as a response to the austere poverty that many of them endured. The Social Security system was not designed to be the main source of income. It was originally intended as a form of insurance against unexpected reductions in income due to retirement, disability, or the death of a wage-earning spouse. However, the system has become a kind of government-administered public pension plan. It is now seen as an earned right for seniors, not a form of welfare. Payments from Social Security have successfully reduced the percentage of seniors who are impoverished.

How Social Security Works

OASDI retirement benefits are financed by a tax on earnings up to a certain level that is set by Congress. For the year 2015, that earnings level is $118,500. Any earnings over that amount are not taxed. The tax is paid by both the employee and the employer at a rate of 6.2 percent each (Social Security Online, 2013). The Social Security tax has been called a regressive tax because it essentially taxes low earners at a higher rate than high earners. For example, say "Bob" earned $118,500 in 2015; therefore, he paid 6.2 percent of his income or $7,347 in Social Security taxes. Meanwhile, "Mary" earned twice that amount, or $237,000, but still paid 6.2 percent only on the first $118,500 she earned, so she also paid $7,347. The rest of Mary's income is free of Social Security tax. Thus, Bob paid 6.2 percent of his *total income* in Social Security tax while Mary paid only 3.1 percent. As a higher wage earner, Mary is, in effect, taxed at a lower rate, and as a lower wage earner, Bob is taxed at a higher rate.

Social Security is a major income source for those who are elderly, and for some it is the only source of retirement income. It is guaranteed for life and adjusted for inflation. It serves 41 million retired workers and their dependents at a cost of $51 billion a year. The average monthly benefit is about $1,300 a month (Social Security Administration, 2014).

Yet it is important to remember that Social Security serves other groups, too. For example, nearly 11 million disabled workers and their dependents receive Social Security benefits, as do about 6 million survivors (widows, widowers, and their dependents). These groups account for about one-quarter of Social Security beneficiaries. However, these groups are not growing in size substantially. In contrast, the size of the elderly population is rapidly increasing, thus the attention on that age group.

Future Prospects

The Social Security program is facing an impending challenge that causes many people to wonder if it actually will be around to help them in old age, as revealed in Table 9–5 (Employee Benefit Research Institute and Greenwald & Associates, 2014). Only 8 percent of workers and 14 percent of retirees in 2014 were "very confident" that Social Security will continue to provide benefits of at least equal value to those today, representing a steep decline in confidence over the past two decades. In contrast, 35 percent of workers and 21 percent of retirees claim that they are "not at all confident" that Social Security will continue to provide benefits at the same level of value.

Their concern stems from the fact that we have an increasing number of people living longer (drawing on Social Security) and have fewer people in the cohort behind them to pay into the system. Thus, over the next two decades as the baby boomers retire, how can Social Security remain solvent? There are a number of options. First, for younger cohorts among the baby boomers, the retirement age for benefits has been raised to 66 or 67 years (depending on birth date). As we go forward, other sacrifices may be needed to keep the program solvent, such as increasing the tax rate above the current 6.2 percent, eliminating the regressive cap so that all income is taxed instead of just the first $118,500, raising the retirement age even further, or changing Social Security to serve only those who are poor or low income rather than all those who are elderly.

Going Beyond Left and Right

Social Security has the tremendous support of virtually all Americans, regardless of political affiliation, age, ethnicity, or gender. It is an extremely popular program and one that most Americans cannot imagine living without. In a recent poll, 89 percent of adults claimed that Social Security benefits are more important now than ever to ensure that retirees have a dependable income. Americans are even willing to increase taxes to keep it solvent. The same poll found that 82 percent of Americans agree it is

Table 9–5 Confidence That "Social Security Will Continue to Provide Benefits of at Least Equal Value to Benefits Received Today"

	Workers	Retirees
Very Confident	8%	14%
Somewhat Confident	24%	38%
Not Too Confident	33%	26%
Not At All Confident	35%	21%

SOURCE: Adapted from Employee Benefit Research Institute and Greenwald & Associates, 2014.

Figure 9–8 Share of Americans Agreeing with "It is critical that we preserve Social Security for future generations, even if it means ..."

SOURCE: Adapted from Tucker, Reno, and Bethell, 2014.

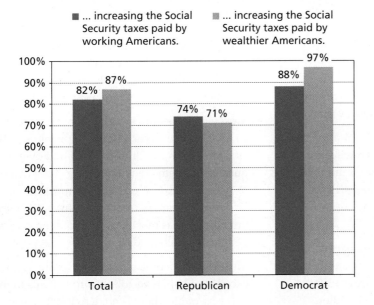

critical to preserve Social Security for future generations even if it means increasing Social Security taxes paid by working Americans, and 87 percent want to preserve Social Security for future generations even if it means increasing taxes paid by wealthier Americans (Tucker, Reno, and Bethell, 2014). As you can see from Figure 9–8, the majority of both Democrats and Republicans agree that a tax increase may be the necessary and prudent thing to do.

This level of agreement does not mean, however, that Democrats and Republicans have no differences on how they would propose saving Social Security for future generations. For example, former President George W. Bush proposed privatizing Social Security. As a privatized program, Social Security would allow workers to control their own retirement money through personal investment accounts. Supporters of private accounts contend that retirees would have the freedom to invest their retirement money in the stock market as they wish, possibly earning higher returns than with government-invested funds. Most Republicans lean in this direction. They believe young Americans especially should be given this opportunity because they would have a longer period of time to recoup any losses resulting from a fluctuating stock market.

Critics of privatizing Social Security, which includes most Democrats, argue that investing retirement money is complicated and risky because individuals can lose their retirement safety net through bad decisions. Social Security was intended to be a secure source of income that is removed from the fluctuations of the stock market. Putting money from Social Security into private accounts means moving retirement savings from a simple, easily understood system to a complex structure of investment portfolios and stock market shares that is more difficult to understand. Americans who do not understand investment strategies would be at a disadvantage. Critics further argue that such a move will not benefit the American economy, but will put billions of dollars in brokerage and management fees into the pockets of Wall Street financial services corporations. Instead of radically altering Social Security, they suggest that future budget shortfalls can be fixed by raising the retirement age and increasing taxes as needed.

Summary

- Aging is a social problem for two reasons. First, aging places stress on society. For example, as the American aging population continues to grow, and the country's number of younger workers does not keep up, how will Americans pay for the programs that those who are elderly use? The second reason aging can be viewed through a social problem lens involves an individual approach. It has to do with the way that elders live their lives and are treated in society.

- Most developed nations have a high and growing *proportion* of elderly people, but in terms of sheer numbers, most elderly people live in developing nations. People are living longer, and fewer babies are being born.

- Today, there are nearly 50 million people age 65 and older in the United States, and the numbers are quickly rising. By 2020, there are likely to be another 6 million elders, and by 2060, when you are likely to still be alive, the number could be about 92 million.

- There are two categories in the physiological aging process: (1) primary aging, the result of molecular and cellular changes, and (2) secondary aging, an accelerated version of normal aging that is caused by environmental factors. Changing self-concept and status are particularly important as psychological processes as aging occurs. Culturally, social gerontologists frequently refer to the elderly as a minority group who can be victims of prejudice, stereotyping, and discrimination.

- Average income among people who are elderly hovers around $36,000 per year. This income comes from a number of sources, such as earnings, pensions, or retirement savings, but the largest single source, at nearly 40 percent, comes from Social Security. Earnings comprise about a quarter of the average income of elders, and pensions account for 20 percent. Assets such as stocks, bonds, or income from rented real estate, and other unknown income sources make up the remainder. Those who have multiple areas of vulnerability, for example, being old, female, and members of a minority, are most likely to be poor.

- Most elderly people have been married for many years. However, over 14 million people are classified as widowed in the United States, and over three-quarters of them are women. The death of a spouse or partner stands as one of life's most stressful events. Widowhood can occur at any point in the life cycle, but because it is most likely to occur among older people, research tends to focus on that population.

- Most elderly people report their health as good or excellent. Despite various improvements in the general way of life, there is no denying that as people age their health declines in a number of ways, such as losing some degree of vision and hearing. Medicare is the program that helps pay the health costs for people who are elderly.

- The Social Security Act was passed in 1935, creating many different kinds of assistance programs. One of them, Old Age, Survivor, and Disability Insurance (OASDI), is the program Americans have come to know as "Social Security." It was not designed to be the main source of income. It was originally intended as a form of insurance against unexpected reductions in income due to retirement, disability, or the death of a wage-earning spouse. However, the system has become a kind of government-administered public pension plan.

Chapter 10
The Changing Family

 ## Learning Objectives

10.1 Define the term *family* and explain why it is important.

10.2 Identify the functions of families.

10.3 Compare and contrast three perspectives on family change.

10.4 Discuss the changing norms of marriage and intimate relationships.

10.5 Review different types of parenting contexts.

10.6 Explain two types of family problems or challenges: violence and divorce.

10.7 Discuss family policy, using the example of maternity leave.

The cultural imagery of American families that we see on television and throughout the media suggests that "normal" families contain a mom, a dad, and siblings, all of whom are expected to behave toward each other in very specific ways. The problem is this cultural imagery is at odds with the reality of life for many families. This family ideology implicitly denigrates those families whose structure or cultural practices are different, and it contributes to negative self-images and even self-derogation among members of such families, as I found in my research. I conducted interviews with 73 grown children of Korean and Vietnamese immigrants and found that when these young adults contrasted behavior in their immigrant families with mainstream images of normalcy, they interpreted their own family life, as well as that of Asians and Asian Americans in general, as deficient. They emphasized Americanized definitions of love that stress expressiveness, such as the display of affection, sentimentality, and close communication. They downplayed their parents' instrumental style of love emphasized in Asian cultures, such as their material support of children well into adulthood and—in the case of many parents—their decision to immigrate in search of a better life and education for their children. However, because their parents did not conform to Americanized notions of expressive love, these children often described them as distant, unloving, uncaring, and not "normal." This ideology puts immense pressure on many of the children of immigrants in this study to assimilate and encourages some to denigrate their own ethnic family styles as deficient in comparison. As Robert, 24, who emigrated from Korea at age 7, explained, "I still find myself envying white American families and wishing that my family was perfect like theirs. So basically I find myself suckered into this ideal image of the American family. And I realize, sadly, that my family is not the American family and never will be."
—*Karen Pyke (referring to Pyke, 2000a, 2000b)*

What Is a Family?

10.1 **Define the term** *family* **and explain why it is important.**

We all probably come from some type of family. Many Americans, especially younger Americans, accept divorce, cohabitation, remaining single, same-sex marriage, and being childfree as legitimate lifestyles, while at the same time, espousing that marriage, children, and a strong family life are important goals toward which they strive (Taylor, 2014).

This chapter explores social and cultural aspects of families, describes how they have changed in recent years, and identifies some of the contemporary social problems that they face. But first ask yourself, "What is a family?" Oddly, despite the often-used term, there is no widespread agreement on its definition.

For example, Edward and Ashley, a young couple, have been dating for several years. Two years ago, they moved in together and are saving money to buy their first house. They love each other very much and plan to marry someday. Are they a family? Would your answer be different if I told you that Edward and Ashley had a child together last year? Meanwhile, Jonathon and Martin, an older same-sex couple, have been happily together for the past 30 years but are not married because, until recently, their state did not allow it. Are they a family? Finally, Valeria and David recently married, and each of them has a child from a previous marriage. David's son lives on the other side of the country and has met Valeria's daughter only a couple of times. What are the family lines here? Are David and Valeria's children family to one another?

The U.S. Census Bureau defines a **family** as two or more people living together who are related by birth, marriage, or adoption. This definition remains the basis for many social programs and policies, including employee fringe benefits, such as health and dental insurance or family and medical leaves. However, this official definition does not really reflect the rich diversity of family life today (Amato, 2014). Some people suggest that if people *feel* that they are a family and *behave* as though they are a family, then they should be recognized as such. The focus should be on greater inclusion of family relationships. This chapter uses a broader and more inclusive definition

family

Relationships by blood, marriage, or affection, in which members may cooperate economically, may care for any children, and may consider their identity to be intimately connected to the larger group.

Slide Show

What Is a Family?

Families play a primary role in all cultures around the world. Family roles, responsibilities, and even membership may vary from one region to another. For example, the United States and most developed countries recognize grandparents, aunts and uncles, and cousins on both the mother's and father's side of the family—called a bilateral approach to family. However, in many parts of the world, only one side is recognized as kin, either those on the father's side (patrilineal) or those on the mother's side (matrilineal). Despite differences like this, there are many similar functions of families. These functions include the regulation of sexual behavior, reproduction and socializing children, providing a path for inheritance, economic cooperation among members, social status placement, and a mechanism for providing warmth, intimacy, and protection.

Families are universal. Although they may vary in size or social roles, they remain a cornerstone of life in all cultures. In less developed countries, families often take the place of social institutions such as schools or health care.

Family size has been shrinking in the United States. Most American families have only two children. However, unlike some countries such as China and India that put significant pressure on families to remain small to control population growth, American families can be as large or small as desired.

Although the teenage pregnancy rate has been steadily declining, the number of older single parents is on the rise. Adoption is a popular mechanism for having a child, although the number of international adoptions has been declining since 2005.

About one in five people today say that they do not want to have children. This couple is very happy with one another and their dog, "Scooby." They think of Scooby as part of the family.

Same-sex couples actively sought the right to marry and be recognized as legitimate families in the eyes of the law. Most people now agree with the position that same-sex couples should be allowed to marry and agree with the Supreme Court's decision in 2015 that allowed them to wed.

Critical Thinking

What is your own personal definition of "family"? What factors influence your views? These factors might include religion, culture, personal experience, or your parents' values.

than that taken from the Census Bureau. Families are defined here as *relationships by blood, marriage, or affection, in which members may cooperate economically, may care for any children, and may consider their identity to be intimately connected to the larger group.*

Why does it matter how we define family? The definition used has important consequences with respect to informal and formal rights (Human Rights Campaign, 2015). For example, neighbors, schools, and other community groups interact with family members differently from ways they interact with other nonrelated groups who live together. Families even get special membership discounts to a wide variety of organizations that roommates or friends do not get. For example, an individual membership to a particular organization may be $25, but a family rate is $30, regardless of family size. However, far more is at stake than simply a few dollars. The agreed-on definition has important consequences that are legally recognized. For example, under most employer insurance plans, only a worker's spouse and legal children can be covered by a health or dental insurance policy. Taxes also favor those who are legally married. It is for these reasons, and many more, that same-sex couples fought for the right to marry.

Functions of Families

10.2 Identify the functions of families.

The family is a vital institution in all societies, although the structure of families and what is expected of parents and children varies widely across different cultures and societies. In India or Pakistan, for example, parents generally select their children's spouses, a practice that most people in Western cultures reject. But perhaps even more surprising than the differences found in families from place to place are the *similarities* across families. Structural functionalists often discuss families in terms of the important functions that they serve for individuals and for society at large.

In general, there are at least six universal functions of families, and although they may play out differently from one culture to another, they are regarded as key features of family life.

- *Regulation of Sexual Behavior:* Every culture, including ours, regulates sexual behavior. Cultural norms make it clear who can have a sexual relationship with whom and under what circumstances. One virtually universal regulation around the world is the incest taboo, which forbids sexual activity (and marriage) among close family members. However, the definition of "close family members" differs, although it usually involves at least parents and their children, and siblings.
- *Reproduction and Socializing Children:* For a society to continue, it must produce new members to replace those who die or move away. Families have the primary responsibility for producing the newest members and for teaching them the culture in which they live. Children learn primarily from their families the language, values, beliefs, interpersonal skills, and general knowledge necessary to adequately function in society.
- *Property and Inheritance:* As families moved from a nomadic lifestyle as hunters and gatherers to one based on agriculture, it became possible for the first time for people to accumulate surplus property beyond what was needed for sheer survival. Friedrich Engels (1884/1902) tied the origin of the family to males' desire to identify heirs so that they could pass down their property to their sons. Monogamy worked in men's favor. Without it, paternity was uncertain. Therefore, men sought to strictly control women sexually, economically, and socially through marriage.
- *Economic Cooperation:* Adults and children have physical needs for food, shelter, and clothing. Families are the first line of defense for providing these necessities to its members. There is usually a gendered division of labor, with certain tasks

primarily performed by men and others by women. However, exactly which tasks are considered masculine or feminine varies from one society to the next.

- *Social Placement, Status, and Roles:* All members of society relate in some way to the basic structure of that society, usually in a way that preserves order and minimizes confusion and conflict. We fit in by way of a complex web of statuses (positions in a group or society) and roles (behaviors that are associated with those positions). Through our families, we are given an identity and position in society. For example, we are born into a certain social class, ethnic or racial group, religious affiliation, or geographic region.

- *Care, Warmth, Protection, and Intimacy:* People need more than food, shelter, and clothing to survive. Families are intended to provide the care, warmth, protection, and intimacy that individuals need. However, cross-culturally, families may give different weights to these features. For example, in many less developed societies, love is not a feature of marriage. Likewise, in more developed countries, families may be less focused on the aspect of protection, leaving that to the local police department.

What Do You Think?

Provide examples of each of these functions in modern American society. How have they changed, if at all, over time?

Perspectives on Family Change

10.3 Compare and contrast three perspectives on family change.

In every recent presidential election campaign, "family values" have been a hot issue, largely because some people are concerned that the family is in trouble and facing a great number of social problems (National Marriage Project, 2012), citing "the neglect of marriage," "lack of commitment by men," "the rise in cohabitation," and "fatherless families." Popular television shows, newspapers, and magazines bombard viewers with stories about the demise of the family and the problems families face: single parenthood, juvenile delinquency, teen pregnancy, family breakups. Some refer to the "good old days," when there were fewer problems, life was easier, family bonds were stronger, families had more authority to fulfill their functions, and people were generally happier. People who believe that today's families are being threatened suggest: (1) Americans are rejecting traditional marriage and family life; (2) family members are not adhering to roles within families; and (3) many social and moral problems result from the changes in families.

In contrast to this pessimistic perspective, others remind us that these golden years of the past never really existed. They argue that families have always faced challenges, including desertion, poverty, children born out of wedlock, alcoholism, unemployment, violence, and child abuse (Coontz, 2007). Yet, despite these long-standing problems, attempts to strengthen families through improved social services and financial assistance have been met with resistance. Ensuring that families have adequate childcare, low-cost educational opportunities, jobs with livable wages, health care regardless of cost, and safe housing is at odds with the emphasis on "rugged individualism." Instead, a theme felt by many Americans is that people should "pull themselves up by their own bootstraps."

Families are changing in composition, expectations, and roles. What is causing these changes? Are these changes good or bad? What are the consequences of family change? These questions are hotly debated—a debate that is woven firmly into the U.S. political discourse, as you can see in any nightly news show, from Fox News to MSNBC. Janet Giele (1996) contrasts three conflicting political viewpoints about the causes and consequences of changes in families, as shown in Figure 10–1.

Conservative Perspective

Conservatives express grave concern that changes in family structure put children at risk (American Enterprise Institute, 2013; Heritage Foundation, 2013; Murray, 1984; National Marriage Project, 2012). They suggest that many challenges families face are linked to

Figure 10–1 Conservative, Liberal, and Feminist Views of Family Change
SOURCE: Giele, 1996.

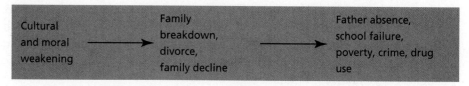

Conservative

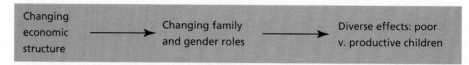

Liberal

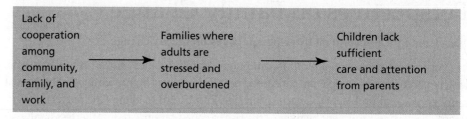

Feminist

cultural and moral weakening. This weakening contributes to father absence and family disorganization through divorce or having children outside of marriage, which ultimately results in greater poverty, crime, drug use, and a host of other social problems.

Conservatives argue that the weakening of the U.S. moral fabric can be traced to the decline of religious practice and affiliation. They suggest that the lack of religious influence has reshaped our cultural norms so that practices such as nonmarital sex, cohabitation, or having a child outside of marriage are no longer seen as immoral. When this shift in norms happens, society witnesses the breakdown of the traditional two-parent family, which conservatives argue is the cornerstone of society. Fathers become increasingly irrelevant in the lives of women and children. Divorce rates and illegitimacy soar. Husbands divorce their wives, leaving their children behind. They form new unions and have additional children, referred to as **multiple partner fertility**, sometimes without providing financially or emotionally for the children they already have. Conservatives suggest that welfare and other social programs actually serve to undermine families, rather than help them, because they make it easy for men to leave their partner and children.

According to conservatives, when families break up and fathers become increasingly marginalized, social problems flourish. Poverty becomes rampant, and children fail to thrive. They do worse in school, and possibly turn to alcohol, drugs, and crime to try to alleviate their suffering. Conservatives suggest that the solution to this downward spiral is to strengthen and support traditional marriage. They propose restoring the ideal of the two-parent family by making other types of families less attractive. For example, the government should minimize its support of single mothers and encourage couples to marry and rely on one another for the care of their children.

Liberal Perspective

Liberals also note that families have changed significantly in recent decades, resulting in many challenges. However, liberals suggest that these challenges result from economic and structural adjustments that place new demands on families

multiple partner fertility

Having children with multiple partners.

without offering additional social supports. These changes include the loss of relatively high-paying manufacturing jobs, an erosion of the minimum wage, a decline in employer-sponsored fringe benefits, and a rise in the number of low-paying service sector jobs. These economic circumstances have influenced a number of changes within families. First, there is an increasing need for both husbands and wives to work to support the family. Second, corresponding with dual-earner households, there is a greater need for childcare assistance. Third, because young women are less inclined to marry men with few good economic prospects, there is a rise in cohabitation and having children outside of marriage. According to William Julius Wilson (1996), a scholar and former president of the American Sociological Association, it is partly the lack of jobs in the inner city that drives up the rate of nonmarital births because the men are not considered "marriageable."

The result, according to liberals, is the creation of an underclass. Poor children face extraordinary challenges because they don't have the social supports to weather these changes. Liberals essentially believe in a market economy, but they ask for sufficient social supports to help families in the lower tiers of the economy or those who face other vulnerablities. Such supports include welfare benefits, job training programs, educational subsidies, expansion of quality childcare programs, and strengthening supports for working families.

Feminist Perspective

The feminist perspective blends elements of both conservative and liberal perspectives. In common with conservatives, feminists share a heightened respect for the often invisible but important caregiving work done in families. With liberals, they share a concern that the changes in economic conditions have had many deleterious consequences for families, particularly those that are most vulnerable. Yet, there are also sharp differences with conservative and liberal perspectives. The feminist perspective criticizes conservatives for exploiting female caregivers, which allows men to be more active in the public realm. Meanwhile, the feminist perspective also criticizes liberals for perpetuating the notion that the best families are those that are somehow self-sufficient.

Feminists attribute the difficulties children face to a lack of cooperation between the community, family, and employers to improve the quality of life. They express concern that a sense of individualism permeates U.S. culture and there is little collective responsibility for one another's welfare. They point to comparative research in other countries that shows that government support for all families causes poverty and its associated problems to plummet, while health, education, and well-being soar. However, in the United States, the lack of collective spirit results in families in which adults feel routinely stressed and overburdened. Although poor families may feel these stresses more acutely than the middle class, all families suffer. Children may suffer because they lack sufficient care and attention from their parents who are expected to fend for themselves with little outside support.

Feminists ask for alternative policies that place higher value on the quality of human relationships. They work for reforms that strengthen neighborhoods and volunteer groups, support caregiving activities, and encourage education and employment among both women and men. They advocate that family policies should be enacted to protect and nurture families, including in the areas of childcare, maternity benefits, health care, work guarantees, and other economic supports. In sum, feminists judge the strength of a family not by its form (dual-parent versus single-parent), but by the social well-being that comes from parents knowing that they have the support necessary to be the best family caregivers and productive workers that they can be (Giele, 1996).

What Do You Think?

Which perspective—conservative, liberal, or feminist—is most popular in our society, and why? Do you think it might vary across social groups, such as by age, education, or sex? Which perspective makes the most sense to you, and why?

Changing Norms of Marriage and Intimate Relationships

10.4 Discuss the changing norms of marriage and intimate relationships.

Many aspects of marriage have changed substantially over the past few decades. For example, fewer people marry, and those who do so marry later and likely cohabit beforehand. Same-sex couples demanded the same right to marry that is afforded to heterosexual couples. Partners are renegotiating their roles with their relationships, including the division of household labor. These issues are discussed in the sections that follow.

The Declining Rates of Marriage

In the United States, most people want to marry and eventually do so. Less than 4 percent of adults remain unmarried throughout their lives. Although the practical necessity of marriage has declined in recent years as more women can support themselves financially and more men know their way around the domestic arena, the symbolic importance of marriage has remained high. Marriage is now a sign of prestige rather than conformity because it often comes *after* a certain level of attainment (after a job, a career, savings, or children) rather than before.

Among the roughly 250 million Americans ages 18 and over, 55 percent are currently married. Asian Americans have the highest percentages of married people over age 18 in the population (63 percent), whereas blacks had the lowest (34 percent). These proportions represent a significant decline over the past generation. Figure 10–2 compares the marital status of adults ages 18 and older in 1970 and 2014 (U.S. Census Bureau, October 30, 2014a). The figure reveals that the likelihood of being married has declined significantly. Instead, more people claim to be never married, divorced, or widowed. In fact, the percentage of the adult population who claim to be divorced is more than triple that in 1970. However, this figure represents a *snapshot* in time; it is likely that most of these unmarried or divorced people will marry.

Figure 10–2 Marital Status of U.S. Population 18 Years and Over, 1970, 2014

SOURCE: U.S. Census Bureau, October 30, 2014a.

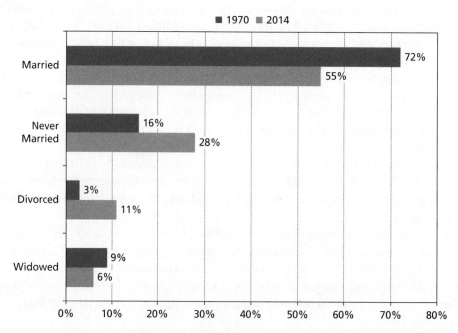

Figure 10–3 Median Age at First Marriage, 1890–2014

SOURCE: U.S. Census Bureau, October 30, 2014a.

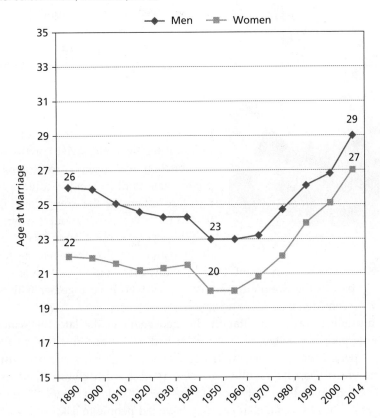

If the vast majority of people marry eventually, why does it look like so few people are married? One reason is that people are delaying the age at which they marry.

The average age at which people marry has fluctuated substantially through time. The age at marriage at the end of the nineteenth century was about what it is today. However, ask your grandparents at what age they married, and don't be surprised if it was by age 20 or 21. One psychiatrist wrote in 1953 that "a girl who hasn't a man in sight by the time she is 20 is not altogether wrong in feeling that she may never get married," and therefore, young women set their sights on finding a husband early (Coontz, 2007). Consequently, as shown in Figure 10–3, the age at marriage dropped to an all-time low during the 1950s to 20 years for women (with the greatest number marrying at age 18) and 23 for men.

Since the 1950s, the age at first marriage has been steadily increasing. Today, the average age for marriage has risen to 27 and 29 years for women and men, respectively, increasing by several years in just a generation, as shown in Figure 10–3 (U.S. Census Bureau, October 30, 2014a). For those people with advanced education, the average age is even higher.

The delay of marriage is occurring among all racial and ethnic groups. This delay is likely due to greater educational and economic opportunities, especially for women. As increasing numbers of women go to college, graduate school, or begin careers, they are more likely to postpone getting married and having children. It is not necessarily that marriage is less appealing; it is just more appealing to wait. Women enjoy an annual income premium if they wait until age 30 or later to marry. For college-educated women in their mid-thirties, this premium amounts to $18,152 (Hymowitz et al., 2013).

Just because people are waiting to marry does not mean that they are not interested in committed relationships. The decline in marriage rates has been accompanied by a rise in unmarried couples living together (Manning, Brown, and Payne, 2014).

Fifty years ago, cohabitation was considered by most people to be either immoral or deviant. Today, it is commonplace. Most people have cohabited before marriage, as is the case with this couple as they move into their new home.

cohabitation

Living with a romantic and sexual partner without being married.

The Rise in Cohabitation

It is tempting to think that the younger generation invented **cohabitation** (living with a romantic and sexual partner without being married), but it has been practiced long before modern times. In the mid-1800s, people may have spoken little of cohabitation, but it was a fact of life for many, especially in rural areas. A couple may have wanted to marry, but perhaps a minister was unavailable, or the couple was waiting until family could arrive for the wedding. Cohabitation was usually considered a temporary state until the couple could marry, and therefore others in the community generally treated them as a married couple (Cott, 2002).

However, as the United States began to develop and urbanize, these reasons for cohabitation became much less relevant. Consequently, cohabitation became less common in the early part of the twentieth century. People who lived together without being married were considered sinful or deviant.

The attitude toward cohabitation changed again in the late 1960s and 1970s, when young people rebelled against established norms and institutions (Popenoe, 2008). This period was one of new freedoms for a large baby-boom youth cohort. It was the era of "sexual revolution," new reliable birth control, and expanded access to education and the workplace for women. People no longer felt the need to marry young. These societal changes may have led people to ask, why not just live together?

Today, the Census Bureau estimates that 8 million U.S. households are maintained by heterosexual cohabiting couples (U.S. Census Bureau, October 30, 2014a), more than twice the number in 2000. People who cohabit span all ages, races, and ethnic groups and are found within all social classes.

Along with changing behavior around cohabitation, there is now a greater acceptance of cohabitation. In a national survey, high school seniors were asked whether they agreed with the statement, "It is usually a good idea for a couple to live together before getting married to find out whether they really get along." Attitudes are considerably more favorable than those of a generation ago, with 69 percent of young men and 63 percent of young women agreeing that cohabitation is a good idea, compared with only 45 and 33 percent, respectively, in the late 1970s (National Marriage Project, 2012). Likewise, the General Social Survey, a large survey based on a nationally representative sample of adults, reports that 44 percent of adults agree or agree strongly with the statement, "Living together is an acceptable option." But "acceptable" doesn't necessarily mean that cohabitation is seen as a "good" thing (Pew Research Center, 2010). Figure 10–4 shows that only 9 percent of adults see cohabitation as a good thing for society, 46 percent believe that it makes no difference, and 43 percent feel it is bad for society. Men, Hispanics, young adults, and those who live in the West are most likely to consider cohabitation as good for society.

COHABITATION AND MARRIAGE More than two-thirds of marriages begin with cohabitation (Copen et al., 2012), but that fact does not necessarily mean that cohabitation leads to marriage. Those are two different issues. In fact, only about half of cohabiting relationships end up in marriage within three years (Goodwin, Mosher, and Chandra, 2010). The others either break up or continue cohabiting.

The belief that living together before marriage is a useful way "to find out whether you really get along" is widespread but not completely accurate. Cohabitation may

Figure 10–4 Percentage Saying Unmarried Couples Living Together Is a Bad Thing for Society, a Good Thing, or Makes No Difference, 2010

SOURCE: Pew Research Center, 2010.

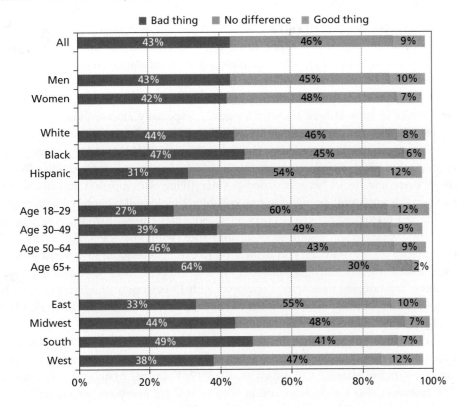

ease roommate problems, and it may make good financial sense, but is cohabitation a good test for marriage? Interestingly, people who cohabit are actually *more* likely to have unhappy marriages and to divorce (Copen et al., 2012; Tach and Halpern-Meekin, 2009).

There are two possible reasons for the positive relationship between cohabitation and divorce. First, a **selection effect** may be operating, meaning that the cohabitors do not represent a random sample and that the type of person who cohabits may be the same type of person who would be more likely to end an unhappy marriage (Copen et al., 2012; Kuperberg, 2014; Lichter and Qian, 2008). For example, someone who values personal freedom may be both more likely to cohabit and more likely to divorce. Or, a less religious person may be more likely to cohabit and more likely to end an unhappy marriage. In other words, it is not the case that cohabitation *causes* the divorce per se; rather, the relationship between cohabitation and divorce is **spurious**, meaning that both cohabitation and divorce are really caused by a third factor—in this case, the high value placed on personal freedom or looser religious values.

The second reason for the relationship of divorce and cohabitation may be cause and effect. Perhaps something about the cohabitation experience weakens a relationship and makes it more prone to divorce. Attitudes and behaviors developed through cohabitation may be at odds with long-term marriage. For example, couples who cohabit are more likely to maintain financial independence and keep their own separate checking accounts (Hamplová, Le Bourdais, and Lapierre-Adamcyk, 2014), possibly emphasizing the couple's degree of separateness and undermining a feeling of unity. It is possible that cohabiting couples are living more like singles, with less of an emphasis on permanence and, therefore, are not really "testing" the relationship as if it were marriage. Consequently, when they do marry, the social expectations that come along with being a husband, wife, son-in-law, and daughter-in-law remain new and uncharted territory.

selection effect

An effect that occurs when the sample is not random and leads to biased inferences about social processes, such as the relationship about cohabitation and divorce.

spurious

A type of apparent relationship between two variables that is really caused by a third factor.

So, which is it: Is the relationship between cohabitation and divorce a spurious relationship, or does cohabitation really cause divorce? It is likely that both operate to some degree, but the most research supports the notion of the relationship between cohabitation and divorce as spurious.

COHABITATION AND CHILDREN About 40 percent of cohabiting couples have children under the age of 18 residing in the home, born to one or both partners. This percentage is about the same as the percentage of married couples who have children in the home (U.S. Census Bureau, October 30, 2014a). Most often, the children are from one partner's previous union. However, there is a growing trend among many cohabiting couples to have at least one child together, especially among those cohabiting couples with less education (Gibson-Davis and Rackin, 2014).

Whether cohabitation is good or bad for children largely depends on what alternatives exist. Possible living arrangements include living with a single mother, living with a parent and his or her unmarried partner, living with a parent and his or her new spouse (stepparent), living with two cohabiting biological parents, or living with two married biological parents. Children can potentially benefit from living with a cohabiting partner when resources are shared with family members. For example, a study by sociologists Manning and Brown found that between 7 and 9 percent of children of cohabiting relationships faced high risk (defined as experiencing poverty, food insecurity, and housing insecurity) compared with 13 percent of children living with a single mother. Further, only 2 percent of children in married biological or married stepparent families faced this risk (Manning and Brown, 2006).

The research suggests that, in general, children receive the most support and do the best academically and socially when they are reared in households with two married biological parents (Crawford et al., 2012; Osborne, Manning, and Smock, 2007). However, this family structure is not possible for everyone. Moreover, some married-couple households are fraught with conflict. Therefore, embracing only one type of family structure as "best" and others as "less than" is not helpful because all families have their strengths and challenges.

Public opinion toward same-sex marriage has changed significantly in recent years. In June 2015, the U.S. Supreme Court ruled 5-4 that it is legal for all Americans, no matter their sex or sexual orientation, to marry the people they love.

equal marriage

Same-Sex Marriage

Many people see same-sex marriage as one of the most important civil rights issue of our times. The Supreme Court ruled in June 2015 that the right for same-sex couples to marry is protected under the 14th Amendment, citing the clauses that guarantee equal protection and due process. In a close 5-4 decision, the justices outlined several reasons same-sex marriage should be allowed. They wrote that the right to marriage is an inherent aspect of individual autonomy and that gay Americans have a right to intimate association beyond merely freedom from laws that ban homosexuality. Extending the right to marry protects families and the children within them.

The battle to give gays and lesbians the right to marry has been long and steeped in controversy. In 1996, the federal Defense of Marriage Act (DOMA) was passed with bipartisan support and defined marriage as a legal union between one man and one woman. It allowed states to refuse to recognize same-sex

Table 10–1 Percentage of U.S. Adults Who Support Same-Sex Marriage, May 2015

Total	57%
Political Affiliation	
Democrat	65%
Independent	65%
Republican	34%
Age	
Millennials born 1981 or later	73%
Generation X born 1965–1980	59%
Baby Boomers born 1946–1964	45%
Silent Generation born 1928–1945	39%
Sex	
Female	60%
Male	53%
Race	
White	59%
Black	41%

SOURCE: Pew Research Center, 2015.

marriages performed under the laws of other states. In June 2013, the Supreme Court struck down DOMA, saying in a 5 to 4 ruling that the federal government cannot disparage marriages recognized by the states (DeSilver, 2013).

Public opinion has continued to move toward supporting same-sex unions. Today, overall, more than half of Americans now support same-sex marriage. As you can see in Table 10–1, younger adults, Democrats, women, and whites are most likely to express support for marriage equality (Pew Research Center, 2015).

Advocates see same-sex marriage as a civil rights issue: Gays and lesbians should not be discriminated against, and forbidding them to legally wed is an overt form of discrimination. Because they generally do not see homosexuality as a choice, they equate restrictions on same-sex marriage with the restrictions on interracial marriage that were strictly enforced in some states and repealed only a generation ago. Advocates believe that allowing same-sex couples to marry does not harm or diminish heterosexual marriage or hurt society in any way. Pointing to the few countries that do allow gays and lesbians to wed, they note no ill effects. Love and public commitment should be encouraged rather than suppressed.

Opponents' views vary, but some suggest that same-sex marriage is immoral and is in violation of God's teaching. For example, the Catholic Church decries homosexual acts because they do not lead to procreation. Early American antisodomy laws discouraged all forms of nonprocreative sex (including heterosexual oral and anal sex). Islam has a similar view. Other opponents simply suggest that marriage has *always* been defined as between a man and a woman and see no need to change it. In particular, there is some concern that allowing gays and lesbians to wed elevates the status of their relationship to that of a heterosexual couple and legitimizes their right to have and raise children. Many of these opponents support civil unions or domestic partnerships for gays and lesbians, but draw the line at legal marriage.

There are many opinions on the subject, steeped in deeply held values. An often raised question is: How will allowing same-sex couples who are in loving and devoted relationships to marry weaken the social institutions of marriage and family? The research shows that same-sex relationships are as fulfilling as heterosexual ones and that children raised in same-sex families grow up happy and well adjusted (American Psychological Association, 2012; Biblarz and Stacey, 2010; Crouch et al., 2014).

The Division of Household Labor

The work at home that feeds, clothes, shelters, and cares for family members is just as important as the work that occurs in the labor market. Yet, household labor has been considered "women's work," and not deemed worthy of scientific study until roughly 30 years ago. Since then, a tremendous amount of research has been done to examine who does what in the home, under what circumstances, and why and how housework is embedded in complex family processes.

How is household labor defined? Generally, it refers to unpaid work that is done to maintain family members and/or a home. It usually excludes childcare and other types of emotional labor and caregiving. According to national surveys, the five most time-consuming major household tasks are (1) meal preparation or cooking; (2) house-cleaning; (3) shopping for groceries and household goods; (4) washing dishes and cleaning up after meals; and (5) laundry, including washing, ironing, and mending clothes. Coltrane (2000) refers to these tasks as **routine household labor** because they are repetitive and less able to be postponed than are other tasks. Although some people enjoy some or all of these activities (Poortman and van der Lippe, 2009), most people say that they do not enjoy routine household work, calling it boring, onerous, and mundane. Other tasks such as gardening, paying bills, household repairs, or servicing the car, called occasional labor, occur less frequently and have more flexibility in timing.

Women do significantly more housework than men. The size of men's and women's contributions vary across studies, but most find that women spend 50–100 percent more time on various household tasks than men do (Bureau of Labor Statistics, 2014; Parker and Wang, 2013). A large survey of how Americans use their time shows this sex difference in the amount of time devoted to housework, as illustrated in Figure 10–5 (Parker and Wang, 2013).

Many women believe this difference is unfair, and one of the most common areas of conflict is household labor. Consequently, many families are now renegotiating how family labor is performed. Childcare is also a large focus of renegotiation. The amount of time both fathers and mothers spend with their children has grown considerably since 1965, but fathers' time has increased threefold from 2.5 hours per week to 7.3 hours per week (Parker and Wang, 2013). Nevertheless, this increase is still much less than the amount of time mothers spend with their children at 13.5 hours per week, as shown in Figure 10–6.

routine household labor

Household work that is repetitive and less able to be postponed than are other tasks.

What Do You Think?

Compare your attitudes toward the division of household labor with those of your parents or grandparents. Are your attitudes and expectations different? If so, what accounts for this change?

Figure 10–5 The Amount of Weekly Hours That Men and Women, Mothers and Fathers Spend on Housework

SOURCE: Parker and Wang, 2013.

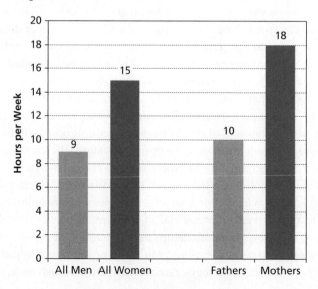

Figure 10–6 Parents' Childcare Time (in hours), 1965–2011

SOURCE: Parker and Wang, 2013.

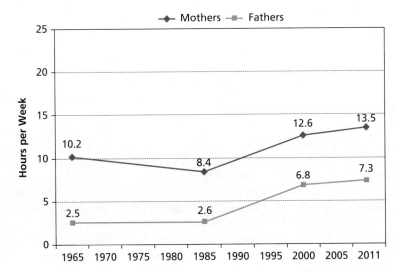

Researchers have been studying the ways that work and family influence each other (Nomaguchi, 2012; Voydanoff, 2008). Out of this research have come several important concepts that help us begin to understand the reciprocal relationship between work and family life.

One such concept is **work–family conflict**, which is the tension people feel when the pressures from paid work and family roles are incompatible. The conflict can go both ways: Work is made more difficult by virtue of participation in family activities (e.g., it is difficult to work the expected overtime at one's job because of needing to pick up one's children from day care), and participation in family activities is made more difficult by work (e.g., it is difficult to get to one's son's baseball practice every Wednesday afternoon because of a 4:00 department meeting). Work–family conflict has increased for both men and women in recent decades.

Another concept, **role overload**, is the feeling of being overwhelmed by many different commitments and not having enough time to meet each commitment effectively. *Perception* of overload is key. What appears to make the difference in role overload is not how many hours a person has worked, but how much support a person has. Role overload can lead to stress and depression. Mothers with higher incomes (who can, presumably, hire more help), people with happier marriages, and those with higher-quality jobs were least likely to feel role overload.

Another related concept, **spillover**, refers to the negative (or sometimes positive) moods, experiences, and demands involved in one sphere that carry over or "spill over" into the other sphere. How does someone purge the rushed and hectic mood at work when he or she now has to grocery shop with a toddler? How does a parent play with his or her children after work, when a boss is still sending him or her e-mails in the evening? With the creation of computers, cell phones, and other important technology, work increasingly encroaches on family time.

work–family conflict

The tension people feel when the pressures from paid work and family roles are somehow incompatible.

role overload

The feeling of being overwhelmed by many different commitments and not having enough time to meet each commitment effectively.

spillover

The negative (or sometimes positive) moods, experiences, and demands involved in one sphere that carry over or "spill over" into the other sphere.

Parenting Contexts

10.5 **Review different types of parenting contexts.**

Most adults become parents one day, although not all adults do, as you can see in the feature, A Personal View: "Children? No Thanks." It is estimated that one in five young adults today will not have children, sometimes because of infertility, but also

A Personal View

"Children? No Thanks."

My husband Michael and I just returned last week from Christmas with the family—mom, dad, grandma, my Aunt Sandra and Uncle Bob, and my older brother and his family. What a depressing experience! Don't get me wrong; I love each and every one of them, but I cannot stand the constant snide comments about the fact that Michael and I don't have children. We've been married for nine years, and the first years were okay because we were in graduate school. No one really expected us to have kids while in school. But after we graduated, the comments started coming in, like "So, when are you going to have a family?" or "Any buns in the oven yet?" I really hate that expression. We just smiled and politely said no, even though I was tempted to say "None of your business, if you don't mind!" They probably thought infertility was the issue. But, last week we did it. Michael and I told them straight out that we were not going to have children because we really did not want them. Aunt Sandra shrieked! My mom started to cry. My brother told me that we were going to miss the best part of life. He and his wife have two preschool-age kids, and, personally, I don't think their life

looks so great. Let me be clear. I honestly do enjoy my nieces in short doses. I can play horsey, use crayons, and push them on the swings as well as anyone can. I'm looking forward to having them spend the weekend when they are a bit older. It's just that I don't want to do those things on a full-time basis. Please don't think I'm heartless! I volunteer for Meals on Wheels and help deliver food to seniors twice a month. Last month Michael and I volunteered for the annual cleanup of the wonderful large park in our city. I donate money for a lot of local causes, and I voted yes on the last school levy. However, I also value my privacy, my work, and my relationship with Michael. I am afraid that I would have to compromise on these values if I had children. I just wish people would support my right to choose whether or not to be a mother.

Critical Thinking

An increasing number of women and men are opting to be childfree. Why do you think they are choosing this path? What social changes have taken place in American culture that might explain this new phenomenon?

because of personal choice. However, for the other four in five adults, children loom on the horizon, and there are different types of parenting contexts.

Teen Parents

Fewer than 250,000 teenagers ages 15–19 had babies in 2014, representing 24 births for every 1,000 adolescent girls. The good news is that the teen pregnancy rate has declined substantially over the past two decades, after reaching its all-time high in 1991 of nearly 62 births per 1,000 girls (Martin et al., 2015). The decline has been large among all racial and ethnic groups, but it has been most steepest among blacks, as shown in Figure 10–7.

The negative biological, social, and economic consequences of early parenting in the United States have been well documented (National Campaign to Prevent Teen and Unplanned Pregnancy, 2013; Office of Adolescent Health, 2015). Teen mothers are 2.5 times as likely to die in childbirth as are older mothers, their infants are twice as likely to be of low birth weight, and the babies are nearly 3 times more likely to die within the first month of life. Many of these biological problems have social roots; teen mothers are more likely to be poor and lack proper nutrition and prenatal care.

Other repercussions are more social and economic in nature. Teen mothers are more likely to drop out of school than are other teens, are considerably poorer, and more likely to receive welfare. Adolescent mothers are also less knowledgeable about child development, are less prepared for childrearing, and are more likely to be depressed than are other mothers. Children born to teen mothers have lower math and reading skills and increased behavioral problems, although many of these differences may be related to the mother's background rather than to her teen pregnancy *per se*. It is therefore not surprising that social workers, health professionals, educators, researchers, and parents remain alarmed at the number of teens—both young women and men—involved in adolescent pregnancies. It has been estimated that teen childbearing costs taxpayers at least $11 billion each year for health care and child welfare, plus lost revenues (National Campaign to Prevent Teen and Unplanned Pregnancy, 2013).

What Do You Think?

If you were given the task of developing a program to prevent teen pregnancy, what would that program look like? Who would you target it to? How would you structure it? What kind of opposition might it face and how would you deal with that?

Figure 10–7 Teenage Fertility Rates per 1,000 Women Aged 15–19 by Race and/or Ethnicity for 1991 and 2013

SOURCE: Martin, Hamilton, Osterman, Curten, and Matthews, 2015.

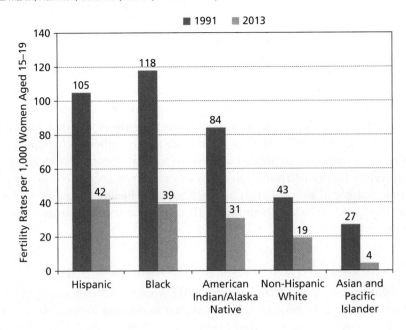

Single Parents

Single-parent families used to be referred to as *broken homes*. Today, many people take exception to that term. The vast majority of single-parent families are single-mother families, and the terms are often used interchangeably; if you say "single parent," people typically think of a single mother. These families have been maligned for causing a wide range of social ills, including poverty. The concern with such a sweeping generalization is that (1) there are different kinds of single-parent families with different kinds of circumstances (a teenager vs. a 40-year-old executive); (2) there are different paths to becoming a single parent (never marrying, divorce, or widowhood); (3) the cause-and-effect relationship is unclear (e.g., does poverty cause single parenthood or does single parenthood cause poverty?); and (4) single parenthood is less problematic in other developed nations because of a wide number of social supports provided to all families, which are largely unavailable in the United States.

The number of single parents has risen in recent generations. In 1950, only 6 percent of households with children were maintained by a mother; by 2014, it was 24 percent. Only 1 percent of households in 1950 were maintained by single fathers, but that number has increased to 4 percent (U.S. Census Bureau, November 6, 2014b). Black children are far more likely to live with a single parent than are children in other racial or ethnic groups. For example, more than half of black children live with a single parent, as compared with just 13 percent of Asian/Pacific Islander children.

There are many different paths to single parenthood. Some women have babies outside of marriage. Some are teenagers and others are older adults. Others become single parents because of divorce or widowhood. Data allow for some generalizations about single parents. They are more likely to be poor or nearly so, and on food stamps (DeNavas-Walt and Proctor, 2014; Hokayem and Heggeness, 2014). They are less likely to own a home and they have lower levels of education (Vespa, Lewis, and Kreider, 2013). Yet, you should guard against sweeping generalizations because the different routes to single parenthood do produce different results.

Much of the concern surrounding single parents is targeted toward young women who forgo education when they have babies outside of marriage. However,

15 percent of single mothers have a bachelor's degree or higher, and one in five is at least 30 years old. If you think about it, unmarried women in their thirties and forties offer a substantially different portrait of single parenthood: They are likely to have completed their education and have jobs, perhaps even well-paying careers.

Single parenthood does not have to be synonymous with poverty. Research from other countries makes this point clear. For example, using data from government agencies, social scientists, and researchers worldwide, a recent study of 16 high-income countries shows that single mothers in the United States—most of whom either are separated or were previously married—work more hours, but also have much higher poverty rates than their peers in other high-income countries (Kaufmann, 2012). Why is poverty so much higher in the United States among single mothers than in peer nations? Most high-income developed nations offer universal family or child cash allowances and an assortment of other cash programs and social policies such as childcare and health insurance specifically designed to help families with children. These programs and policies lift families out of poverty.

Lesbian, Gay, Bisexual, and Transgender Families

Lesbian, gay, bisexual, and transgender (LGBT) women and men are fighting for a basic human right: to be recognized and accepted as families. Because same-sex couples have only recently been allowed to marry in all states, their family relationships have historically been ignored or trivialized, and even less is known about transgender families. The small amount of research on same-sex families tends to focus on lesbians, furthering the stereotype that gay men are not interested in committed relationships or nurturing relationships with children (Biblarz and Stacey, 2010). However, these stereotypes are untrue. Many gays and lesbians are partnered and now married, and almost one-half of lesbian couples and one in five gay male couples are raising children (Gates, 2013; Pawelski et al., 2006). Overall, at least 6 million children (and adults) have an LGBT parent.

For the most part, same-sex parents have a great deal in common with heterosexual parents: They struggle to get their children to school on time, they take their children to soccer practice after school, and they get involved in the local PTA. Their children grow up as well adjusted and happy as do those in heterosexual families (Biblarz and Stacey, 2010; Manning, Fettro, and Lamidi, 2014; Potter, 2012). Yet, although most aspects of raising children are similar, a few differences do arise:

- The decision to parent among gay and lesbian couples is generally a deliberate choice that reflects a strong commitment to raising children. Studies tend to show either no difference among homosexuals and heterosexuals in their fitness to parent or give a slight advantage for same-sex couples. For example, lesbian mothers exhibit more parenting skills and awareness of child development than heterosexual couples, and there is greater similarity between partners' parenting skills. Likewise, compared with heterosexual fathers, gay fathers go to greater lengths to promote their children's cognitive skills, are more responsive to their children's needs, and are more involved in activities with children.
- LGBT families are more likely to be affected by loss. Lacking institutional constraints and support such as legalized marriage in all states, their relationships are somewhat more likely to dissolve than are heterosexual ones. However, because same-sex couples have only recently been allowed to marry anywhere in the United States, their trauma may not be publicly recognized or as easily supported. U.S. society acknowledges the tremendous disruption caused by a divorce; however, a "breakup" may be trivialized.

- Lesbian and gay families must cope with homophobia and discrimination. Although attitudes are shifting, same-sex relationships are stigmatized in some circles, and living openly as a family leaves them vulnerable to ridicule or discrimination. Violence against gays and lesbians is a possibility: One large-scale national survey found that 30 percent of LGBT respondents said that they had been threatened or physically attacked (Pew Research Center, 2013). Just as racial and ethnic minorities must teach their children about racism, gay and lesbian parents, too, must teach their children about prejudice and discrimination.

Lesbians and gay men often have a close network of friends whom they regard as **fictive kin** who provide emotional and social support. Social support is crucial from family and friends as a way to ward off oppression and to create a safe and supportive environment for lesbians, gay men, and their children. They often have developed a close network of friends whom they regard as a sort of extended family. These friends are there to celebrate birthdays; participate in commitment ceremonies; babysit when needed; and in countless ways, offer the love and support that are needed to keep a household and a family running smoothly.

fictive kin

Friends in a close network who provide support.

Grandparents Raising Grandchildren

My grandchildren, Caleb and Helen, came to live with my wife and I when they were 11 and 8 years old. We really didn't know what to do, but there was no other choice. Their mother was just up to no good. She'd leave them home alone when she went out partying. I'm not even sure that she came home at night. I think she's using drugs. And their dad, our son, he's so messed up. He ain't around much. So, I just told their mother, the kids gotta live with us. And she dropped them off one day and didn't even put up a fuss. (William, age 61)

Some children live with and are under the custodial care of their grandparents (Hayslip and Smith, 2013). Eight million children—roughly one in ten—live with their grandparents (Ellis and Simmons, 2014). Sometimes the child's parent(s) also live with the grandparent. The recession has been hard on young families, and multigenerational households are on the rise, especially among single parents, those with little education, and those with low or no earnings. But the greatest growth has occurred among grandchildren living with grandparents on their own, without a parent present. Approximately 5 million children, like Caleb and Helen, live only with their grandparents and are cared for by those grandparents.

Where are these children's parents? Mothers and fathers may be absent for many reasons, including incarceration, drug or alcohol problems, physical or mental illnesses, employment difficulties, child abuse or neglect, desertion, or even death. There are often multiple problems in the homes of the grandchildren's parents that led the grandparents to take over their grandchildren's care. When parents are unable or unwilling to care for their children, grandparents often step in. Most arrangements are done privately, but in about one in six cases, child welfare agencies have intervened on behalf of the child.

Many of these grandparent-headed families experience considerable strain and challenges. First, grandparents face physical exhaustion trying to keep up with their grandchildren. Forty-three percent of grandparents who take care of their grandchildren are 55 years or older, and 15 percent are 65 or older. More than half are single grandparents, yet many are caring for young children who require considerable energy. Second, the grandparents often have physical or mental health problems, which could make caring for a child difficult. Third, many of these families are poor, have difficulty paying housing bills, or are on public assistance (Ellis and Simmons, 2014).

Most grandparents report having loving and fun relationships with their grandchildren. Some grandparents go one step further and are the primary caretakers of their grandchildren. When parents are unable to care for their own children, perhaps because of drugs, incarceration, or child neglect, it is grandparents who often step in to help.

Despite these challenges, a growing number of grandparents continue to assume the responsibilities of caring for their grandchildren (Hayslip and Smith, 2013). As William, the grandfather in the earlier account, said, "There was no other choice." Out of love and out of duty, grandparents step in when parents fall short of their own responsibilities.

Family Problems and Challenges

10.6 Explain two types of family problems or challenges: violence and divorce.

Families face many difficulties over their life course. This next section will discuss two difficulties that plague many families: The first is violence, and the second is divorce.

Violence

What do former talk show host Oprah Winfrey, singer Rihanna, and actress Pamela Anderson have in common? In addition to being celebrities, they all have had the frightening experience of being abused within their families or close relationships. Rihanna and Pamela Anderson were victims of violence by their intimate partners; Oprah Winfrey revealed that several members of her extended family sexually abused her as a child. People find violence in families to be particularly abhorrent because they like to idealize families as safe havens. Yet, for many people, especially women and girls, this safe haven is not the case.

violence among intimates

Violence among family members or intimate partners.

Violence has touched the lives of millions of families. **Violence among intimates**, defined as violence among family members or intimate partners, takes many forms, including intimate partner violence, child abuse, and elder abuse. As you will see, violence is more than simply a personal problem of "he just has a bad temper." Violence among intimates is a *social* problem. First, it affects large numbers of people. Second, violence is not completely random—it is possible to detect particular patterns and risk factors for both victims and perpetrators. Third, the causes, consequences, and solutions of violence must address social, cultural, and economic factors.

Human Rights Watch (2015) and the United Nations (UN Women, 2015), both international organizations dedicated to protecting the human rights of people around the world, report that many countries have horrendous records on addressing violence against women and girls, as you learned in Chapter 5, and much of this violence occurs within families and intimate relationships. The following sections will examine violence against partners and children and will consider what might explain it.

intimate partner violence (IPV)

Violence between those who are physically and sexually intimate, such as spouses or partners.

INTIMATE PARTNER VIOLENCE Intimate partner violence (IPV) refers to violence between those who are physically and sexually intimate, such as spouses or partners. The violence can encompass physical, economic, sexual, or psychological abuse, and many abusive situations include more than one type. But just as important as the type of violence is the underlying premise of that violence. Family violence researcher Michael Johnson distinguishes between four general premises:

- *Common couple violence (CCV)* arises out of a specific argument in which at least one partner lashes out physically. It is less likely to escalate or involve severe injury; yet, it is this type of violence that is usually captured in research studies.
- *Intimate terrorism (IT)* is motivated by a desire to control the other partner. It is more likely than CCV to escalate over time and to cause serious injury, although some cases of IT involve relatively little injury. The primary feature of this type of abuse is the general desire for control.

- *Violent resistance (VR)* is the nonlegal term associated with self-defense. Research on VR is scarce, and it is conducted almost entirely by women. Engaging in violent resistance may be an indicator that a person will soon leave the abusive partner.
- *Mutual violent control (MVC)* refers to a pattern of behavior in which both partners are controlling and violent; they are battling for control. Again, this pattern is an understudied phenomenon.

Until the 1970s, what people knew about spousal and partner abuse was based on small samples from the isolated case files of social workers, psychologists, and police. These data can be very biased because only certain types of abuse and abusers come to the attention of these professionals.

However, since that time, family and social scientists have been using large and representative samples to understand how often spousal and partner violence occurs, who is likely to be a victim, and what are its causes and consequences. Early surveys by Murray Straus and colleagues (Straus, Gelles, and Steinmetz, 1980) showed an alarming rate of IPV in the United States, and more recent studies confirm this trend, as you can see in Table 10–2. This national survey is based on nearly 13,000 interviews with both men and women and is designed to shed light on a wide variety of violent experiences. The table examines the percentage of women and men who have experienced different forms of IPV over the course of their lives (so far). Women are much more likely than men to say they have experienced rape, other sexual violence, and stalking. The difference between women and men with respect to physical violence is not large; however, when broken down by type of violence, it is easy to see that women are more likely to be victims of the most extreme types of violence, such as beating, choking, being slammed against something, or having a weapon used on them.

Intimate partner violence is a serious social problem causing injury and disability to thousands of people (mostly women) throughout the country each year. Issues of power and control are usually involved.

IPV can have tragic results, both emotionally and physically (Hegarty et al., 2013; Lacey et al., 2013). Minor forms of bruises, scratches, and welts are most common, but broken bones, severe bruising, or head trauma are other consequences of violence. In general, victims of repeated violence over time experience more serious consequences than victims of one-time incidents (Breiding et al., 2014).

Table 10–2 Lifetime Prevalence of Intimate Partner Violence (IPV) Victimization, by Sex of Victim, 2011

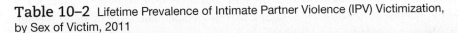

		Women	Men
Rape		8.8%	0.5%
Other Sexual Violence		15.8%	9.5%
Stalking		9.2%	2.5%
Physical Violence		31.5%	27.5%
	Slapped, pushed, shoved	29.7%	25.5%
	Hurt by pulling hair	9.4%	2.6%
	Hit with fist/something hard	13.2%	10.1%
	Slammed against something	15.4%	2.5%
	Choked or suffocated	9.2%	0.7%
	Beaten	10.5%	2.3%
	Threatened or attacked with knife or gun	4.2%	2.3%

SOURCE: Breiding et al., 2014.

Other consequences are not as visible, but just as real. The stress from IPV can wreak havoc on the immune and endocrine systems, causing conditions such as fibromyalgia, gynecological disorders, irritable bowel syndrome, or gastrointestinal problems (Black, 2011). Because physical violence is typically accompanied by emotional or psychological abuse, many victims are depressed and have anxiety, disturbed sleep, and low self-esteem. They often are socially isolated and have thoughts of suicide (Breiding et al., 2014). Victims of IPV are more likely to behave in unhealthy ways, such as engaging in high-risk sexual behavior (e.g., having unprotected sex, trading sex for food or money); using harmful substances (e.g., smoking cigarettes, abusing drugs); or having unhealthy diet-related behaviors (e.g., binging and purging food).

Despite the clear need for mental health care, many women, especially minority women, often experience barriers to getting this care. Barriers include cultural or language differences, or a lack of services and providers in poor or ethnic communities (Bryant-Davis, Chung, and Tillman, 2009; Rodriguez et al., 2009).

In addition to the consequences to the individual, there are also societal consequences. In other words, you are affected by intimate partner violence even if you do not know anyone who is a victim or perpetrator (which is highly unlikely). Victims lose nearly 8 million days of paid work a year, the equivalent of more than 32,000 full-time jobs. Costs exceed $8 billion, most of which goes to medical and mental health care.

CHILD ABUSE   Child abuse is an attack on a child that violates social norms and may result in an injury. Sometimes these social norms are ambiguous; for example, is hitting your child a form of child abuse? Does it sound less violent if it is called "spanking"? Does it matter what you hit your child with, for example, your hand versus a baseball bat? Most parents believe spanking children is appropriate, and surveys generally find that about half of parents report having slapped or spanked a child, a decline in recent years (Smith, 2012). Meanwhile, others suggest that spanking is child abuse because spanked children are more likely to be depressed, to abuse animals, and eventually to assault their own partners (Busby, Holman, and Walker, 2008).

But often, the abuse is so egregious that there is little doubt, and government agencies become involved to protect the child. According to the U.S. government, over 650,000 children are victims of abuse or neglect annually (U.S. Department of Health and Human Services, Administration for Children and Families, 2013). The good news, if there is any, is that the number of substantiated abuse cases has declined by about 25 percent since 2004.

There are several different types of child abuse:

- *Neglect* is the most common form of abuse and involves the failure to provide for the child's basic needs, such as failing to provide adequate food, clothing, shelter, a safe environment, supervision, or medical care to a dependent child.
- *Physical abuse* involves inflicting physical injury and harm on a child and may include hitting, shaking, burning, kicking, or in other ways physically harming a child. Among substantiated child abuse cases, nearly one in six involved physical abuse. The most extreme cases may result in the death of a child. The most common forms of death were skull fracture and internal bleeding.
- *Sexual abuse* involves inappropriate sexual behavior with a child for sexual gratification. It occurs in about 9 percent of substantiated child abuse cases. It could include fondling a child's genitals, making the child fondle the perpetrator's genitals, and progressing to more intrusive sexual acts such as oral sex and vaginal or anal penetration. Sexual abuse also includes acts such as exhibition or in other ways exploiting the child for sexual purposes.
- *Psychological maltreatment* involves about 9 percent of substantiated cases of child abuse and includes verbal, mental, or psychological maltreatment that destroys a child's self-esteem. Abuse of this nature often includes threatening, degrading, or humiliating the child and extreme or bizarre forms of punishment,

What Do You Think?

Most victims of intimate partner violence eventually leave the situation, but for many people, leaving is a long process. Why do you think leaving takes so long? Why would someone stay in an abusive situation? Be sure to identify both cultural and personal characteristics.

Figure 10–8 Who Are the Child Abuse Perpetrators?

NOTE: Analysis counts every relationship for each report; therefore, the percentages total more than 100 percent.
SOURCE: U.S. Department of Health and Human Services, Administration on Children, Youth, and Families, 2015.

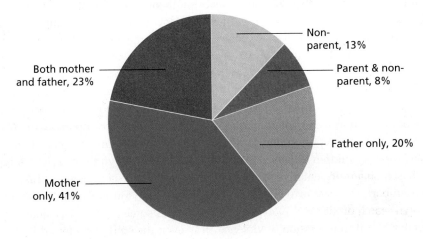

such as confinement to a dark room or being tied to a chair for long periods of time. It is likely that emotional abuse occurs far more frequently than what can be substantiated.

- *Medical neglect* represents a small but important type of abuse, and involves delaying or forgoing a child's needed medical, dental, or prescription care.

There are also other types of abuse, of course, such as congenital drug addiction or threats of harm. Abuse occurs in all income, racial, religious, and ethnic groups and in all types of communities. Female victims outnumber male victims, especially in cases of sexual abuse. Black children have the highest rates of victimization, and Asian Americans have the lowest. Most people who abuse children are not strangers, but are biological family members, as shown in Figure 10–8. Over 90 percent of child abusers are family members (most often the mother).

Child abuse can have serious consequences for the child. In its most extreme forms, it can result in death. Each year, more than 1,500 children die as a result of abuse and neglect; 60 percent were age 1 year or younger, and 80 percent were under age 4 (U.S. Department of Health and Human Services, Administration on Children and Families, 2015). Annually, more children under the age of 4 die from abuse and neglect than from falls, choking, drowning, fires, or motor vehicle accidents.

Perhaps even more insidious are the emotional scars left behind. Abuse is trauma. Physically abused children tend to be more aggressive and more likely to get involved in delinquent activities, have difficulty in school, and be involved in early sexual activity, which can result in teen pregnancy. However, not all physically abused children have these outcomes. One study reviewed the findings of 21 published reports on child abuse to note any trends in children's behavior. The researchers found that the number of abused children having difficulty in educational, behavioral, or emotional domains varied greatly and that a child may do poorly in one domain, but excel in another. About one in five abused children had difficulty and functioned poorly in all domains (Walsh, Dawson, and Mattingly, 2010). The emotional trauma can be long lasting. Even as adults, children who have been abused are more likely to suffer nightmares, depression, panic disorders, and have suicidal thoughts (Hyman, 2000). Former abuse can also affect their relationship with their own children, increasing the likelihood of poor attachment, neglect, and abuse (Briere and Jordan, 2009). The costs of child abuse are far too great to ignore (Fang et al., 2012).

WHAT EXPLAINS VIOLENCE?   A quick survey of your classmates would probably show that virtually everyone abhors violence in families and intimate relationships.

Why then is it so widespread? Three factors contribute to violence: (1) intergenerational transmission of violence; (2) stress; and (3) cultural factors, including patriarchy, cultural tolerance for violence, and norms of family privacy.

Drawing on Bandura's (1977) social learning theory, the idea of intergenerational transmission suggests that people learn norms and behaviors, including violence, by observing others. There is a tendency toward intergenerational transmission of violence: Children who witness or experience abuse are more likely to be in abusive relationships as an adult than are other children. For example, a study based on 45,000 responses to a Web-based survey, the "Relationship Evaluation Questionnaire" (RELATE), found that 10 percent of couples without any reported violence in their family of orientation were violent in their current relationship compared with 32 percent of couples who reported that they had either witnessed or experienced violence in their home as children (Busby et al., 2008). Granted, although the sample is large, it is not based on a representative sample because people who completed RELATE may have been part of a class or workshop, or they may have found the questionnaire on their own search of the Web. Nonetheless, it provides some degree of evidence of the intergenerational transmission of violence. However, the study also found that more than two-thirds of people who witnessed or experienced violence as children were *not* in an abusive relationship as an adult. Therefore, it is very important to note that the intergenerational transmission of violence refers to a greater likelihood of engaging in violence; it does not refer to determinism. Many people who witnessed or experienced abuse as children grow up to be caring and supportive partners and parents.

Inordinate amounts of stress such as chronic under- or unemployment, economic issues, health problems, or other job or family difficulties also may play a role in violent relationships (Straus, 1980). Many stressors are highly correlated with income. Moreover, lower-income families have fewer opportunities available to help them ward off the impact of the stressors, for example, fewer savings or assets. Lower-income families are also more likely to engage in coping mechanisms that jeopardize their health (e.g., drinking, smoking, or eating poorly nutritious foods), whereas wealthier people have other options. Not surprisingly then, violence is more likely to occur in lower-income households, although it does occur at all income levels.

Observations about intergenerational transmission of violence and stress help explain why some people are violent, but they do not place individual actions in their social context. Murray Straus, in the study of stress just described, argued that stress by itself does not necessarily lead to violence, but rather, researchers should look at social and cultural attitudes that perpetuate violence as a response to stressors (Straus, 1980). Three of these attitudes, patriarchy, cultural support for violence, and norms of family privacy help to further explain violence.

In many patriarchal cultures, violence against women is not only tolerated but also holds a wide degree of support (Crittenden and Wright, 2013). For example, 56 percent of men in Turkey stated on a survey that they accepted "wife beating" (Rani and Banu, 2009). Interestingly, because women are socialized in the same patriarchal culture as men, they often support the violence. One study interviewed 450 women living in three cities in the West Bank to assess their attitudes toward "wife beating." Overall, the women perceived violence against wives to be justified if a wife insults her husband (59 percent), if she disobeys her husband (49 percent), if she neglects her children (37 percent), if she goes out without telling her husband (25 percent), if she argues with her husband (11 percent), and if she burns the food (5 percent). Sixty-five percent of the women agreed with at least one reason for wife beating, and those who have less education, who have more than one child, who make few household decisions, and who have been married less than 10 years agreed most strongly (Dhaher et al., 2010).

A second cultural explanation focuses on the fact that some cultures are more tolerant of violence in general than are others. For example, in the United States, violence is very public, readily seen on television or in theaters. Football, hockey, rugby,

Figure 10–9 Power and Control Wheel

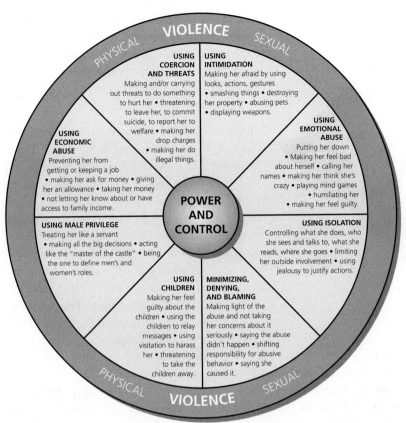

wrestling, and race car driving are notoriously violent sports, and the millions of fans who watch these events expect nothing less, all in the name of fun. Yet at other times, similar aggression is completely inappropriate: Your professor cannot slap you because you failed to read the assigned material; your mother might not be questioned if she were to slap you. The difficulty lies in the fact that sometimes these lines get blurred. When is it okay to hit, and when is it not okay? Or, when does hitting turn into abuse?

You have probably heard the saying, "a man's home is his castle." It refers to the idea that the man is dominant in his home, and what occurs there is no one else's business, a third cultural explanation (Berardo, 1998). The structure of modern society reinforces this sense of privacy. In urban areas, families know few, if any, of their neighbors well and, therefore, are increasingly isolated (Nock, 1998). Moreover, many people genuinely believe violence is a private matter between family members. Neighbors, coworkers, or even friends and other kin can be hesitant to get involved, perhaps saying, "I didn't want to say anything because it's really none of my business."

Although individual and cultural explanations focus on different factors that contribute to violence, both levels of analysis suggest that perpetrators are exerting their domination, power, and control over their victims (Anderson, 2010; Vives-Cases, Gil-González, and Carasco-Portiño, 2009). Likewise, those who feel powerless within their relationships experience higher rates of victimization (Filson et al., 2010). The Power and Control Wheel shown in Figure 10–9 depicts behaviors and privileges that batterers use to dominate and control their partners and/or children.

Divorce

A divorce decree may be granted in a matter of minutes by a judge. However, behind those few tense minutes usually lies a long period in which a couple has analyzed, redefined, and reorganized virtually all aspects of their relationship and their lives. Divorce is not simply the ending of a relationship between two people; it alters or

Married couples in the United States are more likely to divorce than are couples in any other country except for Russia. Why do you think that is the case?

even severs many personal and legal ties. A divorce can end relationships with family members; with friends who find themselves taking sides; with neighbors if one or both of the former couple have moved away; and with community groups of which an ex-spouse is no longer a member or can no longer afford to join. If you are like many college students, you have seen divorce up close.

FREQUENCY OF DIVORCE   We commonly hear that "half of all marriages end in divorce." This phrase, however, is somewhat misleading. Some people interpret it to mean that if 100,000 couples married last year, 50,000 divorces were also granted; on the surface, it looks as though 50 percent of marriages ended in divorce. But this comparison does not really make sense because the 100,000 marriages took place in only one year, whereas the divorces are from marriages that may have continued over many years. Therefore, this comparison is misleading and not very useful.

A better measure is called the crude divorce rate, which examines the frequency of divorce per 1,000 people. In the United States, this rate amounts to about 3.6 divorces per 1,000 people (Centers for Disease Control and Prevention, 2013).

However, the crude divorce rate is still problematic. Not all people have married; therefore, why should they be included in a divorce statistic? A more useful way to measure the frequency of divorce is to talk about the number of divorces that occur out of every 1,000 married women, which is called the refined divorce rate. Using the refined divorce rate, there are 20.9 divorces per 1,000 married women in the United States each year (National Marriage Project, 2012). Thus, within a year, less than 21 out of 1,000 married women, or about 2 percent, received a divorce.

These divorce rates are cross-sectional, meaning that they reflect rates at only one point in time. So, even though a married woman had a 2 percent chance of divorcing last year, she has a far higher chance of divorcing over the course of her married life. If only 21 out of 1,000 married women get divorced this year and the remaining 979 do not, those women could get divorced the following year, or the year after that, or 15 years later. However you measure it, the United States has one of the highest rates of divorce in the world, exceeded only by Russia.

THE IMPACT OF DIVORCE ON ADULTS   Divorce, even when desired by both partners, is almost always accompanied by considerable emotional and financial strain. One or both partners may feel angry, resentful, sad, depressed, or rejected, and divorced people tend to have more health problems than those who are married (Symoens et al., 2013). Generally, one spouse initiates the breakup of the marriage (Hewitt, Western, and Baxter, 2006). A common pattern is that an initiator expresses general discontent at first, but without attributing it to the marriage *per se*. He or she may try to alter the relationship or the other spouse's behavior by suggesting such remedies as a new job, having a baby, or some other substantial change to the nature of the relationship. He or she may even use the threat of leaving as a way to demand change. The other spouse's reaction—anger, resentment, sadness, resolve, or rejection—shapes his or her emotional response.

Men and women often have distinctive challenges after divorce. According to feminist theory, society offers men and women different opportunities and constraints that help explain their gendered experiences. For example, women are more likely than men to have financial problems after a divorce. In contrast, men often have a more difficult time emotionally after a divorce, and in some cases, this stress is so extreme that it can lead to increased illness or an early death. One reason for this emotional difficulty is that men tend to have a weaker network of supportive relationships (Chu, 2005). Additionally, most men lose custody of their children; more than 80 percent of children live with their mother following a divorce (Grall, 2013). For many fathers, moving away from their children is devastating (Kamp Dush, 2013).

With respect to finances, those couples who divorce when young, who are without children, and who have high levels of education and job prospects may fare just fine. However, female-headed families with children are nearly twice as likely as male-headed families, and five times as likely as married-couple families, to live in poverty (DeNavas-Walt and Proctor, 2014). Most mothers do not have the skill set or the work experience to support themselves to the level they had while married. Also, because they usually have children living with them, they may have to restrict the type of job they can take (e.g., one that requires no overtime or travel). Moreover, most husbands do not continue to support their children after divorce at the level decreed by the courts. According to data from the U.S. Census Bureau, in a recent year, only 43 percent of custodial parents (usually mothers) received the full child support payment that is due to them, 31 percent received a partial payment, and 26 percent received no payment at all (Grall, 2013).

Because of all the decisions a divorcing couple faces—for example, who gets the house, should alimony be paid, how the assets should be divided, where will the children live—a couple may hire a mediator to help them. The goal of a mediator is to be a neutral force (unlike an attorney) who helps couples negotiate before having to go to court.

THE IMPACT OF DIVORCE ON CHILDREN   Some people try to brush off the effects of their parents' divorce saying, "Hey, I turned out just fine …," but the truth is that many children are deeply affected by their parents' divorce and remain so for many years (Amato, 2007; Baker and Brassard, 2013). The first year or two after a divorce can be particularly tough for children. During this time, children grieve the loss of their intact family and are dealing with new feelings and fears. They may feel guilty or depressed, suffer from sleep difficulties, and act out aggressively (Guinart and Grau, 2014). In particular, young children are egocentric and often feel that they are responsible for their parents' conflict and divorce—that if they had just behaved better, their parents would not have divorced. During this crisis period, children face many situations with which they must learn to cope, including (1) handling parental conflict; (2) weakened parental bonds, especially to their fathers; (3) coping with a reduced standard of living; and (4) adjusting to many transitions such as a new neighborhood and school.

Although most children adjust adequately over time to the transitions in their lives, some children continue to be plagued by problems (Lindsey et al., 2009). Children whose parents divorce are more likely to become pregnant before marriage or impregnate someone, drop out of school and have lower academic achievement, experience more behavioral problems and aggression toward peers, use alcohol or drugs, have poor health, be more likely to suffer from depression, and tend toward being idle or unemployed. One recent study looked at whether there were any differences in college students' achievement or their persistence at staying in college in terms of whether or not their parents had divorced. Collecting data from a large public university, the research team found that students whose parents were divorced were significantly less likely to continue into their second year of college than their peers. They also had lower cumulative grade point averages. These differences remained after controlling for demographic characteristics or academic indicators before coming to college (Soria and Linder, 2014).

These findings certainly do not mean that all children from divorced households experience these negative outcomes. Many children whose parents have divorced lead happy, well-adjusted, and successful lives; these studies simply show that children of divorced parents are more likely to have these problems than are children from families in which parents have not divorced.

Matt's parents have been arguing for years. Their arguments are not violent physically, but they occur frequently, and his parents call each other terrible names. Matt tries to tune them out, but it is difficult to do so, and his own schoolwork is starting to suffer as a result. Do you think Matt would be better off if his parents divorced?

stepfamilies

Families in which one or both of the adult partners have at least one child, either residing with them or living elsewhere.

The question that people usually want answered is: Are children better off when their unhappily married parents remain married or are children better off when their parents divorce? The answer depends on many things, particularly the severity of the conflict in the marriage.

Children do not fare well when there is tremendous conflict and when they are put in the middle of their parents' struggles (Cummings et al., 2006; Michael, Torres, and Seemann, 2007)—regardless of whether the parents divorce or remain married. In fact, many researchers suggest that it is the amount of conflict rather than a divorce per se that causes the most harm to children. For example, Jekielek (1998) examined data on 1,640 children between the ages of 6 and 14 and found that children in high-conflict but intact families had lower levels of well-being than did children whose highly conflicting parents divorced.

A pioneering study by Amato and Booth (1997), which was based on telephone and in-person interviews conducted in 1980 and 1992 with a nationally representative sample, found that of the children who were in families with high marital conflict in 1980, they were actually doing better in 1992 if their parents had divorced than if they had stayed together. However, Amato and Booth also found that children from relatively low-conflict families were worse off if their parents divorced than if their parents had remained together. Altogether, these findings suggest that the worst situations for children are to be in either (1) a high-conflict marriage that does not end in divorce or (2) a low-conflict marriage that does end in divorce.

STEPFAMILIES   Most people remarry or cohabit after a divorce. Sometimes one or both of these people have children from a previous relationship. Sometimes they have children together. **Stepfamilies** are families in which one or both of the adult partners have at least one child, either residing with them or living elsewhere. Stepfamilies can create an intricate weave of complex relationships. For example, children in stepfamilies can be referred to as (1) siblings (biologically related to same parents); (2) stepsiblings (not biologically related, but parents are married to each other); (3) half-siblings (share one parent biologically); (4) mutual child (a child born to the remarried couple); (5) residential stepchildren (live in the household with the remarried couple more than half of the time); and (6) nonresidential stepchildren (live in the household less than half of the time). There are also multiple part-time and full-time living arrangements.

Despite the prevalence of stepfamilies, the expectations, obligations, and rules within them are ambiguous (Martin-Uzzi and Duval-Tsioles, 2013; Papernow, 2013). No socially prescribed script explains how family members are expected to relate to one another. Should a stepparent behave like a biological parent, like a friend, like an aunt or uncle, or like someone else entirely? To what extent can stepparents discipline their stepchildren? How are stepparents and stepchildren supposed to feel about one another? What names do children call their stepparent? Indeed, do stepparents and their stepchildren even include one another as part of their "family"? For example, if your father remarries when you are an adult and living away from home, and you see his wife once a year or so, would you consider her as "your stepmom" or simply "my dad's wife"? Would you think of her grown children, whom you may have never met, as your "stepsiblings" or are they "her children"?

Nonetheless, stepfamilies can be an enriching experience. Roughly 70 percent of adults who have at least one step relative say they are very satisfied with their family life, and this rating is only slightly less than those who have no step relatives (78 percent very satisfied) (Pew Research Center, 2011). Children living in stepfamilies gain exposure to new behavior patterns and lifestyles. Children may also benefit from an increased standard of living made possible by two incomes and their parents' greater happiness at being involved in another relationship. Stepfamily adoptions are the most common type of adoption in the United States, a testament to the love and commitment that many stepparents and children feel toward one another (Lamb, 2007).

Social Policy

10.7 Discuss family policy, using the example of maternity leave.

The government regulates many aspects of families. For example, the government prohibits certain people from marrying each other, requires people who intend to marry to have a blood test, and requires two witnesses for a legal wedding ceremony. The government also touches the lives of families by an absence of certain policies. For example, U.S. adults have no guaranteed maternity leave, national health insurance, or subsidized childcare. These family policies reflect historical, cultural, political, and social factors in the United States, including norms that favor personal over collective responsibility. The United States has little in the way of a comprehensive and collective vision for families, unlike other developed nations (Dey and Wasoff, 2013).

There are many family policy issues worthy of discussion, but due to space limitations we will focus on just one here: maternity leave. An important way to invest in families is by providing paid maternity (and paternity) leaves after the birth of a child. The box A Closer Look: What a Difference Location Can Make examines the maternity leave policy of the United States versus that of our Canadian neighbor.

A Closer Look

What A Difference Location Can Make

Melinda and Dave, who live in Seattle, Washington, are excited to welcome their first child, a daughter, to their family. They have dreamed of having a child for several years. Melinda works for a mid-sized corporation that, like most corporations, does not offer a paid maternity leave policy. Luckily for her she has two weeks of sick-leave saved, two weeks of paid vacation she can use, and her company agreed to give her another two weeks off of work, unpaid, to care for her baby. Legally she could stay home another six weeks without pay and not fear losing her job, but her family cannot live on Dave's salary alone. So Melinda goes back to work, still sleep-deprived and anxious over their new baby, not to mention the angst of an $800-a-month childcare bill. She takes her breast pump with her to work and uses it in the women's restroom on her breaks. This effort allows her to save her breast milk to feed it to her daughter while she is away at work.

Meanwhile, Janine, across the border in Vancouver, Canada, is enjoying four months of maternity leave, at 55 percent of her pay. She is also considering taking additional time off, knowing that her job is guaranteed for her when she returns. She rests assured knowing that when she does, the cost of childcare will be subsidized by the government, and she will be eligible for a family allowance to help offset the cost of raising her son. There is no stigma in taking maternity leave in Canada. No one will accuse her of not being "serious" about her job. Virtually all women take maternity leave, and the program is held in very high regard in Canada. Likewise, there is no stigma attached to a family allowance. Children are considered a "public good" because all Canadians benefit by having children who are well-tended to. Therefore, the government gives a small sum of money to help the new family with the costs of raising a child. It is available to all families, regardless of income, and is not considered welfare.

The United States and Canada—two countries that are located right next to one another—could not be further apart.

Critical Thinking

Why do you think that neighboring countries have such different views of what is needed after the birth of a baby? Now compare and contrast how a functionalist and conflict theorist would answer this question.

Table 10–3 A Comparison of Maternity Leave Benefits in Developed and Developing Nations

	Length of Maternity Leave	Percentage of Wages Paid in Covered Period
Less Developed Countries		
Afghanistan	90 days	100%
Bangladesh	16 weeks	100%
Cuba	18 weeks	100%
Egypt	90 days	100%
Guatemala	84 days	100%
India	12 weeks	100%
Kenya	3 months	100%
Mozambique	60 days	100%
Republic of Korea	60 days	100%
Developed Countries		
Canada	17–18 weeks	55% for 15 weeks
Denmark	52 weeks	100%
Finland	105 days	80%
Ireland	28 weeks	80% or fixed rate
Italy	5 months	80%
Japan	14 weeks	67%
Netherlands	16 weeks	100%
Spain	16 weeks	100%
Sweden	480 days	80% for 390 days; flat rate afterwards
Switzerland	98 days	80%
United Kingdom	52 weeks	90% for 6 weeks; flat rate afterwards
United States	12 weeks[a]	0%

[a] Applies only to workers in companies with 50 or more workers.

SOURCE: Adapted from United Nations Statistics Division, 2013.

Why are maternity leaves so important? Lengthy maternity leaves are associated with better maternal and child health and with lower family stress. Moreover, with extended leave benefits, women are likely to breastfeed for longer periods, which improves children's immunity and reduces their later risk of obesity. The benefit of longer parental leaves also extends to employers. Women are more likely to return to work after childbirth in those countries that have longer leaves. It is more cost-effective for a company to develop a well-planned parental leave policy than it is to rehire and retrain new employees.

Even fathers now want time off to help bond with and care for a newborn. One-third of fathers stay home more than two weeks, but generally, these fathers work in professional jobs with a higher degree of flexibility and must use their vacation time or take unpaid leave.

The United States has, by far, the least generous family leave policy of any nation in the world, including poor and developing nations, as you can see in Table 10–3. The Family Medical Leave Act of 1993, signed by President Clinton, requires employers with more than 50 employees to offer 12 weeks of unpaid leave for maternity or to care for a sick family member. Many women take only a few weeks off from work after having a baby because they cannot afford unpaid leave. They return to work soon after exhausting any short-term disability, vacation, or sick pay they may have. Among women who worked during their pregnancy, 58 percent returned to work within three months after giving birth, and 72 percent returned within six months.

By way of contrast, consider what other countries offer for maternity leave:

- France offers 16 weeks of paid maternity leave to women at 100 percent of their salary.
- In Denmark, women receive 52 weeks of paid maternity leave at 100 percent of their salary.
- Cuba offers women 18 weeks of leave at 100 percent of their salary.
- The United Kingdom allows maternity pay at 90 percent for 6 weeks and a flat rate after that for up to 1 year.
- Brazil provides 120 days of maternity benefits at 100 percent of the mother's salary (United Nations Statistics Division, 2013).

It is odd to think that a country as wealthy as the United States offers so little to new parents.

Future Prospects

President Obama has reminded Americans that it is the only nation without paid maternity leave. His Secretary of Labor, Thomas Perez, summarized these concerns. "What we're doing here in America is we're making women choose between the family they love and the job that they need. No other nation on the planet is making these choices," Perez said. "In other countries, they've put politics aside and looked at the facts. When women succeed, the world succeeds. We're losing sight of that here in the USA."

In his sixth State of the Union speech in January 2015, President Obama asked a joint session of Congress to pass measures that would allow federal workers to earn up to six weeks of paid sick time a year that could be used as paid family leave. This proposal, while representing a major change in policy, would still leave Americans with one of the weakest maternity leave laws in the world.

Going Beyond Left and Right

As the social institution that organizes intimate relationships among adults and socializes new generations, the family is frequently singled out as the source of many social problems. Americans hear endless debates about how to restore faltering "family values" or about which policies will best support and enhance the family as a social institution. Conservatives attack liberals for their tolerance of a variety of families, especially same-sex families and single parenthood. Conservatives are concerned about poor mothers and their children, but they tend to believe that if more people took responsibility for their own actions, there would be fewer such cases. Liberals assert that the conservatives' attacks are a smoke screen to divert attention from the relatively low levels of assistance given to struggling families by the institutions of government. Meanwhile, feminists argue that that caregiving is devalued, and women and children pay the consequences for this mindset. And so the debate over individual versus social responsibility continues without much resolution.

These debates are not likely to disappear in the foreseeable future, especially as the diversity of family forms in the United States and throughout the world continues to increase. Politics is becoming more polarized than ever. Americans have trouble even agreeing on which family issues constitute social problems. Is cohabitation a social problem? Conservatives say yes, that it contributes to the decline of stable families. Liberals say no, that it is a legitimate family form. Is same-sex marriage a social problem? Conservatives say yes, that it undermines the definition of family based on biblical principles. Liberals say no because marriage is a basic human right. Is the lack of paid maternity leave a social problem? Many conservatives say no because this government intrusion would undermine business. Liberals would argue that maternity leaves are healthy for baby and mother and should be available to all, regardless of financial circumstances.

Sociologists are in the unique position to conduct research and provide data that bear on these questions. Through surveys, in-depth interviews, experiments, observational studies, and analysis of census and other governmental data, they can provide information about what happens when people cohabit, when same-sex couples marry, and when women take maternity leaves. This important information needs a solid "seat at the table" of political discussions about families.

Summary

- Families are defined here as relationships by blood, marriage, or affection, in which members may cooperate economically, may care for any children, and may consider their identity to be intimately connected to the larger group. The definition used has important consequences with respect to informal and formal rights.

- Functions of the family include regulation of sexual behavior; reproduction and socializing children; property and inheritance; economic cooperation; social placement status and roles; and care, warmth, protection, and intimacy.

- Conservatives express grave concern that changes in family structure put children at risk. They suggest that many challenges families face are linked to gross cultural and moral weakening. Liberals suggest that these problems experienced by families result from economic and structural adjustments that place new demands on families without offering additional social supports. Feminists ask for policies that place higher value on the quality of human relationships. They work for reforms that build and strengthen neighborhoods and volunteer groups, support caregiving activities, and encourage education and employment among both women and men.

- Norms surrounding marriage and intimate relationships are changing. For example, fewer people are married today than in the past, including a delay in the age at which they marry; more couples cohabit before or instead of marrying; same-sex couples fought for and won the right to marry; and the division of household labor has become somewhat more equitable.

- Most adults have children at some point in their lives. There are different types of parenting contexts, including a declining number of teenage parents, a growing number of single parents, an increase in gay and lesbian families, and an increase in grandparents raising their grandchildren. Although parenting across these contexts has many similarities, it also has significant differences.

- Families face a number of problems, and two are discussed here. The first is violence, including intimate partner violence (IPV) and child abuse. The second problem discussed is divorce. The number of divorces has declined steadily since the peak in the 1980s, but the United States still has one of the highest divorce rates in the world. Divorce has a variety of negative consequences for adults and children.

- The government regulates many aspects of families by the policies it creates. The government also touches the lives of families by an absence of certain policies. For example, U.S. adults have no guaranteed maternity leave. An important way to invest in families is by providing paid maternity (and paternity) leaves after the birth of a child.

Chapter 11
Problems of Education

Learning Objectives

11.1 Describe the history of the American education system.

11.2 Summarize why education is a social problem.

11.3 Compare and contrast the sociological perspectives on education.

11.4 Identify the educational attainment and achievement of different groups in society.

11.5 Discuss some of the current social problems facing schools.

11.6 Assess the policy issues surrounding early child education for the poor and the Race to the Top educational program.

It's Monday morning, and Mason is just entering his classroom. He is a happy-go-lucky fourth grader and loves school, although he would never admit that to his friends, which include the other 16 students in his class. But he secretly knows that they also enjoy school. When the bell rings, he knows the drill—he picks up his school-issued notebook computer and begins working on a paper that he saved yesterday in Google Docs. Once his file is up and he rereads his work, he combs the Internet for more information for his paper. He knows that if he has any problems finding what he needs, his teacher or the classroom aide can offer individual help. Likewise, if he has any problems with his computer itself, the school's technology department will have it fixed in no time or they will issue him another. Mason works on his project quietly until his teacher informs the class that the science specialist has just walked into the classroom. Mason saves his work, puts his laptop away, and eagerly awaits what they will do in science today. His favorite classes are science, art, music, and P.E., all taught by specialists with expertise in their fields. What school is this, you ask, where class size is 17 students, each student has his or her own computer, and the school's curriculum is so enriching? Where can you sign your child up? Mason attends a private school with tuition costs of $25,000 a year, and your child will likely have to be put on the waiting list to get in.

What Do You Think?

How would you rate the quality of your primary and secondary education, and why?

No Child Left Behind Act of 2001

A major legislative initiative of the Bush administration to improve education in four clearly defined ways: (1) accountability for results; (2) an emphasis on doing what works based on scientific research; (3) expanded parental school choice options; and (4) expanded local control and flexibility.

Unlike many private schools that cater to the wealthy, the issues that affect public schools in the United States are staggering. At present, there is a debate about national education standards; school choice; school privatization; prayer in school; weapons in schools; standards for teachers; the impact of technology; classroom and school size; and much more. School reform figures prominently in presidential and gubernatorial elections, and will no doubt be an issue in every local election for years to come. Yet, the irony in all of the controversies swirling around schools, including in higher education, is that people tend to like their own schools, even if they do not think highly of public schools in general, as shown in Figure 11–1 (Gallup, 2015).

The **No Child Left Behind Act of 2001**, a major legislative initiative of President Bush's administration, was designed to improve education in four clearly defined ways: (1) accountability for results; (2) an emphasis on doing what works based on scientific research; (3) expanded parental school choice options; and (4) expanded local control and flexibility. According to the Act's accountability provisions, states must describe how they will close achievement gaps and make sure all students, including those who are disadvantaged or in special education classes, achieve

Figure 11–1 Overall, How Satisfied Are You with the Quality of Education?, 2014
SOURCE: Gallup, 2015.

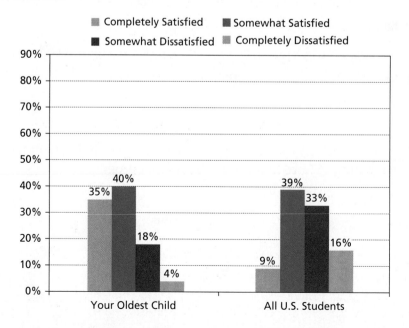

academic proficiency. Schools that do not make progress must provide supplemental services such as free tutoring or after-school assistance; take corrective actions; and, if still not making adequate annual progress after five years, make substantial changes in the way the school is run. Many educators complain, however, that under these strict guidelines schools suffer unfairly by being labeled as failing when they really are not. President Obama and his administration have been trying to improve the legislation by making more resources available to the public schools. Later in this chapter you will read about their **Race to the Top** approach that has proven to be an effective strategy for encouraging state school systems to institute reforms, plus be able to further consider this important legislation.

History of American Education

11.1 Describe the history of the American education system.

Education is the social institution through which a society teaches its members the skills, knowledge, norms, and values they need to learn to become good, productive participants in society. *Formal* education is often referred to as *schooling*, and as this term implies, it occurs in schools under teachers, principals, and other trained professionals. In contrast, *informal* education may occur almost anywhere: at home, on a walk in the woods, or as you read a good book.

In early United States history, education was largely informal. Boys and girls usually learned what they needed to know at home or on the family farm. During the colonial period, the Puritans in Massachusetts required parents to teach their children to read and required larger towns to have an elementary school. However, in general, schooling was not required in the colonies, and only about 10 percent of children, usually just boys from the wealthiest families, went to school. Boys who were not rich or not white were excluded from formal school. Girls were also excluded because their education revolved around homemaking skills and took place informally at home (Urban and Wagoner, 2008).

To help unite the nation after the Revolutionary War, educators created textbooks to standardize spelling and pronunciation. The books were also designed to unify cultural and political views, including patriotism, religion, and distrust of Native Americans. However, school continued to be largely a pastime of boys from wealthy white families.

It took another 75 years, or roughly until the mid-1800s, for people to begin calling for free and compulsory elementary and secondary education, and another 50 years for it to become the law. By the beginning of the twentieth century, most communities of size had schools, and schooling was considered an important development for all children, regardless of sex or social class. Note that blacks were still generally barred from government-subsidized schools that whites attended. Despite this important fact, compulsory education was intended to further national unity and to teach the swarm of new immigrants about "American" values. This period was also the time of the "Industrial Revolution." An industrial economy demanded reading, writing, and math skills at a higher level than was the case in an agrarian society.

Today, schools are open to all young people, regardless of race, ethnicity, sex, and social class. However, you will see that these statuses continue to affect both educational achievement and the type of learning that occurs in schools.

Education as a Social Problem

11.2 Summarize why education is a social problem.

The supposed "failure" of the U.S. educational system is a complex issue that groups in society define differently, depending on the specific goals of each particular group. For example, parents at all social-class levels demand that the schools do a better

Race to the Top

President Obama and his administration have been trying to improve the No Child Left Behind legislation by making more resources available to the public schools for creative ventures.

Table 11–1 Percent Responding to Survey Questions, "How Often Did You ___ This Past Year?" in 2012

	Daily/ Weekly	Monthly	Once or Twice a Semester	Never
Help your child with his or her homework?	80%	7%	7%	6%
Review your child's grades?	57%	27%	15%	1%
Take on a leadership role in any of your child's extracurricular activities?	18%	16%	32%	34%
Meet with your child's teachers?	17%	22%	55%	5%
Volunteer in your child's classroom?	10%	15%	35%	40%
Donate supplies for the school?	7%	21%	55%	17%
Donate money to the school?	5%	20%	53%	22%

SOURCE: Tompson, Benz, and Agiesta, 2013.

What Do You Think?

How involved were your parents in your school when you were a child? Do you think they volunteered too little, too much, or about the right amount? What social factors, including income, jobs, and attitudes affected their level of involvement?

job of preparing students to work and live in a technologically sophisticated society. Various minority groups want schools to prepare their children to compete in American society, yet at the same time, not strip them of their cultural identity—or, in the case of Hispanics, of the language they learn at home. Educational policymakers believe that schools must do more to increase the overall level of student achievement. Many teachers, in contrast, believe that parents should play a greater role in their children's education. Table 11–1 shows what parents are doing from their point of view.

In the face of severe state and federal budget deficits, many school boards have been cutting back on hiring teachers and even laying off some administrators and teachers. This crisis situation does not change the basic debates about school reform, but it does postpone some of the more heated debates as administrators scramble to find ways to retain their programs and staffs. Should schools be more open to new ideas and teaching methods, or should they focus on the traditional curriculum—"the basics"? Indeed, what are the basics? Do they consist simply of reading, writing, and arithmetic, or do they include learning how to get along with others and how to communicate effectively? Are the basics the same for all students? These questions are only some of the fundamental questions being asked about public education in the United States today. There are many others. Should more qualified and effective teachers receive merit pay? Should the school year be longer? Should there be a standardized national curriculum? There is even some question about whether education should be a public institution. Perhaps high-quality private schooling should be encouraged by means of a government-sponsored voucher system that would refund to households the amounts they spend on public education through taxes (Irons, 2007).

The United States has led the world in establishing free public education for its people. Per capita public expenditures on education in the United States are among the highest in the world (National Center for Education Statistics, 2014f). A comparison of the countries in the Organisation for Economic Co-operation and Development (OECD), an organization of 24 countries whose purpose is to promote trade and economic growth, shows that the United States leads the way in postsecondary education funding at nearly $26,000 per full-time-equivalent (FTE) student and is near the top in elementary and secondary education funding, at nearly $12,000 per FTE. Of OECD countries, Luxembourg spends the most on elementary and secondary education, at over $19,000 FTE, more than 50 percent higher than the United States.

Education is compulsory in the United States; the requirements differ from one state to another, but usually children must attend school until age 16. As a result, over 98 percent of all U.S. children between the ages of 7 and 15 are enrolled in school, as are 94 percent of 16- and 17-year-olds (U.S. Census Bureau, 2014). Moreover, the number of students enrolled in higher education increased rapidly in the twentieth century.

So what is wrong? Why is the educational system under attack? How does this impressive record constitute a "failure"? These questions can be answered in different ways, depending on the sociological perspective from which they are viewed.

Sociological Perspectives on Education

11.3 Compare and contrast the sociological perspectives on education.

In democratic nations, education is a primary method of addressing a number of social needs and problems. The schools are expected to prepare new generations of good citizens and reliable, capable workers who can enter the labor force with the necessary skills in literacy, computation, and written expression. Higher education in colleges, universities, and professional training institutions is expected to produce young adults who can become scientists, professionals, and leaders in business and other institutions of society.

But these ambitious goals hardly exhaust the list of demands placed on educators. Schools and institutions of higher education are expected to address and solve problems of inequality. They are not expected to make everyone equal (all societies recognize that people are born with differing interests and abilities), but they are expected to provide equal opportunities to learn and to gain the skills and experiences that society requires. And, as if these demands were not enough, the schools are also expected to address other social problems such as racism, sexism, and violence.

As might be expected, there are vast differences in the analyses of public education by sociologists who approach the subject from different theoretical perspectives. Functionalists stress stability and consensus; in their view, education is, or should be, one of several interdependent parts that work together to create a smoothly functioning society whose members all share the same basic values and beliefs. Conflict theorists argue that schools reproduce the society's system of inequality and class stratification in new generations of children. They see society as divided into dominant and subordinate groups, with education being used as a tool to promote the interests of the dominant group while teaching the subordinate groups to accept their situation. Symbolic Interactionists take still another approach: They examine how expectations of students' performance actually determine that performance and how these expectations can result in labels that shape the students' future. Each of these perspectives gives rise to different approaches to the study of public education and are summarized in Table 11–2 and discussed below.

Table 11–2 Perspectives on Education

Theoretical Perspective	Major Assumptions
Functionalism	• Education serves several manifest functions for society, including (a) socialization, (b) social integration, (c) social placement, and (d) social and cultural innovation. • Latent functions include reduced crime, child care, the establishment of peer relationships, and lowering unemployment by occupying high school students. • Problems in the educational institution harm society because all these functions cannot be completely fulfilled. • Schools are poorly equipped to help students who come from disorganized backgrounds.
Conflict Theory	• Education promotes social inequality of gender, race, and class through the use of tracking and standardized testing and the impact of its "hidden curriculum." • Schools differ widely in their funding and learning conditions, and this type of inequality leads to learning disparities that reinforce social inequality. • Those with wealth and power try to ensure that their children get high-quality education by going to private schools.
Symbolic Interactionism	• This perspective focuses on social interaction in the classroom, on the playground, and in other school venues. • Specific research finds that social interaction in schools affects the development of gender roles and that teachers' expectations of pupils' intellectual abilities affect how much pupils learn. • Certain educational problems have their basis in social interaction and expectations. Schools label students as "achievers," "underachievers," or "rebels," which lead students to fulfill those expectations.

Functionalist Approaches

manifest functions

Those societal functions that are direct and the most obvious.

Functionalists view education as an important social institution because it can lead to the smooth functioning of society and can provide individuals with opportunities for work, fulfillment, and upward social mobility. **Manifest functions** are those that are direct and the most obvious, such as the teaching of academic subjects and the imparting of new knowledge (e.g., reading, writing, and arithmetic). Other manifest functions include:

- *Socialization, which involves enabling students to absorb dominant cultural norms, values, and attitudes.* In the United States, these norms, values, and attitudes include respect for authority (e.g., raise your hand for the teacher to call on you), patriotism (e.g., reciting the Pledge of Allegiance), punctuality (e.g., the ringing of school bells), time management (e.g., homework, deadlines), and competition (e.g., report cards, sports).
- *Social Placement, which involves assigning, or tracking, students into programs based on individual ability and achievement, and providing credentials.* Early on in school, teachers identify students as bright and motivated or as less so. Depending on how they are identified, children are taught at a level that teachers decide suits them best. For example, high schools may offer both a college "prep" curriculum and a trade school curriculum. In this way, students are presumably prepared for their later station in life.
- *Social Control and Integration, which involves imparting to students the knowledge that society shares.* School is compulsory, and the curriculum is relatively standardized from one school to another. A geometry course in Maine will cover the same material as a geometry course in Oregon, and the course is required for graduation, even though these high schools are located 3,000 miles apart. Schools help prepare students for the workforce and integrate them into American life.
- *Social Change and Innovation, which involves learning new information and technologies as they emerge.* Educational programs are designed to train new scientists, artists, and intellectuals who will make new discoveries, solve social problems, and also impart that knowledge to a new generation of students.

latent functions

Indirect by-products of some phenomenon that are less obvious.

In addition to these manifest functions, education also provides latent functions. **Latent functions** are the indirect by-products of education rather than a direct effect of the education itself. For example, schooling reduces crime by keeping children and teenagers busy and off the street; it reduces the costs that parents pay for childcare; it lowers the unemployment rate by occupying teenagers; and it establishes peer relationships and assists with mate selection by integrating young men and women in a variety of social activities such as sports, dances, and parties. Can you think of any other latent functions of education?

From a functionalist perspective, problems in the educational system are a symptom of social disorganization. The educational system is geared to students from stable homes and communities. It is not well equipped to handle the problems of students from disorganized homes—for example, where there is a difficult divorce, extreme poverty, or other challenging circumstances. Such students may be depressed and angry, have trouble concentrating on their schoolwork, and therefore have more difficulty achieving in school (Bastaits, Ponnet, and Mortelmans, 2014; Guinart and Grau, 2014; Soria and Linder, 2014). According to social-disorganization theorists, these students are more likely to join deviant peer groups, such as gangs, that reinforce their negative attitudes toward school.

Additionally, a functionalist perspective sees schools as mechanisms to reinforce society's values and to control deviance through discipline. Educational problems arise when schools fail to do these tasks. Perhaps schools inadequately teach students the values that our society holds dear, or perhaps schools are weak on disciplining those who do not learn the rules. In a multicultural school with large numbers of students, these tasks become more difficult.

Functionalism may also analyze the difficulties experienced by schools when they attempt to change their organization or procedures to improve student performance. How can schools organize themselves to meet the demands of students with special learning needs? How can schools with high levels of student failure on standardized tests recruit better teachers and administrators? How can school systems offer parents and children more choices of schools and educational approaches? These are all issues that hinge to a great extent on how schools, or entire school systems, are performing as they try to meet the demands placed on them. The No Child Left Behind legislation seeks to make schools accountable for students' performance on nationally distributed standardized tests of reading and math achievement. It also imposes penalties on schools and school districts when they fail to meet minimum standards of achievement. This legislation is a functionalist approach to improving the schools because it is based on performance measurements, but many functionalist theorists would point out that the initiative does not provide adequate resources to help schools improve teaching and student performance (Klenk, 2005; Riordan, 2004).

Conflict Approaches

Conflict theory does not dispute the manifest and latent functions described by functionalists. However, it does give these functions a different slant by emphasizing how education also perpetuates social inequality (Ballantine and Hammack, 2012).

One example of this process involves socialization. Conflict theorists point out that compulsory schooling began in part to teach immigrants how to be "American" and prevent immigrants' values from corrupting "American" values. That approach is an example of **ethnocentrism** (the belief that one's own group is superior to another group). Early schools were also designed to teach students the skills they needed to work in the "new" industrial economy of the mid-nineteenth century. Education was not designed to teach students to be managers, leaders, or entrepreneurs, but to be compliant and obedient workers (Cole, 2008). Therefore, compulsory education served the interests of the upper class much more than it served the interests of workers. In a classic statement of this position, Samuel Bowles wrote that compulsory education in the United States developed to meet the needs of a capitalist economy for skilled and disciplined workers and, while doing so, to justify the unequal social status of workers and capitalists (Bowles, Gintis, and Groves, 2005).

Conflict theorists believe that schooling continues to teach a set of values and beliefs, such as conformity and obedience to authority, that support the status quo and perpetuate the existing social hierarchy. This effect is called the hidden curriculum (Booher-Jennings, 2008). Although no one plots this curriculum behind closed doors, our schoolchildren learn obedience and respect for authority from the books they read and from various classroom activities.

Theorist Pierre Bourdieu suggests that education reproduces social class inequities because students come to school with differing amounts and types of **cultural capital** that they bring from home. This resource may include forms of knowledge, skills, education, and other advantages a person has that give him or her a certain status in society (Bourdieu, 1986). One example of this cultural capital is language. Upper class families are more likely to teach their children to speak **Standard American English (SAE)** and to avoid slang or poor grammar. They learn to "speak *well*" (not "speak *good*"). An example of these differences is shown in the box, A Personal View: Learning to Speak SAE.

Social placement is another aspect of education on which conflict theorists focus. Beginning in grade school, students who are thought by their teachers to be bright are placed in the faster tracks (especially in reading and arithmetic), while other students

ethnocentrism

The belief that one's own group is superior to another group.

cultural capital

The resource that a person brings from his or her family, which may include forms of knowledge, skills, education, and other advantages that a person has and which give him or her a certain status in society.

Standard American English (SAE)

A speaking style that avoids slang or poor grammar, used by upper class people.

A Personal View

Learning to Speak SAE

Okay, here's the deal: I'm a working-class girl done good. Please allow me to rephrase that. I would like to share that I am a highly successful woman who has roots in the working class. Do you see the difference in these two ways of speaking? My words, syntax, tones, even gestures change depending on the group I'm with. It hasn't always been that way.

I was raised in a working-class family with notoriously bad grammar. Around them parts we said "ain't," as in "I ain't hungry no more," and "fixin'," as in "Hey Janey, you fixin' to get to the store soon?" We all spoke this way in my family, as did most people within my community, so I really wasn't aware that my grammar was incorrect. I don't even remember my teachers calling me on it.

Things changed drastically when I went to college. Because I did well in high school, I had the fortunate opportunity to attend a prestigious college in the northeast. I would like to say that I loved the experience, but the culture shock was so overwhelming that I might as well have landed on Mars. In particular, I noticed that people did not speak the same way I did. They didn't have my accent, they used different words, and they used those words in a different pattern. I immediately felt inadequate.

One incident stands out in particular: In one of my math classes I wanted to ask the professor to expand on his explanation, so I simply asked, "How come?" He stared at me. "*How come?*" he repeated. Then he said it again more loudly than the first, "HOW COME?" At first I didn't catch what they were laughing about. But then it came to me, "I mean, why?" I gulped. Later that day I withdrew from the class.

That same day I also went to the English department and asked the secretary if the department offered any English tutors, "for, you know, people who talk different." She was a sweet lady, "Oh, you mean for people who have English as a second language? Sure honey, let me give you a list." I didn't dare tell her that I was looking for a tutor for myself. But I contacted the first name on the list, Darcy, and I am forever grateful. She taught me to speak "Standard American English," as she called it. We met twice a week for an entire year, and I practiced daily. The drills included verbal and nonverbal communication.

I can now easily pass as an upper-middle-class student at my college. I know how to "talk the talk." However, when I go back home to see my mama and pa, I'm just one of the working-class girls "done good."

By the way, I think I'll stop by to see my old math professor just to say "hey."

—Janey, Age 20

Critical Thinking

What is it about social class that contributes to different speech patterns? Can you think of specific issues that would cause these differences? Why is an upper-middle-class speech pattern more valued than other speech patterns? How would a conflict theorist answer this question?

are placed in the slower tracks. Tracking may affect not only test scores but also the likelihood of college attendance (Jennings et al., 2015).

Tracking students does have its advantages; it helps ensure that bright students learn as much as their abilities allow them, and it helps ensure that slower students are not taught over their heads. But conflict theorists believe that tracking perpetuates social inequality by locking students into faster and slower tracks. Worse yet, several studies show that students' social class, race, and ethnicity affect the track into which they are placed, even though their intellectual abilities and potential should be the only things that matter. White middle-class students are more likely to be tracked "up," while poorer students and students of color are more likely to be tracked "down."

Once they are tracked, students learn more if they are tracked up and less if they are tracked down. The latter tend to lose self-esteem; they begin to think they have little academic ability and thus do worse in school because they were tracked down (Ansalone, 2010; Chmielewski, Dumont, and Trautwein, 2013).

Conflict theorists add that standardized tests are culturally biased and thus also help perpetuate social inequality (Grodsky, Warren, and Felts, 2008). They suggest that these tests favor white middle-class students whose socioeconomic status and other aspects of their backgrounds have afforded them various experiences that help them answer questions on the tests.

Interactionist Approaches

Symbolic interaction focuses on micro-level social interactions. Interactionists see education as a vital part of socialization and therefore tend to focus not only on the dynamics of the school or classroom but also on the interactions between students and teachers, teachers and administrators, and among students themselves. What are the norms around interaction, and what labels are used?

According to the interactionist perspective, schools label students, and these labels follow them for years (Kirk and Sampson, 2013). Through the formal structure of grades, testing, and tracking, along with the social aspects of cliques, students develop a self-identity, either positive (e.g., "I am a smart person with a talent for basketball") or negative (e.g., "I'm just not good at math"). Self-fulfilling prophecies can become a substantial part of education. That is, when students are labeled in any way—dumb, loser, smart, slut, friendly, jock, cute, learning disabled—they may come to view themselves that way and behave accordingly (Shifrer, Callahan, and Muller, 2013).

According to labeling theorists, teachers form expectations about students early in the school year, and these are communicated to the students in varying ways. The students tend to perform in ways that meet the teacher's expectations, thereby reinforcing them. Sometimes these labels have little to do with reality. An early research study (Rosenthal and Jacobson, 1968) tested this theory by assessing a group of students at the beginning of the school year and telling their teachers which students were smart and which were not. The researchers then tested the students again at the end of the school year. As you might guess, the smarter students had learned more during the year than those students who were not as smart. The truth is, however, that the researchers randomly selected which students would be called smart, and these labels had nothing to do with reality. What would account for these so-called "smart" students to have learned more during the school year, given that they were not necessarily smarter at all? The answers can be found in the teachers' behavior. The teachers of the "smart children" spent more time with them and praised them more often than was true for the "less bright" group.

What Do You Think?

What theoretical perspective do you find most intriguing with respect to education, and why?

Educational Attainment and Achievement

11.4 Identify the educational attainment and achievement of different groups in society.

Today, ever-greater proportions of U.S. students are finishing high school and going on to college. As shown in Figure 11–2, from 1920 to 2013, the nation underwent a transformation in which high school completion, rather than leaving (i.e., dropping out), became the norm. Only 16 percent of people age 25 or older in 1920 had a high school diploma; today, that figure is 88 percent. Likewise, those with at least four years of college have also increased. In 1920, only 3 percent of adults ages 25 and older had earned a college degree, but today, almost a third have done so.

Nonetheless, much work remains in helping young people to finish high school and encouraging them to attend college. For members of most minority groups,

Figure 11–2 Years of School Completed by Persons Age 25 and Over, 1920–2013

SOURCE: National Center for Education Statistics, 2013a, Table 104.10.

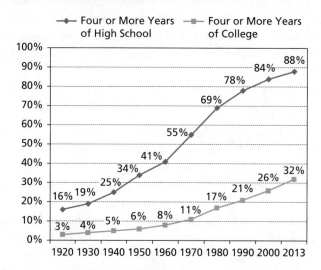

these educational issues continue to be especially pressing, as shown in Figure 11–3. Although the vast majority of Asian/Pacific Islander (93 percent) and white (85 percent) high school students graduated from high school in the 2011–12 school year, only two-thirds of black (68 percent) and American Indian/Alaska Native youths (68 percent) graduated. The rates for Hispanic youth are somewhere between these groups (76 percent), but still remain quite low for a wealthy, industrialized country such as the United States.

The good news is that the gap in **educational attainment** (number of years of school completed) between most minority groups and whites has narrowed considerably since the turn of the century, mainly because of the increase in the minimum amount of education received by almost all Americans. For example, a generation ago, in 1980, 25 percent of whites between the ages of 25 and 29 had completed a bachelor's degree or higher, compared with only 12 percent of blacks, and 8 percent of Hispanics,

Figure 11–3 Graduation Rate for Public High School Students, by Race/Ethnicity: School Year 2011–12

SOURCE: Kena, Aud, Johnson, Wang, Zhang, Rathbun, Wilkinson-Flicker, and Kristapovich, 2014.

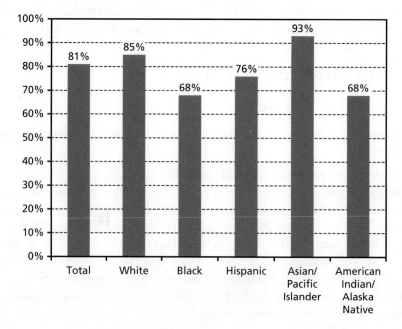

educational attainment

The number of years of school completed.

Figure 11–4 Percentage of Persons Ages 25–29 Who Have Achieved a Bachelor's Degree or Higher by Race/Ethnicity, 1980 and 2013

SOURCE: National Center for Education Statistics, 2013b, Table 104.20.

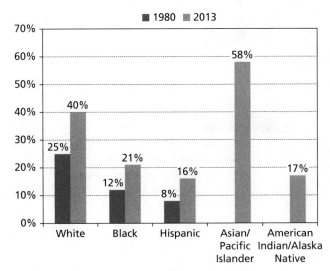

as shown in Figure 11–4 (unfortunately, no data are available for Asian/Pacific Islanders or American Indian/Alaska Natives for that year). However, all groups have seen significant increases over the years. Today, 58 percent of young Asian/Pacific Islanders have at least a bachelor's degree, followed by whites (40 percent), blacks (21 percent), American Indian/Alaska Natives (17 percent), and Hispanics (16 percent).

Why is it so important to close the gap in educational attainment? People with higher levels of education tend to earn more money than those with less education. Figure 11–5 reveals the average earnings of young adults between the ages of 25 and 34 who work full-time (all year). As you can see, educational credentials have a linear effect on earnings. People with a high school diploma (or GED) earn more than those

Figure 11–5 Median Annual Earnings of Full-Time Year-Round Wage and Salary Workers Ages 25–34, by Educational Attainment

SOURCE: Kena, Aud, Johnson, Wang, Zhang, Rathbun, Wilkinson-Flicker, and Kristapovich, 2014.

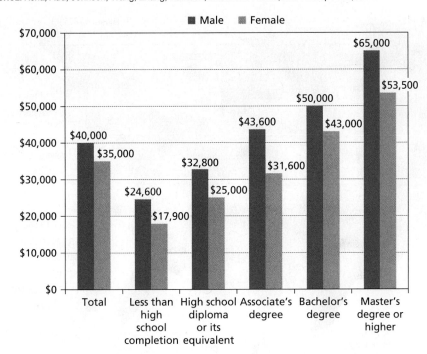

who have not completed high school. People with an associate's two-year degree earn more than those who have completed high school. Those with a bachelor's degree earn more than do those with an associate's degree, and those with a master's degree or higher earn the most of all. However, you will also note that men earn considerably more than do women at all education levels. For example, women with a high school diploma earn about the same, on average, as men who have dropped out of high school. Disparities persist even at the most advanced educational levels. Women with a master's degree or higher earn only slightly more than men with only a bachelor's degree.

These young people did not complete high school. Their job options are very limited, and they have suffered bouts of unemployment. They now work in a packing company, earning $10.50 an hour, with no fringe benefits. It is unlikely that their pay or working conditions will improve significantly; consequently, few people stay at the packing plant for the long term.

Blacks

Before World War I, about 90 percent of all blacks in the United States lived in the southern states (Orfield and Eaton, 1996). The data in Map 11–1 show that most southern states and some western states continue to spend far less per student than school systems in the Northeast. Black students are disproportionately concentrated in the Deep South, where blacks (and poor southern whites) receive only about 70 percent of the amount of schooling received by whites in more advantaged areas of the nation.

In the North, educational opportunities for blacks and whites are more equal, but inequalities between schools in poor black communities and those in more affluent white suburbs tend to perpetuate differences in educational attainment. At the beginning of the twentieth century, northern-born blacks were rapidly closing the educational gap between themselves and whites, but the gap widened again after 1915. The reasons for

Map 11–1 U.S. Expenditures Per Pupil by State, 2012.

SOURCE: National Education Association, 2014.

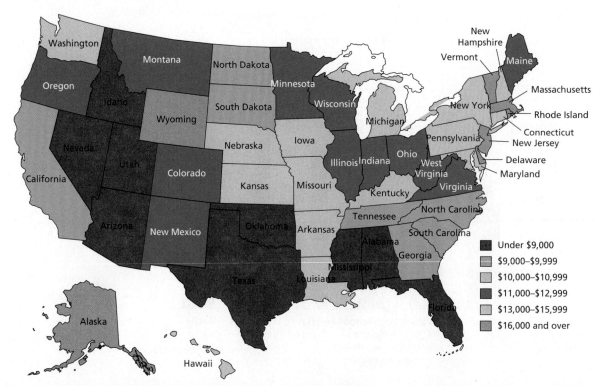

■	Under $9,000
▨	$9,000–$9,999
▧	$10,000–$10,999
■	$11,000–$12,999
▨	$13,000–$15,999
■	$16,000 and over

this reversal are complex. An important factor was the competition between black children and the children of European immigrants, who tended to come from better-educated families and thus enjoyed an advantage over blacks, whose parents had migrated from the South. Another factor, beginning in the Great Depression and continuing to the present, was the higher rate of unemployment among blacks. The employment status of parents has a great deal to do with the educational attainment of their children because children of low-income parents are more likely to drop out of school (Slavin, 1997). A third factor was segregation. Segregation tends to increase disparities between groups, not only because minority schools (which are usually located in central cities) have fewer highly qualified teachers and other resources but also because students in those schools do not learn the values, work habits, and skills they need to compete effectively in the larger society (Darling-Hammond, 1998, 2010; Orfield, 1999).

Hispanics

Another minority group that has faced difficulties in education is Hispanic Americans. The educational attainment of Hispanic students is lower than the average for all students (Kena et al., 2014). But this difference should not be interpreted to mean that Hispanics do not care about education. A recent study of 733 Hispanic registered voters asked them to rate the importance of five issues that might be discussed in an election: education, health care, immigration, jobs and the economy, and conflicts in the Middle East. Education was considered the most important, with 92 percent saying it was "extremely" or "very important." Interestingly, only 73 percent said that immigration was "extremely" or "very important," as shown in Figure 11–6 (Lopez, Gonzalez-Barrera, and Krogstad, 2014).

An especially important factor in the lower educational attainment of Hispanic students to date is that they, like blacks, have experienced the effects of de facto segregation and poor schools. This problem is particularly acute in large metropolitan areas, yet this issue has received minimal attention (Carriuolo, Rodgers, and Stout, 2002; Orfield, 2004/2005).

Another factor that receives greater attention is that some Hispanic students do not speak English at all or do not speak it well enough to succeed in an English-speaking school. A large nationally representative sample of Hispanics in the United States

Figure 11–6 Percentage of Hispanic Registered Voters Who Say This Issue Is "Extremely" or "Very Important" To Them Personally

SOURCE: Lopez, Gonzalez-Barrera, and Krogstad, 2014.

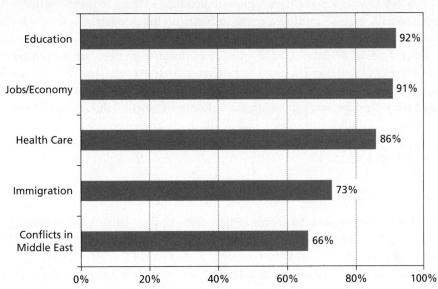

Figure 11–7 Language Spoken at Home and English Speaking Ability by Age Among Hispanics, 2012

SOURCE: Brown and Patten, 2014.

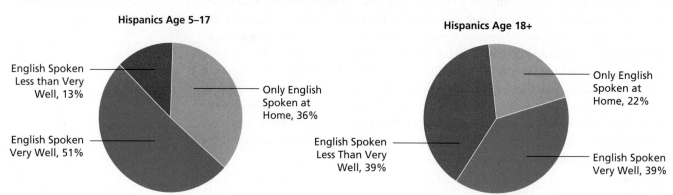

showed that 13 percent of children between the ages of 5 and 17 "speak English less than very well," although the percentage of older Hispanics who do not speak English very well is three times larger (39 percent), as illustrated in Figure 11–7 (Brown and Patten, 2014). If researchers were to look only at young children who are just beginning school, they would likely see that more than 13 percent need substantial help with English to prevent them from falling behind in school.

Since the late 1960s, a primary goal of education for Hispanic students has been to improve their ability to use English without allowing them to fall behind in other subjects. One technique for achieving this goal is bilingual/bicultural education in which students are taught wholly or partly in their native language until they can function adequately in English, and in some cases, longer. This approach has received the support of the federal Office of Civil Rights, which requires that schools take "affirmative steps" to correct minority students' deficiencies in the English language to receive federal funds.

Asian Americans and Pacific Islanders

Students from Chinese, Korean, East Indian, Pacific Islander, and other Asian backgrounds face different problems in U.S. schools. Due to their higher achievement on most measures of school performance, Asian students and their parents are proud of their scholastic achievements but often feel that they are treated as the "model minority" who are expected to be uniformly high achievers and extremely well behaved in schools (Abboud and Kim, 2005; Yu, 2006). Asian Americans make up 4 percent of the U.S. population, but represent 20 percent of the students attending elite U.S. Ivy League schools. This representation has led some to ponder whether Ivy League schools may be putting a quota or limits on the number of Asians admitted (Friedersdorf, 2012; Klein, 2014).

But for Asian students who do not outperform their peers or do not behave according to cultural stereotypes, the extremely high expectations of their families and the larger society can present severe problems. Asian American teenagers and college students experience more stress, harbor more suicidal thoughts, and attempt suicide at higher rates than other racial or ethnic groups, as you can see in Table 11-3 (American Psychological Association, 2012; Wong et al., 2011; Suicide Prevention Resource Center, 2014).

American Indians and Alaska Natives

There are nearly 400,000 American Indian and Alaska Native youths enrolled in public schools in the United States (National Indian Education Association, 2015). A much smaller number, about 47,000 students, attend one of the 184 schools funded by the Bureau of Indian Education (BIE). The BIE school system was created to meet the

Table 11–3 Results of 2011 Youth Risk Behavior Survey of High School Students

Survey Question, "In the past 12 months, have you …"	Asian Youth	Total U.S. Youth
Had serious thoughts of suicide	19%	16%
Made suicide plans	14%	13%
Attempted suicide	11%	8%
Gotten medical attention for a suicide attempt	5%	2%

SOURCE: Suicide Prevention Resource Center, 2014.

federal government's commitment to provide for the education of American Indian and Alaska Native children. The goal of the BIE is "to provide quality education opportunities from early childhood through life in accordance with a tribe's needs for cultural and economic well-being, in keeping with the diversity of Indian tribes and Alaska Native villages as distinct cultural and governmental entities" (Bureau of Indian Education, 2015). The BIE schools consider the spiritual, mental, physical, and cultural aspects of the students within their family and tribal or village context. They strive to contribute to the development of quality American Indian and Alaska Native communities (Northwest Evaluation Association, 2014).

Of the 184 BIE-funded schools, 57 are operated by the BIE and the remaining 127 are tribally controlled. The Bureau also operates two postsecondary schools: Haskell Indian Nations University and Southwestern Indian Polytechnic Institute.

How do the students in BIE-funded schools compare with other students across the country? A large-scale evaluation was conducted for the BIE by the educational research center, the Northwest Evaluation Association (NWEA, 2014). Researchers found that student achievement in both math and reading was below average at all grade levels in 2012–13. In only 29 percent of the BIE-funded schools did students have test scores near the national average. However, a review of data over the four years prior showed that student achievement had improved, particularly among younger students. Math gains were also notable. Therefore, proponents of BIE-funded schools suggest that these improvements, coupled with the social and cultural advantages available to students, indicate the successes and strengths of Indian education.

Can We Find Any Common Themes?

Blacks, Hispanics, and American Indian/Alaska Native youths are less likely to finish high school and less likely to attend college than are their Asian American/Pacific Islander and white counterparts. Whatever the cause, dropping out has serious economic consequences. Those who have less education earn significantly less than people who have completed more years of school.

We have briefly reviewed some of the unique characteristics of these minority groups that could account for some of the educational disparities. But can we find any common themes that could offer us more clues? The following seven ideas offer potential leads in better understanding the disparities. Some of these ideas are structural and others represent individual-level factors:

- *Lack of Cultural Capital:* Students bring their own personal history to school with advantages or disadvantages. For example, if a child was raised by parents who did not read well, chances are these parents had a more limited vocabulary than other parents, they did not have a lot of books in the home, and they may not have valued reading as an activity. Therefore, the child begins school at a distinct disadvantage that can continue throughout a child's educational career, unless schools work to equalize cultural capital by providing enriching material and field trips (Kisida, Greene, and Bowen, 2014).

What Do You Think?

Identify the specific personal and structural factors that shaped your educational attainment to date (and your plans for the future). Personal factors might include intelligence or personal initiative, while structural factors might include your family's educational background or issues related to your culture, social class, or race or ethnic identity.

- *Inferior Teachers:* The first large study of American schools was commissioned by the U.S. Congress and conducted by James Coleman in the 1960s (Coleman, 1966). He noted the factors that contribute to a student's academic performance, including family and neighborhood experiences and, to a lesser degree, school resources. Yet, research suggests that among school-related factors, the quality of teachers matters most (Sadler et al., 2013). When it comes to student performance on reading and math tests, a teacher is estimated to have two to three times the impact of any other school factor, including services, facilities, and even leadership (Rand Education, 2012). Yet classrooms are often segregated into achievement levels, racial composition, and socioeconomic composition, and it is the teachers with less experience who tend to be assigned to the most challenging classes (Kalogrides, Loeb, and Béteille, 2013; Kalogrides and Loeb, 2013).

- *Inferior Schools:* Traditionally, schools reflected the socioeconomic and racial profile of the surrounding neighborhood and were most often segregated. Desegregation effectively began with the Supreme Court's 1954 ruling in *Brown v. Board of Education of Topeka, Kansas*, which found that segregation had negative effects on black students even when their school facilities were "equal" (which they rarely were). Segregation continued, however, because many white or upper-income families transferred to private schools (i.e., "white flight") and politicians gerrymandered districts to change school attendance boundaries (Richards, 2014). In 2007, the Court reversed the 1954 landmark decision, and ruled that policies that selected students based on race to achieve more integrated classrooms are unconstitutional. Consequently, today's typical minority student attends school with fewer whites than his or her counterpart did in 1970 (Fiel, 2013), despite the fact that high-poverty schools and racially segregated schools result in lower educational attainment for the poor and racial minorities (Mickelson, Bottia, and Lambert, 2013; Palardy, 2013).

- *Lack of Help at Home:* It is possible that blacks, Hispanics, and American Indian youths may not receive enough help with their schoolwork at home from their parents. Although minority enrollments in high school and college are higher today than at any time in the past, the parents of these students have less education than the parents of white and Asian American/Pacific Islander students and, therefore, are less able to assist their children.

- *Peer Groups:* Peer groups take on increasing importance as children become teenagers and young adults. Many blacks, Hispanics, and American Indian/Alaska Native youths may not have access to a large peer network of college-bound friends. If you do not have very many friends who are finishing high school or considering college, it is not surprising that you may also have limited educational aspirations.

- *Multiple Obligations:* Although the primary cause of dropping out is poor academic performance, students often drop out of high school because of the difficulties they encounter in trying to cope with school, family, and work roles at the same time. They may be married and/or pregnant or working at a job, all of which increases the likelihood of dropping out of school.

- *Lack of Financial Resources:* Cutbacks in federally funded assistance, particularly the emphasis on loans rather than outright grants, place a college education out of reach for many minority or poor students.

An egalitarian society has a responsibility to provide equal access to high-quality education for all its citizens. Critics claim that U.S. society has failed to meet this responsibility, particularly for minority groups. This criticism has become especially sharp as the composition of student populations has changed. Since the

1960s, increasing numbers of blacks, Hispanics, and other minority groups have become concentrated in central cities, while whites have moved to the suburbs. As a result, in some metropolitan areas, over 90 percent of the students in public schools are black or Hispanic. And because central-city schools often have fewer resources than suburban schools, the quality of education available to black and Hispanic central-city residents tends to be lower than that available to white suburban residents.

How U.S. Students Measure Up in International Comparisons

Throughout the world, education runs in two extremes: Some children receive excellent education, at least as evidenced by their high scores on standardized tests. In contrast, other children receive little or no education at all. This pattern is especially the case for girls, who are often excluded from school on legal grounds, because of religious or cultural traditions, or for economic reasons.

EDUCATION IN DEVELOPED COUNTRIES   One issue that motivates the clamor for educational reform in the United States is the fact that on standardized tests administered throughout the world, the United States lags behind other advanced industrialized nations. Table 11–4 shows the average score of 15-year-olds taking the Program for International Student Assessment, which is a very large cross-national test that measures math, science literacy, and other key skills among 15-year-olds in dozens of developed and developing countries. As you can see, the United States placed a paltry 35th out of 64 countries in math and placed 27th in science (DeSilver, 2015).

The standing of American students is a bit better in other international measures. For example, in the assessment known as the Trends in International Mathematics and Science Study (TIMSS), which tests children in grades four and eight every four years (since 1995), American students fare better. In the most recent test, among the fourth graders, only seven countries (out of 50) had statistically higher math scores, and six countries had higher science scores than the United States. Among eighth graders, only six countries (out of 42) had higher math scores and eight countries had higher science scores (DeSilver, 2015). These results are certainly better, but given what our country spends on education, we should expect even stronger outcomes.

There are a few important things to note with respect to these comparisons, however. First, because of the great diversity of U.S. students and schools, the U.S. students' scores vary quite a bit. Much of this variation is explained by whether the students attend segregated schools in which high proportions of students are poor or of very low income (often measured by whether students are eligible for free lunch in school, a reflection of their family's financial need). The lower the income of students, and the greater the number of low-income students in the schools, the less well they do on standardized international tests.

The second point to note is that American test scores are improving, as shown in Figure 11–8. An assessment of the U.S. Department of Education, the National Assessment of Educational Progress, has found that U.S. students have made substantial gains in their math scores since 1990. Scores have increased slightly every year, although fourth-grade scores have leveled off in recent years (DeSilver, 2015). For example, in 1990, 50 percent of fourth graders scored below a "basic" level in math; by 2013 only 17 percent did so. Likewise, the percentage of eighth graders who scored below "basic" dropped from 48 percent to 26 percent.

These recent national assessments of educational achievement have shown some encouraging improvement in students' math scores. Nevertheless, the level of student achievement remains a subject of widespread debate. In a study of inequalities in

What Do You Think?

What might explain why students in so many other countries have higher test scores than students in the United States? Compare and contrast our culture and American educational system with those found in other countries.

Table 11.4 U.S. Mediocre on Science, Math Scores

Average Scores of 15-Year-Olds Taking the 2012 Program for International Student Assessment

MATHEMATICS				SCIENCE			
Singapore	573	Russian Fed.	482	Hong Kong	555	Luxembourg	491
Hong Kong	561	Slovakia	482	Singapore	551	Croatia	491
Taiwan	560	**United States**	**481**	Japan	547	Portugal	489
South Korea	554	Lithuania	479	Finland	545	Russian Fed.	486
Macao	538	Sweden	478	Estonia	541	Sweden	485
Japan	536	Hungary	477	South Korea	538	Iceland	478
Liechtenstein	535	Croatia	471	Vietnam	528	Slovakia	471
Switzerland	531	Israel	466	Poland	526	Israel	470
Netherlands	523	Greece	453	Liechtenstein	525	Greece	467
Estonia	521	Serbia	449	Canada	525	Turkey	463
Finland	519	Turkey	448	Germany	524	U.A.E.	448
Poland	518	Romania	445	Taiwan	523	Bulgaria	446
Canada	518	Cyprus	440	Netherlands	522	Serbia	445
Belgium	515	Bulgaria	439	Ireland	522	Chile	445
Germany	514	U.A.E.	434	Macao	521	Thailand	444
Vietnam	511	Kazakhstan	432	Australia	521	Romania	439
Austria	506	Thailand	427	New Zealand	516	Cyprus	438
Australia	504	Chile	423	Switzerland	515	Costa Rica	429
Ireland	501	Malaysia	421	Slovenia	514	Kazakhstan	425
Slovenia	501	Mexico	413	United Kingdom	514	Malaysia	420
New Zealand	500	Montenegro	410	Czech Republic	508	Uruguay	416
Denmark	500	Uruguay	409	Austria	506	Mexico	415
Czech Republic	499	Costa Rica	407	Belgium	505	Montenegro	410
France	495	Albania	394	Latvia	502	Jordan	409
United Kingdom	494	Brazil	391	France	499	Argentina	406
Iceland	493	Argentina	388	Denmark	498	Brazil	405
Latvia	491	Tunisia	388	**United States**	**497**	Colombia	399
Luxembourg	490	Jordan	388	Spain	496	Tunisia	398
Norway	489	Colombia	376	Lithuania	496	Albania	397
Portugal	487	Qater	376	Norway	495	Qatar	384
Italy	485	Indonesia	375	Italy	494	Indonesia	382
Spain	484	Peru	368	Hungary	494	Peru	373

SOURCE: DeSilver, 2015.

educational achievement in the United States, researchers with the McKinsey consulting company concluded that:

> *The underutilization of human potential as reflected in the achievement gap is extremely costly. Existing gaps impose the economic equivalent of a permanent national recession— one substantially larger than the deep recession the country is currently experiencing. For individuals, avoidable shortfalls in academic achievement impose heavy and often tragic consequences via lower earnings, poor health, and higher rates of incarceration.*

> (McKinsey and Company, 2010)

EDUCATION IN DEVELOPING NATIONS   Most children around the world do not share in the educational successes noted above. Instead, at best they attend crowded, underfunded schools with teachers who may have little education themselves. Students' attendance may be sporadic, they may have few books for their lessons, and they often quit school after a short number of years because of the long travel distance

Figure 11–8 Math Proficiency Slowly Growing Among U.S. Fourth and Eighth Grade Students 1990 and 2013

SOURCE: DeSilver, 2015.

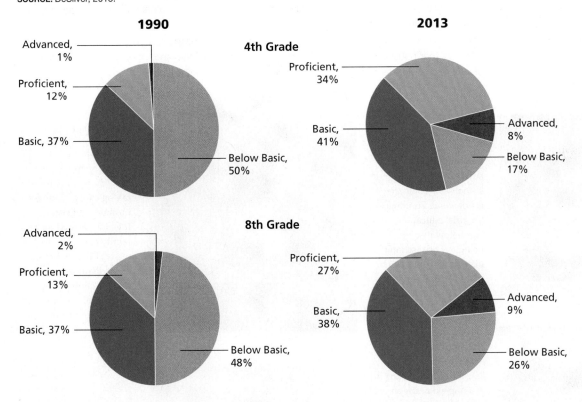

from home, the cost of school, or because they are needed to work at home. For example, in Afghanistan, only 21 percent of girls and 55 percent of the boys complete primary school, as do only 34 percent of girls and 55 percent of boys in Niger (Population Reference Bureau, 2015).

Current Social Problems in Education

11.5 Discuss some of the current social problems facing schools.

There are many contentious issues in education. In the following section, you will read about a few of these, such as the need for quality preschool and early childhood education programs; the growing problem of school violence and issues surrounding it; educational biases based on sex and gender; and issues surrounding school choice.

Preschool and Early Childhood Education

Thomas is a high-spirited 4-year-old who lives with his mother, father, and 2-year-old sister. He is happy, healthy, and very much loved by his family. He and his sister have a playroom of toys, including many books, puzzles, and interactive videos. His mother and father read to Thomas daily, knowing that this activity will increase his vocabulary and help him learn to read. Thomas has been attending a preschool five mornings a week for almost two years. He knows his alphabet, can sound out letters and count to 100, and he can do simple addition such as 2+2. When he begins kindergarten next year, he will have a smooth transition because he likes school, is eager to learn, and already has mastered a strong foundation.

Bobby is a high-spirited 4-year-old who lives with his mother, father, and 2-year-old sister. He is happy, healthy, and very much loved by his family. His family is poor, so Bobby has only a few toys, and many of them are broken or have pieces that

Slide Show

Education for Girls

Globally, girls are often absent from schools. The local culture, religious customs, or economic circumstances may contribute to the opinion that education for girls is unnecessary. Some parents may see it as a waste of time and money, since their daughter will marry young and move to another household. In other regions, education for girls is viewed as dangerous and a threat to "normal" family functioning. Educated girls may start making demands for change. In other regions, educating girls is considered immoral and is in contrast to religious views about right and wrong. But often, the reason comes down to simple economics. Families need the labor of girls. The slideshow provides insight about girls and education in the developing world.

In many countries girls and boys attend separate schools. But separate is not equal. Funding for girls' education lags below that spent on boys. Girls' schools may close to maintain a higher educational standard for boys.

Some girls are not able to go to school because they are busy taking care of younger brothers and sisters. It is not unusual for a family to contain five or six children, a result of inadequate access to birth control and traditional customs that promote large families as beneficial.

Many communities in developing nations lack access to clean drinking water. Family members, usually girls and women, often spend nearly an entire day walking to a water source and walking back home carrying up to 50 pounds on their backs, only to do it again later that day. In addition to keeping them out of school, the walk for water also makes the girls and women vulnerable to predators, both animal and human. Girls are raped on their way to and from their water source.

Some girls do not go to school because they are expected to earn money for their family. They may be required to beg on the street, to steal from shop vendors, or to sell themselves sexually to men. Girls are considered valuable only insofar as what resources they can bring to the family.

Girls and women work very hard in developing nations. This 8-year-old girl already is responsible for gathering firewood for her family. This task takes up much of her day because firewood is used for cooking, bathing, and boiling drinking water. Meanwhile, her younger sister helps her mother clean the house while her two older brothers are at school.

Critical Thinking

Reflecting on the four themes of this text—the importance of using an empirical approach, linking individual experiences with social structure, understanding that social inequality contributes to social problems, and acknowledging that understanding social problems requires a comparative perspective—devise a program in the developing world to help girls attend school. What social, personal, economic, and political factors must be addressed?

have been lost. Neither his mother nor his father read well, and therefore there are no books around the house and neither parent cares much for going to the library across town. Bobby has never been to preschool because his parents cannot afford it. He has been taught the alphabet song, but he does not yet know that it describes letters, nor does he know what letters actually are. He can count to ten, but stumbles after that. He heard that he will begin kindergarten next year, but he is nervous about that because he's never been away from his mother for long periods. He cries at the thought of leaving home.

While ideological controversies have swirled around education in elementary and secondary schools, more pragmatic policies have been developed and tested at the preschool level. **Head Start**, the federally funded preschool program for poor children, and other early-education programs have grown in importance, especially since evidence of their effectiveness in addressing the needs of children from low-income families has accumulated. Evaluations consistently show that children in such programs make gains that continue throughout their later school years and beyond. Head Start offers poor families a comprehensive program that would provide health and nutritional services to preschool children while also developing their cognitive skills and engaging parents (Head Start, 2015). In addition, educational programs for parents are usually included. Many programs are integrated to include children with special physical or cognitive needs.

Head Start
The federally funded preschool program for children from low-income families.

Measuring Head Start's actual success is not a simple matter. Head Start is said to save taxpayers' money because attendees are more likely to improve their academic skills, graduate from high school, and get a job than their peers who did not attend Head Start. Attendees are also healthier and receive preventative medical and dental checkups, also saving taxpayer money (Deming, 2009; Lumeng et al., 2015; Zhai, Brooks-Gunn, and Waldfogel, 2011). The price tag? Over $8.5 billion in 2014 (Head Start, 2015). Not surprisingly, the amount of funding for Head Start is a very polarized issue politically because precise long-term benefits are impossible to gauge.

The United States ranks below almost all the advanced economies of the European Economic Union in funding for early-childhood education. In 2010, the Obama administration signaled its intention to stimulate funding and innovations for a variety of early-childhood education initiatives. The Department of Housing and Urban Development, for example, announced that it would reward applicants for housing renewal grants with additional funds if they also partnered with early-education programs to provide new opportunities to increase their enrollment or begin new programs in low-income neighborhoods. In doing so, the administration's education experts were affirming what the research shows: Early education is a key element in preventing educational deficits, not only among children from disadvantaged backgrounds but also for all children.

Early childhood education and care (ECEC) has become an important issue in many parts of the world because of the rise in labor force participation of mothers, the push for single mothers to work rather than receive public aid, and a growing interest in ensuring that all children begin elementary school with basic skills are ready to learn (Clearinghouse on International Developments in Child, Youth, and Family Policies, 2005). ECEC programs enhance and support children's cognitive, social, and emotional development.

A 3-year study of 12 developed nations compared the availability and structure of ECEC programs. Several interesting points were noted. To begin with, access to ECEC is a statutory right in all countries except the United States. Although compulsory school begins at ages 6 or 7, ECEC availability begins at age one year in Denmark, Finland, and Sweden (after generous maternity and family leave benefits are exhausted); at age 2.5 years in Belgium; at age 3 years in Italy and Germany; and at age 4 years in Britain. Most countries have full coverage of education for 3- to 6-year-olds.

A Global View

Raising My Children in France

My sister and I were born and raised in France, but she moved to the United States for college, met an American who she later married, and now has two children. In contrast, I went to university here in France, later married a native Frenchman, and also have two children, roughly the same age. Although I am separated from my sister by thousands of miles, Skype allows us to share the ups and downs of parenting on a weekly basis. What a difference we are having raising our children!

Each time after I had my babies, my employer gave me four months off, completely paid, so that I could stay at home to bond. A newborn turns your world upside down, so I appreciated this time at home with him. We could sleep, eat, relax, and play whenever we needed to and not have to worry about getting on a tight schedule while I went back to work right away. Law in France requires maternity leave, so every woman has 16 weeks of paid time off. I then decided to stay home for another two months without any pay, and my job was held for me.

France also provides a helper to come to the house for two weeks after a baby is born to check on us and help us out. My helper did the laundry for me and cooked some meals. She also watched the baby so I could go for a walk and have some quiet time, or have lunch with friends. This service was all free.

When my baby was 6 weeks old, I could take him to a childcare center and they would watch him for a very small charge, the equivalent of about a dollar an hour. Since I wasn't yet back to work, I usually just took him there for a couple of hours a day so that I could go to the gym or run my errands. However, after 6 months, I went back to work full-time, and he stayed there from 8:00 until 5:30, and, again,

it was just a nominal charge. I felt that he was in good care because all the childcare workers have a university degree and seem to love their jobs. They are paid well. Also, my husband and I receive a Family Allowance from the government for my child, and that helps with incidental costs. Three years later when I had my second baby, my Family Allowance was even higher.

At the same time, I watched my sister in the United States when she had her baby, and her experience was very different. She had only 6 weeks off of work and it was completely unpaid other than some saved up vacation pay. How can you heal and bond with a new baby in only 6 weeks? She said that legally she could have taken up to 12 weeks off, but since it was all unpaid, she could not afford it. She also had no helper. I think it would be lonely and very difficult to handle a brand new baby all by yourself. When she went back to work after 6 weeks, she had to pay over a thousand dollars a month for childcare! My sister also does not get a Family Allowance from her government. Wow, in France, we think of children as a benefit to our entire society, so the government gives us a little money to offset the costs of raising them. I don't know; I guess the United States doesn't see it that way.

—Sylvie, Age 32

Critical Thinking

The French government provides many services to new parents that are paid for by taxes. Would Americans be willing to pay for higher taxes to provide these services? Why or why not? Are there specific groups of Americans that might be more or less likely to support these types of services? Are children a "public" good? Why or why not?

In contrast, in the United States there is no statutory entitlement until ages 5 to 7, depending on the state. Access to publicly funded ECEC programs such as the Head Start program is generally restricted to at-risk children, usually defined as poor or near-poor. Furthermore, the demand for these programs among vulnerable groups far outstrips their availability.

In most of the 12 countries reviewed, government pays the largest share of the costs, with parents covering only 25–30 percent. Countries may also make arrangements for sliding-scale payments for low-income families to help make programs affordable. Most countries require staff to complete at least three years of training at universities or other institutes of higher education. Their earnings reflect their levels of education. The box, A Global View: Raising My Children in France, describes the French way of delivering early childhood education.

In contrast, U.S. parents pay an average of 60–80 percent of ECEC costs. Some of these costs can be recouped through tax benefits, but many low-income families find the tax system confusing and therefore end up using informal or unregulated childcare. In the United States, there is also no agreed-on set of qualifications for staff. Their status and pay are low, and turnover is high. Other countries make a clear investment in their ECEC. Denmark devotes 2 percent of its gross domestic product (GDP), with Sweden and

Norway close behind. In contrast, the United States devotes less than half of 1 percent of its GDP to early childhood services (Clearinghouse on International Developments in Child, Youth, and Family Policies, 2005). Ironically, the United States is a leader in research on child development, but has not developed the programs that research suggests are needed and that are increasingly available in other developed nations.

Bilingual/Bicultural Education

Over 4 million children participate in English Language Learner programs in school each year (Kena et al., 2014). The states with the largest number of English Language Learners are California, Texas, Florida, New York, and Illinois (National Center for Education Statistics, 2014d). The desirability of teaching non-English-speaking pupils in their native language is a subject of intense debate, particularly in California and other states with large Hispanic populations. On one side are those who believe that preserving the language and culture of minority groups is a worthwhile, even necessary, goal of public education. On the other side are those who believe that minority students must be "immersed" in English-language instruction if they are to be prepared to compete effectively in American society.

Bilingual education has a long history in this country, and it was used to help immigrants learn English in the nineteenth century (National Association for Bilingual Education, 2014). In 1839, Ohio was the first state to pass a law requiring bilingual education if parents requested it from the schools. Many other states and communities gradually followed suit. In 1968, the U.S. Congress passed Title VII of the Elementary and Secondary Education Act, known informally as "the Bilingual Education Act," which mandated bilingual education to give immigrants access to education in their "first" language. Federal spending on bilingual education jumped from only $7.5 million in 1968 before the law was passed to $150 million by 1979 (Frum, 2000).

Bilingual education was implemented in all needed schools by the 1970s and 1980s by teaching children primarily or even exclusively in their native language and then transitioning at some point in elementary school to English-only instruction. Proponents argue that the more schools develop children's native-language skills, especially in reading, the higher the children score academically over the long term in English (August and Shanahan, 2006). It may sound counterintuitive, but they claim that proficiency in a second language does not develop separately in the brain, but

What Do You Think?

Respond to the person who says, "Why should I pay higher taxes to pay for you to educate your young child? S/he is *your* child, therefore you should pay for his or her early education yourself."

Many students come to school with limited or no English skills. What is the best way to integrate them into the school and teach them English? This issue is an important one because of the large number of immigrants from Mexico, Central America, and Asia.

builds on the proficiency of the native language (National Association for Bilingual Education, 2014).

Parents and teachers who believe bilingual education is helpful in keeping their children from falling behind in substantive fields such as math and science face intense pressure from those in the growing English-only movement. Since the 1990s, the political tide has shifted, and many people now wish to eliminate any use of other languages in government, schools (other than specific world language classes), and other public institutions. They argue that bilingual education programs are expensive, that native language instruction interferes with or delays English development, and that these programs segregate children to a second-class status (Rossell and Baker, 1996).

Several states, including California, Massachusetts, and Arizona, have enacted policies to greatly curb bilingual education, and federal policies now restrict the amount of time children can be taught in their native language (Slavin et al., 2010). Often, the discussion deteriorates into political attacks, with opponents arguing that bilingual education threatens our national identity, divides us along ethnic lines, and sends the message to immigrants that they can live in the United States without learning English. In Arizona in 2010, this reasoning allowed Arizona's legislature to ban ethnic studies classes in high school. However, recent careful research on how students with limited English proficiency can best learn English while keeping up with their other studies indicates that bilingual programs in the early grades, and instruction in English as a second language in the primary and middle grades, result in the highest levels of achievement by non-English-speaking students (Genesee et al., 2005).

The Bush administration's No Child Left Behind initiative insists that all students, regardless of their native language or how recent their arrival in U.S. classrooms, must take the standardized proficiency tests. These test scores must be included in calculating school performance scores. This requirement has placed even more pressure on school districts, many of which have increasing numbers of non-English-speaking children registering each year, to create special programs, including bilingual classes and intensive English instruction for nonnative speakers.

School Violence

In December 2012, a young man walked into Sandy Hook Elementary School in Newtown, Connecticut and gunned down 20 children ages 6 and 7, and 6 school faculty and staff, before committing suicide. Investigating police later found the shooter's mother dead from a gunshot wound. The final count was 28 dead, including the shooter.

Sandy Hook brought school violence into homes throughout the world. Yet, this tragedy was only one of a series of devastating episodes of violence; the story continued into schools in Nevada, Colorado, Oregon, Washington, and elsewhere. These senseless acts add to the already long list of violent events within our schools that have shaken Americans' confidence in the security of their children in schools once thought to be safe havens for learning and social development.

To explain why extremely violent episodes are occurring in schools, social scientists and others have cited, among many possible causes: (a) violence in the media; (b) access to guns and other lethal weapons; (c) harassment of students who are nonconformists; (d) the influence of religious cults and "outsider" groups; (e) low self-esteem brought on by social isolation; and (f) the failure of parents to supervise their children.

Although the most extreme forms of school violence grab the media attention, smaller but insidious types of violence such as bullying or fistfights are far more common. Fortunately, most of these types of violence are on the decline, as shown in Table 11–5. In a nationally representative 2013 sample of youth in grades 9–12, 8 percent reported being in a physical fight on school property in the 12 months before the survey, 7 percent reported that they did not go to school at least once in the 30 days

Table 11–5 Trends in Violent Behaviors on School Property: National Youth Risk Behavior Survey, 1993–2013

	1993	1997	2001	2005	2009	2013
Carried a weapon on school property (such as a gun, knife, or club at least once during the 30 days before the survey)						
	12%	9%	6%	7%	6%	5%
Were threatened or injured with a weapon on school property (such as a gun, knife, or club at least once during the 12 months before the survey)						
	7%	7%	10%	8%	8%	7%
Were in a physical fight on school property (at least once during the 12 months before the survey)						
	16%	15%	13%	14%	11%	8%
Did not go to school because they felt unsafe at school or on their way to or from school (at least once during the 30 days before the survey)						
	4%	4%	7%	6%	5%	7%
Were bullied on school property (during 12 months before the survey)						
	-	-	-	-	20%	20%

SOURCE: Centers for Disease Control and Prevention, 2014.

before the survey because they felt unsafe either at school or on their way to or from school, 5 percent reported carrying a weapon (gun, knife, or club) to school at least once in the 30 days before the survey, 7 percent reported being threatened or injured with a weapon on school property at least once in the 12 months before the survey, and 20 percent reported being bullied on school property (Centers for Disease Control and Prevention, 2014). Although these common forms of violence are on the decline, the number of students who did not go to school because they felt unsafe is on the rise.

Solutions such as installing metal detectors and hiring additional security guards have been attempted, and these measures may help prevent violence by outsiders, but they do not convey authority to teachers. Educators are searching for ways to empower teachers. Several possibilities have been suggested: creating smaller high schools, or "schools within schools"; expecting more from students than mere attendance; and encouraging dropouts to return to school as adults. The last suggestion is especially attractive because adult high school students often become role models for younger students, and their presence tends to reduce the amount of disorder in the schools they attend.

School Choice

Efforts to create smaller schools, schools with special approaches to learning, or schools that promote a particular religious orientation invariably become entangled in the ongoing debate over school choice. People who are dissatisfied with the public schools or seek special educational opportunities for their children are often attracted to proposals for expanding the array of parental choices, including parochial and secular private schools.

CHARTER SCHOOLS Members of the movement for smaller schools often advocate the creation of special schools, known as charter schools, which are innovative in their use of resources and yet are funded as public schools. As choices within the public school system widens, they argue, there will be more pressure on the conventional schools to become more competitive and to improve their educational methods.

Nationwide, there are about 5,700 charter schools are in operation, serving 2.1 million students (National Center for Education Statistics, 2014a, Table 216-20). California has the largest number of charter school students (about 430,000), representing 7 percent of students in the state. About two-thirds of charter school students are racial or ethnic minorities, and over half qualify for reduced or free school lunches.

While most students in charter schools do not perform better than other students, on average, there are important exceptions. The Knowledge Is Power Program (KIPP) Academy educates 200 middle-school students, mostly poor black and Latino children, and has the highest test scores in the Bronx, New York. To achieve these impressive results, students attend school for nine-and-a-half hours a day, including Saturdays and throughout the summer, and get two hours of homework a night.

Most charter schools are small, with fewer than 300 students, and they are most often found in the western or southern United States (National Center for Education Statistics, 2014c, Table 216-30). Charter schools are usually units of a local school system, but each charter school reflects its founders' educational philosophies, programs, and organizational structures.

Recent research sponsored by the federal government based on fourth-grade students found that students in charter schools do not perform measurably better on reading and math tests than do students in noncharter public schools with similar student populations. And among disadvantaged students—that is, students who are eligible for a free or reduced-price lunch—fourth graders in charter schools did not score as high in reading or mathematics, on average, as fourth graders in other public schools (National Center for Education Statistics, 2014c). These results are disappointing for advocates of charter schools, but the demand for greater school choice and parents' desire for alternatives to some of the public schools in their communities will continue to stimulate the growth of charter schools and other alternatives to public schooling, such as homeschooling.

SCHOOL VOUCHERS   Proponents of school vouchers ask that parents be allowed to choose among public and private schools that offer all kinds of educational options. The theory is that increased competition among schools to attract students would improve the schools' efficiency or cost-effectiveness while stimulating a more open market for educational practices. The main criticism of voucher plans is that they are likely to be used most effectively by more highly educated and affluent parents, leaving the poorer public schools to less well-equipped parents; this possibility would worsen the existing situation of stratification and inequality in education.

An alternative to school vouchers is reform of the property tax system for funding schools in the United States. Most public school systems are funded through a levy on residential property known as the school tax. In municipalities throughout the nation, property owners have become increasingly loath to pay higher taxes on their homes to fund increases in teachers' pay or improvements in the local schools. In large cities, where revenues from property taxes are lower, this system is largely responsible for inequities in funding between suburban and urban schools and explains why urban schools often lack the art, music, athletic, and science programs usually found in suburban schools. In the past, state education budgets were used to offset these differences, but as states cut back on public spending, the schools in poorer central-city communities suffer inordinately.

HOMESCHOOLING   Homeschoolers are students whose parents report that their children are taught at home rather than in a public or private school. Although many parents in the homeschooling movement are motivated by religious principles and want to include specific religious instruction in their teaching, or wish to avoid the secular aspects of public schooling, many others simply believe that they can do a better job teaching their children than the schools can or wish to emphasize specific language or other skills in their home teaching. Approximately 1.7 million students were being homeschooled in the United States in 2012, an increase from the estimated 850,000 students who were being homeschooled in the spring of 1999 (National Center for Education Statistics, 2003; 2014b, Table 7).

Students who are homeschooled perform as well, if not better, on average than those graduating from public schools. Critics of the movement often argue, however, that while withdrawing students from the public schools may be a good solution to what parents perceive as problems of those schools, homeschooling also takes students out of the school community, perhaps to the detriment of that community, which loses access to the students' talents (and tax dollars). For their part, homeschooling parents argue that their children should be allowed to play on local public school teams and to use other school resources. Some school districts have complied with these requests. Homeschooling is facilitated by the wealth of educational materials and resources now available on the Internet (Clements, 2004).

Sex and Gender Influences in Schooling

Girls do better in school than boys and complete more years of education. For example, from primary school through college, girls average higher grades on all subjects, including math and science. This difference is not just a recent phenomenon, and it occurs in many countries, not just the United States. A large meta-analysis of 369 different studies published between 1914 and 2011 examined the academic grades of over one million boys and girls in more than 30 countries. The analysis found that girls earn higher grades in every subject, even the science-related fields where boys are assumed to surpass them, and girls' higher grades have been consistent over time (Voyer and Voyer, 2014). Therefore, the authors of this study suggest that the recent claim of the "boy crisis" with boys suddenly lagging behind girls' achievements is false.

However, what *has* changed in recent years is young women's likelihood of enrolling and graduating from college. For example, in 1994, women and men who had recently graduated from high school were nearly equally likely to enroll in college, at 63 percent and 61 percent, respectively. But today, women have blown past men, and 71 percent of women enroll, whereas the rate for men remains unchanged at 61 percent. The largest increases in women's college enrollment have been among black and Hispanic women (Lopez and Gonzalez-Barrera, 2014).

In addition to attending college, women now are more likely than men to earn college degrees, including advanced degrees. For example, despite constituting about half of the population, women earn about 57 percent of bachelor's degrees, 63 percent of master's degrees, and 53 percent of Ph.D. and professional degrees, such as medical or law degrees.

Why do girls and women perform better in school than boys and men, on average? We can only speculate. Social, cultural, and economic factors likely operate. Some parents assume that boys are smarter and therefore encourage their girls to put more effort into their studies. Differences in studying styles may affect outcomes; research shows that girls tend to study to understand the material, which tends to produce higher grades, whereas boys emphasize the final performance. Structural conditions are also an important consideration (Lopez and Gonzalez-Barrera, 2014). As labor market barriers to women have been lowered, the benefits of a college education are more obvious for women than they might be for men. In contrast, boys' aspirations may be leveled because of their higher incidence of behavioral and disciplinary problems. To help combat this latter issue, President Obama recently announced a new initiative called "My Brother's Keeper" that aims to improve educational attainment and job prospects and to reduce crime among black and Hispanic men.

Women have made great strides in advancing their education. Yet, something is amiss; the fields that men and women study remain segregated. For example, fewer women major in "STEM" fields (science, technology, engineering, and mathematics) that can be quite lucrative financially. Why? Is it simply that women do not want to be engineers, mathematicians, or scientists?

A slew of research studies give us important insights into why women remain poorly represented in STEM fields. Sex and gender bias by schools, teachers, and professors may play a role beginning in elementary school and then continue through

Despite the fact that women earn the majority of college degrees, college majors remain highly segregated by sex. Few men major in fields traditionally held by women, such as social work or nursing, and it remains that few women major in STEM fields, which tend to pay much higher than average wages. Some schools are brainstorming ways to make these fields more attractive to women.

What Do You Think?

Sex biases in education can go both ways. Why do you think that there are so few men in the fields of nursing, social work, and early childhood education?

college (Lavy and Sand, 2015). One recent study using data from the National Education Longitudinal Study found that high schools with highly gendered extracurricular activities (e.g., sports, clubs) had fewer girls enroll in STEM education programs (Legewie and DiPrete, 2014).

Another study examined the opinions of college science faculty toward women in STEM fields. Yale researchers contacted professors in physics, chemistry, and biology at six major research universities (both public and private) and asked them to evaluate an application (fake) from a recent graduate seeking a position as a laboratory manager. All professors received a one-page application from a candidate who was designed to be "promising," although not particularly stellar. Half of the applications were listed as being from "John," while the other half were from "Jennifer." On a scale of 1 to 7, with 7 being the highest, the professors gave John an average score of 4 for competence, while Jennifer received only a 3.3. The professors described John more favorably as someone they might hire for their labs or would be willing to mentor. They also offered John a starting salary that was 15 percent higher than that offered to Jennifer (Moss-Racusin et al., 2012). Remember, these applications were identical.

Should it surprise us that faculty evaluate the applications differently? Sex and gender biases permeate all aspects of our society, including education. In fact, in an interesting twist that looks not at how faculty evaluate students, but rather *how students evaluate faculty*, this bias is clear. A researcher examined 14 million comments on the website "Rate My Professor" in 25 different disciplines in the Humanities, Social Sciences, Physical Sciences, and STEM fields (Schmidt, 2015). He found that students in all disciplines were far more likely to say that male professors, as compared with female professors, were "brilliant," "smart," "intellectual," "knowledgeable," "important," "funny," "interesting," and students referred to them as "professor." Meanwhile, female professors were more often referred to as "biased," "unfair," "moody," "unhappy," "strict," having "busywork," and were called "teacher." To female professors' credit, they were also described more often as "friendly," "helpful," "caring," and "nice," although they were also more likely to be described as the opposite of these: "unfriendly," "unhelpful," "uncaring," and "mean." Clearly, students tend to focus on female professors' interpersonal skills, and think less of their brilliance or intellect.

Access to Higher Education

The rising cost of college tuition threatens access to public state universities. Taxpayer support for public universities has fallen precipitously over the last several decades and legislators look to tuition, grant funding, and private donations to make up the difference. Several prominent university presidents have stated that the decline amounts to privatization of the institutions that played a crucial role in the creation of the American middle class. During the years after World War II, the United States built the world's greatest system of public higher education. "We're now in the process of dismantling all that," said John D. Wiley, chancellor of the University of Wisconsin–Madison.

He has a point. The share of all public universities' revenues derived from state and local taxes declined to 53 percent in 2013 from 74 percent in 1991. These changes translate into significantly higher tuition costs for students and their parents. Tuition has increased by 28 percent since the 2007–08 school year, even after adjusting for inflation (Mitchell, Palacios, and Leachman, 2014). The decline in government spending on higher education is also responsible for drastic spending cuts at colleges and universities that may diminish the quality of education available to students at a time when a highly educated workforce is more crucial than ever to the nation's economic future. For example, many public colleges and universities have cut faculty positions, eliminated course offerings, increased class sizes, closed campuses, shut computer labs, decreased the number of advisors and student support staff, and reduced library services.

As the recession lifts, some states are reinvesting in higher education once more, although only barely. Eight states are still cutting their appropriations, and in all states except Alaska and South Dakota, higher education funding remains well below pre-recession levels. In fact, per-student funding in Arizona, Louisiana, and South Carolina is down by more than 40 percent since the start of the recession, as shown in Figure 11–9 (Mitchell, Palacios, and Leachman, 2014).

As tuition has soared at public state universities, financial aid has grown, too, although it does not meet the demand. Between the 2007–08 and 2012–13 school years, **Pell Grants**—the nation's primary student grant aid program—more than doubled from $16 billion to nearly $33 billion (College Board, 2013). This funding boost allowed the program to reach a greater number of students and to provide the average recipient with more funding to offset tuition costs and living expenses. However, because tuition varies so much from one state to the other, and the Pell Grant does not, many students in those states with higher tuition found college to be simply unaffordable. In the 1980s, the Pell Grant covered more than half of the cost of a four-year degree from a public college; today, it covers less than a third of that cost (Mayotte, 2014).

Pell Grants

The nation's primary student grant aid program.

Students' families may try to chip in for the cost of college, but incomes have not risen significantly in recent years while tuition has skyrocketed, so families cannot easily absorb these costs. The bottom line is (Mitchell, Palacios, and Leachman, 2014; Valle, Normandeau, and González, 2015):

- *More students are working and going to school part-time,* which prolongs their schooling and delays entry into their career of choice, often at considerable hardship.
- *Students are taking on greater debt.* The average student now owes over $14,000 in student loans by the time he or she graduates.
- *College dropout rates are increasing* as students find they cannot continue to pay tuition costs.

Figure 11–9 Percent Reduction in Higher Education Spending Since the Recession

SOURCE: Mitchell, Palacios, and Leachman, 2014.

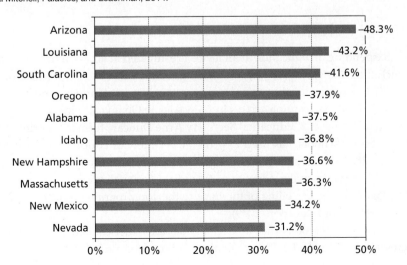

Tuition costs have soared at both private and public universities. Yet, college remains attractive because graduates earn significantly more than do those who have not graduated from college. This photo of Vanderbilt University shows the allure of the college environment.

- *Tuition costs are keeping some students from enrolling, particularly low-income students.* Young people with family incomes in the top 25 percent of incomes (the top quartile) go to four-year colleges at almost twice the rate of equally qualified students from the bottom quartile.

President Obama has taken significant steps toward making all college education more affordable and has expressed particularly strong support for the nation's system of community colleges. In 2010, he signed legislation that ends the bank-based lending system for student loans and pours tens of billions of federal dollars into higher education. At the signing ceremony, held at Northern Virginia Community College, the president also announced that Jill Biden, the wife of Vice President Joseph R. Biden, Jr., and an English instructor at the college, would lead a community college conference at the White House. The president brought the community colleges to national attention during 2009 when he called on them to produce 5 million more graduates by 2020 and proposed a $12 billion plan to improve and expand these educational institutions. In 2015, he proposed a system of free community college tuition to qualifying students.

Social Policy

11.6 Assess the policy issues surrounding early child education for the poor and the Race to the Top educational program.

The public school is the nation's largest educational institution, offering basic education to the greatest number of children. Of all American social institutions, education may be the easiest to change through social policy, if only people could agree on what they want schools to do. Those who believe American society has become too secular may advocate prayer in the schools. Others, who believe that schools have a responsibility to steer children away from the dangers of AIDS or early pregnancy, may advocate more thorough sex education. Still others, who lament the supposed failure of the schools to produce adequately trained students, may come up with proposals for educational reform. Here we discuss President Obama's signature educational program, Race to the Top.

K–12 Race to the Top

Total U.S. spending on education at all levels is estimated at almost a trillion dollars in 2015, including from federal, state, and local governments (USGovernmentSpending.com, 2015). Consequently, the government exerts a powerful influence on how education is carried out. An example of this influence is the Obama administration's Race to the Top Fund, which U.S. Education Secretary Arne Duncan, former superintendent of Chicago's public schools, has used to promote a variety of education reforms among the states. "It's time to stop just talking about education reform and start actually doing it. It's time to make education America's national mission," said President Barack Obama, at the unveiling of the Race to the Top program on November 4, 2009 (U.S. Department of Education, 2009).

President Obama took office at a time when the American education system was at a crossroads. The No Child Left Behind Act, created under President George W.

Bush, focused on issues like accountability and equity for all students, highlighting achievement gaps. The federal No Child Left Behind Act placed heavy stress on achieving its goals through standardized tests in the primary grades. Schools that fall behind national or state averages can be penalized by losing motivated parents and their children, who may be offered voucher incentives to choose other schools. The legislation had unintended and unfortunate consequences, such as creating incentives for states to lower standards, mandating one-size-fits-all remedies, and putting standardized testing ahead of a well-rounded curriculum.

Starting with its signature education reform initiative—Race to the Top—the Obama administration set a new agenda that put state-level innovation at center stage. The Race to the Top Fund set aside over $4 billion in federal education dollars to award states that come up with comprehensive plans for school reform. States take center stage. Race to the Top asks states to submit their best ideas on raising standards to prepare all students for college and careers, investing in America's teachers and school leaders, turning around the lowest-performing schools, and using data to inform support for educators and decision making (White House and U.S. Department of Education, 2014).

These reforms must include, among other innovations, greater school choice, including more charter schools, progress toward implementing national student performance standards and performance-based teacher evaluations, and acceptance of the plans by state teachers' unions (U.S. Department of Education, 2009).

In the Fund's first year, 40 states submitted applications; only Delaware and Tennessee were declared winners. Most of the other states decided to reapply, and in the second round of the "race," many more states won major funding for their reform plans. However, Indiana opted out when its education leadership received insufficient support from teachers' unions. Virginia dropped out because its officials did not want to adopt a set of common standards in English language arts and math. Although some critics see this approach as overly manipulative, most educators agree that Race to the Top is quickly becoming one of the most successful federal education programs ever (Carey, 2010).

Future Prospects

Current trends in educational policy include efforts to improve the quality of public school teaching; create more innovative and engaging programs, especially in the realm of STEM; and eliminate biases so that all students can arrive at kindergarten school-ready and continue to thrive in school regardless of their income, race or ethnic background, sex, and level of physical and mental abilities. Throughout this book you have seen many instances of the importance of education in a technologically advanced and rapidly changing society. But if education is to meet the challenges facing it and if young people are to seriously consider teaching as a vocation, then increased funding is necessary. The state initiatives developed out of the Race to the Top program can offer keen insights into creative programs for the future.

Going Beyond Left and Right

So many hopes are pinned on education, and schools are asked to do so many things to assist in the socialization of the young—from teaching them the "basics" to providing physical and moral education of all kinds—that it is little wonder that education is such a contested area of life in democratic societies. There are, however, some areas of convergence between people on the left and right sides of the debate over school reform. For example, there is increasing consensus that schools need to raise their standards, although as yet there is little consensus about whether the federal or state governments should be the proper enforcers and monitors of these standards. Also, those on the left and the right generally agree that more universal access to higher education is necessary if Americans are to cope with changing economic and technological conditions. But again, as yet there is no consensus on how to fund either elementary education or public colleges and universities. People of all ideological persuasions are seeking alternatives to the inadequate property tax system for funding the schools, and in time we may indeed see political, if not ideological, agreement on pragmatic means to fund the education that our society's students will need in coming decades.

Classroom size is an example of an educational issue that must be addressed through funding, which, in turn, depends on a consensus that the problem needs to be addressed in the first place. In the United States, suburban schools average about 19 students per classroom in the early high school years, while inner-city schools average about 30 students per classroom. Once they become aware of these disparities, people of all political persuasions tend to conclude that this inequality is unfair and are more willing to agree that funds should be invested to balance classroom size in all the nation's schools.

Summary

- In early U.S. history, boys and girls usually learned what they needed to know at home or on the family farm. To help unite the nation after the Revolutionary War, educators created textbooks to standardize spelling and pronunciation and to unify cultural and political views such as patriotism, religion, and distrust of Native Americans. It took until the mid-1800s for people to begin calling for free and compulsory elementary and secondary education, and another 50 years for it to become the law.

- Functionalists view education as an important social institution because it can lead to the smooth functioning of society. They see education as providing individuals with opportunities for work, fulfillment, and upward social mobility. Conflict theorists emphasize how education perpetuates social inequality and supports the status quo. Interactionists see education as a vital part of socialization and, therefore, tend to focus on the dynamics of the school or classroom and the interactions between students and teachers, between teachers and administrators, or among students themselves.

- Today, ever-greater proportions of U.S. students are finishing high school and going on to college. Nonetheless, much work remains in helping young people to finish high school and in encouraging them to attend college. For members of minority groups, these educational issues continue to be especially pressing. People with higher levels of education tend to earn significantly more money than those with less education.

- There are many contentious issues in education. This chapter discussed a few of them, including the need for quality preschool and early childhood education programs, the growing problem of school violence, issues surrounding school choice, biases based on sex and gender, and declining access to higher education.

- Of all American social institutions, education is most subject to intentional change through social policy. This chapter discussed two important educational programs. Head Start is a program designed to intervene on behalf of poor preschoolers and their parents. The Race to the Top Fund awards states that come up with comprehensive plans for school reform. It asks states to submit their best ideas on raising standards to prepare all students for college and careers, investing in America's teachers and school leaders, turning around the lowest-performing schools, and using data to inform support for educators and decision making.

Chapter 12
Problems of Work and the Economy

 ## Learning Objectives

12.1 Compare and contrast Americans' subjective views on the economy with the objective data.

12.2 Describe the principles underlying key trends in the American system of free enterprise.

12.3 Identify the consequences of global markets and corporate power.

12.4 Assess the consequences of globalization for the American worker.

12.5 Evaluate the problems associated with work today.

12.6 Explain the importance of consumerism, credit, and debt in American society.

12.7 Construct an argument about why the minimum wage should be raised.

I climb and inspect cellular phone towers for a living. This means that I climb up a cell tower, maybe 400 feet in the air and do maintenance like changing out transmission lines or antennas or even just fixing light bulbs on the tower, that sort of thing. It's a good job. I made almost $50,000 last year, but I work pretty long hours too—usually 55 or 60 hours a week. Being up that high takes some getting used to. I've seen new hires say how they are mountain climbers and not scared of heights, and then they don't last a day because they can't do it. It's different. When you climb a mountain, you have it in front of you, but when you climb a tower, you can see right through it and everything below you. That can take some getting used to, especially in the winter when it's cold, wet, and sometimes windy. I swear it's ten times colder up there than on the ground. No thunder though; we aren't allowed to climb in the thunder. I've been doing this for a few years now, but last year, we had to have some new training on account of the number of guys falling. OSHA (Occupational Safety and Health Administration) has been spreading the word that 13 workers died in 2013. I knew one of the guys; it was a real shame. He had a wife and two kids. I heard that four more people died in the first few weeks of 2014. OSHA said we weren't properly trained. Maybe. I think it all depends on the specific carrier because they're all pretty different.

Because people work for so much of their lives, it is important to understand the social problems related to work and the economy, and how these problems affect our health and well-being. So far, the twenty-first century has been a tumultuous time for the United States economically (Eichengreen, 2015; Mian and Sufi, 2014; Wolf, 2014). During the first 15 years of the new century, there were a major terrorist attack, a housing foreclosure disaster, a severe economic recession, near record-high unemployment, and a significant downturn in the U.S. stock market. Household net worth dropped by more than $10 trillion during the recession—the largest loss of wealth since the federal government started keeping records of wealth accumulation 50 years ago (Jacobsen and Mather, 2010). Globally, there were areas of growth in China and India, but economies in Europe, Japan, and elsewhere sputtered, while in the United States an anemic job market left millions of job seekers and discouraged workers without much hope of finding good jobs.

Despite the worst economic times since the Great Depression, however, there has been significant growth and renewed economic activity in the past few years. Are these hopeful signs enough to inspire confidence? How do Americans feel about the economy?

Americans' Views on the Economy

12.1 Compare and contrast Americans' subjective views on the economy with the objective data.

When a 2015 Gallup Poll was conducted with a nationally representative sample of adults asking them to identify the most serious problem facing America, the largest single response was "the economy," chosen by 34 percent of respondents (Gallup, 2015). By way of comparison, however, a 2009 Gallup Poll, taken during the throes of the recession, found that 86 percent of respondents said that the economy was the most serious problem, as illustrated in Figure 12–1. This change in only six years represents a remarkable decline and a growing optimism in the economy. However, the concern over the economy is still considerably higher than it was before the recession. As Figure 12–1 shows, in 2007, before the recession began, only 16 percent of American adults rated the economy as the most important problem. Instead, most people at the time felt that our economy was booming and would continue to do so. The recession, beginning in earnest in 2008–2009, caught many people by surprise.

"The economy," however, is a very broad topic. What precisely are Americans concerned about? Table 12–1 indicates that of those who claim that the economy is the

Figure 12–1 Percentage of Americans Mentioning Economic Issues as the Nation's Most Important Problem, 2007, 2009, 2015

SOURCE: Gallup, 2015.

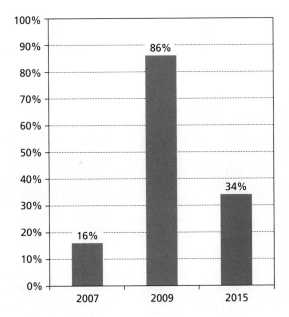

most important problem today, the majority cite "the economy in general," or "unemployment/jobs" as the primary problem (Gallup, 2015). Far fewer refer to the federal debt, the gap between rich and poor, or taxes as the most problematic. This distinction is interesting because national elections often focus on tax issues, yet most Americans do not see taxes as the most serious issue.

Other indicators suggest that Americans are growing more confident in the economy. Figure 12–2 examines the degree of financial worry that people report. These data are from another Gallup Poll, again based on a nationally representative sample of American adults (Saad, 2015). The survey offered a list of seven personal economic issues that many people face, including not having enough money for retirement; not having enough money to pay the medical costs of a serious accident or illness; not being able to maintain the standard of living that they enjoy; not being able to pay medical costs for normal health care; not having enough money to pay monthly bills; not being able to pay their rent, mortgage, or other housing costs; and not being able to pay the minimum amount on their credit cards. Respondents were asked to

Table 12–1 Aspects of the Economy That Are Most Problematic, April 9–12, 2015

What do you think is the most important problem facing this country today?	
ECONOMIC PROBLEMS (NET)	34%
Economy in general	11%
Unemployment/jobs	10%
Federal budget deficit/Federal debt	5%
Gap between rich and poor	3%
Lack of money	2%
Taxes	1%
Wage issues	1%
High cost of living/Inflation	1%

SOURCE: Gallup, 2015.

Figure 12–2 Americans' Financial Worry, 2001–2015

SOURCE: Saad, April 20, 2015.

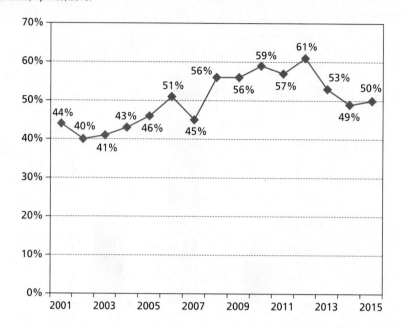

indicate the degree to which they worried about these things. Figure 12–2 shows that 50 percent of adults report being "very" or "moderately" worried about three or more of these financial issues. This proportion represents a decline since the recession, but again, confidence has not yet reached pre-recession levels.

The decline in financial worry is likely related to the fact that fewer Americans feel that their jobs are vulnerable (Riffkin, 2015). Another Gallup Poll asked adults about the likelihood that they would lose their job or be laid off in the next 12 months. As illustrated in Figure 12–3, 13 percent report that it is "very" or "fairly" likely that they would experience job loss, declining substantially from the percentage who were worried about losing their job during the recession. Americans' fear of losing their job has returned to pre-recession levels.

Yet, despite the improved economic outlook of most Americans, not to mention data that show the economy has indeed improved over the past several years, the social class

Figure 12–3 Americans' Concern (Rated as "Very Likely" or "Fairly Likely") for Losing Their Job, 2001–2015

SOURCE: Riffkin, April 23, 2015.

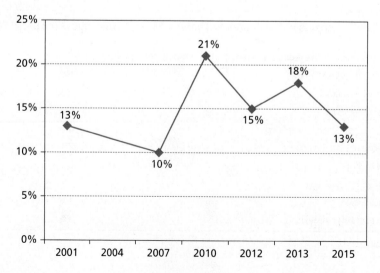

Figure 12–4 Social Class Self-Identification, April 2003, 2008, 2012, 2015

SOURCE: Newport, April 28, 2015.

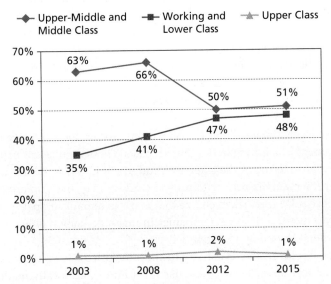

that many Americans assign themselves to has declined (Newport, 2015). As reported in Figure 12–4, the percentage of people who classify themselves as "upper-middle" or "middle" class has declined from 66 percent in 2008 immediately before the recession to only 51 percent in 2015. Correspondingly, those who identify themselves as "working" or "lower" class increased from 41 percent to 48 percent during this period. Many people during the recession dipped into their savings and retirement accounts (or exhausted them), and had trouble paying mortgages and other bills. They are only now beginning to climb out of debt and replenish their savings, and this might explain the decline in self-perceived social class. It will be interesting to watch whether, over the next few years, social class identification eventually begins to trend toward pre-recession levels, as has been the case for the other indicators presented here.

The next few sections move to a broader discussion of the U.S. economic system. Moving away from Americans' opinions about the economy, especially how it affects them personally, these sections review some of the key trends and features of the American free-enterprise system and its connection to the global marketplace.

Principles Underlying Key Trends in the American Free-Enterprise System

12.2   Describe the principles underlying key trends in the American system of free enterprise.

While the U.S. economy remains by many measures the strongest on earth, its institutions are undergoing rapid and dramatic changes that can be grouped into a few master trends:

- Globalization of markets and the rise of major multinational corporations that compete for power on the world stage
- Growth in service-sector jobs in the advanced economies and continued export of manufacturing jobs to regions with lower wage rates
- Increasing reliance of families on the incomes of multiple workers, especially of women and formerly retired people
- Increased reliance on innovations in technology and specialization to increase the productivity and competitiveness of companies and their employees

capitalism

A particular type of economic system found in the United States (and elsewhere); sometimes known as a free-enterprise system.

markets

Institutions that regulate the worldwide flow of an almost infinite array of goods and services. Almost all markets in nations throughout the world are regulated by acts of governments, including the United States.

capital

Both the money used to purchase resources (e.g., raw materials) and the physical assets (e.g., buildings and equipment) used to produce goods and services. Capitalists are people who combine capital with the labor of workers to produce goods and services in the hope of making a profit—that is, selling their product or service at a market price higher than the costs of the equipment and labor used to create it.

entrepreneur

A capitalist who creates a new business venture.

limited liability

A protection by which the assets of the corporation are liable to seizure in the case of economic failure or wrongdoing, but the entrepreneur's personal assets are not liable if the corporation fails.

To better understand these trends shaping the economies of the United States (and other developed nations), it is important to understand the basic principles underlying the system of corporate capitalism as it exists in the United States today.

When people refer to the American free-enterprise system, they are talking about an economic system known as **capitalism**. The central social institutions of capitalism are **markets**, which regulate the worldwide flow of an extensive array of goods and services. Theoretically, markets in a pure free-enterprise system are regulated by the demand for specific goods and services and by the competition among suppliers to furnish them at a price that is attractive to buyers. This is referred to as "supply and demand."

In fact, however, almost all markets in nations around the world are regulated by acts of governments, including in the United States. These regulations usually attempt to protect buyers in terms of the safety of products (e.g., rules about food and drug purity and airline maintenance) or to protect workers (e.g., occupational safety regulations). Other regulations seek to ensure that markets remain competitive and are not dominated by a handful of giant companies in markets, known either as oligopolies (only a few sellers) or monopolies (one seller).

In other cases, governments may try to affect the prices charged for various goods by imposing import taxes. These levies usually seek to give locally made products a price advantage over products imported from outside the nation. The North American Free Trade Agreement of 1993 (NAFTA), for example, is an arrangement in which the United States, Mexico, and Canada agree not to impose import taxes on goods and services flowing among these countries. Congress and the Obama administration continue to negotiate free-trade agreements, most notably with Colombia, Panama, and South Korea (Appelbaum, 2011). Unfortunately, enforcement of the environmental and labor clauses of these agreements remains quite weak (Wells, 2003).

Capital refers to both the money used to purchase resources (e.g., raw materials) and the physical assets (e.g., buildings and equipment) used to produce goods and services. Capitalists combine capital with the labor of workers (whether hourly or salaried) to produce goods and services in the hope of making a profit—that is, selling their product or service at a market price higher than the costs of the equipment and labor used to create it. A capitalist who creates a new business venture is known as an **entrepreneur**. In the pure form of free-enterprise capitalism, the entrepreneur assumes all the business risks and expects to make as much profit as possible with as little regulation as possible. However, in actual practice, most entrepreneurs try to minimize their risks in many different ways.

Formation of a corporation is one major way of minimizing risk. Corporations are chartered by governments to conduct business with limited liability to the owners of the business. **Limited liability** means that only the assets of the corporation are liable to seizure in the case of economic failure or wrongdoing. The entrepreneur's personal assets are not liable if the corporation fails. This protection is vital to the existence of corporations and makes it possible for them to raise funds for expansion by selling shares of their business in the financial markets (stocks and bonds). As shareholders become part owners of the corporation, they are not liable for what the corporation does beyond the risk of losing their investment in the business. The fact that governments grant limited liability to corporations is one way in which the public, through its elected representatives, can try to hold corporations responsible for their actions. Governments can revoke the charters of corporations if they violate federal or state laws.

Not all corporations sell shares to the public, but those that do are among the largest and most powerful economic entities in the world. Indeed, the global reach of large corporations, and their increasing power throughout the world, is often associated with social problems such as environmental pollution, sudden unemployment in specific regions, the use of child labor in poor nations, and many others. It is also true that corporations often create opportunities for economic development and new jobs in formerly impoverished regions.

Inspired by the Marxian dream of a classless society in which the means of production (e.g., capital) are collectively owned, nations like Cuba or North Korea follow the tenets of **communism**. This means they attempt to abolish free enterprise, competitive markets, and profits and replace them with a planned economy in which the central government determines the flow of goods and services. Communists see this approach as one of fairness. However, it also has the potential to create untold opportunities for corruption and waste.

Although most Americans tout capitalism as the preferred economic model, capitalist business practices are by no means free of problems, including ruthless dealings, exploitation of the powerless, and various forms of corruption. Even when they are successful in generating economic growth and new employment opportunities in a global marketplace, success in one region may come at the expense of workers in another.

communism

A system of government that controls a planned economy, determining the flow of goods and services.

Global Markets and Corporate Power

12.3   Identify the consequences of global markets and corporate power.

The effects of globalization are a topic that is receiving a lot of attention today, but the term and its meanings are often not defined. By economic globalization, social scientists refer to the growing tendency for goods and services to be produced in one nation or region and consumed in another. Companies that produce those goods and services engage in business activities in many different regions of the world.

This trend is not new. Commodities such as sugar, coffee, tobacco, and tea were early entrants in the global marketplace of the eighteenth and nineteenth centuries. Sugarcane, for example, was produced on slave plantations in the Caribbean, made into raw sugar and rum, and traded in the northern colonies of what is now the United States and Canada for lumber and other products, which were brought back to the rapidly industrializing nations of Europe. Much of the early economic growth of England, France, and Holland, as well as their competition to establish colonies, was stimulated by this global trade.

In today's global economy, the major changes from older patterns of worldwide economic activity are due to the far greater speed of modern communications and transport. Fish produced in massive salmon farms in Chile, for example, can be on American dinner tables the next day. Information about prices and investment opportunities can travel with electronic speed over computer networks. The Internet can make a corporation such as McDonald's, which has ventures everywhere, lose vast sums of money when there is a health scare about tainted beef from suppliers in Japan and China (Riley, 2014).

Many social problems associated with globalization are due to the overwhelming influence of multinational corporations, both in their home countries and the less developed countries (LDCs), where they increasingly do business (Derber, 2014; Ruggie, 2013).

Multinational Corporations

Few aspects of globalization are more controversial than the operations and even the existence of **multinational (or transnational) corporations**. The definition of these entities is extremely broad. They may produce many different kinds of goods and services, but they are all large corporations (often with many subsidiary corporations) that have their headquarters in one country but pursue business activities and profits in one or more foreign nations (Smelser and Swedberg, 2005). In this sense, multinationals have existed at least since the days of the international banking houses of the

multinational corporations (or transnational corporations)

Corporations that have their headquarters in one country but pursue business activities and profits in one or more foreign nations.

Italian Renaissance. American firms such as Singer, United Fruit, and Firestone have had extensive foreign operations—and political influence—since the late nineteenth century. For the most part, however, these early multinationals were national companies with secondary foreign operations.

The sharp rise in foreign investments and the concentration of financial resources that followed World War II led to the development of transnational corporations. These companies are international organizations that operate across national boundaries, whatever their country of origin may be. Their size, wealth, influence, and diversity of operations have grown enormously. The annual sales of companies such as General Motors, Apple, and the major petroleum corporations exceed the gross national product of many nations—not just the poorer LDCs but also highly industrialized countries such as Switzerland and South Africa. In fact, of the world's largest 150 economic entities in 2012, 87 (58 percent) were corporations (Global Trends, 2015). Increasingly, therefore, the term *multinational* is used to emphasize the fact that these corporations operate outside national boundaries almost as if they were nations unto themselves.

For decades, the multinational auto companies, such as General Motors and Ford, have been producing thousands of cars in Europe for sale in the expanding European markets. They have had less success in the growing Asian markets, which are dominated by Japanese manufacturers. Now, the Japanese multinational manufacturers, especially Toyota, Nissan, and Honda, produce cars in the United States, using Japanese methods and parts. These and other multinational companies try to create an image of themselves, not as Japanese or American, but as world companies that are above nationalistic sentiments.

Although the multinationals will certainly continue to grow and to account for an increasing share of the world's production of goods and services, they are widely criticized for operating outside the control of any nation. One way in which multinational corporations are a source of social problems is that they tend to move quickly to areas where labor costs are lowest, often to the detriment of workers left behind in the nations where they began their operations (Backer, 2009; Ruggie, 2013; Derber, 2014).

Global Factories

Multinational corporations are transforming the world's economy by focusing on rapidly developing markets and on labor forces in the LDCs, which have an oversupply of workers in their manufacturing sectors and an undersupply of highly skilled workers with technological training. No longer confined to generating their products in just one country, the multinationals have created a "global factory" that is made possible by two kinds of technology: high-speed transportation and component production (Martin and Torres, 2004). The first type of technology, high speed transportation, enables companies to get raw materials, finished products, communications, and so on from one point to another anywhere in the world. The second, component production, divides the production process into components that can be carried out anywhere, thereby allowing multinational companies to take advantage of the worldwide supply of cheap labor. For example, U.S. baseball manufacturers send the materials for their product—leather covers, yarn, thread, and cement—to Haiti, where the baseballs are assembled for wages far below those paid for similar work anywhere in the United States.

24/7 Economy

U.S. industries have undergone rapid restructuring in the past few decades in response to technological changes and global competition. First, the widespread use of personal computers (virtually unheard of 35 years ago, believe it or not), smartphones, fax machines, and pagers has changed the way people do business and the way they conduct their personal life. You can buy e-tickets for your flights, order groceries over the Internet, check e-mail on your smartphones, text your friends to see what is on the agenda for the weekend, post your latest happenings on Facebook or Instagram, and Skype your mom when you are on vacation.

Many companies use these technologies to conduct business 24 hours a day, 7 days a week. More and more people can do their "work" from just about anywhere, including the dining room table as their children romp in the living room. Work enters the home. Likewise, home life enters the work arena. Thus, for many people, the boundaries between work and family are blurring. Sometimes this situation works out well (e.g., possibly reducing childcare costs among those who work at home). However, for others, the burst of technology has actually increased stress levels as work encroaches on other dimensions of our lives.

A second form of rapid restructuring is that many jobs are being outsourced to other countries, especially India, Indonesia, and China, as companies search for cheaper labor costs and fewer government regulations (Galinsky, Aumann, and Bond, 2009; Peralta, 2014). Manufacturing jobs, sales, and service are being shipped overseas.

Outsourcing

Critics of U.S. multinationals have been especially vocal in condemning the practice known as **outsourcing**—locating businesses that produce goods for American markets in poor countries where the firm can take advantage of lower wage rates and fewer environmental restrictions. This practice in effect "exports" jobs from the United States to LDCs, greatly reducing the number of jobs available for American workers. The jobs lost by outsourcing may have originally been in the area of manufacturing, but now the lost jobs are often service profession positions. Is your computer on the blink? When you telephone a call center for help, it is quite possible that someone in India will answer the phone. Consumers appreciate the 24/7 economy, and they benefit from the lower cost of goods and services, but outsourcing contributes to widespread job losses in this country. For example, in early 2015, Disney laid off hundreds of information technology workers, outsourcing their positions to other countries (Thibodeau, 2015). They since hired them back, possibly due to the negative publicity this outsourcing caused the Disney company. This issue is described more fully in the box, A Closer Look: Disney: The Happiest Place on Earth?

In recent years, however, there has also been a countertrend: Multinational firms are increasing their investments in the United States. Sony of Japan has purchased CBS Records; Italy's Fiat owns the Chrysler automobile company; Japanese and German automobile manufacturers have opened plants in the United States to assemble their cars, often using parts manufactured abroad. These arrangements are considered preferable to outsourcing because they keep jobs in the United States. But many foreign-based multinationals resist union contracts and the resulting higher wages and benefits (Martin and Torres, 2004).

Global Sweatshops

In addition to engaging in outsourcing, multinational corporations attempt to sell their products in the markets of LDCs. As the populations of those countries increase and their standard of living also begins to slowly rise, they represent a vast untapped source of profits. For example, Coca-Cola is marketed in even the poorest of nations. However, unlike many other corporations, their marketing strategy is to do "good works" in these poor areas, such as investing in infrastructure, providing clean water, providing local residents with jobs, and making investments in women's economic empowerment (Westaway, 2014). But

outsourcing

Locating businesses that produce goods for American (or other Western) markets in poor, developing nations where the firm can take advantage of lower wage rates and fewer environmental restrictions.

Employees dine in a canteen in the Tata Consultancy Services, which provides computer services and back-office support to companies, including Citigroup Inc. and Scandinavian Airline Systems. These jobs have been outsourced to India because of lower labor costs.

A Closer Look

Disney: The Happiest Place on Earth?

Up to several hundred information technology (IT) workers at Walt Disney Parks and Resorts were called into the conference room one by one to receive notice of their layoffs on January 30, 2015. The workers were shocked, tearful, and angry. The company decided to restructure its IT department, according to Disney, claiming that it had nothing to do with displacing workers, but rather to shift more resources to projects involving innovation. The laid-off workers were free to reapply for these jobs. However, from the perspective of workers themselves, they knew few co-workers who had landed one of these new jobs. Disney cut well-paid and longtime staff members and shifted work to contractors who use foreign labor, primarily from India. Known as H-1B or "visa" workers, Disney's CEO claims that "H-1B workers complement—instead of displace—U.S. workers." It also claims that, as more employers use foreign workers to fill more technical and low-level jobs, firms are able to expand and allow U.S. workers "to assume managerial and leadership positions."

The American workers are upset at losing their jobs and feel that a sense of loyalty on the part of Disney had been breached as a cost-saving measure. As one worker said about the new foreign workers, "Some of these folks were literally flown in the day before to take over the exact same job I was doing." He trained his replacement and is angry over the fact that he had to train someone from India "on site, in our country."

Update: In June 2015, Walt Disney Parks and Resorts cancelled its plans to replace employees with workers from an agency known for outsourcing jobs to immigrants on temporary work visas.

SOURCE: Thibodeau, 2015.

Critical Thinking

Should a company be allowed to hire and fire whomever they want? What does a company owe its workers, if anything?

---

it is unlikely that Coca-Cola is turning into a social service agency with a bleeding heart. Rather, they see that a more constructive, organic investment in developing markets is a more cost-effective business strategy than the old way of muscling their way in.

However, most multinationals produce high-technology products and services intended for markets with much greater buying power than that available in poor LDCs. The workers are employed for low pay in **sweatshops**, highly unpleasant factory-like working conditions in which they are essentially forced to endure crowded, hot, and dangerous working conditions with few breaks, conditions that would not be tolerated in affluent nations. Sweatshops are the norm in the global garment industry (International Labor Rights Forum, 2015).

On occasion, usually after a disaster, the world takes note of the condition of sweatshops and fights for their workers. For example, there was headline news around the world when over 1,500 garment workers died in two disasters within one year in 2013. The first incident was a fire that broke out in a sweatshop in Pakistan, and the second involved the collapse of a sweatshop in Bangladesh.

Sometimes American workers and consumers take to the streets in protest, such as a large protest in Seattle a decade ago responding to revelations that major multinational corporations, or local companies under contract to them, hire child labor at extremely low wages. For example, the Nike Corporation subcontracts with overseas employers for about 75,000 Asian workers to make Nike shoes. In some cases, 11-year-old workers who earn about $2.20 a day are producing sneakers at a cost of about $6 a pair. The sneakers are then sold in the United States for $80 or more. Revelations that Nike, McDonald's, and other major global corporations were purchasing goods made by sweatshop labor stimulated the antisweatshop movement and forced these powerful corporations to take strong positions against the use of such labor (Powell, 2014; Wells, 2003).

Some people argue that the United States should apply trade sanctions such as import duties against nations that exploit their workers. They believe that wages in Latin America, Asia, and the Middle East will increase only if the rights of workers are protected from repression by their governments and powerful businesses. Workers must have the right to bargain collectively for wages, pensions, and health and other benefits. But representatives of China, Pakistan, India, and many other LDCs where

sweatshops

Factory-type arrangements, especially in developing nations, with working conditions that would not be tolerated in affluent nations (e.g., crowded, hot spaces; minimal breaks; dangerous work).

Slide Show

A Chinese Sweatshop

This slide show depicts a sweatshop in Guangdong province, China, on the southern coast, where one town, Xintang, nicknamed the "denim jeans center of the world," claims to produce 60 percent of the global output of jeans. Who works here, and why do they tolerate low wages and such poor working conditions?

Liu Xiao (left) and Zhu Cheng pose by the lights of the city that lured them to reach for a better life in Xintang. Both boys are from the rural countryside in interior China, and they are very poor. Neither boy finished high school; most children from their village complete only eighth grade. They did not want to be farmers like their parents—"peasant work," Liu claimed—but other opportunities for work do not exist nearby. He saw a flyer advertising "good jobs" and "good pay" in a garment factory far from home. Together, with his friend Zhu, they decided to make the trek.

Men and women do different work in the garment industry. The female workers sew blue jeans. They are at their sewing machines for 14 hours a day, six days a week. They receive two 20-minute meal breaks, and two 10-minute rest breaks, all unpaid. All workers receive one day off of work; the day rotates because the factory is open seven days per week. The room in which they sew has little ventilation. It is very cold in the winter and stifling hot in the summer months. Song Li chooses to work without a mask that protects her lungs from the damage caused by the cloth fibers. She says that the costs of the masks are deducted from pay, and she would rather keep the money.

Males generally do not sew blue jeans, but they prepare the cloth beforehand and iron the newly manufactured jeans afterwards. They too work long hours for very little pay; however, they are allowed to move around as they work. The female workers are required to sit at their station and can get up only during their breaks. Most people in the factory say that the men's jobs are better for this reason.

The workers live in small dorms located on the company grounds. There are two beds in each room, and each bed sleeps three women. There is a washbasin in the room that the six workers share, and a community bathroom down the hall. Rooms do not have a window or closet. Mei Xiouyun shows off her room. It is crowded when all six young women are there at the same time, but she and her roommates have fixed up the room with posters to make it feel like home. Most workers stay at a factory for only a short time and then move on to a new factory in hopes of a better job or higher pay. In the seven months that Mei has lived here, she has gone through nine different roommates.

Bao Huang, the CEO of the factory, poses in his office. He is a very wealthy man by Chinese standards. He does not feel that his company is exploiting workers. "They come very willingly," he says. "There is nothing for them at home. Here they can earn some money and send it back to their family. Life is better for them here."

Critical Thinking

How often do you think of the person(s) who made your clothes? How about the person who picked the fruit or vegetables that you eat? Why are Americans so removed from the clothes they wear and the food they eat?

multinationals are active argue that insistence on workers' rights and other protections would drive labor costs up and diminish one of the few advantages poor nations have in the global marketplace.

Effects on American Workers

12.4 **Assess the consequences of globalization for the American worker.**

For the American worker, the growth of multinationals, global factories, and outsourcing of jobs means that a steadily decreasing number of employers have come to dominate the labor market. This trend has had several effects. Chief among them is the tendency to export capital and jobs overseas, where labor is cheaper and more plentiful, and environmental regulations are more lax. U.S. manufacturing workers have been most seriously affected by this trend. In 1960, over 28 percent of all U.S. workers were employed in manufacturing jobs. By 2014, this figure had dropped to under 9 percent (Bureau of Labor Statistics, 2015b).

The early part of the twentieth century experienced a manufacturing boom as people around the world desired products made in the United States. However, beginning in earnest in the 1970s and 1980s, U.S. plants, factories, mills, and other industrial facilities began to suffer losses as capital was diverted abroad. Unable to maintain their competitive edge, many manufacturing facilities closed. Especially hard hit were plants in the nation's older, single-industry cities, such as Gary, Indiana, once the nation's most important producer of steel.

Over the past generation, there have been three unprecedented changes in the U.S. labor force, largely because of transformations in the global economy. First is the shift from manufacturing to service employment. Second is the large increase in contingent nonstandard work schedules. Third is the enormous increase in the number of women working outside the home—women of all ages and from all kinds of family backgrounds.

From Manufacturing to Services

As manufacturing jobs declined over the past generation, jobs in the service sector and in sales have increased. These job categories are broad. For example, sales jobs include the clerk at the mom and pop store down the street as well as a high-paid pharmaceutical salesperson with a Ph.D. However, many service and sales jobs are low-paying and may not provide important fringe benefits such as sick leave, vacation pay, retirement, or health insurance. The growth in these low-paying jobs goes a long way in explaining why political and educational leaders constantly emphasize the importance of staying in school and gaining the educational credentials required for better-paying positions.

The momentous shift from an economy dominated by manufacturing employment to one dominated by service jobs has improved some work-related social problems and at the same time has created new ones. In terms of an improvement, it should be noted that accidents and deaths on the job are far less prevalent today than they were when the economy was dominated by manufacturing, agriculture, and extractive industries such as mining and lumbering. For example, the rate of accidental deaths at work in 1960 was 21 per 100,000 workers, but by 2013, with the rise of service work as the leading form of employment, that rate had declined to 3.2 per 100,000 workers (Bureau of Labor Statistics, 2014a).

However, the decline in union membership is often viewed as one of the down sides of the switch to a service-oriented economy. In 1960, at the height of union influence in the United States, about 27 percent of employees in the private sector were members of trade unions. Today, only 11 percent

There has been a sharp decline in manufacturing jobs in the United States. Many of these jobs have been replaced by service jobs, which tend to have significantly lower pay and fewer job benefits.

Figure 12–5 Median Weekly Earnings of Full-Time Workers, by Union Affiliation and Sex, 2014

SOURCE: Bureau of Labor Statistics, 2015d.

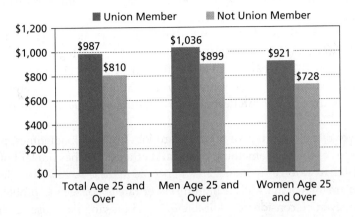

are union members (Bureau of Labor Statistics, 2015d). This change reflects the shift away from manufacturing work, which was always more heavily unionized. The rate of unionization varies from one state to another. New York and Alaska have the highest proportion of their workers unionized, at 25 and 23 percent, respectively, while North and South Carolina have the lowest rates of unionization (both 2 percent). Some states with so-called "right to work" laws make it much harder for unions to organize workers.

These differences in union membership are extremely important because unions help workers obtain higher pay, as shown in Figure 12–5. The financial benefits are particularly strong for unionized women; they average $200 more a week than nonunionized women workers (Bureau of Labor Statistics, 2015d). Unions also are more likely to provide fringe benefits that many nonunion workers often do not have. For example, the proportion of families with health insurance is higher for union families than for nonunion ones. Indeed, the loss of union jobs to global manufacturing sites outside the United States is one of the primary reasons the number of Americans without health insurance skyrocketed to 50 million before the Affordable Care Act was passed, as shown in Chapter 2 (Garfield and Young, 2015).

Contingent Nonstandard Work

Another aspect of the shift from manufacturing to services is the growing importance of what is known as **contingent nonstandard work**, work that does not have a written employment contract, is only temporary, or has irregular hours. Employees working in these types of jobs represent the fastest-growing category of workers in the United States (Gornick, Presser, and Ratzdorf, 2009). Millions of women and men begin the workday not knowing whether, or for how long, their jobs are likely to continue. Women are overrepresented in these arrangements, particularly in those characterized by lower wages and fewer benefits.

Some contingent nonstandard workers prefer this arrangement, especially highly paid professionals who value their freedom and independence on the job, or mothers with young children who would prefer to work only sporadically. However, most Americans do not work such schedules out of personal choice, but because these are the required working conditions of their jobs as cashiers, maids, nursing aids, cooks, and waiters. They prefer the assurance of a steady job with prearranged hours, an established pay scale with fringe benefits, and daytime hours.

Families with nonstandard work schedules may find it difficult to organize childcare because most childcare centers are open only between 7 A.M. and 6 P.M.

contingent nonstandard work

Employment that does not have a written employment contract, is only temporary, has irregular hours, or is some combination of these elements.

Furthermore, childcare centers usually require a paid commitment to a particular schedule such as a Monday through Friday schedule or a Monday, Wednesday, Friday schedule. When a parent works full-time one week, three days the next week, and four half days the next, it wreaks havoc on childcare arrangements, school schedules, and parenting tasks, creating stress for everyone. Children whose parents work evening or nonstandard hours have, on average, more behavioral problems, lower cognitive development, and higher rates of obesity (Gassman-Pines, 2011; Grzywacz et al., 2011; Li et al., 2012). The cause may be due to a reduced quality of the home environment, lack of adequate parental time spent with children, fewer intellectually stimulating activities, and more television viewing.

Turnover rates in contingent nonstandard jobs are high. Sometimes, people quit work in hopes of finding something better, and other times they are laid off; they are an expendable workforce. To management, people in these largely unskilled or semi-skilled jobs are interchangeable. A high turnover rate is not seen as problematic, and in fact, may even be considered desirable to avoid offering pay raises or fringe benefits. These disposable workers earn less than those on the regular payroll and must live with the uncertainty that their jobs may permanently end today when they clock out at 5:00 P.M. Their anxiety is high, and for many, unemployment insurance is not an option.

"Rhonda" is one of many people looking for a stable job with good pay (Seccombe, 2015). She has a high school diploma, but has not gone to college. She is a poor single mother, and would like to raise her young son Bobby without relying on welfare assistance. She wants a permanent full-time job, but she has been stymied by the increase of temporary positions with irregular hours (Seccombe, 2015):

> Hopefully I can get me a job. A permanent job. My sister's trying to get me a job where she works. I put my application in last week. And it would be a permanent job. When you go through those agencies, it's just temporary work. It's just whenever they need you, and it's unfair too. Every job I've found is through this temporary agency, like Manpower, but it's only temporary. And they cut my check and my food stamps, and when my job ends, it's like you're stuck again. So I'm trying to find a permanent steady job. But it's hard around here. I've been out looking for work, and hoping that something comes through. (p. 177)

Rhonda may be surprised to learn that temporary agencies are booming. Manpower is one of the largest private employers in the United States, ranking 144 in the *Fortune* 500 list of large companies, with revenues approximating $20 billion worldwide. They serve over 400,000 employer clients worldwide and placed 3.4 million workers within more than 80 countries (ManpowerGroup, 2015).

Women in the Labor Force

The labor force, as defined by the federal government, consists of all people ages 16 years or over (excluding those in institutions) who worked one hour for pay during one survey week (the employed) plus those who did not work during the survey week, do not have a job, and are actively seeking work (the unemployed). As the shift occurred from manufacturing to service work, one of the most significant changes in the labor force was the enormous increase in the number of married women, especially those with children, as paid workers.

> You can really see how women's opportunities have changed by looking at my family. My grandmother, who never worked outside the home, is pretty adamant that mothers should not be working. She talks about that a lot, and is worried about the state of families today. Meanwhile, my mom thinks it's okay for mothers to work as long as their children are in school. That's what she did—she waited until my brother and I were in

first and third grade. Today, I feel differently. I'm planning to go to medical school, and I just assume that I'll be working when I have my children. I think women can have a fulfilling career and have children at the same time.

— Abby, Age 22

As revealed in Chapter 8, most married women with children did not work outside the home until recently. Work during and after the Industrial Revolution in the late 1800s was often done in factories, and this work was considered dirty and dangerous. Only women in difficult circumstances took jobs there, most likely immigrant women, poor women, and minority women who needed the wages to survive. This situation created and perpetuated a class- and race-based division among women—those who worked, and those who did not work.

Middle-class white women, especially those who were married with children, largely stayed out of the labor market throughout the early twentieth century except during extreme events like World War II when their labor was sought after. But after the war, most women returned to lives of domesticity, pitying their lower-income counterparts who remained employed (Friedan, 1963).

However, beginning in the 1970s, the tide began to change, and women began to see work more favorably. This shift has been due to a variety of cultural events, including the Women's Movement, which helped to expand job and educational opportunities for women; the invention of the birth control pill, which allowed women greater freedom to control their fertility; and the outsourcing of higher-paying manufacturing jobs overseas, which required many families to now earn two paychecks instead of just one. Thus, work became, for some, more available and desirable and, for many others, a sheer necessity.

Today, over two-thirds of married mothers are employed outside the home for pay, as are three-quarters of unmarried mothers. These trends have remained relatively stable over the last decade and show no signs of significant change in the future. Women work for a variety of reasons: to put food on the table, to provide housing, to pay for vacations, or for personal fulfillment.

Women's employment is not a social problem. The social problem occurs when policies and programs do not keep pace with the changing social structure. Many women and men in the United States scramble because of the lack of paid maternity leaves, the high cost of childcare, the low number of subsidized preschool slots, extended summer vacations from school, and the limited availability of part-time jobs with benefits that would allow families to more easily combine work and family. This dearth of programs and policies affects the quality of life of both adults and their children.

CATCH 22: INFLEXIBLE FULL-TIME WORK OR PART-TIME PENALTY Part of parents' tension over balancing work and family is due to an increasing work week with little control over working conditions—when they work, how long of a day they work, or whether they can take time off. Work is demanding more time of employees: The average American works 48 more hours per year—six extra days each year—than did Americans just a generation ago (Morrissey, 2008). For example, a study of over 1,000 employers found that only 55 percent report allowing most workers to take time off during the workday to attend to important family or personal needs without loss of pay. Only 27 percent of employers allow their workers to periodically change their starting and quitting time within some range; most are not given time off to care for sick children without losing pay (Matos and Galinsky, 2012).

Some parents opt to reduce their work hours to part-time, or wish that they could. A survey of working mothers in 2012 found that 37 percent claimed that they would prefer to work part-time (Parker and Wang, 2013). However, people generally pay a steep price for this added flexibility. Workers who go part-time earn much less than

Most part-time jobs in the United States do not provide benefits and the pay is low. This situation is not necessarily the case in other countries, where the government prohibits employers from treating part-time workers less favorably.

What Do You Think?

How do you think your life has been affected by globalization and its effects on American workers? Have these changes been good or bad for you personally? Are they good or bad for society? Why is it that sometimes what is good for you is at odds with what is good for society (and vice versa)?

---

regular full-time workers. They are also less likely to receive retirement benefits, health insurance, or sick leave. For example, full-time workers, as compared with those who work part-time, are twice as likely to receive a retirement benefit, are three times more likely to receive paid sick leave, and are four times more likely to receive health insurance from their employers (Bureau of Labor Statistics, 2014b).

SOLUTIONS IN OTHER COUNTRIES These drawbacks to part-time work have been eliminated in many other countries. For example, as far back as 1997, the European Union drafted a directive "to eliminate discrimination against part-time workers and improve the quality of part-time work" (Official Journal of the European Communities, 1998). The directive prohibits employers from treating part-time workers less favorably than comparable full-time workers (unless they can demonstrate that the differential treatment is justified). It addresses issues of pay equity, Social Security, job benefits, training and promotion opportunities, and collective bargaining rights.

How does this directive actually work? Germany grants the right to work part-time in firms that have more than 15 workers; Belgium grants employees the right to work at 80 percent of full-time for five years; the United Kingdom allows employees the right to request flexible and part-time work to care for a child under age 6 or a disabled child under age 18; and Sweden allows parents to work six hours a day until their children turn eight (Gornick, Heron, and Eisenbrey, 2007). All parents in these nations, rich or poor, have these legal rights.

Problems with Work

12.5 Evaluate the problems associated with work today.

As the economy steadily improves, it remains that a number of social problems continue to plague the work environment. This section will discuss several of these problems: unemployment, insecurity about the decline of "good" jobs, job discrimination, and occupational health and safety.

Unemployment

Until the recession began in 2008, the United States experienced many years of low unemployment. The economy was strong, inflation was low, and people were working. Some level of unemployment is generally considered "normal" because people change jobs and spend time looking for new ones for a variety of reasons. Economists argue about the precise meaning of the term "full employment," but the consensus is that an unemployment rate between 4 percent and 4.5 percent is to be expected in a thriving economy. However, after the global financial crisis of 2008, unemployment rates in the United States soared to about 10 percent. Unemployment rates were particularly high among black and Hispanic people, at nearly 17 percent and 13 percent, respectively.

In response, the Obama administration and Congress used billions of federal dollars to prop up major economic institutions in banking, insurance, and the major auto companies, General Motors and Chrysler—a set of funding priorities commonly known as the stimulus package. The state of the economy began to slowly improve. By 2015, the unemployment rate declined to 5.5 percent, roughly similar to

Table 12–2 Unemployment Rate, by Age, Sex, and Race, March 2005, 2010, 2015

	2005	2010	2015
Total Age 16 and Over	5.2%	9.9%	5.5%
Adult Men Ages 20 and Older	4.6%	10.2%	5.1%
Adult Women Ages 20 and Older	11.6%	8.1%	4.9%
White	4.5%	8.9%	4.1%
Black	10.5%	16.8%	10.1%
Asian	3.9%	7.6%	3.2%
Hispanic	5.8%	12.9%	6.8%

SOURCE: Bureau of Labor Statistics, 2015b.

pre-recession rates, as shown in Table 12–2. However, it remains high for blacks and Hispanics, at 10.1 and 6.8 percent, respectively.

What these unemployment figures mean is that during the recession many breadwinners lost their jobs or had their income reduced, contributing to the rise in home foreclosures, drained savings accounts, and personal bankruptcies. What does it feel like to look for work week after week, and find no job offers? When even the lowest-tier jobs in the economy have stiff competition, many people who would like to work feel psychologically wounded by the lack of employment opportunities. A Gallup Poll based on a nationally representative sample during the height of the recession found that people who had been unemployed more than six months were far more likely than those who were employed to feel stress, sadness, and worry (Marlar, 2010).

Unemployment also affected personal relationships. For example, high unemployment tends to lower marriage rates: People are less likely to marry if they or their potential partner cannot find a job (Edin and Kefalas, 2005). The stress associated with unemployment can also endanger relationships, contribute to domestic violence, and harm children's social well-being. For example, a study based on 4,476 school-age children in 2,569 families across the country found that, when fathers are involuntarily unemployed, children have a greater likelihood of repeating a grade or getting suspended from school (Luo, 2009).

Although more people are employed today than just a few years ago, it is important to realize that bouts of unemployment can have long-term effects. When people lose an income, especially for long periods of time, they likely need to dip into savings, retirement accounts, or their children's college funds. Many people also use their credit cards for basic living expenses. During the recession, some people exhausted their savings, maxed out their credit cards, filed for bankruptcy, and still lost their homes to foreclosure. It takes these people many years to pull themselves out of this crisis and rebuild their financial and personal lives. This difficulty is part of the reason why many people continue to list the economy as the number one social problem facing Americans today, even though the economy has regained considerable strength. For a closer look at what unemployment can do to a family, take a look at the box, A Personal View: Unemployment Up Close and Personal.

Insecurity about the Decline of "Good Jobs"

Although many people are now back at work, *where* are they working? If you were offered a full-time job in the private sector with relatively low wages, without health benefits, without an employer-paid pension plan, and with no sick leave or disability policy, would you consider it a "good job"? Probably not, yet employers are offering workers more jobs like that one every year, according to data from the U.S. Department of Labor survey of employee benefits (Bureau of Labor Statistics, 2014b).

A Personal View

Unemployment Up Close and Personal

I grew up in a typical middle-class family, if there is such a thing. My dad worked as a manager for a medium-sized company, and my mom was a teacher's aide. We had the basic trappings, you know, a three-bedroom house in the suburbs, two cars, and a vacation to the beach every summer. Our lifestyle wasn't fancy, but I never had to worry about whether we had enough money to buy some new school clothes every fall, or whether we would get enough to eat. My parents always stressed that my brother and I would go to college, and they saved a little money toward that goal to help with tuition. In other words, life was secure.

All that changed when I was in high school and my dad lost his job. They gave him a few months of severance pay, but that was it. I remember the frightened look on his face when he came home from work one day and asked my brother and me to leave the room so he could talk to my mom alone. I could hear them talking softly, and then I heard my mother cry. I was dying to know what was wrong.

About 30 minutes later, they called my brother and me back into the room and told us that, after this week, my dad would no longer be working at his company. I didn't really understand what that meant financially. I even thought, "Cool, he'll be home more. Maybe he can go to more of my soccer games." I didn't understand what it meant to be unemployed.

I learned quickly, however. To save money, my parents immediately cut our cable television, and most after-school activities and summer camps. They let me continue the soccer season, since it was already paid for, but the rest had to go. My brother was really upset about giving up his art lessons because art has always been important to him, and he's really pretty good.

There were also no more allowance, dinners out, or 10 dollars here and there when I wanted to go to the movies.

I heard, "no, we can't afford it" daily, and it got old real quickly. By the third month, my parents began to sell some of our possessions—mostly things stored out in the garage that we didn't use, but still, it felt weird to be selling stuff off.

But even more unsettling than the financial issues were the changes I saw in my parents. My father spent the first few months of his unemployment actively seeking work, not finding any, and then it was like he just gave up. He would just sit around the house watching TV and sometimes not even shave or get dressed. He didn't come to my soccer games either, "Sorry son, I just don't feel like it today," he would say. My mom would get upset because when she would come home from her job, the house would be a mess. My brother and I had chores of course, but we didn't think it was our job to clean the whole house! My dad wouldn't even fix dinner most nights. Obviously, this made my mom even more upset and they began to argue a lot. I remember her calling him a "pig" once, and it really broke me up because they never used to talk like that to each other. I'm sure he was depressed, but no one knew what to do about it.

After about 8 months, my father did finally get another job. But things weren't automatically rosy then either. I don't know all the details, but I sense that his bout with unemployment caused them to go into debt. You know, credit cards, home equity loans, and that sort of thing. And our college savings account? That disappeared too. I think their marriage is getting back on track though. Whew, things were rough for a while.

Critical Thinking

Compare and contrast how a functionalist, conflict theorist, and symbolic interactionist would see the issue of unemployment, including its cause and consequence.

They show that worker (and family) benefits are on the wane. Table 12–3 confirms this trend with data from 2010 to 2014, which show a decline in employer-sponsored retirement plans, health care benefits, paid sick leave, and paid holidays, even as the economy has improved (Bureau of Labor Statistics, 2015c).

Table 12–3 Percent of Workers (NonCivilian) Who Have Benefits Provided by Employer, 2010, 2014

Benefit	2010	2014
Defined Retirement Plan	28%	25%
Any Retirement Plan	69%	68%
Health Care Benefits	74%	72%
Paid Sick Leave	67%	65%
Paid Holidays	76%	75%
Paid Vacation	74%	74%

SOURCE: Bureau of Labor Statistics, 2015c.

Job Discrimination

A number of laws exist to protect the rights of workers from job discrimination (U.S. Equal Employment Opportunity Commission, 2015). For example, in 1963, the Equal Pay Act was passed, which makes it illegal to pay different wages to men and women if they perform equal work in the same workplace. The law also makes it illegal to retaliate against a person because of a complaint about discrimination.

More sweeping, the 1964 Civil Rights Act was passed, which makes it illegal to discriminate against someone on the basis of race, color, religion, national origin, or sex (after one of the longest debates in congressional history). Retaliation for filing a complaint is illegal. The law also requires that employers reasonably accommodate employees' religious practices, unless doing so would impose an undue hardship on the operation of the business.

Other protective laws were passed to prevent discrimination on age, disabilities, pregnancy status, and genetic information. However, there is no federal law that consistently protects lesbians, gays, bisexual, or transgender (LGBT) individuals from employment discrimination. On a state-by-state basis, as of late 2015, as this chapter is written, there are no laws in 29 states that explicitly prohibit discrimination based on sexual orientation and no laws in 32 states that prohibit discrimination based on gender identity. Consequently, in many states, LGBT people can be denied a promotion or fired from their jobs. Yet, more than two-thirds of voters, including a majority of Republican voters, support a federal law protecting LGBT people from discrimination in the workplace (Human Rights Campaign, 2015).

While equality in the workplace is an important social justice issue, it is important to remember that laws on the books do not automatically end discrimination. Employers sometimes find ways to circumvent the intent of the law. For example, the 1963 Equal Pay Act requires equal pay for equal work, but some employers assign highly similar jobs a different title, classification, and pay scale. It is not always completely clear whether the jobs are actually equal or not. How much similarity is needed for jobs to be truly equal?

What Do You Think?

How serious of a problem do you think that discrimination in the workplace is today? Is there any evidence that it continues to exist?

Occupational Safety and Health

People have long been concerned about the physical toll exacted by work. Medical writings reveal that even in ancient Rome physicians recognized an unusually high frequency of lung disease among metalworkers, miners, and weavers of asbestos cloth. During the Renaissance, each craft was known to have its unique maladies. But the Industrial Revolution created a new wave of deadly occupational hazards. From the beginning, the American labor movement made safety one of its top priorities at the urging of rank-and-file workers and union activists, yet despite this long history of concern and awareness, occupational health remains a serious problem.

Nearly 4,500 fatal work injuries were recorded in the United States in 2013, which is lower than the revised count of 4,600 fatal work injuries in 2012 (Bureau of Labor Statistics, 2014a). Figure 12–6 presents the most dangerous occupational categories, some of which have fatality rates 10, 20, or even 30 times the average worker. These occupations tend to be male-dominated, which explains why about 90 percent of those killed on the job are men. As the graph shows, loggers, fishers, aircraft pilots and flight engineers, roofers, refuse and recyclable material collectors, mining machine operators, truck drivers and driving sales workers, farmers, electrical power installers and repairers, and construction laborers have the highest fatality rates (Bureau of Labor Statistics, 2014a).

But fatalities are only part of the problem. In 2013, over 1.2 million people experienced injuries or illness from their jobs that did not kill them, but caused serious pain and suffering (Bureau of Labor Statistics, 2014c). These events might include falls, contact with objects, injury from fires, and exposure to harmful substances. These workers miss an average of 8 days of work annually due to these incidents.

Figure 12–6 Occupations with the Highest Work–Related Fatality Rates (per 100,000) Full–Time Workers), 2013

SOURCE: Bureau of Labor Statistics, 2014a.

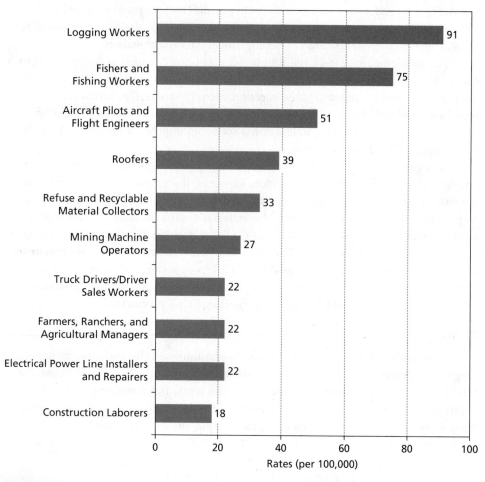

Occupation	Rate
Logging Workers	91
Fishers and Fishing Workers	75
Aircraft Pilots and Flight Engineers	51
Roofers	39
Refuse and Recyclable Material Collectors	33
Mining Machine Operators	27
Truck Drivers/Driver Sales Workers	22
Farmers, Ranchers, and Agricultural Managers	22
Electrical Power Line Installers and Repairers	22
Construction Laborers	18

Rates (per 100,000)

More people die in logging accidents than in any other occupation.

Industrial accidents are only part of the problem. The field of occupational health has widened to include illnesses as well as accidents, and is concentrating on preventing work-related diseases rather than merely treating or compensating workers for them. Perhaps the greatest health hazards come from the chemical industry. Chemicals, which are involved in the manufacture of almost every product we use, can also produce cancer. Workers who are exposed to certain chemicals have an unusually high rate of malignancies. They also frequently suffer from other health problems, such as nervous disorders and sterility; their children may suffer from birth defects.

Occupational health is an issue loaded with moral, medical, and economic questions. Industries claim that further safeguarding the workplace will be expensive and costs will be passed along to consumers in the form of higher prices. Others industries argue that compulsory adherence to proposed health regulations will put them out of business or force them to relocate to other countries. Some workers, more fearful of imminent unemployment than of future illness, side with their employers and agree to take their chances in the workplace. Others, realizing that their interests as consumers and citizens may outweigh their economic stake, join the ranks of consumer activists.

As workers in the United States and other industrialized nations organize to deal with occupational safety issues, there is more incentive for industries to locate in low-wage regions of the world whose impoverished citizens are far less capable of recognizing dangers and are less likely to complain to employers about dangerous working conditions. That even more American workers do not question the conditions in which they work or the desirability of what they produce is perhaps attributable, in part, to their high level of indebtedness, which has resulted from extensive use of consumer credit.

Consumers, Credit, and Debt

12.6 Explain the importance of consumerism, credit, and debt in American society.

The United States is a consumer society, one with an economy that depends on the disposable income, or buying power, of consumers. A consumer society requires a large middle and upper class with enough leisure time to enjoy the use of many goods and services that are not strictly necessary (although they may be perceived as such). Americans are proud of their access to an abundance of consumer goods and often contrast that abundance with the scarcities common in many other nations, especially those in less developed regions of the world.

There are several drawbacks to a consumer-based economy, however. Among these are the dominance of large corporations and franchise operations and the unplanned spread of shopping malls. Smaller businesses find it extremely difficult to compete with chain businesses that are better financed, more efficient, and highly profitable. Indeed, franchise chains such as McDonald's and Burger King have come close to wiping out the mom-and-pop restaurant and the roadside stand, traditional symbols of business independence. These chains have dominated through heavy advertising. Another drawback is that the push to consume encourages some people to spend far beyond their means, sometimes resulting in people losing what they have and filing for bankruptcy. Each of these drawbacks is discussed in the sections that follow.

Advertising and the Consumer Society

The activities of franchise operations and major corporations are accompanied by massive advertising campaigns. "Early to bed, Early to rise, Advertise, Advertise, Advertise" is the advice of McDonald's former advertising director. The media are inundated by advertising messages, so much so that advertising slogans have become part of our everyday conversation. "Getting there is half the fun," an executive may comment ruefully as she arrives late for a meeting. "Don't leave home without it," a father may say to his son as he hands him an umbrella. "Because I'm worth it," a woman may say to justify spending money on things that she may not need. Advertising plays a crucial role in a consumer society (Ritzer, 2012), but some observers are also concerned about its effects on other aspects of social life. For example, to what extent does the dependence of the media on advertisers influence the content of the news and other information they broadcast?

A consumer society leads to excessive materialism, a tendency to judge people by their possessions, and other negative consequences such as waste and planned obsolescence. But perhaps the most serious flaw of a consumer society is that it requires the ready availability of credit. Large-scale production of consumer goods depends on a steady flow of profits, which in turn requires that purchases be made constantly, not just whenever the consumer has a windfall or can accumulate enough through savings—hence the widespread use of consumer credit in the United States.

Advertising is the foundation of a consumer-based society. Advertisers try to create a demand for their products, be it a new car or a Big Mac sandwich.

Table 12–4 American Debt, 2015

U.S. Household Consumer Debt Profile (2015)	
Average credit card debt	$15,609
Average mortgage debt	$156,706
Average student loan debt	$32,956
In total, American consumers owe:	
$11.9 trillion in total debt	
$884.8 billion in credit card debt	
$8.2 trillion in mortgages	
$1.2 trillion in student loans	

SOURCE: Chen, 2015.

What Do You Think?

Direct-to-consumer pharmaceutical advertisements on television have been legal only since 1985, but did not really appear regularly until 1997. What are the pros and cons of these types of ads?

Since the 1950s the United States has been transformed from a cash to a credit society. As credit companies compete fiercely to lend money to credit seekers, they grant more and more loans to individuals. In total, Americans were a little over $11.9 trillion in debt in early 2015, as shown in Table 12–4, which is up nearly 3 percent from a year ago. A typical credit card user has a debt of over $15,000. Average student loan debt averages nearly $33,000, and a typical mortgage holder carries about $157,000 in debt.

Personal Bankruptcy

Although the enormous increase in consumer credit has been a boon to the U.S. economy, it has given rise to a new and pervasive social problem: debt entanglement and bankruptcy. Each year, more than a million workers have their wages garnished to meet their unpaid debts; many others are sued by their creditors for defaulting.

Personal bankruptcies have risen substantially since the recession. During the period from April 1, 2007, to March 31, 2008, there were 696,000 filings for bankruptcy in the United States. Seven years later (April 1, 2014, to March 31, 2015) as the recession was coming to an end, that number had increased to 911,000. People are still suffering from the effects of unemployment even though they may be back to work. This debt is another reason why, even though the economy is improving by objective measures, subjectively people still consider the economy to be the number one social problem.

In 2005 a law was passed making it more difficult for families to erase their debts through bankruptcy. After years of intense pressure from banks and credit card companies, Congress passed legislation that requires a number of steps, including mandatory counseling and agreements to repay some proportion of debts according to a specific schedule, before judges could grant bankruptcy protection. In the House, the Republican leadership allowed no amendments or real debate; in the Senate, one proposed amendment would have protected families declaring bankruptcy for medical reasons, but it failed (Alter, 2005).

Just before this law went into effect in 2006, there was a spike in personal bankruptcy filings as consumers who were in financial trouble hoped to avoid the harsher new regulations by filing quickly. As planned, filings went down precipitously after passage of the law. However, due to the recession and its aftermath, bankruptcies have climbed rapidly again even though they are harder to obtain and the penalties are more stringent. Perhaps the most significant fact about bankruptcies is that over 90 percent are due to divorce, medical bills, and job loss rather than careless or frivolous spending (Warren, 2010).

Social Policy

12.7 **Construct an argument on why the minimum wage should be raised.**

The economy continues to improve, and much of the thanks is due to new, key policies that helped stimulate the economy and helped individuals who were suffering from home and job losses. Another idea has been floating around to help the economy—raising the minimum wage—and people are lining up to support or oppose this proposal.

Minimum Wage

Some U.S. workers earn only the minimum wage or even less. The federal minimum wage in the United States stood at $7.25 per hour in late-2015, and comes nowhere near to lifting even a small family out of poverty. At $7.25 per hour, working 40 hours per week yields $290 per week before taxes (yes, people working at minimum wage still pay taxes). Working 52 weeks a year, without any vacation time, a full-time employee would average around $15,080 per year. How does a person or a family pay for rent, utilities, food, clothing, and other incidentals on a federal minimum wage?

Because this rate is so low, 29 states (and the District of Columbia) have adopted state minimum wages that are higher than the federal wage. Washington State and Oregon have the highest state minimum wages in the nation at $9.47 and $9.25 per hour, respectively (National Conference of State Legislatures, 2015). However, in Georgia, the state minimum wage is $5.15. Employees covered under the federal Fair Labor Standards Act (FLSA) are subject to the federal minimum wage of $7.25, but those not covered under the FLSA (such as many part-time domestic workers) may be paid the state minimum wage of $5.15. In Oklahoma, employers of ten or more full-time employees at any one location and employers with annual gross sales over $100,000 irrespective of the number of full-time employees are subject to the federal minimum wage of $7.25; all others are subject to the state minimum wage of $2.00.

About 77 million workers ages 16 and older are paid hourly wages, and of these, 3 million workers earn the minimum wage or even less (Bureau of Labor Statistics, 2015a). Teenagers and young adults are overrepresented among low-wage workers; however, as indicated in Table 12–5, 52 percent of these workers are adults age 25 and

Table 12–5 Characteristics of Persons Earning the Federal Minimum Wage or Less, 2014 (16 and Older)

Age	
16–24	48%
25 and Over	52%
Sex	
Male	37%
Female	63%
Race/Ethnicity	
White	76%
Black	15%
Asian	4%
Hispanic	17%
Work Status	
Full-Time	35%
Part-Time	65%

SOURCE: Bureau of Labor Statistics, 2015a.

Senator Bernie Sanders, Independent of Vermont, speaks during a rally with striking federal workers on the East Front of the Capitol, in April 2015, to call on President Obama to sign the Model Employer Executive Order that would raise the minimum wage to at least $15 an hour.

over. Females are nearly twice as likely as men to earn the minimum wage or less. The racial and ethnic breakdown roughly parallels their distribution in the population with no one group singled out as being more likely than others to hold this distinction. Most low-wage workers are part-time, and nearly a quarter of them reside in only two states: Texas and California (Bureau of Labor Statistics, 2015a).

The purchasing power of the minimum wage has eroded substantially over the past decades, controlling for inflation. Using today's purchasing power as the benchmark, the minimum wage in 1968 was equal to about $10 an hour, significantly more than today's $7.25 wage. Additionally, the gap between the minimum-wage workers and middle-wage workers, has grown significantly. Increasing the minimum wage would restore its relative value (Bernstein and Parrott, 2014).

Future Prospects

Recognizing that the purchasing power of the minimum wage has eroded, and is far too low to support a family, in the 2014 State of the Union Address, President Obama called on Congress to raise the federal minimum wage to $10.10 an hour. Soon afterwards, he signed an Executive Order to raise the minimum wage to $10.10 for individuals working on new federal service contracts, which will benefit at least 200,000 workers by 2019 (Executive Office of the President, 2014).

Raising the minimum wage to $10.10 would directly boost the wages of about 28 million workers and help low-income parents make ends meet. It would lift 2 million families out of poverty (Executive Office of the President, 2014). Whether or not this proposal will pass Congress, 13 states have agreed to raise their minimum wages substantially, phased in over a few years. For example, California plans to raise its minimum wage to $10 in 2016, benefiting over 3 million workers.

Some people feel that a raise in the minimum wage to $10.10 does not go far enough. U.S. Senator Bernie Sanders from Vermont, a candidate for U.S. President, is an outspoken supporter of raising the minimum wage to $15 an hour. This boost in the minimum wage is beginning to receive some national traction. For example, the city council in Seattle, Washington, passed an ordinance to raise the minimum wage to $15 an hour. The increase will be phased in over a few years; large firms with greater than 500 workers will have until January 1, 2017, while smaller firms will have several years longer to phase up to $15 an hour (Office of the Mayor, 2015). The University of California, the County of Los Angeles, Washington, DC, and some businesses in New York City have also agreed to raise the minimum wage to $15 an hour.

Going Beyond Left and Right

Former House Speaker John Boehner argued against raising the minimum wage, stating: "If you raise the price of something, guess what? You get less of it" (Geewax, 2013). What Mr. Boehner means is, if the cost of low-wage labor rises, employers will lay off workers and hire fewer workers in the future. However, there are numerous ways to accommodate wage increases without layoffs. These methods include more efficient production, higher prices, and lower profits.

In a review of over 60 studies that look for statistical linkages between minimum-wage increases and job losses, some studies find that raising the minimum wage has a small negative effect on employment, a smaller number find that it has a small positive effect, and most find no significant effect at all (Schmitt, 2013). These findings suggest there would likely be few job losses with an increase in the minimum wage. Even those persons whose hours were reduced may still see increases in their weekly earnings. Businesses like Costco, Walmart, and Stride Rite have supported past increases to the minimum wage, in part, because they believe that increasing worker productivity and consumers' purchasing power will also help the overall economy.

The minimum wage was last raised in 2007 with support from both Republicans and Democrats, and the action is an example of how perceptions of fairness cut across ideological lines. In the face of a widening gap between the haves and the have-nots, Congress was unwilling to allow a huge segment of the low-wage labor force to sink into poverty. It raised the minimum wage from $5.15 to $7.25 per hour fully realizing that, even though this advance would not lift all poor households out of poverty, it would at least indicate that the nation's leaders cared about the plight of those at the bottom of the economic ladder. It remains to be seen what will happen as the fight to raise the minimum wage to $10.10, or even $15, intensifies.

Summary

- Objective data indicate that the U.S. economy is recovering from the recession that plagued the country beginning in 2008. Americans are more optimistic than they were a few years ago. Unemployment has declined, there is less financial worry, and fewer Americans are worried about losing their jobs. However, although there has been significant objective and subjective improvement, Americans are still more likely to rate the economy, as compared with anything else, as the most important social problem.

- A number of key trends in America's capitalist system of free enterprise include the globalization of markets and the rise of major multinational corporations that compete for power on the world stage; growth in service-sector jobs in the advanced economies and continued export of manufacturing jobs to regions with lower wage rates; increasing reliance of families on the incomes of multiple workers; and increased reliance on innovations in technology and specialization to increase the productivity and competitiveness of companies and their employees.

- Multinational corporations are transforming the world's economy by focusing on rapidly developing markets and on labor forces in the less-developed nations. Labor is often done 24 hours a day, seven days a week, and many jobs are outsourced to other countries where the labor is cheaper, working conditions are poor, and environmental policies are weak.

- Over the past generation, there have been three unprecedented changes in the U.S. labor force, largely because of transformations in the global economy. First is the shift from manufacturing to service employment. Second is the large increase in contingent nonstandard work schedules. Third is the enormous increase in the number of women working outside the home—women of all ages and from all kinds of family backgrounds.

- As the economy steadily improves, a number of social problems continue to plague the work environment. These include unemployment, especially among minority groups; insecurity about the decline of "good" jobs that provide important benefits; job discrimination, especially among groups currently not covered by anti-discrimination legislation; and health and safety in the workplace.

- The United States is a consumer society. One drawback to being a consumer society is the dominance of large corporations and franchise operations and the near elimination of small mom-and-pop businesses. Large corporations have used the power of advertising to increase their dominance. Another drawback to consumerism is the push to consume, which encourages some people to spend far beyond their means, often leading to filing for bankruptcy.

- Some U.S. workers earn only the minimum wage of $7.25 an hour (in mid-2015) or even less. This wage comes nowhere near to lifting even a small family out of poverty. The purchasing power of the minimum wage, controlling for inflation, has declined significantly over the years, and is now on par with what it was in 1981. There is a movement under way to increase the minimum wage to $10.10 an hour, although some are pushing for an increase to $15 an hour. Critics fear that the minimum wage will cause job cuts, but research suggests that this effect is unlikely.

Chapter 13
Population and Immigration

 Learning Objectives

13.1 Describe the growth in the world's population.

13.2 Explain the demographic transition and its relevance in the world today.

13.3 Analyze the indicators of rising expectations in the less developed world.

13.4 Compare and contrast governments' involvement in population control efforts.

13.5 Sequence and differentiate the history of immigration in the United States.

13.6 Explore the issue of illegal immigration and its consequences for Americans and the immigrants themselves.

13.7 Consider the controversy and the policies associated with children who are fleeing violence in Central America.

Why study population? Population growth can lead to major social problems such as war, famine, political instability, and infanticide. Over 7.3 billion people live in the world today. There may be room for everyone; in fact, all of the world's population standing side by side could fit into the Los Angeles area (Gupton, 2011). However, the issue is about resources. How many people can the earth really sustain, and does our behavior affect that number?

Population changes can be related to high birthrates, low death rates, emigration, or immigration. In the United States, population concerns tend to revolve around immigration, which accounts for much (but by no means all) of the overall growth of the U.S. population. It is often difficult to assimilate new immigrants into U.S. society. The newcomers require education, health care, and other services that may strain already tight local budgets. Yet, if not for immigration, nations like the United States would have growing labor shortages. In other parts of the world, however, population issues are less related to immigration and are more likely due to large numbers of women giving birth to many children. In this chapter, you will look at some of the patterns of world population. In particular, you will be able to compare some of the key differences between less developed countries (LDCs) and those that are more developed, such as the United States. Understanding the dynamics of population is important because population shifts can cause many different social, health, and environmental problems and tensions.

The World's Population

13.1 **Describe the growth in the world's population.**

The world's population is currently growing at a rapid rate, but this rate of growth has not always been the case, as shown in Figure 13–1. Although humans have flourished for 200,000 years, the rapid and problematic rise in population that concerns us in this chapter is a feature of the last 300 years. The population did not reach 1 billion people until about the year 1800. Then, it increased to 1.6 billion only 100 years later. Today, after another century, the world's population as of late

Figure 13–1 World Population Change

SOURCE: Data from Office of Technology Assessment.

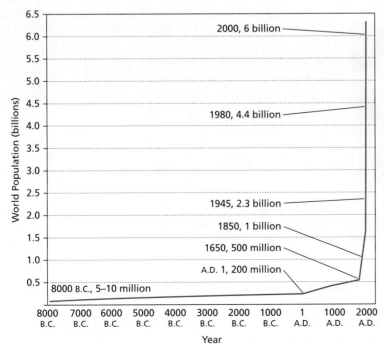

Slide Show

Overpopulation

Overpopulation has less to do with the number of people per se, than it has to do with the number of people who are using precious resources. People require, at a minimum, food, clean water, clothing, and shelter, but certainly most humans want much more than these minimums.

The world contains over 7.3 billion people. It's easy to say "Oh, what's one more," but each beautiful, sleeping, bundle of joy taxes the earth's resources.

Many cities in less developed countries are crowded and do not supply proper sanitation facilities. Diseases easily spread in this environment.

As developing countries attempt to modernize, they are usually lax about pollution standards. Their goal is to industrialize, at whatever the cost. In China, one of the costs of their rapid development is polluted air.

Clean drinking water is a precious commodity and one that is rare in many developing countries. People use the same water to drink as they do to wash clothes, clean the dishes, and relieve themselves. Animals may use the same water source as humans, resulting in a variety of bacteria and diseases. Is it any surprise that the leading cause of death in many developing nations is diarrhea?

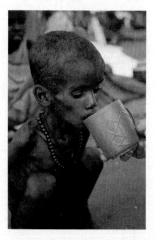

This girl is one of the 800 million people who do not get enough food to eat. She is one of the lucky ones, however, and is receiving assistance from aid workers.

Critical Thinking

If the world now contains about 7.3 million people, what changes might you see if the population reaches 9 million, or even higher? Will the lifestyles of people in developed countries like the United States change, and if so, what type of changes could occur? What about those who live in less developed countries (LDCs); what changes would they likely see?

2015 was over 7.3 billion and, depending on the projection used, could be between 9.2 and 9.6 billion by 2050 (Population Reference Bureau, 2015; Worldwatch Institute, 2013).

If the concept of a billion is difficult to comprehend, consider the following:

- If you were 1 billion seconds old, you would be 31.7 years old.
- The circumference of the earth is 25,000 miles. If you circled the earth 40,000 times, you would have traveled 1 billion miles.

Now, multiply this information by seven or nine, and you can get a good grasp on what we are talking about for today's population and that of the future. Consider another way to think about population growth: The average population growth rate before 1650 is thought to have been about two-thousandths of 1 percent per year. By 1900, the annual growth rate had reached one-half of 1 percent. Between 1900 and 1940, the rate rose to 1 percent, and by 1960, to 2 percent.

Measures of Population Growth

A few definitions might help you better understand the significance of these population growth figures. Several terms are used to describe population changes:

- *Total birth (or fertility) rate.*   The term **total birth (or fertility) rate** refers to the average number of children born to a woman during her lifetime. This indicator is a direct measure of the level of fertility since it refers to births per woman. It shows the potential for population change in the country. A rate of two children per woman is considered the replacement rate for a population, resulting in relative stability in terms of total numbers. Rates above two children indicate populations growing in size. This measure allows for useful historical and international comparisons.
- *General birth (or fertility) rate.*   The term **general birth (or fertility) rate** means the number of children born per 1,000 women ages 15–44 (some countries use 49 as the cutoff age). This refined method allows international or historical comparisons because it relates birth to the age of females likely to give birth.
- *Crude birth (or fertility rate).*   This measure refers to the number of children born per 1,000 of the population. Note that this measure doesn't account for the age of the population. A crude birthrate of 20, for example, means that each year a given group of 1,000 people will produce 20 babies. This figure does not tell what percentage of the population is of childbearing age or what percentage of the population are women. Obviously, if the average age of the population is young (e.g., in Kenya), there will be more children born than if the average age of the population is old (e.g., in Japan).

The differential between the **crude birthrate** and the death rate is called the **rate of population growth (natural increase)** and is usually expressed as a percentage. (In a hypothetical 1,000-person group in which 20 people are added by birth and 10 removed by death, the total population at the end of the year is 1,010—a growth rate of 1 percent.) Note that this figure does not take into account immigration patterns.

Most nations have population growth rates of 0.1 percent to 3.0 percent. If a nation's population growth rate is negative, more people are lost through death than are gained through birth and immigration, and the total population can be expected to decline over time. This negative rate could be a problem economically because it is likely that the population is old, with fewer young adults and children. On the flip side, a nation's population growth rate that reaches 2 percent or more is considered "explosive" population growth. If it were to continue unabated, such a rate would cause the population to double in 35 years or less. As you can imagine, this quick increase would be a problem.

total birth (or fertility) rate

Average number of children born to a woman during her lifetime.

general birth (or fertility) rate

Number of children born per 1,000 women ages 15–44 (some countries use 49 as the cutoff age).

crude birth (or fertility) rate

The number of children born per 1,000 of the population.

rate of population growth (natural increase)

The differential between the crude birthrate and the death rate.

What Do You Think?

How would life in the United States be different if our population doubled in 35 years? Think of our social institutions, for example, our schools, economy, families, health care, education, and political system. What kinds of changes would we see?

Uneven Population Growth: Developed and Less Developed Countries

Population growth occurs unevenly around the world, as shown in Figure 13–2. Growth is particularly pronounced in Africa, where today, a typical woman has about five children. The good news? Fertility has declined in all regions of the world. Only a generation ago, a typical woman in Africa had about seven children.

Less developed countries (LDCs), which include Africa but also parts of South America and Southern Asia, contain about 81 percent of the world's population. In many of these countries, population growth exceeds 2 percent. And, if we look to the future, it is likely that their population will continue to grow explosively. Why? In some countries such as Niger, the median age of the population is only 15 years; therefore, the population is likely to grow rapidly because so many people are, or will soon be, of childbearing age. In other words, lots of young women will be having lots of babies. Although women are having fewer children in LDCs, the massive numbers of young people in the early stage of their childbearing age means that many babies will continue to be born.

In contrast, Russia and many other European nations have been experiencing extremely slow or even negative rates of natural population increase. According to estimates by the United Nations, these nations have such low birthrates that they are experiencing population declines. Japan has the oldest median age—44 years old. Fewer people there are at the age where they want to (or can) have babies, and the country is concerned about significant population decline and the costs of taking care of all the elderly people.

The median age of a population is important because it allows a glimpse into the future to see what is ahead. A low median age means the population will grow significantly, whereas a high median age means the population has stabilized or may decline. The median age reflects two important trends that actually occur at opposite ends of the lifespan, and both have important implications for population size. First, the median age reflects birth (fertility) rates. Second, it reflects mortality (death) rates.

Map 13–1 on pages 370–371 shows birthrates throughout the world using the total birth (fertility) rate, which calculates the average number of children born to a woman during her lifetime. Looking at this map, note that South Korea, China, Taiwan, and much of Western and Eastern Europe have fertility rates below 1.5, well below replacement level. Countries with fertility rates this low must rely on immigration to maintain their population, or else the population will decline (Population Reference Bureau, 2015).

Generally speaking, the fertility rate in developing nations far exceeds the rate in developed nations. In Niger, for example, an average woman bears seven children,

---

Figure 13–2 Total Fertility Rates, 1970–2013

SOURCE: Carl Haub and Toshiko Kaneda, 2014 World Population Data Sheet.

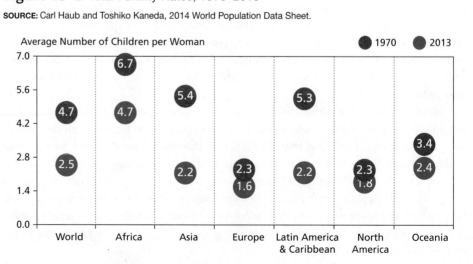

whereas in Taiwan, she has only one (Population Reference Bureau, 2015). One reason for this difference is that, in some LDCs such as Cambodia, Kenya, Pakistan, and Yemen, less than half of married women ages 15–49 use some sort of contraceptive, as shown in Table 13–1 (Population Reference Bureau, 2015). This limited contraceptive use may be due to obstacles such as inadequate funds for supplies and the lack of comprehensive programs to educate couples on their options. Moreover, large families are often valued culturally as a means of social security. With few government aid programs, large numbers of children are believed to be important social, economic, and political resources that can help maintain and provide for families. However, in reality, having many children will likely keep families impoverished.

In addition to indicating fertility rates, the median age also reflects a country's mortality (death) rates. You would think that countries with a high mortality rate (i.e., a greater number of people dying) would grow their populations slowly. However, fertility and mortality rates are often positively related to one another; that is, those countries that have the most births also tend to have the most deaths (e.g., most of Africa). But their births surpass their deaths, and so the population grows rapidly. Conversely, those countries with the lowest fertility rates tend to have lower death rates (e.g., the United States, Canada). In these countries, birth and death rates are more balanced, and therefore the population grows slowly.

However, some interesting exceptions exist. Some countries with low fertility rates also have high death rates, reflecting an aging population (e.g., Japan and much of Europe). Moreover, some countries have high fertility rates but also surprisingly low death rates, reflecting the youthfulness within a relatively healthy population (e.g., much of Central America). In these countries, population grows rapidly, as you might imagine.

However, taken as a whole, fertility rates are declining all over the world. The real issue is that more people are living to the age when they have babies and, in fact, are living well beyond these years. In other words, *mortality rates have started to decline, especially in LDCs.* More people have been exposed to improved vaccinations, sanitation, and modern medicines and have learned new ways to combat the spread of disease. We have also increased ability to compensate for excessive cold, heat, and other dangers to life in our environment. And our power to prevent or quickly counteract the effects of famine, drought, flood, and similar natural disasters has improved considerably. As a result, people are living longer. This development is very good news, but it also exacerbates population growth. In effect, more babies are surviving to produce babies themselves, thus posing significant challenges for food production. Many nations are struggling to feed their rapidly growing population and therefore rely on the aid of wealthier nations such as the United States. In other words, as we look forward, *the world's population will continue to grow, but the primary cause will be declining death rates, not necessarily continued high birthrates.* This forecast has important policy implications, doesn't it?

What Do You Think?

Pretend that you work for a nongovernmental organization that has humanitarian issues as a top concern. Your board of directors believes that overpopulation is the root of many of the social and health problems in the developing world. They ask you to develop a policy that would control population growth. What would your policy look like?

Table 13–1 Percentage of Married Women of Childbearing Age Who Use Modern Contraceptives, Selected Countries, 2014

Contraceptive Use	
Mexico	66%
Bangladesh	52%
Kenya	39%
Cambodia	35%
Haiti	31%
Yemen	29%
Pakistan	25%

SOURCE: Population Reference Bureau, 2015.

Map 13–1 Total Fertility Rates, 2015

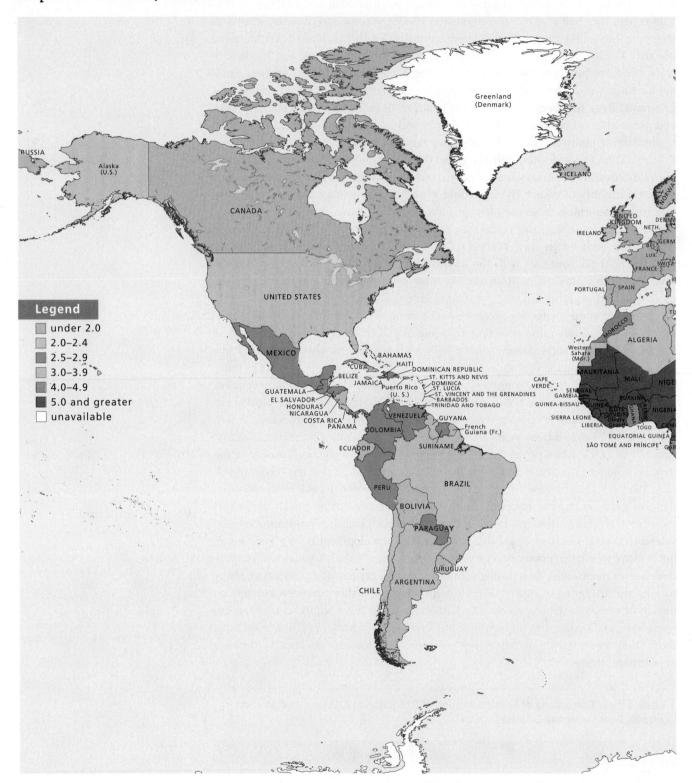

Legend
- under 2.0
- 2.0–2.4
- 2.5–2.9
- 3.0–3.9
- 4.0–4.9
- 5.0 and greater
- unavailable

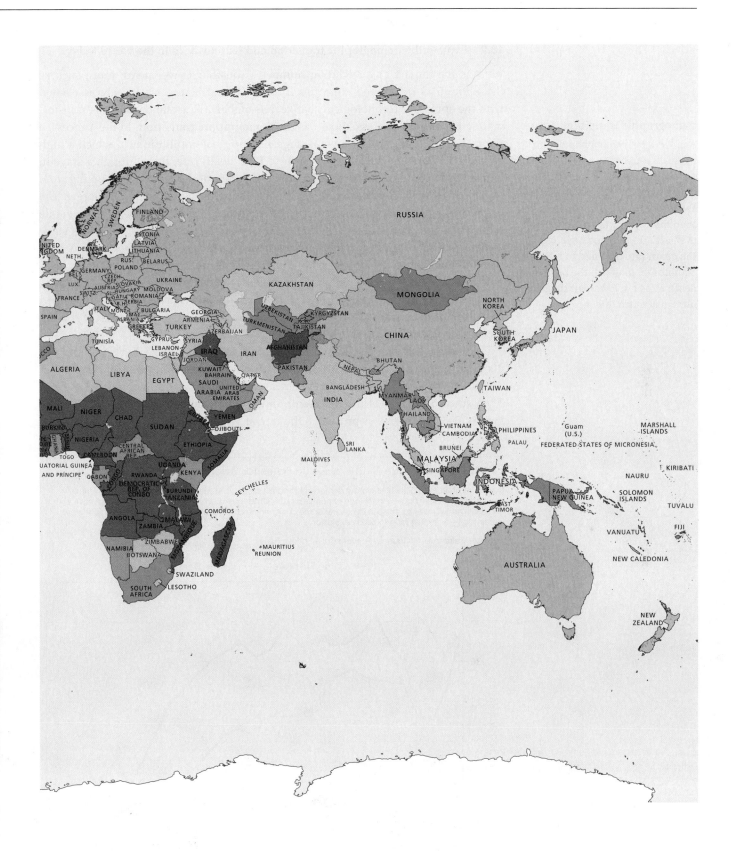

The Demographic Transition

13.2 Explain the demographic transition and its relevance in the world today.

demographic transition

A process by which a population moves through several stages: An original equilibrium in which a high birthrate is more or less canceled out by a high death rate, then through a stage in which the birthrate remains high but the death rate declines, to a final equilibrium in which the birth and death rates are lower but the population is much larger.

What is the impact of a declining number of deaths? Lower death rates, such as those found in developed countries like the United States, are closely associated with the spread of technological change and higher living standards. This transformation is part of a process known as the **demographic transition**. In this process, a population moves through several stages: an original equilibrium in which a high birthrate is more or less canceled out by a high death rate, then through a stage in which the birthrate remains high but the death rate declines, to a final equilibrium in which the birth and death rates are lower but the population is much larger. The first stage is characteristic of peasant and primitive populations before large-scale improvement in sanitation, health care, and other improvements. After this stage comes a period of rapid population growth as traditional values about family size, together with the lack of birth control techniques, keep the birthrate high while technological advances produce a steady decrease in the death rate, especially of infants. Most LDCs are in this stage. In the final stage, which is characteristic of developed industrialized societies, values change, the birthrate declines, and rates of natural increase slow down.

The demographic transition first occurred in northwestern Europe. During a period of about 100 years in the eighteenth and nineteenth centuries, death rates decreased by about 60 percent while birthrates remained at traditionally high levels. Then, toward the end of the nineteenth century, fertility began a long-term decline. Figure 13–3 illustrates this process in the case of Sweden.

Figure 13–3 Crude Birth and Death Rates for Sweden, 1690-1960

NOTE: This chart exemplifies the classic demographic transition, in which death rates and birthrates eventually become more or less equal and the rate of population growth stabilizes. Many less developed nations have birth and death rates similar to those in the center of the chart, where crude death rates are declining and birthrates remain high—a formula for population explosion.

SOURCE: Matras, 1973. Courtesy Armand Colin Éditeur, Paris.

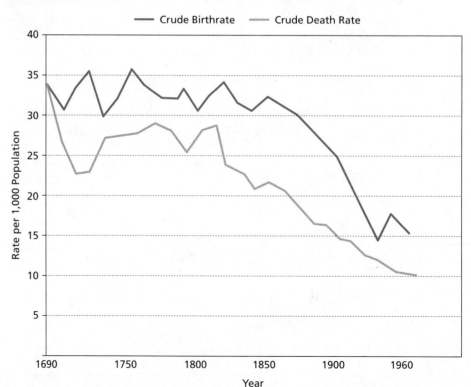

Wherever industrial technology has taken hold on a local level, the third stage of the demographic transition has followed—from Western Europe to North America, Australia, and New Zealand and, later, through the rest of Europe. Today, the populations of Japan, Singapore, Taiwan, Hong Kong, and two or three other such areas have reached the final phase, and they have tended to reach it much more quickly (in about 30 years) than the northern European nations did. However, large areas of Asia, Africa, and Latin America still remain in the middle phase. Their birthrates, although declining, are still relatively high, and people are living longer. In these societies, population growth often outstrips economic and social development, producing poverty and social unrest.

Rising Expectations in the Developing World

13.3 Analyze the indicators of rising expectations in the less developed world.

There are rising expectations in many LDCs. When some people have access to an improved standard of living naturally, there is the expectation among others that if conditions have begun to improve, everyone should be able to share in its benefits. But will that expectation hold true?

This process of rising expectations began in the late 1950s and early 1960s, when many LDCs, particularly in sub-Saharan Africa and Southeast Asia, gained independence from the former colonial powers (Geertz, 2005). Turning their attention to efforts to improve the lives of people in isolated rural populations, governments embarked on campaigns for favorable terms of trade and direct aid from developed nations. Ever greater sums were invested in education, health care, transportation, and communication. These investments ultimately resulted in changing expectations among the populations of the LDCs as newly educated and healthier masses were exposed to the media and all the information about culture and standards of living that they convey.

It is important to distinguish between the **standard of living** of a population, which is what people want or expect in the way of material well-being, and the **level of living**, which is what people actually obtain. In many LDCs, there is a wide gap between the two, which produces frustration, conflict, and political instability. These problems make economic and social development in the poor regions of the world even more problematic, as countries squabble over water rights, borders, and critical resources.

standard of living

What people want or expect in the way of material well-being.

level of living

The level of material well-being that people actually obtain.

Literacy Rates

Literacy rates are a good indicator of the likelihood that traditionally poor and powerless groups may be gaining some ground. Literacy has been increasing steadily, from an estimated 68 percent of the total world population in 1970 to more than 80 percent today. These figures, of course, do not show the tremendous disparities in literacy that continue to persist, as reported in Table 13–2. For example, Cuba enjoys virtually a 100 percent literacy rate, whereas the figure for Chad is 35 percent (United Nations Development Programme, 2014).

Table 13–2 Comparison of Literacy Rates in Selected Less Developed Countries, 2014

Cuba	100%
Chile	99%
India	63%
Pakistan	55%
Chad	35%

SOURCE: CIA World Factbook, 2014.

Significant discrepancies in literacy also exist between women and men, especially in LDCs, but women, too, are gaining ground. For example, in 2000, only about 74 percent of women in Guatemala were literate. Today, that proportion is at least 84 percent, a 10 percent increase. Meanwhile the increase since 2000 among males was only about 3 percent, from 86 percent to 89 percent.

But in many countries, educating girls, including teaching them to read and write, is steeped in controversy. In highly patriarchal countries, education is considered the prerogative of boys, and schools for girls are scarce. For example, in Afghanistan, only about one in three girls now attends elementary school, and about one in six attends high school. Meanwhile, the legal age of marriage for a girl is 15 years, and almost half of girls are married by age 18 (United Nations Girls' Education Initiative, 2014). Pakistan fares a little better. There, almost two in three girls attend primary school, but only one in four attends high school. However, these figures represent sweeping improvements over the time when the Taliban was in control of these regions.

Yet, even today, in many parts of the world, families who send their daughters to school may face substantial risk of attack. Girls have been sexually assaulted, have had acid poured on their faces, or have even been killed, as they walk to or from school. In April 2014, the militant Islamic group Boko Haram kidnapped 270 girls from a boarding school in Nigeria. Believing that Western education is a sin, the soldiers, dressed in camouflage, shot up the school in the middle of the night and abducted the girls. In the first few days, 57 girls managed to escape from their captors. But hundreds remain missing and are feared to have been sold into marriage or slavery. Their abduction sparked global outrage and a huge campaign calling for their rescue, partly propelled by the hashtag #BringBackOurGirls (Alfred, 2014). As of this writing in late 2015, these girls have yet to be returned to their families.

In Pakistan, one young woman, a 17-year-old named Malala Yousafzai, who faced her own grave risks attempting to receive an education, has become an outspoken advocate for the educational rights of women and girls throughout the world. Surviving an attempted assassination attempt, she continues to speak out internationally. For her work, she was awarded the Nobel Peace Prize and is the youngest person ever to win this esteemed award. Her story can be found in A Global View: Malala Yousafzai.

The best way to reduce the birthrate is to educate women. Educating men does not have the same effect. However, it is not always easy for women to get an education in many countries because of cost and safety issues and because patriarchal values promote that girls' education is not important.

Meanwhile, teachers are also at risk of physical violence against them. The situation is so dire and widespread that many international organizations, such as the United Nations and the World Bank, have entire programs designed to intervene, educate, and assist national governments as they fulfill their responsibilities toward ensuring the right to education for all children (United Nations Girls' Education Initiative, 2014; The World Bank 2014).

The education of girls is an important human rights issue. But it is more. It is also a critical population control issue. Girls and young women who receive an education are likely to marry later and to have fewer children. They also are more likely to educate their own daughters and sons equally. Educating girls has a domino effect: It is a gift that keeps on giving (The World Bank, 2014).

Energy Consumption

As expectations rise, so does energy consumption. People want to use energy to heat their homes, cook their food, and, increasingly, drive their cars. Per capita energy consumption is a good indication of the quality of life of a population, and by this measure, stark disparities

A Global View

Malala's Story

She's just a child, really. At age 17, she's also the youngest person ever to win the Nobel Peace Prize. Her name is Malala. Malala Yousafzai. She's become a household name, and a bit of a rock star among preteen and teenage girls. Who is she? She's a girl who fights for the rights of other girls to receive an education.

In many parts of the world, girls are routinely denied access to schools, or if allowed an education, are harassed by others in the community. Educating girls is considered dangerous and against God's will. With education, girls may start speaking out, demanding rights, and disobeying the men in their families. Girls, like their older sisters and mothers, should be kept at home, inside, illiterate, powerless.

The Taliban, a ruling political organization in parts of the Middle East, fervently holds these views, and when its members come into power, they ban education for girls. The Taliban savagely destroys schools and may maim or kill girls who try to circumvent the law. Malala is a girl who spoke up when the Taliban took control of the area in Pakistan where she lived.

Malala's father was a teacher and political activist, and his daughter was his pride and joy. She went to school and had dreams of becoming a doctor. Meanwhile, her father encouraged her to become a politician, believing that she could change the world. When the Taliban took control, they destroyed schools and mandated that women and girls stay indoors. Malala claims that she prayed for a magic wand so she could make the Taliban disappear. But she soon realized that it would take more, much more, than a magic wand.

After her school was closed, at the age of 11 she gave a public speech titled, "How Dare the Taliban Take Away My Basic Right to an Education?" The next year, when she was 12, she began blogging for the BBC about living under the Taliban's threats to deny her an education. To hide her identity, she used a fake name. However, within months, she was revealed to be the BBC blogger. With a growing public platform, Malala continued to speak out about the right of all girls to an education and was awarded Pakistan's National Youth Peace Prize.

The Taliban considered Malala a threat to their mission, and when she was 14, the Taliban issued a death threat against her. However, Malala's family didn't really believe that the Taliban would harm a child; her family was more concerned that the Taliban would harm Malala's father.

Nonetheless, on her way home from school, a man boarded the bus she was riding and demanded to know which girl was Malala. When her friends looked toward Malala, her location on the bus was given away. The gunman fired at her, hitting Malala in the left side of her head; the bullet then traveled down her neck. Mala was flown to a military hospital, in critical condition. A portion of her skull was removed to treat her swelling brain. She was then flown to England to receive further care, which included multiple surgeries to fix the paralyzed left side of her face. Miraculously, Malala suffered no brain damage.

The shooting resulted in an outpouring of support for Malala and her cause. She gave a speech at the United Nations on her sixteenth birthday and published an autobiography, *I Am Malala: The Girl Who Stood Up for Education and Was Shot by the Taliban*. Malala and her family have remained in England where she continues to speak out for the rights of girls to receive an education. The United Nations Secretary-General Ban Ki-moon described Malala as "a brave and gentle advocate of peace who through the simple act of going to school became a global teacher."

Critical Thinking

Why do you think Malala was so intent on getting an education? In what ways would an education change her life? Why do you think the Taliban are so intent on keeping girls uneducated? What is it that the Taliban fears about educating girls?

---

remain. Table 13–3 shows average oil consumption per capita (per person) in selected countries in 1990 and in 2012. As you can see, oil consumption has actually declined in developed nations such as the United Kingdom, Switzerland, and the United States. However, the use of oil has increased in LDCs, sometimes quite substantially. China represents the most extreme case of all: Oil consumption has increased nearly 300 percent during this period, while the population has grown relatively slowly.

Yet, despite the increase in oil consumption in LDCs and the decline in developed countries, the imbalance in its use remains striking. People in developed countries use five to ten times as much oil as do people in LDCs. Americans consume extremely large quantities of oil, reflecting the nature of American lifestyles. The typical middle-class suburban lifestyle consumes considerable gasoline, but also consumes large quantities of paper, steel, synthetic chemicals, aluminum, and so forth, all of which require high levels of oil (and other forms of energy) for their production.

Oil is just one of many forms of energy. Some types of energy are "dirty," such as coal and oil, and others are "clean," such as wind or solar energy because they do not pollute the earth. These clean forms of energy are also renewable.

Table 13–3 Oil Use in Selected Countries: Kg of Oil Per Capita, 1990 and 2012

	1990	2012
Less Developed Countries:		
Haiti	219	320 (2011)
India	357	614 (2011)
Kenya	461	489 (2011)
China	767	2,029 (2011)
Developed Countries:		
United Kingdom	3,626	3,020
Switzerland	3,628	3,189
United States	7,770	6,790

SOURCE: United Nations Statistics Division, 2014.

Perhaps a better way to compare energy consumption among countries is to examine their level of carbon emissions (CO_2). Scientists note that carbon emissions have increased more than 50 percent since 1990, and these emissions have a grave impact on air pollution and climate change. The six largest carbon emitting regions were China (29 percent), the United States (15 percent), the European Union (11 percent), India (6 percent), the Russian Federation (5 percent), and Japan (4 percent) (PBL Netherland Environmental Agency, 2014). The top three carbon emitting regions—China, the United States, and the European Union—account for 55 percent of total global CO_2 emissions. Emissions *increased* by 4.2 percent in China and 2.5 percent in the United States between 2012 and 2013 (even though oil consumption slightly declined in the United States), while in the European Union, emissions *decreased* by 1.4 percent. The growth in emissions in China is particularly striking and has been one of the unfortunate consequences of their incredible economic progress over the last few decades. However, it is important to keep perspective. China may have almost twice the carbon emissions of the United States, but China also has about five times as many people. In other words, the United States still leads the world in carbon emissions per capita, by far.

Naturally, other countries want to emulate the United States. They think, "If Americans can heat or cool their houses, have washing machines, and drive cars, then why shouldn't we?" The social problem lies in the fact that the world's population is too large for everyone to have these things—it would tax our resources and contribute to pollution and climate change beyond what humankind has ever known. But the question remains and is an important one: If Americans can have these things, then why shouldn't the rest of the world? Or maybe the question should be rephrased, "Should Americans have unlimited access to these things?"

Food and Hunger

As expectations rise and populations continue to grow, hunger abounds. It is almost impossible to fathom, but 800 million people in the world today do not get enough food to eat to lead a healthy and active life (Food and Agriculture Organization of the United Nations, 2014). This figure comes to one person in every nine. Look around you; if your classroom was the world, how many people would be chronically undernourished? In Western Europe and North America, the average person's diet supplies over 3,500 calories a day. In much of Africa south of the Sahara and in South Asia, average daily caloric intake is much lower, between 2,000 and 2,500 calories a day. These people are chronically undernourished and experience lowered resistance to diseases that comes with semi-starvation. Every 4 seconds someone, somewhere in the world, dies of hunger-related causes; children account for 75 percent of these deaths.

What Do You Think?

Think about the ways that you used energy over the last week. What would you have to change to reduce your level of energy consumption by one-half to compare with the European Union? Is this reduction feasible? Why or why not?

The sad irony of this situation is that food is actually plentiful in the world today (World Food Programme, 2014). The fundamental problem is the uneven distribution of available food. In most countries in the world food is plentiful, but in other countries, or even areas of countries, it is extremely scarce. There are several reasons for this uneven distribution of food:

- Hungry people are *poor and therefore lack the money to buy food that will nourish them*. Farmers cannot afford to purchase seeds to produce food for their families. As they get hungrier, their bodies weaken, which further affects their ability to earn a living or farm to feed themselves.
- Hungry people *often live in areas that do not invest in agricultural infrastructure*. They may lack adequate roads for transportation or irrigation to water the crops. There may be limited storage facilities, so food that is produced may go to waste.
- Hungry people often *live in regions where the climate is at odds with food production*. Natural disasters such as droughts, tropical storms, and floods are on the increase, and these events can have catastrophic consequences on food production. For example, droughts are widespread in Africa and directly contribute to crop failures and livestock losses. Moreover, climate change is exacerbating already dire conditions.
- *Wars and conflicts can disrupt farming and food production.* Conflict forces millions of people to leave their homes, and the displaced lack food and a way to feed themselves. Soldiers also use food as a weapon by burning crops, killing livestock, or contaminating water wells. Recent examples of the effect of war on hunger can be seen in Syria, Somalia, and the Congo.
- *Food prices are often unstable.* Roller-coaster prices make it difficult for those who are poor to have consistent access to food. When prices spike upward, food may be out of reach, or people may be forced to shift to cheaper and less nutritious foods, increasing the likelihood of malnutrition.

There is some good news in this story, however. The number and percentage of hungry malnourished people in the world has actually declined over the last few decades, as shown in Figure 13–4. There are about 100 million fewer hungry people

Figure 13–4 Percentage of Population Undernourished

SOURCE: Food and Agriculture Organization of the United Nations, 2012, 2014.

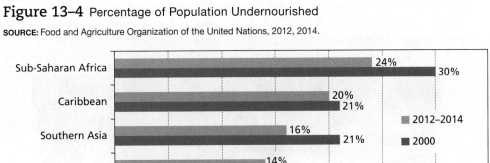

today than there were in 2000, and 200 million fewer hungry people than in 1990. Southeast Asia (China in particular) has made the greatest progress overall. The Caribbean and western Asia, which have experienced a considerable number of natural disasters and political conflicts, have made only modest progress or none at all (Food and Agriculture Organization of the United Nations, 2012, 2014).

Government Involvement in Population Control

13.4 Compare and contrast governments' involvement in population control efforts.

As an outsider looking at the plight of poorer LDCs, it is easy to say that they should simply reduce their birthrates to offset their declining death rates. That is, if people are going to live longer, then LDCs must have fewer of them.

Efforts to control population growth can take any of three basic approaches:

1. *Reduce* the rate of growth of the population,
2. Control fertility to achieve a *zero rate of population growth*, or
3. Achieve a *negative rate of growth* and thus reduce the size of the population.

Obviously, all three of these approaches involve reduction of the birthrate; however, *how much* should births be reduced? And even when it is agreed that births should be limited to some degree, there is much less agreement on how fast and to what extent limits should be imposed—indeed, on whether they should be imposed at all (i.e., whether limits on family size should be voluntary or involuntary). Efforts to limit births raise a number of moral and ethical questions, but the costs of not making such efforts could be catastrophic.

Family-planning programs have been introduced in LDCs, but the programs have only limited success in rural regions where traditions remain strong. China is a notable exception and provides an interesting example of the extent to which a government will go to reduce its fertility rate. Since the late 1970s, through incentives, deterrents, and punishments, China has strongly encouraged families to have only one child. China's current fertility rate is 1.6, and its population is expected to grow only minimally between now and 2025 (Population Reference Bureau, 2015).

Billboards advertising the benefits of having only one child are common in China. The billboards usually display a family that is wealthy and prosperous, trying to show the advantages of having only one child.

China's One-Child Policy

The grandmother wrestled the baby girl from the mother's arms, after hours of arguments that were going nowhere. The decision had been made. Both women were sobbing, but the baby girl slept peacefully, not knowing what was in store for her. The grandmother put several layers of clothing on her granddaughter, despite the warmth on this June night. She then laid the one-week-old girl in a box lined with blankets, a bottle, and an extra package of formula, and carried her off into the night. The grandmother could hear the wails of the baby's mother, her own daughter, as she headed down the road to a nearby village. "My baby, my baby, bring back my baby …," the mother cried, although she felt too, deep in her heart, that this relinquishing must be done. The grandmother quickly scurried with her bundle toward the park, which was eerily deserted in the late night. In the light of the moon she kissed her granddaughter for the very last time, propped up the bottle next to the sleeping baby, and set the baby and her makeshift bed on a bench located in a popular area of the park. The grandmother looked up above with tears in her eyes and prayed to her god that the child be found safely and quickly in the early dawn light. With that, she disappeared alone into the night, never to see or hear of her granddaughter again.

This story is one that has occurred tens, if not hundreds of thousands of times in China. What would prompt a grandmother to take her granddaughter away from her parents and abandon her in a public place? The answer lies in a complex interweaving of government policy and cultural traditions (Dvorsky, 2012; Hays, 2012).

China, like many countries, had a population that was rapidly rising, and the government worried about its people: Would there be enough resources to feed and house everyone sufficiently? To combat tremendous population growth, the Chinese government implemented in the late 1970s what is known as the **one-child policy**. It consists of three main points: (1) delayed marriage and delayed childbearing, (2) fewer and healthier births, and (3) one child per couple (with a few exceptions, such as instances when the first child is disabled). The policy has been slowly modified. For example, a couple living in rural China could have a second child if their first child was a girl. Today, a Chinese couple may have a second child if both of them are single children. Otherwise, the one-child policy remains in force.

Families who follow the one-child policy can be rewarded with extra salary, larger houses, or better jobs. The official sanction for violating the one-child policy is a stiff fine. Second or subsequent children may not be eligible for social, educational, and health care benefits. The government actively promotes the one-child policy through massive media efforts that include newspapers, radio, television, theater, music, local performances, and schools; by a thorough set of laws and policies that govern marriage and fertility; and by strategically placing compliance officers in workplaces and in neighborhoods. For example, each city, county, and township has a family-planning station focused on publicity and education. Most Chinese willingly comply with the policy and see it as good for the country.

The one-child policy has been both praised and condemned around the world (The Economist, 2012; Dvorsky, 2012; Hays, 2010; Jian, 2013). It has been applauded as an effective tool for ensuring that China will be able to support and feed its people, increase their standard of living, and combat widespread poverty. In this regard, it has been highly successful. China's population is about 400 million people less from what it would have been without the policy, relieving some of the obvious stresses of overpopulation. Families are more able to concentrate their limited resources on one child, thereby leading to higher standards of living, higher levels of education, and increased income. Women are able to work outside the home instead of raising multiple children (Rosenberg, 2009). According to Chinese Health Ministry data released in March 2013, there have been 336 million abortions and 220 million sterilizations carried out since 1971 (Jian, 2013).

one-child policy

This Chinese policy has three main points: (1) delayed marriage and delayed childbearing; (2) fewer and healthier births; and (3) one child per couple (with some exceptions).

However, China's one-child policy has also been criticized as an abuse of human rights because of the disappearance of girls, both before and after birth. The sex ratio is highly imbalanced, with at least 32 million more boys than girls under age 20 (Scutti, 2014). Naturally, there are 105 boys for every 100 girls, but in parts of China, the ratio is 130 or even 150 boys per 100 girls. Consequently, many Chinese men will be competing with one another to marry.

What has happened to all of these girls? Some are not recorded in the birth statistics and are therefore uncounted in the census. These girls are "noncitizens," ineligible for any government benefits. Others are abandoned because there is no formal mechanism in China to put a child up for adoption. Still, others are killed in utero or quickly after birth, although the number of deaths is likely declining because Chinese officials have banned elective amniocentesis and restrict the use of ultrasound scanners that would determine the sex of the fetus as one way to stop the selective abortion of female fetuses. Yet, the number of female births continues to be less than what would be expected given the number of male births in the population. Although no one knows exactly how many female infants are aborted or killed, the excess of recorded live male births over female births is far greater in China than in any other society.

Why is it that girls, rather than boys, have disappeared? In China, where generally only one child is allowed, girls are viewed as an economic liability, and parents see boys as a better investment. The traditional culture of China favors boys over girls to such a degree that many couples believe they must have a male child at all costs. Sons are expected to carry on the family lineage and take care of their aging parents. When a woman marries, she turns her focus to her husband's family. Customs like these reinforce the preference for sons; daughters are seen as costing more, wasting precious resources, and providing little or no security for parents in old age. Although the Chinese government has expanded women's opportunities, rights, and obligations in recent decades, long-standing patriarchal attitudes change slowly.

In October 2015, the Chinese government reassessed the one-child policy, noting both the shortage of young women and the growing elderly population with fewer young people to care for them. The one-child policy was officially ended, and married couples are now allowed to have two children, but no more.

What Do You Think?

What do you personally think of China's policy of requiring families to have just one child? Do you think a model like this one could be implemented in other countries that are also facing tremendous population growth?

Japan's Quest for Growth

In contrast to China, in which the government is involved in trying to limit births, the Japanese government is trying to *increase* the country's birthrate (Lee and Lee, 2013). Nearly one-quarter of Japan's population is 65 or older. The rapidly aging population, coupled with a birthrate of only about 1.3 births per woman—far below replacement level—shows a declining population. Projections are that the population of Japan will decline from about 127 million today to about 90 million by 2055 (Haub, 2010). One reason that women in Japan have so few children is because they have the near exclusive responsibility for taking care of them rather than sharing the workload with their partners, as is increasingly the case in other developed nations (Lee, Tufis, and Alwin, 2010). Japanese fathers, especially those who work on salary, spend very little time with their children. This practice is due in part to the demands made on employed men to work very long hours and in part because of the cultural ideas that child care is women's work (Demetriou, 2010).

However, hoping to encourage more births, the government instituted the "Angel Plan" in 1994 to help couples raise their children. The government reasoned that, if it can encourage fathers to become more involved in the lives of their children, then families might choose to have more births. Their campaign profiled a well-known Japanese celebrity playing with his son, with a slogan claiming "A man who doesn't raise his children can't be called a father" (Ishii-Kuntz, 2003; Ishii-Kuntz et al., 2004).

Nevertheless, fertility rates remained low; so in 2009, Japan introduced a much broader version of the Angel Plan. The government recognized that people feel frustrated because jobs are so demanding that they often have to choose between work and having children. In Japanese surveys, over 90 percent of couples said that they did want to marry and would like to have at least two children (Haub, 2010). Therefore, the new program worked to change some aspects of Japanese culture that encourage people to become "workaholics." The goal is to make society more conducive to sharing childrearing and household chores, which also allows mothers to work outside the home. Specifically, the revised Angel Plan includes the following goals (Haub, 2010; Lee and Lee, 2013):

- Encouraging workers to use 100 percent of their paid annual leave (as opposed to the current 47 percent)
- Reducing by half the number of employees who work 60 hours or more per week, currently at 11 percent
- Increasing the amount of time husbands spend on child care and housework from the current 1 hour per day to 2.5 hours per day
- Increasing the proportion of people of ages 60–64 who are working to 60 percent, currently at 53 percent
- Reducing the number of so-called "freeters," or youths who skip from one part-time job to another to 1.5 million or less, from the current 1.9 million, by helping them find permanent employment

Will the Angel Plan succeed in encouraging more births, and will the Japanese be able to support their large number of elderly? Japan's demographic future is uncertain.

Family Planning and Population Growth in the United States

Voluntary efforts to limit births are common in the United States and customarily take the form of personal family planning which allows couples to have the number of children they want, when they want them. The American family planning movement owes much to the energy and dedication of a nurse named Margaret Sanger who hoped to free women from the burdens of unplanned childbearing. In 1916, she opened the nation's first birth control clinic, and was jailed for doing so. Later, court decisions allowed physicians to prescribe birth control for health reasons; these were the first in a series of decisions that eventually permitted the sale and advertisement of contraceptive materials and the dissemination of information about birth control. By 1965, some 85 percent of married women in the United States had used some method of birth control (Ehrlich, Ehrlich, and Holdren, 1977).

As a cautionary note, we should be reminded that family planning and population control are not synonymous. Family planning has historically dealt with the needs of individuals and families, not those of societies. Sociologist Kingsley Davis (1971) has pointed out some fundamental weaknesses of the family planning approach as a means of large-scale population control. Chief among them is its basic assumption that the number of children couples *want* is the actual number they *should* have. Families may want four or five children, but is that number desirable for the economic health of society?

The U.S. population is growing at a rate of about 1 percent per year, far slower than those of the LDCs, but faster than the rate of most other highly developed nations. There are two important sources of this growth: (1) natural increase (just over 60 percent), owing to more births than deaths, and (2) migration (about 40 percent), because more people are immigrating to the United States than are leaving it. By

Figure 13–5 Ten Metro Areas with the Largest Numeric Increase in Population, 2013

SOURCE: Badger, 2014

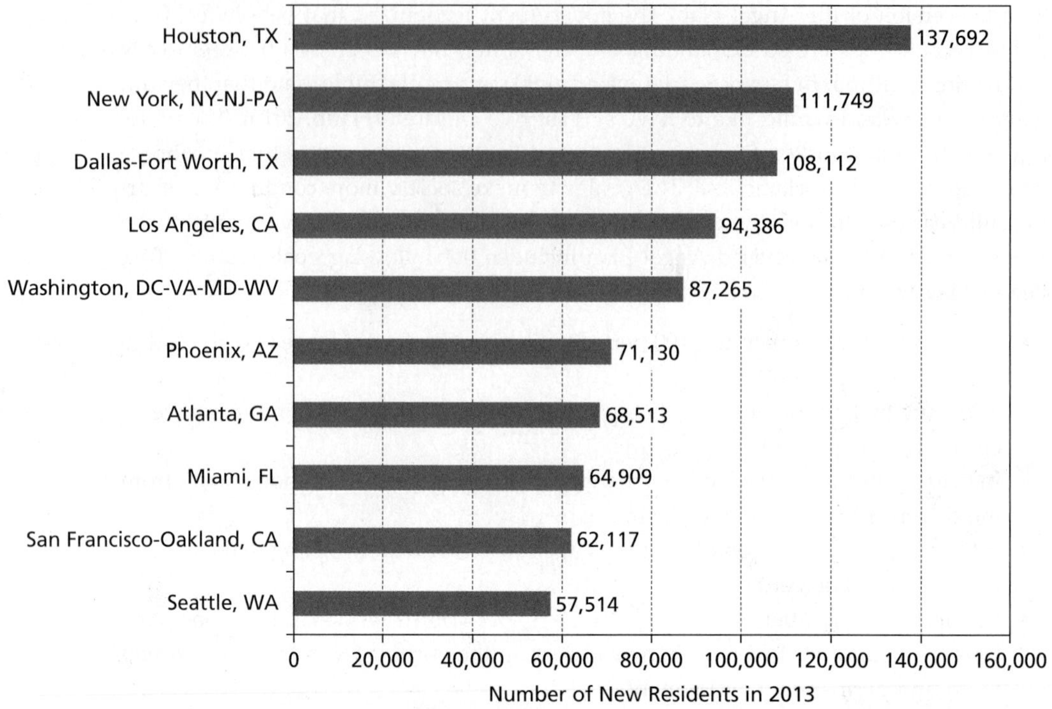

Metro Area	Number of New Residents in 2013
Houston, TX	137,692
New York, NY-NJ-PA	111,749
Dallas-Fort Worth, TX	108,112
Los Angeles, CA	94,386
Washington, DC-VA-MD-WV	87,265
Phoenix, AZ	71,130
Atlanta, GA	68,513
Miami, FL	64,909
San Francisco-Oakland, CA	62,117
Seattle, WA	57,514

2050, the populations of most other developed nations may decrease, while that of the United States may continue to increase, perhaps to as many as 400 million residents (Kochhar, 2014). This estimate assumes that high rates of immigration to the United States will continue over the next two or three decades and that these immigrant populations will have higher birthrates than older, native-born populations.

Steady population growth means that people are continuing to settle in new communities to raise their families, and many migrate in search of new opportunities. Recent decades have seen increased migration to the Sunbelt and western states. In 1950, for example, 26 percent of the population lived in the Northeast, whereas today, only 17 percent live there. Instead, people have moved to sunnier climates. Figure 13–5 shows that many of the fastest-growing metropolitan areas—that is, those with the largest numeric increase—are located in the Southwest and West (Badger, 2014). Note that Seattle, Washington, with its rapidly growing technology industries, which include Microsoft and Amazon, is experiencing quite rapid growth even though it is not in the Sunbelt.

In addition to births, the U.S. population is rising because of immigration. The next section explores this important issue, including its history and recent trends.

Immigration

13.5 **Sequence and differentiate the history of immigration in the United States.**

Throughout the world, people in poor nations dream of moving to richer ones. Most often, they do not wish to uproot themselves entirely but hope to be temporary sojourners, working at better-paying jobs temporarily. If they can save and send money home, they reason, then they may someday be able to return to a better life in their homeland.

Data on the birth origin of the U.S. population were first collected in the 1850 census. That year, there were 2.2 million immigrants in the United States, which represented almost 10 percent of the total population. Between 1860 and 1920, immigrants as a share of the total population fluctuated between 13 and 15 percent, peaking at 15 percent in 1890, mainly due to high levels of European immigration. Restrictive immigration legislation of 1921 and 1924, coupled with the Great Depression and World War II, led to a sharp drop in new arrivals in the United States. As a result, the foreign-born share of the U.S. population continued to decline between the 1930s and 1970s, reaching a record low of only 5 percent in 1970 (9.6 million). Since 1970, however, the share and number have increased rapidly, this time mainly due to large-scale immigration from Latin America and Asia made possible by changes to admission rules adopted by Congress in 1965 (Nwosu, Batalova, and Auclair, 2014). Today, immigration to the United States has reached levels unmatched since early in the twentieth century, approximately 13 percent of the American population (40 million).

But immigration is not just an American phenomenon; the movement of people from poor to richer lands is also occurring in other countries. There has been an influx of people into Germany and France from poorer areas to the south, especially Turkey and northern Africa. In the Middle East, there has been a great movement of temporary workers from Egypt to the richer and underpopulated nations of Saudi Arabia and Kuwait. In Japan, there are Korean immigrants, and in Australia, there are immigrants from many Asian nations. But the United States leads the world in total number of immigrants.

It is often said that the United States is a nation of immigrants. Since the earliest days of settlement by Europeans, North America has brought people together from all over the world. Some, like the black slaves from Africa, were brought against their will. Many other groups came in search of new opportunities and freedom from oppression, bringing together people of different races, different religions, different cultures, and different political views to these shores. This diversity has become one of the most important aspects of U.S. culture.

But immigration has also contributed to some problems that plague U.S. society. Beginning with the exclusion of Native Americans from their original lands, immigration has led to ethnic and racial conflict; competition among nationality groups for a "piece of the pie"; debates about immigration policy, illegal immigration, and the exploitation of illegal immigrants; and the stresses and costs associated with educating and caring for newcomers. These issues can become social problems when they are not adequately addressed in a timely fashion. The summary of the major periods of immigration to the United States in the next section will help you begin to understand the varying contexts in which immigration has occurred in this country.

Immigration to the United States: A Brief History

THE EARLY COLONIAL PERIOD (TO 1790) During the colonial period, the major population groups in North America, other than Native Americans, came from Europe. Most traveled from England and accounted for 77 percent of the total population. African and native-born slaves of African origin accounted for 19 percent, German immigrants for 4 percent, Irish immigrants for 3 percent, and Dutch immigrants for 2 percent (Bogue, 1985; Portes, 2001). There were many other immigrant groups in the population, but their numbers were much smaller and, consequently, so was their influence.

OLD NORTHWEST EUROPEAN MIGRATION (1820–1885) Large-scale immigration to the new nation known as the United States began again in 1820 and was dominated by people from England and other areas of northwestern Europe until about 1885. In this wave of immigrants, the largest groups came from northern and western Europe, especially Germany, Ireland, and England. The proportion of immigrants from Ireland reached high levels in the 1840s and 1850s as a result of severe famine and economic catastrophe in Ireland. German immigration reached a peak in the years after 1848, when popular revolutions in Germany failed and many Germans sought asylum or greater political freedom in the United States.

The most significant nonwhite immigrant group during this period were the Chinese, many of whom settled on the West Coast or in the Rocky Mountain states. Labor contractors who were seeking low-wage workers for the construction of railroads brought in many Chinese immigrants.

THE INTERMEDIATE MIGRATION FROM SOUTHERN AND EASTERN EUROPE (1885–1945) Because of the breakup of the Austro-Hungarian and Ottoman empires and the resulting political upheavals, many thousands of people from southern and eastern Europe found their way to the United States. The major immigrant groups during this period were Italians, Poles, Hungarians, Serbians, Croatians, Greeks, and Jews from all of these nations and from Russia. During this period, waves of **nativist** feeling (anti-immigrant or anti-foreigner sentiment) swept across sections of the United States. Among other things, nativism gave rise to the Asian exclusion movement, which flourished between 1882 and 1907. It resulted in sporadic violence against Chinese and Japanese Americans and the passage of legislation in some states that stopped further immigration of Asians.

At the same time, large numbers of Mexican immigrants began moving into the Southwest, the West, and portions of the Midwest. These immigrants often joined relatives and friends in parts of California and the Southwest, where Mexicans had been living long before these regions became part of the United States.

During this period, there had been no specific limits on immigration to the United States, and well over 20 million immigrants had arrived since the early nineteenth century. However, concerned about immigration, Congress passed the Immigration Act of 1921, which for the first time in American history established quotas and strict controls over the admission of new immigrants. An overall quota of 150,000 immigrants per year was imposed, which curtailed the United States as a realistic destination for most of those persons fleeing the horrors of Nazi Germany.

THE POST–WORLD WAR II REFUGEE PERIOD (TO 1968) By the end of World War II, hundreds of thousands of Europeans had lost their homes and property, and many were refugees. Some, like Jews and Roman Catholic activists, were fleeing religious persecution. In 1945, Congress agreed to admit 185,000 immigrants per year, many of whom would be European refugees. This count remained a very small number of immigrants allowed into the United States, given the millions of people needing resettlement.

THE NEW IMMIGRATION (1968 AND BEYOND) In 1968, Congress again voted to increase immigration quotas, establishing totals of 170,000 per year from the Eastern Hemisphere and 120,000 from the Western Hemisphere. Priority would be given to immigrants who were political or religious refugees or who had close relatives living in the United States—known as the principle of family unification. Between 1975 and 1980, refugees and refugee-related issues dominated immigration more than they had since the years following World War II. Beginning with the fall of Vietnam and Cambodia in April 1975, this five-year period saw the admission of more than 400,000 Indochinese refugees. The Refugee Act was passed in 1980 and made provision for both a regular flow and the emergency admission of refugees. In addition, the law authorized federal assistance for the resettlement of refugees. Shortly after the enactment of the Refugee Act of 1980, large numbers of Cubans entered the United States through southern Florida, totaling an estimated 125,000, along with continuing smaller numbers of Haitians. There have been many tweaks to immigration policy since then. The increases in immigration quotas in recent decades have given rise to a new pattern of immigration to the United States, with the largest flows of people coming from Asia and Latin America (Zolberg, 2008).

nativist

Anti-immigrant or anti-foreigner sentiment.

Ellis Island was the primary destination for immigrants coming from Europe. Immigrants were not welcomed with open arms. They had to pass rigid medical checkups to be allowed to stay.

Recent Trends in Immigration to the United States

Yue Lin Wang. Jose Gonzalez. Min Nguyen. Diego Molina. What do these four people have in common? They have all immigrated to the United States in recent years. Their circumstances vary. Yue Lin Wang was adopted by an American family when she was 9 months old as a result of China's one-child policy. Jose Gonzalez, a journalist from Cuba, came to the United States two generations ago seeking political asylum. Min Nguyen and her family escaped the ravages of the Vietnam War when she was only 8, after surviving for a year in a refugee camp in Laos. Diego Molina walked many days through the desert from Mexico trying to evade detection. A Personal View: Immigrants' Stories provides a close-up experience of immigration.

In the United States today, about 40 million people, or 13 percent of the population, were not born in the United States but immigrated here from elsewhere (Nwosu, Batalova, and Auclair, 2014; Pew Research Center, 2013b). In 1900, the majority of persons immigrating to the United States came from Europe; however, by 1980, four times more Hispanics and Asians migrated to the United States than did Europeans, as they fled persecution in their war-torn countries. The largest number of immigrants today come from Mexico and Southeast Asia, although immigration from Asia has slowed somewhat as political strife there has abated. The percentage of Europeans immigrating to the United States is now a relatively small component of the total.

Characteristics of immigrants vary by their country of origin and length of time in the United States (as well as the personal circumstances surrounding their immigration). For example, many Asians arriving from Cambodia and Vietnam in the 1980s were poor, but they brought with them young children. These children were exposed to U.S. culture early on and are now attending college in large numbers. Their experiences in the United States may be vastly different from migrant farmworkers from Mexico who are coming today. Nonetheless, some generalizations can be made: Immigrants are more likely than native-born residents to be in their childbearing years; they live in larger family households; they earn less money in their jobs; they are more likely to live in poverty; and they tend to reside in central cities within a metropolitan area (Motel and Patten, 2013; Pew Hispanic Center, 2013).

Some groups in U.S. society oppose immigration, and the resulting conflicts and tensions can be a problem for immigrants and for the regions or cities that receive them. Because new immigrants tend to settle near other immigrants, these tensions can run especially high in regions with large immigrant populations.

What Do You Think?

Describe the influence that immigrants have had on American culture in the last century. Can you think of both positive and negative influences?

Urban Concentration of Immigrants

Many of the immigrants who arrive in the United States reside in just a few key cities and regions, including New York City, Los Angeles, Miami, and Chicago (Migration Policy Institute, 2014). Immigrants from Mexico and Central America tend to congregate in California, Texas, Arizona, and New Mexico.

The concentration of new immigrants in a few metropolitan regions greatly adds to the problems of both immigrants and nonimmigrants in those areas. This concentration leads to the formation of large non-English-speaking enclaves, where education becomes more challenging and the economic and social assimilation of the newcomers may create difficulties for native-born citizens. Increasingly, frequent attacks against immigrants and members of minority groups and the rise of nativist and anti-immigrant feelings in many parts of the United States are another consequence of the concentration of immigrants in certain localities.

The phenomenon of **chain migration**, the primary cause of this urban concentration, refers to the tendency of immigrants to migrate to areas where they have kin and others from their home communities. Most prefer to be around other people who share their culture and language and can help them adjust to their new social environment.

chain migration

The tendency of immigrants to migrate to areas where they have kin and others from their home communities.

A Personal View

Immigrants' Stories

Four years ago, I came to America from Greece for holiday—"vacation" as you call it. I was 18 and just graduated from school. This trip was my present before I began college. I got a three-month visa. I planned to return to Greece afterwards; I had no thought that I might overstay my visa. However, life sometimes takes you in new directions. I met the love of my life in Boston, and didn't want to go back to Greece. So I overstayed, figuring how would anyone really know? I thought we would marry and everything would be okay because I could emigrate as his wife. But, we broke up about a year later. As it turned out, he was a bit of a jerk. I'm still here—I like America—although it's sometimes difficult to find good work. I'm 22 now, and figure I'll probably stay another four or five years if I can afford it. Then I'll head back to Greece when I'm ready to settle down.

—*Melania, age 22*

****

When I was younger, I decided I was going to be president of the United States, but my friend laughed at me and told me I couldn't be the president. I didn't understand. I went home and asked my mom, and she said she wasn't sure, but it was a great question.

I was born in China. My birthparents felt that they couldn't keep me. My mom explained to me that families in China can have only one child, and that Chinese parents often prefer to have a son. Personally I think that's crazy because girls are cool, too. As the story goes, I lived in an orphanage for almost a year, and then my parents adopted me and brought me here to California. I have an older sister who was also adopted from China, but we didn't know each other. In fact, she lived in the northern part of China and I lived in the southern part. But now she's my sister. We hang out a lot after school, but she also gets on my nerves because she likes rock instead of pop, and doesn't like Dr. Who or Supernatural. Really? I didn't think that was even possible.

—*Kate, age 15*

****

My mom left our small village in Mexico when I was 8 and my younger sister was 3, and we went to live with my grandmother. My mom said that she was going to the United States and get a good job to earn enough money to bring us there to live with her. I didn't really know what she meant; I was only 8, and I didn't understand that "going to the United States to get a good job" was against the law, and that my mother could

be killed trying to get there. She left quietly one night, and my brother and I cried for many days afterwards. We lived with my grandmother for nearly two years and heard nothing from my mother. Grandma spoke of my mother often, wondering if she made it and what she was doing, but my mother seemed dead to me. Then, suddenly one day Grandma received some cash from my mother. It was enough to smuggle only one of us to America, and since I was the oldest, now 10, I could go. My uncle arranged it all, and the details scared me. I was to leave next month with a small group of other men and boys. We had a leader—a gruff man with piercing eyes—but he said he could get us to the United States, so I forced myself to trust him. He was right. Most of us made it to the United States, but there were many times on the trail that I didn't think we would. One dad and his son turned back because they had bad luck—the dad was robbed and the son got very sick—but after more than a month of walking, hitching, waiting, wading, and belly crawling, I made it to the United States. It took another couple of weeks to be reunited with my mom, but now we are a family. She works in a factory, pressing fruit. I go to school. I like America, but I miss my family in Mexico so much. I don't know if I'll ever see them again.

—*Arturo, age 12*

Critical Thinking

Compare and contrast these stories about immigration. How are they similar, and how are they different? Of the two illegal immigration stories, do either of them seem more compelling than the other? If so, why?

The uneven distribution of immigrants greatly adds to the costs of education and health care in the cities in which they become concentrated. Because many new immigrants arrive without any form of health insurance and do not speak English well, schools and adult education programs are needed to help them. The federal government does not usually compensate the expenses incurred by the cities, even though the entry of immigrants is regulated by federal legislation.

A problem that affects the immigrants in these urban centers is the intense competition and, at times, direct hostility they encounter from nonimmigrants or other immigrants who have lived there for longer periods. For example, Koreans often establish businesses in segregated minority communities where costs are lower. They thus become a new ethnic and racial group in those communities. They may encounter anger and hostility from residents who believe the Koreans are not sensitive to their needs and their local culture (Kim, 2003). Elsewhere in the nation—along the Gulf Coast of Texas, where Vietnamese shrimp fishermen have come into conflict with native-born fishermen, or in the Southwest, where Mexican immigrants are often discriminated against because of language differences—the difficulties of life as a stranger in a strange land are amplified by prejudice and violence.

In response to the hostility they can encounter, children and adolescents in the new groups sometimes form defensive gangs. But some immigrant groups, notably the Chinese and Koreans, attempt to shelter their children from the problems of urban street life by imposing a strict set of values and high expectations for achievement in school. Children of Asian immigrants make rapid strides in U.S. schools, often achieving the highest honors in their high schools and on standardized achievement tests. Indeed, the school achievement of Asian Americans is now so high that many of the brightest Asian students have come to believe they are being penalized by admission quotas in private universities, an experience exactly analogous to that of high-achieving children of Jewish immigrants two generations ago.

Not all immigrants are in the United States legally. This next section explores illegal immigration and its consequences.

Undocumented Illegal Immigrants

13.6 **Explore the issue of illegal immigration and its consequences for Americans and the immigrants themselves.**

No one knows with great accuracy exactly how many illegal (undocumented) immigrants actually live in the United States, but it is estimated to be about 11 million, down from 12 million before the recession (Passel et al., 2014). Almost three-quarters come from Mexico or Central America where they face extreme poverty and limited job prospects in their countries. Nearly half live in married-couple households with children, a rate much higher than among those adults who were born in this country. Sometimes a family has mixed citizenship, with children born in the United States to undocumented immigrants, but despite the media attention, these situations are rare. Illegal immigrants are remaining in the United States for longer periods than they did in the past: In 1995, about 36 percent were in the United States for less than five years. Today, that figure has dropped to only 16 percent. Instead, the median length of stay is now 12.7 years (Passel et al., 2014).

Modes of Entry into the United States

Nearly half (45 percent) of all illegal immigrants actually arrived legally as visitors to the United States, passing through ports of entry where they were processed by the U.S. Immigration and Naturalization Service. They started out as legal visitors, but become *illegal* immigrants when they exceed the time allocated to them to visit or reside in the United States. This group is referred to as **overstayers**.

The remainder, just over half, entered the United States illegally by hiding in vehicles such as cargo trucks, trekking through the desert or northern plains, wading across the Rio Grande, or otherwise eluding the U.S. Border Patrol. We usually associate illegal immigration with the southwestern border states such as Texas, New Mexico, Arizona, and California, but untold numbers of evaders also arrive over the Canadian border and through ports like New York City through various forms of human smuggling.

These illegal immigrants face many horrific and dangerous situations in their trek to the United States to find work and a better life, and many do not make the journey

overstayer

Someone who starts out as a legal visitor, but becomes an *illegal* immigrant when he or she exceeds the time allocated to visit or reside in the United States.

coyotes

Guides who help people immigrate illegally to the United States.

successfully. Ruthless individuals exploit them because they know that immigrants cannot readily go to the authorities when they have been victimized. Immigrants are robbed, raped, and otherwise taken advantage of by guides, or **coyotes**. The U.S. Border Patrol then captures many of those who do make it to the border. As two men who were detected trying to come into the United States from Mexico emotionally explained in their native Spanish: "The Border Patrol treats us like animals, like dirt, like we don't matter. We know we are doing something wrong but it is not to hurt anyone but to feed our families. We have nothing to eat [at our homes]" (Arditti, 2006).

Those who do make it into the United States and make it past U.S. Border Patrol agents find jobs in a variety of occupations; nearly one-third work in low-paying service industries or in construction or agriculture (Passel and Cohn, 2009). Their status is quite precarious because employers must report workers who are discovered to not have proper documents. Thus, employers who continue to hire immigrants without documentation or disregard forgery of their documents can exploit them by paying pitifully low wages and expecting inordinate amounts of work.

Illegal Immigration and the Economy

Until recently, it was not against the law to employ illegal immigrants. This situation changed in 1986, when Congress passed the Immigration Reform and Control Act. Under this law, employers are subject to civil penalties that range from $250 to $10,000 for each illegal alien they hire.

It is not clear exactly what effect illegal residents have on the U.S. economy. They may take some jobs away from native-born residents, but they also perform functions that citizens are reluctant to do—"dirty work" or stoop labor on row crops, for example—and they help maintain some industries by accepting lower wages and inferior working conditions. Their willingness to accept these conditions may hold back progress on wages and working conditions for others, but the survival of such industries stimulates growth in associated services, actually creating more jobs. Indeed, it appears that illegal immigrants—who can generally be laid off or discharged more easily than citizens—play a vital, if equivocal, role in many advanced nations, cushioning the native-born population from economic uncertainty. And when an increasing proportion of adults are retired—as an estimated 20 percent of U.S. adults will be in 2035—the taxes paid by employed illegal immigrants may become extremely important. A little recognized fact is that millions of undocumented workers do indeed pay taxes—taxes that approach nearly $11 billion (Lee, 2014). Many researchers suggest that these taxes offset, or closely offset, the extra costs associated with providing education, health care, and other services to these workers and their families. Moreover, many undocumented workers also pay into Social Security, but will not receive any benefits from that program when they age.

The Great Recession discouraged illegal immigrants from testing their fortunes in the U.S. job market. After reaching an estimated high of over 12 million, unauthorized immigration began decreasing, especially as the recession began to hit the U.S. economy with severe job losses in 2008. For example, in Florida and throughout the Southwest, illegal immigrants were working in new housing construction, often with the full knowledge of developers and contractors, who paid them below the prevailing wage for their work. When the real estate bubble burst and new housing construction almost ceased in many former boom areas, thousands of illegal workers

Do illegal immigrants take jobs away from American citizens, or do they do the work that American citizens do not want to do? This woman stoops in the sun for many hours a day and earns the equivalent of the minimum wage on a good day.

Table 13–4 The Shift in Deportation Countries

Country	FY 2013	FY 2014
El Salvador	21,602	27,180
Guatemala	47,749	54,423
Honduras	37,049	40,695
Mexico	241,493	176,968

SOURCE: Department of Homeland Security, 2015b.

lost their jobs. Similar effects have been felt by immigrant workers in landscaping and other services related to new home construction.

Increased Deportations

As the number of illegal immigrants in the United States grew from about 3 million in 1980 to 11 million today, pressure on government agencies resulted in new waves of enforcement of existing immigration laws, including those that bar undocumented persons from working in most jobs. In recent years, the number of deportations has been in a state of flux. The Department of Homeland Security reports that it "removed" (the official term for *deported*) 316,000 individuals in 2014, including 102,000 within our borders, and 214,000 individuals who were trying to enter the United States illegally (U.S. Department of Homeland Security, 2015b). There has been a substantial increase in the number of deportations to El Salvador, Honduras, and Guatemala, while the number of deportations to Mexico has declined significantly, as you can see in Table 13–4.

Deferred Action for Childhood Arrival

In 2012, the Secretary of Homeland Security announced that certain unauthorized immigrants who entered the United States as children would be able to apply for the Deferred Action for Childhood Arrival (DACA) program, granting relief from deportation and work authorization for two years. Prospective beneficiaries have to meet a series of requirements, including the following:

- Entered the United States before the age of 16
- Have continuously resided in the United States since June 15, 2007
- Are currently in school, have graduated from high school or earned a GED, or are honorably discharged veterans of the U.S. armed forces (including the Coast Guard)
- Have not been convicted of a felony, significant misdemeanor, or three or more misdemeanors or do not otherwise pose a threat to public safety or national security

Over a million unauthorized youths and young adults were eligible to apply because they met both age and education criteria and had no criminal background. Between August 15, 2012 (when the U.S. Citizenship and Immigration Services began accepting applications) and December 2014, 962,000 applications were accepted for consideration by the agency (U.S. Department of Homeland Security, 2015a).

Public Attitudes toward Illegal Immigration

Despite a lot of media attention, only 39 percent of Americans said that dealing with the issue of illegal immigration should be a top priority for the president and Congress. That response placed it seventeenth on a list of policy priorities for the coming year, a significant decline over the past decade. The decline of this national concern has been particularly striking among Republicans (Pew Research Center, 2013a).

The lack of priority given to illegal immigration may be because many people are not really sure what to do about it. In fact, most people favor a path to citizenship, as

What Do You Think?

What are the jobs that many illegal immigrants take? Do you think they are taking away jobs from Americans? Do most Americans want these jobs? Do you?

What Do You Think?

The Department of Defense is letting undocumented immigrants apply for military service under the Military Accessions Vital to National Interest (MAVNI) program. The program recruits up to 1,400 foreigners with specific skill sets needed by the military. Individuals are eligible if they entered the United States illegally as children, have lived in the country for most of their lives, have graduated from high school or earned a GED, have kept a clean legal record, and other stringent requirements. Debate the pros and cons of this program. Keep in mind that these undocumented immigrants are not allowed to vote, collect benefits such as Social Security, or in some states even secure a driver's license.

Figure 13–6 Percent Who Say Illegal Immigrants Should Be Eligible for Citizenship, 2014

SOURCE: Dimock, 2014.

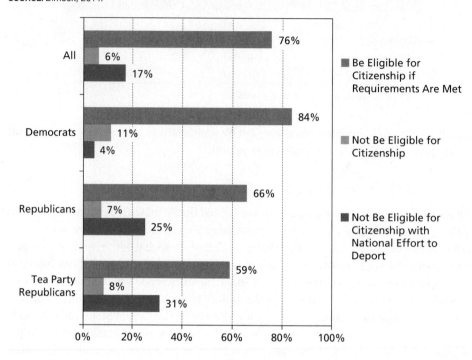

shown in Figure 13–6. Despite what we may hear in the media, even the majority of so-called "tea partiers"—the most conservative component of the Republican Party—favor a path to citizenship. However, it is important to note that almost a third of "tea partiers" prefer a national effort to deport illegal immigrants, which is almost twice the national average who feel this way (Dimock, 2014).

Social Policy

13.7 Consider the controversy and the policies associated with children who are fleeing violence in Central America.

Juan, as usual, was walking the three miles to his home after the school day ended at 3:30 in his small town in Honduras. His mother knew to expect him no later than 4:30. He was always prompt, but on this day he never arrived. His parents, aunts and uncles, and neighbors searched for him all night. The next morning his body was found partially buried in a field outside of town. He had been stabbed several times in the chest and his head had been severed. Juan was 14 years old and in the eighth grade. He was a whiz at math and excelled at art. He also enjoyed playing sports with the other boys in the neighborhood. The police investigated the murder but had no real leads. The police assumed that Juan was killed and beheaded by gang members because he refused to join them. This killing was the ninth of this type by gang members over the past year in this small town, yet Juan's murder was not widely reported within the country. It was simply another act of violence—one of many. Meanwhile, Juan's parents are actively encouraging their other sons, ages 10 and 16, to leave Honduras and find their way to the United States to live with their cousin who is in Texas illegally. There, they pray, their remaining sons will be safe from the drug cartels and gangs that proliferate in their country.

What Do You Think?

If Juan was your son, would you encourage his siblings to try to escape to the United States? Why or why not?

The United Nations identifies Honduras as the most violent country in the world, with 90 murders per 100,000 people. Other countries in Central America are also among the most violent. El Salvador was the fourth most violent; Guatemala, with 40 murders per

100,000 people, the fifth. For context, note that the United Nations considers a rate of 10 murders per 100,000 people to be an epidemic. The rate of violence in Honduras is nearly twice that of America's most violent city, Detroit, which has a homicide rate of 55 per 100,000. Just as striking as these statistics themselves is the consistently young age of the victims. Nearly 40 percent of those murdered in Honduras every year are between the ages of 15 and 24, and a growing number are even younger (Martinez, 2014). The gangs recruit young children, even as young as 8 or 9, to work as messengers or drug runners because young children are better able to evade detection by police. Refusal to work with the gangs can result in death, usually grisly to make maximum impact on the community and to instill maximum fear in other young boys.

Immigrants or Refugees?

To avoid being victims of gang violence, tens of thousands, or perhaps hundreds of thousands of unaccompanied children, mostly boys, have fled to the United States looking for freedom, safety, and a chance to work. The U.S. Customs and Border Protection took more than 60,000 unaccompanied children under 18 into custody in the 10 months between October 2013 and July 2014 (Renwick, 2014), and upwards of 90,000 over the year (Strain, 2014). The numbers of unaccompanied minors entering the United States has been reduced in 2015 because of stepped-up enforcement on the border and Mexico apprehending more of the children before they get to the United States. But the problems in Central America remain very serious.

Lawmakers in Washington have sought to deport these children as quickly as possible. But under current law, it can take many months or even years before the children are processed through the U.S. immigration system and either given asylum (or other legal status) or ordered to be deported back to their home countries. Originally, President Obama wanted the deportation process sped up by bypassing the tradition of having the child appear before an immigration judge. But in 2014, President Obama changed course, referring to the surge as "an urgent humanitarian situation," and asked for $3.7 billion in emergency funds for greater border surveillance, additional detention facilities for youth, and more law enforcement and judges to help shorten the wait time through the legal process. Deportation of these children, however, remained the ultimate goal.

In late 2014, President Obama met with the presidents of Honduras, El Salvador, and Guatemala at the White House to discuss how to stop the flow of child migrants to the United States (Renwick, 2014). The four leaders agreed it was a shared responsibility. The Central American presidents agreed that they must address the underlying causes of migration by reducing criminal activity and violence, and they must promote greater social and economic opportunity for those who are poor. All three Central American countries have launched media campaigns to discourage illegal outward migration. Yet, at the same time, the Central American presidents said that the United States bears some responsibility for the crisis because of our own market for illegal drugs that pass through their region, and our "ambiguity" on immigration reform.

What should be done with these children fleeing horrible violence in Central America? Immigration is a controversial political topic. House Republicans dismissed the president's $3.7 billion proposal by passing a bill for only $700 million targeted toward expediting deportations and increasing security at the border. Consequently, some state governments are taking matters into their own hands. Governor Rick Perry of Texas, whose state has received the majority of migrants, has

These young boys are attempting to sneak into the United States with two other men and their coyote guide. The boys are fleeing gang violence in Nicaragua that has already killed several of their friends. Should they be viewed as illegal immigrants, or as refugees?

sent hundreds of guardsmen into the Rio Grande Valley, with the total of guardsmen expected to reach 1,000. Governor Jan Brewer of Arizona, a Republican who has clashed with the president on immigration issues, has blamed the Obama administration for "failing to send a message" that the U.S. border was closed to illegal immigration (Renwick, 2014).

But with all the political clamor focusing on securing our borders and deporting those who sneak in, little attention is given to the horrific conditions these children are fleeing and their fate if they are sent home. Are these children *illegal immigrants* or are they *refugees*? Is this situation an *immigration problem* or a *humanitarian crisis*? Should these children be immediately deported, detained for a period of time, or allowed to seek asylum in the United States? Given the polarity in today's politics, you would think the answers to these questions would be evenly split along party lines. However, they are not. Surprisingly, even the conservative think tank American Enterprise Institute (AEI) argues that the problem is less about immigrants pouring into the country and more about the social conditions in those countries that inspire people to flee. "The problem isn't Central America's refugees. It's the countries they come from," an AEI researcher writes (Strain, 2014, p. 1).

What is the best way to deal with these unaccompanied children? Figure 13–7 reports the popular opinion of all U.S. adults and among those who identify as Hispanic. A few things stand out in this figure. First, Hispanics are more likely than other adults to have formed an opinion about this issue. Second, Hispanics are about evenly split on whether the government should follow through on the current policy, even though the process could take a long time, or whether the government should speed up the process, possibly deporting children who would otherwise qualify for asylum. Adults in general favor speeding up the processes, even with its risks.

But the real solution to this crisis is far more complex and does not lend itself to a quick fix. In the near term, Americans must face the issue of what to do with these children right now. Advocates call for increasing the centers to care for the children and improving screening to ensure that the United States offers humanitarian protection to children who would truly be in danger if they returned to their home countries. Others suggest quick deportation is in order.

But those who take a longer or mid-range view can see that many of these children are here in hopes of being reunited with their family members, some of whom have come legally and some of whom have slipped in illegally, maybe under different circumstances than escaping violent gangs. Family reconciliation has always

Figure 13–7 How to Best Deal with Surge of Central American Children?, 2014

SOURCE: Krogstad and Gonzalez-Barrera, 2014.

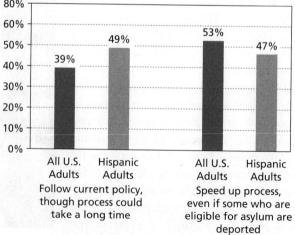

been a central tenet of immigration. What then is America's responsibility to reunite these children with their families? And what is the international responsibility to protect those children who cannot be reunited? And, finally, those who take the long view realize that, ultimately, only improved national and regional economic and security conditions in the children's countries of origin can really stem the flow of these migrant/refugee children. Yet, all of these solutions—whether immediate or long-term—are uphill battles that are expensive to undertake and politically difficult to execute.

Future Prospects

Despite the wave of anti-immigrant feeling that has arisen in the United States in recent years, it is by no means clear what, if any, new policies will emerge in the future. The continuing flow of illegal immigrants, especially across the U.S. border with Mexico, has prompted some political leaders in the Southwest to advocate the construction of a fence along the entire 1,275-mile U.S.–Mexican border. Although this idea appeals to those who want the U.S. government to make a greater effort to prevent illegal immigration, there is no assurance that such a fence would be effective, aside from having a negative effect on international relations (Goldsborough, 2004).

Congress continues to be sharply divided on most issues, and immigration is no different. Former President George W. Bush sponsored an immigration reform bill that was defeated in 2007. That bill would have offered illegal immigrants who have been living in the United States for a certain length of time, and who have paid taxes and not been arrested, a chance to pay a fine and eventually gain permanent status (a "green card"). Another feature of the defeated bill would have placed far greater emphasis on the skills of individuals who seek to immigrate to the United States than on whether they have family members already in the country.

As of this writing, in late 2015, the Obama administration, weakened by recession, war, and electoral defeats, may also be unlikely to be able to muster the support for sweeping reform that will address the issue of what to do about people who are in the United States illegally but are raising families, paying taxes, and otherwise contributing to the growth of the society and economy.

Going Beyond Left And Right

Ironically, there are no clear left and right viewpoints on immigration, but there are people with strong views on the issues involved. Those on the right may be of the opinion that the United States is threatened by hordes of newcomers, some of whom will become burdens on the welfare system. But many other people with conservative views argue that immigrants are needed to provide a needed service and help the economy by doing the work that people born here do not want to do. On the left, there are also divisions. Some liberals argue that immigrants add new vitality to the society and its culture and that they are living reminders of the traditions of American democracy. But others on the left side of the political spectrum voice concern about the possibility that immigrants drive down wages for native-born workers and compete for entry-level jobs with Americans who are poor, especially as welfare policies now push more of those who are poor into the job market.

Clearly, there are subdivisions within the major ideological divisions. In deciding where you stand, these disputes will help you realize that there are no easy solutions. Because immigrants are encouraged in a variety of ways to work in the United States and to strive to become U.S. citizens, it is reasonable to argue that people who are already citizens have some responsibility for helping the newcomers achieve a better life, regardless of one's political ideology.

Summary

- The world's population exceeds 7.3 billion, and continues to grow rapidly, especially in LDCs. There are several ways to measure population growth: total, general, and crude birth (fertility) rates. The differential between the crude birthrate and the death rate is the rate of population growth, or natural increase. Today, more people are living to childbearing age and fewer are dying, so the world's population is growing faster than in the past and putting increased pressure on resources and the environment.

- The demographic transition is a process that consists of three stages: (a) a high birthrate canceled out by a high death rate, (b) a high birthrate coupled with a declining death rate, and (c) low birth and death rates. The process began in northern Europe in the eighteenth century and has occurred in all areas where industrial technology has taken hold on a local level. Today, large areas of Asia, Africa, and Latin America remain in the middle phase of the demographic transition.

- Currently, expectations in LDCs are rising; people have increasing expectations for their own future and that of their children. Literacy rates serve as an indicator of rising expectations. Although literacy rates have increased in many countries, the gaps in living standards between rich and poor societies have widened. Hunger and malnutrition are persistent problems in the less developed regions of the world.

- Governments can and sometimes do get involved in population control. The Chinese government has actively sought to reduce births, while the Japanese government is trying to grow their population. The population of most industrialized nations is growing at a relatively slow rate, and it appears likely that this rate can be maintained through voluntary population control (e.g., family planning).

- The United States is often described as a nation of immigrants; since the earliest years of European settlement, it has attracted people from all over the world. Today, the largest numbers of immigrants have come from Asia and Latin America. A problem related to immigration is the uneven distribution of immigrants among cities and regions in the United States. Immigrants in urban centers encounter intense competition and, at times, direct hostility.

- Millions of undocumented immigrants are currently residing in the United States by either overstaying their visas or sneaking into the country illegally. Undocumented immigrants are easily exploited by employers and others. Their effect on the U.S. economy is not clear, but it appears that they cushion the native-born population from economic uncertainty. Americans are not in agreement about how to address immigration, and popular opinion does not fall neatly along political party lines.

- One issue of current interest is what to do about the flood of children fleeing gang violence in their homes in Central America. Are these children immigrants or refugees?

Chapter 14
Technology and the Environment

Learning Objectives

14.1 Describe the nature of technology, focusing on technological dualism and the digital divide.

14.2 Compare and contrast different ways that technology operates autonomously and is removed from political control.

14.3 Assess the adaptation of technology to changing social institutions.

14.4 Discuss the link between technology and the environment.

14.5 Summarize different types of stressors on the environment.

14.6 Identify the role of the United States in the world's environment.

14.7 Critique the social policy on climate change.

Jackson was 17 years old and looking forward to buying his first car. He passed driver's education class with flying colors last summer. "Driving," he said, "now that's just plain cool." Up until now he walked or rode his bike the mile and a half to school most days, unless his mom could give him a lift on her way to work. But usually she went to work early, and so it just didn't work out for him to ride with her. But now, after working to save money, he would be on the way to having wheels! His big plans went beyond driving to school, and included cruising at night with his friends, driving to the lake with his girlfriend, and offering to drive for every errand for his mother, no matter how close by. Yes, soon he would be driving! Not once did he stop to think about the effects his driving has on the community or the world. After all, his car will be just one of the 1.2 billion cars that are now on the road. How large of an effect can his little car possibly have? He didn't realize that, if he drove in a typical American fashion, each year he would spew 9,700 pounds of carbon dioxide into the air, along with 278 pounds of carbon monoxide, 28 pounds of hydrocarbons, 27 pounds of volatile organic compounds, and 10 pounds of nitrogen oxide. The good news? At least he is not driving a truck.

Of the many ways in which technology has changed our lives, probably none has more far-reaching consequences than its impact on the earth's environment. The problems of climate change, toxic waste disposal, and water and air pollution are direct consequences of technological advances. The way we use energy has an enormous effect on the earth's ecological systems. The technologies of production, climate control, transportation, and agriculture transform the physical shape of the planet and lead to environmental stress. The United States is the world's greatest consumer of natural resources, especially carbon-based energy from fossil fuels (coal, oil, and natural gas). It is also the world's leader in the production and use of technological systems of all kinds. The U.S. government and the nation's citizens therefore bear much of the responsibility for seeking ways to reduce the negative effects of pollution due to energy consumption.

Environmentalists claim that in recent years the United States has shifted its concerns away from environmental protection—especially in relation to such crucial issues as climate change—in favor of deregulation and pro-growth policies that have the effect of increasing pollution. As in any dispute, there are arguments on both sides of this debate (Climate Debate Daily, 2015); these debates are discussed in detail in the chapter.

Energy technologies, including petrochemicals, electricity, nuclear power, hydroelectricity, and others, are basic to everyday life throughout the world, so much so that we often take their availability for granted. But we make that presumption at our peril. The contemporary world has become entirely dependent on energy technologies, but we cannot assume that they will always be at our disposal or that we can recover them after disasters such as earthquakes and hurricanes. To better understand the meanings of technologies and their relation to modern science, we turn to some basic social-scientific definitions.

The Nature of Technology

14.1 Describe the nature of technology, focusing on technological dualism and the digital divide.

technology

The use of science in industry, engineering, etc., to invent useful things or to solve problems.

The dictionary definition of **technology** is "the use of science in industry, engineering, etc., to invent useful things or to solve problems." In this sense, technology is a way of solving practical problems; indeed, it is often viewed as the application of scientific knowledge to the problems of everyday life. But neither the dictionary definition nor the view of technology as applied science places enough emphasis on its organizational aspects. Langdon Winner (2004) has provided a useful set of dimensions for understanding the broader meaning of technology:

- Technological tools, instruments, machines, gadgets, which are used in accomplishing a variety of tasks. These material objects are best referred to as apparatus, the physical devices of technical performance.

- The body of technical skills, procedures, routines—all activities or behaviors that use a purposive, step-by-step, rational method of doing things.
- The organizational networks associated with activities and apparatus.

Technological change refers to changes in any or all of the major dimensions of technology listed in Winner's dimensions. Some technological changes have revolutionary significance in that they alter the basic institutions of society. Thus, the Industrial Revolution—that is, the development of factories and mass production—radically altered the organization of many noneconomic institutions, including the family, religion, the military, and science itself.

Not all technological change is revolutionary, however. Some innovations spur only minor adjustments in other sectors of society or among small numbers of people. Nor does technological change always consist of a single major invention. After all, the technological revolution that took place in American agriculture from the end of the nineteenth century to World War II involved hundreds of major inventions and the skills and organization to support them. The combination of all these factors allowed the United States to make the transition from an agrarian society to an urban industrial society in less than one century.

technological change

Changes in any or all of the major dimensions of technology.

Technological Dualism

The term **technological dualism** refers to the fact that advances in technology can have both positive and negative impacts. This idea is not new; the ancient Greeks believed the god Apollo embodied this dualism because he could bring them new techniques of healing but could also use those techniques to cause death. In our own time, the problem of the good and evil consequences of technologies is ever present. Think of the controversy over guns: Larger numbers of guns in a population are associated with higher rates of violence, but their defenders claim that the violence is not caused by guns but by those who use them for bad purposes. Automotive technology has changed almost every aspect of how we live, but it has also contributed immensely to the problem of global climate change. And nothing illustrates the dual nature of technologies better than nuclear power, which on the one hand has many peaceful uses but, on the other hand, is used in nuclear weapons that could someday destroy entire human societies (Clarke, 2005).

technological dualism

The idea that advances in technology can have both positive and negative impacts.

What Do You Think?

Can you list the positive and negative aspects of technology that you likely use every day, such as a cell phone or computer? Do you think someone in a less developed country would have a different list of positive and negative aspects of these technologies? Why or why not?

The Digital Divide

It is hard to believe, but the World Wide Web will turn only 27 years old in 2016. It is one of the most important and heavily used parts of the linked computer networks that make up the Internet. The invention of the Web was the key to turning the Internet from a geeky data-transfer system used by only a few into a mass-adopted technology used around the world by hundreds of millions of people (Fox and Rainie, 2014).

Most American adults use the Internet (about 88 percent), and claim that the Internet has been good for society (76 percent) and good for them personally (90 percent) (Fox and Rainie, 2014). However, Internet use is correlated with income, education, and age. The gap between those with access to computers and the Internet and those without such access is often referred to as the **digital divide**. Poor families, those with less education, and older people are more likely to be among the 12 percent of Americans who do not use the Internet (Fox and Rainie, 2014; Internet World Stats, 2015).

digital divide

The gap between those with access to computers and the Internet and those without such access.

Efforts to give children time on computers in schools have greatly reduced the income and education aspect of the digital divide gap in the past few years. Today, virtually all schools in the United States give their students Internet access for assignments and projects. This development is encouraging because Internet access is a type of passkey to success in the global economy.

Figure 14–1 Percentage of Internet Users in Selected World Regions, June 2014

SOURCE: Internet World Stats, 2015.

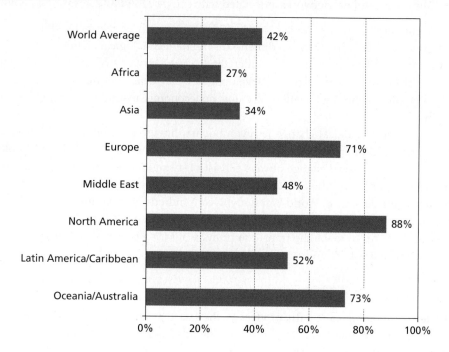

Despite progress in the United States, the global digital divide is still immense in many parts of the world. Figure 14–1 reveals the variation in access to the Internet in parts of the world. North America has the highest rate of use, and Africa has the lowest. As you can imagine, in countries with low use, the digital divide is commonplace; many urban rich people have Internet access while those with less income or education, especially in the rural regions, are without it.

The technologies that convey information can be a positive force for social change, but patterns of inequality may prevent this access to information. People in developing nations, for example, suffer from the most serious infectious diseases. Yet medical personnel in those nations often cannot access the information they need to combat those diseases.

Controlling Technology

14.2   Compare and contrast different ways that technology operates autonomously and is removed from political control.

Some social commentators are convinced that technology has become an autonomous force in society—one that is less and less subject to the control of democratic political institutions. A more hopeful view stresses social adaptation to technological innovation. In this section, you can explore these contrasting views of technology.

Autonomous Technology

The theme of "technology run amok" appears frequently in movies, books, and other fictional works. But these fictional nightmares are based on real experiences or real possibilities for future problems. In the classic film *2001: A Space Odyssey*, a computer named Hal that ran the space mission malfunctioned in ways that suggested it could now think for itself and had to be taken over by its human crew. This plotline is, of course, a satirical view of computers' domination of human life, but how often do we read about computer mistakes that result in bureaucratic disasters affecting hundreds, even thousands, of people? We depend on machines, which are all too frail and fallible, yet we know that machines do not literally have lives of their own. People make machines and operate them, not vice versa. How can it be then that technology has achieved a seeming independence from human control, as many critics argue?

The answer, according to Winner (1986, 1997) and others, is not that individual machines exercise tyranny over human subjects but that the complex web that connects the various sectors of technology—such as communication, transportation, energy, manufacturing, and defense—has enmeshed us in a web of dependency. People who live in simple societies meet their basic survival needs with a fairly small number of tools and a simple division of labor. To accomplish goals such as building a shelter, gathering and growing food, and warding off enemies, they have evolved a set of tools that families and other groups manufacture and use as the need arises. The lives of these people are dominated by the need to survive, and technology simply provides the means for doing so. In modern industrial societies, however, most people spend most of their productive hours working to meet the quotas, deadlines, and other goals of large organizations. Each of the corporations, government bureaucracies, and other organizations produces goods and services that people want or need, not with a few tools, but with a complex array of machines and skills. As a whole, this complex web of technologies supply the basic necessities of life, along with innumerable extras. But in the process, much of the life of society has been diverted from meeting the needs of survival to meeting the requirements of technology (Sernau, 2013).

Most sociologists do not see technology as autonomous. They argue that we have been drawn into the momentum of technological change but are not sure where it is taking us. Future uses of technology and future technological inventions increasingly will be based on human values. The following sections discuss the role of values as it applies to particular technologies.

Automation

A classic example of the difficulty of understanding the interaction between technology and human values is automation, the replacement of workers by a nonhuman means of producing the same product or performing the same task. People may lose jobs because of automation, but should we fight to keep these jobs, many of which may be among the dirtiest and most dangerous ones in industrial facilities? The greatly feared displacement of workers by machines may increase productivity and thus create new wealth, which could be channeled into the "higher" work of humans, such as health care, education, or caring for the aged, but will those who lose their jobs in the process ultimately be hurt or helped?

In fact, the stereotypical image of automation in which a worker is replaced by a mechanical robot is indeed occurring throughout the industrialized world (Sernau, 2013). Each of these machines replaces at least three workers because it can work continuously, whereas human workers must be replaced every eight hours. Thus, automation increases the productivity of the economy because a constant or decreasing number of workers can turn out more of a desired product. The question remains, however, whether the new wealth generated by higher productivity will be used to benefit the entire society or only individuals who are already wealthy.

Whistleblowers

So many of the proposed solutions to technological problems are themselves new technologies that opportunities abound for abuse and personal profit through their application. People who see abuses of technological systems often run grave personal risks when they attempt to expose them. These individuals, and others who expose various kinds of abuses, are known as **whistleblowers**.

whistleblowers

People who see abuses of technological systems and other kinds of abuses and attempt to expose them.

Within any organization, values dictate certain ways of doing things, beliefs about the environment in which the group operates, and ideas about how individuals should behave become established. Whistleblowers challenge some element of this body of procedures, beliefs, and norms in an effort to bring about change. At the least, they must endure snubs or ostracism by fellow workers. At the worst, they may be fired or even subjected to physical violence. An important case illustrates these challenges: the BP Deepwater Horizon oil disaster.

The worst environmental disaster in U.S. history, the BP Deepwater Horizon oil spill in the Gulf of Mexico during the summer of 2010, raises many of the same issues of whistleblowing and lax enforcement that characterized earlier disasters such as the *Challenger* space shuttle explosion (Coy and Reed, 2010). The federal Minerals Management Service (MMS), which regulates offshore oil and gas production and collects reports on all oil spills, had exempted BP from filing an environmental-impact statement for the well that exploded. By the end of the Bush administration, the agency had become essentially a captive of the companies it is supposed to regulate. In September 2010, the Interior Department shut down an oil-royalty program run by the agency for failing to collect millions of dollars' worth of royalties from the oil companies drilling on federally administered seafloor sites. The Interior Department inspector general's office found that several MMS officials had "frequently consumed alcohol at industry functions, had used cocaine and marijuana, and had sexual relationships with oil and gas company representatives." Even before the disaster, 19 members of Congress wrote to the MMS asking for its response to accusations by an anonymous former contractor that BP did not complete crucial engineering drawings and other paperwork for subsea components of its Atlantis project, which began producing oil in 2007.

While investigations of the disaster continue to this day, it is not clear how many chances were missed to forestall the events, or even, given the technological scale of such projects, whether they can ever be managed in such a way as to avoid the risk of disaster, even for future projects. As Lee Clarke (2005) points out in his book *Worst Cases*, modern technological systems are extremely complex, and despite the best intentions of managers and employees, information is often lost or suppressed because of lack of coordination between different parts of the system. The tragic example of the BP disaster illustrates the need for more thorough technology assessment.

Identity Theft and Identity Fraud

In December 2013, just in time for the busy holiday shopping, Target, the nation's third-largest retailer, acknowledged that thieves had obtained credit and debit card information belonging to 40 million customers, along with the customers' names. In January 2014, Target announced that personal contact information for up to 70 million more customers had also been compromised. The method used was not particularly inventive; someone installed malware in Target's security and payments system designed to steal every credit card used at the company's 1,797 U.S. stores. At the critical moment—when the Christmas gifts had been scanned and bagged and the cashier asked for a swipe—the malware would step in, capture the shopper's credit card number, and store it on a Target server commandeered by the hackers. Customers and banks have filed more than 90 lawsuits against Target for negligence and compensatory damages. In addition, other costs related to the hack could run into the billions of dollars. Target set up a customer response operation and, in an effort to regain lost trust, promised that consumers would

Target is an example of a large retailer whose computer was hacked, and thieves stole credit and debit card data from millions of customers. Other retailers, including Home Depot, have faced similar situations.

Table 14–1 SCAM to Avoid Becoming a Victim of Identify Theft or Fraud

S	Be **stingy** about giving out your personal information to others unless you have a reason to trust them. Adopt a "need to know" approach to your personal data. If someone you do not know calls you on the phone asking for your personal data, such as a request for funds for a charity event, ask him or her for a written request. If the person refuses, hang up.
C	**Check** your financial information regularly, and look for what should be there, for example, monthly statements from credit card companies itemizing every transaction. Also look for what should not be there, such as unauthorized purchases or credit cards that you did not request.
A	**Ask** periodically for a copy of your credit report. Your credit report should list all bank and financial accounts under your name, and it will provide other indications of whether someone has wrongfully opened or used any accounts in your name.
M	**Maintain** careful records of your banking and financial accounts. Even though financial institutions are required to maintain copies of your checks, debit transactions, and similar transactions for five years, you should retain your monthly statements and checks for at least one year, preferably longer.

SOURCE: Adapted from the U.S. Department of Justice, 2015a.

not need to pay any fraudulent charges stemming from the breach. People were slow to warm back up to Target; the chain's profit for the holiday shopping period fell 46 percent from the same quarter the year before the breach (Riley et al., 2014).

Identity theft (and identity fraud) are terms used to refer to all types of crime in which someone wrongfully obtains and uses another person's personal data in some way that involves fraud or deception, typically for economic gain (U.S. Department of Justice, 2015b). Unlike your fingerprints, which are yours alone and cannot be taken by another person, identification such as your Social Security number, credit card information, or bank account numbers can fall into the wrong hands and be used by another person for his or her own profit. Thieves may take money out of a bank account; rack up huge debt on credit cards; or in the worst case scenario, take over a person's identity and commit crimes in the person's name. The victim not only may lose vast sums of money but also must then spend the time necessary to clear his or her name.

No one knows exactly how widespread this form of theft is, but approximately 13 million cases were reported to authorities in 2013, costing victims $18 billion (Ellis, 2014). The widespread use of online databases has given computer hackers an incentive to work with conventional criminals to "phish" through millions of online computers in search of openings that will enable them to invade private and corporate computers and steal identity data. As widespread as this computer "phishing" has become, however, experts on identity theft point out that even more identity information is obtained through old-fashioned means like stolen wallets, lost identification cards, and rummaging through trash bins. Nevertheless, much of the effort to develop ways of fighting identity theft focuses on increasing security for critical databases in government and the corporate sector (U.S Department of Justice, 2015b). The U.S. Department of Justice offers tips for avoiding identity theft, listed in Table 14–1.

identity theft (and identity fraud)

All types of crime in which someone wrongfully obtains and uses another person's personal data in some way that involves fraud or deception, typically for economic gain.

Bureaucracy and Morality

Technology consists not only of machines but also of procedures and organizations. Today, much of the productive activity that occurs in complex societies takes place in large bureaucratic organizations. With their orientation toward specified goals, their division of labor into narrowly defined roles, and their hierarchical authority structures, such organizations are supremely efficient. But like technology in general, some qualities of large organizations that make them so productive and valuable can also cause harm. For example, individuals in a hierarchical system may commit immoral acts and may not feel personally responsible for the consequences of those acts because they are carried out under the direction of superiors.

The list of immoral acts committed on the instructions of superiors in large organizations is long. Writing as London was being pounded by Nazi bombs during World War II, George Orwell (quoted in Milgram, 1974) described the irony of one such situation:

> *As I write, highly civilized human beings are flying overhead, trying to kill me. They do not feel any enmity against me as an individual, nor I against them. They are only "doing their duty," as the saying goes. Most of them are kind-hearted law abiding men who would never dream of committing murder in private life. On the other hand, if one of them succeeds in blowing me to pieces with a well-placed bomb, he will never sleep any the worse for it.* (pp. 11–12)

Stanley Milgram called attention to the fact that, when an immoral task is divided up among a number of people in a large organization like an air force or a bomb factory, no one person, acting as an individual, actually decides to commit the act, perceives its consequences, or takes responsibility for it. It is easy for each participant to become absorbed in the effort to perform his or her role competently. It is also psychologically easy to reduce guilt with the rationalization that one's duty requires the immoral behavior and that one's superior is responsible in the end (Blass, 2009).

In a famous series of experiments conducted at Yale University, Milgram (1974) studied the conditions under which people forsake the universally shared moral value against doing harm to another person as part of obeying the instructions of someone in a position of authority. Subjects entered the laboratory assuming that they were to take part in a study of learning and memory. One person was designated a "learner" and the other a "teacher." The experimenter explained that the purpose of the study was to observe the effect of punishment on learning, and then the learner was strapped into a chair and electrodes were attached to his wrist. Next, the learner was told that the task was to learn a list of word pairs and that for every error, he would receive an electric shock of progressively greater intensity. The teacher, who had been present for this interchange, was escorted to another room and seated at the controls of a large shock generator. Each time the learner gave a wrong answer, the teacher was to flip the next in a series of 30 switches designed to deliver shocks in 15-volt increments, from 15 to 450, starting at the lowest level.

In reality, the learner was an actor who received no shock, but pretended greater discomfort as the supposed intensity of the shocks increased. Grunts gave way to verbal complaints, to demands for release from the experiment, and then to screams. The true purpose of the experiment was to study the behavior of the teachers. They were affected by the cries and suffering of the learners but whenever they hesitated to deliver a shock, the experimenter ordered them to continue. In one form of the experiment, almost two-thirds of the subjects administered the maximum shock of 450 volts. Interviews with these subjects (who had been carefully selected to represent a cross section of society) revealed that they justified delivering shocks by absorbing themselves in its technical details, transferring responsibility to the experimenter, and justifying their actions in the name of scientific truth (Milgram, 1974).

Milgram's experiments generated a great deal of controversy and contributed to the establishment of rules for governing federally funded social-science research that uses human subjects. At the same time, there has not been any significant debate about the implications of his findings for society. Should people be taught that disobedience to authority under some conditions is necessary? This issue of disobedience is the situation faced by whistleblowers, who actually overcome their feelings of subservience to bureaucratic hierarchies, which are often technologically oriented (Blass, 2004).

What Do You Think?

How do you think you would respond if you were one of the teachers in the Milgram study? How willing are you to disobey authority to uphold your values? Keep in mind that this "authority" could be as common as a peer group.

Technology and Social Institutions

14.3 **Assess the adaptation of technology to changing social institutions.**

Sociologists who study technology and the effects of technological change most often concern themselves with the adaptation of social institutions to changing technology or, conversely, the adaptation of technology to changing social institutions. The best-known statement of these relationships is William F. Ogburn's **cultural lag** theory, first stated in the 1920s. According to Ogburn (1957), a founder of the study of technology in the United States, "a cultural lag occurs when one of two parts of culture which are correlated changes before or in greater degree than the other part does, thereby causing less adjustment between the two parts than existed previously" (p. 167). In other words, one aspect of culture changes, but a related part of that culture lags behind and causes problems.

A classic example of cultural lag during the nineteenth century involves the introduction of the Industrial Revolution, coupled with the failure of social-welfare legislation to protect workers who were using the new and dangerous industrial machinery. The frequency of industrial accidents was increasing during that period because operators were not adequately protected from the rapidly moving wheels of the new machines. The loss of life and limb generally meant financial disaster for workers' families because, under existing law, employers could not easily be held liable. As a result, compensation was meager and slow to come. Only when worker's compensation and employer liability were introduced early in the twentieth century was this maladjustment, which had led to much impoverishment and suffering, finally corrected (Ogburn, 1957).

Typically, social institutions and technology adjust and readjust to each other in a process that approaches equilibrium, unless one or the other alters so radically that a lag develops. In the history of transportation technology, radical changes have occurred relatively often. Witness the impact of the steamboat, the railroad, the automobile, and the airplane. Sometimes mere refinements in existing technology can devastate the social arrangements that had evolved in response to older machines and procedures, which is what occurred in the railroad town of Caliente (not its real name) when diesel power replaced steam in the 1940s. A classic study by Cottrell (1951) describes the results.

Caliente had been settled at the turn of the twentieth century, when the railroad was built, and it owed its existence almost entirely to the railroad. When the line was put through, the boiler of a steam engine could withstand high pressures and temperatures for only short periods. A locomotive had to be disconnected from service roughly every 100 miles, and Caliente was located in the middle of the desert for this purpose.

Over the years, the community had invested considerable sums in its own future. Railroad workers and others had put their life savings into mortgages; merchants had built stores; and the town had constructed a hospital, a school, and a park. But when the diesel engine was developed, it undermined the economic base of the town, saddling its residents with devalued property and no means of supporting themselves. Diesel engines require much less maintenance and many fewer stops for fuel and water than do steam engines, and a stop in Caliente was no longer necessary. Thus, the railroad employees who lived in Caliente either lost their jobs or were transferred; the town had become irrelevant from the point of view of the railroad. In the U.S. free-enterprise system, the profitability of the railroad determined the fate of the town. The railroad was under no obligation to cushion the social impact of its move, and the state did not offer any assistance, so the town died.

The construction of interstate highways after World War II had the opposite effect. The width, straightness, and limited access of interstates permit greater traffic

cultural lag

A delay that occurs when one aspect of a culture changes more rapidly than another aspect does and thereby causes some maladjustment between the two aspects.

Wind turbines flank the electricity pylons and a coal-fired power plant. Cultural change—the desire for clean energy—occurred long before the technological change, according to Ogburn.

flow and higher speeds than those possible on conventional roads. Initially, there were few towns or services along these highways. However, in time, new jobs were created to service the cars, and then new jobs were created to serve those who serviced the cars. The promise of new jobs attracted new residents from other areas. Thus, a study of the impact of interstate highways on nonmetropolitan counties between 1950 and 1975 was able to establish an association between highway construction and population and economic growth along the interstate corridor (Lichter and Fuguitt, 1980).

Ogburn's (1957) theory of cultural lag and other sociological research on adaptation to technological change are often considered examples of technological determinism, the theory that technological innovation dictates changes in social institutions and culture (Winner, 2004). But Ogburn demonstrated that, in many instances, cultural change occurs long before technological change. Such technological lags are major challenges to modern science and engineering.

An example of Ogburn's ideas can be found in the way American culture has come to depend on the availability of relatively cheap fossil fuels. Yet, as supplies dwindle and become more difficult to secure for political reasons, technological breakthroughs are needed to maintain the supply of low-cost energy (Brown, 2015). America has the know-how to harness the wind and rays of the sun to produce "green" renewable energy sources, and these forms of energy receive overwhelming support (Moore and Nichols, 2014). Table 14–2 shows the results of a survey conducted with a nationally representative sample of adults. Approximately two-thirds of respondents favor green and renewable energy proposals. In other words, America has the will and the capabilities, but green energy outputs remain paltry. Ogburn's theory is played out today: Cultural change occurs before technological change.

Table 14–2 Environmental and Energy Proposals, 2014

Do you generally favor or oppose this proposal?

	Favor	Oppose
Spending more government money on developing solar and wind power	67%	32%
Spending government money to develop alternate sources of fuel for automobiles	66%	33%
Setting higher emissions and pollution standards for business and industry	65%	35%
More strongly enforcing federal environmental regulations	64%	34%
Imposing mandatory controls on carbon dioxide emissions/other greenhouse gases	63%	35%
Setting higher auto emissions standards for automobiles	62%	35%
Opening up land owned by the federal government for oil exploration	58%	41%
Setting stricter standards on the use of techniques to extract natural gas from the earth, including "fracking"	58%	37%
Expanding the use of nuclear energy	47%	51%

SOURCE: Moore and Nichols, 2014.

Technology and the Natural Environment

14.4   Discuss the link between technology and the environment.

Human civilization has been changing and becoming more complex at an accelerating rate. The ideas, facts, and procedures that make up science and technology at any given time serve as a platform for future progress. A single technological advance such as the wheel, the internal combustion engine, or the semiconductor may form the basis of an enormous range of inventions. As the ability of humans to exploit the resources of the earth has grown, so has the size of human populations.

These two developments—accelerated technological and scientific change and rapid population growth—are causing pollution and depletion of the natural environment as never before. Natural cycles of purification can absorb only a limited amount of certain artificial substances before ecological damage is done. Water pollution occurs when streams, rivers, lakes, and oceans can no longer purify themselves. When wind, rain, and snow can no longer remove the particles deposited in the air by machines of various kinds, pollution is the result. In these cases, the speed at which technology creates pollutants exceeds the pace at which nature can absorb them.

Sometimes technologies that seem benign and that we take for granted as part of everyday life have unanticipated consequences. Earlier in this century, pesticides and herbicides revolutionized agriculture, making it much more productive. Subsequent research has linked many of these chemicals to the destruction of fish and birds and to certain cancers in humans. Along the same lines, for years people used aerosol containers for purposes ranging from personal hygiene to applying whipped cream to ice cream sundaes. In the mid-1970s, the suspicion that a propellant used in aerosol cans was eroding the atmospheric ozone layer, which protects us from harmful radiation, led to the use of different propellants.

Perhaps the central question is this: Can we control such harmful effects before it is too late? In many cases, the technology exists to control environmental damage, but powerful interests do not wish to shoulder the cost of doing so. Here, the problem becomes one of creating a political consensus around a solution. In other cases, the technology that is needed to get us out of jams that earlier inventions have helped put us into does not yet exist. Thus, advanced economies around the world are consuming energy in the form of oil, which is becoming depleted and for which an adequate substitute has not yet been found. Any technological solution to this and other problems will almost inevitably contribute to a whole new generation of crises.

Environmental Stress

14.5   Summarize different types of stressors on the environment.

An investigation of winter fish kills in Wisconsin lakes led to the unexpected conclusion that they were caused by snowmobiles. Heavy snowmobile use on a lake during the winter compacts the snow and makes the ice opaque. The opaque ice reduces the amount of sunlight that reaches underwater plants, which need it for photosynthesis. As the plants' oxygen production declines, they die, and their decomposition consumes considerable amounts of the oxygen left in the water. As a result, the fish are asphyxiated.

The term **environmental stress** refers to what society does to the environment. As this example suggests, we can best understand environmental stress as the interaction and conflict of three systems: (a) the natural environment; (b) the technological system; and (c) the social system. The fish, ice, oxygen, and plants are all elements of the

environmental stress

The interaction and conflict of three systems: the natural environment, the technological system, and the social system.

Figure 14–2 Percentage of Americans Who "Worry a Great Deal" About the Environment, 2001–2014

SOURCE: Riffkin, 2014.

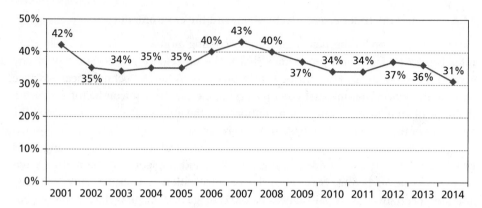

natural system. The snowmobile is an element of the technological system. That this vehicle is produced, marketed, and used is a product of the social system—as is the fact that no one is held responsible for the fish kills.

Taking a broader perspective, we can define the natural system as containing the following elements and their interrelationships: air, water, earth, solar energy, plants, animals, and mineral resources. Our technological system includes transportation, farming, electricity-generating facilities, manufacturing processes and plants, various methods for extracting mineral resources, and the actual consumption and disposal of the products of these processes. Our social system includes attitudes, beliefs and values, and institutional structures. And as with the fish and the snowmobiles, so in larger matters we must look to our social and technological processes for the origins of the problems in the natural system.

However, this effort becomes difficult when our attitudes, beliefs, and values do not recognize the importance of environmental stress and the role of humans in creating that stress. Figure 14–2 indicates the percentage of adults between 2001 and 2014 who say they "worry a great deal" about our environment. These responses are the results of a survey for Gallup, which is based on a large and nationally representative sample. As you can see, the percentage of adults who agree with that statement fluctuates, but it is now at an all-time low for the twenty-first century (Riffkin, 2014).

Origins of the Problem

Examples of environmental stress abound and include discharging substances into the air, water, and soil; producing heat, noise, and radiation; removing plants and animals; and physically transforming the environment through drilling, damming, dredging, mining, pumping, and so on (Brown, 2015). Environmental stress is not synonymous with pollution, although pollution is perhaps its most familiar form. Webster's dictionary defines **pollution** as "the action or process of making land, water, air, etc., dirty and not safe or suitable to use."

Four concepts are basic to understanding environmental stress: interdependence, diversity, limits, and complexity (Ophuls, 1977).

pollution

The action or process of making land, water, air, etc., dirty and not safe or suitable to use.

- *Interdependence,* which literally means that everything is related to and depends on everything else; there is no beginning or end to the web of life.
- *Diversity,* which refers to the existence of many different life and life-support forms. A basic principle of ecology is that the greater the diversity of species, the greater the probability of survival of any given one.

- *Limits,* which includes several kinds. First, there is a finite limit to the growth of any organism. Second, there is a limit to the numbers of a given species that an environment—including other organisms—can support. Finally, there is a finite limit to the amount of materials available in the earth's ecosystem.
- *Complexity,* which refers to the intricacy of the relationships that constitute the web. Because of this complexity, interventions in the environment frequently lead to unanticipated and undesired consequences.

Use of the chemical DDT (dichlorodiphenyltrichloroethane) is an example of complexity. The pesticide was once repeatedly sprayed over large areas of land to eliminate various disease-carrying or crop-destroying insects. To an impressive degree, it succeeded. But DDT is a long-lasting chemical, and its effects are not limited to insects. Much of it was washed from farmlands and forests into rivers and oceans, where it was taken up by smaller organisms at the bottom of the food chain. Eventually, as small creatures consumed tiny plants and larger creatures consumed smaller ones, several species of fish-eating birds accumulated so much of the poison that their eggs developed very thin shells, which consistently broke before hatching. These species were in grave danger of extinction, although the users of DDT never intended such a result (Ehrlich and Ehrlich, 2004). Only federal restrictions on the use of DDT prevented the elimination of these bird species.

One of the major difficulties in dealing with environmental stress, therefore, is the number of problems involved and the extent to which they are interrelated. This complexity will become clear as you explore specific problems, particularly climate change, air pollution, water pollution, and solid-waste disposal, and the efforts that have been made to combat them.

Climate Change and Global Warming

In today's society, terms such as *climate change* and *global warming* have become politicized and controversial. **Global warming** refers to the long-term warming of the planet. Global temperature shows a well-documented rise since the early twentieth century and most notably since the late 1970s. Since 1880, the average worldwide surface temperature has gone up by about 0.8°C (1.4°F), relative to the mid-twentieth-century baseline of 1951–1980. **Climate change** encompasses global warming, but refers to the broader range of changes that are happening to our planet. These changes include rising sea levels; shrinking mountain glaciers; accelerating ice melt in Greenland, Antarctica, and the Arctic; and shifts in flower and plant blooming times. These developments are all consequences of the warming, which is caused mainly by people burning fossil fuels and emitting heat-trapping gases into the air. The two terms are often used interchangeably, although climate change is a more accurate description because the changes involve far more than just an increase in temperatures. Some places will be noticeably hotter, others will be wetter, and others drier.

WHAT IS CLIMATE CHANGE? Of all the many aspects of pollution and environmental stress, perhaps none alarms scientists and environmental groups at present as much as climate change—the dangerous warming of the planet, and the consequences associated with this warming, because of continued high levels of greenhouse gases into the atmosphere from (a) carbon dioxide (CO_2), primarily from burning fossil fuels including coal, oil, and gas; (b) breeding vast numbers of methane-producing livestock; and (c) cutting down forests that naturally absorb carbon dioxide from the

global warming

The long-term warming of the planet.

climate change

A type of environmental change that encompasses global warming, but refers to the broader range of changes that are happening to our planet, including rising sea levels; shrinking mountain glaciers; accelerating ice melt in Greenland, Antarctica, and the Arctic; and shifts in flower and plant blooming times.

Americans have been concerned about water and air pollution for decades. The concern about climate change is much more recent. However, climate change is a problem that must be addressed immediately or the other issues are almost moot.

air (World Wildlife Fund, 2015). Carbon-based gases such as carbon dioxide and methane are natural gases and essential for life on earth—in the right amounts. However, the extra carbon dioxide and methane in the atmosphere traps more of the sun's heat, creating a "greenhouse effect," and raising global temperatures. That is, these gases trap heat near the earth's surface, raising the average temperature of the atmosphere. Fourteen of the 15 hottest years recorded have all been in the twenty-first century (United Nations, 2015).

Such overheating, even by a few degrees, could melt the polar ice caps, with calamitous results. Some scientists believe that globally, the temperature today is 0.8°C above pre-industrial times and that a warming of close to 1.5°C above pre-industrial times is already locked into the earth's atmosphere by past and predicted emissions. Everyone will feel the impact of this warming (World Bank Group, 2014).

Scientists estimate that a rise of just 2°C would cause severe storms and floods in some countries and crippling droughts in others; would cause seas to become more acidic, killing coral and krill and thus disrupting food chains; and would reduce Arctic ice to little or none in the summer, which not only is bad news for polar bears, but also means that the earth would warm even faster because there would be less polar ice to deflect sunlight (World Wildlife Fund, 2015; Union of Concerned Scientists, 2015; United Nations, 2015). A rise beyond 2°C could lead to dying rain forests, increased melting of the ancient ice sheets of Greenland and Antarctica, dramatic sea level rises, and untold suffering among people and animals. Scientists predict that the temperature could rise up to 6°C in this century if the world's people do not drastically cut greenhouse gas emissions.

million tons of oil equivalent (Mtoe)

A standard method of converting different types of energy units into one measure.

Until recently, the United States has been the largest energy consumer and the largest contributor to the production of these gases. In recent years, the United States has been eclipsed by China. Figure 14–3 reports the world's top 10 consumers of energy, which includes the use of coal, gas, oil, electric, heat, and biomass. China is now ranked first, using 3,013 **million tons of oil equivalent (Mtoe)**, which is a standard method

Figure 14–3 World's Top 10 Energy Consumers, 2013 (Mtoe)

NOTE: Mtoe (Million Tons of Oil Equivalent). Energy consumed includes coal, gas, oil, electric, heat, and biomass.

SOURCE: Enerdata, 2014.

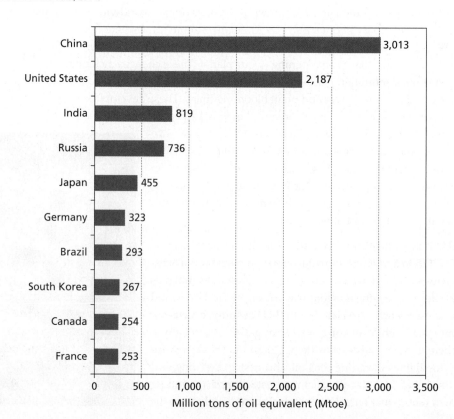

Million tons of oil equivalent (Mtoe)

Table 14–3 Percentage Who Have Expectations That Global Warming Will Seriously Threaten One's Way of Life, by Age Group, 2014

	18 to 29 years	30 to 49 years	50 to 64 years	65+ years
No	57%	57%	63%	82%
Yes	43%	42%	37%	18%

SOURCE: Jones, 2014.

of converting different types of energy units into one measure. The United States uses 2,187 Mtoe units. However, China's population is nearly 5 times that of the United States, so, per person, Americans still use the vast majority of the world's energy.

Less developed countries (LDCs) burn fossil fuels at far lower rates than developed nations, but many LDCs meet their energy needs by burning wood, straw, and similar fuels, which also emit carbon. The felling and burning of forests in tropical countries adds between 1 billion and 2 billion tons of carbon emissions to the worldwide total. Growing populations and the associated demand for energy, land, and other resources will lead to carbon emissions—and hence the amount of carbon dioxide in the atmosphere—that will likely increase for the foreseeable future.

AN INCONVENIENT TRUTH At present, there is widespread consensus among scientists that global warming is a real and present danger (Union of Concerned Scientists, 2015). There is continued debate about it among laypeople. Two-thirds of adults surveyed acknowledge that climate change is occurring; 57 percent of people say it has already begun or will begin in a few years, and another 8 percent believe it will begin in their lifetime. However, most still do not see global warming as a serious threat, as shown in Table 14–3. Even among young people, who will experience the most severe effects during their lifetime of any group, only slightly more than half agreed that "global warming will seriously threaten one's way of life" (Jones, 2014). In another poll, in which Americans ranked the most serious problems facing America today, climate change was not even on the list (McCarthy, 2015).

In other words, most people are aware that climate change is happening, but are not particularly worried about it. This mindset may signal that many people do not understand climate change and feel that the seriousness of it presented in the news is exaggerated, as shown in Figure 14–4 (Dugan, 2014; Jones, 2014). Yet most scientists agree that the consequences of climate change are already here and are having significant and costly effects on our communities and our health. As former Vice President and Nobel Prize winner Al Gore has said, climate change is "an inconvenient truth."

CONSEQUENCES OF CLIMATE CHANGE What are the serious consequences of climate change? Looking only at the United States, we are likely to see (Union of Concerned Scientists, 2015):

- *Accelerated sea level rise and increased coastal flooding.* The average sea level has increased eight inches since 1880 and is rising the fastest in the East Coast and Gulf of Mexico regions, increasing flooding risks to low-lying communities and coastal properties. This increase is due to the rising temperature in the planet's polar regions, which is causing the vast majority of the world's glaciers to melt faster than new snow and ice can replenish them.
- *More frequent and intense heat waves.* Dangerously hot weather is already occurring more frequently in much of the United States, and the last few summers have had record heat. Scientists expect heat waves to become more frequent and severe as global warming intensifies. The heat creates serious health risks, including heat exhaustion, heat stroke, and aggravations of other medical conditions.
- *Longer and more damaging wildfire seasons.* Rising temperatures lead to a longer wildlife season and an increase in the number of wildfires. Spring arrives 10 days

Figure 14–4 Americans Rate the Seriousness of Global Warming, 1998, 2007, 2014

SOURCE: Dugan, 2014.

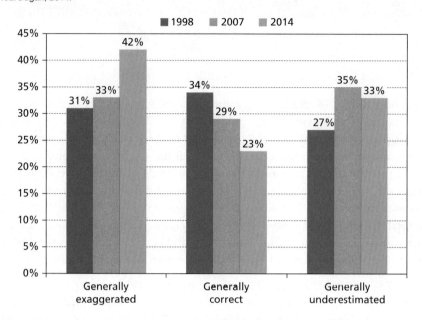

earlier on average in the Northern Hemisphere. Higher temperatures and early spring snowmelt cause forests in the West to be drier for longer periods, priming conditions for wildfires to ignite and spread.

- *Heavier precipitation and flooding.*   As temperatures increase, more rain falls during the heaviest downpours, increasing the risk of flooding. "Very-heavy" rainfalls, defined as the heaviest 1 percent of storms, now drop 67 percent more precipitation in the Northeast, 31 percent more in the Midwest, and 15 percent more in the Great Plains than they did 50 years ago. Snow accumulations are also increasing; Boston had its highest snowfall ever recorded in the 2014–2015 season.

- *More severe droughts in some areas.*   Climate change affects many factors associated with droughts, and has increased the drought risk in the West and Southwest. As of late 2015, California is experiencing the most serious drought ever recorded.

- *Disruption to food supplies.*   Rising temperatures and the lack of water in the West and heavier precipitation in other areas has significant implications for crop and meat production. Global warming has the potential to seriously disrupt the American food supply, drive costs upward, and affect the availability and quality of most foods, from coffee to cattle.

- *Plant and animal range shifts.*   A changing climate affects the range of plants and animals, causing disruptions throughout the food chain. The range of warm-weather species will expand, but the range of those requiring cooler environments will face shrinking habitats and possible extinction.

As serious as these consequences are for Americans, they pale in comparison to other parts of the world where they are likely to occur in more extreme forms. For example, record high temperatures of between 100 and 105 degrees (Fahrenheit) occurred in a number of European cities in the summer of 2015. Torrential rains hit the northern deserts of Chile in spring 2015, normally among the driest places on earth. The monthly precipitation over the Pacific side of western Japan for August 2014 was 301 percent above normal—the highest since area-averaged statistics began in 1946. At the same time, northeast China and parts of the Yellow River basin did not reach half of the summer average, causing severe drought. Africa is one of the most vulnerable continents to

Slide Show

Some Effects of Climate Change

Climate change is not some far-off prophecy. It is real and happening today, as these images reveal.

This is an aerial view of the town of Ilulissat, Greenland. Even though the disappearing ice cap could lead to higher sea levels all over the world, Greenland's Inuit population will be among the first to feel the effects of climate change. Records show that the average air temperature has risen by 4°C over the past decade while the water temperature has climbed by two degrees. Fishermen and hunters now avoid the fjords where the ice has become too thin to travel on. For the first time, they are now beginning to catch cod, which prefer warmer water.

This woman wades through a flooded street in Miami, Florida, to catch a bus. Some of the streets in Miami Beach were flooded because of unusually high tides that some suspect were due to rising sea levels connected with global warming and climate change. Florida ranks as the state most vulnerable to sea-level rise, with some 2.4 million people living on the coast at risk.

Climate change will increase the number and intensity of wildfires, especially in the western United States. Here, a house burns in San Marcos, California. Because of the prolonged and continuing record drought in California, fire agencies are scrambling to prepare for the next season.

The year 2015 was the snowiest on record for many parts of the country. This view is of Lake Shore Drive and a frozen Lake Michigan in March 2015. Some of the coldest temperatures ever recorded have settled onto the Chicago area during 2015.

Donna Johnson distributes drinking water to neighbors as water wells supplying hundreds of residents remain dry in the central California community of East Porterville. Many local residents fill water tanks with free nonpotable water for flushing toilets, bathing, and laundering. Bottled water is used for drinking, cooking, and washing dishes. Many wells in the county stopped flowing during the summer due to the drought. In 2015, some scientists believe that California has only enough water in reservoirs to last about one more year.

Critical Thinking

Think about where you live. How is global warming affecting you today? How do you think it will affect you in five years?

climate change, already suffering from droughts, arid land unsuitable for farming, and severe water shortages. Climate change will intensify these issues, and its poor state of economic development, its high levels of poverty, and its political instability will further worsen this situation (Munang and Andrews, 2014; United Nations, 2015).

All of these issues raise the specter of social and political conflict as people try to adapt to changing conditions. When food and water run short, conflict is inevitable. Will the poor suffer more than the rich, or will the challenges be equally shared? The head of the Catholic Church, Pope Francis, raises this question.

California, which in late 2015 is experiencing its fourth year of drought and perhaps its worst in 1,000 years, provides an interesting test case of the way that social inequality weaves its way through limited resources. At this writing, water in California is not rationed for homeowners, but the governor encourages people to voluntarily reduce their water usage. Who is doing so? The box, A Closer Look: Who's Using the Water? Social Class and Water Usage in California, indicates that not all people are conserving equally.

A Closer Look

Who's Using the Water? Social Class and Water Usage in California

California is in a drought that is considered the worst in recorded history. This region, with a dry Mediterranean climate, is used to little rainfall. However, over the last decade, the winter rains have been unusually light, snowfall in the mountains has been well below average, and water usage by farmers, industry, and private individuals continues to drain the reservoirs.

By 2011, the state began to take serious notice of the low levels of water in the reservoirs and the dreaded "D" word—drought—became a common part of everyday conversations. Many people consider the drought a short-term inconvenience. Scientists, however, know that there have been multiple droughts in California, often lasting hundreds of years. The two most severe droughts that we know of include a 240-year-long drought that started in 850 AD. Fifty years after its conclusion, another one began that stretched at least 180 years. So it may be wishful thinking to assume that this one will be over quickly.

Now in its fourth year of crisis (at least), tempers are heating up. Governor Brown asked households for a voluntary reduction of 20 percent. The state established rules that allowed communities to fine excessive water-wasters up to $500, but enforcement has been rare. In Los Angeles, for instance, only two $200 fines were issued in a service area of about 4 million people. Without serious consequences, many people continued to water lawns, take long showers, wash their cars, and go on day to day as if water were unlimited. Therefore, water usage declined on average only 10 percent by 2014. By 2015, the governor imposed stricter policies in hopes of cutting use by 25 percent.

Should we be surprised to learn that wealthy people and wealthy communities in California used considerably more water than poorer people and poorer communities? The California Department of Water Resources notes that, for example, working-class residents in Bellflower used an average of 128 gallons of water a day in 2014. Per capita, water use in surrounding low-income suburbs was similar. In contrast, water use in nearby posh Palos Verdes and Beverly Hills was markedly higher at 282 and 284 gallons per day, respectively.

What accounts for income differences in water usage? If you don't mind a large water bill, what is the incentive to conserve? As one man in tony Rancho Santa Fe, a wealthy suburb of Los Angeles, said, "I know I am not supposed to be watering my yard so much, but I think brown grass is ugly. Go ahead, fine me if you have to, but I want to keep things looking nice."

This is one of the reasons that in April 2015, Governor Brown ordered mandatory water use restrictions for the first time in California's history. In an executive order, he directed the State Water Resources Control Board to impose a 25 percent reduction over the coming year in California's local water supply agencies, which serve 90 percent of California's residents. This order would impose cutbacks on water use across the board, affecting homeowners, farms, and businesses, regardless of income; however, the size of cuts will vary from community to community, reflecting that some communities have already been better at reducing their water then other communities. Furthermore, the State Water Resources Control Board has the power to impose fines on local water suppliers that fail to meet the reduction targets.

"People should realize we are in a new era," Governor Brown said at an April 2015 news conference, as he stood on a patch of brown and green grass that would normally be under snow at that time of year. "The idea of your nice little green lawn getting watered every day, those days are past."

Critical Thinking

How would a conflict theorist analyze water usage in California? Would a conflict theorist support or oppose mandatory water rationing, and why? What approach to conserving water do you think is best?

SOURCES: Stevens, 2014; Su et al., 2012; Worland, 2015.

Still despite the urgency, many Republicans, including those in Congress, and major energy companies are not convinced that these and similar changes are more than periodic natural fluctuations in the earth's temperature (Jones, 2014). Nor are they convinced that even if climate change is accelerating, all of its consequences will be negative. They question whether there is adequate scientific evidence to justify expensive retrofitting of power plants and more drastic measures to conserve energy (Climate Debate Daily, 2015). However, the scientific evidence that our climate is changing, largely caused by human activity, is overwhelming.

Air Pollution

If the atmosphere is not overburdened, natural processes will cleanse it and preserve its composition. Through photosynthesis, for example, green plants combine water with the carbon dioxide that we and other organisms exhale, and they produce oxygen. But these natural processes, like other resources, have limits. They can remove only a limited quantity of harmful substances from the air; if pollution exceeds their capacity to do so, the air will become progressively more dangerous to those who breathe it.

Human activities are overtaxing the atmosphere. Although the specific nature of air pollution varies from one locality to another (as a function of geography, climate, and type and concentration of industry), we can identify some of the common components, including organic compounds (hydrocarbons); oxides of carbon, nitrogen, and sulfur; lead and other metals; and particulate matter (soot and fly ash).

The Environmental Protection Agency (EPA) says motor vehicles account for three-quarters of the carbon monoxide in the air (Brinson, 2015). The remainder comes from the burning of fossil fuels (oil and coal) in power-generating plants, airplanes, and homes; airborne wastes from manufacturing processes; and the burning of municipal trash. Certain chemical processes frequently render these pollutants more dangerous after they reach the atmosphere. In the presence of sunlight, the emission of hydrocarbons and nitrogen oxides (primarily from cars) produces the photochemical soup called smog that envelops many of our cities, and various oxides combine with water vapor in the atmosphere to produce corrosive acids that eventually become what is known as acid rain, which eats away the surfaces of many buildings.

Pollution is particularly severe in parts of the world where regulations still permit the use of leaded gasoline and where large populations still rely on firewood or other combustibles for cooking. Over parts of China, the air quality has reached hazardous levels. Table 14–4 shows the **Air Quality Index (AQI)**, which is an index of daily air quality that indicates how clean or polluted the air is (Environmental Protection Agency, 2015a). The EPA calculates the AQI for five major air pollutants regulated by the Clean Air Act: ground-level ozone, particle pollution (also known as particulate matter), carbon monoxide, sulfur dioxide, and nitrogen dioxide. Think of the AQI as a measuring stick that runs from 0 to 500. The lower the AQI value, the better the air quality.

Air Quality Index (AQI)

A way of categorizing levels of daily air quality that indicates how clean or polluted the air is.

Table 14–4 Current EPA Air Quality Index (AQI)

AQI Range	EPA Color Scale	EPA Descriptor
0 to 50	Green	Good
51 to 100	Yellow	Moderate
101 to 150	Orange	Unhealthy for Sensitive Groups
151 to 200	Red	Unhealthy
201 to 300	Purple	Very Unhealthy
Over 300	Black	Hazardous

SOURCE: Environmental Protection Agency, 2015a.

Beijing and other cities in China have the most polluted air in the world. President Obama and China's President Xi Jinping met in late 2014 and agreed on a plan to limit carbon emissions by their countries, which are the two biggest polluters.

As you can see in Table 14–4, a value of less than 50 indicates good air quality, while a value between 301 and 500 indicates hazardous air quality that would trigger a health warning of emergency conditions. In the Los Angeles–Long Beach–Santa Ana area, generally known to have some of the most consistently polluted air in the United States, the AQI is most often in the moderate range. There were 12 days in 2014 that were classified as unhealthy, where the AQI was between 151 and 200. In comparison, the air in Beijing, China, is routinely at the unhealthy or very unhealthy level. In 2014, 24 days were recorded as hazardous, having an index higher than 301—often much higher. In fact, the U.S. Embassy recorded one day in 2013 when the pollution reached an index of 755! Because the air in Beijing is so polluted and registered above 500 on the index with some frequency, the U.S. Embassy has created a new category exclusively for China—above 500—and warns everyone to stay indoors with filtered air conditioning turned on high during those days.

EFFECTS ON HUMAN HEALTH The health effects of air pollution can range from headaches, coughs, and dizziness to cancer, birth defects, nervous system damage, and death (Correia et al., 2013; EPA, 2013; Lepeule et al., 2012). Clearly, effects of chronic air pollution are of great significance for human health in the long run. Scientists do not exactly know how much air pollution, for how long a period of time, will cause these most extreme effects. Research that tests the effects of air pollution on humans is difficult to conduct for ethical reasons. Instead, scientists usually conduct studies on laboratory animals such as rats and expose them to pollutants at varied concentrations and for varied time periods. Scientists have learned that continued exposure to air pollutants and their accumulation in the body—essentially a slow poisoning process—causes health problems by interfering with normal body functions. Most commonly, pollutants change chemical reactions within individual cells, the building blocks of living things, resulting in impaired cell function, or even cell death.

ECONOMIC EFFECTS Air pollution also has economic effects. It leads to thousands of illnesses each day, lost days at work, and significantly increased hospital spending. A large-scale study of hospital visits estimates that nearly 30,000 hospital admissions and emergency-room visits could have been avoided throughout California alone during a two-year period if federal clean-air standards had been met. These visits led to hospital care costs in 2009 of approximately $193 million more than typical annual costs. Medicare and Medicaid spent about $132 million on such hospital care while the rest was incurred by private insurance (Romley, Hackbarth, and Goldman, 2010).

Air pollution also leads to accelerated deterioration of property; it increases maintenance and cleaning costs; and it blights crops, which means lost income for farmers and higher food prices for consumers. The bottom line is that air pollution is expensive and everyone pays the price.

Water Pollution

Water is emerging as a leading crisis of our times (Barlow and Clarke, 2005; Black, King, and Lacy, 2009). Water—what so many of us take for granted—is increasingly viewed around the world as "liquid gold." We can no longer take for granted access to fresh water for drinking, for irrigating crops, for cooking or cleaning because it is becoming an increasingly rare commodity. How has this crisis come to be?

Water is constantly moving through what is known as the hydrologic cycle. It is found in the atmosphere as vapor; it condenses and falls to the earth as rain, snow, or dew; it percolates underground or runs off the surface as streams, rivers, and finally oceans; it evaporates into the atmosphere as vapor once again; and the cycle continues. While on the ground, water may be either absorbed into the roots of plants and, through the leaves, eventually evaporate back into the atmosphere or drunk from streams or other sources by animals or people and excreted or evaporated back into the earth or air. Alternately, it may sink into underground reservoirs and be stored for millions of years.

It is quite possible for water to be used more than once as it passes through a single round of the hydrologic cycle if it is sufficiently purified between uses by natural or artificial means. However, we render much of our water unfit for reuse because of various kinds of pollutants: raw and inadequately treated sewage, oil, synthetic organic chemicals (detergents and pesticides), inorganic chemicals and mineral substances, plant nutrients, radioactivity, and heat. We therefore face a dual crisis: The amount of water available to us could be insufficient for our demands, and what is available could be polluted.

Just as air can cleanse itself if not overburdened so too can rivers, lakes, and oceans. But we have been discharging wastes, directly or indirectly, into our waterways in amounts that prohibit natural purification. In fact, nearly 30 percent of the U.S. population is not served by sewage treatment facilities (Center for Sustainable Systems, 2014). The bacteria in untreated sewage render the water unfit for drinking, swimming, and even many industrial uses. Finally, the use of oxygen to decompose the waste reduces the life-support capacity of the water, with a consequent decline in the number and variety of fish. As the human population grows, the problem of waste disposal will become even more acute.

Current farming practices, such as extensive use of nitrate and phosphate fertilizers, also seriously impair water quality. Rain and irrigation cause the runoff of large quantities of these materials into rivers and lakes. The fertilizers work in water much as they do on land, producing algae "blooms"—huge masses of algae that grow very quickly and then die. As with the decomposition of sewage, the decay of these blooms consumes oxygen, thereby killing fish and other animals that have high oxygen requirements. As the algae decay, they settle at the bottom of the water, along with various compounds of nitrogen and phosphorus. At one time, the bottom of Lake Erie was covered by a layer of muck from 20 to 125 feet thick. Only intensive efforts by environmentalists to stop pollutants from being discharged into the lake and adjoining waterways saved Lake Erie from total destruction.

Long-lasting pesticides and radioactive substances are especially dangerous because they accumulate in the tissues of animals that eat food contaminated with them. One reason this accumulation poses such a serious problem is the process known as biological magnification, whereby the concentration of a given substance increases as it ascends the food chain. This process can be an especially serious danger in the vicinity of nuclear plants, where safe levels of radioactivity in the surrounding waters may still produce high levels of radioactivity in plankton. Those levels, in turn, can multiply to produce extremely high levels of radioactive contamination in birds and fish that eat these microorganisms.

Another form of water pollution is thermal pollution. The effluents of many factories and generating plants—especially nuclear power plants—are warmer than the rivers and lakes into which they flow, and when discharged in quantity, they may raise the water temperature by as much as 10°F to 30°F. Such thermal pollution can be ecologically devastating. Because most aquatic animals are cold-blooded, they are at the mercy of the surrounding water temperature. If the temperature rises beyond an organism's capacity for metabolic adjustment, the animal will die. Because larvae and young animals are far more susceptible than mature organisms to slight temperature variations and because increases in temperature also interfere with the spawning and migratory patterns of many organisms, thermal pollution may exterminate some aquatic populations through reproductive failure.

Finally, an important form of water pollution, and one that seems to get the most media attention is that from oil spills. The Exxon oil spill, which released 10 million gallons of oil in pristine Prince William Sound in Alaska, caught media attention as one of the largest American oil spills to date. However, since that time, there have been at least two dozen major oil spills in the United States, ranging in size from a few hundred gallons to hundreds of millions. The largest was the Deepwater Horizon oil rig explosion, introduced earlier, which in 2010 killed 11 people and dumped more than 200 million gallons of crude into the Gulf of Mexico. However, America does not win the "prize" with respect to the largest oil spills. That award goes to Kuwait for oil spills related to the Gulf War in 1991 (240–336 million gallons).

Solid-Waste Disposal

Americans do not really "consume" most products, despite our reputation as a consumer society. It is more accurate to say that we buy things, use them, and then throw them away. Thus, we have had about 250 million tons of municipal solid waste—more commonly known as trash or garbage—to dispose of in recent years (Environmental Protection Agency, 2014). This amount represents a nearly threefold increase since 1960, as illustrated in Figure 14–5. This garbage includes food, paper, glass, plastic, wood, abandoned cars, yard clippings, cans, metals, paints, dead animals, and a host of other things. However, because our population has increased since 1960, it stands to reason that our garbage would, too. Therefore, another useful way to measure solid-waste output is by looking at how much each individual produces. That too has increased, although not as sharply.

There are two pieces of good news about solid-waste production and disposal. First, the amount of waste each person produces is now starting to decline. Second, the amount of this waste that gets recycled is on the increase, as shown in Figure 14–6. In 2012, about 87 tons of the solid waste were recycled out of the 251 tons produced. The percentage of the population that recycles is also increasing, although it still represents only about a third of households.

Figure 14–5 Number of Tons of Total Municipal Solid Waste (MSW) Generated and the Amount of Waste Per Person (Per Capita), 1960–2012

SOURCE: Environmental Protection Agency, 2014.

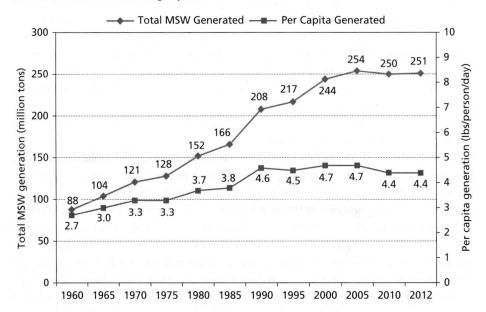

Figure 14–6 Number of Tons of Municipal Solid Waste (MSW) Recycled and Percentage of Households That Recycle, 1960–2012

SOURCE: Environmental Protection Agency, 2014.

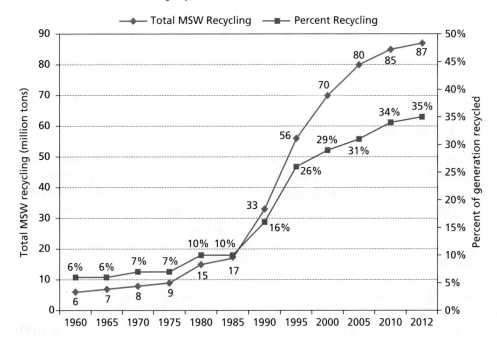

When someone throws something away, he or she rarely thinks of where it goes next. But trash does not just disappear. Most often, it goes into a landfill. In the last few decades, the waste disposal problem has taken on new urgency as many landfill sites have filled up and fears of groundwater contamination caused many communities to forbid the opening of new sites on their land. In 1987, a barge filled with garbage from Long Island became a notorious illustration of the seriousness of the problem as it spent several weeks searching the East Coast for a site that would accept its load of waste. In 2015, there are over 2,400 active landfills in the United States, and another 650 are under construction or are in the planning stage (Environmental Protection Agency, 2015b). Landfills are monitored by the EPA and have been redesigned in recent years to reduce the health hazards associated with them, but nonetheless, no one wants to live near a landfill.

The large-scale introduction of plastics and other synthetics has produced a new waste disposal problem: Whereas organic substances are eventually decomposed through bacterial action, plastics are generally immune to biological decomposition and remain in their original state when they are buried or dumped. If they are burned, they become air pollutants in the form of hydrocarbons and nitrogen oxides. The EPA estimates that plastics now make up nearly 13 percent of our solid waste (Environmental Protection Agency, 2014).

In addition to plastics, another new disposal problem has to do with metals, which now represent 9 percent of solid waste. Every piece of electronic waste, from fluorescent lights to computer parts, contains some kind of metal, and possibly lead. For example, lead is found in most batteries and in the tubes used in television screens and computer monitors. When these items are dumped into landfills, the lead in them can be absorbed into the soil and groundwater.

This aerial view is of a former landfill in West Covina, California. The former landfill site now houses a sports complex, commercial space, and a nature preserve. However, according to the EPA, the landfill accepted hazardous wastes from 1972 to 1984. A multi-million dollar lawsuit filed by nearby residents was settled in 1986.

What Do You Think?

Design a campaign to increase recycling in your community. Be sure to consider what neighborhood or area you want to focus on, and target your campaign specifically to this area. What are some of the challenges that you will face? How will you try to overcome them?

Exposure to high levels of lead is a serious health hazard. It can lead to cancers, brain disorders, and death.

The EPA encourages all people to reduce the amount of waste needing to be disposed of. They suggest three broad measures:

- *Source reduction.* Choose products that are designed and packaged to reduce the amount of waste that will be thrown away.
- *Recycle.* Separate materials that can be recycled, such as paper, glass, plastic, and metals, from the trash. These materials can be used to make new products.
- *Compost organic wastes.* Compost food scraps and yard trimmings and use the result as a natural fertilizer. In a landfill environment, these materials emit large doses of methane, a contributor to climate change.

TOXIC WASTES Toxic wastes or residues from the by-products of manufacturing, construction, laboratories, hospitals, and other systems, including the production of plastics, pesticides, and other products, are a particularly serious problem. These residues have typically been buried in ditches or pits, but they can spread easily into the land and water resources and cause many serious health problems.

The famous case of Love Canal, near Niagara Falls, brought toxic waste hazards to national attention. The crisis arose when toxic residues that had been dumped into the unfinished canal seeped into the surrounding area and contaminated both the soil and the water, causing cancers, leukemia, birth defects, and other health issues for local residents. In 1978, Love Canal was declared an environmental disaster area, and more than 200 families were evacuated from the neighborhood. In early 1985, after more than six years of litigation, 1,300 former residents were awarded payments totaling $20 million in compensation for health problems suffered as a result of the contamination of their neighborhood by toxic wastes. In 1991, 13 years after the discovery of the contamination and the beginning of cleanup efforts, some houses in the Love Canal area were declared habitable again. The EPA and state environmental departments oversee the rules that regulate hazardous waste, requiring extra precautions and disposal at a special facility rather than the landfill. Some communities have collection day events, where people are encouraged to bring their paint, motor oil, batteries, or other hazardous materials.

RADIOACTIVE WASTES The United States currently produces about 20 percent of its electricity in nuclear power plants. These plants pose a problem because the radioactive fuel in the reactor's core must be replaced periodically. The spent fuel must be deposited somewhere under extremely well-protected conditions because it is highly dangerous and can contaminate surrounding water and lands. In the last two decades, as tons of nuclear waste have accumulated in temporary storage sites, the U.S. government has spent several billions of dollars on efforts to create a system for permanent storage. The United States currently has over 72,000 metric tons of spent nuclear fuel and other nuclear wastes (Nuclear Energy Institute, 2015).

Radioactive wastes must be stored safely for up to 1,000 years before they become harmless. During that time, any alteration in the seismological conditions of the burial site could disturb the radioactive material and contaminate the area. A large facility under Yucca Mountain in Nevada is ready, but disputes about its safety (e.g., in an earthquake), transportation of radioactive wastes, and protest by environmentalists caused President Obama to eliminate federal funding for the site. Most people who think about the problem want the wastes to be disposed of properly, but few are willing to have trucks or trains carry these hazardous materials through their communities.

In 2011, when an earthquake damaged significant quantities of radioactive waste material stored at a Japanese nuclear plant, people around the world were reminded of the growing danger posed by these wastes in a world hungry for energy. The incident was also a reminder of how much radioactive material is stored at locations throughout the world.

ENVIRONMENTAL RACISM, ENVIRONMENTAL JUSTICE Landfills and toxic waste dumpsites are disproportionally located near low-income and minority neighborhoods on the outskirts of metropolitan regions or in rural areas (Hind et al., 2013). Many local activists and residents of these neighborhoods label such dumping **environmental racism** or "environmental justice." This issue is increasingly recognized as a serious social problem. Low-income people—especially blacks and Mexicans who are poor—have far higher levels of illnesses because of contamination of their water, land, and air by toxic chemicals from these dump sites.

An Indian woman passes by the Union Carbide plant in Bhopal, India. On a night in December 1984, deadly gas leaked from the plant, instantly killing 3,500 people and thousands more over subsequent months. Tens of thousands of people were injured. Thirty years after one of the world's worst industrial disasters, the Union Carbide plant still stands.

environmental racism

The act of disproportionally placing landfills and toxic waste dumpsites near low-income and minority neighborhoods.

Thirty years ago, the Union Carbide chemical spill in Bhopal, India, killed thousands of poor people living around the facility and injured possibly 100,000 more. The spill drew international attention to the need for improved safety at chemical facilities. Yet no U.S. federal law adopted since the tragedy requires companies to fully assess and substantiate whether the toxic chemicals they use or store are truly necessary—or whether safer alternatives could be used instead.

This lax oversight has led to many more catastrophic chemical hazards in communities. In the United States, there are several serious toxic chemical releases every week, most of which do not hit the news. However, in 2012, an explosion at the Chevron refinery in Richmond, California, sent 15,000 people to hospitals seeking treatment. In 2013, a fertilizer storage facility explosion in West, Texas, killed 15 people and leveled an entire neighborhood. In a typical year, the U.S. Chemical Safety Board screens more than 250 high-consequence chemical incidents involving death, injury, evacuation, or serious environmental or property damage, and these are only the very worst incidents (Orum et al., 2014).

One recent study examined the demographic profile of people living near 3,433 facilities for several common industries that store or use highly hazardous chemicals. There are 134 million people who live within range of a worst-case chemical release. In particular, the researchers want to know about the 3.8 million people who live at the "fenceline" closest to the chemical plants because these people would face the highest concentrations of poisons and would have the least time to react in a catastrophe. They found that minorities and poor people are greatly overrepresented among this vulnerable group who live closest to the chemical plants (Orum et al., 2014):

- Residents of the fenceline zone have incomes that are 22 percent below the national average.
- The poverty rate for those at the fenceline zone is 50 percent higher than the national average.
- The percentage of blacks at the fenceline zone is 75 percent higher than the percentage of blacks in the United States as a whole.
- The percentage of Hispanics at the fenceline zone is 60 percent higher than for the percentage of Hispanics in the United States as a whole.
- The percentage of adults at the fenceline zone who have less than a high school education is 46 percent higher than the national average, while the percentage of adults with a college diploma is 27 percent lower.

This study reveals that environmental racism indeed exists, and activists suggest that greater justice is warranted.

The United States and the World Environment

14.6 Identify the role of the United States in the world's environment.

Americans are among the wealthiest, the most educated, and the most polluting of the earth's peoples. Therefore, environmental scientists often argue that Americans bear a large share of the responsibility for the problem; however, Americans also are capable of wise management of the planet.

The difference in living standards between the United States and most other countries is enormous. You have learned that America (and China) are top energy consumers. In addition, in stark contrast to the hunger that prevails in many poor LDCs, the increased affluence of the United States, and to a lesser extent other developed countries, has made possible a steady increase in per capita consumption of meat and other foods. In fact, Americans consume, on the average, four times as much food per person as people in poor nations (Brown, 2012).

The dominant position of the United States can be seen not only in how much we eat but also in *what* we eat. The food eaten by Americans includes a much larger proportion of meat than is the case in other countries. Vast quantities of grain—one-third of total world production—are fed to livestock in the United States and other developed countries to produce meat. This grain fed to livestock could be used to nourish hungry people elsewhere in the world (Lappé, 1971).

It is true that the United States exports large amounts of grain to all parts of the world. Some of these exports are part of international aid programs that help alleviate the problem of hunger in the poorer nations; in fact, some of the world's least developed nations depend heavily on this aid. But it remains true that the developed nations, particularly the United States, consume a disproportionate share of the world's food resources, and feeding large quantities of grain to livestock is not a very efficient way of producing food.

The significance of these facts is twofold. First, the United States consumes a disproportionate share of total food and energy resources, leaving comparatively little for the majority of the world's population. This imbalance partially explains the desperate plight of people in the least developed nations. The other major effect of the dominant position of the United States is that our food production and consumption contributes to environmental problems both at home and abroad. It turns out that producing half a pound of hamburger for someone's lunch patty of meat the size of two decks of cards releases as much greenhouse gas into the atmosphere as driving a 3,000-pound car nearly 10 miles.

As populations increase in size and affluence, the complexity of social organization, the imbalances in energy and food budgets, the depletion of resources, and the difficulty of correcting these problems also increase. If the United States is to maintain its position as a world leader, it must take the lead in developing a way to control environmental problems, starting at home. Along with other developed nations, it can use its resources to help control the growth of the world's population and encourage sustainable farming and energy practices. Through its own aid and through cooperation with agencies of the United Nations and the World Bank, the United States can also help poorer nations develop more adequate and sustainable water supplies.

Social Policy

14.7 Critique the social policy on climate change.

With record heat waves throughout the world, record rain and snow in many places, devastating floods and droughts, and stunning levels of air pollution, this century will face an environmental crisis. Equally as serious a threat is the apparent inability of

A Global View

Is it Too Late to Prevent Climate Change?

Humans have caused major climate changes that have already occurred, and we have set in motion more changes still. Even if we completely stopped emitting greenhouse gases today, climate change would continue to happen for at least several more decades, if not centuries. The lag occurs because it takes a while for the planet and the oceans to respond and because carbon dioxide—the predominant heat-trapping gas—lingers in the atmosphere for hundreds of years. In other words, there is a time lag between what improvements we might make and when we see the results.

In the absence of major action to reduce emissions, global temperature is on track to rise by an average of 6°C (10.8°F) in this century, according to the latest estimates. Some scientists argue that a "global disaster" is already unfolding at the poles of the planet; the Arctic, for example, could be ice-free in the summer in the near future. Some express concern about the earth having passed one or more "tipping points"—abrupt, irreversible changes that tip our climate into a new state.

But it may not be too late to avoid or limit some of the worst effects of climate change. Responding to climate change will involve a two-tier approach: (1) "mitigation"—reducing the flow of greenhouse gases into the atmosphere;

and (2) "adaptation"—learning to live with, and adapt to, the climate change that has already been set in motion.

The key question is: What will our emissions of carbon dioxide and other pollutants be in the years to come? Recycling and driving more fuel-efficient cars are examples of important behavioral changes that will help, but they will not be enough. Because climate change is a truly global, complex problem with economic, social, political, and moral ramifications, the solution will require both a globally coordinated response (such as strict international policies and agreements between countries and a push to cleaner forms of energy) and local efforts on the city and regional levels (for example, public transport upgrades, energy efficiency improvements, and sustainable city planning). It is up to people themselves as to what happens next.

Critical Thinking

Why has national and global action toward climate change been so slow? How might the reasons for this slow reaction differ across regions of the world?

SOURCE: NASA Global Climate Change and Global Warming: Vital Signs of the Planet website. 2015. http://climate.nasa.gov/vital-signs/

---

global and national political institutions to cope with the uncertainties and potential costs of significant action. Although modest gains can be claimed for global efforts, on the domestic front, the United States is not doing enough to address the central issues of energy technologies and environmental threats.

The Obama administration's environmental agenda covers an immense range of policy initiatives directed at making the hoped-for transition to a clean economy. Through the American Recovery and Reinvestment Act—often called as the "stimulus package" of legislation—$80 billion was included for the generation of renewable energy sources, expanding manufacturing capacity for clean energy technology, and advancing vehicle and fuel technologies. While these achievements are laudable and were not easy to win, even greater substantial structural and personal changes are quickly needed if the world is going to make progress on stopping the earth from continuing to warm. Is it too late to prevent climate change? Yes, it is too late to prevent it, but there is still much we can do now to avoid the worst of the potential crisis.

The consensus among earth scientists is that climate change poses a genuine threat and needs to be addressed immediately through increased efforts to curb emissions of greenhouse gases. They argue that further study of the situation is always needed, but that, in this instance, it represents a cynical effort to delay the responsibility to do anything about the crisis. Climate change is not a vague concern in the far-off future. Climate change is happening right now.

Most experts agree that, without U.S. leadership, global efforts to reduce emissions will be ineffective. Yet, the United States has not emerged as a world leader on fighting climate change and has in fact been accused of dragging its feet. While the Obama administration tried to provide leadership in convincing a record number of nations (including China) to sign the 2010 Copenhagen Accords on global warming, the accords failed to win support either in the United States Congress or in China for a set of mandatory emission limits and a stricter system of enforcement. However, 190 nations that did sign the pacts agreed that each will determine its own target for reducing greenhouse gas emissions rather than follow one standard mandate. If every nation makes good on its pledges, they will certainly reduce the emissions, but unfortunately, this degree of reduction will not be enough to hold temperatures to levels that scientists say are necessary to minimize risks of drought, flooding, and other catastrophic natural events (Tankersley, 2010).

Americans are generally not supportive of mandates. Voluntary compliance was the strategy promoted by the George W. Bush administration. President Obama had hoped to convince conferees at Copenhagen and legislators in the United States of the need for stricter enforcement of mandatory emission limits, but he was unable to do so at the international conference and had even less success at home with Congress. Yet, few experts on energy policy expect that voluntary compliance will yield significant reductions in the coming years. They are far more optimistic about the idea of creating markets for emission credits. The most likely policy to achieve lower emissions is what is known as a system of **cap and trade**, a mix of environmentalism with free market tendencies.

cap and trade

A program that would create markets for emission credits, representing a mix of environmentalism with free market tendencies.

Cap and trade has been referred to "as the most environmentally and economically sensible approach to controlling greenhouse gas emissions" (Environmental Defense Fund, 2015). Companies that pollute could acquire credits from the agency in charge of regulating that particular industry by reducing their emissions below the levels set by the agency. They could then sell the credits to other companies whose emissions exceed regulatory maximums (Pooley, 2010).

This approach rewards industries that clean up their act while allowing those that do not reduce emissions to continue to operate without society as a whole exceeding global limits on greenhouse gases. In other words, the "cap" sets a limit on emissions, which is lowered over time to reduce the amount of pollutants released into the atmosphere. Meanwhile, the "trade" creates a market for carbon allowances, helping companies innovate to meet, or come in under, their allocated limit. It is an environmental policy tool that can deliver results with a mandatory cap on emissions while providing sources flexibility in how they comply.

According to the EPA (2012), successful cap-and-trade programs can reward innovation, efficiency, and early action and provide strict environmental accountability without inhibiting economic growth. A cap-and-trade approach worked extremely well to reduce chlorofluorocarbons in aerosol sprays that destroy the ozone layer in the atmosphere and for reducing sulfur dioxide emissions that cause acid rain. But energy lobbyists and their allies, many of whom are oil producers, have campaigned effectively to prevent anything but relatively weak voluntary enforcement.

Although a cap-and-trade approach is generally thought to be a more conservative measure to control greenhouse emissions and had the support of former Republican President George W. Bush and former Republican presidential candidate John McCain, Republicans in Congress have now largely eschewed it (Open Congress, 2015; Skocpol, 2013). Most Republicans in the House and Senate have moved away from environmental protections more generally, and many deny the existence of human-generated climate change altogether. When a cap-and-trade bill came before a vote in the House of Representatives in 2009, Republican opponents demonized the pending legislation as "cap and tax" and proclaimed that, if the bill passed, families would have to spend up to $3,100 more per year for gas and electricity. Opponents also claimed it would be bad for business and discourage job creation. As cap-and-trade supporters in the Senate were making final efforts to assemble votes, American public support also waned. Most people were scared by the claims of it being a tax because few understood the issues. In May 2009, just before the House acted on the bill, only 24 percent of respondents to a national poll told the polling firm Rasmussen that they understood what *cap and trade* meant (Rasmussen Reports, 2009). The final

Table 14–5 Results of a Meta-Analysis of 25 Surveys That Asked Adults How to Best
Control Greenhouse Gases

• Favor EPA Regulation	75–80%
• Favor Cap and Trade	44–55%
• Favor a Carbon Tax	25–44%

SOURCE: Ansolabehere and Konisky, 2014.

vote on the cap-and-trade bill in 2009, officially known as H.R. 2454 American Clean
Energy and Security Act of 2009, was narrowly passed in the House (although only
eight Republicans voted for it); however, it failed in the Senate (Open Congress, 2015).

Future Prospects

How do people feel about cap and trade several years later? A meta-analysis, which summarized the results of 25 different surveys of American public opinion, found that about
half of people support a cap-and-trade approach (Ansolabehere and Konisky, 2014).
However, as you can see in Table 14–5, even more people favor having the EPA regulate
greenhouse gases (with no specific details provided), and far fewer people approve of
a tax. In other words, people want the EPA to regulate the environment in some vague
way, but they are not willing to do the things they would need to do at a personal consumption level, such as pay a higher gas price or pay a higher electricity price.

> **What Do You Think?**
> Make a list of all the ways that indi-
> viduals can reduce their contributions
> to global warming. Now, from this list,
> which of these changes would you
> personally be willing to make? Which
> ones would you not make, and why?

Going Beyond Left and Right

Do companies have the right to pollute or exterminate endangered species to save
jobs? What is the best way to conserve water—through volunteer efforts or rationing?
What types of policies are needed to reduce the amount of solid waste going into
landfills? What can be done now to limit the effects of climate change? People on the
ideological right and left often have different opinions on vexing questions like these.
Those on the right tend to focus on the free market and suggest that government mandates will stagnate our economy. People on the left often say that environmental resto-
ration will add new, less damaging jobs to the economy. In some parts of the country
(and the world), these debates are extremely rancorous.

An integrative way to think about environmental problems may be that, no
matter what our politics are, humans are the problem and humans can be the solution. Most people who live in affluent nations consume large quantities of gasoline
and other consumer goods, and those in LDCs want to do the same. Unless those
who live in developed nations begin to understand the global consequences of their
consumption, it is argued, the level of stress on the environment will never be sufficiently reduced. This argument is based on facts. It is not really a right or left debate.
However, although the argument goes beyond left–right debates, it is not very popular with large segments of the American public. Naturally, no one is particularly eager
to make the changes and sacrifices that seem to be needed, but needed they are.

Summary

- Technology is the use of science in industry, engineering, etc., to invent useful things or to solve problems.
  Technology comprises (1) apparatuses such as tools,
  instruments, machines, and gadgets, which are used
  in accomplishing a variety of tasks; (2) all activities or

  behaviors that use a purposive, step-by-step, rational
  method of doing things; and (3) the organizational
  networks associated with activities and apparatuses.
  Advances in technology can have both positive and
  negative impacts. Important advances in technology,

such as computers and the Internet, are not equally shared, a situation known as the digital divide.

- Some social commentators are convinced that technology has become an autonomous force in society—one that is less and less subject to the control of democratic political institutions. Social scientists suggest that future uses of technology and future technological inventions be based on human values.

- Sociologists are concerned with the ways in which social institutions adapt to changing technology or, conversely, how technology adapts to changing social institutions. The best-known statement of these relationships is William F. Ogburn's cultural lag theory.

- Two developments—accelerated technological and scientific change and rapid population growth—are causing widespread pollution and depletion of the natural environment. Natural cycles of purification can absorb only a limited amount of certain artificial substances before ecological damage is done.

- Environmental stress is the interaction and conflict of three systems: the natural environment, the technological system, and the social system. There are many different environmental stressors in the world today. This chapter discusses climate change, air and water pollution, and solid waste and its disposal.

- Americans are among the wealthiest, the most educated, and the most polluting of the earth's peoples, and therefore environmental scientists often argue that Americans not only should bear a large share of the responsibility for the problem but also are capable of wise management of the planet.

- The consensus among earth scientists is that climate change poses a genuine threat and needs to be addressed immediately through increased efforts to curb emissions of greenhouse gases. Few experts on energy policy anticipate that voluntary compliance will yield significant reductions in the coming years. They are far more positive about a system of cap and trade, a mix of environmentalism with free market tendencies that creates markets for emission credits.

Chapter 15
Summing Up the Sociological Imagination: War and Global Insecurity

Learning Objectives

15.1 Discuss the direct and indirect effects of war.

15.2 Identify various forms of weapons of mass destruction.

15.3 Review modern-day terrorism in the United States and around the world.

15.4 Explain terrorism's impact on society.

15.5 Compare and contrast sociological theories on war and terrorism.

15.6 Describe policy approaches to dealing with terrorism.

I am a long-distance runner. I started before my children were born, then took a break from it when they were little, but found that I was calmer and less stressed out when I went for long runs. In other words, I was a better mother when I ran. So my husband, James, bought me some excellent running shoes for my birthday and took care of the kids when I was off on my own running for a couple of hours. I love the breeze, the sweat, and the endorphins! I ran a couple of local marathons, and then I had a crazy idea about trying to qualify for the Boston Marathon. I wasn't fast enough yet, and it would take some work, but I felt that it was in reach. So, I set up a training program, and my two-hour runs and weekend races became more frequent. After a couple of years of this program, I got a qualifying score! Boston, here I come. I saved money for months so I could afford airfare for James and me, and my sister offered to take the kids for the weekend. The day before the race, I drank lots of water, went for a very short run just to keep the legs moving a bit, and ate all the right foods. I even got a decent night's sleep; I was so nervous I think I just crashed! The day of the race, I woke up early and refreshed. "I am ready for this," I told myself. James told me how proud he was of me.

The race itself is almost a blur as I try to remember it. I paced myself well, but also ran hard. But as I was on the last leg of the run, I heard an incredibly loud, earsplitting noise. And then another one. Oh my God, what was it, I wondered? I saw smoke up ahead, and there seemed to be a lot of commotion and screaming, but I was too far away to see exactly what was going on. I kept running toward the finish line, but some people were coming toward me shouting at me to hide, to stop, and they were yelling other words that I couldn't understand. Clearly they were fleeing what was up ahead. Within seconds, large groups of people were running away from the race course, crying in sheer terror. I couldn't make out what they were saying, but it was obvious that something horrible had just happened. I joined them and we ran off the course, away from the finish line. I huddled with a group of people under some bleachers; we were all shaking in fright. It was minutes later that I learned that bombs had just exploded.

A discussion of war and terrorism might seem like a "heavy" way to end a book. Yet, these issues offer an essential opportunity to reexamine the premise of the sociological imagination, introduced in Chapter 1. The results of war and terrorism are deeply felt on a personal level. Lives are lost, people are injured, property is destroyed, and immense fear can spread throughout the land.

Yet, war is hardly just a personal issue. C. Wright Mills stressed the importance of understanding the relationship between individuals and the society in which they live (Mills, 1959). The sociological imagination reveals that problems associated with war and terrorism represent far more than personal troubles experienced by a few isolated people. They are issues that affect large numbers of people and originate in society's institutional arrangements.

Using war and terrorism as a case study, this chapter revisits the premise of the sociological imagination and underlines the four themes of the book. The tragic topics of war and terrorism challenge you not only to explicitly see the connections between personal lived experience and broader social problems, but also to understand the importance of these four themes: (*Theme 1*) using an empirical approach; (*Theme 2*) linking individual experiences with social structure; (*Theme 3*) recognizing that social inequality contributes to social problems; and (*Theme 4*) understanding social problems requires a comparative perspective.

War and Its Effects

15.1   Discuss the direct and indirect effects of war.

The twenty-first century began on a note of great hope for world peace. The fall of the Soviet Empire and the destruction of the Berlin Wall ended the long period of superpower conflict known as the Cold War. But the spread of advanced weapons around the globe; the rise in racial, ethnic, and religious conflict; and the worsening of environmental problems and limitations of natural resources have increased the threat of wars of all kinds in many parts of the world.

For those who experience its tragic devastation, war is among the most serious social problems one can imagine. The sections that follow discuss both its direct and indirect effects.

Direct Effects of War

Over the centuries, warfare has taken many millions of lives and has caused untold suffering. According to one early estimate (Sorokin, 1937), between 1100 and 1925, about 35 million soldiers were killed in some 862 wars in Europe. However, by any standard, the twentieth century was the deadliest in human history. During World War I, eight million soldiers and another one million civilians died. The casualties of World War II were even higher: almost 17 million soldiers and 35 million civilians were killed. In the Soviet Union alone, the generation of men old enough to fight in World War II was nearly decimated. Later, the Korean War, the Vietnam War, the Gulf War (in Kuwait), the war in Iraq, the war in Afghanistan, and so on, caused the death toll to continue to rise. As of May 14, 2015, deaths of U.S. personnel serving in Iraq (since 2003) and in Afghanistan (since 2001) totaled 4,493 and 2,357, respectively (Antiwar.org, 2015). As of October 30, 2014 (the most recent date available), those wounded in action in Iraq and Afghanistan totaled 32,244 and 20,037, respectively (Fischer, 2014). And, these numbers exclude deaths to noncombatants, such as local citizens, journalists, and military contractors, or "nonhostile" injuries and deaths, such as suicides, vehicle crashes, heat stroke, or respiratory problems.

PHYSICAL INJURIES   Long after peace is declared, many soldiers bear the scars of their battlefield experiences. Using an empirical approach (*Theme 1*) allows us to fully understand the extent of these physical injuries. For every U.S. soldier who died in battle in World Wars I and II, almost two people were injured. Today in the Middle East, seven men and women are injured for every person killed. About 50,000 people have been injured in recent military conflicts (Wounded Warrior Project, 2015).

Many of the wounded have required medical care for months or years, and many have been so badly injured that they have not been able to hold a job or return to a normal way of life. Almost 4 million veterans are receiving compensation from the U.S. government for war-related disabilities. Of these, over one million have been evaluated to be 70 to 100 percent disabled (U.S. Department of Veterans Affairs, 2014c). When so many individuals require government assistance for the same reason—war-related injuries—you can see the link between personal experience and social structure (*Theme 2*).

MENTAL HEALTH AND PTSD   Not all war-related disabilities are physical. War also takes a psychological toll. During and after World War II, Harvard sociologist Samuel Stouffer and his colleagues (1949) conducted the first major study of war stress. They found correlations between psychological stress and several types of combat experience. For example, soldiers stationed close to the front lines—who were constantly exposed to the threat of injury or death to themselves and their friends, to the hardships of life on the battlefield, to the value conflicts involved in killing others, and to the inability to control their own actions—suffered psychological stress to a greater extent than others.

In the decades since Stouffer's research, mental-health experts have identified **post-traumatic stress disorder (PTSD)**, a disorder in which a person experiences severe stress reactions after a traumatic event; it is a common aftereffect of battle (U.S. Department of Veterans Affairs, 2014a). Other factors in a combat situation can add even more stress to an already stressful situation. These factors include what a person does in the war, the politics around the war, where the war is fought, and the type of enemy a soldier faces. For example, the psychological impact of the Vietnam War may have differed from that of earlier U.S. wars because it was a guerrilla war. That is, the enemy blended with the civilian population and therefore seemed to be

post-traumatic stress disorder (PTSD)

Severe stress reactions after a traumatic event such as war.

everywhere and nowhere at the same time. These conditions may have been responsible for the unusually high levels of violence against civilians that characterized the war, as well as for the mistreatment of prisoners and the use of such weapons as napalm, which killed civilians and the enemy indiscriminately. Soldiers who saw or engaged in these forms of violence suffered from psychological disorders to a greater extent than those who did not. As one Vietnam veteran said of his experience, forty years afterwards:

> *I'm shocked at what I did. … I hurt innocent people. Hurt? What am I saying? I killed them. I killed innocent civilians who didn't even want this war in the first place. I shot a mom with her two young sons because they may have been the enemy. May have … I don't even know. To this day I see those children's faces, and I hear the mom pleading for their lives. She offered to let us rape her if we would just let her children live. We raped her, and still killed them all. When I think about it I get a panicky feeling inside. I can barely breathe.*

Recent data from the U.S. Department of Veterans Affairs suggest that the number of veterans with PTSD varies by service era (U.S. Department of Veterans Affairs, 2014a).

- *Operation Iraqi Freedom (OIF) and Operation Enduring Freedom (OEF):* About 11 to 20 of every 100 veterans who served in OIF or OEF have PTSD in a given year.
- *Gulf War (Desert Storm):* About 12 of every 100 Gulf War veterans have PTSD in a given year.
- *Vietnam War:* About 15 of every 100 Vietnam veterans were diagnosed with PTSD in the late 1980s at the time of the most recent study, the National Vietnam Veterans Readjustment Study (NVVRS). It is estimated that about 30 out of every 100 Vietnam veterans have had PTSD in their lifetime.

MILITARY SEXUAL TRAUMA Another cause of PTSD in the military can be **military sexual trauma (MST)**, which is any sexual harassment or sexual assault that occurs to a veteran while serving in the military. MST can happen to both men and women and can occur during peacetime, training, or war. How common is MST? Data are collected from the national screening program run by the Veterans Administration (VA). Through that program, every veteran seen for health care is asked whether he or she experienced MST. National data from this program reveal that, when screened by their VA provider, about one in four women and one in a hundred men respond that they experienced MST. Although rates of MST are far higher among women, because there are many more men than women in the military, there are actually significant numbers of both women and men seen in VA facilities who have experienced MST (U.S. Department of Veterans Affairs, 2014b).

One aspect of these casualties, injuries, and traumas that is rarely discussed is the fact that social inequality plays a significant role in who will become a victim, a premise of *Theme 3*. Men and women who are poor are especially likely to be recruited into dangerous military roles. Several studies have shown that, during the Vietnam War, battle deaths and injuries were more common among lower-class soldiers than among those from the middle and upper classes (Janowitz, 1978; Moskos, 2005).

Indirect Effects of War

In addition to the killing, wounding, and mental health effects, war disrupts the lives of the veterans themselves and their families. In addition, war disrupts the lives of civilians whose homeland has become a battleground.

---

military sexual trauma (MST)

Any sexual harassment or sexual assault that occurs to a veteran while serving in the military.

What Do You Think?

Using the sociological imagination, can you explain why PTSD is a social problem rather than just a personal issue?

U.S. First Lady Michelle Obama speaks about the "Joining Forces" initiative, calling on Americans to rally around service members, veterans, and their families. Encouraging greater support of military families has been one of Ms. Obama's signature issues.

INDIRECT EFFECTS ON MILITARY PERSONNEL AND VETERANS   Men and women who serve in the military face many significant disruptions in their personal lives, including multiple moves across the country or around the world, long periods away from home, and possibly multiple deployments. Some of these soldiers are married or partnered and have children, which makes the disruptions in their lives even more complicated. First Lady Michelle Obama and Jill Biden, wife of U.S. Vice President Joe Biden, have taken on the support of military families as one of their primary roles.

During periods of deployment, family members may have a range of feelings and experiences, including loneliness, sadness, worry, or panic. Coupled with these emotions, the spouse or partner left behind must assume new family responsibilities and may experience financial difficulties, either of which can feel overwhelming.

A growing area of research shows the negative impact on children, youth, and families of U.S. military personnel. Children of military families often experience multiple stressors before and during their parent's deployment and when they come home. They have more school-, family-, and peer-related emotional difficulties (Substance Abuse and Mental Health Services Administration, 2014). Without appropriate mental health support systems, children of military personnel may be at a significant disadvantage compared with their peers in nonmilitary families.

INDIRECT EFFECTS ON CIVILIANS   War often leads to mass migrations of people trying to escape from danger or persecution or looking for new opportunities. A look at the causes and consequences of this migration, and social policies around it, using *Theme 4* of this text, should be of interest to the United States. The United Nations High Commissioner for Refugees reports that more people in 2014 became refugees or internally displaced people than at any time since 1994. War is the main cause for this displacement, with more than 60 percent of all refugees coming from five war-affected countries: The Democratic Republic of the Congo, Iraq, Nigeria, South Sudan, and Syria. Afghanistan has been the world's "top producer" of refugees for 32 years. About one-half of refugees are children under age 18. A record 34,000 asylum applications were submitted in 2014 from children who were unaccompanied or separated from their parents (United Nations High Commissioner for Refugees, 2015). What is the United States' role in producing so many migrants, and is it the United States' responsibility to help them?

Men and women in the military, especially those with children, make great personal sacrifices for their country. Here, a father on leave hugs his son whom he has not seen in almost five months.

Another major cause of wartime migration is government policy. During and after World War II, a number of European states forced whole populations to move. During the war, the German government ordered hundreds of thousands of ethnic Germans to move back to Germany from the eastern European nations that Germany had invaded. After the war, under the terms of the Potsdam Treaty, many more Germans were required to move from various eastern European nations to areas within the redrawn borders of Germany.

Some of the indirect effects of war are not as easy to calculate as the numbers of refugees. For example, it is impossible to measure the economic damage caused by war. Billions of dollars must be diverted from productive uses, first into arms and then into the effort to repair the damage caused by arms. Even less quantifiable is the impact of war on how people think. The Vietnam War left in its wake widespread disillusionment with traditional values. To many men in the trenches, patriotism lost much of its appeal. After the war, some people were pessimistic about the future of civilization and were alienated from their former way of life.

Liberated Iraq is a good example of the longer-term political and social effects of even a "successful" war. The nation's people remain badly divided in their feelings about what kind of government—secular or religious—should be established. At this writing, Iraq has a prime minister and parliament and is nominally considered a representative democracy. However, Iraq has also been called the most corrupt state in the Middle East and a hybrid between a "flawed democracy" and an "authoritarian regime" (Costsofwar.org, 2014b). Recent captures of Iraqi territory by ISIL make the challenges of effectively governing Iraq much more difficult (Arango, 2015). It is clear that no lasting peace is likely as long as the many ethnic and religious factions of the Iraqi population cannot work together to ensure peace and the rule of law on their own. What can the United States learn from this experience?

Weapons of Mass Destruction

15.2 Identify various forms of weapons of mass destruction.

In the past 100 years, wars have become more intense as military technology has become more lethal. **Weapons of mass destruction**, such as nuclear weapons and biological agents, have the potential to annihilate millions of people quickly.

Nuclear Weapons

The development of nuclear weapons in the 1940s contributed to peace among the major powers because each was fearful of unleashing nuclear devastation on a large scale. However, today, if peace breaks down, a war of almost unimaginable destructiveness could ensue. Nine nations—the United States, Russia, United Kingdom, France, China, India, Pakistan, Israel, and North Korea—possess approximately 16,300 nuclear weapons in total.

Some idea of the nature of the destruction that could occur is provided by accounts of the bombing of Hiroshima and Nagasaki, Japan, during World War II, although today's warheads are far more powerful than those used on Japan. The box, A Closer Look: The Story Behind the Bomb, provides the historical context of the bomb's creation.

On the morning of August 6, 1945, as the people of Hiroshima were preparing to go to work, a U.S. aircraft flew over the city. Seconds later, a nuclear bomb exploded 2,000 feet above the center of the city. Even though the 12.5 kiloton device was tiny by modern standards, its effect was devastating. The force and heat of the blast annihilated 70,000 to 80,000 people almost instantly and delivered a deadly dose of radiation to hundreds of thousands of others. Three days later, another bomb was dropped on Nagasaki, immediately killing another 40,000 citizens. Over the course of months and years, the death toll reached at least 100,000 more due to burns and radiation.

Many of those who survived were burned and maimed. One woman, who had been with some junior high school boys about a mile from the center of the blast, was knocked unconscious. "When I came to, I looked around," she said in a recent interview. "The boys had been so cute before, but now their clothes were burned off and they were nearly naked. Their skin was cut up and ripped off. Their faces were peeling off as well." She herself was so hideously deformed that her own parents urged her to show mercy to her husband and leave him. "At that time, I cried every day, wishing that I had died immediately," she said. She added that she did not seek compensation from the United States. "I just want [Americans] to feel sorry and to try to abolish nuclear weapons" (quoted in Kristof, 1995, pp. 1, 12).

In the years since nuclear weapons were developed, war has become much riskier than ever before because local wars fought with conventional weapons can escalate into much wider destruction. The possibility that countries with unstable political regimes could produce nuclear bombs and missiles, and the fear that these and other weapons of mass destruction such as biological agents like the smallpox virus could be sold to terrorist organizations, have become part of the fearful post–9/11 global scene. These scenarios keep the threat of nuclear war alive. Even a limited nuclear war would create human catastrophes on a scale not hitherto experienced, to say nothing

weapons of mass destruction

Nuclear weapons and biological agents that have the potential to annihilate thousands or even millions of people quickly.

A Closer Look

The Story Behind the Bomb

In 1939, President Roosevelt and Congress authorized a secret project to expand research on nuclear fission and use uranium and plutonium to generate nuclear chain reactions as atomic weapons. This project, known as the Manhattan Project, was under the military authority of General Leslie Groves and was headed by chief civilian scientist Robert Oppenheimer. Most of the scientists, civilian leaders, and military officials responsible for the development of the bomb assumed that its military use, however unpleasant, was the inevitable outcome of the project.

Work continued at a variety of locations around the United States throughout World War II, and three bombs were finished by July 1945, then field-tested in the New Mexico desert. By this time, President Roosevelt had passed away (April) and Germany had surrendered (May), but the war in the Pacific continued.

The news of the test was sent to President Truman, who was attending an important meeting in Germany with Great Britain's Prime Minister Winston Churchill and Soviet leader Joseph Stalin. Churchill had been kept informed about the bomb's development all along, and Stalin—who had detailed knowledge of the project through espionage—feigned indifference. Stalin also affirmed the idea to attack the Japanese no later than mid-August. Some historians would later argue that the bomb on Japan was used in the hope of securing Japan's surrender before the Soviet Union could enter the Pacific War.

American soldiers were weary after years of war, but the Japanese military was a strong opponent and would not give up the fight. Truman issued one final warning to Japan, asking for an immediate unconditional surrender, and stating that refusal would result in total destruction. He did not mention that the United States had nuclear bombs. The Japanese rejected the request for unconditional surrender, although there were some indications that a conditional surrender was possible.

Nonetheless, on August 6, 1945, a plane called the *Enola Gay* dropped a nuclear bomb on the city of Hiroshima. Two days later, the Soviet Union declared war on Japan. One day after the Soviet Union's declaration of war, on August 9, another American nuclear bomb was dropped on the city of Nagasaki. Between these two bombs, at least 100,000 people were immediately annihilated, and tens of thousands of others died in the ensuing days, weeks, and months due to widespread radiation and burns over their bodies. Japan's Emperor Hirohito announced his country's unconditional surrender in World War II in a radio address on August 15, 1945, citing the devastating power of "a new and most cruel bomb."

Critical Thinking

Using the sociological imagination, do you believe that using a nuclear bomb was the right or wrong action to take against Japan? Explain your reasoning.

SOURCES: Hall, 2013; History.com, 2015; U.S. History.org, 2014.

---

of the environmental damage and destruction such wars would cause for years afterward, even in regions beyond the boundaries of the original conflict.

Still, it remains that the United States is the only nation that has ever used nuclear bombs in war, and it has threatened to use nuclear weapons at least 11 times since 1946, including the Berlin crisis of 1961, the Cuban missile crisis of 1962, and twice during the Vietnam War. Because warfare has become so dangerous and the world's military powers have built up huge stockpiles of both conventional and nuclear arms, many people have begun to study the causes of war in the hope of promoting peace.

Biological Weapons

Perhaps an even greater threat to the world are biological toxins or infectious germs that can more easily get into the hands of terrorist groups. These types of weapons include things such as anthrax, botulinum toxins, cholera, smallpox, and ricin, among many other substances.

As one example, botulinum toxins are the most deadly substances known. Because botulinum toxin is so lethal and easy to manufacture, it represents a credible threat as a biological warfare agent. Exposure could occur following inhalation of aerosolized toxin or ingestion of food contaminated with the toxin or its microbial spores. Iraq has admitted to active research on the offensive use of botulinum toxins and to deploying more than 100 munitions with botulinum toxin (Hooker, 2014). The toxin produces similar effects whether ingested, inhaled, or applied to a wound. Symptoms may occur hours to several days after exposure. Initial signs and symptoms include blurred vision, dilated pupils, difficulty swallowing, difficulty speaking, an altered voice, and muscle weakness. After 24 to 48 hours, muscle weakness and paralysis may cause the person to be unable to breathe.

Terrorism, Global and Domestic

15.3 Review modern-day terrorism in the United States and around the world.

Terrorism is defined as the threatened or actual use of illegal force and violence by a non-state actor to attain a political, economic, religious, or social goal through fear, coercion, or intimidation (Institute for Economics and Peace, 2014). This definition recognizes that terrorism includes not only the physical attack itself but also the long-term psychological effect it has on society.

Terrorism was a serious social problem in the world long before the suicide bombing of the World Trade Center and the Pentagon on September 11, 2001. One need only think of the years of terrorist bombings in Northern Ireland or Sri Lanka, the deadly bombing in Oklahoma City, sniper attacks against abortion clinic doctors, and the episodes of terror attacks in Israel and elsewhere in the Middle East or on the Indian subcontinent or in Russia and Chechnya. But since 9/11 and the declaration by the U.S. government of a "war against terrorism," the world has entered a new era in which terrorism and armed responses against suspected terrorists have become dominant issues. Terrorism in the post–9/11 world has enormous impacts on global economic conditions, on the ability to travel and maintain open borders, on civil rights and the protection of basic freedoms, and much else.

Violent terrorist acts—kidnapping, torture, bombings, beheadings, and the like—are often committed by a nation or a political movement to call attention to its cause and to shake people's faith in their government's ability to eliminate the threat. The movement may be a revolutionary one that seeks far-reaching change in the government or hopes to gain control over the nation. But not all terrorism is revolutionary in nature. The terrorism of cocaine barons in Colombia is designed to take revenge on the authorities and to intimidate them into lax enforcement of the law. Terrorism of governments like that of Nigeria against its own people (known as repressive terrorism or state terrorism) is also not associated with revolutionary movements (Mazrui, 1996).

But the most common type is **revolutionary terrorism**, which involves acts of violence against civilians that are carried out by enemies of a government. The 1995 bombing of a federal office building in Oklahoma City by Timothy McVeigh and Terry Nichols; the lethal letter bombs mailed to universities and airlines by Ted Kaczynski, the so-called Unabomber, during the 1980s and 1990s; and the 9/11 attacks on the World Trade Center in New York City and on the Pentagon are only a few recent examples of terrorism. Two brothers with extremist Islamic beliefs carried out the 2013 bombings at the Boston Marathon in which three people were killed and over 260 people were injured, as profiled in the opening vignette. These brothers detonated two pressure cooker bombs, set a few hundred feet apart near the finish line of the marathon. In their attempt to escape, they killed a policeman from the Massachusetts Institute of Technology and injured another officer. The older brother was shot by police (and inadvertently run over by his younger brother as he fled in a stolen vehicle) and died at the scene. The younger brother was captured within a few days. Convicted in April 2015, he was given the death penalty.

What Do You Think?

The United States is the only country that has ever used a weapon of mass destruction on innocent civilians in another country, and it did so twice. Can you think of a context in which the United States would use it a third time? Would the United States be justified in doing so?

terrorism

The threatened or actual use of illegal force and violence by a non-state actor to attain a political, economic, religious, or social goal through fear, coercion, or intimidation.

revolutionary terrorism

Acts of violence against civilians that are carried out by enemies of a government.

United Flight 175 flies directly into the World Trade Center Tower 2 during a terrorist attack on September 11, 2001, a day that will always be remembered as "9/11."

Modern Terrorist Groups

Since 9/11, terrorism has become among the most dangerous threats to world order. It destabilizes governments, preys on innocent victims, and involves large amounts of financial and human resources. Yet unlike war, which openly pits opponents against each other in a recognized trial of strength, terrorism is covert. It seeks to sway the masses through intimidation and fear.

Four groups—(1) the Islamic State of Iraq and the Levant (ISIL), also called ISIS; (2) Boko Haram; (3) the Taliban; and (4) al Qaeda—"took credit" for 66 percent of all claimed terrorism-related deaths in 2013 (Institute for Economics and Peace, 2014). ISIL is one of the largest active terrorist groups in the Middle East. It was originally a part of al Qaeda in Iraq (AQI), but after the death of AQI's head and after tactical disagreements, ISIL split from AQI. ISIL became known for extreme violence and terror during the Syrian civil war in 2013, rapidly expanding into Syria and then Iraq in 2014. In February 2014, al Qaeda formally broke ties with ISIL, claiming that ISIL disobeyed directions from al Qaeda to kill fewer civilians.

Boko Haram (one translation is "Western education is sin") is a Nigeria-based terrorist group founded in 2002 to create a separatist community within Nigeria under Wahhabi Islamic principles. Originally, the group was not very violent, but since the 2009 death of its leader while in police custody, Boko Haram has been responsible for at least 3,500 civilian deaths. The group is also responsible for the April 2014 kidnapping of 276 female students ages 16 to 18 from a school in northeastern Nigeria. The students' fate remains unknown as this book goes to press.

Founded in 1994, the Taliban was originally a mixture of "Mujahedeen," who fought against the 1980s Soviet invasion of Afghanistan, and a group of Pashtun tribesmen. The Taliban took control of Afghanistan in 1996 and ruled until 2001, when they were overthrown by the United States. The Taliban has since regrouped as an insurgency movement to fight the Afghan government and Western security forces. The Taliban strives to retake control of Afghanistan and has rebranded itself an independence movement.

Al Qaeda was formed in 1988 by Osama bin Laden, a Saudi killed by U.S. troops in 2011, and Abdullah Azzam, a Palestinian Sunni scholar who was killed in 1989. Al Qaeda, like the Taliban, arose during the Soviet war in Afghanistan. Its goal is international jihad (i.e., struggle against Islam's enemies), and it is the only group to have successfully conducted large-scale attacks in the West, including the 9/11 attacks in the United States. Many of al Qaeda's leaders have since been killed, and the group now adopts a decentralized structure of regional cells and affiliates. While direct terrorism attributed to al Qaeda has been relatively low since 2011, activity by its affiliated groups has risen.

Although the histories and strategic objectives of these groups differ, they share a focus on religious ideology based on extreme interpretations of Wahhabi Islam and strict adherence to Sharia law. Wahhabism is an austere form of Islam that insists on literal interpretation of the Koran. Strict Wahhabis believe that anyone who does not practice their form of Islam is a heathen and enemy. Sharia law is the body of Islamic law that governs all aspects of daily life from politics and economics to sexual and social issues. Yet, despite the power of religious ideology as a motivation for terrorism among these groups, it is not universal. Outside the Middle East, North and Sub-Saharan Africa, and South Asia, terrorism is more likely driven by local separatist, political, or nationalistic movements.

Despite the differing motivations, countries with higher levels of terrorism do seem to share certain characteristics:

- Greater hostilities between different ethnic, religious, and linguistic groups, lack of intergroup cohesion, and high levels of group grievances
- Presence of state-sponsored (i.e., government) violence such as extrajudicial killings, political terror, and gross human rights abuses

- Higher levels of other violence, including deaths from organized conflict, likelihood of violent demonstrations, levels of violent crime, and perceptions of criminality

Contrary to what some may assume, poverty and other economic factors do little to explain the sources of terrorism within a country. Measures such as life expectancy or average levels of education do not matter very much. Instead, weak political systems, a lack of political legitimacy, and government-sponsored violence are much more influential in nurturing terrorism than is the overall economic environment.

Measuring Terrorism

The Institute for Economics and Peace has developed a Global Terrorism Index (GTI), which is the first index to systematically rank and compare 162 countries according to the impact of terrorism (Institute for Economics and Peace, 2014). The GTI uses four indicators to measure the impact of terrorism: number of terrorist incidents, number of deaths, number of casualties, and level of property damage.

On a 0 to 10 scale, with 10 indicating the highest impact of terrorism, the five countries with the highest GTI values in 2014 were Iraq (10.00), Afghanistan (9.39), Pakistan (9.37), Nigeria (8.58), and Syria (8.12), as shown in Table 15–1. For context, 2014 GTI values for selected countries were China (5.21), United States (4.71), Israel (4.66), Ukraine (2.95), Saudi Arabia (2.71), Jordan (1.76), Canada (0.95), United Arab Emirates (0.29), Kuwait (0.04), and Japan (0.01).

These values suggest two interesting issues. First, Ukraine's GTI is much lower than Iraq's GTI, or even that of the United States. Yet, few would argue that Ukraine, in serious conflict with internal rebel groups likely supported by Russia, is safer or less violent than the United States. In other words, terrorism's impact in a country may differ quite a lot from the impact of violence from war or other sources. A nation can have a low terrorism score but also be very violent.

Second, the GTIs for Saudi Arabia, Jordan, United Arab Emirates, and Kuwait are quite low. This finding indicates that the impact of terrorism is not universal across Arab countries, a fact sometimes forgotten. Arab countries should not be lumped together and seen as one large force.

Table 15–1 Top Five Countries with Highest Global Terrorism Index Scores, 2014

Iraq	10.00
Afghanistan	9.39
Pakistan	9.37
Nigeria	8.58
Syria	8.12
Other Selected Countries	
China	5.21
United States	4.71
Israel	4.66
Ukraine	2.95
Saudi Arabia	2.71
Jordan	1.76
Canada	0.95
United Arab Emirates	0.29
Kuwait	0.04
Japan	0.01

NOTE: Scale is 0 to 10, with 10 representing the greatest effect of terrorism.
SOURCE: Institute for Economics and Peace, 2014.

Table 15–2 Ten Countries with the Most Terrorist Attacks, 2013

Country	Total Attacks	Total Killed	Total Wounded	Average Number Killed per Attack
Iraq	2,495	6,378	14,956	2.56
Pakistan	1,920	2,315	4,989	1.21
Afghanistan	1,144	3,111	3,717	2.72
India	622	405	717	0.65
Philippines	450	279	413	0.62
Thailand	332	131	398	0.39
Nigeria	300	1,817	457	6.06
Yemen	295	291	583	0.99
Syria	212	1,074	1,773	5.07
Somalia	197	408	485	2.07

SOURCE: U.S. Department of State, 2014.

Although the number of terrorist acts fluctuates from year to year, since 2000, the number of terrorism-related deaths has grown fivefold, rising from 3,400 to nearly 18,000 in 2013. The good news is that the number of deaths in 2013 is a reduction from the 2007 high of nearly 23,000 killed. However, the bad news is that, since the Syrian civil war began, there has been a jump in terrorist activity. Terrorism-related deaths increased 61 percent between 2012 and 2013, from roughly 11,000 to 18,000. Moreover, during this period, the number of countries suffering at least 50 terrorism-related deaths rose from 15 to 24, and another 55 countries had at least one such death (Institute for Economics and Peace, 2014).

Table 15–2 indicates the 10 countries with the most terrorist attacks in 2013, and reports the total killed, the total wounded, and the average number of people killed per attack. As shown, Iraq, Pakistan, Afghanistan, India, and the Philippines had the largest *number of attacks*, but attacks in India and the Philippines tended to kill few people. Consequently, it is the terrorist attacks in Nigeria and Syria, along with Iraq, Pakistan, and Afghanistan, that killed the most people, over 80 percent of lives lost to terrorism in 2013 (U.S. Department of State, 2014).

Figure 15–1 illustrates the tactics used in terrorist attacks worldwide in 2014. The use of bombings and explosives were the most common, occurring in over half of terrorist attacks. Armed assaults were the primary method in nearly one quarter of attacks around the world.

Terrorism in the United States and throughout the world shows no signs of abating. The number of Taliban fighters is estimated at between 36,000 and 60,000, with

Figure 15–1 Tactics Used in Terrorist Attacks Worldwide, 2014

SOURCE: U.S. Department of State, 2015. Annex of Statistical Information Country Reports on Terrorism 2014, June 2015. http://www.state.gov/documents/organization/239628.pdf

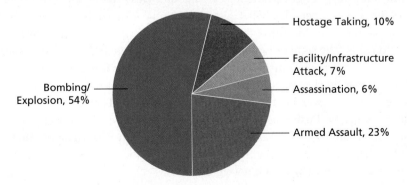

ISIL at 20,000, with al Qaeda at between 3,700 and 19,000, and with Boko Haram at between 500 and 9,000. As individuals, terrorists want to save the world, but salvation is based on a few rigid beliefs. The purity of their "end" justifies any means to achieve social change, even at the cost of their own lives, which are essentially meaningless relative to the greater goal (Dershowitz, 2002).

In this process, the victim, who in the terrorist's mind is merely a pawn in the struggle for societal reform, is stripped of human rights and identity. The terrorist wants to punish society, to force it to accept his or her demands. The terrorist preys on both known and unknown victims, convinced that—as representatives of an abhorrent society—the victims are responsible for society's wrongs and are unworthy of compassion. Because any society is the combined achievement of thousands of individuals and many generations, the injustice of terrorist thinking is obvious. Terrorists' victims are innocent people whose lives are destroyed by fanatical intolerance.

Terrorism, Religion, and ISIS/ISIL

That so many terrorist individuals and groups are motivated by extreme religious beliefs and feelings is one of the chief ironies of the present war on terrorism. Religion as a factor in terrorism has grown in importance since 2000 (Arnett, 2014; Institute of Economics and Peace, 2014). All major religions seek peace and understanding among people everywhere. But religions may also have a group of radical segments within them. Some domestic terrorists, such as the anti-abortion organization Army of God, are members of radical Christian groups. Al Qaeda and other contemporary Islamic terrorist groups espouse various forms of fundamentalist Islam—even though, as numerous Islamic leaders have pointed out, terrorism violates basic foundations of Islamic law. But in his analysis of the contribution of religious radicalism to contemporary terrorism, sociologist Amitai Etzioni (2002: 3) notes:

> It is sad but true that Islam, like Christianity and Judaism, has both temperate and virulent strands. Christianity in earlier ages not only had an Inquisition but also those who justified it in religious terms. The Catholic Church supported the mass torture and murder that occurred during military dictatorship in Argentina, deeming them necessary to "excise the cancer of communism." Terrorism in Northern Ireland has religious roots, and Operation Rescue claims religious justifications. Militant Judaism not merely claims a right to the West Bank and finds scriptural support for a still Greater Israel, but also blessed those who assassinated Yitzhak Rabin, the peacemaker.

In other words, *just like other world religions*, Islam has its aggressive and extreme forms. Wahhabism is the version of Islam that is most dominant in Saudi Arabia and is a leading influence on Muslim fundamentalists elsewhere. Wahhabism pushes for the return to original Islam, rejects innovations, stresses literal belief in the Koran and the Hadith (the sayings or traditions of Mohammad), and calls for the formation of states to be governed strictly according to Islamic law. It rejects all notions of human rights and democratic forms of government as secular and Western notions.

Like many fundamentalist belief systems, extreme forms of Islam tend to be totalitarian in that they seek to control the person's total life: what she or he eats, listens to, wears, and reads. The sight of women in their burkas is a well-defined representation of these views. Extreme Islamists seek to achieve these goals through coercion and the use of fear rather than by persuasion or democratic decision-making. Thus, in trying to distance the U.S. war on terrorism from conflict with Islamic civilization itself, President George W. Bush was correct in stating, "The face of terror is not the true faith of Islam. Islam is peace." Yet extremists of Islam or any other religion can become persuaded that the "end justifies the means" and then may resort to terror or other illegitimate uses of force against innocent civilians.

Slide Show

Victims of Terrorism

Terrorists thrive on anonymity. They want to remain nameless and faceless. Their victims, however, are very real. This slide show introduces you to several victims of terrorism in the United States and abroad.

This picture shows Nazli holding a picture of her son Erdal Elbistan, 26, who died during a battle against ISIL insurgents in the Kurdish Syrian town of Kobane. The city has been under siege from ISIL for months, with brutal abuses against the local population. More than 1,000 people have been killed in the fighting. ISIL succeeded in capturing hundreds of Kurdish villages and towns, creating a wave of more than 300,000 displaced Kurds, most of whom fled across the border into Turkey.

Matt Smith (left) of Boston, and Zach Mione of Portland, Oregon, helped Sydney Corcoran on the Boylston Street sidewalk at the scene of the first bomb explosion near the finish line of the 117th Boston Marathon in 2013. These two strangers applied pressure and tried to stop the bleeding of her injured leg. Sydney was standing next to her mother, who lost both legs, as they were waiting for her sister to finish the race when the attack happened. In the opening photo for this chapter, all three women approach the finish line one year later during the 118th Boston Marathon.

A young man carries a young neighbor girl who was injured in a barrel-bomb attack in the northern city of Aleppo, the largest city in Syria. More than 2,000 civilians, including at least 500 children, have been killed in regime air strikes in war-torn Aleppo. Thousands more have been wounded, often seriously, with limbs blown off or burned.

Of all the horrific sights associated with the attacks on the World Trade Center on September 11, 2001, one that is forever etched into the minds of those who were nearby are the sounds of bodies smashing into the concrete below. Hundreds of people leapt to their death after the two planes hit the twin towers rather than die in the ensuing inferno.

Congregants of St. Mary Ethiopian Orthodox Church held a vigil for more than 30 Ethiopian Christians who were shot and beheaded by ISIL militants in Libya in 2015. The killings were videotaped for propaganda and show two groups of men, one in orange jumpsuits and one in black, being killed at different locations.

Critical Thinking

Compare and contrast traditional war and terrorism. What are the similarities and differences? Which is more effective, and why? What can be done to stop terrorism?

Those who suffer as a result of terrorist acts can be divided into two groups. The first are random victims, people who are simply in the wrong place at the wrong time. Bombings, hijackings, and the spontaneous seizure of hostages victimize whoever happens to be available. Other members of society are intimidated by the casualness of this kind of terror, and the terrorist hopes that they will pressure the government to meet his or her demands.

The second category of victims includes individuals who are singled out because of their prominence. They, too, become dehumanized symbols: All politicians are blamed for whatever political injustices the terrorist perceives; all businesspeople are held personally responsible for commercial waste and greed. Civilians who have been killed or injured in bombings by terrorist groups as part of the ongoing Palestinian–Israeli conflict or the four French Jews murdered by Islamic extremists at a Paris kosher market in January 2015 are an example of the first category of random victims. (Walt, 2015). The 11 employees of the prominent French satirical newspaper Charlie Hebdo who were murdered by members of al Qaeda's Yemen branch, also in January 2015, are examples of the second group of victims (BBC News Europe, 2015).

Terrorism's Impact on Society

15.4   Explain terrorism's impact on society.

One reason that terrorism is becoming so common is that terrorism can be extremely effective. As a form of warfare waged by the relatively powerless against powerful states, contemporary global terrorism has had significant effects on world trade and on the institutions of the United States and other nations.

Social, Economic, and Political Impacts

When terrorism strikes, it can be felt in a variety of ways. The effects of recent terrorist activity include the following.

- *Increased fear* of attack and heightened security at airports, ports, and major landmarks and federal buildings
- *Erosion of civil liberties,* including heightened government secrecy, limitations of habeas corpus, and curtailments of freedom of speech in the interests of security
- *Economic consequences,* including drastic curtailments in international tourism and trade, especially due to attacks on airlines
- *Health consequences,* such as fear of bioterrorism
- *Political consequences,* including terrorism's threat to polarize the world between Islamic and Christian civilizations, thus increasing the chances of war not only in Iraq but also elsewhere in the Middle East and on the Korean peninsula and increasing tensions between the United States and its European allies who worry that the United States is seeking to extend its power over the Middle East and other regions of the world (Jurkowitz, 2010; Pew Research Center, 2002)

It is too early to fully understand or assess the potential consequences of terrorism or the war on terrorism for people in the United States and elsewhere in the world. While war clouds gather and threats of major terrorist attacks continue, it is difficult to find anything positive in the current situation. But if the current world crisis yields improvements in the ability of nations to cooperate in combating terrorism, and if the Islamic nations begin to solve some of their problems related to political instability, then the war against terrorism will have had some positive consequences together with the negative ones.

At the same time, the world's major powers, and especially the United States, find their military and logistical resources stretched thin as they struggle to confront threats of terrorism and other sources of violence. Their concerns of overextending leave them less inclined to intervene militarily in situations such as the current presence of ISIL and al Qaeda in Syria. Although the United States has led a multinational coalition against these groups in Syria since September 2014, U.S. involvement has been limited largely to airstrikes and the training and arming of selected Syrian opposition groups. To date, involvement of American soldiers in combat (i.e., "boots on the ground") has been extremely limited in large part because of U.S. weariness after more than a decade of war in Iraq and Afghanistan (Brooks, 2014).

What Do Americans Believe about Terrorism?

There has been growing concern about terrorism among the American public. For example, a 2014 Gallup Poll revealed that 39 percent of adults surveyed have "a great deal of concern" about the possibility of future terrorist attacks in the United States; however, by early 2015, that figure had jumped up to 51 percent (McCarthy, 2015). News of terrorism fills the airways, newspapers, and online news sources.

The public has grown more supportive of the U.S. attempts to fight ISIL, as shown in Figure 15–2a–c (Pew Research Center, 2015). More than twice as many people

Figure 15–2a Percentage Saying They Approve or Disapprove of U.S. Campaign against Islamic Militants in Iraq and Syria, 2014–2015

SOURCE: Pew Research Center, 2015.

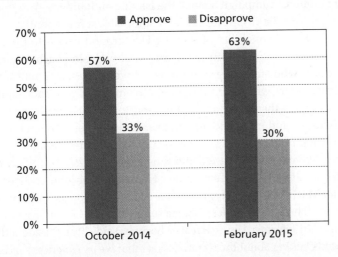

Figure 15–2b Percentage Saying They Favor or Oppose the Use of Ground Troops to Fight against Islamic Militants in Iraq and Syria, 2014–2015

SOURCE: Pew Research Center, 2015.

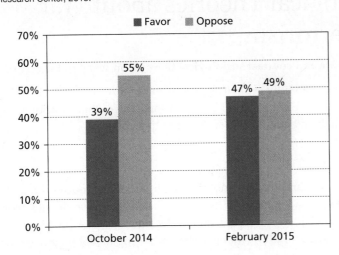

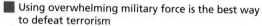

Figure 15–2c Percentage Who Say That Military Force Is the Best Way to Defeat Terrorism vs. Too Much Reliance on Military Force Creates Hatred and More Terrorism, 2014–2015

SOURCE: Pew Research Center, 2015.

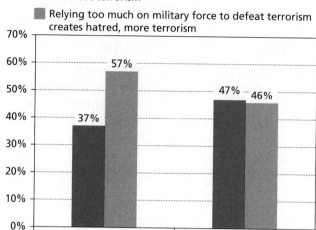

approve of the military campaign against the Islamic militant group in Iraq and Syria compared with those who disapprove, a large jump in just four months.

The reaction to the possibility of sending U.S. ground troops to the area is more divisive, with about an equal number favoring and opposing such action. However, again the numbers who support ground troops have increased significantly in just a few short months. Men, whites and Hispanics, the middle aged, and Republicans are more likely to support the possible use of ground forces than are women, blacks, the young or the elderly, and Independent and Democratic voters. The public is also split over whether using military force is the best way to defeat terrorism or whether military force actually creates more hatred and thus more terrorism.

Republican Senators John McCain, former House Speaker John Boehner, and Senate Majority Leader Mitch McConnell have been particularly outspoken in favor of a stronger military approach than what President Obama suggests. After Obama's State of the Union Address in early 2015, former House Speaker Boehner said, "The President didn't spend but a few seconds talking about the terrorist threat that we as Americans face. This problem is growing all over the world, and the President is trying to act like it's not there. It's going to be a threat to our homeland if we don't address it in a bigger way" (Pianin, 2015).

Sociological Theories about War and Terrorism

15.5   Compare and contrast sociological theories on war and terrorism.

No single theory can fully explain any given war or terrorist act. Nevertheless, various sociological perspectives have shed light on some forces that contribute to global conflict and can help to better understand war and terrorism.

Functionalism

Functionalism is particularly concerned with social organization and the ways in which interconnected parts of a society work together or do not work together. Several early sociologists have examined the functions associated with war (Coser, 1956; Mills, 1958; Park, 1941; Simmel, 1904), including the following functions.

What Do You Think?

Why do you think that Americans have grown more supportive of U.S. attempts to fight terrorism over the past year, including the willingness to send in ground troops? Has there been an objective change in terrorism, or is the media more vocal, or is there something else that might affect public opinion?

- *The Expansion of Territory*—Countries come into being because of conflicts over boundaries. For example, the United States went to war with France, Spain, Great Britain, and Mexico to establish the borders that currently exist.
- *Economic Benefits*—War can provide economic gains through land, crops, treasures, and natural resources such as oil. War also has an unintended economic benefit; it puts millions of unemployed people to work. For example, World War II was largely responsible for ending the Great Depression in the United States.
- *Advancing Ideology*—Conflict is often about advancing religious or political ideology. The Taliban, al Qaeda and ISIL, all hope to advance their extremist religious ideology. In these and similar situations, rather than push for peaceful reforms, acts of war and terrorism bond groups of people together in a fever pitch; the outgroup is dehumanized, and revenge is sought. Alternatively, some groups fight to disseminate ideology; the largest wars that the United States have entered have been about defending a democratic form of government.
- *Social Change*—Wars are fought in the name of change, but changes also happen to facilitate war itself. For example, our national highway system was developed in the 1950s under President Eisenhower, who pushed to create highways across the United States so that we could move military supplies quickly in case of an attack from the Soviet Union.
- *Social Integration*—Conflicts can bring people together and create a strong sense of nationalism or group solidarity, which can have either negative or positive consequences. The 1994 war in Rwanda pitted two groups against each other, the Tutsi and Hutu. Group identification during the war was so strong that former neighbors, coworkers, and friends turned on members of the other group in a mass slaughter of epic portions. Within only a three-month span, roughly 800,000 Tutsi and politically moderate Hutu were killed: wiping out roughly three-quarters of the Tutsi population in Rwanda.

Conflicts, war, and terrorism also have many obvious dysfunctions. Innocent people are killed or injured, cities are destroyed, children are orphaned, people are impoverished, and the social fabric is damaged.

The Vietnam war was particularly unpopular. Service men and women were often booed or ridiculed after returning home from war. The memorial honoring those who died reflects this tense time in American history. Designed by a graduate student from Yale, Maya Lin, the memorial contains two long black walls, sunken partially into the ground, with the names of those who died etched in the stone.

Conflict Perspective

Conflict theorists are concerned about tensions and power differentials in society. They suggest that war occurs when interests of nations or groups collide with one another for power, control, resources, and markets. Nations tend to use their military to advance their objectives, while smaller factions may resort to terrorist actions.

Marx predicted that as capitalist economies grew, their need for raw materials, labor, and new markets in which to sell finished goods also would increase. In the early twentieth century, Vladimir Lenin claimed that the competition among Britain, France, Germany, and other major powers to establish colonies around the world during the nineteenth and early twentieth centuries was evidence that Marx's prediction was correct. It was this competition for colonies that led to World War I, according to Lenin. In essence, the war pitted the national ruling classes against one another; the workers had nothing to gain by taking up arms (Rapoport, 1968). According to Lenin, then, the basis of war is economic competition among national ruling classes.

Marx and Lenin believed that economic interests shape most social phenomena, including warfare, but a number of social scientists have argued that noneconomic factors must also be considered. These explanations can be grouped into two types.

The first takes the individual nation as the unit of analysis and looks inside societies at the relationships among institutions such as the military, government, and business. The second group of explanations focuses on institutions and patterns of behavior that cut across national boundaries. According to this perspective, organizations such as the United Nations, as well as international treaties and trade networks, are among the factors that influence the likelihood of war or peace.

INSTITUTIONAL FORCES WITHIN NATIONS   Most social scientists believe that during much of the twentieth and twenty-first centuries the influence of military leaders on government policy has grown in the United States and elsewhere. This growth may be seen as a threat to peace. Keeping a large, well-equipped military force at the ready makes it easier for political leaders to choose war rather than negotiation as a tactic for handling international conflicts (Barton, 1981). In contrast, supporters of military interests argue that a powerful military actually discourages other nations from starting wars.

After World War II, a few critics voiced alarm at the newly won power of the military in the United States. In *The Power Elite*, C. Wright Mills (1956) argued that by the mid-1950s military leaders were "more powerful than they have ever been in the history of the American elite; they have now more means of exercising power in many areas of American life which were previously civilian domains; they now have more connections; and they are now operating in a nation whose elite and whose underlying population have accepted what can only be called a military definition of reality" (198).

In effect, the U.S. economy never returned to its pre–World War II production patterns. Military and industrial leaders have ensured that a significant portion of the national budget is allocated to preparation for war. Today, the defense budget of the United States is three to five times larger than China's, the second largest defense budget. The United States has used this investment to become the world's most powerful military force by far, with weapons that no other nation possesses. With a federal government that intends to maintain this military superiority and use it wherever it believes American security is threatened, defense budgets in the United States are likely to remain extremely high for the foreseeable future, despite tax cuts and increasing levels of federal debt.

In addition to elites, another actor affects the likelihood of war—the public. During the twentieth century, many countries became much more democratic. As a result, political leaders must take public opinion into account in setting foreign policy. In some cases, public opinion actually favors war, especially when sentiments of **nationalism**—identification with, and exaltation of, the nation's culture and interests above those of all other nations—are strong. During the 1930s and 1940s, powerful nationalistic feelings in Germany helped make peace seem dishonorable and war seem a feasible option.

Today, renewed nationalism in Southeast Asia, Taiwan and China, Russia, and the Middle East poses a serious threat to prospects for world peace because the possibility of civil wars and nationalist movements leads to increased fear of terrorism and greater political instability. Moreover, local wars can draw in the larger nations, as occurred during World War I and could occur again in the Middle East. A more recent area of concern is the East and South China Seas where China has been involved in sometimes tense confrontations with many of its neighbors, including Japan, the Philippines, Taiwan, Malaysia, and Vietnam. Island ownership and other maritime disputes between these countries raise fears that mishandling of even a minor dispute could result in armed clashes that eventually draw in other countries, for example, the United States because of its commitment to Taiwan's defense (Council on Foreign Relations, 2013).

THE INTERNATIONAL CONTEXT OF WAR AND PEACE   Although national institutions and domestic forces can either preserve or threaten peace, no discussion of

nationalism

Identification with, and exaltation of, the nation's culture and interests above those of all other nations.

war and peace would be complete without some attention to the international context. The world is composed largely of independent sovereign countries, each with its own interests. Because the supply of natural resources, power, prestige, and other valued commodities is limited, nations inevitably compete with one another. There is no central authority powerful enough to resolve all international conflicts peacefully. Nevertheless, a number of forces do reduce incentives to wage war.

One such force to promote peace is international cooperation embodied in organizations such as the League of Nations and the United Nations. In 1919, after World War I, the League of Nations was founded and was the first international organization whose principal mission was to maintain world peace. However, despite President Woodrow Wilson's strong support, the United States never joined the League; the American Congress wanted to avoid the United States being drawn into future conflicts because of the League's commitment to mutual defense. Ultimately, the onset of World War II showed that the League had failed in its mission, and it was replaced at the end of the war in 1945 by the United Nations, which now includes 193 member states.

Flags wave outside the entrance to the United Nations Building, located in Geneva, Switzerland. It was created in 1945 to promote peace and human rights, and currently 193 countries are members.

A key function of these organizations is the settlement of disputes. The United Nations, for example, has helped restore peace in three wars between Israel and the Arabs, in the Korean conflict, in the Greek civil war, in Bosnia, and in a number of other conflicts. It has often failed to resolve clashes that involve the superpowers, however. The United States, Russia, and other major nations are often unwilling to give up some of their power to arbitrators, especially on issues of vital national interest (Raghavan, 2014).

Although the United States and other nations are often drawn into global conflicts in the role of peacekeepers, they usually achieve only limited success. Almost invariably, the peacekeeping force has difficulty withdrawing because of (1) explosiveness of the conflicts themselves; (2) the problems faced by peacekeepers in attempting to maintain neutrality; (3) the difficulty of coordinating in-the-field mediation with diplomacy; and (4) the lack of a workable model for peacekeeping. All of these problems were encountered in Bosnia, Rwanda, Somalia, Sierra Leone, Sri Lanka, and the Democratic Republic of the Congo. But the desire to do something to ease bloody conflicts and to provide humanitarian aid continues to motivate third-party peacekeeping efforts and to improve their effectiveness in some instances.

International trade is another force that tends to promote peace. When influential citizens benefit economically from peaceful relations, support for war is diminished. Moreover, trade promotes a common outlook and common interests; trading partners are usually political partners. Today, the volume of world trade is still dominated by market economies like those of the United States, Japan, and the European Union. However, global competition is increasing as economic growth transforms the developing world, whether in East and South Asia, the Middle East, Africa, or Eastern Europe. For example, the 4.5 percent growth of merchandise exports in 2012 was greater in the "BRIC" countries (Brazil, Russia, India, and China) than in either the European Union or the North American Free Trade Agreement (NAFTA) countries (United States, Canada, and Mexico). And, in 2013, with imports and exports totaling $4.159 billion, China passed the United States ($3.909 billion) as the world's largest merchandise trader (World Trade Organization, 2014). These and related trends make it even more necessary to have international peacekeeping institutions and effective international law, which is especially true as the renewed influence of nationalism throughout the world threatens to produce greater instability and terrorism.

Symbolic Interactionism

The symbolic interactionist perspective looks at the symbols people use in everyday interaction, such as words, gestures, or appearances, and explores the meanings they attach to these symbols. A person's behavior with and among other people (their interaction) is the result of their shared understanding of cultural symbols.

Symbolic interactionist writing on war features several emphases. One theme explores the symbolic meaning behind the military or terrorist attack. According to the symbolic interactionist paradigm, the September 11, 2001, terrorists used the symbols of American power—the World Trade Center, New York City, the Pentagon, Washington, D.C.—to deliver a message to the world concerning their perception that the United States is the cause of the misery of Muslims in the Middle East and throughout the world. The actions of the terrorists were a form of language, a method of communication that was extreme because the message was extreme.

A second emphasis of symbolic interactionists concerns the perceptions and experiences of people involved in war: soldiers, civilians, and others. How are they affected by war? Many moving accounts, for example, both real and fictitious, have been offered of soldiers' lives both on the battlefield and at home after returning from war. A cursory search in May 2015 found 156 entries on the goodreads.com list of best books on the Iraq and Afghanistan wars. In the popular book, *The Long Walk*, Brian Castner describes his three tours of duty in the Middle East, two of them in Iraq as the head of an Explosive Ordnance Disposal unit. Whenever bombs were discovered, he and his men would lead the way in either disarming the deadly devices or searching through rubble and remains for clues to the identities of those who made the bombs. Although robots and other remote means were used for safety, when these methods failed, one technician would suit up and take "the long walk" to disarm the bomb by hand. This lethal task expresses the real war in the Middle East. And movies such as *American Sniper, The Hurt Locker*, and *Zero Dark Thirty* among many others help shape Americans' current perceptions of the war experience.

A third emphasis concerns the use of symbols to marshal support for war or protest against war. Symbols such as the flag evoke feelings of patriotism, perhaps especially when a nation is at war. The president and other politicians typically display a flag when they give major speeches, and it would be unthinkable for a flag not to be showing when the speech is about war or the threat of war. During the Vietnam War, protesters sometimes flew the American flag upside down (the international symbol of distress) to show their hatred of the war, and some protesters also burned the flag—an act that is almost guaranteed to provoke outrage and hostility from onlookers. Another ubiquitous symbol during the Vietnam War was the so-called international peace symbol, originally designed in the late 1950s to symbolize concern over nuclear weapons. Vietnam War protesters wore this symbol on their clothing, and many put peace symbol decals on their motor vehicles, book bags, and other possessions. More recently, when the United States invaded Iraq in 2003, millions of Americans put magnetic yellow ribbons on their cars, SUVs, and pickup trucks to show their support for the troops.

Another emphasis of symbolic interactionism concerns how concepts related to war and terrorism come to be defined in ways that advance the goals of various parties. For example, a key goal of the military in basic training is to convince trainees that people they may face on the battlefield are "the enemy" and, as such, the killing is justified and is not murder. Similarly, the military often refers to civilian deaths or wounding as "collateral damage" in a conscious or unconscious attempt to minimize public horror at civilian casualties. This attempt backfired in Vietnam where, as a guerilla war, Americans were on the ground fighting for and against people who looked alike. Many innocent victims were shot at, killed, and injured. The My Lai massacre is the most common example of this dissonance. However, in his book *Kill Anything That Moves: The Real War in Vietnam*, author Nick Turse argues that the intentional killing of civilians was common in a war that claimed 2 million civilian lives, left 5.3 million civilians wounded, and generated 11 million refugees. The ongoing conflicts in Iraq, Afghanistan, and Pakistan have continued this legacy, with at least 174,000 civilians through April 2014 having died violently because of direct military action and many times more who died from indirect causes such as damaged infrastructure and environmental disruptions (Costsofwar.org, 2014a). And, according to the World Health Organization, the recent Saudi Arabia–led military assault in Yemen has already killed 643 civilians and wounded 2,226 between March 19 and April 8, 2015 (Lazare, 2015).

Social Policy

15.6 Describe policy approaches to dealing with terrorism.

The wars in Iraq and Afghanistan, continuing violence and terrorism in Syria and elsewhere in the Middle East, the continuing instability of the nuclear-armed North Korean government, China's increasing economic and military assertiveness, Russian activities in Ukraine and other former satellites—these and other challenges to peace make the world situation precarious. After an outpouring of sympathy and support for the United States and its people after the 9/11 attacks, the perception in Europe and elsewhere was that the United States pursued a unilateralist, "go-it-alone" set of policies that subverted international bodies such as the United Nations and sought to enhance U.S. control of Middle Eastern oil resources.

The rise of negative feelings about the United States is quite evident from State Department and Pew Research Center international survey results, as shown in Table 15–3. In many nations, the percentage of citizens with favorable views of the United States declined dramatically in the mid-2000s after invading Iraq, including America's closest allies in Western Europe. The most common negative attitude has been the belief that the United States does not take into account the interests of others outside its borders when making international policies. In most countries where the surveys were conducted, many people see American policies as contributing to the growing gap between rich and poor nations. Large numbers of people are convinced that the war on terrorism and against Iraq masks American economic and political ambitions and that the United States is not doing enough to solve global problems.

President Obama renounced the unilateral policies of the Bush administration and, in his first year as president, went out of his way to speak reassuringly to leaders of other nations, and to the press, about his intentions to seek cooperation and collaboration among nations to address terrorism and nuclear threats. His efforts bore fruit, as shown in the recently improved ratings of American policies in Europe and China, but they still rate low in much of the Middle East and Russia (Pew Research Center, 2014).

But as the president's standing increased abroad, his poll numbers at home declined, and the administration's policies suffered severe setbacks in the 2012 elections. A wave of anti-Islamic feeling spread throughout many parts of America, and many people continue to believe that Obama is a Muslim. When a late 2014 poll asked a representative sample of American adults, "Which of these [religious traditions] do you think most likely describes what Obama believes deep down?" 54 percent of Republicans responded with "Muslim" (Theodoridis, 2015).

Dealing with Terrorism

Terrorist acts, especially suicide bombings, kidnappings, and the holding (and more recently, beheadings) of hostages, often attract worldwide attention. Indeed, terrorists use violence and drastic actions not only to attract media attention to their cause

In this well-known tragedy, 504 defenseless Vietnamese civilians, mostly women and children, were slaughtered by American soldiers during the war in what has become known around the world as the My Lai massacre. Before being killed, some of the victims were raped, gang-raped, sodomized, beaten, tortured, maimed, or stabbed. Some of the dead bodies were mutilated. The incident prompted widespread outrage throughout the world and reduced American support at home for the war.

Table 15–3 U.S. Favorability, 1999–2014

	1999/2000	2002	2003	2004	2005	2006	2007	2008	2009	2010	2011	2012	2013	2014
Europe														
France	62%	62%	42%	37%	43%	39%	39%	42%	75%	73%	75%	69%	64%	75%
Germany	78%	60%	45%	38%	42%	37%	30%	31%	64%	63%	62%	52%	53%	51%
UK	83%	75%	70%	58%	55%	56%	51%	53%	69%	65%	61%	60%	58%	66%
Middle East														
Turkey	52%	30%	15%	30%	23%	12%	9%	12%	14%	17%	10%	15%	21%	19%
Egypt	-	-	-	-	-	30%	21%	22%	27%	17%	20%	19%	16%	10%
Jordan	-	25%	1%	5%	21%	15%	20%	19%	25%	21%	13%	12%	14%	12%
Lebanon	-	36%	27%	-	42%	-	47%	51%	55%	52%	49%	48%	47%	41%
Palestinian territory	-	-	0%	-	-	-	13%	-	15%	-	18%	-	16%	30%
Asia														
China	-	-	-	-	42%	47%	34%	41%	47%	58%	44%	43%	40%	50%
Russia	37%	61%	37%	46%	52%	43%	41%	46%	44%	57%	56%	52%	51%	23%
Pakistan	23%	10%	-	21%	23%	27%	15%	19%	16%	17%	12%	12%	11%	14%

SOURCE: Pew Research Center, July 11, 2014.

but also to intimidate civilians and show governments that they can exert power. Although public sentiment often favors negotiating with terrorists to win the release of captives, the usual official policy is not to give in to terrorist demands (Clawson, 1988; Spector, 2003). Policies that have proven somewhat effective include the following: imposing boycotts and other measures to put pressure on countries that sponsor terrorism; negotiators making promises but not keeping them after the captives have been released because promises made under threat are not valid; treating terrorists as criminals; enlisting the cooperation of journalists and media personnel in depriving terrorists of media attention; offering substantial rewards for information about and capture of terrorists; and developing an international campaign against terrorists with the help of a network of experts on the subject.

An informed public that will cooperate with antiterrorist policies is extremely important in combating this social problem. Since 9/11, for example, there have been predictions of widespread terrorism, especially against air travelers, and public cooperation with searches and stringent antiterrorist measures at airports was credited with preventing even more violence. However, although these policies may have helped to diminish specific terrorist acts, much larger forces are at work that seem to be increasing the likelihood of terrorism.

The Oklahoma City terrorism trial raised questions about why the United States does not pass laws that require tagging explosives with an identifying chemical that would make it far more difficult to use commonplace materials like fertilizer as explosives for mass destruction. The National Rifle Association and other pro-weapons groups oppose such laws on grounds of individual freedom and self-protection (Guterl, 1996). Other experts on domestic terrorism argue that the United States should ban private armies and militias, but given the fierce lobbying that accompanies any effort to control sales of personal weapons, it is doubtful that the nation has the political will to accomplish this goal.

Given the rise in terrorist acts, the passage of the Homeland Security Act in 2002 represents the largest reorganization of the federal government in over 50 years. The Department of Homeland Security's mission is to prevent terrorism and enhance security, secure and manage the borders, enforce and administer immigration laws, safeguard and secure cyberspace, and ensure resilience to disasters (U.S. Department of Homeland Security, 2012).

This mission includes preventing terrorist attacks within the United States, reducing America's vulnerability to terrorism, minimizing the damage from attacks that do occur, and aiding in the recovery from such attacks. The director of Homeland Security has jurisdiction over airport security, port security, border surveillance and management, and a wide variety of antiterror initiatives. The Department includes the Coast Guard, the Federal Emergency Management Agency, the U.S. Customs Service, and the Immigration and Naturalization Service.

Future Prospects

What can be done to reduce the likelihood of war and terrorism? No one can answer this question with certainty. Much may depend on how well individual citizens understand its causes and consequences and on how effectively they participate in debates over policies designed to control and limit the use of force in settling national differences.

The continuing political instability in many parts of the world makes it certain that international diplomacy will be a matter of continuing urgency. It is also quite clear that, as they face the continuing threat of international terrorist groups, the United States and other Western targets of terrorist attacks will continue to improve their intelligence capabilities. Strengthening intelligence entails developing more effective undercover operations, hiring agents with world language skills, improving international cooperation, upgrading computer tracking systems, and gaining a more sophisticated understanding of why individuals become motivated to commit acts of suicidal violence.

But going beyond government intelligence, it is important to take a step back and ask why so many people around the world dislike the United States. There is a perception that Americans are rude; they think of themselves as the center of the universe; they believe that money entitles them to everything; they brag; they are greedy and exploit others for their own gain; they are immoral; they spy on other countries; they get involved where they have no business; they fight unfairly (e.g., drones); and they are fanatical.

Before jumping in to say "What a lie!" perhaps Americans could stop and take stock of their social policies and social and political ethos. Is there a kernel of truth in these allegations? Given America's tremendous resources, more than one person has asked "Why are we dropping bombs on Middle Eastern countries instead of building schools there? Wouldn't that be a more effective way to fight terrorism?"

What Do You Think?

Considering the themes of this text presented in Chapter 1 (using an empirical approach; linking individual experiences with social structure; recognizing that social inequality contributes to social problems; and acknowledging that understanding social problems requires a comparative perspective), describe how these themes help inform your understanding of war and terrorism.

Going Beyond Left and Right

Republicans and Democrats have substantially different views on the best ways to fight terrorism in the world. Most Republicans express the view that force is the best way to defeat terrorism. Many support the use of "enhanced interrogation techniques" that some would refer to as torture (Condon, 2014). They say that the use of harsh interrogation techniques helped bring down Osama bin Laden and disrupt terrorist plots.

In contrast, most Democrats disagree with the premise that force is the best way to fight terrorism. Instead, they believe that such force creates hatred that fuels even more terrorism. They suggest that harsh interrogation techniques are tantamount to torture and remind Americans that the United States has long had a record of forbidding torture under any circumstances.

These differences in perspectives between the parties over the right approach to terrorism are hard to reconcile. However, most people do not favor greater military intervention overseas, and do not want a foreign policy in the next presidential administration that is more hawkish than President Obama's (only 25 percent overall favor a more hawkish option). Even among Republicans, the support for more military interventions around the world is just 47 percent (YouGov, 2015). Perhaps the greater disconnect over the appropriate use of the military is not between Democratic and Republican voters but between the general public and a bipartisan "elite" of government officials, military leaders, public intellectuals, and journalists that advocates a much more interventionist foreign policy (Beauchamp, 2015).

Summary

- The direct effects of war are obvious. Millions of men and women are killed in war, and many more millions are injured. War also takes a psychological toll, and many soldiers and veterans suffer from post-traumatic stress disorder (PTSD). Another cause of PTSD in the military can be military sexual trauma. War also has many indirect effects. Soldiers experience significant disruptions in their personal lives, and war often leads to mass migrations of people trying to escape from danger or persecution or looking for new opportunities.

- In modern times, wars have become more intense as military technology has become more lethal. Nuclear weapons (which are held by nine countries) and biological agents have the potential to annihilate millions of people quickly.

- Since 9/11, terrorism has become the most dangerous threat to world order. It destabilizes governments, preys on innocent victims, and involves large amounts of financial and human resources. Yet unlike war, which openly pits opponents against each other in a recognized trial of strength, terrorism is covert. It seeks to sway the masses through intimidation and fear. Many terrorist individuals and groups are motivated by extreme religious beliefs, and religion as a factor in terrorism has grown in importance.

- The effects of recent terrorist activity include increased fear of attack and heightened security; erosion of civil liberties; economic consequences and curtailments in international tourism and trade; fear of bioterrorism; and polarized Islamic and Christian civilizations. There is a growing concern about terrorism among Americans, with over half of adults surveyed responding that they have a "great deal of concern."

- Several early sociologists have examined the functions associated with war, including the expansion of territory, social integration, social change, advancing ideology, and economic benefits. Conflict theorists suggest that war occurs when interests of nations or groups collide with one another for power, control, resources, and markets. Symbolic interactionist writing on war features several emphases, including the symbolic meaning behind the military or terrorist attack; the war experience by those directly involved; the symbols used to promote or protest the war; and how concepts related to war and terrorism come to be defined in ways that advance the goals of various parties.

- No one method of dealing with terrorists has universal support. The traditional policy is not to give in to terrorist demands. Other policies that have proven somewhat effective include the following: imposing boycotts and other measures to put pressure on countries that sponsor terrorism; negotiators making promises but not keeping them after the captives have been released because promises made under threat are not valid; treating terrorists as criminals; enlisting the cooperation of journalists and media personnel in depriving terrorists of media attention; offering substantial rewards for information about and capture of terrorists; and developing an international campaign against terrorists with the help of a network of experts on the subject.

Glossary

addiction   A complex phenomenon that involves the drug user's physical and psychological dependence, the type of drug, and the amount and frequency of use.

advance directive   A written statement that explains the patient's wishes for medical care should the person be unable to communicate them to the physician.

affirmative action   Controversial policies that require institutions that have engaged in discriminatory practices to increase opportunities for women and members of minority groups.

Affordable Care Act (ACA)   Legislation developed by President Obama and passed in 2010 that is the first major overhaul of the U.S. health care system since the creation of Medicare and Medicaid in 1967.

agents of socialization   The people, social institutions, and organizations that teach boys and girls their gendered expectations.

Air Quality Index (AQI)   A way of categorizing levels of daily air quality that indicates how clean or polluted the air is.

alcohol abuse   An overuse of alcohol to an extent that interferes with normal social roles, such as the roles of spouse, parent, or worker.

alcoholism   The state of being addicted to alcohol with the following four symptoms: craving, loss of control, physical dependence, and tolerance.

anomie   The feeling of being adrift that arises from the disparity between goals and means.

antimiscegenation laws   Laws banning marriage between whites and other races.

assimilation   A process through which a racial or an ethnic minority group slowly ceases being "different" by taking on the characteristics of the mainstream culture.

aversion therapy/behavior conditioning   A form of treatment that applies nausea-producing drugs or electric shock to condition the patient against alcohol.

baby-boom generation   The large number of people who were born between the mid-1940s and the early 1960s who are now reaching retirement age.

binge drinking   A pattern of drinking that brings blood alcohol concentration (BAC) levels to 0.08 g/dL. Although the quantity of alcohol required to reach this level can vary, in general, it amounts to a consumption of five or more drinks in a single session for males, and to four or more drinks for females.

cap and trade   A program that would create markets for emission credits, representing a mix of environmentalism with free market tendencies.

capital   Both the money used to purchase resources (e.g., raw materials) and the physical assets (e.g., buildings and equipment) used to produce goods and services. Capitalists are people who combine capital with the labor of workers to produce goods and services in the hope of making a profit—that is, selling their product or service at a market price higher than the costs of the equipment and labor used to create it.

capitalism   A particular type of economic system found in the United States (and elsewhere); sometimes known as a free-enterprise system.

chain migration   The tendency of immigrants to migrate to areas where they have kin and others from their home communities.

civil law   Laws that deal with noncriminal acts in which one individual injures another.

class stratification   The stratification of individuals and groups according to their access to various occupations, incomes, skills, and opportunities.

climate change   A type of environmental change that encompasses global warming, but refers to the broader range of changes that are happening to our planet, including rising sea levels; shrinking mountain glaciers; accelerating ice melt in Greenland, Antarctica, and the Arctic; and shifts in flower and plant blooming times.

clitoridectomy   A procedure in which the clitoris is cut out of the body.

codependency   A relationship pattern in which a person assumes the responsibility for meeting others' needs, often to the detriment of their own needs.

cohabitation   Living with a romantic and sexual partner without being married.

communism   A system of government that controls a planned economy, determining the flow of goods and services.

community psychology   The idea of easily accessible, locally controlled facilities that could care for mentally ill people in their own communities.

comparative perspective   A process to learn about other cultures and other historical periods to better understand social problems within one's own culture.

conflict perspective   A way of thinking that is based on the belief that social problems arise out of major contradictions in the way societies are organized, contradictions that lead to large-scale conflict between those who have access to the good life and those who do not.

contingent nonstandard work   Employment that does not have a written employment contract, is only temporary, has irregular hours, or is some combination of these elements.

coyotes   Guides who help people immigrate illegally to the United States.

crime   Any act or omission of an act for which the state can apply sanctions.

criminal law   The practice wherein society prohibits certain acts and prescribes the punishments to be meted out to violators.

crude birth (or fertility) rate   The number of children born per 1,000 of the population.

cultural capital   The resource that a person brings from his or her family, which may include forms of knowledge, skills, education, and other advantages that a person has and which give him or her a certain status in society.

cultural lag   A delay that occurs when one aspect of a culture changes more rapidly than another aspect does and thereby causes some maladjustment between the two aspects.

cyberstalking   Stalking and harassment that occurs electronically, such as through e-mail, texts, bulletin boards, chat rooms, or other types of media.

date-rape drugs   Drugs such as gamma hydroxybutyrate (GHB), Rohypnol (popularly known as "roofies" or "roofenol"), or ketamine hydrochloride (ketamine), which can immobilize a person to facilitate an assault.

de facto segregation   Segregation that is not required by law, but results from housing patterns, economic inequalities, or gerrymandered school districts.

de jure segregation   Segregation that is required by law.

deinstitutionalization   The act of discharging patients from mental hospitals directly into the community.

dementia   An overall term that describes a wide range of symptoms associated with a decline in memory or other thinking skills severe enough to reduce a person's ability to perform everyday activities.

demographic transition   A process by which a population moves through several stages: An original equilibrium in which a high birthrate is more or less canceled out by a high death rate, then through a stage in which the birthrate remains high but the death rate declines, to a final equilibrium in which the birth and death rates are lower but the population is much larger.

demographic transition   The process in which a society moves from a situation of high fertility rates and low life expectancy to one of low fertility rates and high life expectancy.

detoxify   To keep a person off alcohol or another substance until none shows in blood samples.

differential association   A theory that suggests that criminal behavior is a result of a learning process that occurs chiefly within small, intimate groups—family, friends, neighborhood peer groups, and the like.

digital divide   The gap between those with access to computers and the Internet and those without such access.

discrimination   The differential treatment of individuals considered to belong to a particular social group.

drift hypothesis   A concept that argues that social class is not a cause but a consequence of mental disorder.

drug abuse   The use of societally unacceptable drugs and/or the excessive or inappropriate use of acceptable drugs in ways that can lead to physical, psychological, or social harm.

drug   Any substance, other than food, that chemically alters the structure or function of a living organism.

educational attainment   The number of years of school completed.

empirical approach   A method that answers questions through a systematic collection and analysis of data.

enabling behaviors   Behaviors that a codependent person will do to cover for, support, and enable an alcoholic to continue to drink (or to enable another type of abuser to continue toxic behaviors).

entrepreneur   A capitalist who creates a new business venture.

environmental racism   The act of disproportionally placing landfills and toxic waste dumpsites near low-income and minority neighborhoods.

environmental stress   The interaction and conflict of three systems: the natural environment, the technological system, and the social system.

epidemiologists   Social scientists who study the course of diseases in human populations.

ethnic minorities   Groups of people who share cultural features, such as language, religion, national origin, dietary practices, and a common history, and who regard themselves as a distinct group.

ethnocentrism   The belief that one's own group is superior to another group.

euthanasia   The painless killing of a patient suffering from a terminal illness or irreversible coma.

family   Relationships by blood, marriage, or affection, in which members may cooperate economically, may care for any children, and may consider their identity to be intimately connected to the larger group.

fee-for-service   A type of health care system in which patients are expected to pay for their own medical care.

fetal alcohol spectrum disorders (FADS)   A group of conditions that can occur in a person whose mother consumed alcohol during pregnancy. These effects can include physical abnormalities and problems with cognition, behavior, and learning that last a lifetime.

fictive kin   Friends in a close network who provide support.

food insecurity   A condition described by the United States Department of Agriculture (USDA) as not having enough nourishing food available on a regular basis.

functionalist perspective   A way of thinking that considers the way major social institutions such as the family, the military, the health care system, and the police and courts actually operate.

gender socialization   A process whereby people learn to behave according to the gendered norms of a culture.

gender-based violence   Any act of gender violence that results in or is likely to result in physical, sexual, or psychological harm and suffering to women, including threats of such acts, coercion, or arbitrary deprivations of liberty, whether occurring in public or private life.

gender   The culturally and socially constructed differences between males and females, which are found in the meanings, beliefs, and practices associated with femininity and masculinity.

general birth (or fertility) rate   Number of children born per 1,000 women ages 15–44 (some countries use 49 as the cutoff age).

global warming   The long-term warming of the planet.

halfway house   A small, privately run residential community, usually located in an urban area, in which ex-patients are helped to make the transition from the hospital to normal life.

Head Start   The federally funded preschool program for children from low-income families.

hidden curriculum   An undocumented teaching approach that informally teaches gendered norms.

homogamy   The expectation that one must marry a person similar to oneself with respect to such characteristics as religion, social class, and race or ethnicity.

hospice   An institution that offers care to a dying person, with the goal of maintaining or improving quality of life; the focus is on caring, not curing.

human capital   Skills and capabilities.

human trafficking   The illegal and highly profitable business of recruitment, transport, or sale of human beings into all forms of forced labor and servitude.

identity theft (and identity fraud)   All types of crime in which someone wrongfully obtains and uses another person's personal data in some way that involves fraud or deception, typically for economic gain.

infant mortality   The number of deaths of children in their first year of life, for every 1,000 live births.

infibulation   A procedure in which the clitoris is cut out of the body, the vaginal lips are cut or scraped away, and the outer labia are stitched together, leaving only a miniscule opening for menstrual blood and urine to escape the body.

institution building   A modern version of the functionalist perspective, which attempts to show how people reorganize their lives to cope with new conditions.

institution A more or less stable structure of statuses and roles devoted to meeting the basic needs of people in a society, for example, the health care system.

institutional discrimination An unconscious result of the structure and functioning of the public institutions and policies themselves.

intersexed Individuals with anatomical categories that are not easily identifiable.

intimate partner violence (IPV) Violence between those who are physically and sexually intimate, such as spouses or partners.

latent functions Indirect by-products of some phenomenon that are less obvious.

level of living The level of material well-being that people actually obtain.

life expectancy How long a person can expect to live, usually calculated at birth.

limited liability A protection by which the assets of the corporation are liable to seizure in the case of economic failure or wrongdoing, but the entrepreneur's personal assets are not liable if the corporation fails.

long-term care Care for chronic physical or mental conditions that will likely never go away.

lumpenproletariat Members of capitalist societies who are poor and not in the labor force, according to Karl Marx.

manifest functions Those societal functions that are direct and the most obvious.

manslaughter Unlawful homicide without malice aforethought.

markets Institutions that regulate the worldwide flow of an almost infinite array of goods and services. Almost all markets in nations throughout the world are regulated by acts of governments, including the United States.

Medicaid The federal-state health care program for certain categories of people living in poverty.

medical sociology The subfield of sociology that specializes in research on the health care system and its impact on the public, especially access to health care.

Medicare A federal health insurance program for people age 65 and older (and for younger people receiving Social Security Disability Insurance payments or suffering from specified conditions).

mental health A state of well-being in which the individual realizes his or her own abilities, can cope with the normal stresses of life, can work productively and fruitfully, and is able to make a contribution to his or her community.

mental illness A mental, behavioral, or emotional disorder (excluding developmental or substance abuse disorders), diagnosable currently or within the past year and of sufficient duration to meet diagnostic criteria specified within the fifth edition of the *Diagnostic and Statistical Manual of Mental Disorders (DSM-V)*.

military sexual trauma (MST) Any sexual harassment or sexual assault that occurs to a veteran while serving in the military.

million tons of oil equivalent (Mtoe) A standard method of converting different types of energy units into one measure.

Mothers Against Drunk Driving (MADD) A nonprofit organization working to protect families from drunk driving and underage drinking through education and support of victims and survivors.

multinational corporations (or transnational corporations) Corporations that have their headquarters in one country but pursue business activities and profits in one or more foreign nations.

multiple jeopardy Having multiple minority statuses that include being old, female, and black (or Hispanic or Native American), which may cause more hardships than a person would face if he or she were in just one or two of these categories.

multiple partner fertility Having children with multiple partners.

murder Unlawful killing of a human being with malice aforethought.

nationalism Identification with, and exaltation of, the nation's culture and interests above those of all other nations.

nativist Anti-immigrant or anti-foreigner sentiment.

natural history approach The idea that social problems develop in a series of phases or stages.

net worth For a person or entity, the value of savings and checking accounts, real estate, automobiles, stocks and bonds, and other assets (minus debts).

No Child Left Behind Act of 2001 A major legislative initiative of the Bush administration to improve education in four clearly defined ways: (1) accountability for results; (2) an emphasis on doing what works based on scientific research; (3) expanded parental school choice options; and (4) expanded local control and flexibility.

one-child policy This Chinese policy has three main points: (1) delayed marriage and delayed childbearing; (2) fewer and healthier births; and (3) one child per couple (with some exceptions).

organized crime Crime that is committed by various types of criminal organizations, from large global crime syndicates to smaller local organizations whose membership may be more transient.

outsourcing Locating businesses that produce goods for American (or other Western) markets in poor, developing nations where the firm can take advantage of lower wage rates and fewer environmental restrictions.

overstayer Someone who starts out as a legal visitor, but becomes an *illegal* immigrant when he or she exceeds the time allocated to visit or reside in the United States.

patriarchy A form of social organization that supports male authority.

Pell Grants The nation's primary student grant aid program.

pollution The action or process of making land, water, air, etc., dirty and not safe or suitable to use.

post-traumatic stress disorder (PTSD) Severe stress reactions after a traumatic event such as war.

prejudice An emotional, rigid attitude toward members of the subordinate group.

projection The act of attributing the unwanted traits of themselves onto others.

psychotherapy Interaction between a patient and a therapist or among patients in groups that is intended to foster insight and change.

qualitative methods A research strategy that focuses on narrative description with words rather than numbers to analyze patterns and their underlying meanings.

quantitative methods A research strategy in which data can be measured numerically.

Race to the Top President Obama and his administration have been trying to improve the No Child Left Behind legislation by making more resources available to the public schools for creative ventures.

racial minorities Groups of people who share certain inherited characteristics, such as eye folds or brown skin.

racism Behavior, in word or deed, that is motivated by the belief that human races have distinctive characteristics that determine abilities.

rate of population growth (natural increase)   The differential between the crude birthrate and the death rate.

recidivism   The tendency that a former inmate will break the law after release and be arrested again.

revolutionary terrorism   Acts of violence against civilians that are carried out by enemies of a government.

role overload   The feeling of being overwhelmed by many different commitments and not having enough time to meet each commitment effectively.

role   The performance of a certain set of behaviors that go with a status.

routine household labor   Household work that is repetitive and less able to be postponed than are other tasks.

sandwich generation   Adults who are caring for an aging parent while also caring for their own children under age 18.

secondary deviance   A state in which a person who is labeled "deviant" may then adopt elements of what is popularly viewed as a deviant lifestyle.

selection effect   An effect that occurs when the sample is not random and leads to biased inferences about social processes, such as the relationship about cohabitation and divorce.

sex   Biological differences and one's role in reproduction for example, male and female.

sexism   The entire range of attitudes, beliefs, policies, laws, and behaviors discriminating against women (or against men) on the basis of their sex or gender.

social construction   The process by which some claims about social problems become dominant and others remain weak or unheeded; these claims develop through the activities of actors and institutions in society that shape our consciousness of the social world.

social control   The capacity of a social group, which could be an entire society, to regulate itself according to a set of higher moral principles beyond those of self-interest.

social disorganization   The result when rules break down; it is manifested in three major ways: normlessness, culture conflict, and breakdown.

social norm   A commonly accepted standard that specifies the kind of behavior appropriate in a given situation.

social policies   Formal procedures designed to remedy a social problem; can be designed by officials of government at the local, state, or federal level or by private citizens in voluntary associations, by corporations, and by nonprofit foundations.

social problem   Widespread agreement that a condition threatens the quality of life and cherished values and that something should be done to remedy that condition.

social stratification   A pattern in which individuals and groups find themselves in different positions in the social order, positions that enjoy varying amounts of access to desirable goods and services.

social structure   The organized arrangements of relationships and institutions that together form the basis of society.

spillover   The negative (or sometimes positive) moods, experiences, and demands involved in one sphere that carry over or "spill over" into the other sphere.

spurious   A type of apparent relationship between two variables that is really caused by a third factor.

stalking   Repeated and obsessive contact or tracking of another person—attention that is unwanted and causes a reasonable concern for one's safety.

Standard American English (SAE)   A speaking style that avoids slang or poor grammar, used by upper class people.

standard of living   What people want or expect in the way of material well-being.

status   A social position.

stepfamilies   Families in which one or both of the adult partners have at least one child, either residing with them or living elsewhere.

stereotyping   Attributing a fixed and usually unfavorable or inaccurate conception to a category of people.

sweatshops   Factory-type arrangements, especially in developing nations, with working conditions that would not be tolerated in affluent nations (e.g., crowded, hot spaces; minimal breaks; dangerous work).

symbolic interactionist perspective   A way of thinking that offers an explanation that gets closer to the individual level of behavior by looking at the symbols people use in everyday interaction—words, gestures, appearances—and how these symbols are interpreted by others. People's interactions with others are based on how they interpret these symbols.

technological change   Changes in any or all of the major dimensions of technology.

technological dualism   The idea that advances in technology can have both positive and negative impacts.

technology   The totality of means used by a people to provide themselves with the objects of material culture, and includes various apparatuses, skills, procedures, and related organizational networks.

terrorism   The threatened or actual use of illegal force and violence by a non-state actor to attain a political, economic, religious, or social goal through fear, coercion, or intimidation.

total birth (or fertility) rate   Average number of children born to a woman during her lifetime.

total institution   A place of residence and work where a large number of like-situated individuals are cut off from the wider society for an appreciable period of time and together lead an enclosed life.

violence among intimates   Violence among family members or intimate partners.

weapons of mass destruction   Nuclear weapons and biological agents that have the potential to annihilate thousands or even millions of people quickly.

welfare state   A type of country in which a significant portion of the GDP is taken by the government to provide certain minimum levels of social welfare for those who are poor, elderly, or disabled, among others.

whistleblowers   People who see abuses of technological systems and other kinds of abuses and attempt to expose them.

work–family conflict   The tension people feel when the pressures from paid work and family roles are somehow incompatible.

working poor   Individuals who, within a year, spent at least 27 weeks in the labor force (working or looking for work), but whose incomes fell below the official poverty level.

References

Indicates references new to this edition.

Chapter 1

*Alcaly, R. E. 2010. "How They Killed the Economy." 25 March. New York Review of Books.

*Berger, P. 1963. *Invitation to Sociology.* New York: Doubleday.

*Caplan, R. 2005. "Political Institution-Building." In *International Governance of War-Torn Territories*, Ch. 6. New York: Oxford University Press.

*Centers for Disease Control and Prevention. 2014. "Understanding Suicide: Fact Sheet." Retrieved 27 April 2015 (www.cdc.gov/violenceprevention/pdf/suicide_factsheet-a.pdf).

*Coontz, S. 2005. *Marriage, a History: From Obedience to Intimacy, or How Love Conquered Marriage.* New York: Penguin.

*DeNavas-Walt, C., and B. D. Proctor. 2015. "Income and Poverty in the United States: 2014." Current Population Reports. P60-252. September. Washington, DC: U.S. Census Bureau.

Durkheim, É. 1897/1951. *Suicide, a Study in Sociology.* New York: Free Press.

*Edin, K., and M. Kefalas. 2005. *Promises I Can Keep: Why Poor Women Put Motherhood Before Marriage.* Berkeley, CA: University of California Press.

Edwards, L. P. 1927. *The Natural History of Revolution.* Chicago: University of Chicago Press.

*Fiel, J. E. 2013. "Decomposing School Resegregation: Social Closure, Racial Imbalance, and Racial Isolation." *American Sociological Review*, 78, 828–48.

*Funk, C., and L. Rainie. 2015. "Chapter 3: Attitudes and Beliefs on Science and Technology Topics." Public and Scientists' Views on Science and Society. Pew Research Center. 29 January. Retrieved 27 April 2015 (www.pewinternet.org/2015/01/29/chapter-3-attitudes-and-beliefs-on-science-and-technology-topics/).

*Garcia-Moreno, C., A. H. Jansen, F. M. Ellseberg, L. Heise, and C. Watt. 2005. WHO Multicultural Study on Women's Health and Domestic Violence Against Women. Retrieved 21 May 2015 (http://www.who.int/gender/violence/who_multicountry_study/Introduction-Chapter1-Chapter2.pdf).

*Griswold, W. 2012. *Cultures and Societies in a Changing World*, 4th ed. Thousand Oaks, CA: Pine Forge Press.

*Jones, J. M. 2014. "In U.S., Most Do Not See Global Warming as Serious Threat." Gallup. 13 March. Retrieved 15 March 2015 (www.gallup.com/poll/167879/not-global-warming-serious-threat.aspx).

*Kalogrides, D., and S. Loeb. 2013. "Different Teachers, Different Peers: The Magnitude of Student Sorting within Schools." *Educational Researcher*, 42, 304–16.

*Kalogrides, D., S. Loeb, and T. Béteille. 2013. "Systematic Sorting: Teacher Characteristics and Class Assignments." *Sociology of Education*, 86, 103–23.

Larana, E., H. Johnston, and J. R. Gusfield, eds. 1994. *New Social Movements: From Ideology to Identity.* Philadelphia: Temple University Press.

*Lasswell, H. D. 1941. "The Garrison State." *American Journal of Sociology*, 46:455–68.

*Leeder, E. 2004. *The Family in Global Perspective: A Gendered Journey.* Thousand Oaks, CA: Sage Publications.

*Marx, K. 1867/1971. *Das Kapital* (*Capital*). New York: International Publishers.

*Marx, K., and F. Engels. 1848/1971. *Manifesto of the Communist Party.* New York: International Publishers.

*Mills, C. W. 1959. *The Sociological Imagination.* New York: Oxford University Press.

*Mindfully.org. 2015. "Consumption in the United States." Retrieved 28 April 2015 (http://www.mindfully.org/Sustainability/Americans-Consume-24percent.htm).

*Mintz, S. 2004. *Huck's Raft: A History of American Childhood.* Cambridge, MA: Belknap Press.

*National League for Nursing. 2015. "Nursing Student Demographics." Retrieved 27 April 2015 (www.nln.org/newsroom/nursing-education-statistics/nursing-student-demographics).

*Palazzolo, J. 2013. "Racial Gap in Men's Sentencing." *The Wall Street Journal*, February 14. Retrieved 21 May 2015 (http://www.wsj.com/articles/SB10001424127887324443200457830 4463789858002).

Park, R. E. 1955. "The Natural History of the Newspaper." In *Society: The Collected Papers of Robert Ezra Park, Vol. III.* New York: Free Press.

*Pew Research Center. 2014. "Beyond Red vs. Blue." 26 June. Retrieved 27 April 2015 (http://www.people-press.org/files/2014/06/6-26-14-Political-Typology-release1.pdf).

*RAND Education. 2012. "Teachers Matter: Understanding Teachers' Impact on Student Achievement." Retrieved 9 February 2015 (www.rand.org/education/projects/measuring-teacher-effectiveness/teachers-matter.html).

*Realty Trac. 2015. "Foreclosure Trends." Retrieved 28 April 2015 (http://www.realtytrac.com/statsandtrends/foreclosuretrendsatti).

*Richards, M. P. 2014. "The Gerrymandering of School Attendance Zones and the Segregation of Public Schools: A Geospatial Analysis." *American Educational Research Journal*, 51, 1119–57.

Rubington, E., and M. S. Weinberg. 2003. *The Study of Social Problems: Seven Perspectives*, 6th ed. New York: Oxford University Press.

*Saul, L. 2015. "Cluster of Concerns Vie for Top U.S. Problem in 2014." Gallup. 2 January. Retrieved 27 April 2015 (www.gallup.com/poll/180398/cluster-concerns-vie-top-problem-2014.aspx).

*Seccombe, K. 2015. *"So You Think I Drive a Cadillac?" Welfare Recipients' Perspectives on the System and Its Reform*, 4th ed. Boston: Pearson.

Shaw, C. R. 1929. *Delinquency Areas: A Study of the Geographic Distribution of School Truants, Juvenile Delinquents, and Adult Offenders in Chicago.* Chicago: University of Chicago Press.

Spector, M., and J. Kitsuse. 1987. *Constructing Social Problems.* Hawthorne, NY: Aldine de Gruyter.

Thomas, W. I., and F. Znaniecki. 1922. *The Polish Peasant in Europe and America.* New York: Knopf.

*Wilson, W. J. 1987. *The Truly Disadvantaged: The Inner City, the Underclass, and Public Policy.* Chicago: University of Chicago Press.

*Wilson, W. J. 1996. *When Work Disappears: The World of the New Urban Poor.* New York: Knopf.

Wirth, L. 1927. "The Ghetto." *American Journal of Sociology,* 23, 57–71.

*World Health Organization. 2014. "Domestic Violence: Factsheet." Retrieved 21 May 2015 (http://www.who.int/mediacentre/factsheets/fs239/en/).

Chapter 2

*Agency for Healthcare Research and Quality. 2011. "The Number of Practicing Primary Care Physicians in the United States: Primary Care Workforce Facts and Stats No. 1." October. Retrieved 17 April 2014 (www.ahrq.gov/research/findings/factsheets/primary/pcwork1/index.html).

*Altman, D. 1987. *AIDS in the Mind of America.* New York: Anchor Press/Doubleday.

*Altman, D. 2014. "Health Cost Growth Is Down, Or Not. It Depends Who You Ask." Kaiser Family Foundation Perspectives. 5 March. Retrieved 16 April 2014 (kff.org/health-costs/perspective/health-cost-growth-is-down-or-not-it-depends-who-you-ask/).

*American Cancer Society. 2015. Lung Cancer. Retrieved 3 March 2015 (www.cancer.org/cancer/lungcancer/index).

*Aon. 2013. "Medical Malpractice Claim Costs Remain Stable, According to Annual AON/ASHRM Report." 7 November. Retrieved 17 April 2014 (aon.mediaroom.com/2013-11-07-Medical-malpractice-claim-costs-remain-stable-according-to-annual-Aon-ASHRM-report).

*Blumenthal, D. 2006. "Employer-Sponsored Health Insurance in the United States—Origins and Implications." *New England Journal of Medicine,* 355, 82–88.

*Centers for Disease Control and Prevention. 2012. "Defining Overweight and Obesity." 27 April. Retrieved 17 April 2014 (www.cdc.gov/obesity/adult/defining.html).

*Centers for Disease Control and Prevention. 2014. "Overweight and Obesity." 28 March. (www.cdc.gov/obesity/data/adult.html).

*Cockerham, W. C. 2012. *Medical Sociology,* 12th ed. Boston: Pearson.

*Dlugacz, Yosef D. 2006. *Measuring Health Care: Using Quality Data for Operational, Financial, and Clinical Improvement.* San Francisco: Jossey-Bass.

*Ekos Research Associates, Inc. 2011. "Shifting Public Perceptions of Doctors and Health Care: FINAL REPORT." February. Retrieved 17 April 2014 (www.afmc.ca/future-of-medical-education-in-canada/postgraduate-project/pdf/EKOS-Final-Report.pdf).

*Ferdinand, A. O., Epane, J. P., and Menachemi, N. 2014. "Community Benefits Provided by Religious, Other Nonprofit, and For-Profit Hospitals: A Longitudinal Analysis 2000-2009." *Health Care Management Review,* 39, 145–153.

*The Fistula Foundation. 2015 "Fistula Fast Facts and Frequently Asked Questions." Retrieved 16 April 2015 (www.fistulafoundation.org/what-is-fistula/fast-facts-faq/).

*Gandhi, S. O. 2012. "Differences Between Non-Profit and For-Profit Hospices: Patient Selection and Quality." *International Journal of Health Care Finance and Economics,* 12, 107–127.

*Garfield, R., and Young, K. 2015. "Adults who Remained Uninsured at the End of 2014." The Henry J. Kaiser Family Foundation. Executive Summary. 29 January. Retrieved 25 February 2015 (kff.org/health-reform/issue-brief/adults-who-remained-uninsured-at-the-end-of-2014/).

*Health Canada. 2014. "Health Care System." Retrieved 17 April 2015 (www.hc-sc.gc.ca/hes-sss/index-eng.php).

*Hirst, E.J. 2014. "Generic Drug Prices Skyrocket in Past Year." Retrieved 28 April 2015 (www.huffingtonpost.com/2014/09/03/health-care-spending-2013_n_5759800.html).

*Kaiser Family Foundation. 2007. "Snapshots: How Changes in Medical Technology Affect Health Care Costs." 2 March. Retrieved 17 April 2014 (kff.org/health-costs/issue-brief/snapshots-how-changes-in-medical technology-affect/).

*Kaiser Family Foundation. 2012. "Health Care Costs: A Primer." May. Retrieved 28 April 2015 (kff.org/health-costs/issue-brief/health-care-costs-a-primer/).

*Kaiser Family Foundation. 2015. "ACA 101: What You Need to Know." Retrieved 29 April 2015. (kff.org/health-reform/event/aca-101-what-you-need-to-know-2015/).

*Kaiser Family Foundation and Health Research & Educational Trust. 2014. "Employer Health Benefits 2014 Annual Survey." Retrieved 29 April 2015. (kff.org/health-costs/issue-brief/health-care-costs-a-primer/).

*Kutscher, B. 2014. "For-Profit Hospitals: More Cost-Cutting…Acquisitions to Build Scale or Diversify…Robust Environment for IPOs." *Modern Healthcare,* 44, 16–17.

*Jajerol, M., Newkirk, V, and R. Garfield. 2015. "The Uninsured: A Primer-Key Facts about Health Insurance and the Uninsured in America." Retrieved 28 April 2015 (kff.org/uninsured/report/the-uninsured-a-primer/).

*Martinez, M. E., and Cohen, R. A. 2014. "Health Insurance Coverage: Early Release of Estimates from the National Health Interview Survey, January–June 2014." National Center for Health Statistics. December. Retrieved 25 February 2015 (www.cdc.gov/nchs/nhis/releases.htm).

*National Center for Health Statistics. 2014. "Health, United States, 2013: With Special Feature on Prescription Drugs." Hyattsville, MD.

*Organisation for Economic Co-Operation and Development. 2013. "Health at a Glance: OECD Indicators." Retrieved 27 February 2015 (www.oecd.org/els/health-systems/Health-at-a-Glance-2013.pdf).

*Ortman, J.M., Velkoff, V.A., and Hogan, H. 2014. "An Aging Nation: The Older Population in the United States." U.S. Census Bureau. Current Population Reports. P25-1140. May. Retrieved 28 April 2015 (www.census.gov/prod/2014pubs/p25-1140.pdf).

*Pollitz, K., Cox, C., Lucia, K., and Keith, K. 2014. "Medical Debt Among People With Health Insurance." Henry J. Kaiser Family Foundation. 7 January. Retrieved 27 February 2015 (kff.org/report-section/

medical-debt-among-people-with-health-insurance-incidence-of-medical-debt/).

*Population Reference Bureau. 2015. "2014 World Population Data Sheet." Retrieved 1 May 2015. (www.prb.org/Publications/Datasheets/2014/2014-world-population-data-sheet.aspx).

*Proctor, R. N. 2012. *Golden Holocaust: Origins of the Cigarette Catastrophe and the Case for Abolition*. Berkeley, CA: University of California Press.

Rainwater, L. 1974. "The Lower Class: Health, Illness, and Medical Institutions." In L. Rainwater, ed., *Inequality and Justice*. Hawthorne, NY: Aldine.

*Rosenthal, E. 2014. "Even Small Medical Advances Can Mean Big Jumps in Bills." *New York Times*. 5 April. Retrieved 17 April 2014 (www.nytimes.com/2014/04/06/health/even-small-medical-advances-can-mean-big-jumps-in-bills.html).

*Smith, J. C., and Medalia, C. 2014. Health Insurance Coverage in the United States: 2013. Current Population Reports. P60-250. Washington, DC: U.S. Census Bureau.

*Stanford Research into the Impact of Tobacco Advertising. 2014. "Slogans." Retrieved 17 April 2014 (tobacco.stanford.edu/tobacco_main/slogans.php).

Starr, P. 2010. March 4. "A Health Insurance Mandate with a Choice." *New York Times*, p. 35.

Wangsness, L. 2009. June 21. "Health Debate Shifting to Public vs. Private." *Boston Globe*.

*Stolberg, S. G., and Pear, R. 2010. "Obama Signs Health Care Overhaul Bill, With a Flourish." NYTimes.com. 23 March. Retrieved 27 February 2015 (www.nytimes.com/2010/03/24/health/policy/24health.html).

*Tejada, S., Darnell, J. S., Cho, Y. I., Stolley, M. R., Markossian, T. W., and Calhoun, E. A. 2013. "Patient Barriers, to Follow-Up Care for Breast and Cervical Cancer Abnormalities." *Journal of Women's Health*, 22, 507–517.

*Ungar, L., and J. O'Donnell. 2014. "Health Care Grows at Lowest-Ever Rate." Retrieved 29 April 2015. (www.huffingtonpost.com/2014/09/03/health-care-spending-2013_n_5759800.html) United Nations Development Programme. 2013. "Humanity Divided: Confronting Inequality in Developing Countries." November. Retrieved 1 March 2014 (www.undp.org/content/undp/en/home/librarypage/poverty-reduction/humanity-divided-confronting-inequality-in-developing-countries/).

*U.S. Census Bureau. 2014a. "2014 National Population Projections." 18 December. Retrieved 3 February 2015 (www.census.gov/population/projections/data/national/2014.html).

*U.S. Census Bureau. 2014b. "Census Bureau News—Profile America Facts for Features: Older Americans Month: May 2014." 25 March. Retrieved 17 April 2014 (www.prnewswire.com/news-releases/census-bureau-news—profile-america-facts-for-features-older-americans-month-may-2014-252306191.html).

*U.S. Census Bureau. 2014c. "American's Families and Living Arrangements: 2014." 30 October. Retrieved 28 April 2015 (www.census.gov/hhes/families/data/cps2014A.html).

*U.S. Department of Health and Human Services. 2014. "The Health Consequences of Smoking—50 Years of Progress: A Report of the Surgeon General." Atlanta, GA: U.S. Department of Health and Human Services, Centers for Disease Control and Prevention, National Center for Chronic Disease Prevention and Health Promotion, Office on Smoking and Health.

*Weiss, G. L., and L. E. Lonnquist. 2015. *The Sociology of Health, Healing, and Illness*, 8th ed. Boston: Pearson.

*World Health Organization. 2014. "10 Facts on Obstetric Fistula." Retrieved 16 April 2015 (www.who.int/features/factfiles/obstetric_fistula/en/).

Chapter 3

*Alzheimer's Association. 2014. "2014 Alzheimer's Disease Facts and Figures." Retrieved 11 April 2014 (www.alz.org/downloads/Facts_Figures_2014.pdf).

*American Psychiatric Association. 2015. "DSM-5 Implementation and Support." Retrieved 11 April 2015 (www.dsm5.org/Pages/Default.aspx).

Barry, P. 2002. *Mental Health and Mental Illness*. Philadelphia: Lippencott.

*Brown, R. A., G. N. Marshall, J. Breslau, C. Farris, K. C. Osilla, H. A. Pincus, T. Ruder, P. Voorhies, D. Barnes-Proby, K. Pfrommer, L. Miyashiro, Y. Rana, and D. M. Adamson. 2015. "Far from Care: Increasing Access to Behavioral Health Care for Remote Service Members and Their Families." RAND Corporation Research Brief. Retrieved 11 April 2015 (www.rand.org/content/dam/rand/pubs/research_briefs/RB9700/RB9790/RAND_RB9790.pdf).

*Centers for Disease Control and Prevention. 2015a. "Autism Spectrum Disorder: Data & Statistics." Retrieved 11 April 2015 (www.cdc.gov/ncbddd/autism/data.html).

*Centers for Disease Control and Prevention. 2015b. "Suicide Prevention." Retrieved 11 April 2015 (http://www.cdc.gov/violenceprevention/pub/youth_suicide.html).

*Clark, T. T., C. P. Salas-Wright, M. G. Vaughn, and K. E. Whitfield. 2015. "Everyday Discrimination and Mood and Substance Use Disorders: A Latent Profile Analysis with African Americans and Caribbean Blacks." *Addictive Behaviors*, 40, 119–25.

Cockerham, W. C. 2006. *Medical Sociology*, 13th ed. Boston: Pearson.

*Cockerham, W. C. 2014. *Sociology of Mental Disorder*, 9th ed. Boston: Pearson.

*Cokes, C., and W. Kornblum. 2010. "Experiences of Mental Distress by Individuals During an Economic Downturn." *Western Journal of Black Studies*, 34, 24–35.

Curtis, W. R. 1986. "The Deinstitutionalization Story." *Public Interest*, 85, 34–49.

*Drake, R. E., and E. Latimer. 2012. "Lessons Learned in Developing Community Mental Health Care in North America." *World Psychiatry*, 11, 47–51.

Elhai, J. D., J. D. Ford, K. J. Ruggiero, and B. C. Frueh. 2009. "Diagnostic Alterations for Post-Traumatic Stress Disorder: Examining Data from the National Comorbidity Survey Replication and National Survey of Adolescents." *Psychological Medicine*, 39, 1957–66.

Faris, R. E. L., and H. W. Dunham. 1938. *Mental Disorders in Urban Areas*. Chicago: University of Chicago Press.

*Giang, V. 2012. "Untreated Mental Illnesses Are Costing American Companies Billions Every Year." *Business Insider*. 29 September. Retrieved 11 April 2015 (www.businessinsider.com/you-dont-even-know-how-many-mentally-ill-people-youre-working-with-2012-9).

Goffman, E. 1961. *Asylums: Essays on the Social Situation of Mental Patients and Other Inmates.* Garden City, NY: Doubleday.

Greenley, J. R. 1972. "Alternative Views of the Psychiatrist's Role." *Social Problems,* 20, 252–62.

*Harvey, S. B., M. Hotopf, S. Overland, and A. Mykletun. 2010. "Physical Activity and Common Mental Disorders." *British Journal of Psychiatry,* 197, 357–64.

Hazlett, S. B., M. L. McCarthy, M. S. Londner, and C. U. Onyike. 2004. "Epidemiology of Adult Psychiatric Visits to U.S. Emergency Departments." *Academic Emergency Medicine,* 11, 193–95.

*Hendryx, M., C. A. Green, and N. A. Perrin. 2009. "Social Support, Activities, and Recovery from Serious Mental Illness: STARS Study Findings." *Journal of Behavioral Health Services Research,* 36, 320–29.

*Hoven, C. W., C. S. Duarte, C. P. Lucas, P. Wu, D. J. Mandell, R. D. Goodwin, M. Cohen, V. Balaban, B. A. Woodruff, F. Bin, G. J. Musa, L. Mei, P. A. Cantor, J. L. Aber, P. Cohen, and E. Susser. 2005. "Psychopathology Among New York City Public School Children 6 Months After September 11." *Archives of General Psychology,* 62, 545–51.

*Hudson, C. G. 2005. "Socioeconomic Status and Mental Illness: Tests of the Social Causation and Selection Hypotheses." *American Journal of Orthopsychiatry,* 75, 3–18.

*Hudson, C. G. 2012. "Patterns of Residential Mobility of People with Schizophrenia: Multi-Level Tests of Downward Geographic Drift." *Journal of Sociology & Social Welfare,* 39, 149–79.

*Hurst, C. 2013. *Social Inequality: Forms, Causes, and Consequences,* 8th ed. Boston: Pearson.

Jamison, K. R. 2000. *Night Falls Fast: Understanding Suicide.* New York: Knopf, Vintage.

Kessler, R. C., O. Demler, R. G. Frank, M. Olfson, H. A. Pincus, E. E. Walters, P. Wang, K. B. Wells, and A. M. Zaslavsky. 2005. *Prevalence and Treatment of Mental Disorders, 1990 to 2003.* World Health Organization.

Kozol, J. 1988. "The Homeless and Their Children." *The New Yorker.* 25 January, pp. 65ff; 1 February, pp. 36ff.

McEwen, C. 1988. "Continuities in the Study of Total and Non-total Institutions." In: *Annual Review of Sociology.* Newbury Park, CA: Sage.

*National Alliance on Mental Illness. 2015. "Mental Health Medications." Retrieved 11 April 2015 (www.nami.org/Learn-More/Treatment/Mental-Health-Medications).

*National Institute of Mental Health. 2015. "Statistics." Retrieved 11 April 2015 (www.nimh.nih.gov/health/statistics/index.shtml).

*Pascoe, E. A., and L. S. Richman. 2009. "Perceived Discrimination and Health: A Meta-Analytic Review." *Psychological Bulletin,* 135, 531–54.

*Perou, R., R. H. Bitsko, S. J. Blumberg, P. Pastor, R. M. Ghandour, J. C. Gfroerer, S. L. Hedden, A. E. Crosby, S. N. Visser, L. A. Schieve, S. E. Parks, J. E. Hall, D. Brody, C. M. Simile, W. W. Thompson, J. Baio, S. Avenevoli, M. D. Kogan, and L. N. Huang. 2013. "Mental Health Surveillance Among Children—United States, 2005–2011." *Morbidity and Mortality Weekly Report (MMWR),* 62, 1–35.

*RAND Center for Military Health Policy Research. 2008. "Invisible Wounds: Mental Health and Cognitive Care Needs of America's Returning Veterans." RB-9336. Retrieved 11 April 2015 (http://www.rand.org/content/dam/rand/pubs/research_briefs/2008/RAND_RB9336.pdf).

Rosenhan, D. L. 1973. "On Being Sane in Insane Places." *Science,* 179, 250–58.

Salize, H. J., H. Schanda, and H. Dressing. 2008. "From the Hospital into the Community and Back Again—A Trend towards Reinstitutionalization in Mental Health Care?" *International Review of Psychiatry,* 20, 527–34.

Scheff, T. J. 1963. "The Role of the Mentally Ill and the Dynamics of Mental Disorder." *Sociometry,* 26, 436–53.

*Schoenbaum, M., R. C. Kessler, S. E. Gilman, L. J. Colpe, S. G. Heeringa, M. B. Stein, R. J. Ursano, and K. L. Cox. 2014. "Predictors of Suicide and Accident Death in the Army Study to Assess Risk and Resilience in Servicemembers (Army STARRS)." *JAMA Psychiatry,* 71, 493–503.

Schulte, B., and C. L. Jenkins. 2007. "Cho Didn't Get Court-Ordered Treatment." *Washington Post.* 7 May. P. A1.

*Scull, A. T. 1988. "Deviance and Social Control." In: *The Handbook of Sociology,* edited by N. J. Smelser. Newbury Park, CA: Sage.

Sheehan, S. 1982. *Is There No Place on Earth for Me?* New York: Scribner.

Sperry, L. 1995. *Pharmacology and Psychotherapy: Strategies for Maximizing Treatment Outcomes.* New York: Brunner/Mazel.

Squire, S. 1987. "Shock Therapy's Return to Respectability." *New York Times Magazine.* 22 November. Pp. 78ff.

Srole, L., T. S. Langner, S.T. Michael, P. Kirkpatrick, M. K. Opler, and T. A. C. Rennie. 1978. *Mental Health in the Metropolis: The Midtown Manhattan Study,* rev. ed. New York: New York University Press.

Szasz, T. S. 2003. *The Myth of Mental Illness: Foundations of a Theory of Personal Conduct,* rev. ed. New York: Perennial.

*Treatment Advocacy Center, 2012. "No Room at the Inn: Trends and Consequences of Closing Public Psychiatric Hospitals 2005–10." Retrieved 13 April 2015 (http://tacreports.nonprofitsoapbox.com/storage/documents/no_room_at_the_inn-2012.pdf)

*Treatment Advocacy Center, 2015. "Consequences of Nontreatment." Retrieved 15 April 2015 (http://www.treatmentadvocacycenter.org/problem/consequences-of-non-treatment).

*U.S. Army, National Institute of Mental Health, Uniformed Services University of Health Sciences, Harvard Medical School, University of Michigan, and University of California San Diego School of Medicine. 2015. "Army STARRS." Retrieved 11 April 2015 (www.armystarrs.org/).

*U.S. Department of Housing and Urban Development, 2014. "The 2104 Annual Homeless Assessment Report (AHAR) to Congress." Retrieved 14 April 2015 (https://www.hudexchange.info/resources/documents/2014-AHAR-Part1.pdf).

*U.S. Department of Veterans Affairs. 2014. "PTSD: National Center for PTSD." Retrieved 11 April 2015 (www.ptsd.va.gov/public/PTSD-overview/reintegration/overview-mental-health-effects.asp).

*World Health Organization. 2010. "Mental Health and Development: Targeting People with Mental Health Conditions as a Vulnerable Group." Retrieved 11 April 2015 (whqlibdoc.who.int/publications/2010/9789241563949_eng.pdf?ua=1).

*World Health Organization. 2012. "Media Centre: Depression." Fact Sheet No. 369. October. Retrieved 11 April 2015 (www.who.int/mediacentre/factsheets/fs369/en/).

*World Health Organization. 2014. "Media Centre: Suicide."
Fact Sheet No. 398. September. Retrieved 11 April 2015
(www.who.int/mediacentre/factsheets/fs398/en/).

*World Health Organization. 2015. "Gender and Women's
Mental Health: Gender Disparities and Mental Health:
The Facts." Retrieved 11 April 2015 (www.who.int/
mental_health/prevention/genderwomen/en/).

*World Health Organization and the Calouste Gulbenkian
Foundation. 2014. "Social Determinants of Mental Health."
Retrieved 20 July 2015. (http://www.who.int/mental_
health/publications/gulbenkian_paper_social_
determinants_of_mental_health/en/)

*Zschucke, E., K. Gaudlitz, and A. Ströhle. 2013. "Exercise
and Physical Activity in Mental Disorders: Clinical and
Experimental Evidence." *Journal of Preventive Medicine &
Public Health*, 46, S12–S21.

Chapter 4

*Alcoholics Anonymous. 2012. "2011 Membership Survey."
Retrieved 15 April 2015 (www.aa.org/assets/en_US/
p-48_membershipsurvey.pdf).

Becker, H. S. 1963. "Becoming a Marijuana User." In:
Outsiders: Studies in the Sociology of Deviance. New York:
Basic Books.

*Boyette, C., and J. Wilson. 2015. "It's 2015: Is Weed Legal in
Your State?" CNN.com. Retrieved 20 April 2015 (www.cnn
.com/2015/01/07/us/recreational-marijuana-laws/).

Brick, J., ed. 2004. *Handbook of the Medical Consequences of
Alcohol and Drug Abuse*. New York: Haworth Press.

Campbell, E. 2005. "Injection Drug Use, Global HIV/
AIDS, and Human Rights." *Journal of Ambulatory Care
Management*, 28, 286–87.

*Catalano, S. 2007. "Intimate Partner Violence in the United
States." Bureau of Justice Statistics, Office of Justice
Programs, U.S. Department of Justice. Retrieved 20 April
2015 (www.bjs.gov/content/pub/pdf/ipvus.pdf).

*Centers for Disease Control and Prevention. 2014a.
"Excessive Alcohol Use and Risks to Women's Health."
19 November. Retrieved 15 April 2015 (www.cdc.gov/
alcohol/fact-sheets/womens-health.htm).

*Centers for Disease Control and Prevention. 2014b.
"Excessive Drinking Costs U.S. $223.5 Billion." 17 April.
Retrieved 20 April 2015 (www.cdc.gov/features/
alcoholconsumption/).

*Centers for Disease Control and Prevention. 2014c. "Fact
Sheets - Alcohol Use and Your Health." 7 November.
Retrieved 15 April 2015 (www.cdc.gov/alcohol/fact-
sheets/alcohol-use.htm).

*Centers for Disease Control and Prevention. 2014d.
"Fact Sheets—Binge Drinking." 16 January. Retrieved
20 April 2015 (www.cdc.gov/alcohol/fact-sheets/
binge-drinking.htm).

*Centers for Disease Control and Prevention. 2014e.
"Unintentional Drowning: Get the Facts." 15 May.
Retrieved 15 April 2015 (www.cdc.gov/Homeand
RecreationalSafety/Water-Safety/waterinjuries-
factsheet.html).

*Centers for Disease Control and Prevention. 2015a. "Impaired
Driving: Get the Facts." 13 January. Retrieved 15 April 2015
(www.cdc.gov/Motorvehiclesafety/impaired_driving/
impaired-drv_factsheet.html).

*Centers for Disease Control and Prevention. 2015b. "Injury
Prevention & Control: Prescription Drug Overdose."
3 April. Retrieved 15 April 2015 (www.cdc.gov/
drugoverdose/index.html).

*Dayton, T. 2010. "The Hidden Pain of the Addicted Family."
Huffington Post. 21 September. Retrieved 20 April 2015
(www.huffingtonpost.com/dr-tian-dayton/the-hidden-
pain-of-the-ad_b_732753.html).

*Dayton, T. 2011. "What is an ACOA?" Huffington Post. 13
February. Retrieved 20 April 2015 (www.huffingtonpost
.com/dr-tian-dayton/what-is-an-acoa_b_822493.html).

*Fetal Alcohol Spectrum Disorders Center for Excellence. 2015.
"About FASD." 1 April. Retrieved 15 April 2015
(fasdcenter.samhsa.gov/aboutus/AboutFASD.aspx).

*Glaser, G. 2013. "Why She Drinks: Women and Alcohol
Abuse." *The Wall Street Journal*. 21 June. Retrieved 20 April
2015 (www.wsj.com/articles/SB10001424127887323893504
578555270434071876).

Green, K. M., E. E. Doherty, H. S. Reisinger, H. D. Chilcoat,
and M. Ensminger. 2010. "Social Integration in Young
Adulthood and the Subsequent Onset of Substance Use
and Disorders among a Community Population of Urban
African Americans." *Addiction*, 105, 484–93.

*Grucza, R. A., K. K. Bucholz, J. P. Rice, and L. J. Bierut. 2008.
"Secular Trends in the Lifetime Prevalence of Alcohol
Dependence in the United States: A Re-evaluation." *Alcohol:
Clinical and Experimental Research*, 32, 763–70.

Han, B., J. C. Gfroerer, and J. D. Colliver. 2010. "Associations
between Duration of Illicit Drug Use and Health
Conditions: Results from the 2005–2007 National Surveys on
Drug Use and Health." *Annals of Epidemiology*, 20, 289–97.

Inciardi, J. A. 1999. *Criminal Justice*, 6th ed. Fort Worth, TX:
Harcourt.

*Ingraham, C. 2014. "Think You Drink a Lot? This Chart Will
Tell You." *Washington Post*. 25 September. Retrieved
15 April 2015 (www.washingtonpost.com/blogs/
wonkblog/wp/2014/09/25/think-you-drink-a-lot-this-
chart-will-tell-you/).

*Johnston, L. D., P. M. O'Malley, R. A. Miech, J. G. Bachman,
and J. E. Schulenberg. 2015. *Monitoring the Future National
Survey Results on Drug Use: 1975–2014: Overview, Key
Findings on Adolescent Drug Use*. Ann Arbor: Institute for
Social Research, The University of Michigan.

*McGaha, J. E., J. L. Stokes, and J. Nielson. 1990. "Children of
Alcoholism: Implications For Juvenile Justice." *Juvenile &
Family Court Journal*, 41, 19–24.

*Motel, S. 2015. "6 Facts About Marijuana." Pew Research
Center. Retrieved 14 April 2015 (www.pewresearch.org/
fact-tank/2015/04/14/6-facts-about-marijuana/).

*National Council on Alcohol and Drug Dependence,
Inc. 2015a. "Alcohol and Crime." Retrieved 20
April 2015 (ncadd.org/learn-about-alcohol/
alcohol-and-crime/202-alcohol-and-crime).

*National Council on Alcohol and Drug Dependence, Inc.
2015b. "Drugs and Crime." Retrieved 20 April 2015 (ncadd.
org/learn-about-drugs/drugs-and-crime).

*National Highway Traffic Safety Administration. 2014.
"Alcohol-Impaired Driving." U.S. Department of
Transportation. DOT HS 812 102. Retrieved 20 April 2015
(www-nrd.nhtsa.dot.gov/Pubs/812102.pdf).

*National Institute on Alcohol Abuse and Alcoholism. 2013a.
"Alcohol Use Disorder: A Comparison Between DSM–IV
and DSM–5." NIH Publication No. 13–7999. November.
Retrieved 20 April 2015 (pubs.niaaa.nih.gov/publications/
dsmfactsheet/DSMfact.pdf).

*National Institute on Alcohol Abuse and Alcoholism. 2013b. "Women and Alcohol." August. Retrieved 15 April 2015 (pubs.niaaa.nih.gov/publications/womensfact/womensfact.htm).

*National Institute on Alcohol Abuse and Alcoholism. 2015a. "Alcohol's Effects on the Body." Retrieved 20 April 2015 (www.niaaa.nih.gov/alcohol-health/alcohols-effects-body).

*National Institute on Alcohol Abuse and Alcoholism. 2015b. "Alcohol Facts and Statistics." Retrieved 20 April 2015 (www.niaaa.nih.gov/alcohol-health/overview-alcohol-consumption/alcohol-facts-and-statistics).

*National Institute on Alcohol Abuse and Alcoholism. 2015c. "Fetal Alcohol Exposure." April. Retrieved 20 April 2015 (pubs.niaaa.nih.gov/publications/FASDFactsheet/FASD.pdf).

*National Institute on Drug Abuse. 2014. "DrugFacts: Nationwide Trends." January. Retrieved 20 April 2015 (www.drugabuse.gov/publications/drugfacts/nationwide-trends).

*National Institute on Drug Abuse. 2015a. "Commonly Abused Drugs." February. Retrieved 20 April 2015 (www.drugabuse.gov/drugs-abuse/commonly-abused-drugs).

*National Institute on Drug Abuse. 2015b. "Drugs of Abuse." Retrieved 20 April 2015 (www.drugabuse.gov/drugs-abuse).

Neff, J. A., and A. M. Dassori. 1998. "Age and Maturing Out of Heavy Drinking Among Anglo and Minority Male Drinkers: A Comparison of Cross-sectional Data and Retrospective Drinking History Techniques." *Hispanic Journal of Behavioral Sciences*, 20, 225–41.

Police Foundation of the United Kingdom. 2000. "Drugs and the Law: Report of the Independent Inquiry into the Misuse of Drugs Act of 1971." 4 April. Retrieved 17 April 2015 (www.drugscope.org.uk/Resources/Drugscope/Documents/PDF/virtuallibrary/runcimanreport.pdf).

*Prescott, C. A. 2003. "Sex Differences in the Genetic Risk for Alcoholism." National Institute on Alcohol Abuse and Alcoholism. Retrieved 15 April 2015 (pubs.niaaa.nih.gov/publications/arh26-4/264-273.htm).

*Swift, A. 2013. "For First Time, Americans Favor Legalizing Marijuana." Gallup. 22 October. Retrieved 20 April 2015 (www.gallup.com/poll/165539/first-time-americans-favor-legalizing-marijuana.aspx).

Szasz, T. S. 1992. "The Fatal Temptation: Drug Prohibition and the Fear of Autonomy." *Daedalus*, pp. 161–65.

*United Nations Office on Drugs and Crime. 2014. "World Drug Report 2014." (United Nations publication, Sales No. E.14.XI.7).

*U.S. Census Bureau. 2010. *The 2010 Statistical Abstract: The National Data Book*. Retrieved 20 April 2015 (www.census.gov/compendia/statab/2010/2010edition.html).

*U.S. Department of Health and Human Services. 2014. "The Health Consequences of Smoking—50 Years of Progress: A Report of the Surgeon General." Atlanta, GA: U.S. Department of Health and Human Services, Centers for Disease Control and Prevention, National Center for Chronic Disease Prevention and Health Promotion, Office on Smoking and Health.

*Wechsler, H., and T. F. Nelson. 2008. "What We Have Learned From the Harvard School of Public Health College Alcohol Study: Focusing Attention on College Student Alcohol Consumption and the Environmental Conditions That Promote It." *Journal of Studies on Alcohol and Drugs*, 69, 481–90.

*Wilsnack, S. C., R. W. Wilsnack, and L. W. Kantor. 2014. "Focus On: Women and Costs of Alcohol Use." *Alcohol Research: Current Reviews*, 35, 219–28.

*World Health Organization. 2015. "Management of Substance Abuse: Facts and Figures." Retrieved 15 April 2015 (www.who.int/substance_abuse/facts/en/).

Chapter 5

Anderson, E. 1992. *Streetwise*. Chicago: University of Chicago Press.

Barlow, H. D., and D. Kauzlarich. 2002. *Introduction to Criminology*, 6th ed. Upper Saddle River, NJ: Prentice Hall.

Belluck, P. 1996. "The Youngest Ex-cons: Facing a Difficult Road Out of Crime." *New York Times*. 17 November, pp. 1, 40.

Brown, M. K. 1988. *Working the Street: Police Discretion and Dilemmas of Reform*. New York: Russell Sage.

Califano, J. A. 1998. "A Punishment-only Prison Policy." *America*. 21 February, pp. 3–6.

Chambliss, W. 1973. "The Saints and the Roughnecks." *Society*, 2, 24–31.

Chambliss, W. J. 2000. *Power, Politics, and Crime*. Boulder, CO: Westview Press.

Cohen, A. K. 1971. *Delinquent Boys*. New York: Free Press.

Conklin, J. E. 2007. *Criminology*, 9th ed. Boston: Pearson/Allyn & Bacon.

*Dunaway, R. G., F. T. Cullen, V. S. Burton, Jr., and T. D. Evans. 2000. "The Myth of Social Class and Crime Revisited: An Examination of Class and Adult Criminality." *Criminology*, 38, 589–632.

Durkheim, É. 1897/1951. *Suicide, a Study in Sociology*. New York: Free Press.

Duster, T. 2003. "In Memoriam: Dorothy Nelkin." July-August. *Hastings Center Report*, p. 20.

*Federal Bureau of Investigation, Uniform Crime Reports. 2013a. "Crime in the United States, 2012: Arrest Data." Retrieved 30 March 2015 (http://www.fbi.gov/about-us/cjis/ucr/crime-in-the-u.s/2012/crime-in-the-u.s.-2012/persons-arrested/persons-arrested).

*Federal Bureau of Investigation, Uniform Crime Reports. 2013b. "Crime in the United States, 2012: Expanded Homicide Data." Fall. Retrieved 25 March 2015 (www.fbi.gov/about-us/cjis/ucr/crime-in-the-u.s/2012/crime-in-the-u.s.-2012/offenses-known-to-law-enforcement/expanded-homicide/expandhomicidemain.pdf).

*Federal Bureau of Investigation, Uniform Crime Reports. 2014a. "2013 Hate Crime Statistics: Incidents and Offenses." Retrieved 29 March 2015 (www.fbi.gov/about-us/cjis/ucr/hate-crime/2013/topic-pages/incidents-and-offenses/incidentsandoffenses_final).

*Federal Bureau of Investigation, Uniform Crime Reports. 2014b. "Crime in the United States 2013: Property Crime." Retrieved 21 March 2015 (www.fbi.gov/about-us/cjis/ucr/crime-in-the-u.s/2013/crime-in-the-u.s.-2013/property-crime/property-crime-topic-page/propertycrimemain_final).

*Federal Bureau of Investigation, Uniform Crime Reports. 2014c. "Crime in the United States 2013: Violent Crime." Retrieved 21 March 2015 (www.fbi.gov/

about-us/cjis/ucr/crime-in-the-u.s/2013/crime-in-the-u.s.-2013/violent-crime/violent-crime-topic-page/violentcrimemain_final).

*Federal Bureau of Investigation. 2015. "Hate Crime Data Collection Guidelines and Training Manual, Version 2.0." Law Enforcement Support Section, Crime Statistics Management Unit. 27 February. Retrieved 29 March 2015 (www.fbi.gov/about-us/cjis/ucr/hate-crime-data-collection-guidelines-and-training-manual.pdf).

*Gallup. 2014. "Crime." Retrieved 26 March 2015 (www.gallup.com/poll/1603/crime.aspx).

Gardner, A. M. 2005. "Boot Camp: No Pain, No Gain." *New York Times Style Magazine*. 15 May, p. 70.

Garland, D. 2005. "Cruel and Unusual: Punishment and U.S. Culture." *Social and Legal Studies*, 14, 299–302.

*Garrett, B. L. 2014. *Too Big to Jail: How Prosecutors Compromise with Corporations*. Cambridge, MA: Harvard University Press.

*Harrell, E. 2012. "Violent Victimization Committed by Strangers, 1993–2010." Bureau of Justice Statistics, Office of Justice Programs. 11 December. Retrieved 25 March 2015 (www.bjs.gov/index.cfm?ty=pbdetail&iid=4557).

*Human Rights Watch, 2011. *He Loves You, He Beats You: Family Violence in Turkey and Access to Protection*. Retrieved 29 March 2015 (http://www.hrw.org/node/98418).

*Human Rights Watch, 2013. *Rape Victims as Criminals: Illegal Abortion After Rape in Ecuador*. Retrieved 29 March 2015 (http://www.hrw.org/sites/default/files/reports/ecuador0813_ForUpload_1.pdf).

*Human Rights Watch, 2014a. *Here Rape is Normal: A Five Point Plan to Curtail Rape in Somalia*. Retrieved 29 March 2015 (http://www.hrw.org/sites/default/files/reports/somalia0214_ForUpload.pdf).

*Human Rights Watch, 2014b. "Malawi: End Widespread Child Marriages." Retrieved 29 March 2015 (http://www.hrw.org/news/2014/03/06/malawi-end-widespread-child-marriage).

*Human Rights Watch, 2014c. *Written Statement of Amanda Klasing, Women's Rights Researcher, Human Rights Watch, to U.S. Senate Foreign Relations Subcommittee on International Operations and Organizations, Human Rights, Democracy, and Global Women's Issues*. Retrieved 29 March 2015 (http://www.hrw.org/news/2014/06/24/written-statement-amanda-klasing-women-s-rights-researcher-human-rights-watch-us-sen).

Jacobs, M. D. 1990. *Screwing the System and Making It Work*. Chicago: University of Chicago Press.

Janowitz, M. 1978. *The Last Half Century: Societal Change and Politics in America*. Chicago: University of Chicago Press.

Kobrin, S. 1959. "The Chicago Area Project—A 25-Year Assessment." *Annals of the American Academy of Political and Social Sciences*, 322, 20–29.

*Kristof, N. D., and S. WuDunn. 2009. *Half the Sky: Turning Oppression into Opportunity for Women Worldwide*. New York: Knopf.

*Kristof, N. D., and S. WuDunn. 2014. *A Path Appears: Transforming Lives, Creating Opportunity*. New York: Random House.

*Lee, H., M. S. Vaughn, and H. Lim. 2014. "The Impact of Neighborhood Crime Levels on Police Use of Force: An Examination at Micro and Meso Levels." *Journal of Criminal Justice*, 42, 491–99.

Martinson, R. 1972. "Planning for Public Safety." *New Republic*. 29 April, pp. 21–23.

*Matulich, S., and D. M. Currie, eds. 2008. *Handbook of Frauds, Scams, and Swindles: Failures of Ethics in Leadership*. Boca Raton, FL: CRC Press.

Merton, R. K. 1968. *Social Theory and Social Structure*, 3rd ed. New York: Free Press.

*Miller, W. B. 2001. *The Growth of Youth Gang Problems in the United States: 1970–98: Report*. Darby, PA: Diane Pub Co.

*National Institute of Justice. 2010. "Rape and Sexual Violence: Victims and Perpetrators." 26 October. Retrieved 25 March 2015 (www.nij.gov/topics/crime/rape-sexual-violence/Pages/victims-perpetrators.aspx).

Nelkin, D. 1995. "Biology Is not Destiny." *New York Times*. 28 September, p. A27.

*Pew Research Center. 2014. "Growing Public Support for Gun Rights." 10 December. Retrieved 26 March 2015 (www.people-press.org/2014/12/10/growing-public-support-for-gun-rights/).

*Pew Research Center/USA Today Survey. 2014. "Sharp Racial Divisions in Reactions to Brown, Garner Decisions." 8 December. Retrieved 26 March 2015 (www.people-press.org/2014/12/08/sharp-racial-divisions-in-reactions-to-brown-garner-decisions/).

Quinney, R. 1979. *Criminology*, 2nd ed. Boston: Little, Brown.

Radzinowicz, L. R., and J. King. 1977. *The Growth of Crime: The International Experience*. New York: Basic Books.

Reiss, A. J., Jr., and J. A. Roth, eds. 1993. *Understanding and Preventing Violence*. Washington, DC: National Academy of Sciences Press.

Salinger, L. M., ed. 2004. *Encyclopedia of White Collar and Corporate Crime*. Thousand Oaks, CA: Sage.

Sanchez-Jankowski, M. 2008. *Cracks in the Pavement: Social Change and Resilience in Poor Neighborhoods*. Berkeley: University of California Press.

Schmalleger, F. 2000. *Criminal Justice Today*. Upper Saddle River, NJ: Prentice Hall.

Snyder, H. W., and M. Sickmund. 2006. *Juvenile Offenders and Victims: 2006 National Report*. Washington, DC: U.S. Department of Justice.

*Stewart, J. B. 2015. "In Corporate Crimes, Individual Accountability is Elusive." February 19. *New York Times*. Retrieved 29 March 2015 (http://nyti.ms/1zRG1BJ).

Sutherland, E. H., and D. R. Cressey. 1960. *Principles of Criminology*. Philadelphia: Lippincott.

Suttles, G. 1970. *The Social Order of the Slum*. Chicago: University of Chicago Press.

*Territo, L., and G. Kirkham, eds. 2010. *International Sex Trafficking of Women & Children*. Flushing, NY: Looseleaf Law.

*Truman, J. L., and L. Langton. 2014. "Criminal Victimization, 2013." NCJ 247648. Bureau of Justice Statistics, U.S. Department of Justice. September. Retrieved 21 March 2015 (www.bjs.gov/content/pub/pdf/cv13.pdf).

*United Nations Office on Drugs and Crime. 2013. "Homicide Counts and Rates, Time Series 2000–2012." Global Study on Homicide. Retrieved 25 March 2015 (www.unodc.org/gsh/en/data.html).

*United Nations Population Fund. 2013. "Addressing Gender-Based Violence." Retrieved 29 March 2015 (www.unfpa.org/resources/addressing-gender-based-violence).

*UN Women, 2015. "In Focus CSW59: Implementing the Beijing Platform for Action." Retrieved 29 March 2015 (http://www.unwomen.org/en/news/in-focus/csw).

*U.S. Census Bureau. 2006. *Statistical Abstract of the United States*. Washington, DC.

*U.S. Department of State, 2014. *Trafficking in Persons Report, June 2014.* Retrieved 29 March 2015. (http://www.state.gov/documents/organization/226844.pdf).

*Violence Policy Center. 2015. "States with Weak Gun Laws and Higher Gun Ownership Lead Nation in Gun Deaths, New Data for 2013 Confirms." Retrieved 25 March 2015 (www.vpc.org/press/1501gundeath.htm).

von Lampe, K. 2009. "Trends in Organized Crime." *Recent Publications on Organized Crime*, pp. 208–10. June.

Wacquant, L. 2003. "Toward a Dictatorship Over the Poor?" *Punishment and Society*, 5, 197–205.

*Walker-Rodriguez, A., and R. Hill. 2011. "Human Sex Trafficking." FBI Law Enforcement Bulletin. March. Retrieved 14 May 2013 (http://leb.fbi.gov/2011/march/human-sex-trafficking).

Wilkinson, R., and K. Pickett. 2010. *The Spirit Level: Why Greater Equality Makes Society Stronger.* New York: Bloomsbury Press.

Wilson, J. Q. 1977. *Thinking About Crime.* New York: Vintage Books.

Wilson, J. Q. 1993. *The Moral Sense.* New York: Basic Books.

*Wilson, J. Q., and R. J. Herrnstein. 1985. *Crime and Human Nature.* New York: Simon & Schuster.

Wilson, W. J. 1996. *When Work Disappears: The World of the New Urban Poor.* Chicago: University of Chicago Press.

Chapter 6

*Administration for Children and Families, Office of Family Assistance. 2015. "TANF Caseload Data 2014." U.S. Department of Health & Human Services. 5 February. Retrieved 15 March 2015 (www.acf.hhs.gov/programs/ofa/resource/caseload-data-2014).

*Avert. 2015. "Children Orphaned by HIV and AIDS." Retrieved 6 March 2015 (http://www.avert.org/children-orphaned-hiv-and-aids.htm).

*Bean, J. A. 2011. "Reliance on Supplemental Nutrition Assistance Program Continued to Rise Post-Recession." Issue Brief No. 39. Durham, NH: Carsey Institute, University of New Hampshire.

*Bloom, B., L. I. Jones, and G. Freeman. 2013. "Summary Health Statistics for U.S. Children: National Health Interview Survey, 2012." National Center for Health Statistics. *Vital Health Stat*, 10, 258.

Blumberg, D. 1980. *Inequality in an Age of Decline.* New York: Oxford University Press.

*Bolen, E. 2015. "Who Are the People Who Will Lose SNAP Next Year?" Off the Charts Blog: Center on Budget and Policy Priorities. 13 January. Retrieved 17 March 2015 (www.offthechartsblog.org/who-are-the-people-who-will-lose-snap-next-year/).

Briggs, X. de S., S. J. Popkin, and J. Goering. 2010. *Moving to Opportunity: The Story of an American Experiment to Fight Ghetto Poverty.* Oxford and New York: Oxford University Press.

*Brooks-Gunn, J., and G. J. Duncan. 1997. "The Effects of Poverty on Children." *The Future of Children (Children and Poverty)*, 7, 55–71.

*Browning, E. K. 2008. *Stealing from Each Other: How the Welfare State Robs Americans of Money and Spirit.* New York: Praeger Publishers.

*Bureau of Labor Statistics. 2014. "A Profile of the Working Poor, 2012." BLS Report 1047. March. Retrieved 17 March 2015 (www.bls.gov/cps/cpswp2012.pdf).

*Bureau of Labor Statistics. 2015a. "Characteristics of Minimum Wage Workers, 2014." Retrieved 8 July 2015 (http://www.bls.gov/opub/reports/cps/characteristics-of-minimum-wage-workers-2014.pdf)

*Bureau of Labor Statistics. 2015b. "Unemployment Rate Falls From May to June." Retrieved 8 July 2015 (http://www.bls.gov/opub/ted/2015/unemployment-rate-falls-from-may-to-june-2015.htm).

*Burgard, S. A., and M. M. King. 2014. "National Report Card: Health Inequality." Stanford Center on Poverty and Inequality. January.

*Cancian, M., K. S. Slack, and M. Y. Yang. 2010. "The Effect of Family Income on Risk of Child Maltreatment." Discussion Paper No. 1385-10. August. Madison, WI: Institute for Research on Poverty.

*Centers for Disease Control and Prevention. 2015. "Child Maltreatment Prevention." Retrieved 5 March 2015 (http://www.cdc.gov/violenceprevention/childmaltreatment).

*ChildCare Aware of America. 2014. "Parents and the High Cost of Child Care, 2014." no. 47810-1672-0001. Retrieved 20 March 2015 (cca.worksmartsuite.com/UserContentStart.aspx?category=25).

*Children's Defense Fund. 2005. "Defining Poverty and Why It Matters for Children." Retrieved 6 July 2007 (www.childrensdefensefund.org).

*Children's Defense Fund. 2014. "Progress on Child and Teen Gun Deaths Has Stalled." Retrieved 5 March 2015. (http://www.childrensdefense.org/library/data/2014-gun-report-fact-sheet.pdf).

Clampet-Lundquist, S., K. Edin, J. R. Kling, and G. J. Duncan. 2006. "Moving At-Risk Teenagers Out of High-Risk Neighborhoods: Why Girls Fare Better Than Boys." Working Paper no. 509, Industrial Relations Section, Princeton University.

*Coleman-Jensen, A., C. Gregory, and A. Singh. 2014. "Household Food Security in the United States in 2013." ERR-173. September. Washington, DC: U.S. Department of Agriculture, Economic Research Service.

*Conger, R. D., and K. J. Conger. 2008. "Understanding the Processes Through Which Economic Hardship Influences Families and Children." In *Handbook of Families and Poverty*, edited by D. R. Crane and T. B. Heaton, 64–81. Thousand Oaks, CA: Sage Publications.

Crosnoe, R., T. Leventhal, R. J. Wirth, K. M. Pierce, R. C. Pianta, and NICHD Early Child Care Research Network. 2010. "Family Socioeconomic Status and Consistent Environmental Stimulation in Early Childhood." *Child Development*, 81, 972–87.

*Dean, S., and D. Rosenbaum. 2014. "SNAP Benefits Will Be Cut for Nearly All Participants in November 2013." Center on Budget and Policy Priorities. 9 January. Retrieved 27 February 2014 (www.cbpp.org/cms/?fa=view&id=3899).

*DeNavas-Walt, C., and B. D. Proctor. 2015. "Income and Poverty in the United States: 2014." Current Population Reports, P60-252. Washington, DC: U.S. Census Bureau.

*Domhoff, G. W. 2013. *Who Rules America: Power, Politics, and Social Change.* 7th ed. New York: McGraw-Hill.

*Edin, K., and M. Kefalas. 2005. *Promises I Can Keep: Why Poor Women Put Motherhood Before Marriage.* Berkeley, CA: University of California Press.

*Ermisch, J., M. Jäntti, T. Smeeding, and J. Wilson. 2012. "Thinking about Cross-National Research on the Intergenerational Transmission of Advantage." In *From*

Parents to Children: The Intergenerational Transmission of Advantage, edited by J. Ermisch, M. Jäntti, and T. Smeeding, Chapter 1. New York: Russell Sage Foundation.

*Federal Interagency Forum on Child and Family Statistics. 2014. "At A Glance: America's Children: Key National Indicators of Well-Being." Washington, DC: U.S. Government Printing Office. Retrieved 20 March 2015 (http://www.childstats.gov/pdf/ac2014/ac_14.pdf).

*Fry, R., and P. Taylor. 2013. "A Rise in Wealth for the Wealthy; Declines for the Lower 93%: An Uneven Recovery, 2009–2011." Pew Research Center. 23 April. Retrieved 3 February 2015 (www.pewsocialtrends.org/2013/04/23/a-rise-in-wealth-for-the-wealthydeclines-for-the-lower-93/).

Galbraith, J. K. 1958. *The Affluent Society*. Boston: Houghton Mifflin.

*Gans, H. J. 1995. *The War Against the Poor: The Underclass and Antipoverty Policy*. New York: Basic Books.

Gilbert, D., and J. A. Kahl. 1993. *The American Class Structure: A New Synthesis*. 4th ed. Belmont, CA: Wadsworth.

*Grall, T. S. 2013. "Custodial Mothers and Fathers and Their Child Support: 2011." Current Population Reports, 60–246. October. Washington, DC: U.S. Census Bureau.

*International Monetary Fund World Economic Outlook Database. 2014. "Public Data: GDP Per Capita, Current Prices." October. Retrieved 1 March 2015 (www.google.com/publicdata/explore?ds=k3s92bru78li6_#!ctype=l&strail=false&bcs=d&nselm=h&met_y=ngdpdpc&scale_y=lin&ind_y=false&rdim=world&idim=world:Earth&ifdim=world&hl=en_US&dl=en_US&ind=false).

Jackman, M. R., and R. W. Jackman. 1983. *Class Awareness in the United States*. Berkeley: University of California Press.

*Jansson, B. S. 2012. *The Reluctant Welfare State: A History of American Social Welfare Policies*. 7th ed. Boston: Cengage Learning.

*Jusko, K., and K. Weisshaar. 2014. "National Report Card: Safety Net." Stanford Center on Poverty and Inequality. January.

*Kaplan, T. 2002. "TANF Programs in Nine States: Incentives, Assistance, and Obligation." *Focus*, 22, 36–41.

*Kroll, L., and K. A. Dolan. 2013. "The Richest People on the Planet 2013." Forbes.com. Retrieved 16 February 2014 (www.forbes.com/billionaires/).

*Laughlin, L. 2013. "Who's Minding the Kids? Child Care Arrangements: Spring 2011." Household Economic Studies, 70–135. April. Washington, DC: U.S. Census Bureau.

Lewis, O. 1968. *The Study of Slum Cultures—Backgrounds for La Vida*. New York: Random House.

*Li, J., S. Johnson, W-J. Han, S. Andrews, G. Kendall, L. Stradzins, and A. M. Dockery. 2012. "Parents' Nonstandard Work and Child Wellbeing: A Critical Review of the Existing Literature." CLMR Discussion Paper Series 2012/02. February. Perth, Australia: Centre for Labour Market Research.

Lister, R. 2004. *Poverty*. Malden, MA: Policy.

Ludwig, J., and J. R. Kling. 2006. "Is Crime Contagious?" NBER Working Paper no. 12409. August. National Bureau of Economic Research.

*ManpowerGroup. 2015. "About ManpowerGroup." Retrieved 1 March 2015 (http://www.manpowergroup.com/wps/wcm/connect/manpowergroup-en/home/#.VQj1vWTF-Q5).

*Marlar, J. 2010. "Worry, Sadness, Stress Increase with Length of Unemployment." Gallup. 8 June. Retrieved 1 March 2015 (www.gallup.com/poll/139604/worry-sadness-stress-increase-length-unemployment.aspx).

Massey, D. S., and N. A. Denton. 1993. "American Apartheid: Segregation and the Making of the Underclass." *City and Community*, 3, 221–41.

*McClam, E. 2013. "Americans Blame Poverty on 'Too Much' Welfare, NBC/WSJ Poll Shows." thegrio.com. 6 June. Retrieved 1 March 2015 (thegrio.com/2013/06/06/americans-blame-poverty-on-too-much-welfare-nbcwsj-poll-shows/).

*Motel, S., and E. Patten. 2013. "Statistical Portrait of Hispanics in the United States, 2011." Pew Hispanic Center. 15 February. Retrieved 3 March 2013 (www.pewhispanic.org/2013/02/15/statistical-portrait-of-hispanics-in-the-united-states-2011/).

*Murray, C. 1984. *Losing Ground: American Social Policy, 1950–1980*. New York: Basic Books.

*National Opinion Research Center. 2009. "Mnemonic Index." Retrieved 24 June 2009 (www.norc.org/GSS+ Website/Browse+GSS+Variables/Mnemonic+Index/).

*Patel, T. 2014. "SeaTac's $15 Minimum Wage Goes Into Effect." Q13Fox.com. 1 January. Retrieved 26 February 2014 (q13fox.com/2014/01/01/seatacs-15-minimum-wage-goes-into-effect/#axzz2urAWgN2Q).

*Pew Research Center. 2013. "The Rise of Asian Americans." 4 April. Retrieved 8 March 2015 (http://www.pewsocialtrends.org/files/2013/04/Asian-Americans-new-full-report-04-2013.pdf).

*Pew Research Center. 2014. "Most See Inequality Growing, but Partisans Differ over Solutions." 23 January. Retrieved 1 March 2015 (www.people-press.org/files/legacy-pdf/1-23-14%20Poverty_Inequality%20Release.pdf).

*Pew Research Center for People and the Press. 2012. "Partisan Polarization Surges in Bush, Obama Years: Trends in American Values: 1987–2012." 4 June. Retrieved 1 March 2015 (www.people-press.org/2012/06/04/partisan-polarization-surges-in-bush-obama-years/).

*Reardon, S. F. 2014. "National Report Card: Education." Stanford Center on Poverty and Inequality. January.

Reich, R. B. 1998. "Broken Faith: Why We Need to Renew the Social Compact." *Generations*. Winter, 19.

Riesman, D., N. Glazer, and R. Denney. 1950. *The Lonely Crowd*. New Haven, CT: Yale University Press.

*Sauter, M. B., A. E. M. Hess, and T. C. Froelich. 2013. "America's Richest (and Poorest) States." 247wallst.com. 19 September. Retrieved 1 March 2015 (247wallst.com/special-report/2013/09/19/americas-richest-and-poorest-states/).

*Scaramella, L. V., T. K. Neppl, L. L. Ontai, and R. D. Conger. 2008. "Consequences of Socioeconomic Disadvantage Across Three Generations." *Journal of Family Psychology*, 22, 725–33.

*Schott, L., and L. Pavetti. 2011. "Many States Cutting TANF Benefits Harshly Despite High Unemployment and Unprecedented Need." Center on Budget and Policy Priorities. 3 October. Retrieved 1 March 2015 (www.cbpp.org/cms/index.cfm?fa=view&id=3498).

*Seccombe, Karen. 2007. *Families in Poverty*. Boston: Allyn & Bacon.

*Seccombe, Karen. 2015. *So You Think I Drive a Cadillac?: Welfare Recipients' Perspectives on the System and Its Reform*. 4th ed. Boston: Pearson.

*Seccombe, K., and K. A. Hoffman. 2007. *Just Don't Get Sick: Access to Health Care in the Aftermath of Welfare Reform.* Piscataway, NJ: Rutgers University Press.

*Shaefer, H. L., and K. Edin. 2012. "Extreme Poverty in the United States, 1996 to 2011." February. National Poverty Center Policy Brief no. 28.

*Sherter, A. 2013. "Millions on Food Stamps Facing Benefits Cuts." cbs.com/moneywatch. 3 November. Retrieved 1 March 2015 (www.cbsnews.com/news/millions-on-food-stamps-facing-benefits-cuts/).

*Siebens, J. 2013. "Extended Measures of Well-Being: Living Conditions in the United States: 2011." Household Economic Studies, 70–136. September. Washington, DC: U.S. Census Bureau.

*Stein, R. 2010. "Study Finds That Effects of Low-Quality Child Care Last Into Adolescence." washingtonpost.com. 14 May. Retrieved 1 March 2015 (www.washingtonpost.com/wp-dyn/content/article/2010/05/14/AR2010051400043.html).

*Strong-Jekely, L. 2006. Letter to the Editor. *Brain, Child*, 2. Budapest, Hungary, Winter.

*Swedberg, R. 2007. *Principles of Economic Sociology.* Princeton, NJ: Princeton University.

*Tax Policy Center. 2013. "Tax Facts: Corporate Income Taxes as a Percent of GDP, 1946–2012." Retrieved 15 March 2015 (www.taxpolicycenter.org/taxfacts/displayafact.cfm?Docid=263).

*Thompson, J., and T. Smeeding. 2014. "National Report Card: Income Inequality." Stanford Center on Poverty and Inequality. January.

*Trisi, D., and L. Pavetti. 2012. "TANF Weakening as a Safety Net For Poor Families." Center for Budget and Policy Priorities. 13 March. Retrieved 1 March 2015 (www.cbpp.org/cms/?fa=view&id=3700).

Turney, K., S. Clampet-Lundquist, K. Edin, J. R. Kling, and G. J. Duncan. 2006. "Neighborhood Effects on Barriers to Employment: Results from a Randomized Housing Mobility Experiment in Baltimore." Working Paper no. 511. April. Industrial Relations Section, Princeton University.

*U.S. Census Bureau. 2015. "Educational Attainment in the United States: 2014—Detailed Tables." 5 January. Retrieved 15 February 2015. (www.census.gov/hhes/socdemo/education/data/cps/2014/tables.html).

*U.S. Conference of Mayors. 2015. "Hunger and Homelessness Survey: A Status Report on Hunger and Homelessness in America's Cities: A 25-City Survey." Retrieved 8 July 2015 (http://www.usmayors.org/pressreleases/uploads/2014/1211-report-hh.pdf)

*U.S. Department of Housing and Urban Development. 2015. "Final FY 2015 Fair Market Rent Documentation System." Retrieved 8 July 2015 (http://www.huduser.org/portal/datasets/fmr/fmrs/docsys.html&data=fmr15).

*UNICEF Innocenti Research Centre. 2013. "Child Well-Being in Rich Countries: A Comparative Overview." Report Card 11. April. Retrieved 26 February 2014 (www.unicef-irc.org/publications/pdf/rc11_eng.pdf).

*United Nations Children's Fund and UNAIDS. 2006. "Africa's Orphaned and Vulnerable Generations: Children Affected by AIDS." Retrieved 1 March 2015 (www.unicef.org/publications/files/Africas_Orphaned_and_Vulnerable_Generations_Children_Affected_by_AIDS.pdf).

*United Nations Children's Fund and UNAIDS. 2014. Homepage. Retrieved 2 March 2015 (http://www.childrenandaids.org/).

*U.S. Department of Agriculture, Food and Nutrition Service, Office of Policy Support. 2014. "Supplemental Nutrition Assistance Program Participation Rates: Fiscal Years 2010 and 2011." February.

*U.S. Department of Agriculture, Economic Research Service. 2013. "Rural America At A Glance: 2013 Edition." Economic Brief No. 24. November. Retrieved 27 February 2014 (www.ers.usda.gov/publications/eb-economic-brief/eb24.aspx).

*White, L., and S. J. Rogers. 2000. "Economic Circumstances and Family Outcomes: A Review of 1990's." *Journal of Marriage and Family*, 62, 1035–51.

*Wilkenfeld, B., K. A. Moore, and L. Lippman. 2008. "Neighborhood Support and Children's Connectedness" (Child Trends Fact Sheet). Baltimore, MD: The Annie E. Casey Foundation.

*Williams, G. 2013. "The Heavy Price of Losing Weight." USNews.com. 2 January. Retrieved 1 March 2015 (money.usnews.com/money/personal-finance/articles/2013/01/02/the-heavy-price-of-losing-weight).

*Wilson, W. J. 1987. *The Truly Disadvantaged: The Inner City, the Underclass, and Public Policy.* Chicago: University of Chicago Press.

*Wolff, E. N. 2014. "National Report Card: Wealth Inequality." Stanford Center on Poverty and Inequality. January.

*World Bank. 2014. "Voice and Agency: Empowering Women and Girls for Shared Prosperity." Retrieved 9 October 2014 (www.worldbank.org/en/topic/gender/publication/voice-and-agency-empowering-women-and-girls-for-shared-prosperity).

*Yeung, W. J., M. R. Linver, and J. Brooks-Gunn. 2002. "How Money Matters for Young Children's Development: Parental Investment and Family Processes." *Child Development*, 73, 1861–79.

Chapter 7

*Badger, E. 2014. "The Rapid Demographic Shift of American Public Schools." Washingtonpost.com. 18 August. Retrieved 15 March 2015 (www.washingtonpost.com/blogs/wonkblog/wp/2014/08/18/the-rapid-demographic-shift-of-american-public-schools/).

*Beckett, K., and H. Evans. 2014. "The Role of Race in Washington State Capital Sentencing, 1981-2014." Law, Societies, & Justice Program. University of Washington. Retrieved 3 March 2015 (lsj.washington.edu/sites/lsj/files/research/capital_punishment_beckette-vans_10-1.6.14.pdf).

Bozorgmehr, M., and A. Bakalian. 2009. *Backlash 9/11: Middle Eastern and Muslim Americans Respond.* Los Angeles: University of California Press.

*Bureau of Labor Statistics. 2007. "Access to Historical Data for the Tables of the Union Membership News Release." Labor Force Statistics from the Current Population Survey. 21 June. Retrieved 3 March 2015 (www.bls.gov/cps/cpslutabs.htm).

*Bureau of Labor Statistics. 2015. "Union Members—2014." Economic News Release. 23 January. Retrieved 24 February 2015 (www.bls.gov/news.release/union2.nr0.htm).

*Butler, D. M., and D. E. Brockman. 2011. "Do Politicians Racially Discriminate Against Constituents? A Field Experiment on State Legislators." *American Journal of Political Science*, 55, 463–77.

*Colby, S. L., and J. M. Ortman. 2015. "Projections of the Size and Composition of the U.S. Population: 2014 to 2060:

Population Estimates and Projections." Current Population Reports, 25–1143. March. U.S. Census Bureau. Retrieved 9 March 2015 (www.census.gov/content/dam/Census/library/publications/2015/demo/p25-1143.pdf).

*Coles, R. 2003 *Children of Crisis*. New York: Back Bay Books.

Conley, D. 1999. *Being Black, Living in the Red: Race, Wealth and Social Policy in America*. Berkeley: University of California Press.

*Death Penalty Information Center. 2015. "Facts About the Death Penalty." 11 February. Retrieved 3 March 2015 (www.deathpenaltyinfo.org/documents/FactSheet.pdf).

*DeNavas-Walt, C., and B. D. Proctor. 2015. "Income and Poverty in the United States: 2014." Current Population Reports, P60-252. Washington, DC: U.S. Census Bureau.

*Doleac, J. L., and L. C. D. Stein. 2013. "The Visible Hand: Race and Online Market Outcomes." *The Economic Journal*, 123, F469–92.

*Drake, B. 2014. "Public Strongly Backs Affirmative Action Programs on Campus." Pew Research Center. 22 April. Retrieved 3 March 2015 (www.pewresearch.org/fact-tank/2014/04/22/public-strongly-backs-affirmative-action-programs-on-campus/).

Eckholm, E. 1995. February 24. "Studies Find Death Penalty Tied to Race of Victims." *New York Times*, pp. B1–4.

*The Economist. 2013. "Affirmative Action: Is Affirmative Action a Good Idea?" 29 June. Retrieved 29 June 2013 (www.economist.com/debate/overview/251).

*Edin, K., and M. Kefalas. 2005. *Promises I Can Keep: Why Poor Women Put Motherhood Before Marriage*. Berkeley: University of California Press.

*Epp, C. R., S. Maynard-Moody, and D. Haider-Harkel. 2014. *Pulled Over: How Police Stops Define Race and Citizenship*. Chicago: University of Chicago Press.

*Feagin, J. 2013. *The White Racial Frame: Centuries of Racial Framing and Counter-Framing*, 2nd ed. New York: Routledge.

*Federal Bureau of Investigation (FBI). 2013. "Expanded Homicide Data Table 6." Crime in the United States 2013: About Crime in the U.S. (CIUS). Retrieved 3 March 2015 (www.fbi.gov/about-us/cjis/ucr/crime-in-the-u.s/2013/crime-in-the-u.s.-2013).

*Gaylord-Harden, N. K., and J. A. Cunningham. 2009. "The Impact of Racial Discrimination and Coping Strategies on Internalizing Symptoms in African American Youth." *Journal of Youth and Adolescence*, 38, 532–43.

*Glink, I. 2012. "U.S. Housing Market Remains Deeply Segregated." CBS Moneywatch. 20 June. Retrieved 3 March 2015 (www.cbsnews.com/news/us-housing-market-remains-deeply-segregated/).

*Kelley, R. 2010. "Why We Still Need Affirmative Action." Newsweek.com. 17 February. Retrieved 3 March 2015 (www.newsweek.com/why-we-still-need-affirmative-action-75297).

*Kena, G., S. Aud, F. Johnson, X. Wang, J. Zhang, A. Rathbun, S. Wilkinson-Flicker, and P. Kristapovich. 2014. "The Condition of Education 2014." NCES 2014-083. U.S. Department of Education, National Center for Education Statistics. Retrieved 15 March 2015 (nces.ed.gov/pubsearch).

*Kwate, N. O., and M. S. Goodman. 2015. "Cross-Sectional and Longitudinal Effects of Racism on Mental Health Among Residents of Black Neighborhoods in New York City." *American Journal of Public Health*, 105, 711–18.

*Lamont, M. 2003. "Who Counts as 'Them?': Racism and Virtue in the United States and France." *Contexts*, 2, 36–41.

*Lempert, R. 2014. "The Schuette Decision: The Supreme Court Rules on Affirmative Action." Brookings Institution. 25 April. Retrieved 3 March 2015 (www.brookings.edu/blogs/fixgov/posts/2014/04/25-schuette-affirmative-action-supreme-court-comment-lempert).

Lieberson, S. 1990. *From Many Strands*, 2nd ed. New York: Russell Sage.

*Logan, J. R. 2011. "Separate and Unequal: The Neighborhood Gap for Blacks, Hispanics, and Asians in Metropolitan America." US2010 Project. Brown University. July. Retrieved 3 March 2015 (www.s4.brown.edu/us2010/Data/Report/report0727.pdf).

MacDonald, H. 2001. "The Myth of Racial Profiling." *City Journal*. Spring.

*Massey, D. S., and J. J. Fischer. 2004. "The Ecology of Racial Discrimination." *City and Community*, 3, 221–24.

*McKernan, S.-M., and C. Ratcliffe. 2013. "The Racial Wealth Gap Was Wide In 1963 And It Remains Large Today." Urban Institute/Metro Trends. 6 August. Retrieved 10 March 2015 (blog.metrotrends.org/2013/08/racial-wealth-gap-wide-1963-remains-large-today/).

*McKernan, S.-M., C. Ratcliffe, E. Simms, and S. Zhang. 2013. "Less Than Equal: Racial Disparities in Wealth Accumulation." Urban Institute. April. Retrieved 10 March 2015 (www.urban.org/UploadedPDF/412802-Less-Than-Equal-Racial-Disparities-in-Wealth-Accumulation.pdf).

Merton, R. K. 1949. *Social Theory and Social Structure*. New York: Free Press.

*Milkman, K. L., M. Akinola, and D. Chugh. 2014. "What Happens Before? A Field Experiment Exploring How Pay and Representation Differentially Shape Bias on the Pathway into Organizations." Social Science Research Network. 13 December. Retrieved 12 March 2015 (papers.ssrn.com/sol3/papers.cfm?abstract_id=2063742).

National Advisory Commission on Civil Disorders. 1968. *Report of the National Advisory Commission on Civil Disorders*. Washington, DC: U.S. Government Printing Office.

*National Association for the Advancement of Colored People (NAACP). 2015. "Criminal Justice Fact Sheet." Retrieved 3 March 2015 (www.naacp.org/pages/criminal-justice-fact-sheet).

*National Association of School Psychologists. 2012. "Racism, Prejudice, and Discrimination." Position Statement. Retrieved 15 March 2015 (www.nasponline.org/about_nasp/positionpapers/RacismPrejudice.pdf).

*National Center for Education Statistics. 2013. "Median annual earnings of full-time year-round workers 25 to 34 years old and full-time year-round workers as a percentage of the labor force, by sex, race/ethnicity, and educational attainment: Selected years, 1995 through 2012." Table 502.30. Digest of Education Statistics. October. Retrieved 9 March 2015 (nces.ed.gov/programs/digest/d13/tables/dt13_502.30.asp).

*National Center for Education Statistics. 2014. "Rates of high school completion and bachelor's degree attainment among persons age 25 and over, by race/ethnicity and sex: Selected years, 1910 through 2013." Table 104-10. Digest of Education Statistics. February. Retrieved 15 March 2015 (nces.ed.gov/programs/digest/d13/tables/dt13_104.10.asp).

*National Conference of State Legislatures. 2014. "Affirmative Action: Overview." 7 February. Retrieved 15 March 2015 (www.ncsl.org/research/education/affirmative-action-overview.aspx).

Newport, F. 2008. "Americans See Obama Election as Race Relations Milestone." Gallup.com. 7 November. Retrieved 15 March 2015 (www.gallup.com/poll/111817/americans-see-obama-election-race-relations-milestone.aspx).

*Newport, F. 2013. "In U.S. 87 Percent Approve of Black-White Marriage, As Opposed to 4 Percent in 1958." Gallup.com. 25 July. Retrieved 8 April 2015 (http://www.gallup.com/poll/163697/approve-marriage-blacks-whites.aspx).

Ore, T. E. 2006. *The Social Construction of Difference and Inequality: Race, Class, Gender, and Sexuality*, 3rd ed. Boston: McGraw-Hill.

*Orfield, G., E. Frankenberg, J. Ee, and J. Kuscera. 2014. "Brown at 60: Great Progress, a Long Retreat and an Uncertain Future." The Civil Rights Project. 15 May. Retrieved 9 March 2015 (civilrightsproject.ucla.edu/research/k-12-education/integration-and-diversity/brown-at-60-great-progress-a-long-retreat-and-an-uncertain-future/Brown-at-60-051814.pdf).

*Pager, D., B. Western, and B. Bonikowski. 2009. "Discrimination in a Low-Wage Labor Market: A Field Experiment." *American Sociological Review*, 74, 777–99.

*Parrillo, V. N. 2016. *Understanding Race and Ethnic Relations*, 5th ed. Boston: Pearson.

*Pierce, G. L., and M. L. Radelet. 2005. "Impact of Legally Inappropriate Factors on Death Sentencing for California Homicides, 1990–1999, The Empirical Analysis." 46 *Santa Clara Law Review* 1. 1 January. Retrieved 3 March 2015 (digitalcommons.law.scu.edu/cgi/viewcontent.cgi?article=1174&context=lawreview).

*Pierce, G. L., and M. Radelet. 2011. "Death Sentencing in East Baton Rouge Parish, 1990–2008." *Louisiana Law Review*, 71, 647–73.

*Pew Research Center. 2013. "King's Dream Remains an Elusive Goal; Many Americans See Racial Disparities." Social & Demographic Trends. 22 August. Retrieved 9 March 2015 (www.pewsocialtrends.org/2013/08/22/kings-dream-remains-an-elusive-goal-many-americans-see-racial-disparities/).

Plous, S., ed. 2003. *Understanding Prejudice and Discrimination*. Boston: McGraw-Hill.

*Schaefer, R. T. 2016. *Race and Ethnicity in the United States*, 8th ed. Boston: Pearson.

Sears, D. O., J. Sidanius, and L. Bobo, eds. 2000. *Racialized Politics: The Debate About Racism in America*. Chicago: University of Chicago Press.

*Seccombe, K. 2015. *"So You Think I Drive a Cadillac?" Welfare Recipients' Perspectives on the System and Its Reform*, 4th ed. Boston: Pearson.

*The Sentencing Project. 2013. "Felony Disenfranchisement." Retrieved 10 March 2015 (www.sentencingproject.org/template/page.cfm?id=133).

*The Sentencing Project. 2015. "Black Lives Matter: Eliminating Racial Inequity in the Criminal Justice System." Retrieved 15 March 2015 (sentencingproject.org/doc/publications/rd_Black_Lives_Matter.pdf).

Simpson, G. E., and J. M. Yinger. 1985. *Racial and Ethnic Minorities: An Analysis of Prejudice and Discrimination*, 5th ed. New York: Plenum.

U.S. Commission on Civil Rights, Ohio Advisory Committee. 2001. "Briefing on Civil Rights Issues Facing Muslims and Arab Americans" in Ohio Post–September 11. 14 November.

*U.S. Department of Housing and Urban Development, Office of Policy Development and Research. 2013. "Housing Discrimination Against Racial and Ethnic Minorities 2012." Retrieved 12 March 2015 (www.huduser.org/portal/Publications/pdf/HUD-514_HDS2012.pdf).

*U.S. Equal Employment Opportunity Commission. 2015. "Charge Statistics FY 1997 Through FY 2014." Retrieved 11 March 2015 (eeoc.gov/eeoc/statistics/enforcement/charges.cfm).

*Wang, W. 2012. "Chapter 4: Public Attitudes on Intermarriage." Pew Research Center: Social & Demographic Trends. 16 February. Retrieved 3 March 2015 (www.pewsocialtrends.org/2012/02/16/chapter-4-public-attitudes-on-intermarriage/).

*Watson, E. D. 2014. "Interracial Couples and Marriage More Accepted Among Americans." Huffington Post/Black Voices. 27 January. Retrieved 11 March 2015 (www.huffingtonpost.com/elwood-d-watson/interracial-couples-and-m_b_4663479.html).

*West, C. 1994. *Race Matters*. New York: Vintage.

Chapter 8

*American Bar Association. 2014. "A Current Glance at Women in the Law." July. Retrieved 25 November 2014 (www.americanbar.org/women).

*American Society of Plastic Surgeons. 2015. "News & Resources." Retrieved 12 July 2015 (http://www.plasticsurgery.org/Documents/news-resources/statistics/2014-statistics/plastic-surgery-statistics-full-report.pdf).

*Anderson, D., and M. Hamilton. 2006. "Sex Stereotyping and Under-Representation of Female Characters in 200 Popular Children's Picture Books: A 21st Century Update." *Sex Roles*, 55, 757–65.

*APA Task Force on Gender Identity and Gender Variance. 2008. *Report of the Task Force on Gender Identity and Gender Variance*. Washington, DC: American Psychological Association.

*Association of American Medical Colleges. 2013. *2013 State Physician Workforce Data Book*. Retrieved 6 April 2015 (https://members.aamc.org/eweb/upload/State%20Physician%20Workforce%20Data%20Book%202013%20(PDF).pdf).

*Auster, C. J., and C. S. Mansbach. 2012. "The Gender Marketing of Toys: An Analysis of Color and Type of Toy on the Disney Store Website." *Sex Roles*, 67, 375–88.

*Banaszak, L. A., ed. 2006. *The U.S. Women's Movement in Global Perspective*. Lanham, MD: Rowman and Littlefield.

*Becker, J. B., K. J. Berkley, N. Geary, E. Hampson, J. P. Herman, and E. A. Young, eds. 2008. *Sex Differences in the Brain: From Genes to Behavior*. New York: Oxford University Press.

*Bernard, J. 1987. *The Female World from a Global Perspective*. Bloomington, Indiana: Indiana University Press.

*Biddulph, S., and P. Stanish. 2008. *Raising Boys: Why Boys Are Different—and How to Help Them Become Happy and Well-Balanced Men*. Berkeley, CA: Celestial Arts.

*Black, M. C., K. C. Basile, M. J. Breiding, S. G. Smith, M. L. Walters, M. T. Merrick, J. Chen, and M. R. Stevens. 2011. "The National Intimate Partner and Sexual Violence Survey (NISVS)": 2010 Summary Report. Atlanta, GA: National Center for Injury Prevention and Control, Centers for Disease Control and Prevention.

*Bureau of Labor Statistics. 2012. "Wives Who Earn More Than Their Husbands, 1987–2011." Labor Force Statistics from the Current Population Survey. 20 November. Retrieved 24 June 2013 (www.bls.gov/cps/wives_earn_more.htm).

*Bureau of Labor Statistics. 2013a. "Women in the Labor Force: A Databook." Report 1040. *BLS Reports.* February. Retrieved 24 June 2013 (www.bls.gov/cps/wlf-databook2013.htm).

*Bureau of Labor Statistics. 2013b. "Employment Characteristics of Families Summary." Economic News Release. 26 April. Retrieved 24 June 2013 (www.bls.gov/news.release/famee.nr0.htm).

*Bureau of Labor Statistics. 2014. "Women in the Labor Force: A Databook." BLS Report 1049. May. Retrieved 25 November 2014 (www.bls.gov/cps/wlf-databook-2013.pdf).

*Bureau of Labor Statistics. 2015. "Usual Weekly Earnings of Wage and Salary Workers First Quarter 2015." News Release. 21 April. Retrieved 9 July 2015 (http://www.bls.gov/news.release/pdf/wkyeng.pdf).

Carbine, R. P. 2010. "From the Pews in the Back: Young Women and Catholicism." *Theological Studies*, 71, 497.

*Centers for Disease Control and Prevention. 2012. "Sexual Violence: Facts at a Glance." National Center for Injury Prevention and Control, Division of Violence Prevention.

Chancer, L. S. 2005. *High-Profile Crimes: When Legal Cases Become Social Causes.* Chicago: University of Chicago Press.

*Colwell, E. W., and M. Lindsey. 2005. "Preschool Children's Pretend and Physical Play and Sex of Peer Play Partner." *Sex Roles*, 52, 497–509.

Connell, R. W. 1995. *Masculinities.* Berkeley: University of California Press.

*Coontz, S. 2000. *The Way We Never Were: American Families and the Nostalgia Trap.* New York: Basic Books.

*Council of Graduate Schools. 2013. "Graduate Enrollment and Degrees: 2002 to 2012." Retrieved 4 December 2014 (cgsnet.org/ckfinder/userfiles/files/GEDReport_2012.pdfSeptember).

DeBraganza, N., and H. A. Hausenblas. 2010. "Media Exposure of the Ideal Physique on Women's Body Dissatisfaction and Mood: The Moderating Effects of Ethnicity." *Journal of Black Studies*, 40, 700–16.

*Downs, E., and S. Smith. 2010. "Keeping Abreast of Hypersexuality: A Video Game Character Content Analysis." *Sex Roles*, 62, 721–33.

*Eliot, L. 2009. *Pink Brain, Blue Brain: How Small Differences Grow Into Troublesome Gaps—And What We Can Do About It.* New York: Houghton Mifflin.

*Encyclopedia of Surgery. 2015. "Sex Reassignment Surgery." Retrieved 9 July 2015 (http://www.surgeryencyclopedia.com/Pa-St/Sex-Reassignment-Surgery.html).

*Endendijk, J. J., M. G. Groenveld, S. R. van Berkel, E. T. Hallers-Haalboom, J. Mesman, and M. J. Bakermans-Kranenburg. 2013. "Gender Stereotypes in the Family Context: Mothers, Fathers, and Siblings." *Sex Roles*, 68, 577–90.

*England, D. E., L. Descartes, and M. A. Collier-Meek. 2011. "Gender Role Portrayals and the Disney Princesses." *Sex Roles*, 64, 555–67.

*Entertainment Software Association. 2015. "Essential Facts About the Computer and Video Game Industry." Retrieved 7 April 2015 (www.theesa.com/facts/pdfs/ESA_EF_2014.pdf).

*Equal Employment Opportunity Commission. 2014. "Sex-Based Discrimination." Retrieved 26 November 2014 (http://www.theesa.com/wp-content/uploads/2015/03/ESA-2014-Annual-Report.pdf).

*Etaugh, C. A., and J. S. Bridges. 2013. *Women's Lives: A Psychological Exploration*, 3rd ed. Boston: Pearson.

*Fine, C. 2010. *Delusions of Gender: The Real Science Behind Sex Differences.* London: Icon Books Ltd.

*Fisher, B. S., F. T. Cullen, and M. G. Turner. 2000. *The Sexual Victimization of College Women.* Technical Report no. NCJ 182369. Washington, DC: U.S. Department of Justice, National Institute of Justice.

*Forger, N. G., G. J. Rosen, E. M. Waters, D. Jacob, R. B. Simerly, and G. J. de Vries. 2004. "Deletion of Bax Eliminates Sex Differences in the Mouse Forebrain." *PNAS*, 101, 13666–71.

*Gerding, A., and N. Signorielli. 2014. "Gender Roles in Tween Television Programming: A Content Analysis of Two Genres." *Sex Roles*, 70, 43–56.

Giroux, H. A. 2005. "The Passion of the Right: Religious Fundamentalism and the Crisis of Democracy." *Cultural Studies/Critical Methodologies*, 5, 309–17.

*Gonzales, L. M., J. R. Allum, and R. S. Sowell. 2013. "Graduate Enrollment and Degrees: 2002 to 2012." September. Washington, DC: Council of Graduate Schools and Graduate Record Examinations Board.

*Helgeson, V. S. 2012. *Psychology of Gender*, 4th ed. Boston: Pearson.

*Hines, M. 2005. *Brain Gender.* New York: Oxford University Press.

*Kaufman, R. L. 2010. *Race, Gender, and the Labor Market: Inequalities at Work.* Boulder, CO: Lynne Rienner Publishers.

*Kenney-Benson, G. A., E. M. Pomerantz, A. M. Ryan, and H. Patrick. 2006. "Sex Differences in Math Performance: The Role of Children's Approach to Schoolwork." *Developmental Psychology*, 42, 11–26.

*Kimmel, M. S., and M. A. Messner. 2013. *Men's Lives*, 9th ed. Boston: Pearson.

*Kimura, D. 2002. "Sex Differences in the Brain." *Scientific American.* 15 May. Retrieved 23 June 2006 (www.sciam.com/print_version.cfm?articleID=00018E9D-879D-1D06-8E49809EC5).

*Kindlon, D., and M. Thompson. 2000. *Raising Cain: Protecting the Emotional Life of Boys.* New York: Ballantine Books.

*Koss, M. P., and S. L. Cook. 1993. "Facing the Facts: Date and Acquaintance Rape Are Significant Problems for Women." In *Current Controversies in Family Violence*, edited by R. J. Gelles and D. R. Loseke. Newbury Park, CA: Sage Publications.

*Koss, M. P., C. Gidycz, and N. Wisniewski. 1987. "The Scope of Rape: Incidence and Prevalence in a National Sample of Higher Education Students." *Journal of Consulting and Clinical Psychology*, 55, 162–70.

*Kristof, N., and S. WuDunn. 2010. *Half the Sky: Turning Oppression into Opportunity for Women Worldwide.* New York: Vintage Books.

*Kristof, N., and S. WuDunn. 2014. *A Path Appears: Transforming Lives, Creating Opportunity.* New York: Alfred A. Knopf.

*Kwon, K., A. M. Lease, and L. Hoffman. 2012. "The Impact of Clique Membership on Children's Social Behavior and Status Nominations." *Social Development*, 21, 1, 150–69.

*Leaper, C., and C. K. Friedman. 2006. "The Socialization of Gender." In *The Handbook of Socialization: Theory and Research*, edited by J. E. Grusec and P. D. Hastings, pp 561–87. New York: Guilford Press.

*Leonard, L. 2000. "Interpreting Female Genital Cutting: Moving Beyond the Impasse." *Annual Review of Sex Research*, 11, 158–91.

*Lewis, T. 2015. "Bruce Jenner's Transition: How Many Americans Are Transgender?" LiveScience. Retrieved 9 July 2015 (http://www.livescience.com/50635-bruce-jenner-transgender-prevalence.html).

*Lindsey, L. 2011. *Gender Roles: A Sociological Perspective, 5th ed.* Upper Saddle River, NJ: Prentice Hall.

*Logan, T. K., and R. Walker. 2009. "Partner Stalking." *Trauma, Violence, & Abuse*, 10, 247–70.

*Maccoby, E. E. 1998. *The Two Sexes: Growing Up Apart, Coming Together.* Cambridge, MA: Harvard University Press.

*Mackie, G. 2000. "Female Genital Cutting: The Beginning of the End." In *Female "Circumcision" in Africa: Culture, Controversy, and Change*, edited by B. Shell-Duncan and Y. Hernlund, pp. 253–82. Boulder, CO: Lynne Reinner.

*Markey, C. N., and P. M. Markey. 2009. "Correlates of Young Women's Interest in Obtaining Cosmetic Surgery." *Sex Roles*, 61, 158–66.

*Marks, J. L., C. B. Lam, and S. M. McHale. 2009. "Family Patterns of Gender Role Attitudes." *Sex Roles*, 61, 221–34.

*Martin, J. A., B. E. Hamilton, and M. J. K. Osterman. 2014. "Births in the United States, 2013." NCHS Data Brief no. 175. December. National Center for Health Statistics.

*McCarthy, M. M., A. P. Arnold, G. F. Ball, J. D. Blaustein, and G. J. De Vries. 2012. "Sex Differences in the Brain: The Not So Inconvenient Truth." *The Journal of Neuroscience*, 32, 2241–47.

*Messner, M. A. 2009. *It's All for the Kids: Gender, Families, and Youth Sports.* Berkeley, CA: University of California Press.

Mills, V. K. 1972. "The Status of Women in American Churches." *Churches and Society*, 63, 50–55.

*Mo, C. 2012. "What? Me Sexist?" 5 November. Gender News. The Clayman Institute for Gender Research. Retrieved 31 March 2015 (gender.stanford.edu/news/2011/what-me-sexist).

*Mosley, M. 2014. "Is Your Brain Male or Female?" BBC News. 29 September. Retrieved 15 April 2015 (http://www.bbc.com/news/science-environment-29405467).

*Mulvey, K. L., and M. Killen. 2014. "Challenging Gender Stereotypes: Resistance and Exclusion." *Child Development.* doi: 10.1111/cdev.12317.

*Murdock, G. 1949. *Social Structure.* New York: Macmillan.

*Murdock, G. 1957. "World Ethnographic Sample." *American Anthropologist*, 59, 664–87.

*National Center for Education Statistics. 2014. "Enrollment, staff, and degrees/certificates conferred in degree-granting and non-degree-granting postsecondary institutions, by control and level of institution, sex of student, type of staff, and level of degree: Fall 2010, fall 2011, and 2011–12." Digest of Education Statistics 2013, Table 301.10. Retrieved 26 November 2014 (nces.ed.gov/programs/digest/d13/tables/dt13_301.10.asp).

*National Institute on Media and the Family. 2009. "Fact Sheet: Media's Effect on Girls: Body Image and Gender Identity." Retrieved 16 April 2010 (www.mediafamily.org/facts/facts_mediaeffect.shtml).

*National Institute of Mental Health. 2013. "Statistics." Retrieved 23 June 2013 (www.nimh.nih.gov/statistics/index.shtml).

*Near, C. E. 2013. "Selling Gender: Associations of Box Art Representation of Female Characters With Sales for Teen- and Mature-rated Video Games." *Sex Roles*, 68, 252–69.

*Newport, F. 2011. "Americans Prefer Boys to Girls, Just as They Did in 1941." Gallup. 23 June. Retrieved 31 March 2015 (www.gallup.com/poll/148187/americans-prefer-boys-girls-1941.aspx).

*Onion, A. 2005. "Scientists Find Sex Differences in Brain." *ABC News: Technology & Science*, 19 January. Retrieved 23 June 2006 (abcnews.go.com/Technology/ Health/story?id=424260&page=1).

*Orenstein, P. 1994. *School Girls.* New York: Anchor Books.

*Panet, S. 2013. "Rising Up for Rights for Women and Girls: Abandoning Female Genital Mutilation and Cutting in the Fouta of Senegal." United Nations Population Fund. Retrieved 23 June 2013 (www.unfpa.org/public/home/publications/pid/13042).

*Pardo, T. 2008. "Growing up Transgender: Research and Theory." In *Research Facts and Findings*. ACT for Youth Center of Excellence. Retrieved 14 August 2009 (www.actforyouth.net/documents/GrowingUpTransPt1_March08.pdf).

*Parker, K., and W. Wang. 2013. "Modern Parenthood: Roles of Moms and Dads Converge as They Balance Work and Family." Pew Social & Demographic Trends. 14 March. Retrieved 29 June 2013 (www.pewsocialtrends.org/2013/03/14/modern-parenthood-roles-of-moms-and-dads-converge-as-they-balance-work-and-family/).

*Pascoe, C. J. 2011. *Dude, You're a Fag: Masculinity and Sexuality in High School.* Berkeley, CA: University of California Press.

*Peter, J., and P. M. Valkenburg. 2007. "Adolescents' Exposure to a Sexualized Media Environment and Their Notions of Women as Sex Objects." *Sex Roles*, 56, 381–95.

*PFLAG: Parents, Families, & Friends of Lesbians and Gays. 2013. Home Page. Retrieved 23 June 2013 (Community.pflag.org/Page.aspx?pid=194&srcid=2).

*Population Reference Bureau. 2014. "World Population Data Sheet 2014." Retrieved 25 November 2014 (www.prb.org/Publications/Datasheets/2014/2014-world-population-data-sheet/data-sheet.aspx).

*Riegle-Crumb, C., and M. Humphries. 2012. "Exploring Bias in Math Teachers' Perceptions of Students' Ability by Gender and Race/Ethnicity." *Gender & Society*, 26, 290–322.

*Roudsari, B. S., M. M. Leahy, and S. T. Walters. 2009. "Correlates of dating violence among male and female heavy-drinking college students." *Journal of Interpersonal Violence*, 24, 1892–2905.

Safilios-Rothschild, C. 1974. *Women and Social Policy.* Upper Saddle River, NJ: Prentice Hall.

*Shipherd, J. C., K. E. Green, and S. Abramovitz. 2010. "Transgender Clients: Identifying and Minimizing Barriers to Mental Health Treatment." *Journal of Gay & Lesbian Mental Health*, 14, 94–108.

*Stacey, A. M., and C. Spohn. 2006. "Gender and the Social Costs of Sentencing: An Analysis of Sentences Imposed on Male and Female Offenders in Three U.S. District Courts." 11 *Berkeley Journal of Criminal Law* 43. Retrieved 4 March 2015 (scholarship.law.berkeley.edu/cgi/viewcontent.cgi?article=1001&context=bjcl).

*Stalking Resource Center. 2012. Home Page. Retrieved 26 March 2013 (www.victimsofcrime.org/our-programs/stalking-resource-center).

*Stansell, C. 2010. *The Feminist Promise: 1792–Present.* New York: Modern Library.

*Starr, S. B. 2012. "Estimating Gender Disparities in Federal Criminal Cases." University of Michigan Law and Economics Research Paper, no. 12-018. Retrieved 31 March 2015 (papers.ssrn.com/sol3/papers.cfm?abstract_id=2144002##).

*Steiner, S. 2014. "Credit Card Debt Hits All Incomes—Big and Small." Bankrate.com. Retrieved 26 November 2014 (www.bankrate.com/finance/consumer-index/credit-card-debt-hits-all-income-big-and-small.aspx).

*Stevens, J. 1999. *Reproducing the State.* Princeton, NJ: Princeton University Press.

Susser, I., and T. C. Patterson, eds. 2001. *Cultural Diversity in the United States: A Critical Reader.* Malden, MA: Blackwell.

*Terlecki, M. S., J. Brown, L. Harner-Steciw, J. Irvin-Hannum, N. Marchetto-Ryan, L. Ruhl, and J. Wiggins. 2011 "Sex Differences and Similarities in Video Game Experience, Preferences, and Self-Efficacy: Implications for the Gaming Industry." *Current Psychology*, 30, 22–33.

*UNICEF. 2013. "Child Protection: Female Genital Mutilation and Cutting." Retrieved 15 March 2015 (data.unicef.org/child-protection/fgmc).

*U.S. Department of Health and Human Services, Office of Women's Health. 2012. "Date Rape Drugs Fact Sheet." 16 July. Womenshealth.gov. Retrieved 10 May 2013 (www.womenshealth.gov/publications/our-publications/fact-sheet/date-rape-drugs.html).

*U.S. Department of Labor, Women's Bureau. 2014. "Women in the Labor Force: Data and Statistics." Retrieved 4 March 2015 (www.dol.gov/wb/stats/stats_data.htm).

*Ward, B. W., J. S. Schiller, G. Freeman, and T. C. Clarke. 2014. "Early Release of Selected Estimates Based on Data From the January–March 2014 National Health Interview Survey." National Health Interview Survey Early Release Program. September. Washington, DC: National Center for Health Statistics.

*Ward, M., and M. Edelstein. 2014. *A World Full of Women*, 6th ed. Boston: Allyn & Bacon.

*Williams, L., and T. Sobieszczyk. 1997. "Attitudes Surrounding the Continuation of Female Circumcision in the Sudan: Passing the Tradition to the Next Generation." *Journal of Marriage and the Family*, 59, 966–81.

*World Health Organization. 2011. "An Update on WHO's Work on Female Genital Mutilation (FGM): Progress Report."

*World Health Organization. 2014. "Female Genital Mutilation." Fact Sheet no. 241. February. Retrieved 31 March 2015 (www.who.int/mediacentre/factsheets/fs241/en/).

*Yount, K. M. 2002. "Like Mother, Like Daughter? Female Genital Cutting in Minia, Egypt." *Journal of Health and Social Behavior*, 43, 336–58.

*Zweig, J., and M. Dank. 2013. "Teen Dating Abuse and Harassment in the Digital World: Implications for Prevention and Intervention." Urban Institute. February. Retrieved 26 January 2015 (www.urban.org/UploadedPDF/412750-teen-dating-abuse.pdf).

Chapter 9

Achenbaum, W. A. 2010. "An Historian Interprets the Future of Gerontology." *The Gerontologist*, 50, 142–48.

*Administration on Aging. 2014. "A Profile of Older Americans: 2013." Retrieved 3 March 2015 (www.aoa.acl.gov/Aging_Statistics/Profile/2013/docs/2013_Profile.pdf).

*Albom, M. 1998. *Tuesdays with Morrie.* New York: Broadway Books.

*Alzheimer's Association. 2014. Home page. Retrieved 27 October 2014 (www.alz.org).

*Alzheimer's Association. 2015a. "Alzheimer's Disease: Facts and Figures." Retrieved 17 March 2015 (www.alz.org/alzheimers_disease_facts_and_figures.asp).

*Alzheimer's Association. 2015b. "What is Dementia?" Retrieved 17 March 2015 (www.alz.org/what-is-dementia.asp).

*American Foundation for Suicide Prevention. 2014. "Facts and Figures." Retrieved 24 October 2014 (www.afsp.org/understanding-suicide/facts-and-figures).

*American Society for Aesthetic Plastic Surgery. 2015. "2014 Cosmetic Surgery National Data Bank Statistics." Retrieved 19 July 2015 (http://www.surgery.org/media/statistics).

*Berardo, F. M., and D. H. Berardo. 2000. "Widowhood." In *Encyclopedia of Sociology*, 2nd ed., edited by E. F. Borgatta and R. J. V. Montgomery, pp. 3255–61. New York: Macmillan.

*Bureau of Labor Statistics. 2014. "The Last Private Industry Pension Plans." *TED: The Economics Daily*. 3 January. Retrieved 23 October 2014 (www.bls.gov/opub/ted/2013/ted_20130103.htm).

*Calvo, E., K. Haverstick, and S. A. Sass. 2009. "Gradual Retirement, Sense of Control, and Retirees' Happiness." *Research on Aging*, 31, 112–35.

*Carr, D. 2004. "The Desire to Date and Remarry Among Older Widows and Widowers." *Journal of Marriage and the Family*, 66, 1051–68.

*Central Intelligence Agency. 2014. "The World Factbook." Retrieved 8 December 2014 (www.cia.gov/library/publications/yhr-world-factbook/fields/2103.html).

*Cubanski, J., C. Swoope, A. Damico, and T. Neuman. 2014. "How Much Is Enough? Out-of-Pocket Spending Among Medicare Beneficiaries: A Chartbook." 21 July. The Henry J. Kaiser Family Foundation. Retrieved 26 October 2014 (kff.org/medicare/report/how-much-is-enough-out-of-pocket-spending-among-medicare-beneficiaries-a-chartbook/).

*DeNavas-Walt, C., and B. D. Proctor. 2015. "Income and Poverty in the United States: 2014." *Current Population Reports*, P60-252. Washington, DC: U.S. Census Bureau.

*Durkheim, É. 1897/1951. *Suicide, a Study in Sociology.* New York: Free Press.

*Ellis, S. R., and T. G. Morrison. 2005. "Stereotypes of Ageing: Messages Promoted By Age-Specific Paper Birthday Cards Available in Canada." *International Journal of Aging and Human Development*, 61, 57–73.

*Elwert, F., and N. A. Christakis. 2006. "Widowhood and Race." *American Sociological Review*, 71, 16–41.

*Employee Benefit Research Institute. 2014. "Reasons for a Change in Retirement Age." Fast Facts No. 277. 17 April. Retrieved 27 October 2014 (www.ebri.org/pdf/FF.277.Age.17Apr14.pdf).

*Employee Benefit Research Institute and Greenwald & Associates. 2014. "Attitudes About Current Social Security and Medicare Benefit Levels." RCS Fact Sheet No. 7. Retrieved 27 October 2014 (www.ebri.org/pdf/surveys/rcs/2014/RCS14.FS-7.SS-Med.Final.pdf).

* U.S. Equal Employment Opportunity Commission. 2014. "Age Discrimination." Retrieved 27 October 2014 (www.eeoc.gov/laws/types/age.cfm).

*Family Caregiver Alliance. 2012. "Fact Sheet: Selected Caregiver Statistics." November. Retrieved 29 May 2013 (www.caregiver.org/caregiver/jsp/content_node .jsp?nodeid=439&big_font=true).

*Fox, S., and J. Brenner. 2012. "Family Caregivers Online." Pew Internet & Family Life Project. 12 July. Retrieved 29 May 2013 (pewinternet.org/Reports/2012/Caregivers-online.aspx).

*Fredriksen-Goldsen, K. I., L. Cook-Daniels, H.-J. Kim, E. A. Erosheva, C. A. Emlet, C. P. Hoy-Ellis, J. Goldsen, and A. Muraco. 2014. "Physical and Mental Health of Transgender Older Adults: An At-Risk and Underserved Population." *The Gerontologist*, 54, 488–500.

*Fredriksen-Goldsen, K. I., C. A. Emlet, H.-J. Kim, A. Muraco, E. A.Erosheva, J. Goldsen, and C. P. Hoy-Ellis. (2013). "The Physical and Mental Health of Lesbian, Gay Male and Bisexual (LGB) Older Adults: The Role of Key Health Indicators and Risk and Protective Factors." *The Gerontologist*, 53, 664–75.

Friedan, B. 1993. *The Fountain of Age.* New York: Simon & Schuster.

*Grant, J. M. 2009. "Outing Age: Public Policy Issues Affecting Gay, Lesbian, Bisexual, and Transgender Elders." National Gay and Lesbian Task Force Policy Institute.

*Hardy, M. A., and K. Shuey. 2000. "Retirement." In *Encyclopedia of Sociology*, 2nd ed., edited by E. F. Borgatta and R. J. Montgomery, pp. 2401–10. New York: Macmillan.

*He, W., M. Sengupta, V. A. Velkoff, and K. A. DeBarros. 2005. "65+ in the United States: 2005." *Current Population Reports: Special Studies*, pp. 23–209. Washington, DC: U.S. Census Bureau.

*The Heritage Foundation. 2013. "The Number of Workers Per Medicare Beneficiary Is Falling." Retrieved 30 March 2015 (http://www.heritage.org/multimedia/ infographic/2012/05/medicare-at-risk/the-number-of-workers-per-medicare-beneficiary-is-falling).

*Heumann, L. F., M. E. McCall, and D. P. Boldy. 2001. *Empowering Frail Elderly People: Opportunities and Impediments in Housing, Health, and Support Services Delivery.* Westport, CT: Praeger.

*Holmes, T. H., and R. H. Rahe. 1967. "The Social Readjustment Rating Scale." *Journal of Psychosomatic Research*, 11, 213–18.

*Hooyman, N., K. Kawamoto, and H. A. Kiyak. 2015. *Aging Matters: An Introduction to Social Gerontology.* Boston: Pearson.

*Hooyman, N., and H. A. Kiyak. 2011. *Social Gerontology: A Multidisciplinary Perspective*, 9th ed. Boston: Pearson.

*Hospice Foundation of America. 2014. "What Is Hospice?" Retrieved 27 October 2014 (hospicefoundation.org/End-of-Life-Support-and-Resources/Coping-with-Terminal-Illness/ Hospice-Services).

*Human Rights Campaign. 2015. "Health and Aging." Retrieved 17 March 2015 (http://www.hrc.org/topics/ health-and-aging).

Japan Times News. 2014. "Japan Population Drops for Third Year Straight; 25% Are Elderly." Retrieved 3 March 2015 (www.japantimes.co.jp/news/2014/04/15/national/ japans-population-drops-for-third-straight-year-25-are-elderly/#.VQTOK2cU-HM).

*Kaiser Family Foundation. 2014. "The Facts on Medicare Spending and Financing." 28 July. Retrieved 3 March 2015 (kff.org/medicare/fact-sheet/ medicare-spending-and-financing-fact-sheet/).

*Kinsella, K., and W. He. 2009. "An Aging World: 2008." U.S. Census Bureau, International Population Reports No. P95/09-1. Washington, DC: U.S. Government Printing Office.

*Kinsella, K., and V. A. Velkoff. 2001. "An Aging World: 2001." U.S. Census Bureau No. P-95-001. Washington, DC: U.S. Government Printing Office.

*Klein, E. 2013. "Feds Spend $7 on Elderly for Every $1 on Kids." 15 February. Washingtonpost.com. Retrieved 27 October 2014 (www.washingtonpost. com/blogs/wonkblog/wp/2013/02/15/ feds-spend-7-on-elderly-for-every-1-on-kids/).

Kübler-Ross, E. 1969. *On Death and Dying.* New York: Macmillan.

*McArdle, F., T. Neuman, and J. Huang. 2014. "Overview of Health Benefits for Pre-65 and Medicare-Eligible Retirees." 14 April. Retrieved 26 October 2014 (kff.org/report-section/retiree-health-benefits-at-the-crosswords-overview-of-health-benefits-for-pre-65-and-medicare-eligible-retirees/).

*MedPAC. 2014. "A Data Book: Health Care Spending and the Medicare Program." June. Retrieved 3 March 2015 (www.medpac.gov/documents/publications/ jun14databookentirereport.pdf?sfvrsn=1).

*MetLife Mature Market Institute. 2012. "Market Survey of Long-Term Care Costs." November. Retrieved 5 March 2015 (www.metlife.com/assets/cao/mmi/publications/ studies/2012/studies/mmi-2012-market-survey-long-term-care-costs.pdf).

*Morgan, L., and S. Kunkel. 1998. *Aging: The Social Context.* Thousand Oaks, CA: Pine Forge Press.

*Morin, R., and R. Fry. 2012. "More Americans Worry about Financing Retirement: Adults in Their Late 30s Most Concerned." Pew Research Social & Demographic Trends. 22 October. Retrieved 28 May 2013 (www.pewsocialtrends.org/2012/10/22/ more-americans-worry-about-financing-retirement/).

*Munnell, A. H. 2011. "What Is the Average Retirement Age?" No. 11-11. August. Boston: Center for Retirement Research at Boston College.

*National Center for Health Statistics. 2013. "Health, United States, 2012: With Special Feature on Emergency Care." Hyattsville, MD.

*National Hospice and Palliative Care Organization. 2014. "NHPCO's Hospice Facts and Figures: Hospice Care in America: 2014 Edition." Retrieved 3 March 2014 (www.nhpco.org/sites/default/files/public/Statistics_ Research/2014_Facts_Figures.pdf).

*Ortman, J. M., V. A. Velkoff, and H. Hogan. 2014. "An Aging Nation: The Older Population in the United States." Current Population Reports, pp. 25–1140. May. Washington, DC: U.S. Census Bureau.

*Pew Research Center. 2010. "The Decline of Marriage and the Rise of New Families." 18 November. Retrieved 3 March 2015 (www.pewsocialtrends.org/files/2010/11/pew-social-trends-2010-families.pdf).

*Population Reference Bureau 2015. "2015 World Population Data Sheet." Accessed 22/9/15. Available at http://www .prb.org/pdf15/2015-world-population-data-sheet_ eng.pdf.

Quadagno, J. S. 2002. *Aging and the Life Course*, 2nd ed. New York: McGraw-Hill.

*Riffkin, R. 2014. "Average U.S. Retirement Age Rises to 62." Gallup. 28 April. Retrieved 23 October 2014 (www.gallup.com/poll/168707/average-retirement-age-rises.aspx).

Riley, M. W. 1996. "Discussion: What Does It All Mean?" *The Gerontologist*, 36, 256–58.

Riley, M. W., and J. W. Riley, Jr. 2000. "Age Integration: Conceptual and Historical Background." *The Gerontologist*, 40, 266–69.

*Rosenfeld, D., B. Bartlam, and R. D. Smith. 2012. "Out of the Closet and Into the Trenches: Gay Male Baby Boomers, Aging, and HIV/AIDS." *The Gerontologist*, 52, 255–64.

Slevin, K. F. 2010. "If I Had a Lot of Money… I'd Have a Body Makeover. Managing the Aging Body." *Social Forces*, 88, 1003–20.

*Social Security Administration. 2014. "Fact Sheet: Social Security." 2 April. Baltimore, MD: SSA Press Office.

*Social Security Online. 2013. "Social Security and Medicare Tax Rates; Maximum Taxable Earnings." Retrieved 15 July 2013 (ssa-custhelp.ssa.gov/app/answers/detail/a_id/240/~/social-security-and-medicare-tax-rates%3B-maximum-taxable-earnings).

*Span, F. 2013. "Suicide Rates Are High Among the Elderly." NYTimes.com. 7 August. Retrieved 24 October 2014 (newoldage.blogs.nytimes.com/2013/08/07/high-suicide-rates-among-the-elderly).

*Tucker, J. V., V. P. Reno, and T. N. Bethell. 2014. "Strengthening Social Security: What Do Americans Want?" National Academy of Social Insurance. Retrieved 27 October 2014 (www.nasi.org/sites/default/files/research/What_Do_Americans_Want.pdf).

*Uhlenberg, P. 2009. "Children in an Aging Society." *The Journals of Gerontology: Series B*, 64B, 489–96.

*UNAIDS. 2013. "HIV and Aging: A Special Supplement to the UNAIDS Report on the Global AIDS Epidemic 2013." Retrieved 27 October 2014 (www.unaids.org/en/media/unaids/contentassets/documents/unaidspublication/2013/20131101_JC2563_hiv-and-aging_en.pdf).

*United Nations. 2011. "World Population Prospects: The 2010 Revision." Retrieved 27 October 2014 (esa.un.org/unpd/wpp).

*United Nations, Department of Economic and Social Affairs, Population Division. 2015. "World Population Prospects: The 2014 Revision, Key Findings and Advance Tables." ESA/P/WP.227.

*U.S. Census Bureau. 2013 "International Programs." Retrieved 17 March 2015 (http://www.census.gov/population/international/data/idb/informationGateway.php).

*U.S. Census Bureau, October 30, 2014. "America's Families and Living Arrangements: 2014." Retrieved 17 March 2015 (http://www.census.gov/hhes/families/data/cps2014.html).

*U.S. Equal Employment Opportunity Commission. 2014. "Enforcement and Litigation Statistics." Retrieved 8 December 2014 (www.eeoc.gov/eeoc/statistics/enforcement/index.cfm).

*Utz, R. L., M. Caserta, and D. Lund. 2012. "Grief, Depressive Symptoms, and Physical Health Among Recently Bereaved Spouses." *The Gerontologist*, 52, 460–71.

*Waid, M. 2014. "Social Security Is a Critical Income Source for Older Americans: State-Level Estimates, 2010–2012." Fact Sheet 300. January. Washington, DC: AARP Public Policy Institute.

Whitbourne, S. K. 2005. *Adult Development and Aging: Biopsychosocial Perspectives*, 2nd ed. Hoboken, NJ: Wiley.

Chapter 10

*Allen, M., and C. DeWitt. 2012. "Intimate Partner Violence and Belief Systems in Liberia." *Journal of Interpersonal Violence*, 27, 3514–31.

*Amato, P. R. 2007. "Divorce and the Well-being of Adults & Children." *National Council on Family Relations Report*, 52, F3–F4, F18.

*Amato, P. 2014. "What Is a Family?" National Council on Family Relations Report. Volume 59.2. Summer.

*Amato, P. R., and A. Booth. 1997. *A Generation at Risk: Growing up in an Era of Family Upheaval.* Cambridge, MA: Harvard University Press.

*American Enterprise Institute. 2013. "Policy Studies—Society and Culture—Race and Gender." Retrieved 20 June 2013 (www.aei.org/policy/society-and-culture/race-and-gender/).

*American Psychological Association. 2012. "APA Files Two Briefs in Support of Same-Sex Couples." Vol. 43, No. 2. February. Retrieved 2 March 2015 (www.apa.org/monitor/2012/02/same-sex.aspx).

*Anderson, K. L. 2010. "Conflict, Power, and Violence in Families." *Journal of Marriage and Family*, 72, 726–42.

*Baker, A. J. L., and M. R. Brassard. 2013. "Adolescents Caught in Parental Loyalty Conflicts." *Journal of Divorce & Remarriage*, 54, 393–413.

*Bandura, A. 1977. *Social Learning Theory.* New York: General Learning Press.

*Berardo, F. M. 1998. "Family Privacy: Issues and Concepts." *Journal of Family Issues*, 19, 4–19.

*Biblarz, T. J., and J. Stacey. 2010. "How Does the Gender of Parents Matter?" *Journal of Marriage and Family*, 72, 3–22.

*Black, M. C. 2011. "Intimate Partner Violence and Adverse Health Consequences: Implications for Clinicians." *American Journal of Lifestyle Medicine*, 5, 428–39.

*Breiding, M. J., S. G. Smith, K. C. Basile, M. L. Walters, J. Chen, and M. T. Merrick. 2014. "Prevalence and Characteristics of Sexual Violence, Stalking, and Intimate Partner Violence Victimization—National Intimate Partner and Sexual Violence Survey, United States, 2011." *Morbidity & Mortality Weekly Report.* 5 September. 63(SS08):1–18. Retrieved 27 February 2015 (www.cdc.gov/mmwr/preview/mmwrhtml/ss6308a1.htm?s_cid=ss6308a1_e).

*Briere, J., and C. E. Jordan. 2009. "Childhood Maltreatment, Intervening Variables, and Adult Psychological Difficulties in Women." *Trauma, Violence, & Abuse*, 10, 375–88.

*Bryant-Davis, T., H. Chung, and S. Tillman. 2009. "From the Margins to the Center." *Trauma, Violence, & Abuse*, 10, 330–57.

*Bureau of Labor Statistics. 2014. "American Time Use Survey—2013 Results." 18 June. Retrieved 27 February 2015 (www.bls.gov/news.release/atus.nr0.htm).

*Busby, D. M., T. B. Holman, and E. Walker. 2008. "Pathways to Relationship Aggression between Adult Partners." *Family Relations*, 57, 72–83.

*Centers for Disease Control and Prevention. 2013. "National Marriage and Divorce Rate Trends." 19 February. Retrieved 6 July 2013 (www.cdc.gov/nchs/nvss/marriage_divorce_tables.htm).

*Chu, J. 2005. "Adolescent Boys' Friendships and Peer Group Culture." *New Directions for Child and Adolescent Development*, 107, 7–22.

*Coltrane, S. 2000. "Research on Household Labor: Modeling and Measuring the Social Embeddedness of Routine Family Work." *Journal of Marriage and Family*, 62, 1208–33.

*Coontz, S. 2007. "The Family Revolution." Greater Good: The Science of a Meaningful Life." 1 September. Retrieved 27 February 2015 (greatergood.berkeley.edu/article/item/the_family_revolution).

*Copen, C. E., K. Daniels, J. Vespa, and W. D. Mosher. 2012. "First Marriages in the United States: Data From the 2006–2010 National Survey of Family Growth." *National Health Statistics Reports*, No. 49. 22 March. Washington, DC: National Center for Health Statistics.

*Cott, N. F. 2002. *Public Vows: A History of Marriage and the Nation.* Cambridge, MA: Harvard University Press.

*Crawford, C., A. Goodman, E. Greaves, and R. Joyce. 2012. "Cohabitation, Marriage and Child Outcomes: An Empirical Analysis of the Relationship between Marital Status and Child Outcomes in the UK Using the Millennium Cohort Study." *Child and Family Law Quarterly*, 4, 176–98.

*Crittenden, C. A., and E. M. Wright. 2013. "Predicting Patriarchy: Using Individual and Contextual Factors to Examine Patriarchal Endorsement in Communities." *Journal of Interpersonal Violence*, 28, 1267–88.

*Crouch, S. R., E. Waters, R. McNair, J. Power, and E. Davis. 2014. "Parent-Reported Measures of Child Health and Well-Being in Same-Sex Parent Families: A Cross-Sectional Survey." *BMC Public Health*, 14, 635.

*Cummings, E. M., A. C. Schermerhorn, P. T. Davies, M. C. Goeke-Morey, and J. S. Cummings. 2006. "Interparental Discord and Child Adjustment: Prospective Investigations of Emotional Security as an Explanatory Mechanism." *Child Development*, 77, 132–52.

*DeNavas-Walt, C., and B. D. Proctor. 2014. "Income and Poverty in the United States: 2013." *Current Population Reports.* P60-249. Washington, DC: U.S. Census Bureau.

*DeSilver, D. 2013. "Supreme Court's DOMA ruling comes as majority now supports same-sex marriage." 26 June. Pew Research Center. Retrieved 27 February 2015 (www.pewresearch.org/fact-tank/2013/06/26/supreme-courts-doma-ruling-comes-as-majority-now-supports-same-sex-marriage/).

*Dey, I., and F. Wasoff. 2013. *Family Policy.* New York: Routledge.

*Dhaher, E. A., R. T. Mikolaczyk, A. E. Maxwell, and A. Krämer. 2010. "Attitudes toward Wife Beating among Palestinian Women of Reproductive Age from Three Cities in West Bank." *Journal of Interpersonal Violence*, 25, 518–37.

*Ellis, R. R., and T. Simmons. 2014. "Coresident Grandparents and Their Grandchildren: 2012." *Population Characteristics.* P20-576. October. U.S. Census Bureau. Retrieved 27 February 2015 (www.census.gov/content/dam/Census/library/publications/2014/demo/p20-576.pdf).

*Engels, F. 1902, original 1884. *The Origin of the Family.* Chicago: Charles H. Kerr & Co.

*Fang, X., D. S. Brown, C. S. Florence, and J. A. Mercy. 2012. "The Economic Burden of Child Maltreatment in the United States and Implications for Prevention." *Child Abuse & Neglect*, 36, 156–65.

*Filson, J., Ulloa, E. Ulloa, C. Runfola, and A. Hokoda. 2010. "Does Powerlessness Explain the Relationship between Intimate Partner Violence and Depression?" *Journal of Interpersonal Violence*, 25, 400–415.

*Gates, G. J. 2013. "LGBT Parenting in the United States." February. The Williams Institute. Retrieved 27 February 2015 (williamsinstitute.law.ucla.edu/research/census-lgbt-demographics-studies/lgbt-parenting-in-the-united-states/).

*Gibson-Davis, C., and H. Rackin. 2014. "Marriage or Carriage? Trends in Union Context and Birth Type by Education." *Journal of Marriage and Family*, 76, 506–19.

*Giele, J. Z. 1996. "Decline of the Family: Conservative, Liberal, and Feminist Views." In *Promises to Keep: Decline and Renewal of Marriage in America*, edited by D. Popenoe, J. B. Elshtain, and D. Blankenhorn. Lanham, MD: Rowman & Littlefield.

*Goodwin, P. Y., W. D. Mosher, and A. Chandra. 2010. "Marriage and Cohabitation in the United States: A Statistical Portrait Based on Cycle 6 (2002) of the National Survey of Family Growth." *Vital Health Stat* 23 (28). Washington, DC: National Center for Health Statistics.

Grall, T. 2013. "Custodial Mothers and Fathers and Their Child Support: 2011." *Current Population Reports.* P60-246. October. Washington, DC: U.S. Census Bureau.

*Guinart, M., and M. Grau. 2014. "Qualitative Analysis of the Short-Term and Long-Term Impact of Family Breakdown on Children: Case Study." *Journal of Divorce & Remarriage*, 55, 408–22.

*Hamplová, D., C. LeBourdais, and É. Lapierre-Adamcyk. 2014. "Is the Cohabitation-Marriage Gap in Money Pooling Universal?" *Journal of Marriage and Family*, 76, 983–97.

*Hayslip, B., and G. C. Smith, eds. 2013. *Resilient Grandparent Caregivers: A Strengths-Based Perspective.* New York: Routledge.

*Hegarty, K. L., L. J. O'Doherty, P. Chondros, J. Valpied, A. J. Taft, J. Astbury, S. J. Brown, L. Gold, A. Taket, G. S. Feder, and J. M. Gunn. 2013. "Effect of Type and Severity of Intimate Partner Violence on Women's Health and Service Use: Findings from a Primary Care Trial of Women Afraid of Their Partners." *Journal of Interpersonal Violence*, 28, 273–94.

*Heritage Foundation. 2013. FamilyFacts.org. Retrieved 20 June 2013.

*Hewitt, B., M. Western, and J. Baxter. 2006. "Who Decides? The Social Characteristics of Who Initiates Marital Separation." *Journal of Marriage and Family*, 68, 1165–77.

*Hokayem, C., and M. L. Heggeness. 2014. "Living in Near Poverty in the United States: 1966–2012." *Current Population Reports.* P60-248. Washington, DC: U.S. Census Bureau.

*Human Rights Campaign. 2015. "Resources: LGBT-Inclusive Definitions of Family." Retrieved 14 April 2015 (www.hrc.org/resources/entry/lgbt-inclusive-definitions-of-family).

*Human Rights Watch. 2015. "UN: Sexual Violence a 'Tactic of War.'" 14 April. Retrieved 14 April 2015 (www.hrw.org/news/2015/04/14/un-sexual-violence-tactic-war).

*Hyman, B. 2000. "The Economic Consequences of Child Sexual Abuse for Adult Lesbian Women." *Journal of Marriage and the Family*, 62, 199–211.

*Hymowitz, K., J. S. Carroll, W. B. Wilcox, and K. Kaye. 2013. "Knot Yet: The Benefits and Costs of Delayed Marriage In America." The National Marriage Project at the University of Virginia, The National Campaign to Prevent Teen and Unplanned Pregnancy, and The Relate Institute.

*Jekielek, S. M. 1998. "Parental Conflict, Marital Disruption, and Children's Emotional Well-Being." *Social Forces*, 76, 905–36.

*Kamp Dush, C. M. 2013. "Marital and Cohabitation Dissolution and Parental Depressive Symptoms in Fragile Families." *Journal of Marriage and Family*, 75, 91–109.

*Kaufmann, G. 2012. "This Week in Poverty: U.S. Single Mothers—'The Worst Off.'" TheNation.com. 21 December. Retrieved 6 July 2013 (www.thenation .com/blog/171886/week-poverty-us-single-mothers-worst#ixzz2YK8GuGqn).

*Kuperberg, A. 2014. "Age at Coresidence, Premarital Cohabitation, and Marriage Dissolution: 1985–2009." *Journal of Marriage and Family*, 76, 352–69.

*Lacey, K. K., M. D. McPherson, P. S. Samuel, K. Powell Sears, and D. Head. 2013. "The Impact of Different Types of Intimate Partner Violence on the Mental and Physical Health of Women in Different Ethnic Groups." *Journal of Interpersonal Violence*, 28, 359–85.

*Lamb, K. A. 2007. "'I Want to Be Just Like Their Real Dad.'" *Journal of Family Issues*, 28, 1162–88.

*Lichter, D. T., and Z. QIan. 2008. "Serial Cohabitation and the Marital Life Course." *Journal of Marriage and Family*, 70, 861–78.

*Lindsey, E. W., J. C. Chambers, J. M. Frabutt, and C. Mackinnon-Lewis. 2009. "Marital Conflict and Adolescents' peer Aggression: The Mediating and Moderating Role of Mother-Child Emotional Reciprocity." *Family Relations*, 58, 593–606.

*Manning, W. D., and S. Brown. 2006. "Children's Economic Well-Being in Married and Cohabiting Parent Families." *Journal of Marriage and Family*, 68, 345–62.

*Manning, W. D., S. L. Brown, and K. K. Payne. 2014. "Two Decades of Stability and Change in Age at First Union Formation." *Journal of Marriage and Family*, 76, 247–60.

*Manning, W., M. N. Fettro, and E. Lamidi. 2014. "Child Well-Being in Same-Sex Parent Families: Review of Research Prepared for American Sociological Association Amicus Brief." *Population Research and Policy Review*, 33, 485–502

*Martin, J. A., B. E. Hamilton, J. J. K. Osterman, S. C. Curtin, and T. J. Matthews. 2015. "Births: Final Data for 2013." National Vital Statistics Report. Vol. 64, No. 1. Retrieved 19 July 2015 (http://www.cdc.gov/nchs/data/nvsr/nvsr64/nvsr64_01.pdf).

Martin-Uzzi, M., and D. Duval-Tsioles. 2013. "The Experience of Remarried Couples in Blended Families." *Journal of Divorce & Remarriage*, 54, 43–57.

*Michael, K. C., A. Torres, and E. A. Seemann. 2007. "Adolescents' Health Habits, Coping Styles and Self-Concept Are Predicted by Exposure to Interparental Conflict." *Journal of Divorce & Remarriage*, 48, 155–74.

Murray, C. 1984. *Losing Ground: American Social Policy, 1950–1980.* New York: Basic Books.

*National Campaign to Prevent Teen and Unplanned Pregnancy. 2013. "Counting It Up: The Public Costs of Childbearing." Retrieved 6 July 2013 (www.thenationalcampaign.org/costs).

*National Marriage Project. 2012. "The State of Our Unions: Marriage in America 2012." Retrieved 6 July 2013 (national-marriageproject.org/wp-content/uploads/2012/12/SOOU2012.pdf).

*Nomaguchi, K. M. 2012. "Marital Status, Gender, and Home-to-Job Conflict Among Employed Parents." *Journal of Family Issues*, 33, 271–94.

*Nock, S. L. 1998. *Marriage in Men's Lives.* New York: Oxford University Press.

*Office of Adolescent Health. 2015. "Trends in Teen Pregnancy and Childbearing: Teen Births." U.S. Department of Health & Human Services. 25 February. Retrieved 2 March 2015 (www.hhs.gov/ash/oah/adolescent-health-topics/reproductive-health/teen-pregnancy/trends.html).

*Osborne, C., W. D. Manning, and P. J. Smock. 2007. "Married and Cohabiting Parents' Relationship Stability: A Focus on Race and Ethnicity." *Journal of Marriage and Family*, 69, 1345–66.

*Papernow, P. L. 2013. *Surviving and Thriving in Stepfamily Relationships: What Works and What Doesn't.* New York: Routledge.

*Parker, K., and W. Wang. 2013. "Modern Parenthood: Roles of Moms and Dads Converge as They Balance Work and Family." *Pew Social and Demographic Trends.* 14 March. Retrieved 29 June 2013 (www.pewsocialtrends.org/2013/03/14/modern-parenthood-roles-of-moms-and-dads-converge-as-they-balance-work-and-family/).

*Pawelski, J. G., E. C. Perrin, J. M. Foy, C. E. Allen, J. E. Crawford, M. Del Monte, M. Kaufmann, J. D. Klein, K. Smith, S. Springer, J. L. Tanner, and D. L. Vickers. 2006. "The Effects of Marriage, Civil Union, and Domestic Partnership Laws on the Health and Well-Being of Children." *Pediatrics*, 118, 349–64.

*Pew Research Center. 2010. "The Decline of Marriage and Rise of New Families." *Social & Demographic Trends.* 18 November. Retrieved 14 April 2015 (www.pewsocialtrends.org/2010/11/18/the-decline-of-marriage-and-rise-of-new-families/).

*Pew Research Center. 2011. "A Portrait of Stepfamilies." *Social & Demographic Trends.* 13 January. Retrieved 27 February 2015 (www.pewsocialtrends.org/2011/01/13/a-portrait-of-stepfamilies/).

*Pew Research Center. 2013. "A Survey of LGBT Americans: Attitudes, Experiences and Values in Changing Times." 13 June. Retrieved 27 February 2015 (www.pewsocialtrends.org/files/2013/06/SDT_LGBT-Americans_06-2013.pdf).

Pew Research Center. 2015. "Support for Same-Sex Marriage at Record High, but Key Segments Remain Opposed." June 8. Retrieived 19 July 2015. (http://www.cdc.gov/nchs/data/nvsr/nvsr64/nvsr64_01.pdf).

*Poortman, A-R., and T. van der Lippe. 2009. "Attitudes toward Housework and Child Care and the Gendered Division of Labor." *Journal of Marriage and Family*, 71, 526–41.

*Popenoe, D. 2008. "Cohabitation, Marriage and Child Well-Being: A Cross-National Perspective." National Marriage Project. Piscataway, NJ: Rutgers, The State University of New Jersey.

*Potter, D. 2012. "Same-Sex Parent Families and Children's Academic Achievement." *Journal of Marriage and Family*, 74, 556–71.

*Pyke, K. 2000a. "Ideology of 'Family' Shapes Perception of Immigrant Children." Minneapolis, MN: National Council on Family Relations.

*Pyke, K. 2000b. "'The Normal American Family' as an Interpretive Structure of Family Life among Grown

Children of Korean and Vietnamese Immigrants." *Journal of Marriage and Family,* 62, 240–45.

*Rani, M., and S. Banu. 2009. "Attitudes toward Wife Beating." *Journal of Interpersonal Violence,* 24, 1371–97.

*Rodriguez, M., J. M. Valentine, J. B. Son, and M. Muhammad. 2009. "Intimate Partner Violence and Barriers to Mental Health Care for Ethnically Diverse Populations of Women." *Trauma, Violence, & Abuse,* 10, 358–74.

*Smith, B. L. 2012. "The Case Against Spanking." American Psychological Association. April. Retrieved 10 April 2013 (www.apa.org/monitor/2012/04/spanking.aspx).

*Soria, K. M., and S. Linder. 2014. "Parental Divorce and First-Year College Students' Persistence and Academic Achievement." *Journal of Divorce & Remarriage,* 55, 103–16.

*Straus, M. A. 1980. "Social Stress and Marital Violence in a National Sample of American Families." *Annals of the New York Academy of Sciences,* 347, 229–50.

*Straus, M. A., R. J. Gelles, and S. K. Steinmetz. 1980. *Behind Closed Doors: Violence in the American Family.* New York: Anchor Books.

*Symoens, S., K. Bastaits, D. Mortelmans, and P. Bracke. 2013. "Breaking Up, Breaking Hearts? Characteristics of the Divorce Process and Well-Being after Divorce." *Journal of Divorce & Remarriage,* 54, 177–96.

*Tach, L., and S. Halpern-Meekin. 2009. "How Does Premarital Cohabitation Affect Trajectories of Marital Quality?" *Journal of Marriage and Family,* 71, 298–317.

*Taylor, P. 2014. *The Next America.* New York: Public Affairs.

*United Nations Statistics Division. 2013. "UN Data: Maternity Benefits." Retrieved 5 March 2015 (http://data.un.org/DocumentData.aspx?id=344).

*UN Women. 2015. "Facts and Figures: Ending Violence against Women." Retrieved 14 April 2015 (www.unwomen.org/en/what-we-do/ending-violence-against-women/facts-and-figures).

*U.S. Census Bureau. 2014a. "America's Families and Living Arrangements:" 2014: Adults. 30 October. Retrieved 2 March 2015 (http://www.census.gov/hhes/families/data/cps2014.html).

*U.S. Census Bureau. 2014b. "America's Families and Living Arrangements:" 2014: Children. 6 November. Retrieved 28 February. 2015 (http://www.census.gov/hhes/families/data/cps2014C.html).

*U.S. Department of Health and Human Services, Administration for Children and Families, Administration on Children, Youth, and Families, Children's Bureau. 2013. "Child Maltreatment 2013." Retrieved 27 February 2015 (www.acf.hhs.gov/programs/cb/research-data-technology/statistics-research/child-maltreatment).

*U.S. Department of Health and Human Services, Administration for Children and Families, Administration on Children, Youth & Families, Children's Bureau. 2015. "Fewer Child Abuse and Neglect Victims for Seventh Consecutive Year." 15 January. Retrieved 27 February 2015 (www.acf.hhs.gov/media/press/2015/fewer-child-abuse-and-neglect-victims-for-seventh-consecutive-year).

*Vespa, J., J. M. Lewis, and R. M. Kreider. 2013. "America's Families and Living Arrangements: 2012." *Population Characteristics.* P20-570. August. U.S. Census Bureau. Retrieved 27 February 2015 (www.census.gov/prod/2013pubs/p20-570.pdf).

*Vives-Cases, C., D. Gil-González, and M. Carasco-Portiño. 2009. "Verbal Marital Conflict and Male Domination in the Family as Risk Factors of Intimate Partner Violence." *Trauma, Violence, & Abuse,* 10, 171–80.

*Voydanoff, P. 2008. "A Conceptual Model of Work-Family Interface." In *Handbook of Work-Family Integration: Research, Theory, and Best Practices,* edited by K. Korabik, D. S. Lero, and D. L. Whitehead, pp. 37–56. Burlington, MA: Elsevier.

*Walsh, W. A., J. Dawson, and M. J. Mattingly. 2010. "How Are We Measuring Resilience following Childhood Maltreatment? Is the Research Adequate and Consistent? What Is the Impact on Research, Practice, and Policy?" *Trauma, Violence, & Abuse,* 11, 27–41.

Wilson, W. J. 1996. *When Work Disappears: The World of the New Urban Poor.* New York: Alfred A. Knopf.

*Yount, K.M. 2005. "Resources, Family Organization, and Domestic Violence against Married Women in Minya, Egypt." *Journal of Marriage and Family,* 67, 579–96.

Chapter 11

**Abboud, S. K., and J. Y. Kim. 2005. *Top of the Class: How Asian Parents Raise High Achievers—And How You Can Too.* Berkeley, CA: Berkeley Trade.

*American Psychological Association. 2012. "Suicides among Asian Americans." May. Retrieved 2 February 2015 (www.apa.org/pi/oema/resources/ethnicity-health/asian-american/suicide-fact-sheet.pdf).

*Ansalone, G. 2010. "Tracking: Educational Differentiation or Defective Strategy." *Educational Research Quarterly,* 34, 3–17.

*August, D., and T. Shanahan. 2006. "Executive Summary: Developing Literacy in Second-Language Learning: Report on the National Literacy Panel on Language-Minority Children and Youth." Mahwah, NJ: Lawrence Erlbaum Associates, Inc. Retrieved 31 March 2015 (www.bilingualeducation.org/pdfs/PROP2272.pdf).

*Ballantine, J. H., and F. M. Hammack. 2012. *The Sociology of Education,* 7th ed. Boston: Pearson.

*Bastaits, K., K. Ponnet, and D. Mortelmans. 2014. "Do Divorced Fathers Matter? The Impact of Parenting Styles of Divorced Fathers on the Well-Being of the Child." *Journal of Divorce & Remarriage,* 55, 363–90.

*Booher-Jennings, J. 2008. "Learning to Label: Socialisation, Gender, and the Hidden Curriculum of High-States Testing." *British Journal of Sociology of Education,* 29, 149–60.

*Bourdieu, P. 1986. "The Forms of Capital." In *Handbook of Theory and Research for the Sociology of Education,* edited by J. Richardson. New York: Greenwood.

**Bowles, S., H. Gintis, and M. O. Groves, eds. 2005. *Unequal Chances: Family Background and Economic Success.* New York: Russell Sage.

*Brown, A., and E. Patten. 2014. "Statistical Portrait of Hispanics in the United States, 2012." Pew Research Center. 29 April. Retrieved 31 March 2015 (www.pewhispanic.org/2014/04/29/statistical-portrait-of-hispanics-in-the-united-states-2012/).

*Bureau of Indian Education. 2015. Home page. Retrieved 31 March 2015 (www.bie.edu/index.htm).

**Carey, K. 2010. "A Race to the Top." *Chronicle of Higher Education.* Retrieved 7 March 2015 (jobs.chronicle.com).

**Carriuolo, N. E., A. Rodgers, and C. M. Stout. 2002. "Valuing and Building from Strengths of Hispanic Students: An Interview with Juliet Garcia." *Journal of Developmental Education,* 25, 20–24.

*Centers for Disease Control and Prevention. 2014. "Understanding Bullying: Fact Sheet." 16 October. Retrieved 31 March 2015 (www.cdc.gov/violenceprevention/pub/understanding_bullying.html).

*Chmielewski, A. K., H. Dumont, and U. Trautwein. 2013. "Tracking Effects Depend on Tracking Type: An International Comparison of Students' Mathematics Self-Concept." *American Educational Research Journal*, 50, 925–57.

*Clearinghouse on International Developments in Child, Youth, and Family Policies. 2005. "Section 1.2: Early Childhood Education and Care." Retrieved 15 April 2015 (www.childpolicyintl.org/ecec.html).

*Clements, A. D. 2004. *Homeschooling: A Research-Based How-To Manual*. Lanham, MD: Scarecrow Education.

*Cole, M. 2008. *Marxism and Educational Theory: Origins and Issues*. New York: Routledge.

*Coleman, J. S. 1966. "Equality of Educational Opportunity." National Center for Educational Statistics. Report Number OE-38001. Retrieved 31 March 2015 (files.eric.ed.gov/fulltext/ED012275.pdf).

*College Board. 2013. "Trends in Student Aid 2013." Retrieved 9 February 2015 (trends.collegeboard.org/sites/default/files/student-aid-2013-full-report.pdf).

Darling-Hammond, L. 1998. "Unequal Opportunity: Race and Education." *Brookings Review*, Spring, pp. 28–33.

Darling-Hammond, L. 2010. "Restoring Our Schools." *The Nation*, 14 June, pp. 14–20.

*Deming, D. 2009. "Early Childhood Intervention and Life-Cycle Skill Development:" Evidence from Head Start. *American Economic Journal: Applied Economics*, 1:3, 111–34.

*DeSilver, D. 2015. "U.S. Students Improving—Slowly—In Math and Science, But Still Lagging Internationally." Pew Research Center. Retrieved 9 February 2015 (www.pewresearch.org/fact-tank/2015/02/02/u-s-students-improving-slowly-in-math-and-science-but-still-lagging-internationally/).

*Fiel, J. E. 2013. "Decomposing School Resegregation: Social Closure, Racial Imbalance, and Racial Isolation." *American Sociological Review*, 78, 828–48.

*Friedersdorf, C. 2012. "Is The Ivy League Fair to Asian Americans?" *The Atlantic*. 21 December. Retrieved 2 February 2015 (www.theatlantic.com/politics/archive/2012/12/is-the-ivy-league-fair-to-asian-americans/266538/).

*Frum, D. 2000. *How We Got Here: The '70s*. New York: Basic Books.

*Gallup. 2015. "Education." Retrieved 4 April 2015 (www.gallup.com/poll/1612/education.aspx).

Genesee, F., K. Lindholm-Leary, W. Saunders, and D. Christian. 2005. "Language Learners in U.S. Schools: An Overview of Research Findings." *Journal of Education for Students Placed at Risk*, 10, 363–86.

*Grodsky, E., J. R. Warren, and E. Felts. 2008. "Testing and Social Stratification in American Education." *Annual Review of Sociology*, 34, 385–404.

*Guinart, M., and M. Grau. 2014. "Qualitative Analysis of the Short-Term and Long-Term Impact of Family Breakdown on Children: Case Study." *Journal of Divorce & Remarriage*, 55, 408–22.

*Head Start. 2015. "Head Start Program Facts Fiscal Year 2014." Retrieved 16 April 2015 (heclkc.ohs.acf.hhs.gov/hslc/data/factsheets/2014-hs-program-factsheet.html).

Irons, E. J. 2007. *The Challenges of No Child Left Behind: Understanding the Issues of Excellence, Accountability, and Choice*. Lanham, MD: Rowman & Littlefield.

*Jennings, J. L., D. Deming, C. Jencks, M. Lopuch, and B. E. Schueler. 2015. "Do Differences in School Quality Matter More Than We Thought? New Evidence on Educational Opportunity in the Twenty-First Century." *Sociology of Education*, 88, 56–82.

*Kalogrides, D., and S. Loeb. 2013. "Different Teachers, Different Peers: The Magnitude of Student Sorting within Schools." *Educational Researcher*, 42, 304–16.

*Kalogrides, D., S. Loeb, and T. Béteille. 2013. "Systematic Sorting: Teacher Characteristics and Class Assignments." *Sociology of Education*, 86, 103–23.

*Kena, G., S. Aud, F. Johnson, X. Wang, J. Zhang, A. Rathbun, S. Wilkinson-Flicker, and P. Kristapovich. 2014. *The Condition of Education 2014*. NCES 2014-083. Washington, DC: U.S. Department of Education, National Center for Education Statistics. Retrieved 26 January 2015 (nces.ed.gov/pubsearch).

*Kirk, D. S., and R. J. Sampson. 2013. "Juvenile Arrest and Collateral Educational Damage in the Transition to Adulthood." *Sociology of Education*, 86, 36–62.

*Kisida, B., J. P. Greene, and D. H. Bowen. 2014. "Creating Cultural Consumers: The Dynamics of Cultural Capital Accumulation." *Sociology of Education*, 87, 281–95.

*Klein, M. C. 2014. "Are Ivy League Schools Biased against Asians?" *Bloomberg View*, 3 April. Retrieved 2 February 2015 (www.bloombergview.com/articles/2014-04-03/are-ivy-league-schools-biased-against-asians).

Klenk, J. 2005. *Choosing a School for Your Child*. Washington, DC: Office of Innovation and Improvement, U.S. Department of Education.

*Lavy, V., and E. Sand. 2015. "On the Origins of Gender Human Capital Gaps: Short and Long Term Consequences of Teachers' Stereotypical Biases." National Bureau of Economic Research. NBER Working Paper No. 20909. January. Retrieved 9 February 2015 (www.nber.org/papers/w20909).

*Legewie, J., and T. DiPrete. 2014. "The High School Environment and the Gender Gap in Science and Engineering." *Sociology of Education*, 87, 259–80.

*Lopez, M. H., and A. Gonzalez-Barrera. 2014. "Women's College Enrollment Gains Leave Men Behind." 6 March. Pew Research Center. Retrieved 31 March 2015 (www.pewresearch.org/fact-tank/2014/03/06/womens-college-enrollment-gains-leave-men-behind/).

*Lopez, M. H., A. Gonzalez-Barrera, and J. M. Krogstad. 2014. "Latino Support for Democrats Falls, but Democratic Advantage Remains." Pew Research Center. Retrieved 6 February 2015 (www.pewhispanic.org/2014/10/29/latino-support-for-democrats-falls-but-democratic-advantage-remains/).

*Lumeng, J., N. Kaciroti, J. Sutrza, A. M. Krusky, A. L. Miller, K. E. Peterson, R. Lipton, and T. M. Reischl. 2015. "Changes in Body Mass Index Associated with Head Start Participation." *Pediatrics*, 135, 1–8.

*Mayotte, B. 2014. "Past, Future Pell Grant Changes Offer Hope for Families." USNews.com. 24 September. Retrieved 9 February 2015 (www.usnews.com/education/blogs/student-loan-ranger/2014/09/24/past-future-pell-grant-changes-offer-hope-for-families/).

McKinsey and Company. 2010. "How the World's Most Improved School Systems Keep Getting Better." Retrieved 9 February 2015 (www.mckinsey.com/clientservice/ Social_Sector/our_practices/Education/Knowledge_ Highlights/Economic_impact.aspx).

*Mickelson, R. A., M. C. Bottia, and R. Lambert. 2013. "Effects of School Racial Composition on K–12 Mathematics Outcomes: A Metaregression Analysis." *Review of Educational Research*, 83, 121–58.

*Mitchell, M., V. Palacios, and M. Leachman. 2014. "States Are Still Funding Higher Education Below Pre-Recession Levels." Center for Budget and Policy Priorities. 1 May. Retrieved 9 February 2015 (www.cbpp.org/ cms/?fa=view&id=4135).

*Moss-Racusin, C. A., J. F. Dovidio, V. L. Brescoll, M. J. Graham, and J. Handelsman. 2012. "Science Faculty's Subtle Gender Biases Favor Male Students." *Proceedings of the National Academy of Sciences*, 109, 16474–79.

*National Association for Bilingual Education. 2014. "What Is Bilingual Education?" Retrieved 31 March 2015 (www .nabe.org/BilingualEducation).

National Center for Education Statistics. 2003. *Homeschooling in the United States: 2003.* Statistical Analysis Report. Retrieved 23 July 2015 (nces.ed.gov/pubs2006/homeschool).

*National Center for Education Statistics. 2013a. "Table 104.10. Rates of High School Completion and Bachelor's Degree Attainment among Persons Age 25 and Over, by Race/ Ethnicity and Sex: Selected Years, 1910 through 2013." *Digest of Education Statistics.* Retrieved 15 April 2015 (nces. ed.gov/programs/digest/d13/tables/dt13_104.10.asp).

*National Center for Education Statistics. 2013b. "Table 104.20. Percentage of Persons 25 to 29 Years Old with Selected Levels of Educational Attainment, by Race/Ethnicity and Sex: Selected Years, 1920 through 2013." *Digest of Education Statistics.* Retrieved 15 April 2015 (nces.ed.gov/programs/ digest/d13/tables/dt13_104.20.asp).

*National Center for Education Statistics. 2014a. "Table 216.20. Number and Enrollment of Public Elementary and Secondary Schools, by School Level, Type, and Charter and Magnet Status: Selected Years, 1990–91 through 2011–12." *Digest of Education Statistics.* Retrieved 31 March 2015 (nces.ed.gov/programs/digest/d13/tables/dt13_216.20. asp?current=yes).

*National Center for Education Statistics. 2014b. "Table 7. Number and Percentage Distribution of All Children Ages 5–17 Who Were Homeschooled and Homeschooling Rate, by Selected Characteristics: 2011–12." *Digest of Education Statistics.* August. Retrieved 31 March 2015 (nces.ed.gov/ pubs2013/2013028/tables/table_07.asp).

*National Center for Education Statistics. 2014c. "Table 216.30. Number and Percentage Distribution of Public Elementary and Secondary Students and Schools, by Traditional or Charter School Status and Selected Characteristics: Selected Years, 1999–2000 through 2011–12." *Digest of Education Statistics.* Retrieved 31 March 2015 (nces.ed.gov/pro- grams/digest/d13/tables/dt13_216.30.asp?current=yes).

*National Center for Education Statistics. 2014d. "Table 204.20. Number and Percentage of Public School Students Participating in Programs for English Language Learners, by State: Selected Years, 2002–03 through 2011–12." *Digest of Education Statistics.* Retrieved 2 February 2015 (nces.ed.gov/programs/digest/d13/ tables/dt13_204.20.asp).

*National Center for Education Statistics. 2014e. "Table 302.60. Percentage of 18- to 24-Year-Olds Enrolled in Degree- Granting Institutions, by Level of Institution and Sex and Race/Ethnicity of Student: 1967 through 2012." *Digest of Education Statistics.* Retrieved 9 December 2014 (nces. ed.gov/programs/digest/d13/tables/dt13_302.60.asp).

*National Center for Education Statistics. 2014f. "The Condition of Education: Education Expenditures by Country." *Digest of Education Statistics.* January. Retrieved 16 April 2015 (nces. ed.gov/programs/coe/indicator_cmd.asp).

*National Education Association. 2014. "Rankings and Estimates." Retrieved 4 April 2015. (www.nea.org/assets/ docs/NEA-Rankings-and-Estimates-2013-2014.pdf).

*National Indian Education Association. 2015. "Statistics on Native Students." Retrieved 31 March 2015 (niea.org/ Research/Statistics.aspx).

*Northwest Evaluation Association. 2014. "Bureau of Indian Education Report on Student Achievement and Growth: 2009–10 to 2012–13." February. Retrieved 9 February 2015 (bie.edu/cs/groups/webteam/documents/document/ idc1-028067.pdf).

Orfield, G. 1999. "Policy and Equity: A Third of a Century of Educational Reforms in the United States." December. *Prospects* (Paris, France), pp. 579–94.

Orfield, G. 2004/2005. "Why Segregation Is Inherently Unequal: The Abandonment of *Brown* and the Continuing Failure of *Plessy.*" *New York Law School Law Review*, 49, 1041–52.

Orfield, G., and S. E. Eaton. 1996. *Dismantling Desegregation: The Quiet Reversal of* Brown v. Board of Education. New York: Free Press.

*Palardy, G. J. 2013. "High School Sociological Segregation and Student Attainment." *American Educational Research Journal*, 50, 714–54.

*Population Reference Bureau. 2015. "World Population Data Sheet 2014." Retrieved 16 April 2015 (www.prb.org/ Publications/Datasheets/2014/2014-world-population- data-sheet.aspx).

*RAND Education. 2012. "Teachers Matter: Understanding Teachers' Impact on Student Achievement." Retrieved 9 February 2015 (www.rand.org/education/projects/ measuring-teacher-effectiveness/teachers-matter.html).

*Richards, M. P. 2014. "The Gerrymandering of School Attendance Zones and the Segregation of Public Schools: A Geospatial Analysis." *American Educational Research Journal*, 51, 1119–57.

Riordan, C. 2004. *Equality and Achievement: An Introduction to the Sociology of Education*, 2nd ed. Upper Saddle River, NJ: Pearson/Prentice Hall.

*Rosenthal, R., and L. Jacobson. 1968. *Pygmalion in the Classroom: Teacher Expectation and Pupils' Intellectual Development.* New York: Rinehart and Winston.

*Rossell, C., and K. Baker. 1996. "The Educational Effectiveness of Bilingual Education." *Research in the Teaching of English*, 30, 7–74.

*Sadler, P. M., G. Sonnert, H. P. Coyle, N. Cook-Smith, and J. L. Miller. 2013. "The Influence of Teachers' Knowledge on Student Learning in Middle School Physical Science Classrooms." *American Educational Research Journal*, 50, 1020–49.

*Schmidt, B. M. 2015. "Rate My Professor." Retrieved 16 April 2015 (benschmidt.org/2015/02/06/rate-my- professor/).

*Shifrer, D., R. M. Callahan, and C. Muller. 2013. "Equity or Marginalization? The High School Course-Taking of Students Labeled with a Learning Disability." *American Educational Research Journal*, 50, 656–82.

Slavin, R. E. 1997. "Can Education Reduce Social Inequality?" *Educational Leadership*, December 6–11.

*Slavin, R. E., N. Madden, M. Calderon, A. Chamberlain, and M. Hennessy. 2010. *Reading and Language Outcomes of a Five-Year Randomized Evaluation of Transitional Bilingual Education.* January. Baltimore, MD: Johns Hopkins University, Center for Data-Driven Reform in Education.

*Soria, K. M., and S. Linder. 2014. "Parental Divorce and First-Year College Students' Persistence and Academic Achievement." *Journal of Divorce & Remarriage*, 55, 103–16.

*Suicide Prevention Resource Center. 2014. "Suicide Among Racial/Ethnic Populations in the U.S.: Asians, Pacific Islanders, and Native Hawaiians." Retrieved 2 February 2015 (www.sprc.org/sites/sprc.org/files/library/API%20 Sheet%20August%2028%202013%20Final.pdf).

*Tompson, T., J. Benz, and J. Agiesta. 2013. "Parents' Attitudes on the Quality of Education in the United States." The Associated Press–NORC Center for Public Affairs Research. Retrieved 15 April 2015 (www.apnorc.org/PDFs/ Parent%20Attitudes/AP_NORC_Parents%20Attitudes%20 on%20the%20Quality%20of%20Education%20in%20 the%20US_FINAL_2.pdf).

*Urban, W. J., and J. L. Wagoner, Jr. 2008. *American Education: A History*, 4th ed. New York: Routledge.

*U.S. Census Bureau. 2014. "Current Population Data on School Enrollment." 24 September. Retrieved 31 March 2015 (www.census.gov/hhes/school/data/cps/).

*U.S. Department of Education. 2009. "Race to the Top Program Executive Summary." November. Retrieved 9 February 2015 (www2.ed.gov/programs/racetothetop/ executive-summary.pdf).

*USGovernmentSpending.com. 2015. "US Education Spending." Retrieved 16 April 2015 (www. usgovernmentspending.com/us_education_spending_20 .html).

*Valle, R. C., S. Normandeau, and G. R. González. 2015. "Education at a Glance Interim Report: Update of Employment and Educational Attainment." Organisation for Economic Co-Operation and Development. January. Retrieved 31 March 2015 (www.oecd.org/edu/EAG- Interim-report.pdf).

*Voyer, D., and S. D. Voyer. 2014. "Gender Differences in Scholastic Achievement: A Meta-Analysis." *Psychological Bulletin*, 140, 1174–204.

*White House and U.S. Department of Education. 2014. "Setting the Pace: Expanding Opportunity for America's Students under Race to the Top." March. Retrieved 9 February 2015 (www.whitehouse.gov/sites/default/files/ docs/settingthepacerttreport_3-2414_b.pdf).

*Wong, Y. J., K. Koo, K. K. Tran, Y.-C. Chiu, and Y. Mok. (2011). "Asian American College Students' Suicide Ideation: A Mixed-Methods Study." *Journal of Counseling Psychology*, 58, 197–209.

Yu, T. 2006. "Challenging the Politics of the 'Model Minority' Stereotype: A Case for Educational Equality." *Equity and Excellence in Education*, 39, 325–33.

*Zhai, F., J. Brooks-Gunn, and J. Waldfogel. 2011. "Head Start and Urban Children's School Readiness: A Birth Cohort Study in 18 Cities." *Developmental Psychology*, 47, 134–52.

Chapter 12

Alter, J. 2005. "A Bankrupt Way to Do Business." April 25. *Newsweek.*

*Appelbaum, B. 2011. "White House Ties Trade Pacts to Unemployment Benefits." *New York Times.* 16 May. Retrieved 25 May 2015 (thecaucus.blogs.nytimes.com).

*Backer, L. C. 2009. "Small Steps Towards an Autonomous Transnational Legal System for the Regulation of Multinational Corporations." *Melbourne Journal of International Law*, 10, 258–307.

*Bernstein, J., and S. Parrott. 2014. "Proposal to Strengthen Minimum Wage Would Help Low-Wage Workers, with Little Impact on Employment." Center on Budget and Policy Priorities. 7 January. Retrieved 6 May 2015 (www .cbpp.org/research/proposal-to-strengthen-minimum- wage-would-help-low-wage-workers-with-little-impact-on).

*Bureau of Labor Statistics. 2014a. "Census of Fatal Occupational Injuries Summary 2013." Economic News Release. 11 September. Retrieved 3 May 2015 (www.bls .gov/news.release/cfoi.nr0.htm).

*Bureau of Labor Statistics. 2014b. "Employee Benefits in the United States." News Release. USDL-14-1348. 25 July. Retrieved 6 May 2015 (http://www.bls.gov/news.release/ pdf/ebs2.pdf).

*Bureau of Labor Statistics. 2014c. "Nonfatal Occupational Injuries and Illnesses Requiring Days Away from Work, 2013." Economic News Release. USDL-14-2246. 16 December. Retrieved 6 May 2015 (www.bls.gov/news .release/osh2.nr0.htm).

*Bureau of Labor Statistics. 2015a. "Characteristics of Minimum Wage Workers, 2014." Report 1054. April. Retrieved 6 May 2015 (www.bls.gov/opub/reports/cps/ characteristics-of-minimum-wage-workers-2014.pdf).

*Bureau of Labor Statistics. 2015b. "Current Employment Statistics. Establishment Data: Table B-1a." 3 April. Retrieved 3 May 2015 (www.bls.gov/web/empsit/ ceseeb1a.htm).

*Bureau of Labor Statistics. 2015c. "Top Picks: National Compensation Survey—Benefits." Retrieved 6 May 2015 (data.bls.gov/cgi-bin/surveymost?nb).

*Bureau of Labor Statistics. 2015d. "Union Members Summary: Union Members—2014." Economic News Release. 23 January. Retrieved 3 May 2015 (www.bls.gov/ news.release/union2.nr0.htm).

*Chen, T. 2015. "American Household Credit Card Debt Statistics: 2015." Nerdwallet. Retrieved 6 May 2015 (www.nerdwallet.com/blog/credit-card-data/ average-credit-card-debt-household/).

*Derber, C. 2014. *Corporation Nation: How Corporations Are Taking Over Our Lives—and What We Can Do about It.* New York: St. Martin's Press.

*Edin, K., and M. Kefalas. 2005. *Promises I Can Keep: Why Poor Women Put Motherhood before Marriage.* Berkeley, CA: University of California Press.

*Eichengreen, B. 2015. *Hall of Mirrors: The Great Depression, The Great Recession, and the Uses—and Misuses—of History.* New York: Oxford University Press.

*Executive Office of the President. 2014. "A Year of Action: Progress Report on Raising the Minimum Wage." August. Retrieved 6 May 2015 (www.whitehouse.gov/sites/ default/files/docs/minimum_wage_report2.pdf).

*Friedan, B. 1963. *The Feminine Mystique.* New York: Dell.

*Galinsky, E., K. Aumann, and J. T. Bond. 2009. *Times Are Changing: Gender and Generation at Work and at Home.* New York: Families and Work Institute.

*Gallup, 2015. "Most Important Problem." Retrieved 9 May 2015 (http://www.gallup.com/poll/1675/most-important-problem.aspx).

*Garfield, R., and K. Young. 2015. "Adults Who Remained Uninsured at the End of 2014." The Henry J. Kaiser Family Foundation. Executive Summary. 29 January. Retrieved 25 February 2015 (kff.org/health-reform/issue-brief/adults-who-remained-uninsured-at-the-end-of-2014/).

*Gassman-Pines, A. 2011. "Low-Income Mothers' Nighttime and Weekend Work: Daily Associations with Child Behaviour, Mother-Child Interactions, and Mood." *Family Relations*, 60, 15–29.

*Geewax, M. 2013. "Obama's Call for Higher Minimum Wage Could Have Ripple Effect." February 13. Retrieved 25 May 2015 (http://www.npr.org/2013/02/13/171897858/obamas-call-for-higher-minimum-wage-could-have-ripple-effect).

*Global Trends. 2015. "Corporate Clout 2013: Time for Responsible Capitalism." Retrieved 10 May 2015 (www.globaltrends.com/knowledge-center/features/shapers-and-influencers/190-corporate-clout-2013-time-for-responsible-capitalism).

*Gornick, J. C., A. Heron, and R. Eisenbrey. 2007. "The Work-Family Balance: An Analysis of European, Japanese, and U.S Work-Time Policies." Technical Report No. Briefing Paper 189. Washington, DC: Economic Policy Institute.

*Gornick, J. C., H. Presser, and C. Ratzdorf. 2009. "Outside the 9-to-5." *The American Prospect*, 20, 21–24.

*Grzywacz, J. G., S. S. Daniel, J. Tucker, J. Walls, and E. Leerkes. 2011. "Nonstandard Work Schedules and Developmentally Generative Parenting Practices: An Application of Propensity Score Techniques." *Family Relations*, 60, 45–59.

*Human Rights Campaign. 2015. "Employment Non-Discrimination Act." Retrieved 6 May 2015 (www.hrc.org/resources/entry/employment-non-discrimination-act).

*International Labor Rights Forum. 2015. "Sweatfree Communities." Retrieved 9 May 2015 (http://www.laborrights.org/industries/apparel).

Jacobsen, L. A., and M. Mather. 2010. "U.S. Economic and Social Trends since 2000." Population Reference Bureau Report.

*Li, J., S. Johnson, W-J. Han, S. Andrews, G. Kendall, L. Stradzins, and A. M. Dockery. 2012. "Parents' Nonstandard Work and Child Well-Being: A Critical Review of the Existing Literature." CLMR Discussion Paper Series 2012/02. February. Perth, Australia: Centre for Labour Market Research.

*Luo, M. 2009. "Job Woes Exacting a Toll on Family Life." *New York Times*. 12 November. Retrieved 30 December 2009 (www.nytimes.com/2009/11/12/us/12families.html?_r=1&pagewanted=print).

*ManpowerGroup. 2015. "What Sets Us Apart." Retrieved 25 May 2015 (http://www.manpowergroup.com/wps/wcm/connect/manpowergroup-en/home/why-manpowergroup/what-sets-us-apart/#.VV_NodpVhBc).

*Marlar, J. 2010. "Worry, Sadness, Stress Increase with Length of Unemployment." Gallup. 8 June. Retrieved 3 May 2015 (www.gallup.com/poll/139604/worry-sadness-stress-increase-length-unemployment.aspx).

Martin, E., and R. D. Torres. 2004. *Savage State: Welfare Capitalism and Inequality.* Lanham, MD: Rowman and Littlefield.

*Matos, K., and E. Galinsky. 2012. "2012 National Study of Employers." Families and Work Institute. Retrieved 3 May 2015 (familiesandwork.org/site/research/reports/NSE_2012_.pdf).

*Mian, A., and A. Sufi. 2014. *House of Debt: How They (and You) Caused the Great Recession, and How We Can Prevent It from Happening Again.* Chicago: University of Chicago Press.

*Morrissey, T. W. 2008. "Familial Factors Associated with the Use of Multiple Child-Care Arrangements." *Journal of Marriage and the Family*, 70, 549–63.

*National Conference of State Legislatures. 2015. "State Minimum Wages: 2015 Minimum Wage by State." 24 February. Retrieved 6 May 2015 (www.ncsl.org/research/labor-and-employment/state-minimum-wage-chart.aspx).

*Newport, F. 2015. "Fewer Americans Identify as Middle Class in Recent Years." Gallup. 28 April. Retrieved 3 May 2015 (www.gallup.com/poll/182918/fewer-americans-identify-middle-class-recent-years.aspx).

*Office of the Mayor (City of Seattle). 2015. "$15 Minimum Wage." Seattle.gov. Retrieved 6 May 2015 (murray.seattle.gov/minimumwage/#sthash.YslR1Cmf.dpbs).

*Official Journal of the European Communities. 1998. "Council Directive 97/81/EC of 15 December 1997 Concerning the Framework Agreement on Part-Time Work Concluded by UNICE, CEEP and the ETUC." Retrieved 5 January 2010. (Eur-Lex) (eur-lex.europa.eu/LexUriServ/LexUriServ.do?uri=CELEX): 31997L0081: EN: HTML.

*Parker, K., and W. Wang. 2013. "Modern Parenthood: Roles of Moms and Dads Converge as They Balance Work and Family." Pew Social & Demographic Trends. 14 March. Retrieved 29 June 2013 (www.pewsocialtrends.org/2013/03/14/modern-parenthood-roles-of-moms-and-dads-converge-as-they-balance-work-and-family/).

*Peralta, K. 2014. "Outsourcing to China Costs U.S. 3.2 Million Jobs since 2001." *U.S. News and World Report*. Retrieved 10 May 2015 (http://www.usnews.com/news/blogs/data-mine/2014/12/11/outsourcing-to-china-cost-us-32-million-jobs-since-2001).

*Powell, B. 2014. *Out of Poverty: Sweatshops in the Global Economy.* Cambridge, MA: Cambridge University Press.

*Riffkin, R. 2015. "U.S. Workers Job Loss Fears Down to Pre-Recession Levels." 23 April. Retrieved 25 May 2015 (http://www.gallup.com/poll/182840/workers-job-loss-fears-back-pre-recession-levels.aspx).

*Riley, C. 2014. "Asia Consumers Shun McDonald's after Food Scare." 10 September. CNN.com. Retrieved 3 May 2015 (money.cnn.com/2014/09/10/news/mcdonalds-food-scare/).

*Ritzer, G. 2012. *The McDonaldization of Society*, 7th ed. Thousand Oaks, CA: Sage.

*Ruggie, J. G. 2013. *Just Business: Multinational Corporations and Human Rights.* New York: W.W. Norton.

*Saad, L. 2015. "Americans' Money Worries Unchanged From 2014." Gallup. 20 April. Retrieved 3 May 2015 (www.gallup.com/poll/182768/americans-money-worries-unchanged-2014.aspx?utm_source=position3&utm_medium=related&utm_campaign=tiles).

*Schmitt, J. 2013. "Why Does the Minimum Wage Have No Discernible Effect on Employment?" Center for Economic and Policy Research. February. Retrieved 6

May 2015 (www.cepr.net/documents/publications/min-wage-2013-02.pdf).

*Seccombe, K. 2015. *"So You Think I Drive a Cadillac?" Welfare Recipients Perspective on the System and its Reform,* 4th ed. Boston, MA: Pearson.

*Smelser, N. J., and R. Swedberg, eds. 2005. *The Handbook of Economic Sociology,* 2nd ed. Princeton, NJ: Princeton University Press.

*Thibodeau, P. 2015. "Fury Rises at Disney Over Use of Foreign Workers." *Computer World.* Retrieved 9 May 2015 (http://www.computerworld.com/article/2915904/it-outsourcing/fury-rises-at-disney-over-use-of-foreign-workers.html).

*U.S. Equal Employment Opportunity Commission. 2015. "Laws Enforced by EEOC." Retrieved 6 May 2015 (www.eeoc.gov/laws/statutes/index.cfm).

Warren, E. 2010. *The Fragile Middle Class: Americans in Debt.* Laurel, MD: Smith Business Solutions.

Wells, D. 2003. "Global Sweatshops and Ethical Buying Codes." September–October. *Canadian Dimension,* 37, 9.

*Westaway, K. 2014. *Profit and Purpose.* Hoboken, NJ: Wiley.

*Wolf, M. 2014. *The Shifts and the Shocks: What We've Learned—and Have Still to Learn—from the Financial Crisis.* London: Penguin.

Chapter 13

*Alfred, C. 2014. "Remember #BringBackOurGirls? This Is What Has Happened in the 5 Months Since." Huffington Post. 19 September. Retrieved 27 February 2015 (www.huffingtonpost.com/2014/09/14/nigeria-girls-kidnapped-5-months_n_5791622.html).

*Arditti, J. A. 2006. "Editor's Note." *Family Relations,* 55, 263–65.

*Badger, E. 2014. "Metropolitan Areas Are Now Fueling Virtually All of America's Population Growth." Washingtonpost.com. 27 March. Retrieved 3 February 2015 (www.washingtonpost.com/blogs/wonkblog/wp/2014/03/27/metropolitan-areas-are-now-fueling-virtually-all-of-americas-population-growth/).

Bogue, D. J. 1985. *The Population of the United States: Historical Trends and Future Projections.* New York: Free Press.

*Central Intelligence Agency World Factbook. 2014. Home page. Retrieved 27 February 2015 (www.cia.gov/library/publications/the-world-factbook/geos/in.html).

Davis, K. 1971. "Population Policy: Will Current Programs Succeed?" In *American Popular Debate,* edited by D. Callahan. Garden City, NY: Doubleday.

*Demetriou, D. 2010. "'Fathering School' Opens for Japan's Time-Pressed Salarymen Parents." *The Telegraph.* Retrieved 23 May 2010 (www.telegraph.co.uk/news/worldnews/asia/japan/7101692).

*Dimock, M. 2014. "Tea Partiers Are Not All Immigration Hawks." Pew Research Center. 11 June. Retrieved 3 February 2015 (www.pewresearch.org/fact-tank/2014/06/11/tea-partiers-are-not-all-immigration-hawks/).

*Dvorsky, G. 2012. "The Unintended Consequences of China's One-Child Policy." io9.com. 3 October. Retrieved 23 June 2013 (io9.com/5948528/the-unintended-consequences-of-chinas-one-child-policy).

*The Economist. 2012. "Consequences of the One-Child Policy: Perils of Motherhood." 23 June. Retrieved 29 June 2013 (www.economist.com/blogs/analects/2012/06/consequences-one-child-policy/print).

Ehrlich, P. R., A. H. Ehrlich, and J. P. Holdren. 1977. *Ecoscience: Population, Resources, Environment.* San Francisco, Freeman.

*Food and Agriculture Organization of the United Nations. 2012. "Undernourishment around the World in 2012." Retrieved 5 December 2014 (www.fao.org/docrep/016/i3027e/i3027e02.pdf).

*Food and Agriculture Organization of the United Nations. 2014. "The State of Food Insecurity in the World 2014." Retrieved 5 December 2014 (www.fao.org/publications/sofi/2014/en/).

Geertz, C. 2005. Winter. "What Was the Third World Revolution?" *Dissent,* pp. 35–45.

Goldsborough, J.O. 2004. February 19. "A Fence Won't Stem the Tide of Immigration." *San Diego Union-Tribune,* p. B11.

*Gupton, N. 2011. "Quiz: Population 7 Billion—Could We All Fit in One City?" NationalGeographic.com. Retrieved 27 February (news.nationalgeographic.com/news/2011/10/111031-population-7-billion-earth-world-un-seven/).

*Haub, C. 2010. "Japan's Demographic Future." Population Reference Bureau. Retrieved 23 May 2010 (www.prb.org/Articles/2010/japandemography.aspx).

*Hays, J. 2010. "One-Child Policy in China." *China/Facts and Details.* Retrieved 23 May 2010. (factsanddetails.com/china.php?itemid=128&catid=4&subcatid=15).

*Hays, J. 2012. "One-Child Policy in China." *China/Facts and Details.* April. Retrieved 27 February 2015 (factsanddetails.com/china/cat4/sub15/item128.html).

*Ishii-Kuntz, M. 2003. "Balancing Fatherhood and Work: Emergence of Diverse Masculinities in Contemporary Japan." In *Men and Masculinities in Contemporary Japan: Dislocating the Salaryman Doxa,* edited by J. E. Roberson and N. Suzuki, pp. 198–216. New York: Routledge.

*Ishii-Kuntz, M., K. Makino, K. Kato, and M. Tsuchiya. 2004. "Japanese Fathers of Preschoolers and Their Involvement in Child Care." *Journal of Marriage and Family,* 66, 779–91.

*Jian, M. 2013. "China's Brutal One-Child Policy." *The New York Times,* 21 May 2013. Retrieved 19 February 2015 (www.nytimes.com/2013/05/22/opinion/chinas-brutal-one-child-policy.html?_r=0).

Kim, C. J. 2003. *Bitter Fruit: The Politics of Black-Korean Conflict in New York City.* New Haven, CT: Yale University Press.

*Kochhar, R. 2014. "10 Projections for the Global Population in 2050." Pew Research Center. 3 February. Retrieved 27 February 2015 (www.pewresearch.org/fact-tank/2014/02/03/10-projections-for-the-global-population-in-2050/).

*Krogstad, J. M., and A. Gonzalez-Barrera. 2014. "Hispanics Split on How to Address Surge in Central American Child Migrants." Pew Research Center. 29 July. Retrieved 3 February 2015 (www.pewresearch.org/fact-tank/2014/07/29/hispanics-split-on-how-to-address-surge-in-central-american-child-migrants/).

*Lee, E. Y-H. 2014. "On Tax Day, a Reminder That Undocumented Immigrants Pay Billions in Taxes." ThinkProgress.org. 15 April. Retrieved 27 February 2015 (thinkprogress.org/immigration/2014/04/15/3426680/tax-day-undocumented-immigrants-pay-taxes/).

*Lee, G. H. Y., and S. P. Lee. 2013. "Childcare Availability, Fertility, and Female Labor Force Participation in Japan." Monash University Department of Economics, ISSN 1441-5429 Discussion Paper 36/13. Retrieved 27 February

2015 (www.buseco.monash.edu.au/eco/research/papers/2013/3613childcareleelee.pdf).

*Lee, K. S., P. A. Tufis, and D. F. Alwin. 2010. "Separate Spheres or Increasing Equality? Changing Gender Beliefs in Postwar Japan." *Journal of Marriage and Family*, 72, 184–201.

*Martinez, O. 2014. "Why the Children Fleeing Central America Will Not Stop Coming." thenation.com. 30 July. Retrieved 27 February 2015 (www.thenation.com/article/180837/why-children-fleeing-central-america-will-not-stop-coming#).

*Migration Policy Institute. 2014. "U.S. Immigrant Population by Metropolitan Area." Retrieved 27 February 2015 (www.migrationpolicy.org/programs/data-hub/us-immigration-trends#source).

*Motel, S., and E. Patten. 2013. "Statistical Portrait of Hispanics in the United States, 2011." Pew Hispanic Center. 15 February. Retrieved 3 March 2013 (www.pewhispanic.org/2013/02/15/statistical-portrait-of-hispanics-in-the-united-states-2011/).

*Nwosu, C., J. Batalova, and G. Auclair. 2014. "Frequently Requested Statistics on Immigrants and Immigration in the United States." ILW.com. Retrieved 27 February 2015 (discuss.ilw.com/content.php?3080-Article-Frequently-Requested-Statistics-on-Immigrants-and-Immigration-in-the-United-States-By-Chiamaka-Nwosu-Jeanne-Batalova-and-Gregory-Auclair).

*Passel, J. S., and D. Cohn. 2009. "A Portrait of Unauthorized Immigrants in the United States." Washington, DC: Pew Hispanic Center.

*Passel, J. S., D. Cohn, J. M. Krogstad, and A. Gonzalez-Barrera. 2014. "As Growth Stalls, Unauthorized Immigrant Population Becomes More Settled." Pew Research Center. 3 September. Retrieved 27 February 2015 (www.pewhispanic.org/2014/09/03/as-growth-stalls-unauthorized-immigrant-population-becomes-more-settled/).

*PBL Netherlands Environmental Assessment Agency. 2014. "Trends in Global CO2 Emissions: 2014 Report." PBL publication number 1490. The Hague. PBL Publishers.

*Pew Hispanic Center. 2013. "A Nation of Immigrants: A Portrait of the 40 Million, Including 11 Million Unauthorized." 29 January.

*Pew Research Center. 2013a. "Immigration Rises on Washington's Agenda, Not the Public's." 28 January. Retrieved 27 February 2015 (www.pewresearch.org/2013/01/28/immigration-rises-on-washingtons-agenda-not-the-publics/).

*Pew Research Center. 2013b. "The Rise of Asian Americans." 4 April. Retrieved 5 May 2015 (www.pewsocialtrends.org/2012/06/19/the-rise-of-asian-americans/).

*Population Reference Bureau. 2015. "2014 World Population Data Sheet." Retrieved 24 July 2015 (http://www.prb.org/Publications/Datasheets/2014/2014-world-population-data-sheet.aspx).

Portes, A. 2001. *Ethnicities: Children of Immigrants in America.* Berkeley: University of California Press.

Renwick, D. 2014. "The U.S. Child Migrant Influx." Council on Foreign Relations. Retrieved 21 February 2015 (www.cfr.org/immigration/us-child-migrant-influx/p33380).

*Rosenberg, M. 2009. "China's One Child Policy." About.com. Retrieved 9 November 2009 (geography.about.com/od/populationgeography/a/onechild.htm).

*Scutti, S. 2014. "One-Child Policy Is One Big Problem for China." Newsweek.com. 24 January. Retrieved 27 February 2015 (www.highbeam.com/doc/1G1-356435644.html).

*Strain, M. R. 2014. "The Problem Isn't Central America's Child Refugees. It's the Countries They Come From." Washingtonpost.com. 1 August. Retrieved 27 February 2015 (www.washingtonpost.com/posteverything/wp/2014/08/01/the-problem-isnt-central-americas-child-refugees-its-the-countries-they-come-from/).

*United Nations Development Programme. 2014. "Human Development Report." 1 UN Plaza, New York, New York.

*United Nations Girls' Education Initiative. 2014. "Global Section." Retrieved 5 March 2015 (www.ungei.org/infobycountry/247_289.html).

United National Statistics Division. 2014. "Statistics: Energy Use (kg of oil equivalent per capita)." Retrieved 27 February 2015 (data.un.org/Data.aspx?d=WDI&f=Indicator_Code%3AEG.USE.PCAP.KG.OE).

*U.S. Department of Homeland Security, 2015a. "Data Set: Deferred Action for Childhood Arrivals." Retrieved 5 March 2015 (www.uscis.gov/tools/reports-studies/immigration-forms-data/data-set-deferred-action-childhood-arrivals).

*U.S. Department of Homeland Security. 2015b. "Immigration Enforcement: FY 2014 ICE Immigration Removals." Retrieved 5 March 2015 (www.ice.gov/removal-statistics).

*World Bank. 2014. "Girls' Education." 3 December. Retrieved 27 February 2015 (www.worldbank.org/en/topic/education/brief/girls-education).

*World Food Programme. 2014. "What Causes Hunger?" Retrieved 27 February 2015 (www.wfp.org/hunger/causes).

*Worldwatch Institute. 2013. "U.N. Raises 'Low' Population Projection in 2050." Retrieved 19 April 2013 (www.worldwatch.org/node/6038).

Zolberg, A. 2006. *A Nation by Design: Immigration Policy in the Fashioning of America.* New York: Russell Sage.

*Zolberg, A. R. 2008. *A Nation by Design.* Boston, MA: Harvard University Press.

Chapter 14

*Ansolabehere, S., and D. M. Konisky. 2014. *Cheap and Clean.* Cambridge, MA: The MIT Press.

*Barlow, M., and T. Clarke. 2005. *Blue Gold: The Fight to Stop the Corporate Theft of the World's Water.* New York: New Press.

*Black, M., J. King, and C. Lacey. 2009. *The Atlas of Water*, 2nd ed. Berkeley: University of California Press.

*Blass, T. 2004. *The Man Who Shocked the World: The Life and Legacy of Stanley Milgram.* New York: Basic Books.

Blass, T. 2009. "A Historical Perspective on the Milgram Obedience Experiments." *American Psychologist*, 64, 37–45.

*Brinson, L. C. 2015. "How Much Air Pollution Comes from Cars?" HowStuffWorks. Retrieved 15 March 2015 (auto.howstuffworks.com/air-pollution-from-cars.htm).

*Brown, L. R. 2012. *Full Planet, Empty Plates.* New York: W.W. Norton.

*Brown, L. R. 2015. *The Great Transition.* New York: W.W. Norton.

*Center for Sustainable Systems. 2014. "U.S. Wastewater Treatment Factsheet." No. CSS04-14. University of Michigan. October. Retrieved 20 March 2015 (css.snre.umich.edu/css_doc/CSS04-14.pdf).

Clarke, L. 2005. *Worst Cases: Terror and Catastrophe in the Popular Imagination.* Chicago: University of Chicago Press.

*Climate Debate Daily. 2015. Home page. Retrieved 15 March 2015 (climatedebatedaily.com/).

*Correia, A. W., C. A. Pope, III, D. W. Dockery, Y. Wang, M. Ezzati, and F. Dominici. 2013. "Effect of Air Pollution Control on Life Expectancy in the United States: An Analysis of 545 U.S. Counties for the Period from 2000 to 2007." *Epidemiology,* 24, 23–31.

Cottrell, W. F. 1951. "Death by Dieselization: A Case Study in the Reaction to Technological Change." *American Sociological Review,* 16, 358–65.

*Dugan, A. 2014. "Americans Most Likely to Say Global Warming Is Exaggerated." 17 March. Retrieved 15 March 2015 (www.gallup.com/poll/167960/americans-likely-say-global-warming-exaggerated.aspx).

*Duke Center for Sustainability & Commerce. 2015. "How Much Do We Waste Daily?" Durham, NC: Duke University. Retrieved 15 March 2015 (center.sustainability.duke.edu/resources/green-facts-consumers/how-much-do-we-waste-daily).

Ehrlich, P. R., and A. H. Ehrlich. 2004. *One with Nineveh: Politics, Consumption, and the Human Future.* Washington, DC: Island Press.

*Ellis, B. 2014. "Identity Fraud Hits New Victim Every Two Seconds." CNNMoney. 6 February. Retrieved 15 March 2015 (money.cnn.com/2014/02/06/pf/identity-fraud/).

*Enerdata. 2014. "Global Energy Statistical Yearbook 2014." Retrieved 15 March 2015 (yearbook.enerdata.net).

*Environmental Defense Fund. 2015. "How Cap and Trade Works." Retrieved 15 March 2015 (www.edf.org/climate/how-cap-and-trade-works).

*Environmental Protection Agency. 2012. "Quick Facts about Cap and Trade." 10 May. Retrieved 16 March 2015 (www.epa.gov/captrade/).

*Environmental Protection Agency. 2014. "Municipal Solid Waste." 28 February. Retrieved 16 March 2015 (www.epa.gov/epawaste/nohaz/municipal/).

*Environmental Protection Agency. 2015a. "Information about the Air Quality Index (AQI)." Retrieved 15 March 2015 (airnow.gov/index.cfm?action=aqibasics.aqi).

*Environmental Protection Agency. 2015b. "Landfill Methane Outreach Program." Retrieved 17 March 2015 (http://www.epa.gov/outreach/lmop/index.html_).

*Fox, S., and L. Rainie. 2014. "The Web at 25 in the U.S." Pew Research Center. 27 February. Retrieved 20 March 2015 (www.pewinternet.org/2014/02/27/the-web-at-25-in-the-u-s/).

*Hind, R., C. Papathanasoupoulos, R. Moore, M. Roberts, M. Harden, and J. Kim. 2013. "The Danger in Our Backyards: The Threat of Chemical Facilities to Millions." New Brunswick, NJ: New Jersey Public Interest Research Group. Retrieved 20 March 2015 (www.njpirg.org/sites/pirg/files/reports/Danger%20In%20Our%20Backyards%20The%20Threat%20of%20Chemical%20Facilities%20to%20Americas%20Families-2013%20update.pdf).

*Internet World Stats. 2015. "Internet Usage Statistics: The Internet Big Picture." Retrieved 15 March 2015 (www.internetworldstats.com/stats.htm).

*Jones, J. M. 2014. "In U.S., Most Do Not See Global Warming as Serious Threat." Gallup. 13 March. Retrieved 15 March 2015 (www.gallup.com/poll/167879/not-global-warming-serious-threat.aspx).

*Lappé, F. M. 1971. *Diet for a Small Planet.* New York: Ballantine Books.

*Lepeule, J., F. Laden, D. Dockery, and J. Schwartz. 2012. "Chronic Exposure to Fine Particles and Mortality: An Extended Follow-Up of the Harvard Six Cities Study from 1974 to 2009." *Environmental Health Perspectives,* 120, 965–70.

Lichter, D. T., and G. V. Fuguitt. 1980. "Demographic Response to Transportation Innovation: The Case of the Interstate Highway." *Social Forces,* 59, 492–511.

*McCarthy, J. 2015. "Americans Name Government as No. 1 U.S. Problem." Gallup. 12 March. Retrieved 15 March 2015 (www.gallup.com/poll/181946/americans-name-government-no-problem.aspx).

Milgram, S. 1974. *Obedience to Authority: An Experimental View.* New York: HarperCollins.

*Moore, B., and S. Nichols. 2014. "Americans Still Favor Energy Conservation over Production." Gallup. 2 April. Retrieved 15 March 2015 (www.gallup.com/poll/168176/americans-favor-energy-conservation-production.aspx).

*Munang, R., and J. Andrews. 2014. "Despite Climate Change, Africa Can Feed Africa." AfricaRenewal. Retrieved 15 March 2015 (www.un.org/africarenewal/magazine/special-edition-agriculture-2014/despite-climate-change-africa-can-feed-africa).

*Nagourney, A. 2015. "California Drought Imposes First Mandatory Water Restrictions to Deal with Drought." *New York Times.* 1 April. Retrieved 23 April 2015 (www.nytimes.com/2015/04/02/us/california-imposes-first-ever-water-restrictions-to-deal-with-drought.html).

*Nuclear Energy Institute. 2015. "Used Nuclear Energy in Storage." Retrieved 20 March 2015 (http://www.nei.org/getmedia/1b50e6a4-9da9-44fe-af41-7eb1dc0c4e74/Used-Fuel-Map-2013?width=1100&height=850&ext=.png).

Ogburn, W. F. 1957. "Cultural Lag as Theory." *Sociology and Social Research,* 41, 167–74.

*OpenCongress. 2015. "On Passage: H R 2454 American Clean Energy and Security Act." Retrieved 16 March 2015 (www.opencongress.org/vote/2009/h/477).

Ophuls, W. 1977. *Ecology and the Politics of Scarcity.* San Francisco: Freeman.

*Orum, P., R. Moore, M. Roberts, and J. Sánchez. 2014. "Who's in Danger? Race, Poverty, and Chemical Disasters. A Demographic Analysis of Chemical Disaster Vulnerability Zones." Environmental Justice and Health Alliance for Chemical Policy Reform. May. Retrieved 16 March 2015 (comingcleaninc.org/assets/media/images/Reports/Who's%20in%20Danger%20Report%20FINAL.pdf).

*Pooley, E. 2010. *The Climate War: True Believers, Power Brokers, and the Fight to Save the Earth.* New York: Hachette Books.

*Rasmussen Reports. 2009. "Congress Pushes Cap and Trade, But Just 24% Know What It Is." 11 May. Retrieved 15 March 2015 (www.rasmussenreports.com/public_content/politics/current_events/environment_energy/congress_pushes_cap_and_trade_but_just_24_know_what_it_is).

*Riffkin, R. 2014. "Climate Change Not a Top Worry in U.S." Gallup. 12 March. Retrieved 15 March 2015 (www.gallup.com/poll/167843/climate-change-not-top-worry.aspx).

*Riley, M., B. Elgin, D. Lawrence, and C. Matlack. 2014. "Missed Alarms and 40 Million Stolen Credit Card Numbers: How Target Blew It." Bloomberg

Business. 13 March. Retrieved 15 March 2015 (www.bloomberg.com/bw/articles/2014-03-13/target-missed-alarms-in-epic-hack-of-credit-card-data).

*Romley, J. A., A. Hackbarth, and D. P. Goldman. 2010. "The Impact of Air Quality on Hospital Spending." RAND Health Technical Report. Santa Monica, CA: RAND Corporation.

*Sernau, S. R. 2013. *Global Problems: The Search for Equity, Peace, and Sustainability*, 3rd ed. Boston: Pearson.

*Skocpol, T. 2013. "Naming the Problem: What It Will Take to Counter Extremism and Engage Americans in the Fight against Global Warming." Harvard University. January. Retrieved 15 March 2015 (www.scholarsstrategynetwork.org/sites/default/files/skocpol_captrade_report_january_2013_0.pdf).

*Stevens, M. 2014. "In California, Water Use Is All Over the Map." 4 November. *Los Angeles Times*. Retrieved 16 March 2015 (www.latimes.com/local/california/la-me-1105-california-water-20141106-story.html).

*Su, J. G., M. Jerrett, R. Morello-Frosch, B. M. Jesdale, and A. D. Kyle. 2012. "Inequalities in Cumulative Environmental Burdens among Three Urbanized Counties in California." *Environment International*, 40, 79–87.

Tankersley, J. 2010. "U.S., China, Others Join Copenhagen Accord on Climate." *Los Angeles Times*. 2 February. Retrieved 15 March 2015 (articles.latimes.com/2010/feb/02/world/la-fg-climate-accord2-2010feb02).

*Union of Concerned Scientists. 2015. "Global Warming: Confronting the Realities of Climate Change." Retrieved 15 March 2015 (www.ucsusa.org/global_warming#.VQYTjmcU-HM).

*United Nations. 2015. "21st Century 'Hottest' on Record as Global Warming Continues – UN." UN and Climate Change. 2 February. Retrieved 15 March 2015 (www.un.org/climatechange/blog/2015/02/21st-century-hottest-record-global-warming-continues-un/).

*U.S. Department of Justice. 2015a. "Identity Theft and Identity Fraud: What Should I Do to Avoid Becoming a Victim of Identity Theft?" Retrieved 15 March 2015 (www.justice.gov/criminal/fraud/websites/idtheft.html).

*U.S. Department of Justice. 2015b. "What Are Identity Theft and Identity Fraud?" Retrieved 15 March 2015 (www.justice.gov/criminal/fraud/websites/idtheft.html).

Winner, L. 1986. *The Whale and the Reactor: A Search for Limits in an Age of High Technology*. Chicago: University of Chicago Press.

Winner, L. 1997. "Look Out for the Luddite Label." *MIT's Technology Review*. November–December, p. 62.

Winner, L. 2004. "Trust and Terror: the Vulnerability of Complex Socio-Technical Systems." *Science as Culture*, 13, 155–72.

*Worland, J. 2015. "California May Crack Down Further This Week on Water-Wasters." Time.com. 15 March. Retrieved 16 March 2015 (time.com/3745247/california-drought-water-state-regulators/).

*World Bank Group. 2014. *Turn Down the Heat: Confronting the New Climate Normal*. Washington, DC: World Bank. Retrieved 15 March 2015 (openknowledge.worldbank.org/handle/10986/20595).

*World Wildlife Fund. 2015. "What Are Climate Change and Global Warming?" Retrieved 15 March 2015 (www.wwf.org.uk/what_we_do/tackling_climate_change/climate_change_explained/).

Chapter 15

*Antiwar.org. 2015. "Casualties in Iraq." Retrieved 14 May 2015 (antiwar.com/casualties/).

*Arango, T. 2015. "Fall of Ramadi to ISIS Highlights Iraqi Premier's Weakening Authority." *New York Times*. 18 May. Retrieved 18 May 2015 (www.nytimes.com/2015/05/19/world/middleeast/fall-of-ramadi-to-isis-highlights-iraqi-premiers-weakening-authority.html?ref=topics).

*Arnett, G. 2014. "Religious Extremism Main Cause of Terrorism, According to Report." *The Guardian*. Retrieved 17 May 2015 (http://www.theguardian.com/news/datablog/2014/nov/18/religious-extremism-main-cause-of-terrorism-according-to-report).

Barton, J. H. 1981. *The Politics of Peace: An Evaluation of Arms Control*. Stanford, CA: Stanford University Press.

*BBC News Europe. 2015. "Charlie Hebdo Attack: Three Days of Terror." 14 January. Retrieved 17 May 2015 (www.bbc.com/news/world-europe-30708237).

*Beauchamp, S. 2015. "The Bipartisan War Consensus." Al Jazeera America. 2 January. Retrieved 18 May 2015 (america.aljazeera.com/opinions/2015/1/democrats-republican-swarhawks.html).

*Brooks, R. 2014. "Why Obama's Assurance of 'No Boots on the Ground' Isn't So Reassuring." Washington Post.com. 26 September. Retrieved 15 May 2015 (www.washingtonpost.com/opinions/why-obamas-assurance-of-no-boots-on-the-ground-isnt-so-reassuring/2014/09/26/c56d859e-44bf-11e4-9a15-137aa0153527_story.html).

Clawson, P. 1988. "Terrorism in Decline?" *Orbis*, 32, 263–76.

*Condon, S. 2014. "GOP Report Defends CIA Interrogation Tactics." CBS.com. 9 December. Retrieved 8 May 2015 (www.cbsnews.com/news/gop-report-defends-cia-interrogation-tactics/).

*Coser, L. 1956. *The Function of Social Conflict*. New York: Free Press.

*Costsofwar.org. 2014a. "Civilians Killed and Wounded." May. Retrieved 17 May 2015 (costsofwar.org/article/civilians-killed-and-wounded).

*Costsofwar.org. 2014b. "Did the Wars Bring Democracy to Afghanistan and Iraq?" October. Retrieved 17 May 2015 (costsofwar.org/article/did-wars-bring-democracy-afghanistan-and-iraq).

*Council on Foreign Relations. 2013. "China's Maritime Disputes." Retrieved 18 May 2015 (www.cfr.org/asia-and-pacific/chinas-maritime-disputes/p31345#!/).

Dershowitz, A. 2002. *Why Terrorism Works*. New Haven, CT: Yale University Press.

*Etzioni, A. 2002. "Opening Islam." *Society*, July–August. Pp. 29–35.

*Fischer, H. 2014. "A Guide to U.S. Military Casualty Statistics: Operation Inherent Resolve, Operation New Dawn, Operation Iraqi Freedom, and Operation Enduring Freedom." U.S. Department of Defense. 20 November. Retrieved 14 May 2015 (www.fas.org/sgp/crs/natsec/RS22452.pdf).

*Goodreads.com. 2015. "Best Iraq and Afghanistan War Books." May. Retrieved 17 May 2015 (www.goodreads.com/list/show/16945.Best_Iraq_and_Afghanistan_War_Books).

Guterl, F. 1996. "The Chemistry of Mass Murder." January. *Discover*, p. 7.

*Hall, Michelle. 2013. "By the Numbers: WW II's Atomic Bombs." Retrieved 20 May 2015 (http://www.cnn.com/2013/08/06/world/asia/btn-atomic-bombs/).

*History.com. 2015. "Bombing of Hiroshima and Nagasaki." Retrieved 20 May 2015 (http://www.history.com/topics/world-war-ii/bombing-of-hiroshima-and-nagasaki).

*Hooker, E. 2014. "Bioterrorism and Biowarfare Today." Emedicinehealth. 3 December. Retrieved 8 May 2015 (www.emedicinehealth.com/biological_warfare/page2_em.htm#bioterrorism_and_biowarfare_today).

*Institute for Economics and Peace. 2014. "Global Terrorism Index Report 2014." Retrieved 8 May 2015 (www.visionofhumanity.org/sites/default/files/Global%20Terrorism%20Index%20Report%202014.pdf).

Janowitz, M. 1978. *The Last Half Century: Societal Change and Politics in America*. Chicago: University of Chicago Press.

Jurkowitz, M. 2010. "Terrorism Tops Disasters." 11 May. Philadelphia: Pew Research Center.

Kristof, N. D. 1995. "The Bomb: An Act That Haunts Japan and America." 6 August. *New York Times*, pp. 1, 12.

*Lazare, S. 2015. "Enough War: Living Beneath Bombs, Yemenis Refuse to be Collateral Damage." Common Dreams. 8 April. Retrieved 17 May 2015 (www.commondreams.org/news/2015/04/08/enough-war-living-beneath-bombs-yemenis-refuse-be-collateral-damage).

Mazrui, A. A. 1996. "The New Dynamics of Security: The United Nations and Africa." *World Policy Journal*, 13, 37–42.

*McCarthy, J. 2015. "In U.S., Worries about Terrorism, Race Relations Up Sharply." Gallup. 17 March. Retrieved 12 May 2015 (www.gallup.com/poll/182018/worries-terrorism-race-relations-sharply.aspx).

Mills, C. W. 1956. *The Power Elite*. New York: Oxford University Press.

*Mills, C. W. 1958. *The Causes of World War Three*. New York: Simon & Shuster.

*Mills, C. W. 1959. *The Sociological Imagination*. New York: Oxford University Press.

Moskos, C. C. 2005. "Saving the All-Volunteer Force." *Military Review*, May–June, pp. 6–7.

*Park, R. 1941. "The Social Functions of War." *American Journal of Sociology*, 46, 551–70.

*Pew Research Center. 2002. "What the World Thinks in 2002." 4 December.

*Pew Research Center. 2014. "U.S. Favorability." Global Attitudes & Trends. 11 July. Retrieved 8 May 2015 (www.pewglobal.org/2014/07/14/global-opposition-to-u-s-surveillance-and-drones-but-limited-harm-to-americas-image/pg-2014-07-14-balance-of-power-1-02/).

*Pew Research Center. 2015. "Growing Support for Campaign Against ISIS—and Possible Use of U.S. Ground Troops." 24 February. Retrieved 12 May 2015 (www.people-press.org/2015/02/24/growing-support-for-campaign-against-isis-and-possible-use-of-u-s-ground-troops/).

*Pianin, E. 2015. "McCain: Get Ready for U.S. Troops on the Ground in Iraq and Syria." *The Fiscal Times*, January 27. Retrieved 18 May 2015 (http://www.thefiscaltimes.com/2015/01/27/McCain-Get-Ready-US-Troops-Ground-Iraq-and-Syria).

*Raghavan, S. 2014. "Record Number of U.N. Peacekeepers Fails to Stop African Wars." *Washington Post*. 3 January. Retrieved 26 May 2015 (www.washingtonpost.com/world/record-number-of-un-peacekeepers-fails-to-stop-african-wars/2014/01/03/17ed0574-7487-11e3-9389-09ef9944065e_story.html).

Rapoport, A. 1968. "Introduction." In C. von Clausewitz, *On War*. Harmondsworth, England: Penguin Books.

*Simmel, G. 1904. "The Sociology of Conflict." *American Journal of Sociology*, 9, 490–525.

Sorokin, P. 1937. *Social and Cultural Dynamics: Vol. 3. Fluctuations of Social Relationships, War, and Revolution*. New York: American Book.

Spector, B. I. 2003. "Negotiating with Villains Revisited: Research Note." *International Negotiation*, 8, 613–21.

Stouffer, S. A., E. A. Suchman, L. C. DeVinney, S. A. Starr, and R. M. Williams. 1949. *The American Soldier*. Princeton, NJ: Princeton University Press.

*Substance Abuse and Mental Health Services Administration. 2014. "Veterans and Military Families." 29 September. Retrieved 8 May 2015 (www.samhsa.gov/veterans-military-families).

*Theodoridis, A. 2015. "Scott Walker's View of Obama's Religion Makes Him a Moderate." *Washington Post*. 25 February. Retrieved 8 May 2015 (www.washingtonpost.com/blogs/monkey-cage/wp/2015/02/25/scott-walkers-view-of-obamas-religion-makes-him-a-moderate/).

*United Nations High Commissioner for Refugees. 2013. "New UNHCR Report Says Global Forced Displacement at 18-year High." 19 June. Retrieved 18 May 2015 (www.unhcr.org/51c071816.html).

*U.S. Department of Homeland Security. 2012. "Our Mission." 17 December. Retrieved 8 May 2015 (www.dhs.gov/our-mission).

*U.S. Department of State. 2014. "Country Reports on Terrorism: 2013." Retrieved 16 May 2015 (http://www.state.gov/j/ct/rls/crt/2013/index.htm).

*U.S. Department of Veterans Affairs. 2014a. "PTSD: National Center for PTSD. How Common Is PTSD?" 10 November. Retrieved 8 May 2015 (www.ptsd.va.gov/public/PTSD-overview/basics/how-common-is-ptsd.asp).

*U.S. Department of Veterans Affairs. 2014b. "PTSD: National Center for PTSD. Rape of Women in a War Zone." 10 October. Retrieved 8 May 2015 (www.ptsd.va.gov/public/pages/rape-women-war-zone.asp).

*U.S. Department of Veterans Affairs. 2014c. "Service-Connected Disabled Veterans by Disability Rating Group: FY1986 to FY2013." Retrieved 8 May 2015 (www.va.gov/vetdata/Utilization.asp).

*U.S. History.org. 2014. "The Decision to Drop the Bomb." Retrieved 20 May 2015 (http://www.ushistory.org/us/51g.asp).

*Walt, V. 2015. "Paris Jews Reel after Deadly Kosher-Supermarket Attack." Time.com. 11 January. Retrieved 17 May 2015 (time.com/3663060/paris-terror-attack-jews-kosher-supermarket-siege/).

*World Trade Organization. 2014. "International Trade Statistics 2014." Retrieved 17 May 2015 (www.wto.org/english/res_e/statis_e/its2014_e/its2014_e.pdf).

*Wounded Warrior Project. 2015. "Who We Serve." 1 May. Retrieved 8 May 2015 (www.woundedwarriorproject.org/mission/who-we-serve.aspx).

*YouGov. 2015. "Obama Should Go to Congress for ISIS War, But Probably Doesn't Need To." Retrieved 18 May 2015 (today.yougov.com/news/2015/02/18/obama-should-got-congress-over-iraqsyria-probably-/).

Credits

Text Credits

Chapter 1

p. 5, Figure 1-1: Graph: "Most Important Problems Facing the United States, 2001–2014" Saul, L. 2015. "Cluster of Concerns Vie for Top U.S. Problem in 2014." Gallup. 2 January. Retrieved 27 April 2015 www.gallup.com/poll/180398/cluster-concerns-vie-top-problem-2014.aspx; **p. 8,** PQ: "Politics Is the Study of Who Gets What, When, and How" Lasswell. 1941. "The Garrison State." American Journal of Sociology, 46:455-468; **p. 13,** PQ: "Conditions That Are Incompatible with Group Values" Rubington, E., & M.S. Weinberg. 2003. The Study of Social Problems: Seven Perspectives, 6th ed. New York: Oxford University Press; **p. 15,** "Situations people define as real....are real in their consequences" Thomas, W.I., & F. Znaniecki. 1922. The Polish Peasant in Europe and America. New York: Knopf; **p. 18,** "Stage 1—Problem definition. Groups in society....press their claims and enact reforms" Spector, M., & J. Kitsuse. 1987. Constructing Social Problems. Hawthorne, NY: Aldine de Gruyter; **p. 26,** "PQ: "global warming will seriously threaten one's way of life" Jones, J.M. 2014. "In U.S., Most Do Not See Global Warming as Serious Threat." Gallup. 13 March. Retrieved 15 March 2015 www.gallup.com/poll/167879/not-global-warming-serious-threat.aspx; **p. 26,** PQ: "much broader than anything I could have imagined" Alcaly, R.E. 2010, p. 43. "How They Killed the Economy." 25 March. New York Review of Books

Chapter 2

p. 31, Table 2-1: "Health Indicators for Selected Nations, 1970-2013" from Population Reference Bureau, 2014; **p. 32, Box:** "A Global View: Fistulas" Adapted from The Fistula Foundation 2013; World Health Organization March 2010; **p. 34, Chart:** "Number of Uninsured in the United States, 2012 (millions)" Based on DeNavas-Walt, C., and Proctor, B.D. 2014. "Income and Poverty in the United States: 2013." Current Population Reports. P60-249. Washington, DC: U.S. Census Bureau.; Martinez, M.E., and Cohen, R.A. 2014. "Health Insurance Coverage: Early Release of Estimates from the National Health Interview Survey, January-June 2014." National Center for Health Statistics. December. Retrieved 25 February 2015 (www.cdc.gov/nchs/nhis/releases.htm); **p. 36, Chart:** "Characteristics of the Non-elderly Uninsured: Family Work Status, Fall 2014" Garfield, R., and Young, K. 2015. "Adults who Remained Uninsured at the End of 2014." The Henry J. Kaiser Family Foundation. Executive Summary. 29 January. Retrieved 25 February 2015 (kff.org/health-reform/issue-brief/adults-who-remained-uninsured-at-the-end-of-2014/); **p. 36, Chart:** "Characteristics of the Non-elderly Uninsured: Family Income, Fall 2014" Garfield, R., and Young, K. 2015. "Adults who Remained Uninsured at the End of 2014." The Henry J. Kaiser Family Foundation. Executive Summary. 29 January. Retrieved 25 February 2015 (kff.org/health-reform/issue-brief/adults-who-remained-uninsured-at-the-end-of-2014/); **p. 36, Chart:** "Characteristics of the Non-elderly Uninsured: Race, Fall 2014" Garfield, R.,

and Young, K. 2015. "Adults who Remained Uninsured at the End of 2014." The Henry J. Kaiser Family Foundation. Executive Summary. 29 January. Retrieved 25 February 2015 (kff.org/health-reform/issue-brief/adults-who-remained-uninsured-at-the-end-of-2014/); **p. 37, Chart:** "Major Health Indicators, by Race and Ethnicity: Life Expectancy 2012" Based on National Center for Health Statistics. 2013. "Health, United States, 2012: With Special Feature on Emergency Care." Hyattsville, MD; **p. 37,** Chart: "Major Health Indicators, by Race and Ethnicity: Infant Mortality Rate 2012" Based on National Center for Health Statistics. 2013. "Health, United States, 2012: With Special Feature on Emergency Care." Hyattsville, MD; **p. 37, Chart:** "Major Health Indicators, by Race and Ethnicity: Only Fair or Poor Health (Self-Assessment), 2012" Based on National Center for Health Statistics. 2013. "Health, United States, 2012: With Special Feature on Emergency Care." Hyattsville, MD; **p. 38,** "Heart Disease. Blacks are less likely...glasses and hearing aids" Based on Agency for Healthcare Research and Quality. 2000. Addressing Racial and Ethnic Disparities in Health Care. Rockville, MD: Agency for Healthcare Research and Quality; **p. 39, Chart:** "Major Health Indicators, by Income (Federal poverty level): Only Fair or Poor Health (Self-Assesment), 2012" Based on National Center for Health Statistics. 2013. "Health, United States, 2012: With Special Feature on Emergency Care." Hyattsville, MD; **p. 39, Chart:** "Major Health Indicators, by Income (Federal Poverty Level): Serious Psychological Distress, 2012" Based on National Center for Health Statistics. 2013. "Health, United States, 2012: With Special Feature on Emergency Care." Hyattsville, MD; **p. 40, Chart:** "Major Health Indicators, by Income (Federal Poverty Level): Disability Among Elderly, 2012" Based on National Center for Health Statistics. 2013. "Health, United States, 2012: With Special Feature on Emergency Care." Hyattsville, MD; **p. 41, Chart:** "Percentage of Non-Elderly Adults with Difficulty Paying Medical Bills, 2012" Pollitz, K., Cox, C., Lucia, K., and Keith, K. 2014. "Medical Debt Among People With Health Insurance." Henry J. Kaiser Family Foundation. 7 January. Retrieved 27 February 2015 (kff.org/report-section/medical-debt-among-people-with-health-insurance-incidence-of-medical-debt/); **p. 42, Chart:** "Distribution of National Health Expenditures, by Type of Service (in Billions), 2010" Based on Kaiser Family Foundation. 2012. "Health Care Costs: A Primer." May; **p. 45, Table:** "An Example of Calculating BMI to Determine Weight Category"

Chapter 3

p. 60, "a state of well-being in which the individual realizes....contribution to his or her community" World Health Organization. 2014. "Media Centre: Suicide." Fact Sheet No. 398. September. Retrieved 11 April 2015 (www.who.int/mediacentre/factsheets/fs398/en/); **p. 60,** "A mental, behavioral, or emotional disorder..... Manual of Mental Disorders" National Institute of Mental Health. 2015. "Statistics." Retrieved 11 April 2015 (www.nimh.nih.gov/health/statistics/index.shtml); **p. 61, Figure 3-1:** "Chart: Prevalence of Any Mental Illness among U.S. Adults, 2012 National Institute of Mental Health. 2015" "Statistics." Retrieved 11 April 2015 (www.nimh

.nih.gov/health/statistics/index.shtml); **p. 63**, "As I write, I can see the lower.....suicide since the building opened in 1931" Kornblum, one of the authors of this textbook; **p. 66, Box:** "A Personal View—My Brain Works Differently" Marshall, age 11; **p. 70, Figure 3-2:** "Chart: Military Service Members with a Mental Health Condition or Who Reported Experiencing a Traumatic Brain Injury, 2008" Based on RAND Center for Military Health Policy Research. 2008. "Invisible Wounds: Mental Health and Cognitive Care Needs of America's Returning Veterans." RB-9336. Retrieved 11 April 2015 (http://www.rand.org/content/dam/rand/pubs/research_briefs/2008/RAND_RB9336.pdf); **p. 71, Figure 3-3:** "Chart: Top Five Barriers among Military Service Members to Seeking Mental Health Care, 2008" RAND Center for Military Health Policy Research. 2008. "Invisible Wounds: Mental Health and Cognitive Care Needs of America's Returning Veterans." RB-9336. Retrieved 11 April 2015 (http://www.rand.org/content/dam/rand/pubs/research_briefs/2008/RAND_RB9336.pdf); **p. 71, Box:** "A Closer Look: 9/11 and Schoolchildren" Based on Hoven, C.W., Duarte, C.S.; Lucas, C.P.; P. Wu, Mandell,D.J.; Goodwin, R.D.; Cohen, M.; Balaban, V.; Woodruff, B.A.; Bin, F.; Musa, G.J, ; Mei, L, Cantor, P.A., Aber, J.L, Cohen, P.; Susser, E., 2005. "Psychopathology Among New York City Public School Children 6 Months After September 11." Archives of General Psychology, 62: 545-551; **p. 75, Figure 3-4:** "Line Art: The Vicious Cycle of Poverty and Mental Disorders" World Health Organization, 2001; **p. 75, Figure 3-5:** "Chart: Prevalence of Any Mental Illness among U.S. Adults by race/Ethnicity 2012" National Institute of Mental Health. 2015. "Statistics." Retrieved 11 April 2015 (www.nimh.nih.gov/health/statistics/index.shtml); **p. 76,** "Genetics. If a woman has a family history of depression.....with similar challenges do not." Based on National Institute of Mental Health. 2015. "Statistics." Retrieved 11 April 2015 (www.nimh.nih.gov/health/statistics/index.shtml).; World Health Organization. 2015. "Gender and Women's Mental Health: Gender Disparities and Mental Health: The Facts." Retrieved 11 April 2015 (www.who.int/mental_health/prevention/genderwomen/en/); **p. 77,** Table 3-1: " Prevalence of Specific Mental Disorders among Children, 2011" Perou, R., R.H. Bitsko, S.J. Blumberg, P. Pastor, R.M. Ghandour, J.C. Gfroerer, S.L. Hedden, A.E. Crosby, S.N. Visser, L.A. Schieve, S.E. Parks, J.E. Hall, D. Brody, C.M. Simile, W.W. Thompson, J. Baio, S. Avenevoli, M.D. Kogan, & L.N. Huang. 2013. "Mental Health Surveillance Among Children—United States, 2005–2011." Morbidity and Mortality Weekly Report (MMWR), 62, 1-35; **p. 81,** PQ: "recovery assessment scale" Hendryx, M., C.A. Green, & N.A. Perrin. 2009. "Social Support, Activities, and Recovery from Serious Mental Illness: STARS Study Findings." Journal of Behavioral Health Services Research, 36, 320-329; **p. 85,** PQ: "disorganized, depressed, disordered...immobilized by pain and traumatized by fear" Kozol, J. 1988. "The Homeless and Their Children." The New Yorker. 25 January, pp. 65ff; 1 February, pp. 36ff

Chapter 4

p. 91, Table 4-1: "Estimated Number of Drug-Related Deaths (Non-Alcohol) and Mortality Rates Per Million Persons Ages 15–64, 2012" United Nations Office on Drugs and Crime. 2014. World Drug Report 2014 (United Nations publication, Sales No. E.14.XI.7); **p. 94, Table 4-2:** "Lifetime Prevalence Rates of Use of Different Drugs among High School Seniors, 2014" National Institute on Drug Abuse. 2015b. "Drugs of Abuse." Retrieved 20 April 2015 (www.drugabuse.gov/drugs-abuse); **p. 94, Figure 4-1:** Graph: "Trends in Lifetime Prevalence of Any Illegal

Drug, 8th, 10th, and 12th Graders, 1992–2014" Johnston, L.D., P.M. O'Malley, R.A. Miech, J.G. Bachman, & J.E. Schulenberg. 2015. Monitoring the Future National Survey Results on Drug Use: 1975-2014: Overview, Key Findings on Adolescent Drug Use. Ann Arbor: Institute for Social Research, The University of Michigan; **p. 95, Figure 4-2:** Chart: "Average Number of Drinks Per Person Consumed Weekly by Decile, Adults Age 18 and Over, 2014" Ingraham, C. 2014. "Think You Drink a Lot? This Chart Will Tell You." Washington Post. 25 September. Retrieved 15 April 2015 (www.washingtonpost.com/blogs/wonkblog/wp/2014/09/25/think-you-drink-a-lot-this-chart-will-tell-you/); **p. 97, Table 4-3:** "Sex Differences in Alcohol Consumption, 2013" National Institute on Alcohol Abuse and Alcoholism. 2013b. "Women and Alcohol." August. Retrieved 15 April 2015 (pubs.niaaa.nih.gov/publications/womensfact/womensfact.htm); **p. 101, Figure 4-3:** Chart: "Fatalities and Fatality Rate per 100 Million VMT in Alcohol-Impaired-Driving Crashes, 2004–2013" National Highway Traffic Safety Administration. 2014. "Alcohol-Impaired Driving." U.S. Department of Transportation. DOT HS 812 102. Retrieved 20 April 2015 (www-nrd.nhtsa.dot.gov/Pubs/812102.pdf); **p. 101,** "37% of rapes and sexual assaults......25% of simple assaults" National Council on Alcohol and Drug Dependence, Inc. 2015a. "Alcohol and Crime." Retrieved 20 April 2015 (ncadd.org/learn-about-alcohol/alcohol-and-crime/202-alcohol-and-crime); **p. 103,** "Chief Enabler. A child may put aside his.....members, but does not really help the mascot" McGaha, J.E., J.L. Stokes, & J. Nielson. 1990. "Children of Alcoholism: Implications For Juvenile Justice." Juvenile & Family Court Journal, 41, 19-24; **p. 103, Box:** "A Personal View—'My Dad Is an Alcoholic'" Chris, age 13; **p. 106, Table 4-4:** "Percentage of Persons 12 or Over, and 26 or Over Who Have Used a Drug during Their Lifetime" National Institute on Drug Abuse. 2015b. "Drugs of Abuse." Retrieved 20 April 2015 (www.drugabuse.gov/drugs-abuse); **p. 112, Figure 4-4:** Graph: "Percentage of Persons Age 12 and Older Who Have Used the Most Common Drugs Over the Past Month, 2002–2012" National Institute on Drug Abuse. 2014. "DrugFacts: Nationwide Trends." January. Retrieved 20 April 2015 (www.drugabuse.gov/publications/drugfacts/nationwide-trends); **p. 112, Figure 4-5:** Chart: "Percentage Using Drugs in Past Month, by Age, 2011–2012" National Institute on Drug Abuse. 2014. "DrugFacts: Nationwide Trends." January. Retrieved 20 April 2015 (www.drugabuse.gov/publications/drugfacts/nationwide-trends); **p. 116, Figure 4-6:** Graph: "Americans' Views on Legalizing Marijuana" Swift, A. 2013. "For First Time, Americans Favor Legalizing Marijuana." Gallup. 22 October. Retrieved 20 April 2015 (www.gallup.com/poll/165539/first-time-americans-favor-legalizing-marijuana.aspx); **p. 117,** "Our conclusion is that the present law on cannabis.....including the risks of cannabis itself" Police Foundation of the United Kingdom. 2000. "Drugs and the Law: Report of the Independent Inquiry into the Misuse of Drugs Act of 1971." 4 April. Retrieved 17 April 2015 (www.drugscope.org.uk/Resources/Drugscope/Documents/PDF/virtuallibrary/runcimanreport.pdf)

Chapter 5

p. 120, "Crime is present....is the existence of criminality" Durkheim, É. 1897/1951. Suicide, a Study in Sociology. New York: Free Press; **p. 120, Table 5-1:** "Number of Violent Crimes, and Rate of Violent Crime per 100,000 People, 1994, 2000, 2013" Federal Bureau of Investigation, Uniform Crime Reports. 2014a. "2013 Hate Crime Statistics: Incidents and Offenses." Retrieved 29 March 2015 (www.fbi.gov/about-us/cjis/ucr/hate-crime/2013/

topic-pages/incidents-and-offenses/incidentsandoffenses_final); **p. 121, Table 5-2:** "Number of Property Crimes, and Rate of Property Crime per 100,000 People, 1994, 2000, 2013" Federal Bureau of Investigation, Uniform Crime Reports. 2014b. "Crime in the United States 2013: Property Crime." Retrieved 21 March 2015 (www.fbi.gov/about-us/cjis/ucr/crime-in-the-u.s/2013/crime-in-the-u.s.-2013/property-crime/property-crime-topic-page/propertycrimemain_final); **p. 121, Table 5-3:** "Percentage of Victimizations That Are Reported to the Police, 2013" Truman, J.L., & L. Langton. 2014. "Criminal Victimization, 2013." NCJ 247648. Bureau of Justice Statistics, U.S. Department of Justice. September. Retrieved 21 March 2015 (www.bjs.gov/content/pub/pdf/cv13.pdf); **p. 122,** "is something that threatens....is an essential starting point" Radzinowicz, L.R., & J. King. 1977. The Growth of Crime: The International Experience. New York: Basic Books; **p. 123,** "a police bureaucracy has a significant....law in the same circumstances" Brown, M.K. 1988. Working the Street: Police Discretion and Dilemmas of Reform. New York: Russell Sage; **p. 125, Figure 5-1:** Chart: "Violent Crime Rate, per 100,000 People, 2013" Based on Federal Bureau of Investigation, Uniform Crime Reports. 2014a. "2013 Hate Crime Statistics: Incidents and Offenses." Retrieved 29 March 2015 (www.fbi.gov/about-us/cjis/ucr/hate-crime/2013/topic-pages/incidents-and-offenses/incidentsandoffenses_final); **p. 126, Figure 5-2:** Chart: "Murder by Relationship" Based on Federal Bureau of Investigation, Uniform Crime Reports. 2014b. "Crime in the United States 2013: Property Crime." Retrieved 21 March 2015 (www.fbi.gov/about-us/cjis/ucr/crime-in-the-u.s/2013/crime-in-the-u.s.-2013/property-crime/property-crime-topic-page/propertycrimemain_final); **p. 127, Map 5-1:** "Homicide Rates, by Country or Territory, 2012 or latest year" United Nations Office on Drugs and Crime. 2013. "Homicide Counts and Rates, Time Series 2000-2012." Global Study on Homicide. Retrieved 25 March 2015 (www.unodc.org/gsh/en/data.html); **p. 128,** "We have never hesitated to investigate....advantage of the American people" Remarks for Attorney General Eric Holder Press Conference Announcing Settlement with S&P, Washington, February 3, 2015; **p. 133, Figure 5-3:** Chart: "Types of Hate Crimes (N = 6,933), 2013" Based on Federal Bureau of Investigation, Uniform Crime Reports. 2014a. "2013 Hate Crime Statistics: Incidents and Offenses." Retrieved 29 March 2015 (www.fbi.gov/about-us/cjis/ucr/hate-crime/2013/topic-pages/incidents-and-offenses/incidentsandoffenses_final); **p. 136,** "if two persons fell under suspicion of crime the uglier or more deformed was to be regarded as more probably guilty" Ellis, 1914 quoted in Wilson, J.Q., & R.J. Herrnstein. 1985. Crime and Human Nature. New York: Simon & Schuster; **p. 137,** "biology is not destiny....racism might become violent" Nelkin, D. 1995. "Biology is not Destiny." New York Times. 28 September. P. A27; **p. 140, Figure 5-4:** Chart: "Percentage who say race was a factor in the Grand Jury's Decision Not to Charge in the Michael Brown" Based on Pew Research Center/USA Today Survey. 2014. "Sharp Racial Divisions in Reactions to Brown, Garner Decisions." 8 December. Retrieved 26 March 2015 (www.people-press.org/2014/12/08/sharp-racial-divisions-in-reactions-to-brown-garner-decisions/); **p. 141,** "a person becomes delinquent because of the excess of definitions favorable to violation of law over definitions unfavorable to violation of law" Sutherland, E.H., & D.R. Cressey. 1960. Principles of Criminology. Philadelphia: Lippincott; **p. 142,** "takes its norms from the larger culture...of the larger culture" Cohen, A.K. 1971. Delinquent Boys. New York: Free Press; **p. 142,** "Trouble. Trouble is important to the.....to mental hospitals or prisons" Based on Miller, W.B. 2001. The Growth of Youth Gang Prob-

lems in the United States: 1970-98 : Report. Darby, PA: Diane Pub Co.; **p. 142,** PQ: "higher moral principles beyond those of self-interest" Janowitz, M. 1978. The Last Half Century: Societal Change and Politics in America. Chicago: University of Chicago Press; **p. 144,** "To destigmatize crime would be to lift.... society has no business making it a crime" Wilson, J.Q. 1977. Thinking About Crime. New York: Vintage Books; **p. 148, Figure 5-5:** Chart: "Percentage of Adults Expressing Support for Protecting Rights of Americans to Own Guns vs. Support for Controlling Gun Ownership" Based on Pew Research Center. 2014. "Growing Public Support for Gun Rights." 10 December. Retrieved 26 March 2015 (www.people-press.org/2014/12/10/growing-public-support-for-gun-rights/)

Chapter 6

p. 153, Box 6-1: "A Global View: Adeola's Story" Based on International Fund for Agricultural Development, 2014; United Nations Children's Fund and UNAIDS; **p. 153, Figure 6-1,** Chart: "Increase in Children Orphaned by AIDS in Sub-Saharan Africa, 1990–2015" Based on AVERT, 2015; United Nations Children's Fund and UNAIDS, 2006, 2014; **p. 156, Figure 6-2:** "Chart: Corporate Income Taxes as a percentage of Gross Domestic Product, 1942-2013" Based on Tax Policy Center. 2013. "Tax Facts: Corporate Income Taxes as a Percent of GDP, 1946-2012." Retrieved 15 March 2015 (www.taxpolicycenter.org/taxfacts/displayafact.cfm?Docid=263); **p. 157, Table 6-1:** "Share of Income Received by Each Fifth and Top 5 Percent of Households" DeNavas-Walt, C., & B.D. Proctor. 2014. "Income and Poverty in the United States: 2013." Current Population Reports. P60-249. Washington, DC: U.S. Census Bureau; **p. 157, Table 6-2:** "Mean Household Income Received by Each Fifth and Top 5 Percent, 2013" DeNavas-Walt, C., & B.D. Proctor. 2014. "Income and Poverty in the United States: 2013." Current Population Reports. P60-249. Washington, DC: U.S. Census Bureau; **p. 158,** "people are poverty stricken when their income, even if adequate for survival, falls markedly behind that of the community" Galbraith, J.K. 1958. The Affluent Society. Boston: Houghton Mifflin; **p. 158, Figure 6-3a:** Chart: "Number in Poverty, 1959-2013 (Millions)" DeNavas-Walt, C., & B.D. Proctor. 2014. "Income and Poverty in the United States: 2013." Current Population Reports. P60-249. Washington, DC: U.S. Census Bureau; **p. 159, Figure 6-3b:** Chart: "Poverty Rate, 1959-2013" DeNavas-Walt, C., & B.D. Proctor. 2014. "Income and Poverty in the United States: 2013." Current Population Reports. P60-249. Washington, DC: U.S. Census Bureau; **p. 160, Table 6-3:** "People and Families in Poverty (15% of Total Population) by Selected Characteristics, 2013" DeNavas-Walt, C., & B.D. Proctor. 2014. "Income and Poverty in the United States: 2013." Current Population Reports. P60-249. Washington, DC: U.S. Census Bureau; **p. 160,** "Some nights were really hard...babies go hungry" © Pearson Education, Inc.; **p. 161, Figure 6-4:** Chart: "Relative child poverty rates, Percentage of children Aged 0-17 Living in households with Equivalent incomes below 50% of National Median" UNICEF Innocenti Research Centre. 2013. "Child Well-Being in Rich Countries: A Comparative Overview." Report Card 11. April. Retrieved 26 February 2014 (www.unicef-irc.org/publications/pdf/rc11_eng.pdf); **p. 162, Figure 6-5:** Chart: "Level of child support payment among custodial parents with a formal agreement or court orders, 1995, 2005, 2011" Based on Grall, T.S. 2013. "Custodial Mothers and Fathers and Their Child Support: 2011." Current Population Reports P60-246. October. Washington, D.C.: U.S. Census Bureau; **p. 163, Figure 6-6:** Chart: Educational Extremes, by Race and etnicity, age 18 and older 2014 U.S

Census Bureau, jan 5,2015 (Educational Attainment in the united states: 2014 detailed tables); **p. 164,** "Hopefully I can get me a job….something comes through" Seccombe, Karen. 2015. So You Think I Drive a Cadillac?: Welfare Recipients' Perspectives on the System and Its Reform,4th ed. Boston: Pearson; **p. 168,** "Inadequate health and nutrition…. Poor-quality neighborhoods" Seccombe, Karen. 2007. Families in Poverty. Boston: Allyn & Bacon; **p. 168, Figure 6-7:** Chart: "Pathway from poverty to Adverse Child outcomes" Adapted from Children's Defense Fund. 2005. "Defining Poverty and Why It Matters for Children." Retrieved 6 July 2007 (www.childrensdefensefund.org); Brooks-Gunn, J. & G.J. Duncan. 1997. "The Effects of Poverty on Children." The Future of Children (Children and Poverty), 7, 55–71; and Seccombe, Families and their social worlds, 3e @2016 pearson; **p. 171, Table 6-4:** "Comparisons of Home and Neighborhood by Income" Based on Siebens, J. 2013. "Extended Measures of Well-Being: Living Conditions in the United States: 2011." Household Economic Studies P70-136. September. Washington, D.C.: U.S. Census Bureau; **p. 173,** "I think a lot of them are on it…abusing the system." © Pearson Education, Inc.; **p. 174,** "I live in Hungary, where the benefits for families….life easier for families" Based on Strong-Jekely, L. 2006. Letter to the Editor. Brain, Child, p. 2. Budapest, Hungary, Winter; **p. 175,** "Which of the following reasons…. welfare that prevents initiative" McClam, E. 2013. "Americans Blame Poverty on 'Too Much' Welfare, NBC/WSJ Poll Shows." thegrio.com. 6 June. Retrieved 1 March 2015 (thegrio.com/2013/06/06/americans-blame-poverty-on-too-much-welfare-nbcwsj-poll-shows/); **p. 177, Table 6-5:** "Reasons for Poverty, 2013" McClam, E. 2013. "Americans Blame Poverty on 'Too Much' Welfare, NBC/WSJ Poll Shows." thegrio.com. 6 June. Retrieved 1 March 2015 (thegrio.com/2013/06/06/americans-blame-poverty-on-too-much-welfare-nbcwsj-poll-shows/); **p. 178, Figure 6-8:** Chart: "Number of Families Receiving cash welfare Benefits for every 100 families with children in poverty" Based on Trisi, D., & L. Pavetti. 2012. "TANF Weakening as a Safety Net For Poor Families." Center for Budget and Policy Priorities. 13 March. Retrieved 1 March 2015 (www.cbpp.org/cms/?fa=view&id=3700); **p. 178,** "There's all these doctor's offices…grand's not worth it." © Pearson Education, Inc.; **p. 180,** "We fought a war on poverty, and poverty won" President Ronald Reagan

Chapter 7

p. 183, Figure 7-1: Line Art: "Percentage saying situation of Black people is better today than five year ago, 2007, 2009, 2013" Pew Research Center. 2013. "King's Dream Remains an Elusive Goal; Many Americans See Racial Disparities." Social & Demographic Trends. 22 August. Retrieved 9 March 2015 (www.pewsocialtrends.org/2013/08/22/kings-dream-remains-an-elusive-goal-many-americans-see-racial-disparities/); **p. 184,** "We have a choice in this country…help all of America prosper" Barack Obama's Speech on Race, The New York Times, March 18, 2008; **p. 184, Figure 7-2:** Chart: "U.S Population by Race and Hispanic origin 2014, 2060" Based on Colby, S.L., & J.M. Ortman. 2015. "Projections of the Size and Composition of the U.S. Population: 2014 to 2060: Population Estimates and Projections." Current Population Reports. P25-1143. March. U.S. Census Bureau. Retrieved 9 March 2015 (www.census.gov/content/dam/Census/library/publications/2015/demo/p25-1143.pdf); **p. 185,** "separate educational facilities are inherently unequal…separate cannot be equal" Brown v. Board of Education of Topeka; **p. 185,** "The first is surely the continuing…problem of racial disorder. 'our nation

is moving toward two societies, one black, one white—separate and unequal'" National Advisory Commission on Civil Disorders. 1968. Report of the National Advisory Commission on Civil Disorders. Washington, DC: U.S. Government Printing Office; **p. 186,** "For those of Middle Eastern descent …and airline personnel" U.S. Commission on Civil Rights, Ohio Advisory Committee. 2001. Briefing on Civil Rights Issues Facing Muslims and Arab Americans in Ohio Post-September 11. 14 November. P.203, 1; **p. 187,** "Minorities are subordinate…marry within their group" Based on Feagin, J. 2013. The White Racial Frame: Centuries of Racial Framing and Counter-Framing, 2nd ed. New York: Routledge; Simpson, G.E. & J.M. Yinger. 1985. Racial and Ethnic Minorities: An Analysis of Prejudice and Discrimination, 5th ed. New York: Plenum; **p. 190, Table 7-1:** "A Typology of Prejudice and Discrimination" Adapted with the permission of The Free Press, a Division of Simon & Schuster Adult Publishing Group, from Social Theory and Social Structure by Robert K. Merton. Copyright © 1949, 1957 by The Free Press. Copyright © renewed 1977, 1985 by Robert K. Merton. All rights reserved; **p. 193, Table 7-2:** "Percentage Who Approve of Racial Intermarriage, 2013" Newport, F. 2013. "IN U.S. 87 Percent Approve of Black-White Marriage, As Opposed to 4 Percent in 1958. Gallup.com. 25 July. Retrieved 8 April 2015 (http://www.gallup.com/poll/163697/approve-marriage-blacks-whites.aspx); **p. 195, Table 7-3:** "Number of Individual Filings of Discrimination Based on Race, National Origin, or Color, 2000, 2014" U.S. Equal Employment Opportunity Commission. 2015. "Charge Statistics FY 1997 Through FY 2014." Retrieved 11 March 2015 (eeoc.gov/eeoc/statistics/enforcement/charges.cfm); **p. 198, Figure 7-3:** Chart: "Median Annual Earnings of Full-Time Year-Round Workers, Ages 25–34, by Educational Attainment and Race/Ethnicity, 2012" Based on National Center for Education Statistics. 2013. "Median annual earnings of full-time year-round workers 25 to 34 years old and full-time year-round workers as a percentage of the labor force, by sex, race/ethnicity, and educational attainment: Selected years, 1995 through 2012." Table 502.30. Digest of Education Statistics. October. Retrieved 9 March 2015. (nces.ed.gov/programs/digest/d13/tables/dt13_502.30.asp); **p. 198,** "with all deliberate speed 'separate but equal'" Brown v. Board of Education of Topeka; **p. 199, Figure 7-4:** Graph: "Percentage of Black Students in Majority-White Schools" Orfield, G., E. Frankenberg, J. Ee, & J. Kuscera. 2014. "Brown at 60: Great Progress, a Long Retreat and an Uncertain Future." The Civil Rights Project. 15 May. Retrieved 9 March 2015 (civilrightsproject.ucla.edu/research/k-12-education/integration-and-diversity/brown-at-60-great-progress-a-long-retreat-and-an-uncertain-future/Brown-at-60-051814.pdf); **p. 200, Figure 7-5:** Chart: "Percentage of Hispanics Enrolled in 'Intensely Segregated' Schools (90%–100% Minority)" Based on Orfield, G., E. Frankenberg, J. Ee, & J. Kuscera. 2014. "Brown at 60: Great Progress, a Long Retreat and an Uncertain Future." The Civil Rights Project. 15 May. Retrieved 9 March 2015 (civilrightsproject.ucla.edu/research/k-12-education/integration-and-diversity/brown-at-60-great-progress-a-long-retreat-and-an-uncertain-future/Brown-at-60-051814.pdf); **p. 201, Table 7-4:** "Percentage of Employed People Who Are Members of Unions, by Race/Ethnicity, 2000, 2014" Based on Bureau of Labor Statistics. 2007. "Access to Historical Data for the Tables of the Union Membership News Release." Labor Force Statistics from the Current Population Survey. 21 June. Retrieved 3 March 2015 (www.bls.gov/cps/cpslutabs.htm); **p. 201,** "I want a house with a nice yard…care of no man, that's for sure." © Pearson Education, Inc.; **p. 202,** "I was stopped on fake charges…Nun. Let's go, nigger" West, C. 1994. Race Matters. New York: Vintage; **p. 203, Figure 7-6a:** Chart: "Race and Ethnicity of U.S. Defendants Executed, 1976–2015" Based on Death Penalty Information Center. 2015. "Facts About the Death Penalty." 11 February. Retrieved 3 March 2015 (www.deathpenaltyinfo.org/documents/FactSheet.pdf); **p. 203, Figure 7-6b:** Chart: "U.S. Death Row Inmates by Race, 1976–2015" Based on Death Penalty Information Center. 2015. "Facts About the Death Penalty." 11 February. Retrieved 3 March 2015 (www.deathpenaltyinfo.org/documents/FactSheet.pdf); **p. 203,** "Some people are being sentenced to death based on race, and I find that morally and legally objectionable." Eckholm, E. 1995. "Studies Find Death Penalty Tied to Race of Victims." New York Times. 24 February. Pp. B1-B4. P.B1; **p. 204,** "She drew white people larger . . . . even absent or truncated" Coles, R. 2003 Children of Crisis. New York: Back Bay Books. P.47; **p. 205, Box:** "A Personal View—Everyday Racism" © Pearson Education, Inc.; **p. 206,** "reverse discrimination'"The best way to stop discrimination on the basis of race,' 'is to stop discriminating on the basis of race'" The Economist. 2013. "Affirmative Action: Is Affirmative Action a Good Idea?" 29 June. Retrieved 29 June 2013 (www.economist.com/debate/overview/251); **p. 208,** "[R]ace matters for reasons. . . . I do not belong here" Lempert, R. 2014. "The Schuette Decision: The Supreme Court Rules on Affirmative Action." Brookings Institution. 25 April. Retrieved 3 March 2015 (www.brookings.edu/blogs/fixgov/posts/2014/04/25-schuette-affirmative-action-supreme-court-comment-lempert); **p. 208,** "We expect that 25 years from now, the use of racial preferences will no longer be necessary to further the interest approved today." Justice O'Connor, Grutter v. Bollinger, 539 U.S. 306 (2003); **p. 209, Figure 7-7:** Chart: "Share of Americans Supporting Affirmative Action on College Campuses, 2014" Based on Drake, B. 2014. "Public Strongly Backs Affirmative Action Programs on Campus." Pew Research Center. 22 April. Retrieved 3 March 2015 (www.pewresearch.org/fact-tank/2014/04/22/public-strongly-backs-affirmative-action-programs-on-campus/)

Chapter 8

p. 217, "entire range of attitudes. . . .their [sex or] gender" Safilios-Rothschild, C. 1974. Women and Social Policy. Upper Saddle River, NJ: Prentice Hall; **p. 220, Figure 8-1:** Chart: "Percentage of Girls and Women in Selected African Countries Who Have Undergone Female Genital Mutilation/Cutting" Based on UNICEF. 2013. "Child Protection: Female Genital Mutilation and Cutting." Retrieved 15 March 2015 (data.unicef.org/child-protection/fgmc); **p. 221, Table 8-2:** "Top Five Surgical Cosmetic Procedures in 2013" American Society of Plastic Surgeons. 2013. "News & Resources." Retrieved 3 March 2013 (www.plasticsurgery.org/news-and-resources.html); **p. 224, Table 8-3:** "Women's Earnings as a Percentage of Men's Earnings" Bureau of Labor Statistics. 2014. "Women in the Labor Force: A Databook." BLS Report 1049. May. Retrieved 25 November 2014 (www.bls.gov/cps/wlf-databook-2013.pdf); **p. 225, Table 8-4:** "Median Weekly Earnings of Full-Time Workers, by Sex and Educational Attainment" Bureau of Labor Statistics. 2014. "Women in the Labor Force: A Databook." BLS Report 1049. May. Retrieved 25 November 2014 (www.bls.gov/cps/wlf-databook-2013.pdf); **p. 226, Table 8-5:** "Twenty Most Prevalent Occupations for Employed Women" U.S. Department of Labor, Women's Bureau. 2014. "Women in the Labor Force: Data and Statistics." Retrieved 4 March 2015 (www.dol.gov/wb/stats/stats_data.htm); **p. 227, Figure 8-2:** "Chart: Lifetime Reports of Sexual Violence Among Female Victims by Type of Perpetrator, 2010" Based on Black, M.C., K.C. Basile, M.J. Breiding, S.G. Smith, M.L. Walters, M.T. Merrick, J. Chen, & M.R. Stevens. 2011. The National Intimate Partner and Sexual Violence Survey (NISVS): 2010 Summary Report. Atlanta, GA: National Center for Injury Prevention and Control, Centers for Disease Control and Prevention; **p. 233,** "A woman must be a learner. . .yielding to deception, fell into sin" © Pearson Education, Inc.; **p. 235,** "to take action to bring women into full participation in the mainstream of American society now, exercising all the privileges and responsibilities thereof in truly equal partnership with men" National organization for women, Adopted at the organizing conference in Washington, D. C., October 29, 1966

Chapter 9

p. 243, Table 9-2: "Top Five and Bottom Five Countries with Population Age 60 and Over" United Nations, Department of Economic and Social Affairs, Population Division. 2015. "World Population Prospects: The 2014 Revision, Key Findings and Advance Tables." ESA/P/WP.227; **p. 244, Map 9-1:** "Aging Map" Kinsella, K. & V.A. Velkoff. 2001. "An Ageing World: 2001. U.S. Census Bureau No. P-95-001. Washington, DC; U.S. Government Printing Office; **p. 246, Map 9-2:** "Aging Map" Based on Kinsella, K., & W. He. 2009. "An Aging World: 2008." U.S. Census Bureau, International Population Reports No. P95/09-1. Washington, DC: U.S. Government Printing Office; **p. 248, Figure 9-1:** Chart: "Oldest-Old as a Percentage of All People, 2013 and 2050" U.S. Census Bureau. 2013 "International Programs." Retrieved 17 March 2015. (http://www.census.gov/population/international/data/idb/information Gateway.php); **p. 248, Figure 9-2:** Chart: "Percentage Change in the World's Population by Age, 2010–2050" United Nations. 2011. "World Population Prospects: The 2010 Revision." Retrieved 27 October 2014 (esa.un.org/unpd/wpp); **p. 250, Figure 9-3:** "Population Pyramids from Families and Their Social Worlds 3rd Ed. Figure 12–3" from "Families and Their Social Worlds", Pearson Education, 3rd edition, **Figure 12.3,** page 242; **p. 252, Figure 9-4:** Chart: "Number of Persons 65+, 1960–2060, United States (Millions)" Administration on Aging. 2014. "A Profile of Older Americans: 2013." Retrieved 3 March 2015 (www.aoa.acl.gov/Aging_Statistics/Profile/2013/docs/2013_Profile.pdf); **p. 253, Map 9-3:** "Percent of Residents Age 65 and Over: 2010" U.S. Census Bureau, Census 2010 Summary Fig. 1; **p. 254,** "60?! Don't worry-we're. . . . I knew a minute ago" Ellis, S.R., & T.G. Morrison. 2005. "Stereotypes of Ageing: Messages Promoted By Age-Specific Paper Birthday Cards Available in Canada." International Journal of Aging and Human Development, 61, 57-73; **p. 255, Table 9-3:** "Top Three Surgical Cosmetic Procedures for Middle Age and Elderly People in the United States in 2013" Adapted from American Society for Aesthetic Plastic Surgery. 2014. "2013 Cosmetic Surgery National Data Bank Statistics." Retrieved 26 October 2014 (www.surgery.org/sites/default/files/Stats2013_4.pdf); **p. 258, Figure 9-5:** Chart: "Percentage of Private Industry Employees Participating in Defined Benefit Pension Plans, Selected Years, 1990–2011" Bureau of Labor Statistics. 2013. "The Last Private Industry Pension Plans." TED: The Economics Daily. 3 January. Retrieved 23 October 2014 (www.bls.gov/opub/ted/2013/ted_20130103.htm); **p. 260,** "A society must produce an economic. . .other members of society" Based on Morgan, L., & S. Kunkel. 1998. Aging: The Social Context. Thousand Oaks, CA: Pine Forge Press; **p. 260, Figure 9-6:** Graph: "Trends in Actual and Expected Age at Retirement, 2002–2014" Adapted from Riffkin, R. 2014. "Average U.S. Retirement Age Rises to 62." Gallup. 28 April.

Retrieved 23 October 2014 (www.gallup.com/poll/168707/average-retirement-age-rises.aspx); **p. 267, Figure 9-7:** Chart: "Ways in Which Medicare Beneficiaries Supplement Their Medicare, 2010" Based on McArdle, F., T. Neuman, & J. Huang. 2014. "Overview of Health Benefits for Pre-65 and Medicare-Eligible Retirees." 14 April. Retrieved 26 October 2014 (kff.org/report-section/retiree-health-benefits-at-the-crosswords-overview-of-health-benefits-for-pre-65-and-medicare-eligible-retirees/); **p. 270, Table 9-4:** "Characteristics of Hospice Users" Based on National Hospice and Palliative Care Organization. 2014. "NHPCO's Hospice Facts and Figures: Hospice Care in America: 2014 Edition." Retrieved 3 March 2014; **p. 272, Table 9-5:** "Confidence That 'Social Security Will Continue to Provide Benefits of At Least Equal Value to Benefits Received Today'" Adapted from Employee Benefit Research Institute and Greenwald & Associates. 2014. "Attitudes About Current Social Security and Medicare Benefit Levels." 2014 RCS Fact Sheet #7. Retrieved 27 October 2014 (www.ebri.org/pdf/surveys/rcs/2014/RCS14.FS-7.SS-Med.Final.pdf); **p. 273, Figure 9-8:** Chart: "Share of Americans Agreeing with 'It is critical that we preserve Social Security for future generations, even if it means'" Based on Tucker, J.V., V.P. Reno, & T.N. Bethell. 2014. "Strengthening Social Security: What Do Americans Want?" National Academy of Social Insurance. Retrieved 27 October 2014 (www.nasi.org/sites/default/files/research/What_Do_Americans_Want.pdf)

Chapter 10

p. 276, "The cultural imagery of American families…American family and never will be" Based on Pyke, K. 2000a. "Ideology of 'Family' Shapes Perception of Immigrant Children." Minneapolis, MN: National Council on Family Relations.

Pyke, K. 200b. "'The Normal American Family' as in Interpretive Structure of Family Life Among Grown Children of Korean and Vietnamese Immigrants." Journal of Marriage and Family, 62:240-245; **p. 280, Figure 10-1:** Chart: "Conservative, Liberal, and Feminist Views of Family Change" Giele, J.Z. 1996. "Decline of the Family: Conservative, Liberal, and Feminist Views." In Promises to Keep: Decline & Renewal of Marriage in America, Popenoe, D., Elshtain, J.B., & Blankenhorn, D., eds. Lanham, MD: Rowman & Littlefield; **p. 282, Figure 10-2:** Chart: "Marital Status of U.S. Population 18 Years and Over, 1970, 2014" U.S. Census Bureau, October 30, 2014a. America's Families and Living Arrangements: 2014: Adults. Retrieved 2 March 2015 (http://www.census.gov/hhes/families/data/cps2014.html); **p. 283, Figure 10-3:** Chart: "Median Age at First Marriage, 1890–2014" U.S. Census Bureau, October 30, 2014a. America's Families and Living Arrangements: 2014: Adults. Retrieved 2 March 2015 (http://www.census.gov/hhes/families/data/cps2014.html); **p. 285, Figure 10-4:** Chart: "Percentage Saying Unmarried Couples Living Together Is a Bad Thing for Society, a Good Thing, or Makes No Difference, 2010" Based on Pew Research Center. 2010. "The Decline of Marriage And Rise of New Families." Social & Demographic Trends. 18 November. Retrieved 14 April 2015 (www.pewsocialtrends.org/2010/11/18/the-decline-of-marriage-and-rise-of-new-families/); **p. 287, Table 10-1:** "Percentage of U.S. Adults Who Favor Same-Sex Marriage, May, 2014" McCarthy, J. 2014. "Same-Sex Marriage Support Reaches New High at 55%." Gallup. 21 May. Retrieved 27 February (www.gallup.com/poll/169640/sex-marriage-support-reaches-new-high.aspx); **p. 288, Figure 10-5:** Chart: "The Amount of Weekly Hours That Men and Women, Mothers and Fathers Spend on Housework" Based on Parker, K., & Wang, W. 2013.

"Modern Parenthood: Roles of Moms and Dads Converge as They Balance Work and Family." Pew Social and Demographic Trends. 14 March. Retrieved 29 June 2013 (www.pewsocialtrends.org/2013/03/14/modern-parenthood-roles-of-moms-and-dads-converge-as-they-balance-work-and-family/); **p. 289, Figure 10-6:** Line Art: "Parents' Childcare Time, 1965–2011" Based on Parker, K., & Wang, W. 2013. "Modern Parenthood: Roles of Moms and Dads Converge as They Balance Work and Family." Pew Social and Demographic Trends. 14 March. Retrieved 29 June 2013 (www.pewsocialtrends.org/2013/03/14/modern-parenthood-roles-of-moms-and-dads-converge-as-they-balance-work-and-family/); **p. 291, Figure 10-7:** Chart: "Teenage Fertility Rates per 1,000 Women Aged 15–19 by Race and/or Ethnicity, 1991, 2013" Hamilton, B.E., Martin, J.A., Osterman, M.J.K., & Curtin, S.C. 2014. "Births: Preliminary Data for 2013." National Vital Statistics Reports, v. 63, no. 2. 29 May. National Center for Health Statistics; **p. 293,** "My grandchildren, Caleb and Helen …. didn't even put up a fuss" © Pearson Education, Inc.; **p. 295, Table 10-2:** "Lifetime Prevalence of Intimate Partner Violence (IPV) Victimization" Breiding, M.J., Smith, S.G., Basile, K.C., Walters, M.L., Chen, J., & Merrick, M.T. 2014. "Prevalence & Characteristics of Sexual Violence, Stalking, and Intimate Partner Violence Victimization—National Intimate Partner and Sexual Violence Survey, United States, 2011." Morbidity & Mortality Weekly Report. 5 September. 63(SS08):1-18. Retrieved 27 February 2015 (www.cdc.gov/mmwr/preview/mmwrhtml/ss6308a1.htm?s_cid=ss6308a1_e); **p. 297, Figure 10-8:** Chart: "Who Are the Child Abuse Perpetrators?" Based on U.S. Department of Health and Human Services, Administration for Children and Families, Administration on Children, Youth & Families, Children's Bureau. 2015. "Fewer child abuse and neglect victims for seventh consecutive year." 15 January. Retrieved 27 February 2015 (www.acf.hhs.gov/media/press/2015/fewer-child-abuse-and-neglect-victims-for-seventh-consecutive-year); **p. 304, Table 10-3:** "A Comparison of Maternity Leave Benefits in Developed and Developing Nations" Adapted from United Nations Statistics Division, 2013 UN Data Maternity Benefits Retrieved 5 March 2015 (http://data.un.org/DocumentData.aspx?id=344); **p. 305,** "France offers 16 weeks of paid maternity…at 100 percent of the mother's salary" Based on United Nations Statistics Division, 2013 UN Data Maternity Benefits Retrieved 5 March 2015 (http://data.un.org/DocumentData.aspx?id=344); **p. 305,** "What we're doing here in America is we're making women choose…. We're losing sight of that here in the USA" Secretary of Labor, Thomas Perez On Maternity Leave

Chapter 11

p. 308, Figure 11-1: Chart: "Overall, How Satisfied Are You With the Quality of Education? 2014" Based on Gallup, 2015. "Education." Retrieved 4 April 2015. (www.gallup.com/poll/1612/education.aspx); **p. 310, Table 11-1:** "Share responding to Survey question, 'How often Did you_This past year?' in 2012" Tompson, T., J. Benz, & J. Agiesta. 2013. "Parents' Attitudes on the Quality of Education in the United States." The Associated Press-NORC Center for Public Affairs Research. Retrieved 15 April 2015 (www.apnorc.org/PDFs/Parent%20Attitudes/AP_NORC_Parents%20Attitudes%20on%20the%20Quality%20of%20Education%20in%20the%20US_FINAL_2.pdf); **p. 314, Box 11-1:** "A Personal View—Learning to Speak SAE" © Pearson Education, Inc.; **p. 316, Figure 11-2:** Line Art: "Years of School Completed by Persons Age 25 and Over, 1920–2013" Based on National Center for Education Statistics.

2013a. "Table 104.10. Rates of high school completion and bachelor's degree attainment among persons age 25 and over, by race/ethnicity and sex: Selected years, 1910 through 2013." Retrieved 15 April 2015 (nces.ed.gov/programs/digest/d13/tables/dt13_104.10.asp); **p. 316, Figure 11-3:** Chart: "Graduation rate for public high school students, by race/ethnicity: School year 2011–12" Kena, G., Aud, S., Johnson, F., Wang, X., Zhang, J., Rathbun, A., Wilkinson-Flicker, S., and Kristapovich, P. 2014. The Condition of Education 2014. NCES 2014-083. Washington, DC: U.S. Department of Education, National Center for Education Statistics. Retrieved 26 January 2015 (nces.ed.gov/pubsearch); **p. 317, Figure 11-4:** Chart: "Percentage of Persons Ages 25–29 Who Have Achieved a Bachelor's Degree or Higher by Race/Ethnicity, 1980 and 2013" Based on National Center for Education Statistics. 2013b. "**Table 104.20.** Percentage of persons 25 to 29 years old with selected levels of educational attainment, by race/ethnicity and sex: Selected years, 1920 through 2013." Retrieved 15 April 2015 (nces.ed.gov/programs/digest/d13/tables/dt13_104.20.asp); **p. 317, Figure 11-5:** Chart: "Median annual earnings of full-time year-round wage and salary workers ages 25–34, by educational attainment" Kena, G., Aud, S., Johnson, F., Wang, X., Zhang, J., Rathbun, A., Wilkinson-Flicker, S., and Kristapovich, P. 2014. The Condition of Education 2014. NCES 2014-083. Washington, DC: U.S. Department of Education, National Center for Education Statistics. Retrieved 26 January 2015 (nces.ed.gov/pub search); **p. 318, Map 11-1:** "U.S. Expenditures Per Pupil by State, 2012" Based on National Education Association. 2014. "Rankings and Estimates." Retrieved 4 April 2015. (www.nea.org/assets/docs/NEA-Rankings-and-Estimates-2013-2014.pdf); **p. 319, Figure 11-6:** Chart: "Percentage of Hispanic Registered Voters Who Say This Issue Is 'Extremely' or 'Very Important' To Them Personally" Based on Lopez, M.H., A. Gonzalez-Barrera, & J.M. Krogstad. 2014. "Latino Support for Democrats Falls, but Democratic Advantage Remains." Pew Research Center. Retrieved 6 February 2015 (www.pewhispanic.org/2014/10/29/latino-support-for-democrats-falls-but-democratic-advantage-remains/); **p. 321, Table 11-3:** "Results of 2011 Youth Risk Behavior Survey of High School Students" Suicide Prevention Resource Center. 2014. "Suicide among Racial/Ethnic Populations in the U.S.: Asians, Pacific Islanders, and Native Hawaiians." Retrieved 2 February 2015 (www.sprc.org/sites/sprc.org/files/library/API%20Sheet%20August%2028%202013%20Final.pdf); **p. 321,** "to provide quality education opportunities….distinct cultural and governmental entities" Bureau of Indian Education. 2015. Home page. Retrieved 31 March 2015 (www.bie.edu/index.htm); **p. 320, Figure 11-7:** Chart: "Language Spoken at Home and English Speaking Ability by Age Among Hispanics, 2012" Based on Brown, A., & E. Patten. 2014. "Statistical Portrait of Hispanics in the United States, 2012." Pew Research Center. 29 April. Retrieved 31 March 2015 (www.pewhispanic.org/2014/04/29/statistical-portrait-of-hispanics-in-the-united-states-2012/); **p. 324, Table 11-4:** "U.S Mediocre on Science, Math Scores" Based on DeSilver, D. 2015. "U.S. Students Improving—Slowly—In Math and Science, But Still Lagging Internationally." Pew Research Center. Retrieved 9 February 2015 (www.pewresearch.org/fact-tank/2015/02/02/u-s-students-improving-slowly-in-math-and-science-but-still-lagging-internationally/); **p. 325, Figure 11-8:** Chart: "Math Proficiency Slowly Growing Among U.S. 4th and 8th Grade Students" DeSilver, D. 2015. "U.S. Students Improving—Slowly—In Math and Science, But Still Lagging Internationally." Pew Research Center. Retrieved

9 February 2015 (www.pewresearch.org/fact-tank/2015/02/02/u-s-students-improving-slowly-in-math-and-science-but-still-lagging-internationally/); **p. 324,** "The underutilization of human potential….higher rates of incarceration" McKinsey & Company. 2010. "How the World's Most Improved School Systems Keep Getting Better." (www.mckinsey.com/clientservice/Social_Sector/our_practices/Education/Knowledge_Highlights/Economic_impact.aspx); **p. 328, Box 11-3:** "Thinking Globally: Raising My Children in France" © Pearson Education, Inc.; **p. 331, Table 11-5:** "Trends in Violent Behaviors on School Property: National Youth Risk Behavior Survey, 1993-2013" Centers for Disease Control and Prevention. 2014. "Understanding Bullying: Fact Sheet." 16 October. Retrieved 31 March 2015 (www.cdc.gov/violenceprevention/pub/understanding_bullying.html); **p. 334, PQ:** "We're now in the process of dismantling all that" John D. Wiley, chancellor of the University of Wisconsin–Madison; **p. 335, Figure 11-9:** Chart: "Ten States With Largest Percentage Cuts to Higher Education Funding" Mitchell, M., V. Palacios, & M. Leachman. 2014. "States Are Still Funding Higher Education Below Pre-Recession Levels." Center for Budget and Policy Priorities. 1 May. Retrieved 9 February 2015 (www.cbpp.org/cms/?fa=view&id=4135); **p. 335,** "More students are working and going to school part-time…students from the bottom quartile" Based on Mitchell, M., V. Palacios, & M. Leachman. 2014. "States Are Still Funding Higher Education Below Pre-Recession Levels." Center for Budget and Policy Priorities. 1 May. Retrieved 9 February 2015 (www.cbpp.org/cms/?fa=view&id=4135).

Valle, R.C., S. Normandeau, & G.R. González. 2015. "Education at a Glance Interim Report: Update of Employment and Educational Attainment." Organisation for Economic Co-Operation and Development. January. Retrieved 31 March 2015 (www.oecd.org/edu/EAG-Interim-report.pdf).Voyer, D. & S.D. Voyer, 2014. "Gender Differencdes in Scholastic Achievement: A Meta-Analysis>" Psychological Bulletin, 140, 1174-1204; **p. 336,** "It's time to stop just talking about education…education America's national mission" U.S. Department of Education. 2009. "Race to the Top Program Executive Summary." November. Retrieved 9 February 2015 (www2.ed.gov/programs/racetothetop/executive-summary.pdf)

Chapter 12

p. 341, Figure 12-1: Chart: "Percentage of Americans Mentioning Economic Issues as the Nation's Most Important Problem, 2007, 2009, 2015" Gallup, 2015. "Most Important Problem" Retrieved 9 May 2015 http://www.gallup.com/poll/1675/most-important-problem.aspx; **p. 341, Table 12-1:** "Aspects of the Economy That Are Most Problematic, April 9–12, 2015 Gallup, 2015" "Most Important Problem" Retrieved 9 May 2015 http://www.gallup.com/poll/1675/most-important-problem.aspx; **p. 342, Figure 12-2:** Graph: "Americans' Financial Worry, 2011–2015" Saad, L. 2015. "Americans' Money Worries Unchanged From 2014." Gallup. 20 April. Retrieved 3 May 2015 www.gallup.com/poll/182768/americans-money-worries-unchanged-2014.aspx?utm_source=position3&utm_medium=related&utm_campaign=tiles; **p. 342, Figure 12-3:** Graph: "Americans' Concern (Rated as 'Very Likely' or 'Fairly Likely') of Losing Their Job, 2001–2015" Riffkin, R. 2015. "U.S. Workers Job Loss Fears Down to Pre-Recession Levels." Retrieved 25 May 2015 http://www.gallup.com/poll/182840/workers-job-loss-fears-back-pre-recession-levels.aspx; **p. 343,**

Figure 12-4: Graph: "Social Class Self-Identification, April 2003, 2008, 2012, 2015" Newport, F. 2015. "Fewer Americans Identify as Middle Class in Recent Years." Gallup. 28 April. Retrieved 3 May 2015 www.gallup.com/poll/182918/fewer-americans-identify-middle-class-recent-years.aspx; **p. 348,** Box: "A Closer Look: Disney: The Happiest Place on Earth?" Based on Thibodeau, P. 2015 "Fury Rises at Disney Over Use of Foreign Workers." Computer World. Retrieved 9 May 2015 http://www.computerworld.com/article/2915904/it-outsourcing/fury-rises-at-disney-over-use-of-foreign-workers.html; **p. 351, Figure 12-5:** Chart: "Median Weekly Earnings of Full-Time Workers, by Union Affiliation and Sex, 2014" Bureau of Labour Statistics, 2015e; **p. 352,** "Hopefully I can get me a job. A permanent job.....that something comes through" Seccombe, K. 2015, p.177 'So You Think I Drive A Cadillac?' Welfare Recipients Perspective on the System and its Reform. 4th ed. Boston, MA: Pearson; **p. 352,** "You can really see how women's opportunities have....and have children at the same time" Abby, age 22; **p. 354, PQ:** "to eliminate discrimination against part-time workers and improve the quality of part-time work" Official Journal of the European Communities. 1998. "Council Directive 97/81/EC of 15 December 1997 Concerning the Framework Agreement on Part-Time Work Concluded by UNICE, CEEP and the ETUC"; **p. 355, Table 12-2:** "Unemployment Rate, by Age, Sex, & Race, March 2005, 2010, 2015" Bureau of Labor Statistics. 2015b. "Current Employment Statistics. Establishment Data: Table B-1a." 3 April. Retrieved 3 May 2015 www.bls.gov/web/empsit/ceseeb1a.htm; **p. 356, Table 12-3:** "Benefits Provided to Workers (Non–Civilian) by Employer, 2010, 2014" Bureau of Labor Statistics. 2015c. "Top Picks: National Compensation Survey—Benefits." Retrieved 6 May 2015 data.bls.gov/cgi-bin/surveymost?nb; **p. 358, Figure 12-6:** Chart: "Occupations with the Highest Work–Related Fatality Rates (per 100,000 Full–Time Workers), 2013" Bureau of Labor Statistics. 2014a. "Census of Fatal Occupational Injuries Summary 2013." Economic News Release. 11 September. Retrieved 3 May 2015 www.bls.gov/news.release/cfoi.nr0.htm; **p. 360, Table 12-4:** "American Debt, 2015" Chen, T. 2015. "American Household Credit Card Debt Statistics: 2015." Nerdwallet. Retrieved 6 May 2015 www.nerdwallet.com/blog/credit-card-data/average-credit-card-debt-household/; **p. 361, Table 12-5:** "Characteristics of Persons Earning the Federal Minimum Wage or Less, 2014 (16 and Older)" Bureau of Labor Statistics. 2015a. "Characteristics of Minimum Wage Workers, 2014." Report 1054. April. Retrieved 6 May 2015 www.bls.gov/opub/reports/cps/characteristics-of-minimum-wage-workers-2014.pdf; **p. 362, PQ:** "If you raise the price of something, guess what? You get less of it" Geewax, M. 2013. "Obama's Call for Higher Minimum Wage Could Have Ripple Effect." February 13. Retrieved 25 May 2015 http://www.npr.org/2013/02/13/171897858/obamas-call-for-higher-minimum-wage-could-have-ripple-effect

Chapter 13

p. 365, Figure 13-1: Line Art: "World Population Change" Data from Office of Technology Assessment; **p. 368, Figure 13-2:** Chart: "Total Fertility Rates" Carl Haub and Toshika Kaneda, 2014 World population data sheet (Washington, DC: Population Reference Bureau 2014). © 2014 Population reference bureau all rights reserved; **p. 369, Table 13-1:** "Percentage of Married Women Of Childbearing Age Who Use Modern Contraceptives, Selected Countries, 2012" Population Reference Bureau. 2013 "2013 World Population Fact Sheet." Retrieved 20 April 2013

(www.prb/org/); **p. 372, Map 13-1:** "Total Fertility Rates, 2012" from "Families and Their Social Worlds", Pearson Education, 3rd edition, figure 9.1, page 178-179; **p. 373, Table 13-2:** "Comparison of Literacy Rates in Selected Less Developed Countries, 2014" Based on Central Intelligence Agency World Factbook. 2014. Home page. Retrieved 27 February 2015 (www.cia.gov/library/publications/the-world-factbook/geos/in.html); **p. 375,** "a brave and gentle advocate of peace who through the simple act of going to school became a global teacher." Statement of the Secretary-General on the Awarding of the Nobel Prize for Peace to Malala Yousafzai and Kailash Satyarthi, 10 October 2014; **p. 376, Table 13-3:** "Energy Use in Selected Countries: Kg of Oil Per Capita, 1990 and 2012" Based on United National Statistics Division 2014. "Statistics: Energy use (kg of oil equivalent per capita)." Retrieved 27 February 2015 (data.un.org/Data.aspx?d=WDI&f=Indicator_Code%3AEG.USE.PCAP.KG.OE); **p. 372, Figure 13-3:** Graph: "Crude Birth and Death Rates for Sweden 1690-1960" Matras, 1973. Courtesy Armand Colin Éditeur, Paris; **p. 381,** "Encouraging workers to use....find permanent employment" Based on Haub, C. 2010. "Japan's Demographic Future." Population Reference Bureau. Retrieved 23 May 2010 (www.prb.org/Articles/2010/japandemography.aspx).

Lee, G.H.Y., and Lee, S.P. 2013. "Childcare Availability, Fertility, and Female Labor Force Participation in Japan." Monash University Department of Economics ISSN 1441-5429 Discussion Paper 36/13. Retrieved 27 February 2015; **p. 377, Figure 13-4:** Chart: "Percentage of population undernourished" Food and Agriculture organization of the United Nations, 2012, 2014; **p. 382, Figure 13-5:** Chart: "Ten Metro Areas with the Largest Numeric Increase in Population, 2013" Badger, E. 2014. "Metropolitan Areas Are Now Fueling Virtually All of America's Population Growth." Washingtonpost.com. 27 March. Retrieved 3 February 2015 (www.washingtonpost.com/blogs/wonkblog/wp/2014/03/27/metropolitan-areas-are-now-fueling-virtually-all-of-americas-population-growth/); **p. 386,** "Four years ago, I came to America... I'm ready to settle down" © Pearson Education, Inc.; **p. 386,** "When I was younger, I decided I was going ... that was even possible" © Pearson Education, Inc.; **p. 386,** "My mom left our small village in Mexico ... if I'll ever see them again" © Pearson Education, Inc.; **p. 388,** "The Border Patrol treats us .... nothing to eat [at our homes]" Arditti, J.A. 2006. "Editor's Note." Family Relations, 55, 263–65; **p. 389, Table 13-4:** "The Shift in Deportation Countries" U.S. Department of Homeland Security, 2015b. Immigration Enforcement: FY 2014 ICE Immigration Removals. Retrieved 5 March 2015 (www.ice.gov/removal-statistics); **p. 390, Figure 13-6:** Chart: "Percent Who Say Illegal Immigrants Should Be Eligible for Citizenship, 2014" Based on Dimock, M. 2014. "Tea Partiers Are Not All Immigration Hawks." Pew Research Center. 11 June. Retrieved 3 February 2015 (www.pewresearch.org/facttank/2014/06/11/tea-partiers-are-not-all-immigration-hawks/); **p. 392,** "The problem isn't Central America's refugees. It's the countries they come from" Strain, M.R. 2014. "The Problem Isn't Central America's Child Refugees. It's the Countries They Come From." Washingtonpost.com. 1 August. Retrieved 27 February 2015 (www.washingtonpost.com/posteverything/wp/2014/08/01/the-problem-isnt-central-americas-child-refugees-its-the-countries-they-come-from/); **p. 392, Figure 13-7:** Based on Krogstad, J.M., & Gonzalez-Barrera, A. 2014. "Hispanics Split on How to Address Surge in Central American Child Migrants." Pew Research Center. 29 July. Retrieved 3 February

Chapter 14

p. 398, Figure 14-1: Line Art: "Percentage of Internet Users in Selected World Regions, June 2014" Based on Internet World Stats. 2015. "Internet Usage Statistics: The Internet Big Picture." Retrieved 15 March 2015 (www.internetworldstats.com/stats .htm); **p. 400,** "frequently consumed alcohol at industry functions, had used cocaine and marijuana, and had sexual relationships with oil and gas company representatives" The Interior Department, Office of Inspector General; **p. 401, Table 14-1:** "SCAM to Avoid Becoming a Victim of Identify Theft or Fraud" Adapted from the U.S. Department of Justice. 2015a. "Identity Theft and Identity Fraud: What Should I Do to Avoid Becoming a Victim of Identity Theft?" Retrieved 15 March 2015 (www.justice.gov/criminal/fraud/websites/ idtheft.html); **p. 402,** "As I write, highly civilized human beings....sleep any the worse for it" Milgram, S. 1974. Obedience to Authority: An Experimental View. New York: HarperCollins (11-12); **p. 403,** "a cultural lag occurs when one of two parts of culture...parts than existed previously" Ogburn, W.F. 1957. "Cultural Lag as Theory." Sociology and Social Research, 41, 167-174; **p. 404, Table 14-2:** "Environmental and Energy Proposals, 2014" Moore, B., & S. Nichols. 2014. "Americans Still Favor Energy Conservation Over Production." Gallup. 2 April. Retrieved 15 March 2015 (www.gallup.com/poll/168176/ americans-favor-energy-conservation-production.aspx); **p. 406, Figure 14-2:** Graph: "Percentage of Americans Who Worry About the Environment, 2001–2014" Based on Riffkin, R. 2014. "Climate Change Not a Top Worry in U.S." Gallup. 12 March. Retrieved 15 March 2015 (www.gallup.com/poll/167843/ climate-change-not-top-worry.aspx); **p. 408, Figure 14-3:** Chart: "World's Top 10 Energy Consumers, 2013 (Mtoe)" Based on Enerdata. 2014. "Global Energy Statistical Yearbook 2014." Retrieved 15 March 2015 (yearbook.enerdata.net); **p. 409,** "global warming will seriously threaten one's way of life" Jones, J.M. 2014. "In U.S., Most Do Not See Global Warming as Serious Threat." Gallup. 13 March. Retrieved 15 March 2015 (www .gallup.com/poll/167879/not-global-warming-serious-threat .aspx); **p. 409, Table 14-3:** "Percentage Who Have Expectations That Global Warming Will Seriously Threaten One's Way of Life, by Age Group, 2014" Jones, J.M. 2014. "In U.S., Most Do Not See Global Warming as Serious Threat." Gallup. 13 March. Retrieved 15 March 2015 (www.gallup.com/poll/167879/not -global-warming-serious-threat.aspx); **p. 410, Figure 14-4:** Chart: "Americans Rate the Seriousness of Global Warming, 1998, 2007, 2014" Based on Dugan, A. 2014. "Americans Most Likely to Say Global Warming Is Exaggerated." 17 March. Retrieved 15 March 2015 (www.gallup.com/poll/167960/americans -likely-say-global-warming-exaggerated.aspx); **p. 409,** "Accelerated sea level rise and increased coastal flooding. The average....habitats and possible extinction" Based on Union of Concerned Scientists. 2015. "Global Warming: Confronting the Realities of Climate Change." Retrieved 15 March 2015 (www .ucsusa.org/global_warming#.VQYTjmcU-HM); **p. 412, Box 14-1:** "A Closer Look: Who's Using the Water? Social Class and Water Use in California" Stevens, M. 2014. "In California, Water Use is All Over the Map." 4 November. Los Angeles Times. Retrieved 16 March 2015 (www.latimes.com/local/california/la-me-1105 -california-water-20141106-story.html).

Su, J.G., M. Jerrett, R. Morello-Frosch, B.M. Jesdale, & A.D. Kyle. 2012. "Inequalities in Cumulative Environmental Burdens Among Three Urbanized Counties in California." Environment International, 40, 79-87.

Worland, J. 2015. "California May Crack Down Further This Week on Water-Wasters." Time.com. 15 March. Retrieved 16 March 2015 (time.com/3745247/california-drought-water-state -regulators/); **p. 413, Table 14-4:** "Current EPA Air Quality Index" Environmental Protection Agency. 2015a. "Information about the Air Quality Index (AQI)." Retrieved 15 March 2015 (airnow.gov/index.cfm?action=aqibasics.aqi); **p. 416, Figure 14-5:** Graph: "Number of Tons of Total Municipal Solid Waste Generated and the Amount of Waste Per Person (Per Capita), 1960–2012" Environmental Protection Agency. 2014. "Municipal Solid Waste." 28 February. Retrieved 16 March 2015 (www .epa.gov/epawaste/nohaz/municipal/); **p. 417, Figure 14-6:** Graph: "Number of Tons of Municipal Solid Waste Recycled and Percentage of Households That Recycle, 1960–2012" Environmental Protection Agency. 2014. "Municipal Solid Waste." 28 February. Retrieved 16 March 2015 (www.epa.gov/epawaste/ nohaz/municipal/); **p. 419,** "Residents of the fenceline zone have incomes.....diploma is 27 percent lower" Orum, P., R. Moore, M. Roberts, & J. Sánchez. 2014. "Who's in Danger? Race, Poverty, and Chemical Disasters. A Demographic Analysis of Chemical Disaster Vulnerability Zones." Environmental Justice and Health Alliance for Chemical Policy Reform. May. Retrieved 16 March 2015 (comingcleaninc.org/assets/media/images/Reports/Who's%20in%20Danger%20Report%20FINAL. pdf); **p. 421, Box 14-1:** "A Global View: Is It Too Late to Prevent Climate Change?" Based on NASA Global Climate Change and Global Warming: Vital Signs of the Planet website. 2015. http://climate.nasa.gov/vital-signs/; **p. 422,** "as the most environmentally and economically sensible approach to controlling greenhouse gas emissions" Environmental Defense Fund. 2015. "How Cap and Trade Works." Retrieved 15 March 2015 (www.edf.org/climate/how-cap-and-trade-works); **p. 423, Table 14-5:** "Results of a Meta-Analysis of 25 Surveys That Asked Adults How to Best Control Greenhouse Gases" Ansolabehere, S., & D.M. Konisky. 2014. Cheap and Clean. Cambridge, MA: The MIT Press

Chapter 15

p. 428, "Operation Iraqi Freedom (OIF) and Operation Enduring Freedom.....veterans have had PTSD in their lifetime" U.S. Department of Veterans Affairs. 2014a. "PTSD: National Center for PTSD. How Common is PTSD?" 10 November. Retrieved 8 May 2015 (www.ptsd .va.gov/public/PTSD-overview/basics/how-common-is-ptsd .asp); **p. 431,** Box: "A Closer Look: The Story behind the Bomb" Based on Hall, Michelle. 2013. "By the Numbers: WW II's Atomic Bombs." Retrieved 20 May 2015. (http://www.cnn.com/2013/ 08/06/world/asia/btn-atomic-bombs/);

History.com. 2015. "Bombing of Hiroshima and Nagasaki." Retrieved 20 May 2015 (http://www.history.com/topics/world -war-ii/bombing-of-hiroshima-and-nagasaki); U.S. History.org. 2014. "The Decision to Drop the Bomb." Retrieved 20 May 2015. (http://www.ushistory.org/us/51g.asp); **p. 430,** "When I came to, I looked around The boys had been....try to abolish nuclear weapons" Quoted in Kristof, N.D. 1995. "The Bomb: An Act That Haunts Japan and America." 6 August. New York Times, pp. 1, 12; **p. 432,** "the threatened or actual use of illegal force....fear, coercion, or intimidation" Institute for Economics and Peace. 2014. "Global Terrorism Index Report 2014." Retrieved 8 May 2015 (www.visionofhumanity.org/sites/default/ files/Global%20Terrorism%20Index%20Report%202014.pdf); **p. 434, Table 15-1:** "Top Five Countries with Highest Global

Terrorism Index Scores, 2014" Institute for Economics and Peace. 2014. "Global Terrorism Index Report 2014." Retrieved 8 May 2015 (www.visionofhumanity.org/sites/default/files/Global%20Terrorism%20Index%20Report%202014.pdf); **p. 435, Table 15-2:** "Ten Countries with the Most Terrorist Attacks, 2013" U.S. Department of State, 2014. Country Reports on Terrorism: 2013. Retrieved 16 May 2015 (http://www.state.gov/j/ct/rls/crt/2013/index.htm); **p. 435, Figure 15-1:** Chart: "Tactics used in Terrorist Attacks Worldwide, 2012" U.S. Department of State, 2014. Country Reports on Terrorism: 2013. Retrieved 16 May 2015 (http://www.state.gov/j/ct/rls/crt/2013/index.htm); **p. 436,** "It is sad but true that Islam, like Christianity and Judaism..... Yitzhak Rabin, the peacemaker" Etzioni, A. 2002:3. "Opening Islam." Society, July-August. Pp. 29-35; **p. 436,** "The face of terror is not the true faith of Islam. Islam is peace" "Islam is Peace" Says President Remarks by the President at Islamic Center of Washington, D.C. Washington, D.C.; **p. 438,** "Increased fear of attack and heightened security at airports...regions of the world" Based on Jurkowitz, M. 2010. "Terrorism Tops Disasters." 11 May. Philadelphia: Pew Research Center.; Pew Research Center. 2002. "What the World Thinks in 2002." 4 December; **p. 439, Figure 15-2a:** Chart: "Percentage Saying They Approve or Disapprove of U.S. Campaign against Islamic Militants in Iraq and Syria, 2014–2015" Pew Research Center. 2015. "Growing Support for Campaign Against ISIS—and Possible Use of U.S. Ground Troops." 24 February. Retrieved 12 May 2015 (www.people-press.org/2015/02/24/growing-support-for-campaign-against-isis-and-possible-use-of-u-s-ground-troops/); **p. 439, Figure 15-2b:** Chart: "Percentage Saying They Favor or Oppose the Use of Ground Troops to Fight against Islamic Militants in Iraq and Syria, 2014–2015" Pew Research Center. 2015. "Growing Support for Campaign Against ISIS—and Possible Use of U.S. Ground Troops." 24 February.

Retrieved 12 May 2015 (www.people-press.org/2015/02/24/growing-support-for-campaign-against-isis-and-possible-use-of-u-s-ground-troops/); **p. 440, Figure 15-2c:** Chart: Percentage Who Say That Military Force Is the Best Way to Defeat Terrorism vs. Too Much Reliance on Military Force Creates Hatred and More Terrorism, 2014–2015 Pew Research Center. 2015. "Growing Support for Campaign Against ISIS—and Possible Use of U.S. Ground Troops." 24 February. Retrieved 12 May 2015 (www.people-press.org/2015/02/24/growing-support-for-campaign-against-isis-and-possible-use-of-u-s-ground-troops/); **p. 440,** "The President didn't spend but a few....we don't address it in a bigger way" Pianin, E. 2015. "McCain: Get Ready for U.S. Troops on the Ground in Iraq and Syria." The Fiscal Times, January 27. Retrieved 18 May 2015 (http://www.thefiscaltimes.com/2015/01/27/McCain-Get-Ready-US-Troops-Ground-Iraq-and-Syria); **p. 441,** "The Expansion of Territory—Countries come......quarters of the Tutsi population in Rwanda" Based on Coser, L. 1956. The Function of Social Conflict. New York: Free Press.; Mills, C.W. 1958. "The Causes of World War three. New York: Simon & Schuster.; Park, R. 1941. "The Social Functions of War. American Journal of Sociology, 46, 551-570.; Simmel, G. 1904. "The Sociology of Conflict." American Journal of Sociology: 9, 490-525; **p. 442,** "more powerful than they have ever been in....can only be called a military definition of reality", "come to shape much of the economic life of the United States" Mills, C.W. 1956. The Power Elite. New York: Oxford University Press. (P.198-222); **p. 446, Table 15-3:** "U.S. Favorability, 1999–2014" Pew Research Center. 2014. "U.S. Favorability." Global Attitudes & Trends. 11 July. Retrieved 8 May 2015 (www.pewglobal.org/2014/07/14/global-opposition-to-u-s-surveillance-and-drones-but-limited-harm-to-americas-image/pg-2014-07-14-balance-of-power-1-02/).

Photo Credits

Chapter 1

Chapter 2

Chapter 3

Chapter 4

Chapter 5

Images; p. 141: Paolese/Fotolia; p. 143: iStock; p. 147: John Moore/Staff/Getty Images

Chapter 6

p. 151: Jeff Swensen/Getty Images; p. 153: Tony Karumba/Afp/Getty Images; p. 155: Kevin Mazur/WireImage/Getty Images; p. 166: Andrew Toth/Getty Images Entertainment/Getty Images; p. 169 (top, left): Spencer Platt/Getty Images News/Getty Images; p. 169 (top, right): Nolte Lourens/Fotolia; p. 169 (middle): Rafael Ben-Ari/Fotolia; p. 169 (bottom, left): Mark Ralston/Afp/Getty Images; p. 169 (bottom, right): Justin Sullivan/Getty Images News/Getty Images; p. 173: Artisticco/Fotolia; p. 176: Steluta Sabau/Fotolia; p. 179: Nito/Fotolia

Chapter 7

p. 182: SOURCE NEEDED; p. 187: National Archives/Handout/Newsmakers/Hulton Archive/Getty Images; p. 189: DK Images; p. 191: SOURCE NEEDED; p. 194 (top, left): 9lives/Shutterstock; p. 194 (top, right): Anton Lunkov/Shutterstock; p. 194 (bottom, left): Robert Miu/Shutterstock; p. 194 (bottom, middle): Patrimonio designs ltd/Shutterstock; p. 194 (bottom, right): Tsirik/Shutterstock; p. 199: Glen Jones/Fotolia; p. 205: Shutterstock; p. 206: Etien/Fotolia

Chapter 8

p. 211: Diamondforce/Fotolia; p. 215 (left): Tony Duffy/Allsport/Getty Images; p. 215 (center, left): p. 215 (center, right): SOURCE NEEDED; p. 215 (right): SOURCE NEEDED; p. 219: NCP/Star Max/GC Images/Getty Images; p. 222 (top, left): Per-Anders Pettersson/Hulton Archive/Getty Images; p. 222 (right): Angelo Giampiccolo/Fotolia; p. 222 (bottom): Print Collector/Hulton Archive/Getty Images; p. 223 (left): Karwai Tang/WireImage/Getty Images; p. 223 (right): Tracy Whiteside/Fotolia; p. 230 (top): Timur1970/Fotolia; p. 230 (bottom): Alexandra/Fotolia; p. 235: John Olson/The Life Picture Collection/Getty Images

Chapter 9

p. 239: Universal Images Group/Getty Images; p. 242: Visions of America/UIG/Getty Images; p. 249: Karen Seccombe; p. 251: Darren Baker/Fotolia; p. 256: Gldcreations/Fotolia; p. 263 (top, left): iStock; p. 263 (top, right): iStock; p. 263 (middle, left): Bst2012/Fotolia; p. 263 (middle, right): Diego cervo/Fotolia; p. 263 (bottom): Frederic J. Brown/Afp/Getty Images; p. 265: Ysbrandcosijn/Fotolia; p. 269: Vbaleha/Fotolia

Chapter 10

p. 275: RetroClipArt/Fotolia; p. 277 (top, left): Eric Isselée/Fotolia; p. 277 (top, right): Vitalinka/Fotolia; p. 277 (middle, left): Andi.es/Fotolia; p. 277 (middle, right): Scott Griessel/Fotolia; p. 277 (bottom): Eugenio Marongiu/Fotolia; p. 284: Viacheslav Iakobchuk/Fotolia; p. 286: Nito/Fotolia; p. 293: NEED SOURCE; p. 295: Ondrooo/Fotolia; p. 300: Bramgino/Fotolia; p. 302: Three Rocksimages/Fotolia

Chapter 11

p. 307: WavebreakMediaMicro/Fotolia; p. 314: iStock; p. 318: NEED SOURCE; p. 326 (top, left): iStock; p. 326 (top, right): Monkey Business/Fotolia; p. 326 (middle, left): iStock; p. 326 (middle, right): Imaginando/Fotolia; p. 326 (bottom): Somwaya/Fotolia; p. 329: Renate Wefers/Fotolia; p. 332: NH7/Fotolia; p. 334: Highwaystarz/Fotolia; p. 336: SeanPavonePhoto/Fotolia

Chapter 12

p. 339: Justin Sullivan/Getty Images News/Getty Images; p. 347: Dhiraj Singh/Bloomberg/Getty Images; p. 349 (top, left): Lucas Schifres/Getty Images News/Getty images; p. 349 (top, right): Lucas Schifres/Getty Images News/Getty images; p. 349 (bottom, left): Lucas Schifres/Getty Images News/Getty images; p. 349 (bottom, middle): Lucas Schifres/Getty Images News/Getty images; p. 349 (bottom, right): Lucas Schifres/Getty Images News/Getty images; p. 350: iStock; p. 354: iStock; p. 358: iStock; p. 359: Revelpix/Fotolia; p. 362: Tom Williams/Cq-Roll Call/Getty Images

Chapter 13

p. 364: Tom Williams/Cq-Roll Call/Getty Images; p. 366 (top, left): Aynur_sh/Fotolia; p. 366 (top, right): lazyllama/Fotolia; p. 366 (middle, left): Wusuowei/Fotolia; p. 366 (middle, right): Bernard Foubert/Photononstop/Getty Images; p. 366 (bottom): Bruce Brander/Science Source/Getty Images; p. 374: Bruce Brander/Science Source/Getty Images; p. 378: Danita Delimont/Getty Images; p. 384: Keren Su/China Span/Getty Images; p. 386: Joshua Resnick/Fotolia; p. 388: Hill Street Studios/Blend Images/Getty Images; p. 391: Per-Anders Pettersson/Photonica World/Getty Images

Chapter 14

p. 395: Marcovarro/Fotolia; p. 400: Patrick T.Fallon/Bloomberg/Getty Images; p. 404: Sean Gallup/Getty Images News/Getty Images; p. 407: Greg Wood/Afp/Getty Images; p. 411 (top, left): Uriel Sinai/Getty Images News/Getty Images; p. 411 (top, right): Joe Raedle/Getty Images News/Getty Images; p. 411 (bottom, left): David McNew/Getty Images News/Getty Images; p. 411 (bottom, middle): George Rose/Getty Images News/Getty Images; p. 411 (bottom, right): David McNew/Getty Images News/Getty Images; p. 414: Xiao Lu Chu/Getty Images News/Getty Images; p. 417: Robert Alexander/Archive Photos/Getty Images; p. 419: Huriah Niazi/Anadolu Agency/Getty Images

Chapter 15

p. 425: John Tlumacki/The Boston Globe/Getty Images; p. 428: Paul J.Richards/Afp/Getty Images; p. 429: Sandra Manske/Fotolia; p. 432: Carmen Taylor/WireImage/Getty Images; p. 437 (top, left): Aris Messinis/Afp Photo/Getty Images; p. 437 (top, right): Baraa Al-Halabi/Afp/Getty Images; p. 437 (bottom, left): John Tlumacki/The Boston Globe/Getty Images; p. 437 (bottom, middle): Jose Jimenez/Primera Hora/Getty Images News/Getty Images; p. 437 (bottom, right): AAron Ontiveroz/The Denver Post /Getty Images; p. 441: Fotolia; p. 443: Gregory Adams/Moment/Getty Images; p. 445: Ronald S. Haeberle//Time Life Pictures/Getty Images

Name Index

Subject Index